2011 SUPPLEMENT

CASES AND MATERIALS

D1373280

CRIMINAL JUSTICE ADMINISTRATION

FIFTH EDITION

by

FRANK W. MILLER
The late James Carr Professor Emeritus of Criminal Jurisprudence,
Washington University

ROBERT O. DAWSON
The late Bryant Smith Chair in Law,
University of Texas

GEORGE E. DIX
George R. Killam, Jr. Chair of Criminal Law,
University of Texas

RAYMOND I. PARNAS
The late Professor of Law Emeritus,
University of California, Davis

FOUNDATION PRESS
2011

THOMSON REUTERS

© 2000–2004 FOUNDATION PRESS
© 2005–2010 THOMSON REUTERS/FOUNDATION PRESS
© 2011 By THOMSON REUTERS/FOUNDATION PRESS

      195 Broadway, 9th Floor
      New York, NY 10007
      Phone Toll Free 1–877–888–1330
      Fax (212) 367–6799
      foundation–press.com
Printed in the United States of America

ISBN 978–1–59941–969–5

Mat #41127033

PREFACE

Continuing developments, most significantly decisions of the Supreme Court of the United States, make supplementation of the text necessary. This supplement presents primarily decisions of the Supreme Court. Relevant cases decided before the summer recess of the Court's October, 2010 term are included.

Many of the footnotes from reprinted decisions have been omitted. Where this has been done, those footnotes retained in the text have been renumbered. We made deletions of footnotes and textual citations to authorities without specific indications of those omissions.

G.E.D.

July 4, 2011

TABLE OF CONTENTS

CHAPTER 6. Electronic Surveillance

CHAPTER 7. Interrogation and Confessions

TABLE OF CASES

Principal cases are in bold type. Non-principal cases are in roman type. References are to Pages.

2011 SUPPLEMENT

CASES AND MATERIALS

CRIMINAL JUSTICE ADMINISTRATION

PART ONE

INVESTIGATION OF CRIME

EDITORS' INTRODUCTION: FEDERAL AND STATE
CONSTITUTIONAL PROVISIONS AFFECTING LAW ENFORCEMENT
CONDUCT

Page 12. Add the following before the last paragraph of Editors' Introduction: Federal and State Constitutional Provisions Affecting Law Enforcement Conduct:

State courts' independence applies only to matters of *state* law. In Arkansas v. Sullivan, 532 U.S. 769, 121 S.Ct. 1876, 149 L.Ed.2d 994 (2001) (per curiam), the Arkansas Supreme Court reasoned that even if the officer's conduct in the case did not violate the Fourth Amendment as interpreted in United States Supreme Court case law, "there is nothing that prevents this court from interpreting the U.S. Constitution more broadly than the United States Supreme Court, which has the effect of providing more rights." Summarily reversing, the Supreme Court explained:

> The Arkansas Supreme Court's alternative holding, that it may interpret the United States Constitution to provide greater protection than this Court's own federal constitutional precedents provide, is foreclosed by Oregon v. Hass, 420 U.S. 714, 95 S.Ct. 1215, 43 L.Ed.2d 570 (1975). There, we observed that the Oregon Supreme Court's statement that it could " 'interpret the Fourth Amendment more restrictively than interpreted by the United States Supreme Court' " was "not the law and surely must be inadvertent error." We reiterated in *Hass* that while "a State is free as a matter of its own law to impose greater restrictions on police activity than those this Court holds to be necessary upon federal constitutional standards," it "may not impose such greater restrictions as a matter of federal constitutional law when this Court specifically refrains from imposing them."

1

532 U.S. at 770, 121 S.Ct. at 1878, 149 L.Ed.2d at 998–99.

On remand, the Arkansas court explicitly rested its result on *state* constitutional law. State v. Sullivan, 348 Ark. 647, 74 S.W.3d 215 (2002).

CHAPTER 1

THE EXCLUSIONARY SANCTION

Page 14.   Insert the following new Note after the Editors' Introduction:

NOTE: TREATIES AS AFFECTING CRIMINAL PROCEDURE

American criminal procedure may be affected by other law, including international treaties such as the Vienna Convention on Consular Relations.

The Convention provides in Article 36(1) that that if a national of one member nation is detained in another member nation, and the national so requests, the local consular post of the national's home nation is to be notified. A detained national of a member nation detained in another nation is to be informed of this right "without delay." The second paragraph of Article 36 provides:

> 2.   The rights referred to in paragraph 1 of this Article shall be exercised in conformity with the laws and regulations of the receiving State, subject to the proviso, however, that the said laws and regulations must enable full effect to be given to the purposes for which the rights accorded under this Article are intended.

The United States and Mexico have signed the treaty. Both were previously signatories of the Optional Protocol to the Convention, which gave jurisdiction to disputes arising out of the Convention to the International Court of Justice (ICJ); the United States has since withdrawn from the Protocol.

In 2004, the International Court of Justice decided Case Concerning Avena and Other Mexican Nationals (Mexico v. United States), 2004 I.C.J. 12 (Judgment of Mar. 31). This was an action brought by Mexico against the United States, claiming Convention violations concerning specific Mexican nationals facing the death penalties in the United States. Mexico claimed that its nationals were harmed in a variety of ways by United States authorities' failures to provide timely notices of their right to have the Mexican consulate notified of their arrests. This delay prevented some from taking advantage of the consulate's help in securing representation and thus they were unable to make effective cases against the death penalty, Mexico contended. Further, it argued that the exclusionary rule is a "general principle of law," applicable in both common law and civil law jurisdictions. Under the Convention, this required the exclusion from evidence of any statement or confession given by Mexican nationals to United States law enforcement officers prior to the nationals being advised of their consular rights.

Avena held that the United States was obligated to provide a forum in which Mexican nationals not given timely advice concerning their consular rights could secure review and reconsideration of their convictions. This process must guarantee that violations of the Convention and possible prejudice caused by those violations are "fully examined" and "taken into account in the review and reconsideration

3

process." Contentions that statements must be excluded from evidence are to be "examined under the concrete circumstances of each case." The review and reconsideration must be conducted without enforcement of a procedural default rule barring the defendants from securing relief because they failed to raise the matter in the trial court during their original prosecutions.

In 2005, President Bush issued a memorandum stating the United States would discharge its international obligations under the *Avena* judgment "by having State courts give effect to the [ICJ] decision in accordance with general principles of comity in cases filed by the 51 Mexican nationals addressed in that decision." George W. Bush, Memorandum for the Attorney General (Feb. 28, 2005).

The Supreme Court addressed generally the effect of the Convention and *Avena* on state criminal procedure in Sanchez–Llamas v. Oregon, 548 U.S. 331, 126 S.Ct. 2669, 165 L.Ed.2d 557 (2006). *Sanchez–Llamas* involved two consolidated cases in which state defendants sought judicial relief in state courts on the basis of use in their trials of out-of-court statements they maintained were tainted by authorities' noncompliance with the Convention. Neither state defendant had been a party to *Avena* itself and neither was covered by the President's memorandum.

The Court assumed in *Sanchez–Llamas*—but carefully did not decide—that the Convention creates rights that may be invoked by individuals in judicial proceedings. If it does create such rights, the Court held, neither defendant before it was entitled to any relief because of those rights.

Since the Convention itself does not mandate suppression of evidence in a criminal proceeding, the Supreme Court reasoned, any right to suppression must come from United States law. The only possible source in United States law for a right to suppression would be the treaty itself. A majority of the Court found no such right in the Convention. That majority first expressed doubt that the treaty requires any judicial remedy. If it does, however, that remedy must—according to the terms of the Convention—conform to the laws and regulations of the United States. Under United States law, the Court explained in resolving *Sanchez–Llamas*, suppression of evidence would not be an appropriate remedy:

> Under our domestic law, the exclusionary rule is not a remedy we apply lightly. * * * Because the rule's social costs are considerable, suppression is warranted only where the rule's " 'remedial objectives are thought most efficaciously served.' "

> We have applied the exclusionary rule primarily to deter constitutional violations. * * *

> The few cases in which we have suppressed evidence for statutory violations do not help Sanchez–Llamas. In those cases, the excluded evidence arose directly out of statutory violations that implicated important Fourth and Fifth Amendment interests. * * *

> The violation of the right to consular notification, in contrast, is at best remotely connected to the gathering of evidence. Article 36 has nothing whatsoever to do with searches or interrogations. Indeed, Article 36 does not guarantee defendants any assistance at all. The provision secures only a right of foreign nationals to have their consulate informed of their arrest or detention—not to have their consulate intervene, or to have law enforcement authorities cease their investigation pending any such notice or intervention. In

most circumstances, there is likely to be little connection between an Article 36 violation and evidence or statements obtained by police.

Moreover, the reasons we often require suppression for Fourth and Fifth Amendment violations are entirely absent from the consular notification context. We require exclusion of coerced confessions both because we disapprove of such coercion and because such confessions tend to be unreliable. We exclude the fruits of unreasonable searches on the theory that without a strong deterrent, the constraints of the Fourth Amendment might be too easily disregarded by law enforcement. The situation here is quite different. The failure to inform a defendant of his Article 36 rights is unlikely, with any frequency, to produce unreliable confessions. And unlike the search-and-seizure context—where the need to obtain valuable evidence may tempt authorities to transgress Fourth Amendment limitations—police win little, if any, practical advantage from violating Article 36. Suppression would be a vastly disproportionate remedy for an Article 36 violation.

* * *

[S]uppression is not the only means of vindicating Vienna Convention rights. A defendant can raise an Article 36 claim as part of a broader challenge to the voluntariness of his statements to police. If he raises an Article 36 violation at trial, a court can make appropriate accommodations to ensure that the defendant secures, to the extent possible, the benefits of consular assistance. Of course, diplomatic avenues—the primary means of enforcing the Convention—also remain open.

In sum, neither the Vienna Convention itself nor our precedents applying the exclusionary rule support suppression of Sanchez–Llamas' statements to police.

548 U.S. at 347–50, 126 S.Ct. at 2680–82.

The other case, *Bustillo*, posed the question of whether the Convention requires state courts to disregard ordinary procedural default rules. The state courts had failed to reach Bustillo's contentions made on post-conviction habeas corpus because he had not raised his claimed Convention rights at trial or on direct appeal. Bustillo attacked this position, pointing out that in *Avena* and another case the International Court of Justice held that the Convention barred full enforcement of procedural default rules. The *Sanchez–Llamas* majority, however, responded that decisions of the ICJ are not binding on United States federal courts.

Addressing Bustillo's contention on its merits, the Court concluded that despite the reasoning of the ICJ, "Bustillo cannot show that normally applicable procedural default rules should be suspended in light of the type of right he claims." It explained:

The ICJ concluded that where a defendant was not notified of his rights under Article 36, application of the procedural default rule failed to give "full effect" to the purposes of Article 36 because it prevented courts from attaching "legal significance" to the Article 36 violation. This reasoning overlooks the importance of procedural default rules in an adversary system, which relies chiefly on the parties to raise significant issues and present them to the courts in the appropriate manner at the appropriate time for adjudication. Procedural default rules are designed to encourage parties to raise their claims promptly and to vindicate "the law's important interest in the finality of judgments." The consequence of failing to raise a claim for adjudication at the proper time is generally forfeiture of that claim. As a result, rules such as procedural default routinely deny "legal significance" * * * to otherwise viable legal claims.

Procedural default rules generally take on greater importance in an adversary system such as ours than in the sort of magistrate-directed, inquisitorial legal system characteristic of many of the other countries that are signatories to the Vienna Convention. * * * In an inquisitorial system, the failure to raise a legal error can in part be attributed to the magistrate, and thus to the state itself. In our system, however, the responsibility for failing to raise an issue generally rests with the parties themselves.

The ICJ's interpretation of Article 36 is inconsistent with the basic framework of an adversary system. * * *

548 U.S. at 356–57, 126 S.Ct. at 2685–86.

The effect of *Avena* and the President's memorandum on those state defendants who were parties to the *Avena* case was addressed in Medellin v. Texas, 552 U.S. 491, 128 S.Ct. 1346, 170 L.Ed.2d 190 (2008). Medellin had been among the 51 named state defendants whose status was at issue in *Avena*. After the ICJ's decision in *Avena*, Medellin sought relief in the Texas courts. The state tribunals refused to reach the merits of his claim on the ground that by failing to raise it earlier he had procedurally defaulted the claim under Texas law. It refused to disregard that law in compliance with the President's memorandum.

The Supreme Court affirmed the Texas courts' refusal to reach the merits of Medellin's contentions. First, it determined that the ICJ's decision in *Avena* itself is not binding federal law the state courts are required to enforce. Second, it held that the President's memorandum did not transform *Avena* into such binding federal law. Only Congress has the power to transform an international obligation arising from a non-self-executing treaty into domestic law. The treaties relied upon by Medellin are non-self-executing treaties. Finally, the President's foreign affairs authority to resolve claims disputes with foreign nations did not give the President power to compel state courts to ignore state procedural default law. This authority has never been used to reach "deep into the heart of the State's police powers" to compel state tribunals "to reopen final criminal judgments and set aside neutrally applicable state laws." 552 U.S. at 532, 128 S.Ct. at 1372.

A. ADOPTION OF THE FEDERAL CONSTITUTIONAL EXCLUSIONARY SANCTION

Page 25.   Add the following to the Notes after *Mapp*:

8. **Constitutional regulation of law enforcement inaction**. Whatever impact exclusion of evidence may have in preventing inappropriate law enforcement *action*, it obviously cannot be expected to address a problem of law enforcement *inaction*. A federal constitutional response to law enforcement inaction was considered in Town of Castle Rock v. Gonzales, 545 U.S. 748, 125 S.Ct. 2796, 162 L.Ed.2d 658 (2005).

Gonzales obtained a restraining order against her husband in Colorado state court. A state statute stated that a peace officer shall enforce a valid restraining order and shall arrest or seek an arrest warrant if the officer has probable cause to believe a person violated a restraining order. When her husband took her three children in violation of the order and she notified police, the officers refused to respond. Her husband killed the children. She sued the officers' employing city under 42 U.S.C. § 1983, and the District Court dismissed for failure to state a claim. The Court of Appeals reversed, holding that Gonzales had a protected property interest in the enforcement of her restraining order and the city deprived her of this without procedural due process when it failed to act on her complaint.

The Supreme Court reversed. It expressed some doubt that "an individual entitlement to enforcement of a restraining order could constitute a 'property' interest for purposes of the Due Process clause." But it held that despite the language of the statute, Colorado law did not create a personal entitlement to enforcement of restraining orders. It read the statutory terms against the background of "[a] well established tradition of police discretion [that] has long coexisted with apparently mandatory arrest statutes." The language of the statute, the Court reasoned, was not a sufficiently strong indication that the Colorado legislature intended to deprive Colorado peace officers of all discretion "to determine that—despite probable cause to believe a restraining order has been violated—the circumstances of the violation or the competing duties of that officer or his agency counsel decisively against enforcement in a particular instance."

The majority added:

[T]he benefit that a third party may receive from having someone else arrested for a crime generally does not trigger protections under the Due Process Clause, neither in its procedural nor in its "substantive" manifestations. This * * * does not mean States are powerless to provide victims with personally enforceable remedies. Although the framers of the Fourteenth Amendment and the Civil Rights Act of 1871, 17 Stat. 13 (the original source of § 1983), did not create a system by which police departments are generally held financially accountable for crimes that better policing might have prevented, the people of Colorado are free to craft such a system under state law.

545 U.S. at 768–69, 125 S.Ct. at 2810.

Justice Stevens, joined by Justice Ginsburg, dissented:

[T]he Court gives short shrift to the unique case of "mandatory arrest" statutes in the domestic violence context; States passed a wave of these statutes in the 1980's and 1990's with the unmistakable goal of eliminating police discretion in this area. * * *

In 1994, the Colorado General Assembly passed omnibus legislation targeting domestic violence. The part of the legislation at issue in this case mandates enforcement of a domestic restraining order upon probable cause of a violation, while another part directs that police officers "shall, without undue delay, arrest" a suspect upon "probable cause to believe that a crime or offense of domestic violence has been committed." In adopting this legislation, the Colorado General Assembly joined a nationwide movement of States that took aim at the crisis of police underenforcement in the domestic violence sphere by implementing "mandatory arrest" statutes. The crisis of underenforcement had various causes, not least of which was the perception by police departments and police officers that domestic violence was a private, "family" matter and that arrest was to be used as a last resort. Sack, Battered Women and the State: The Struggle for the Future of Domestic Violence Policy, 2004 Wis. L. Rev. 1657, 16621663 (hereinafter Sack); *id.*, at 1663 ("Because these cases were considered noncriminal, police assigned domestic violence calls low priority and often did not respond to them for several hours or ignored them altogether"). In response to these realities, and emboldened by a wellknown 1984 experiment by the Minneapolis police department, "many states enacted mandatory arrest statutes under which a police officer must arrest an abuser when the officer has probable cause to believe that a domestic assault has occurred or that a protection order has been violated." Developments in the Law: Legal Responses to Domestic Violence, 106 Harv. L. Rev. 1498, 1537 (1993). The purpose of these statutes was precisely to "counter police resistance to arrests in domestic violence cases by removing or restricting police officer discretion; mandatory arrest policies would increase police response and reduce batterer recidivism." Sack 1670.

* * *

While Colorado case law does not speak to the question, it is instructive that other state courts interpreting their analogous statutes have not only held that they eliminate the police's traditional discretion to refuse enforcement, but have also recognized that they create rights enforceable against the police under state law. * * *

545 U.S. at 779–84, 125 S.Ct. at 2816–18 (Stevens, J., dissenting). Further, he argued, Gonzales' right to have the restraining order enforced is a legitimate and concrete property right "worthy of constitutional protection."

B.   SCOPE OF EXCLUSIONARY SANCTIONS: STANDING, FRUIT OF THE POISONOUS TREE, INDEPENDENT SOURCE, AND ATTENUATION OF THE TAINT

Page 37. Add the following to Note 7 after Wong Sun v. United States:

In Kaupp v. Texas, 538 U.S. 626, 123 S.Ct. 1843, 155 L.Ed.2d 814 (2003) (per curiam), the Court—citing *Wong Sun*—summarized the law as requiring exclusion of a confession "unless that confession was 'an act of free will [sufficient] to purge the primary taint of the unlawful invasion.'" The giving of *Miranda* warnings, *Kaupp* reiterated, is not alone enough to establish such an act of free will.

C.   EXCEPTIONS TO EXCLUSIONARY REQUIREMENTS

Page 40.   Add the following to the Editors' Introduction at the end of the unit, "Impeachment of Testifying Defendant":

The Supreme Court's application of the impeachment exception to evidence obtained in violation of a defendant's Sixth Amendment right to representation by counsel is addressed in the material supplementing page 503 of the text.

Page 51.   Add the following new Note after United States v. Leon:

1a.   **Unreasonable Reliance on Defective Search Warrant.** What would make a search warrant so clearly defective that a reasonable officer could not rely on it? The matter was addressed in Groh v. Ramirez, 540 U.S. 551, 124 S.Ct. 1284, 157 L.Ed.2d 1068 (2004). Although *Groh* involved whether an officer who executed a warrant had qualified immunity from civil liability for the search, the Court made clear that both qualified immunity and the *Leon–Sheppard* "good faith" exception to the exclusionary rule demand the same objective reasonableness of officers.

In *Groh*, a federal officers prepared an application for a search warrant for the Ramirez residence. In that application, he described in detail various weapons, explosive devices, and receipts pertaining to the purchase or manufacture of such weapons and devices for which the officer sought authority to search. The officer also used a form to prepare a warrant. In that portion of the form calling for a description of the person or property to be seized, the officer mistakenly inserted a description of the premises to be searched. The warrant form did not purport to incorporate the application. Then the officer presented the application, an affidavit, and the warrant form to a Magistrate Judge who signed the filled-in warrant form.

As a result, the warrant contained no description of any things for which the search was to be conducted. Could a reasonable officer nevertheless believe the warrant and search valid? A majority of the Court held not. That majority explained:

> Given that the particularity requirement is set forth in the text of the Constitution, no reasonable officer could believe that a warrant that plainly did not comply with that requirement was valid. Moreover, because [Groh] himself prepared the invalid warrant, he may not argue that he reasonably relied on the Magistrate's assurance that the warrant contained an adequate description of the things to be seized and was therefore valid. In fact, the guidelines of [Groh's] own department placed him on notice that he might be liable for executing a manifestly invalid warrant. * * * And even a cursory reading of the warrant in this case—perhaps just a simple glance—would have revealed a glaring deficiency that any reasonable police officer would have known was constitutionally fatal.

540 U.S. at 563–64, 124 S.Ct. at 1293–94.

Page 56.   Add the following new case and Note after United States v. Leon and the Notes to that case:

Herring v. United States

Supreme Court of the United States, 2009.
555 U.S. 135, 129 S.Ct. 695, 172 L.Ed.2d 496.

■ CHIEF JUSTICE ROBERTS delivered the opinion of the Court.

The Fourth Amendment forbids "unreasonable searches and seizures," and this usually requires the police to have probable cause or a warrant before making an arrest. What if an officer reasonably believes there is an outstanding arrest warrant, but that belief turns out to be wrong because of a negligent bookkeeping error by another police employee? * * *

I

On July 7, 2004, Investigator Mark Anderson learned that Bennie Dean Herring had driven to the Coffee County Sheriff's Department to retrieve something from his impounded truck. Herring was no stranger to law enforcement, and Anderson asked the county's warrant clerk, Sandy Pope, to check for any outstanding warrants for Herring's arrest. When she found none, Anderson asked Pope to check with Sharon Morgan, her counterpart in neighboring Dale County. After checking Dale County's computer database, Morgan replied that there was an active arrest warrant for Herring's failure to appear on a felony charge. Pope relayed the information to Anderson and asked Morgan to fax over a copy of the warrant as confirmation. Anderson and a deputy followed Herring as he left the impound lot, pulled him over, and arrested him. A search incident to the arrest revealed methamphetamine in Herring's pocket, and a pistol (which as a felon he could not possess) in his vehicle.

There had, however, been a mistake about the warrant. The Dale County sheriff's computer records are supposed to correspond to actual arrest warrants, which the office also maintains. But when Morgan went to the files to retrieve the actual warrant to fax to Pope, Morgan was unable to find it. She called a court clerk and learned that the warrant had been recalled five months earlier. Normally when a warrant is recalled the court clerk's office or a judge's chambers calls Morgan, who enters the information in the sheriff's computer database and disposes of the physical copy. For whatever reason, the information about the recall of the warrant for Herring did not appear in the database. Morgan immediately called Pope to alert her to the mixup, and Pope contacted Anderson over a secure radio. This all unfolded in 10 to 15 minutes, but Herring had already been arrested and found with the gun and drugs, just a few hundred yards from the sheriff's office.

Herring was indicted in the District Court for the Middle District of Alabama for illegally possessing the gun and drugs * * *. He moved to suppress the evidence on the ground that his initial arrest had been illegal because the warrant had been rescinded. The Magistrate Judge recommended denying the motion because the arresting officers had acted in a good-faith belief that the warrant was still outstanding. * * * The District Court adopted the Magistrate Judge's recommendation, and the Court of Appeals for the Eleventh Circuit affirmed.

* * *

Other courts have required exclusion of evidence obtained through similar police errors, so we granted Herring's petition for certiorari to resolve the conflict. * * *

II

[W]e accept the parties' assumption that there was a Fourth Amendment violation. The issue is whether the exclusionary rule should be applied.

A

The Fourth Amendment protects "[t]he right of the people to be secure in their persons, houses, papers, and effects, against unreasonable searches and seizures," but "contains no provision expressly precluding the use of evidence obtained in violation of its commands." Nonetheless, our decisions establish an exclusionary rule that, when applicable, forbids the use of improperly obtained evidence at trial. We have stated that this judicially created rule is "designed to safeguard Fourth Amendment rights generally through its deterrent effect." *United States v. Calandra,* 414 U.S. 338, 348, 94 S.Ct. 613, 38 L.Ed.2d 561 (1974).

In analyzing the applicability of the rule, [United States v. Leon, 468 U.S. 897, 104 S.Ct. 3405 (1984),] admonished that we must consider the actions of all the police officers involved. The Coffee County officers did nothing improper. Indeed, the error was noticed so quickly because Coffee County requested a faxed confirmation of the warrant.

The Eleventh Circuit concluded, however, that somebody in Dale County should have updated the computer database to reflect the recall of the arrest warrant. The court also concluded that this error was negligent, but did not find it to be reckless or deliberate. That fact is crucial to our holding that this error is not enough by itself to require "the extreme sanction of exclusion."

B

1. The fact that a Fourth Amendment violation occurred—*i.e.,* that a search or arrest was unreasonable—does not necessarily mean that the exclusionary rule applies. Indeed, exclusion "has always been our last resort, not our first impulse," *Hudson v. Michigan,* 547 U.S. 586, 591, 126 S.Ct. 2159, 165 L.Ed.2d 56 (2006), and our precedents establish important principles that constrain application of the exclusionary rule.

First, the exclusionary rule is not an individual right and applies only where it " 'result[s] in appreciable deterrence.' " We have repeatedly rejected the argument that exclusion is a necessary consequence of a Fourth Amendment violation. Instead we have focused on the efficacy of the rule in deterring Fourth Amendment violations in the future.[2]

In addition, the benefits of deterrence must outweigh the costs. * * * The principal cost of applying the rule is, of course, letting guilty and

2. Justice GINSBURG's dissent champions what she describes as " 'a more majestic conception' of . . . the exclusionary rule," which would exclude evidence even where deterrence does not justify doing so. Majestic or not, our cases reject this conception * * *.

possibly dangerous defendants go free-something that "offends basic concepts of the criminal justice system."

* * *

2. The extent to which the exclusionary rule is justified by these deterrence principles varies with the culpability of the law enforcement conduct. As we said in *Leon,* "an assessment of the flagrancy of the police misconduct constitutes an important step in the calculus" of applying the exclusionary rule. Similarly, * * * we [later] elaborated that "evidence should be suppressed 'only if it can be said that the law enforcement officer had knowledge, or may properly be charged with knowledge, that the search was unconstitutional under the Fourth Amendment.' "

Anticipating the good-faith exception to the exclusionary rule, Judge Friendly wrote that "[t]he beneficent aim of the exclusionary rule to deter police misconduct can be sufficiently accomplished by a practice ... outlawing evidence obtained by flagrant or deliberate violation of rights." The Bill of Rights as a Code of Criminal Procedure, 53 Calif. L.Rev. 929, 953 (1965) (footnotes omitted).

Indeed, the abuses that gave rise to the exclusionary rule featured intentional conduct that was patently unconstitutional. * * * [F]lagrant conduct was at issue in *Mapp v. Ohio,* 367 U.S. 643, 81 S.Ct. 1684, 6 L.Ed.2d 1081 (1961) * * *. Officers forced open a door to Ms. Mapp's house, kept her lawyer from entering, brandished what the court concluded was a false warrant, then forced her into handcuffs and canvassed the house for obscenity. An error that arises from nonrecurring and attenuated negligence is thus far removed from the core concerns that led us to adopt the rule in the first place. And in fact since *Leon,* we have never applied the rule to exclude evidence obtained in violation of the Fourth Amendment, where the police conduct was no more intentional or culpable than this.

3. To trigger the exclusionary rule, police conduct must be sufficiently deliberate that exclusion can meaningfully deter it, and sufficiently culpable that such deterrence is worth the price paid by the justice system. As laid out in our cases, the exclusionary rule serves to deter deliberate, reckless, or grossly negligent conduct, or in some circumstances recurring or systemic negligence. The error in this case does not rise to that level.[4]

* * *

4. We do not suggest that all recordkeeping errors by the police are immune from the exclusionary rule. In this case, however, the conduct at issue was not so objectively culpable as to require exclusion. In *Leon* we

---

4. We do not quarrel with Justice GINSBURG's claim that "liability for negligence ... creates an incentive to act with greater care," and we do not suggest that the exclusion of this evidence could have *no* deterrent effect. But our cases require any deterrence to "be weighed against the 'substantial social costs exacted by the exclusionary rule,' "and here exclusion is not worth the cost.

held that "the marginal or nonexistent benefits produced by suppressing evidence obtained in objectively reasonable reliance on a subsequently invalidated search warrant cannot justify the substantial costs of exclusion." The same is true when evidence is obtained in objectively reasonable reliance on a subsequently recalled warrant.

If the police have been shown to be reckless in maintaining a warrant system, or to have knowingly made false entries to lay the groundwork for future false arrests, exclusion would certainly be justified under our cases should such misconduct cause a Fourth Amendment violation. We said as much in *Leon,* explaining that an officer could not "obtain a warrant on the basis of a 'bare bones' affidavit and then rely on colleagues who are ignorant of the circumstances under which the warrant was obtained to conduct the search." Petitioner's fears that our decision will cause police departments to deliberately keep their officers ignorant, are thus unfounded.

The dissent also adverts to the possible unreliability of a number of databases not relevant to this case. In a case where systemic errors were demonstrated, it might be reckless for officers to rely on an unreliable warrant system. But there is no evidence that errors in Dale County's system are routine or widespread. Officer Anderson testified that he had never had reason to question information about a Dale County warrant, and both Sandy Pope and Sharon Morgan testified that they could remember no similar miscommunication ever happening on their watch. * * * Because no such showings were made here, the Eleventh Circuit was correct to affirm the denial of the motion to suppress.

* * *

Petitioner's claim that police negligence automatically triggers suppression cannot be squared with the principles underlying the exclusionary rule, as they have been explained in our cases. In light of our repeated holdings that the deterrent effect of suppression must be substantial and outweigh any harm to the justice system, we conclude that when police mistakes are the result of negligence such as that described here, rather than systemic error or reckless disregard of constitutional requirements, any marginal deterrence does not "pay its way." In such a case, the criminal should not "go free because the constable has blundered."

The judgment of the Court of Appeals for the Eleventh Circuit is affirmed.

It is so ordered.

■ JUSTICE GINSBURG, with whom JUSTICE STEVENS, JUSTICE SOUTER, and JUSTICE BREYER join, dissenting.

* * *

I would * * * hold the [exclusionary] rule dispositive of this case: "[I]f courts are to have any power to discourage [police] error of [the kind here at issue], it must be through the application of the exclusionary rule." *Arizona v. Evans,* 514 U.S. 1, 22–23, 115 S.Ct. 1185, 131 L.Ed.2d 34 (1995) (STEVENS, J., dissenting). The unlawful search in this case was contested in court because the police found methamphetamine in Herring's pocket and a pistol in his truck. But the "most serious impact" of the Court's holding will be on innocent persons "wrongfully arrested based on erroneous information [carelessly maintained] in a computer data base."

* * *

II

A

The Court states that the exclusionary rule is not a defendant's right; rather, it is simply a remedy applicable only when suppression would result in appreciable deterrence that outweighs the cost to the justice system.

* * *

B

Others have described "a more majestic conception" of the Fourth Amendment and its adjunct, the exclusionary rule. *Evans,* 514 U.S., at 18, 115 S.Ct. 1185 (STEVENS, J., dissenting). Protective of the fundamental "right of the people to be secure in their persons, houses, papers, and effects," the Amendment "is a constraint on the power of the sovereign, not merely on some of its agents." I share that vision of the Amendment.

The exclusionary rule is "a remedy necessary to ensure that" the Fourth Amendment's prohibitions "are observed in fact." The rule's service as an essential auxiliary to the Amendment earlier inclined the Court to hold the two inseparable.

Beyond doubt, a main objective of the rule "is to deter—to compel respect for the constitutional guaranty in the only effectively available way—by removing the incentive to disregard it." But the rule also serves other important purposes: It "enabl[es] the judiciary to avoid the taint of partnership in official lawlessness," and it "assur[es] the people—all potential victims of unlawful government conduct—that the government would not profit from its lawless behavior, thus minimizing the risk of seriously undermining popular trust in government." *United States v. Calandra,* 414 U.S. 338, 357, 94 S.Ct. 613, 38 L.Ed.2d 561 (1974) (Brennan, J., dissenting).

The exclusionary rule, it bears emphasis, is often the only remedy effective to redress a Fourth Amendment violation. Civil liability will not lie for "the vast majority of [F]ourth [A]mendment violations—the frequent infringements motivated by commendable zeal, not condemnable malice." Criminal prosecutions or administrative sanctions against the offending officers and injunctive relief against widespread violations are an even farther cry.

III

The Court maintains that Herring's case is one in which the exclusionary rule could have scant deterrent effect and therefore would not "pay its way." I disagree. *

A

The exclusionary rule, the Court suggests, is capable of only marginal deterrence when the misconduct at issue is merely careless, not intentional or reckless. The suggestion runs counter to a foundational premise of tort law—that liability for negligence, *i.e.,* lack of due care, creates an incentive to act with greater care. * * *

B

Is the potential deterrence here worth the costs it imposes? In light of the paramount importance of accurate recordkeeping in law enforcement, I would answer yes * * *.

Electronic databases form the nervous system of contemporary criminal justice operations. In recent years, their breadth and influence have dramatically expanded. Police today can access databases that include not only the updated National Crime Information Center (NCIC), but also terrorist watchlists, the Federal Government's employee eligibility system, and various commercial databases. Moreover, States are actively expanding information sharing between jurisdictions. As a result, law enforcement has an increasing supply of information within its easy electronic reach.

The risk of error stemming from these databases is not slim. Herring's *amici* warn that law enforcement databases are insufficiently monitored and often out of date. Government reports describe, for example, flaws in NCIC databases, terrorist watchlist databases, and databases associated with the Federal Government's employment eligibility verification system.

Inaccuracies in expansive, interconnected collections of electronic information raise grave concerns for individual liberty. * * *

C

The Court assures that "exclusion would certainly be justified" if "the police have been shown to be reckless in maintaining a warrant system, or to have knowingly made false entries to lay the groundwork for future false arrests." This concession provides little comfort.

First, by restricting suppression to bookkeeping errors that are deliberate or reckless, the majority leaves Herring, and others like him, with no remedy for violations of their constitutional rights. There can be no serious assertion that relief is available under 42 U.S.C. § 1983. The arresting officer would be sheltered by qualified immunity, and the police department itself is not liable for the negligent acts of its employees. Moreover, identifying the department employee who committed the error may be impossible.

Second, I doubt that police forces already possess sufficient incentives to maintain up-to-date records. The Government argues that police have no desire to send officers out on arrests unnecessarily, because arrests consume resources and place officers in danger. The facts of this case do not fit that description of police motivation. Here the officer wanted to arrest Herring and consulted the Department's records to legitimate his predisposition.

Third, even when deliberate or reckless conduct is afoot, the Court's assurance will often be an empty promise: How is an impecunious defendant to make the required showing? If the answer is that a defendant is entitled to discovery (and if necessary, an audit of police databases), then the Court has imposed a considerable administrative burden on courts and law enforcement.

IV

Negligent recordkeeping errors by law enforcement threaten individual liberty, are susceptible to deterrence by the exclusionary rule, and cannot be remedied effectively through other means. Such errors present no occasion to further erode the exclusionary rule. The rule "is needed to make the Fourth Amendment something real; a guarantee that does not carry with it the exclusion of evidence obtained by its violation is a chimera." In keeping with the rule's "core concerns," suppression should have attended the unconstitutional search in this case.

* * *

For the reasons stated, I would reverse the judgment of the Eleventh Circuit.

■ JUSTICE BREYER, with whom JUSTICE SOUTER joins, dissenting.

* * *

Distinguishing between police recordkeeping errors and judicial ones not only is consistent with our precedent, but also is far easier for courts to administer than THE CHIEF JUSTICE's case-by-case, multifactored inquiry into the degree of police culpability. I therefore would apply the exclusionary rule when police personnel are responsible for a recordkeeping error that results in a Fourth Amendment violation.

The need for a clear line, and the recognition of such a line in our precedent, are further reasons in support of the outcome that Justice GINSBURG's dissent would reach.

NOTE: RELIANCE ON PRECEDENT

In Arizona v. Gant, 556 U.S. ___, 129 S.Ct. 1710, 173 L.Ed.2d 485 (2009) (reprinted in the material supplementing page 199 of the text), the Supreme Court overruled prior case law and limited searches of vehicles rendered reasonable because of the arrest of occupants of those vehicles. Davis v. United States, 564 U.S. ___, 131 S.Ct. 2419, ___ L.Ed.2d ___ (2011), addressed the admissibility in an Eleventh Circuit federal prosecution of evidence obtained before *Gant* in a search by state officers that under pre-*Gant* Eleventh Circuit case law was constitutionally permissible. By 7–2 vote, the Court held that under the good faith exception such evidence was admissible.

Justice Alito's majority *Davis* opinion explained:

> The search incident to Davis's arrest in this case followed the Eleventh Circuit's * * * precedent to the letter. Although the search turned out to be unconstitutional under *Gant,* all agree that the officers' conduct was in strict compliance with then-binding Circuit law and was not culpable in any way.

> Under our exclusionary-rule precedents, this acknowledged absence of police culpability dooms Davis's claim. Police practices trigger the harsh sanction of exclusion only when they are deliberate enough to yield "meaningfu[l]" deterrence, and culpable enough to be "worth the price paid by the justice system." The conduct of the officers here was neither of these things. The officers who conducted the search did not violate Davis's Fourth Amendment rights deliberately, recklessly, or with gross negligence. Nor does this case involve any "recurring or systemic negligence" on the part of law enforcement. The police acted in strict compliance with binding precedent, and their behavior was not wrongful. Unless the exclusionary rule is to become a strict-liability regime, it can have no application in this case.

> Indeed, in 27 years of practice under *Leon* 's good-faith exception, we have "never applied" the exclusionary rule to suppress evidence obtained as a result of nonculpable, innocent police conduct.

564 U.S. at ___, 131 S.Ct. at 2428–29. The majority noted that in the future it might nevertheless—to foster the development of Fourth Amendment law—apply the exclusionary rule to a litigant who persuades the Court in that litigant's case to overrule precedent. *Davis,* however, was not such a case.

Justice Sotomayor wrote separately to address the dissenters' view that the majority's analysis would lead to extension of the good faith exception to officers who conduct a search in the face of unsettled precedent. She observed:

> The Court does not address this issue. In my view, whether an officer's conduct can be characterized as "culpable" is not itself dispositive. We have never refused to apply the exclusionary rule where its application would appreciably deter Fourth Amendment violations on the mere ground that the officer's conduct could be characterized as nonculpable. Rather, an officer's culpability is relevant because it may inform the overarching inquiry whether exclusion would result in appreciable deterrence. Whatever we have said about culpability, the ultimate questions have always been, one, whether exclusion would result in appreciable deterrence and, two, whether the benefits of exclusion outweigh its costs.

As stated, whether exclusion would result in appreciable deterrence in the circumstances of this case is a different question from whether exclusion would appreciably deter Fourth Amendment violations when the governing law is unsettled. The Court's answer to the former question in this case thus does not resolve the latter one.

564 U.S. at ___, 131 S.Ct. at 2435–36 (Sotomayor, J., concurring in the judgment).

Justice Breyer, joined by Justice Ginsburg, commented in dissent that the majority's position portends even more dramatic restriction of the Fourth Amendment exclusionary rule:

[A]n officer who conducts a search that he believes complies with the Constitution but which, it ultimately turns out, falls just outside the Fourth Amendment's bounds is no more culpable than an officer who follows erroneous "binding precedent." Nor is an officer more culpable where circuit precedent is simply suggestive rather than "binding," where it only describes how to treat roughly analogous instances, or where it just does not exist. Thus, if the Court means what it now says, if it would place determinative weight upon the culpability of an individual officer's conduct, and if it would apply the exclusionary rule only where a Fourth Amendment violation was "deliberate, reckless, or grossly negligent," then the "good faith" exception will swallow the exclusionary rule. Indeed, our broad dicta in *Herring*—dicta the Court repeats and expands upon today—may already be leading lower courts in this direction. Today's decision will doubtless accelerate this trend.

Any such change (which may already be underway) would affect * * * a very large number of cases, potentially many thousands each year. And since the exclusionary rule is often the only sanction available for a Fourth Amendment violation, the Fourth Amendment would no longer protect ordinary Americans from "unreasonable searches and seizures." It would become a watered-down Fourth Amendment, offering its protection against only those searches and seizures that are *egregiously* unreasonable.

564 U.S. at ___, 131 S.Ct. at 2439–40 (Breyer, J., dissenting).

CHAPTER 2

CONSTITUTIONAL DOCTRINES RELATING TO LAW ENFORCEMENT CONDUCT

B. THE FOURTH AMENDMENT'S PROHIBITION AGAINST UNREASONABLE SEARCHES AND SEIZURES

1. POLICE ACTIVITY CONSTITUTING A "SEARCH"

Page 75. Insert the following in Editors' Introduction: The *Katz* Criterion for Identifying Searches and The Reasonableness of Searches, after *Examination of Trash as a Search*:

Manipulation of Luggage as a Search

A law enforcement officer's manipulation of a bus passenger's luggage was held a search in Bond v. United States, 529 U.S. 334, 120 S.Ct. 1462, 146 L.Ed.2d 365 (2000). The Court set out the facts:

> * * * Steven Dewayne Bond was a passenger on a Greyhound bus that left California bound for Little Rock, Arkansas. The bus stopped, as it was required to do, at the permanent Border Patrol checkpoint in Sierra Blanca, Texas. Border Patrol Agent Cesar Cantu boarded the bus to check the immigration status of its passengers. After reaching the back of the bus, having satisfied himself that the passengers were lawfully in the United States, Agent Cantu began walking toward the front. Along the way, he squeezed the soft luggage which passengers had placed in the overhead storage space above the seats.

> [Bond] was seated four or five rows from the back of the bus. As Agent Cantu inspected the luggage in the compartment above [Bond's] seat, he squeezed a green canvas bag and noticed that it contained a "brick-like" object. [Bond] admitted that the bag was his and agreed to allow Agent Cantu to open it. Upon opening the bag, Agent Cantu discovered a "brick" of methamphetamine. The brick had been wrapped in duct tape until it was oval-shaped and then rolled in a pair of pants.

The Government conceded that Bond had a privacy interest in the bag. It argued, however, that by placing the bag in the overhead compartment he lost any reasonable expectation that the bag would not be physically manipulated. Bond, in response, argued that Cantu's manipulation exceeded the "casual contact" a reasonable person expects as a result of placing a bag in such a location.

Siding with Bond, the Supreme Court first stressed that the visual observation decisions, considered in the first subsection that follows, were not controlling because the case before it involved tactile observation. "Physically invasive inspection," it explained, "is simply more intrusive than purely visual inspection." Further, passengers have a particularly important privacy interest in carry-on luggage used to transport personal items desired to be close at hand, although not as important an interest as individuals have in being free of tactile exploration of their bodies and clothing.

The Court then turned to whether, under *Katz*, the Fourth Amendment protected Bond's expectation that his carry-on bag would not be manipulated as Cantu manipulated it:

> When a bus passenger places a bag in an overhead bin, he expects that other passengers or bus employees may move it for one reason or another. Thus, a bus passenger clearly expects that his bag may be handled. He does not expect that other passengers or bus employees will, as a matter of course, feel the bag in an exploratory manner. But this is exactly what the agent did here. We therefore hold that the agent's physical manipulation of petitioner's bag violated the Fourth Amendment.

529 U.S. at 338–39, 120 S.Ct. at 1464, 146 L.Ed.2d at 370.

JUSTICE BREYER, joined by JUSTICE SCALIA, disagreed that Cantu's actions exceeded what a reasonable person would anticipate in Bond's situation:

> Agent Cantu [testified he] "felt a green bag" which had "a brick-like object in it." He explained that he felt "the edges of the brick in the bag," and that it was a "[b]rick-like object ... that, when squeezed, you could feel an outline of something of a different mass inside of it." Although the agent acknowledged that his practice was to "squeeze [bags] very hard," he testified that his touch ordinarily was not "[h]ard enough to break something inside that might be fragile." * * *
>
> How does the "squeezing" just described differ from the treatment that overhead luggage is likely to receive from strangers in a world of travel that is somewhat less gentle than it used to be? I think not at all. The trial court, which heard the evidence, saw nothing unusual, unforeseeable, or special about this agent's squeeze. It found that Agent Cantu simply "felt the outside of Bond's softside green cloth bag," and it viewed the agent's activity as "minimally intrusive touching." The Court of Appeals also noted that, because "passengers often handle and manipulate other passengers" luggage, the substantially similar tactile inspection here was entirely "foreseeable."

529 U.S. at 339–40, 120 S.Ct. at 1465–66, 146 L.Ed.2d at 371 (Breyer, J., dissenting). "At best," he added, "this decision will lead to a constitutional jurisprudence of 'squeezes,' thereby complicating further already complex Fourth Amendment law, increasing the difficulty of deciding ordinary criminal matters, and hindering the administrative guidance (with its potential for control of unreasonable police practices) that a less complicated jurisprudence might provide."

b. AERIAL AND OTHER OBSERVATIONS

Page 94. Add an additional note to Notes, following Florida v. Riley:

4. **Thermal Imaging Surveillance.** The Supreme Court returned to questions of enhanced surveillance in Kyllo v. United States, 533 U.S. 27, 121 S.Ct. 2038, 150 L.Ed.2d 94 (2001). Its analysis suggested somewhat more emphasis upon privacy—at least in the home—than the earlier case law. *Kyllo* itself involved use of a thermal imaging device:

> In 1991 Agent William Elliott of the United States Department of the Interior came to suspect that marijuana was being grown in the home belonging to * * * Danny Kyllo, part of a triplex on Rhododendron Drive in Florence, Oregon. Indoor marijuana growth typically requires high-intensity lamps. In order to determine whether an amount of heat was emanating from [Kyllo]'s home consistent with the use of such lamps, at 3:20 a.m. on January 16, 1992, Agent Elliott and Dan Haas used an Agema Thermovision 210 thermal imager to scan the triplex. Thermal imagers detect infrared radiation, which virtually all objects emit but which is not visible to the naked eye. The imager converts radiation into images based on relative warmth—black is cool, white is hot, shades of gray connote relative differences; in that respect, it operates somewhat like a video camera showing heat images. The scan of Kyllo's home took only a few minutes and was performed from the passenger seat of Agent Elliott's vehicle across the street from the front of the house and also from the street in back of the house. The scan showed that the roof over the garage and a side wall of [Kyllo]'s home were relatively hot compared to the rest of the home and substantially warmer than neighboring homes in the triplex. Agent Elliott concluded that [Kyllo] was using halide lights to grow marijuana in his house, which indeed he was.

Did Elliot engage in a search of Kyllo's home?

> [T]he District Court found that the Agema 210 "is a non-intrusive device which emits no rays or beams and shows a crude visual image of the heat being radiated from the outside of the house"; it "did not show any people or activity within the walls of the structure"; "[t]he device used cannot penetrate walls or windows to reveal conversations or human activities"; and "[n]o intimate details of the home were observed."

Consequently, the District Court determined that no search resulted from use of the device. This was upheld by the Court of Appeals. A 5-to-4 majority of the Supreme Court reversed. Justice Scalia explained for the Court:

> The present case involves officers on a public street engaged in more than naked-eye surveillance of a home. We have previously reserved judgment as to

how much technological enhancement of ordinary perception from such a vantage point, if any, is too much. * * *

It would be foolish to contend that the degree of privacy secured to citizens by the Fourth Amendment has been entirely unaffected by the advance of technology. For example, * * * technology enabling human flight has exposed to public view (and hence, we have said, to official observation) uncovered portions of the house and its curtilage that once were private. The question we confront today is what limits there are upon this power of technology to shrink the realm of guaranteed privacy.

* * *

We think that obtaining by sense-enhancing technology any information regarding the interior of the home that could not otherwise have been obtained without physical "intrusion into a constitutionally protected area," constitutes a search—at least where (as here) the technology in question is not in general public use. This assures preservation of that degree of privacy against government that existed when the Fourth Amendment was adopted. On the basis of this criterion, the information obtained by the thermal imager in this case was the product of a search.

* * *

The Government * * * contends that the thermal imaging was constitutional because it did not "detect private activities occurring in private areas." * * * The Fourth Amendment's protection of the home has never been tied to measurement of the quality or quantity of information obtained. * * * In the home, our cases show, all details are intimate details, because the entire area is held safe from prying government eyes. Thus, in [United States v. Karo, 468 U.S. 705, 104 S.Ct. 3296, 82 L.Ed.2d 530 (1984)], the only thing detected was a can of ether in the home; and in Arizona v. Hicks, 480 U.S. 321, 107 S.Ct. 1149, 94 L.Ed.2d 347 (1987), the only thing detected by a physical search that went beyond what officers lawfully present could observe in "plain view" was the registration number of a phonograph turntable. These were intimate details because they were details of the home, just as was the detail of how warm—or even how relatively warm—Kyllo was heating his residence.

Limiting the prohibition of thermal imaging to "intimate details" would not only be wrong in principle; it would be impractical in application, failing to provide "a workable accommodation between the needs of law enforcement and the interests protected by the Fourth Amendment." To begin with, there is no necessary connection between the sophistication of the surveillance equipment and the "intimacy" of the details that it observes—which means that one cannot say (and the police cannot be assured) that use of the relatively crude equipment at issue here will always be lawful. The Agema Thermovision 210 might disclose, for example, at what hour each night the lady of the house takes her daily sauna and bath—a detail that many would consider "intimate"; and a much more sophisticated system might detect nothing more intimate than the fact that someone left a closet light on. We could not, in other words, develop a rule approving only that through-the-wall surveillance which identifies objects no smaller than 36 by 36 inches, but would have to develop a jurisprudence specifying which home activities are "intimate" and which are not. And even when (if ever) that jurisprudence were fully developed, no police officer would be able to know in advance whether his through-the-wall surveillance picks up "intimate" details—and thus would be unable to know in advance whether it is constitutional.

527 U.S. at 533–37, 121 S.Ct. at 2042–46, 150 L.Ed.2d at 102–05.

Justice Stevens, writing for four dissenters, stressed that the device used by Agent Elliot only "passively measure[d] heat emitted from the exterior surfaces of [Kyllo]'s home * * *." This "off-the-wall" technique—unlike some present or future "through-the-wall" techniques—accomplished no penetration into the premises and gave the agent no information that could not have been obtained by observation from beyond the curtilage of the house. Rejecting the approach fashioned by the majority, Justice Stevens indicated:

> I would not erect a constitutional impediment to the use of sense-enhancing technology unless it provides its user with the functional equivalent of actual presence in the area being searched.

533 U.S. at 47, 121 S.Ct. at 2050, 150 L.Ed.2d at 110 (Stevens, J., dissenting, joined by the Chief Justice and Justices O'Connor and Kennedy).

The majority was clearly influenced by its perception of future dangers to interests protected by the Fourth Amendment. "While the technology used in the present case was relatively crude," Justice Scalia noted, "the rule we adopt must take account of more sophisticated systems that are already in use or in development." He then added in a footnote:

> The ability to "see" through walls and other opaque barriers is a clear, and scientifically feasible, goal of law enforcement research and development. The National Law Enforcement and Corrections Technology Center, a program within the United States Department of Justice, features on its Internet Website projects that include a "Radar–Based Through–the–Wall Surveillance System," "Handheld Ultrasound Through the Wall Surveillance," and a "Radar Flashlight" that "will enable law officers to detect individuals through interior building walls." www.nlectc.org/techproj/ (visited May 3, 2001). Some devices may emit low levels of radiation that travel "through-the-wall," but others, such as more sophisticated thermal imaging devices, are entirely passive, or "off-the-wall" as the dissent puts it.

533 U.S. at 36 n. 3, 121 S.Ct. at 2044 n. 3, 150 L.Ed.2d at 103 n. 3.

5. **Dog Sniff at Residence Door.** In State v. Rabb, 881 So.2d 587 (Fla.App. 2004), a police officer and "Chevy," a drug sniffing dog, walked from the public roadway up to the door of Rabb's residence, where the dog alerted. Was this a search? A split state court held that despite *Place*, discussed at page 73 of the text, and considering *Kyllo*, it was. The majority explained:

> [L]uggage located in a public airport is quite different from a house, not only in physical attributes but also in the historical protection granted by law. * * * [T]he use of the dog, like the use of a thermal imager, allowed law enforcement to intrude into the constitutionally protected area of Rabb's house * * *. [I]t is of no importance that a dog sniff provides limited information, because as in *Kyllo*, the quality or quantity of information obtained through the search is not the feared injury. Rather, it is the fact that law enforcement endeavored to obtain the information at all * * *. Because of smell of marijuana had its source in Rabb's house, it was an "intimate detail" of that house, no less than the relative warmth of Kyllo's house.

881 So.2d at 592–93.

On petition for writ of certiorari, the United States Supreme Court summarily vacated the judgment and remanded the case to the state court "for further consideration in light of Illinois v. Caballes, 543 U.S. 405, 125 S.Ct. 834, 160 L.Ed.2d 842 (2005) [reprinted later in this supplement]." Florida v. Rabb, 544 U.S. 1028, 125 S.Ct. 2246, 161 L.Ed.2d 1051 (2005).

On remand, the state court—again split—held that in light of *Kyllo* a search occurred:

> The use of the dog, like the use of a thermal imager, allowed law enforcement to use sense-enhancing technology to intrude into the constitutionally-protected area of Rabb's house, which is reasonably considered a search violative of Rabb's expectation of privacy in his retreat. Likewise, it is of no importance that a dog sniff provides limited information regarding only the presence or absence of contraband, because as in *Kyllo,* the quality or quantity of information obtained through the search is not the feared injury. Rather, it is the fact that law enforcement endeavored to obtain the information from inside the house at all, or in this case, the fact that a dog's sense of smell crossed the "firm line" of Fourth Amendment protection at the door of Rabb's house. Because the smell of marijuana had its source in Rabb's house, it was an "intimate detail" of that house, no less so than the ambient temperature inside Kyllo's house. Until the United States Supreme Court indicates otherwise, therefore, we are bound to conclude that the use of a dog sniff to detect contraband inside a house does not pass constitutional muster. The dog sniff at the house in this case constitutes an illegal search.

State v. Rabb, 920 So.2d 1175, 1184 (Fla.App.), review denied 933 So.2d 522 (Fla.), cert. denied 549 U.S. 1052, 127 S.Ct. 665, 166 L.Ed.2d 513 (2006). The result in *Rabb* was approved by the Florida Supreme Court in Jardines v. State, ___ So.3d ___, 2011 WL 1405080 (Fla.2011).

3.   Applying the "Standing" Requirement

Page 114.   Insert the following additional Note after Rakas v. Illinois:

3. **Standing to challenge a "stop."** Could Rakas have challenged the *stop* made by the officers? Almost certainly he could have under Brendlin v. California, 551 U.S. 249, 127 S.Ct. 2400, 168 L.Ed.2d 132 (2007). *Brendlin* pointed out that—as is developed in Chapter 4—whether a passenger in an automobile that is pulled over by a police officer is seized for Fourth Amendment purposes depends on whether a reasonable person in the passenger's position would feel free to decline the officer's requests or otherwise terminate the encounter with the officer. Under this standard, Brendlin—a front seat passenger in a car driven by another—was seized when an officer signaled the driver to pull over:

> A traffic stop necessarily curtails the travel a passenger has chosen just as much as it halts the driver, diverting both from the stream of traffic to the side of the road, and the police activity that normally amounts to intrusion on "privacy and personal security" does not normally (and did not here) distinguish between passenger and driver. An officer who orders one particular car to pull over acts with an implicit claim of right based on fault of some sort, and a sensible person would not expect a police officer to allow people to come and go freely from the physical focal point of an investigation into faulty behavior or wrongdoing.

551 U.S. at 257, 127 S.Ct. at 2407.

CHAPTER 3

ISSUANCE AND EXECUTION OF ARREST AND SEARCH WARRANTS

Page 119. Insert the following in the Editors' Introduction after the material on *The Foundation Requirement—A Neutral and Detached Magistrate*:

Need for a "Local" Magistrate

Traditionally, a judicial officer is sometimes authorized to issue warrants permitting law enforcement action only in the judge's jurisdiction. For example, prior to 2001 Rule 41(a) of the Federal Rules of Criminal Procedure authorized a federal magistrate judge to issue a warrant "for a search of property or for a person within the [magistrate judge's federal] district." A warrant could issue for law enforcement action beyond the judge's district "if the property or person is within the district when the warrant is sought but might move outside the district before the warrant is executed."

The Uniting and Strengthening America by Providing Appropriate Tools Required to Intercept and Obstruct Terrorism (USA PATRIOT) Act of 2001, Public Law 107–56, is discussed in the material supplementing Chapter 6 because of its impact on the federal statutes authorizing electronic surveillance. But in addition it added to Rule 41(a) authorization for issuance of a warrant:

"in an investigation of domestic terrorism or international terrorism * * * by a Federal magistrate judge in any district in which activities related to the terrorism may have occurred, for a search of property or for a person within or outside the district".

A. THE SHOWING OF PROBABLE CAUSE

1. THE INITIAL SHOWING BEFORE THE MAGISTRATE

Page 122. Insert the following before the last paragraph of the Editors' Introduction:

Underlying the *Aguilar–Spinelli* line of cases was undoubtedly the Court's perception that law enforcement's use of informants often themselves involved in criminal activity presents special problems of reliability. These reliability concerns were effectively illustrated by the reported comments of several persons involved in an investigation into questionable reliance by Dallas, Texas narcotics officers upon informants. An informant told a reporter that he had "signed a contract" to work as an officer's "snitch." The contract provided for him to make seven cases against others in return for probation on a pending charge. According to the informant, he withdrew from the arrangement after an incident in which he entered a house to confirm the officer's suspicion that the premises contained drugs. Then:

> I come out of the house and I said, "No, there's no dope in there," the ex-informant said. [The officer] kind of got upset. He goes, "No, that's the wrong answer. Read between the lines." And . . . I said, "OK, there is dope in there," and he goes, "That's better." . . . He never told me plain-out lie; he just said read between the lines.

When the reporter told the officer of the informant's story, the officer gave the reporter a much different version of the incident:

> "That's completely false." * * * "I know exactly which case he's refer-ring to . . . and there were no [search] warrants run on that house. . . . To be quite honest with you, I kind of had my doubts. That's why I didn't run a warrant on that particular location. I was afraid what might be happening is he was doing everything he could do to get his contract completed."

Holley Becka and Todd Bensman, Ex-informant allegedly lied about status, Dallas Morning News, Feb. 8, 2002.

Page 132.   Insert the following additional Note after Illinois v. Gates:

NOTE: "ANTICIPATORY" WARRANTS AND PROBABLE CAUSE

So-called "anticipatory" search warrants were addressed in United States v. Grubbs, 547 U.S. 90, 126 S.Ct. 1494, 164 L.Ed.2d 195 (2006). Defining the warrants at issue, the Court explained:

> An anticipatory warrant is "a warrant based upon an affidavit showing proba-ble cause that at some future time (but not presently) certain evidence of crime will be located at a specified place." 2 W. LaFave, Search and Seizure § 3.7(c), p. 398 (4th ed. 2004). Most anticipatory warrants subject their execution to some condition precedent other than the mere passage of time—a so-called "triggering condition."

547 U.S. at 94, 126 S.Ct. at 1498.

In *Grubbs*, defendant Grubbs ordered a videotape containing child pornography from a Web site actually operated by federal agents. Federal officers arranged for a "controlled delivery" of the videotape to his residence and then—but before the delivery—applied for a warrant for those premises. The affidavit submitted in support of the application provided:

Execution of this search warrant will not occur unless and until the parcel has been received by a person(s) and has been physically taken into the residence * * *. At that time, and not before, this search warrant will be executed * * *.

A warrant issued simply authorizing a search of the residence. It made no reference to the delivery of the videotape as a prerequisite to the search.

The Court of Appeals held that the results of the search should have been suppressed because the warrant itself failed to specify the condition precedent to the search authorization. A unanimous Supreme Court reversed, holding the warrant and search reasonable.

First, the Court rejected the proposition that anticipatory warrants are categorically unconstitutional because they issue on less than the constitutionally-required probable cause:

Because the probable-cause requirement looks to whether evidence will be found *when the search is conducted,* all warrants are, in a sense, "anticipatory." In the typical case where the police seek permission to search a house for an item they believe is already located there, the magistrate's determination that there is probable cause for the search amounts to a prediction that the item will still be there when the warrant is executed. * * * Thus, when an anticipatory warrant is issued, "the fact that the contraband is not presently located at the place described in the warrant is immaterial, so long as there is probable cause to believe that it will be there when the search warrant is executed."

Anticipatory warrants are, therefore, no different in principle from ordinary warrants. They require the magistrate to determine (1) that it is *now probable* that (2) contraband, evidence of a crime, or a fugitive *will be* on the described premises (3) when the warrant is executed. It should be noted, however, that where the anticipatory warrant places a condition (other than the mere passage of time) upon its execution, the first of these determinations goes not merely to what will probably be found *if* the condition is met. (If that were the extent of the probability determination, an anticipatory warrant could be issued for every house in the country, authorizing search and seizure *if* contraband should be delivered—though for any single location there is no likelihood that contraband will be delivered.) Rather, the probability determination for a conditioned anticipatory warrant looks also to the likelihood that the condition will occur, and thus that a proper object of seizure will be on the described premises. In other words, for a conditioned anticipatory warrant to comply with the Fourth Amendment's requirement of probable cause, two prerequisites of probability must be satisfied. It must be true not only that *if* the triggering condition occurs "there is a fair probability that contraband or evidence of a crime will be found in a particular place," but also that there is probable cause to believe the triggering condition *will occur.* The supporting affidavit must provide the magistrate with sufficient information to evaluate both aspects of the probable-cause determination.

547 U.S. at 95–97, 126 S.Ct. at 1499–1500 (emphasis in original).

Second, the Court rejected the reasoning of the court below that the Fourth Amendment's particularity requirement demands that the triggering condition of an anticipatory warrant be set out in the warrant itself. The Fourth Amendment, it held, "specifies only two matters that must be 'particularly describ[ed]' in the warrant: 'the place to be searched' and 'the persons or things to be seized.' " Thus the triggering condition need not be in the warrant itself and of course need not be described particularly. 547 U.S. at 97–98, 126 S.Ct. at 1500–01.

B.   ENTERING THE PREMISES AND OTHER LIMITS ON EXECUTION OF WARRANTS

Page 146.   Insert the following in Editors' Introduction: Announcement Demands and Other Requirements for Execution of Warrants, after the paragraph beginning, "In *Miller* and *Sabbath* * * *":

The matter was addressed in Hudson v. Michigan, 547 U.S. 586, 126 S.Ct. 2159, 165 L.Ed.2d 56 (2006), reprinted later in this supplement.

Page 153.   Add the following new case after Richards v. Wisconsin:

United States v. Banks

Supreme Court of the United States, 2003.
540 U.S. 31, 124 S.Ct. 521, 157 L.Ed.2d 343.

■ JUSTICE SOUTER delivered the opinion of the Court.

Officers executing a warrant to search for cocaine in respondent Banks's apartment knocked and announced their authority. The question is whether their 15–to–20–second wait before a forcible entry satisfied the Fourth Amendment * * *.

I

With information that Banks was selling cocaine at home, North Las Vegas Police Department officers and Federal Bureau of Investigation agents got a warrant to search his two-bedroom apartment. As soon as they arrived there, about 2 o'clock on a Wednesday afternoon, officers posted in front called out "police search warrant" and rapped hard enough on the door to be heard by officers at the back door. There was no indication whether anyone was home, and after waiting for 15 to 20 seconds with no answer, the officers broke open the front door with a battering ram. Banks was in the shower and testified that he heard nothing until the crash of the door, which brought him out dripping to confront the police. The search produced weapons, crack cocaine, and other evidence of drug dealing.

In response to drug and firearms charges, Banks moved to suppress evidence, arguing that the officers executing the search warrant waited an unreasonably short time before forcing entry, and so violated * * * the Fourth Amendment * * *. The District Court denied the motion, and Banks pleaded guilty, reserving his right to challenge the search on appeal.

A divided panel of the Ninth Circuit reversed and ordered suppression of the evidence found. * * * The majority held the 15–to–20–second delay after knocking and announcing to be "[in]sufficient . . . to satisfy the constitutional safeguards."

* * *

We granted certiorari to consider how to go about applying the standard of reasonableness to the length of time police with a warrant must wait before entering without permission after knocking and announcing their intent in a felony case. * * *

II

There has never been a dispute that these officers were obliged to knock and announce their intentions when executing the search warrant, an obligation they concededly honored. Despite this agreement, we start with a word about standards for requiring or dispensing with a knock and announcement, since the same criteria bear on when the officers could legitimately enter after knocking.

The Fourth Amendment says nothing specific about formalities in exercising a warrant's authorization, speaking to the manner of searching as well as to the legitimacy of searching at all simply in terms of the right to be "secure . . . against unreasonable searches and seizures." Although the notion of reasonable execution must therefore be fleshed out, we have done that case by case, largely avoiding categories and protocols for searches. Instead, we have treated reasonableness as a function of the facts of cases so various that no template is likely to produce sounder results than examining the totality of circumstances in a given case; it is too hard to invent categories without giving short shrift to details that turn out to be important in a given instance, and without inflating marginal ones. We have, however, pointed out factual considerations of unusual, albeit not dispositive, significance.

In *Wilson v. Arkansas*, 514 U.S. 927, 115 S.Ct. 1914, 131 L.Ed.2d 976 (1995), we held that the common law knock-and-announce principle is one focus of the reasonableness enquiry; and we subsequently decided that although the standard generally requires the police to announce their intent to search before entering closed premises, the obligation gives way when officers "have a reasonable suspicion that knocking and announcing their presence, under the particular circumstances, would be dangerous or futile, or . . . would inhibit the effective investigation of the crime by, for example, allowing the destruction of evidence," *Richards v. Wisconsin*, 520 U.S. 385, 394, 117 S.Ct. 1416, 137 L.Ed.2d 615 (1997). When a warrant applicant gives reasonable grounds to expect futility or to suspect that one or another such exigency already exists or will arise instantly upon knocking, a magistrate judge is acting within the Constitution to authorize a "no-knock" entry. And even when executing a warrant silent about that, if circumstances support a reasonable suspicion of exigency when the officers arrive at the door, they may go straight in.

Since most people keep their doors locked, entering without knocking will normally do some damage, a circumstance too common to require a heightened justification when a reasonable suspicion of exigency already justifies an unwarned entry. We have accordingly held that police in exigent circumstances may damage premises so far as necessary for a no-knock entrance without demonstrating the suspected risk in any more detail than the law demands for an unannounced intrusion simply by lifting the latch. *United States v. Ramirez,* 523 U.S. 65, 70–71, 118 S.Ct. 992, 140 L.Ed.2d 191 (1998). Either way, it is enough that the officers had a reasonable suspicion of exigent circumstances.[3]

III

Like *Ramirez,* this case turns on the significance of exigency revealed by circumstances known to the officers, for the only substantive difference between the two situations goes to the time at which the officers reasonably anticipated some danger calling for action without delay.[4] Whereas the *Ramirez* Magistrate Judge found in advance that the customary warning would raise an immediate risk that a wanted felon would elude capture or pose a threat to the officers, here the Government claims that a risk of losing evidence arose shortly after knocking and announcing. Although the police concededly arrived at Banks's door without reasonable suspicion of facts justifying a no-knock entry, they argue that announcing their presence started the clock running toward the moment of apprehension that Banks would flush away the easily disposable cocaine, prompted by knowing the police would soon be coming in. While it was held reasonable for the police in *Ramirez* to enter forcibly upon arrival, the Government argues it was equally reasonable for the officers to go in with force here as soon as the danger of disposal had ripened.

[T]he issue comes down to whether it was reasonable to suspect imminent loss of evidence after the 15 to 20 seconds the officers waited prior to forcing their way. Though * * * this call is a close one, we think that after 15 or 20 seconds without a response, police could fairly suspect that cocaine would be gone if they were reticent any longer. Courts of

---

3. The standard for a no-knock entry stated in *Richards* applies on reasonable suspicion of exigency or futility. Because the facts here go to exigency, not futility, we speak of that alone.

4. *Ramirez* and *Richards,* our cases addressing the role of exigency in assessing the reasonableness of a no-knock entry, involved searches by warrant for evidence of a felony, as does this case. In a different context governed by the Fourth Amendment, we have held that the risk of losing evidence of a minor offense is insufficient to make it reasonable to enter a dwelling to make a warrantless arrest. See *Welsh v. Wisconsin,* 466 U.S. 740, 104 S.Ct. 2091, 80 L.Ed.2d 732 (1984). Courts of Appeals have applied *Welsh* to warrantless entries simply to search for evidence, considering the gravity of the offense in determining whether exigent circumstances exist. We intimate nothing here about such warrantless entry cases. Nor do we express a view on the significance of the existence of a warrant in evaluating whether exigency justifies action in knock-and-announce cases when the reason for the search is a minor offense.

Appeals have, indeed, routinely held similar wait times to be reasonable in drug cases with similar facts including easily disposable evidence (and some courts have found even shorter ones to be reasonable enough).

A look at Banks's counterarguments shows why these courts reached sensible results, for each of his reasons for saying that 15 to 20 seconds was too brief rests on a mistake about the relevant enquiry: the fact that he was actually in the shower and did not hear the officers is not to the point, and the same is true of the claim that it might have taken him longer than 20 seconds if he had heard the knock and headed straight for the door. As for the shower, it is enough to say that the facts known to the police are what count in judging reasonable waiting time, and there is no indication that the police knew that Banks was in the shower and thus unaware of an impending search that he would otherwise have tried to frustrate.

And the argument that 15 to 20 seconds was too short for Banks to have come to the door ignores the very risk that justified prompt entry. True, if the officers were to justify their timing here by claiming that Banks's failure to admit them fairly suggested a refusal to let them in, Banks could at least argue that no such suspicion can arise until an occupant has had time to get to the door, a time that will vary with the size of the establishment, perhaps five seconds to open a motel room door, or several minutes to move through a townhouse. In this case, however, the police claim exigent need to enter, and the crucial fact in examining their actions is not time to reach the door but the particular exigency claimed. On the record here, what matters is the opportunity to get rid of cocaine, which a prudent dealer will keep near a commode or kitchen sink. The significant circumstances include the arrival of the police during the day, when anyone inside would probably have been up and around, and the sufficiency of 15 to 20 seconds for getting to the bathroom or the kitchen to start flushing cocaine down the drain. That is, when circumstances are exigent because a pusher may be near the point of putting his drugs beyond reach, it is imminent disposal, not travel time to the entrance, that governs when the police may reasonably enter; since the bathroom and kitchen are usually in the interior of a dwelling, not the front hall, there is no reason generally to peg the travel time to the location of the door, and no reliable basis for giving the proprietor of a mansion a longer wait than the resident of a bungalow, or an apartment like Banks's. And 15 to 20 seconds does not seem an unrealistic guess about the time someone would need to get in a position to rid his quarters of cocaine.

Once the exigency had matured, of course, the officers were not bound to learn anything more or wait any longer before going in, even though their entry entailed some harm to the building. *Ramirez* held that the exigent need of law enforcement trumps a resident's interest in avoiding all property damage, and there is no reason to treat a post-knock exigency differently from the no-knock counterpart in *Ramirez* itself.

IV

Our emphasis on totality analysis necessarily rejects positions taken on each side of this case. *Ramirez,* for example, cannot be read with the breadth the Government espouses, as "reflect[ing] a general principle that the need to damage property in order to effectuate an entry to execute a search warrant should not be part of the analysis of whether the entry itself was reasonable." One point in making an officer knock and announce * * * is to give a person inside the chance to save his door. That is why, in the case with no reason to suspect an immediate risk of frustration or futility in waiting at all, the reasonable wait time may well be longer when police make a forced entry, since they ought to be more certain the occupant has had time to answer the door. It is hard to be more definite than that, without turning the notion of a reasonable time under all the circumstances into a set of sub-rules * * *. Suffice it to say that the need to damage property in the course of getting in is a good reason to require more patience than it would be reasonable to expect if the door were open. Police seeking a stolen piano may be able to spend more time to make sure they really need the battering ram.

* * *

V

* * * Absent exigency, the police must knock and receive an actual refusal or wait out the time necessary to infer one. But in a case like this, where the officers knocked and announced their presence, and forcibly entered after a reasonable suspicion of exigency had ripened, their entry satisfied * * * the Fourth Amendment, even without refusal of admittance.

The judgment of the Court of Appeals is reversed.

So ordered.

Pages 153. Add the following to Note 2 after Richards v. Wisconsin:

In Groh v. Ramirez, 540 U.S. 551, 124 S.Ct. 1284, 157 L.Ed.2d 1068 (2004), addressed in detail in the material supplementing page 161 of the text, the Court observed:

It is true * * * that neither the Fourth Amendment nor Rule 41 of the Federal Rules of Criminal Procedure requires the executing officer to serve the warrant on the owner before commencing the search. Rule 41(f)(3) provides that "[t]he officer executing the warrant must: (A) give a copy of the warrant and a receipt for the property taken to the person from whom, or from whose premises, the property was taken; or (B) leave a copy of the warrant and receipt at the place where the officer took the property." Quite obviously, in some circumstances—a surreptitious search by means of a wiretap, for example, or the search of empty or abandoned premises—it will be impracticable or impru- dent for the officers to show the warrant in advance. Whether it would be unreasonable to refuse a request to furnish the warrant at the outset of the search when, as in this case, an occupant of the premises is present and poses no threat to the officers' safe and effective performance of their mission, is a question that this case does not present.

540 U.S. at 562 n. 5, 124 S.Ct. at 1290 n. 5.

Page 153. Insert the following new Note in the Notes after Richards v. Wisconsin:

2a. The Uniting and Strengthening America by Providing Appropriate Tools Required to Intercept and Obstruct Terrorism (USA PATRIOT) Act of 2001, Public Law 107–56, is discussed in the material supplementing Chapter 6 because of its impact on the federal statutes authorizing electronic surveillance. But it also appeared to have some impact on the execution of ordinary search warrants. 18 U.S.C. § 3103a previously provided that "[i]n addition to [other] grounds for issuing a warrant * * *, a warrant may be issued to search for and seize any property that constitutes evidence of a criminal offense in violation of the laws of the United States." The 2001 legislation and further amendments in 2006 added the following to section 3103a:

(b) Delay.—With respect to the issuance of any warrant or court order under this section, or any other rule of law, to search for and seize any property or material that constitutes evidence of a criminal offense in violation of the laws of the United States, any notice required, or that may be required, to be given may be delayed if—

(1) the court finds reasonable cause to believe that providing immediate notification of the execution of the warrant may have an adverse result (as defined in section 2705, except if the adverse results constitute only of unduly delaying a trial);

(2) the warrant prohibits the seizure of any tangible property, any wire or electronic communication * * *, or * * * any stored wire or electronic information, except where the court finds reasonable necessity for the seizure; and

(3) the warrant provides for the giving of such notice within a reasonable period not to exceed 30 days after the date of its execution, or on a later date certain if the facts of the case justify a longer period of delay.

(c) Extensions of delay.—Any period of delay authorized by this section may be extended by the court for good cause shown, subject to the condition that extensions should only be granted upon an updated showing of the need for further delay and that each additional delay should be limited to periods of 90 days or less, unless the facts of the case justify a longer period of delay.

Under 18 U.S.C. § 2705:

(2) An adverse result * * * is—

(A) endangering the life or physical safety of an individual;

(B) flight from prosecution;

(C) destruction of or tampering with evidence;

(D) intimidation of potential witnesses; or

(E) otherwise seriously jeopardizing an investigation or unduly delaying a trial.

The amended statute authorizes so-called "sneak and peek" search warrants, which permit officers to enter, search, and leave without providing notice to the occupants of the premises. See United States v. Espinoza, 2005 WL 3542519 (E.D.Wash.2005) (warrant authorizing delayed notice must "strictly comply with the requirements of [section 3103a]").

The 2006 amendments added a requirement that federal judges issuing or denying warrants authorizing delayed notice make reports to the Administrative Office of the United States Courts. After 2007, that office is to make annual reports to Congress concerning the use of delayed notice warrants.

Page 158. Insert the following new case after the notes following Richards v. Wisconsin:

Hudson v. Michigan

Supreme Court of the United States, 2006.
547 U.S. 586, 126 S.Ct. 2159, 165 L.Ed.2d 56.

■ JUSTICE SCALIA delivered the opinion of the Court, except as to Part IV.

We decide whether violation of the "knock-and-announce" rule requires the suppression of all evidence found in the search.

I

Police obtained a warrant authorizing a search for drugs and firearms at the home of petitioner Booker Hudson. They discovered both. Large quantities of drugs were found, including cocaine rocks in Hudson's pocket. A loaded gun was lodged between the cushion and armrest of the chair in which he was sitting. Hudson was charged under Michigan law with unlawful drug and firearm possession.

This case is before us only because of the method of entry into the house. When the police arrived to execute the warrant, they announced their presence, but waited only a short time—perhaps "three to five seconds"—before turning the knob of the unlocked front door and entering Hudson's home. Hudson moved to suppress all the inculpatory evidence, arguing that the premature entry violated his Fourth Amendment rights.

The Michigan [courts refused to suppress the evidence, reasoning] that suppression is inappropriate when entry is made pursuant to warrant but without proper " 'knock and announce.' " * * * We granted certiorari.

II

[Wilson v. Arkansas, 514 U.S. 927, 931–932, 115 S.Ct. 1914, 131 L.Ed.2d 976 (1995)] * * * specifically declined to decide whether the exclusionary rule is appropriate for violation of the knock-and-announce requirement. That question is squarely before us now.

III

A

* * *

Suppression of evidence * * * has always been our last resort, not our first impulse. The exclusionary rule generates "substantial social costs," which sometimes include setting the guilty free and the dangerous at large. We have therefore been "cautio[us] against expanding" it, and "have repeatedly emphasized that the rule's 'costly toll' upon truth-seeking and law enforcement objectives presents a high obstacle for those urging [its] application." We have rejected "[i]ndiscriminate application" of the rule, and have held it to be applicable only "where its remedial objectives are thought most efficaciously served,"—that is, "where its deterrence benefits outweigh its 'substantial social costs.' "

* * *

[E]xclusion may not be premised on the mere fact that a constitutional violation was a "but-for" cause of obtaining evidence. Our cases show that but-for causality is only a necessary, not a sufficient, condition for suppression. In this case, of course, the constitutional violation of an illegal manner of entry was not a but-for cause of obtaining the evidence. Whether that preliminary misstep had occurred or not, the police would have executed the warrant they had obtained, and would have discovered the gun and drugs inside the house. But even if the illegal entry here could be characterized as a but-for cause of discovering what was inside, we have "never held that evidence is 'fruit of the poisonous tree' simply because 'it would not have come to light but for the illegal actions of the police.' " Rather, but-for cause, or "causation in the logical sense alone," can be too attenuated to justify exclusion. * * *

Attenuation can occur, of course, when the causal connection is remote. Attenuation also occurs when, even given a direct causal connection, the interest protected by the constitutional guarantee that has been violated would not be served by suppression of the evidence obtained. * * *

[C]ases excluding the fruits of unlawful warrantless searches say nothing about the appropriateness of exclusion to vindicate the interests protected by the knock-and-announce requirement. Until a valid warrant has issued, citizens are entitled to shield "their persons, houses, papers, and effects," U.S. Const., Amdt. 4, from the government's scrutiny. Exclusion of the evidence obtained by a warrantless search vindicates that entitlement. The interests protected by the knock-and-announce requirement are quite different—and do not include the shielding of potential evidence from the government's eyes.

One of those interests is the protection of human life and limb, because an unannounced entry may provoke violence in supposed self-defense by the surprised resident. Another interest is the protection of property. * * *

The knock-and-announce rule gives individuals "the opportunity to comply with the law and to avoid the destruction of property occasioned by a forcible entry." And thirdly, the knock-and-announce rule protects those elements of privacy and dignity that can be destroyed by a sudden entrance. It gives residents the "opportunity to prepare themselves for" the entry of the police. "The brief interlude between announcement and entry with a warrant may be the opportunity that an individual has to pull on clothes or get out of bed." In other words, it assures the opportunity to collect oneself before answering the door.

What the knock-and-announce rule has never protected, however, is one's interest in preventing the government from seeing or taking evidence described in a warrant. Since the interests that were violated in this case have nothing to do with the seizure of the evidence, the exclusionary rule is inapplicable.

B

Quite apart from the requirement of unattenuated causation, the exclusionary rule has never been applied except "where its deterrence benefits outweigh its 'substantial social costs.' " The costs here are considerable. In addition to the grave adverse consequence that exclusion of relevant incriminating evidence always entails (viz., the risk of releasing dangerous criminals into society), imposing that massive remedy for a knock-and-announce violation would generate a constant flood of alleged failures to observe the rule, and claims that any asserted * * * justification for a no-knock entry, had inadequate support. The cost of entering this lottery would be small, but the jackpot enormous: suppression of all evidence, amounting in many cases to a get-out-of-jail-free card. Courts would experience as never before the reality that "[t]he exclusionary rule frequently requires extensive litigation to determine whether particular evidence must be excluded." * * *

Another consequence of the incongruent remedy Hudson proposes would be police officers' refraining from timely entry after knocking and announcing. As we have observed, the amount of time they must wait is necessarily uncertain. If the consequences of running afoul of the rule were so massive, officers would be inclined to wait longer than the law requires—producing preventable violence against officers in some cases, and the destruction of evidence in many others. * * *

Next to these "substantial social costs" we must consider the deterrence benefits, existence of which is a necessary condition for exclusion. To begin with, the value of deterrence depends upon the strength of the incentive to commit the forbidden act. Viewed from this perspective, deterrence of knock-and-announce violations is not worth a lot. Violation of the warrant requirement sometimes produces incriminating evidence that could not otherwise be obtained. But ignoring knock-and-announce can realistically be expected to achieve absolutely nothing except the prevention of destruction of evidence and the avoidance of life-threatening resistance by occupants of the premises-dangers which, if there is even "reasonable suspicion" of their existence, suspend the knock-and-announce requirement anyway. Massive deterrence is hardly required.

It seems to us not even true, as Hudson contends, that without suppression there will be no deterrence of knock-and-announce violations at all. * * *

We cannot assume that exclusion in this context is necessary deterrence simply because we found that it was necessary deterrence in different contexts and long ago. That would be forcing the public today to pay for the sins and inadequacies of a legal regime that existed almost half a century ago. Dollree Mapp could not turn to 42 U.S.C. § 1983 for meaningful relief; Monroe v. Pape, 365 U.S. 167, 81 S.Ct. 473, 5 L.Ed.2d 492 (1961), which began the slow but steady expansion of that remedy, was decided the same Term as [Mapp v. Ohio, 367 U.S. 643, 81 S.Ct. 1684, 6 L.Ed.2d 1081 (1961)]. It would be another 17 years before the § 1983 remedy was extended to reach the deep pocket of municipalities. Citizens whose Fourth Amendment rights were violated by federal officers could not bring suit until 10 years after *Mapp,* with this Court's decision in Bivens v. Six Unknown Fed. Narcotics Agents, 403 U.S. 388, 91 S.Ct. 1999, 29 L.Ed.2d 619 (1971).

* * *

Another development over the past half-century that deters civil-rights violations is the increasing professionalism of police forces, including a new emphasis on internal police discipline. * * * [W]e now have increasing evidence that police forces across the United States take the constitutional rights of citizens seriously. There have been "wide-ranging reforms in the education, training, and supervision of police officers." S. Walker, Taming the System: The Control of Discretion in Criminal Justice 1950–1990, p. 51 (1993). Numerous sources are now available to teach officers and their supervisors what is required of them under this Court's cases, how to respect constitutional guarantees in various situations, and how to craft an effective regime for internal discipline. Failure to teach and enforce constitutional requirements exposes municipalities to financial liability. Moreover, modern police forces are staffed with professionals; it is not credible to assert that internal discipline, which can limit successful careers, will not have a deterrent effect. There is also evidence that the increasing use of various forms of citizen review can enhance police accountability.

In sum, the social costs of applying the exclusionary rule to knock-and-announce violations are considerable; the incentive to such violations is minimal to begin with, and the extant deterrences against them are substantial—incomparably greater than the factors deterring warrantless entries when *Mapp* was decided. Resort to the massive remedy of suppressing evidence of guilt is unjustified.

* * *

For the foregoing reasons we affirm the judgment of the Michigan Court of Appeals.

It is so ordered.

■ JUSTICE KENNEDY, concurring in part and concurring in the judgment.

* * *

Today's decision does not address any demonstrated pattern of knock-and-announce violations. If a widespread pattern of violations were shown, and particularly if those violations were committed against persons who lacked the means or voice to mount an effective protest, there would be reason for grave concern. * * *

In this case the relevant evidence was discovered not because of a failure to knock-and-announce, but because of a subsequent search pursuant to a lawful warrant. The Court in my view is correct to hold that suppression was not required. * * * [T]he Court's holding is fully supported by Parts I through III of its opinion. I accordingly join those Parts and concur in the judgment.

■ JUSTICE BREYER, with whom JUSTICE STEVENS, JUSTICE SOUTER, and JUSTICE GINSBURG join, dissenting.

* * *

[T]he driving legal purpose underlying the exclusionary rule, namely, the deterrence of unlawful government behavior, argues strongly for suppression. * * * Indeed, this Court in *Mapp* held that the exclusionary rule applies to the States in large part due to its belief that alternative state mechanisms for enforcing the Fourth Amendment's guarantees had proved "worthless and futile."

Why is application of the exclusionary rule any the less necessary here? Without such a rule, as in *Mapp,* police know that they can ignore the Constitution's requirements without risking suppression of evidence discovered after an unreasonable entry. As in *Mapp,* some government officers will find it easier, or believe it less risky, to proceed with what they consider a necessary search immediately and without the requisite constitutional (say, warrant or knock-and-announce) compliance.

Of course, the State or the Federal Government may provide alternative remedies for knock-and-announce violations. But that circumstance was true of *Mapp* as well. What reason is there to believe that those remedies (such as private damages actions under 42 U.S.C. § 1983), which the Court found inadequate in *Mapp,* can adequately deter unconstitutional police behavior here?

The cases reporting knock-and-announce violations are legion. Indeed, these cases of reported violations seem sufficiently frequent and serious as to indicate "a widespread pattern." Yet the majority, like Michigan and the United States, has failed to cite a single reported case in which a plaintiff has collected more than nominal damages solely as a result of a knock-and-announce violation. * * *

* * * The majority's "substantial social costs" argument is an argument against the Fourth Amendment's exclusionary principle itself. And it is an argument that this Court, until now, has consistently rejected.

III

* * *

A

The majority * * * argues that "the constitutional violation of an illegal manner of entry was not a but-for cause of obtaining the evidence." But taking causation as it is commonly understood in the law, I do not see how that can be so. See W. Keeton, D. Dobbs, R. Keeton, & D. Owen, Prosser and Keeton on Law of Torts 266 (5th ed.1984). Although the police might have entered Hudson's home lawfully, they did not in fact do so. Their unlawful behavior inseparably characterizes their actual entry; that entry was a necessary condition of their presence in Hudson's home; and their presence in Hudson's home was a necessary condition of their finding and seizing the evidence. At the same time, their discovery of evidence in Hudson's home was a readily foreseeable consequence of their entry and their unlawful presence within the home.

Moreover, separating the "manner of entry" from the related search slices the violation too finely. * * * [W]e have described a failure to comply with the knock-and-announce rule, not as an independently unlawful event, but as a factor that renders the search "constitutionally defective."

The Court nonetheless accepts Michigan's argument that the requisite but-for-causation is not satisfied in this case because, whether or not the constitutional violation occurred (what the Court refers to as a "preliminary misstep"), "the police would have executed the warrant they had obtained, and would have discovered the gun and drugs inside the house." As support for this proposition, Michigan rests on this Court's inevitable discovery cases.

This claim, however, misunderstands the inevitable discovery doctrine. Justice Holmes in [Silverthorne Lumber Co. v. United States, 251 U.S. 385, 40 S.Ct. 182, 64 L.Ed. 319 (1920)], in discussing an "independent source" exception, set forth the principles underlying the inevitable discovery rule. That rule does not refer to discovery that would have taken place if the police behavior in question had (contrary to fact) been lawful. The doctrine does not treat as critical what hypothetically could have happened had the police acted lawfully in the first place. Rather, "independent" or "inevitable" discovery refers to discovery that did occur or that would have occurred (1) despite (not simply in the absence of) the unlawful behavior and (2) independently of that unlawful behavior. The government cannot, for example, avoid suppression of evidence seized without a warrant (or pursuant to a defective warrant) simply by showing that it could have obtained a valid warrant had it sought one. Instead, it must show that the same evidence "inevitably would have been discovered by lawful means." "What a man could do is not at all the same as what he would do." Austin, Ifs And Cans, 42 Proceedings of the British Academy 109, 111–112 (1956).

* * *

Of course, had the police entered the house lawfully, they would have found the gun and drugs. But that fact is beside the point. The question is not what police might have done had they not behaved unlawfully. The question is what they did do. Was there set in motion an independent chain of events that would have inevitably led to the discovery and seizure of the evidence despite, and independent of, that behavior? The answer here is "no."

* * *

C

The majority * * * says that evidence should not be suppressed once the causal connection between unlawful behavior and discovery of the evidence becomes too "attenuated." But the majority then makes clear that it is not using the word "attenuated" to mean what this Court's precedents have typically used that word to mean, namely, that the discovery of the evidence has come about long after the unlawful behavior took place or in an independent way, i.e., through " 'means sufficiently distinguishable to be purged of the primary taint.' " Wong Sun v. United States, 371 U.S. 471, 487–488, 83 S.Ct. 407, 9 L.Ed.2d 441 (1963).

Rather, the majority gives the word "attenuation" a new meaning * * *. "Attenuation," it says, "also occurs when, even given a direct causal connection, the interest protected by the constitutional guarantee that has been violated would not be served by suppression of the evidence obtained." The interests the knock-and-announce rule seeks to protect, the Court adds, are "human life" (at stake when a householder is "surprised"), "property" (such as the front door), and "those elements of privacy and dignity that can be destroyed by a sudden entrance," namely, "the opportunity to collect oneself before answering the door." Since none of those interests led to the discovery of the evidence seized here, there is no reason to suppress it.

* * *

[But] whether the interests underlying the knock-and-announce rule are implicated in any given case is, in a sense, beside the point. * * * [F]ailure to comply with the knock-and-announce rule renders the related search unlawful. And where a search is unlawful, the law insists upon suppression of the evidence consequently discovered, even if that evidence or its possession has little or nothing to do with the reasons underlying the unconstitutionality of a search. * * *

IV

There is perhaps one additional argument implicit in the majority's approach. The majority says * * * that the "cost" to a defendant of "entering this lottery," i.e., of claiming a "knock-and-announce" violation, "would be small, but the jackpot enormous"—namely, a potential "get-out-of-jail-free card." It adds that the "social costs" of applying the exclusionary rule here are not worth the deterrence benefits. * * * [O]ne is left with a simple unvarnished conclusion, namely, that in this kind of case, a knock-and-announce case, "[r]esort to the massive remedy of suppressing evidence of guilt is unjustified." Why is that judicial judgment, taken on its own, inappropriate? Could it not be argued that the knock-and-announce rule, a subsidiary Fourth Amendment rule, is simply not important enough to warrant a suppression remedy? Could the majority not simply claim that the suppression game is not worth the candle?

The answer, I believe, is "no." That "no" reflects history, a history that shows the knock-and-announce rule is important. That "no" reflects precedent, precedent that shows there is no pre-existing legal category of exceptions to the exclusionary rule into which the knock-and-announce cases might fit. That "no" reflects empirical fact, experience that provides confirmation of what common sense suggests: without suppression there is little to deter knock-and-announce violations.

* * *

[W]ith respect, I dissent.

C. Particularity Demanded of Warrants and Related Limits on Execution of Warrants

Page 161. Insert the following in the Editors' Introduction at the end of the material on "Things to be Seized":

The mechanics of complying with the precision requirement were addressed by the Supreme Court in Groh v. Ramirez, 540 U.S. 551, 124 S.Ct. 1284, 157 L.Ed.2d 1068 (2004).

A federal officer prepared an application for a search warrant for the Ramirez residence. In that application he described in detail various weapons, explosive devices, and receipts pertaining to the purchase or manufacture of such weapons and devices for which the officer sought authority to search. The officer also used a form to prepare a warrant. In that portion of the form calling for a description of the person or property to be seized, the officer mistakenly inserted a description of the premises to be searched. The warrant form did not purport to incorporate the application. Then the officer presented the application, an affidavit, and the warrant form to a Magistrate Judge who signed the warrant form.

Federal officers executed the warrant but found no contraband. Members of the Ramirez family then brought a civil action for damages, claiming that the search violated their Fourth Amendment rights. The District Court entered summary judgment for the defendants but on appeal the Court of Appeals held that the plaintiffs were entitled to proceed to trial.

The Supreme Court affirmed. Since the warrant contained no description of any things to be searched for, the majority noted, "[t]he warrant was plainly invalid." It explained:

> This warrant did not simply omit a few items from a list of many to be seized, or misdescribe a few of several items. Nor did it make what fairly could be characterized as a mere technical mistake or typographical error. Rather, * * * the warrant did not describe the items to be seized *at all*. In this respect the warrant was so obviously deficient that we must regard the search as "warrantless" within the meaning of our case law.

540 U.S. at 558, 124 S.Ct. at 1290. It rejected the argument that the search was reasonable despite the deficiency in the warrant because in actual fact the search made did not exceed what would have been permissible had the language in the application been placed in the warrant:

> [U]nless the particular items described in the affidavit are also set forth in the warrant itself (or at least incorporated by reference, and the affidavit present at the search), there can be no written assurance that the Magistrate actually found probable cause to search for, and to seize, every item mentioned in the affidavit. In this case, for example, it is at least theoretically possible that the Magistrate was satisfied that the search for weapons and explosives was justified by the showing in the affidavit, but not convinced that any evidentiary basis existed for rummaging through respondents' files and papers for receipts pertaining to the purchase or manufacture of such items. Or, conceivably, the Magistrate might have believed that some of the weapons mentioned in the affidavit could have been lawfully possessed and therefore should not be seized. The mere fact that the Magistrate issued a warrant does not necessarily establish that he agreed that the scope of the search should be as broad as the affiant's request. * * *

We have long held, moreover, that the purpose of the particularity requirement is not limited to the prevention of general searches. A particular warrant also "assures the individual whose property is searched or seized of the lawful authority of the executing officer, his need to search, and the limits of his power to search." *United States v. Chadwick,* 433 U.S. 1, 9, 97 S.Ct. 2476, 53 L.Ed.2d 538 (1977) * * *.

540 U.S. at 560, 124 S.Ct. at 1291–92.

The defendant contended that he orally described the objects of the search to persons present when the officers arrived and to the absent Ramirez by telephone. Thus the goals of the particularity requirement were met and the search was reasonable. The Court did not reach whether such oral notice might make the search reasonable. Since the specific issue in the case was whether summary judgment should have been granted and the plaintiffs contended that the defendant orally stated only that he was seeking "an explosive device in a box," the Court had to assume the plaintiffs' version was correct. 540 U.S. at 562–63, 124 S.Ct. at 1293.

Page 169.   Add the following to Note 2 following Garrison:

Summers was applied in Muehler v. Mena, 544 U.S. 93, 125 S.Ct. 1465, 161 L.Ed.2d 299 (2005), arising out of an investigation of a gang-related shooting. Officers obtained a search warrant for the residence of one gang member for deadly weapons and evidence of gang membership. The suspect was believed armed and dangerous. Executing the warrant at 7:00 a.m., officers found four persons in the premises including Iris Mena. Mena was asleep in her bed when the officers entered. She was handcuffed at gunpoint and taken to a converted garage where she and the others were kept in the handcuffs and guarded by one or two officers while the search was made. This took from 2 to 3 hours. During that time, an Immigration and Naturalization Service officer questioned her and requested her immigration documentation. Mena later, invoking 42 U.S.S. § 1983, sued the officers who conducted the search on the ground that they had used excessive force in detaining her and detained her longer than was reasonable. She obtained a jury verdict and judgment and this was affirmed on appeal to the court of appeals. The Supreme Court held that the court of appeals erred in upholding the judgment on the grounds that it specified.

The Court first held that the detention and initial handcuffing were reasonable under Fourth Amendment law:

Mena's detention was, under *Summers,* plainly permissible. An officer's authority to detain incident to a search is categorical; it does not depend on the "quantum of proof justifying detention or the extent of the intrusion to be imposed by the seizure." Thus, Mena's detention for the duration of the search was reasonable under *Summers* because a warrant existed to search 1363 Patricia Avenue and she was an occupant of that address at the time of the search.

Inherent in *Summers'* authorization to detain an occupant of the place to be searched is the authority to use reasonable force to effectuate the detention. Indeed, *Summers* itself stressed that the risk of harm to officers and occupants is minimized "if the officers routinely exercise unquestioned command of the situation."

The officers' use of force in the form of handcuffs to effectuate Mena's detention in the garage, as well as the detention of the three other occupants, was reasonable because the governmental interests outweigh the marginal intrusion. The imposition of correctly applied handcuffs on Mena, who was already being lawfully detained during a search of the house, was undoubtedly a separate intrusion in addition to detention in the converted garage. The detention was thus more intrusive than that which we upheld in *Summers*.

But this was no ordinary search. The governmental interests in not only detaining, but using handcuffs, are at their maximum when, as here, a warrant authorizes a search for weapons and a wanted gang member resides on the premises. In such inherently dangerous situations, the use of handcuffs minimizes the risk of harm to both officers and occupants. Though this safety risk inherent in executing a search warrant for weapons was sufficient to justify the use of handcuffs, the need to detain multiple occupants made the use of handcuffs all the more reasonable.

544 U.S. at 98–100, 125 S.Ct. at 1470–71. Nor could the court of appeals have held that the jury verdict was supportable on the ground that the duration of the use of the handcuffs made the detention unreasonable:

The duration of a detention can, of course, affect the balance of interests * * *. However, the 2 to 3 hour detention in handcuffs in this case does not outweigh the government's continuing safety interests. * * * [T]his case involved the detention of four detainees by two officers during a search of a gang house for dangerous weapons. We conclude that the detention of Mena in handcuffs during the search was reasonable.

544 U.S. at 100, 125 S.Ct. at 1471.

The court of appeals also erred in concluding that the questioning of Mena about her immigration status violated the Fourth Amendment:

This holding, it appears, was premised on the assumption that the officers were required to have independent reasonable suspicion in order to question Mena concerning her immigration status because the questioning constituted a discrete Fourth Amendment event. But the premise is faulty. We have "held repeatedly that mere police questioning does not constitute a seizure." *Florida v. Bostick,* 501 U.S. 429, 434, 111 S.Ct. 2382, 115 L.Ed.2d 389 (1991) "[E]ven when officers have no basis for suspecting a particular individual, they may generally ask questions of that individual; ask to examine the individual's identification; and request consent to search his or her luggage." *Bostick, supra,* at 434 435, 111 S.Ct. 2382 (citations omitted). As the Court of Appeals did not hold that the detention was prolonged by the questioning, there was no additional seizure within the meaning of the Fourth Amendment. Hence, the officers did not need reasonable suspicion to ask Mena for her name, date and place of birth, or immigration status.

544 U.S. at 100–01, 125 S.Ct. at 1471.

Mena argued further that she was extended beyond the time the officers completed the tasks incident to the search. The court of appeals had not addressed this contention, and the Supreme Court also declined to reach it.

Actions during execution of a search warrant were also at issue in Los Angeles County, California v. Rettele, 550 U.S. 609, 127 S.Ct. 1989, 167 L.Ed.2d 974 (2007).

Sheriff's deputies investigating a fraud and identity-theft ring had four African–American suspects, one of whom had registered a handgun. The deputies also had information that the suspects resided in a specific home and obtained a warrant authorizing a search of that residence. Unknown to the deputies, the residence had been sold. At 7:15 a.m., the deputies knocked on the door. When one Chase Hall answered, the deputies ordered him to lie face down on the ground. The deputies entered a bedroom and found Judy Sadler and Max Rettle in bed. Despite protests by Sadler and Rettle that they were not clothed, the deputies required them to get out of the bed. Several minutes later, Sadler and Rettle were permitted to dress. Hall, Sadler and Rettle were Caucasian.

The Supreme Court held that the deputies acted constitutionally:

> In executing a search warrant officers may take reasonable action to secure the premises and to ensure their own safety and the efficacy of the search. The test of reasonableness under the Fourth Amendment is an objective one. Unreasonable actions include the use of excessive force or restraints that cause unnecessary pain or are imposed for a prolonged and unnecessary period of time.

> The orders by the police to the occupants, in the context of this lawful search, were permissible, and perhaps necessary, to protect the safety of the deputies. Blankets and bedding can conceal a weapon, and one of the suspects was known to own a firearm, factors which underscore this point. The Constitution does not require an officer to ignore the possibility that an armed suspect may sleep with a weapon within reach.

> The deputies needed a moment to secure the room and ensure that other persons were not close by or did not present a danger. Deputies were not required to turn their backs to allow Rettele and Sadler to retrieve clothing or to cover themselves with the sheets. Rather, "[t]he risk of harm to both the police and the occupants is minimized if the officers routinely exercise unquestioned command of the situation."

> This is not to say, of course, that the deputies were free to force Rettele and Sadler to remain motionless and standing for any longer than necessary. * * * [But] there is no allegation that the deputies prevented Sadler and Rettele from dressing longer than necessary to protect their safety. Sadler was unclothed for no more than two minutes, and Rettele for only slightly more time than that.

550 U.S. at 613, 127 S.Ct. at 1993.

CHAPTER 4

DETENTIONS OF PERSONS AND RELATED SEARCHES

A. DETERMINING WHETHER A PERSON IS DETAINED OR SEIZED

Page 179.   Add the following new Note after Hodari D.:

NOTE

Law enforcement conduct that under *Hodari D.* does not constitute a seizure may become a seizure by means other than submission or capture in the ordinary sense of the latter term. In Scott v. Harris, 550 U.S. 372, 381, 127 S.Ct. 1769, 1776, 167 L.Ed.2d 686 (2007), for example, the parties agreed (and the Court apparently accepted) that an officer's decision to terminate a car chase by ramming the officer's vehicle into the suspect's vehicle constituted a seizure.

Law enforcement pursuit that does not constitute a seizure may be subject to other federal constitutional limits. See text at page 67, note 8.

Page 179.   Add the following to Note: Seizure of a Stationary Suspect:

The Court returned to bus encounters in United States v. Drayton, 536 U.S. 194, 122 S.Ct. 2105, 153 L.Ed.2d 242 (2002). It first set out the facts:

> On February 4, 1999, respondents Christopher Drayton and Clifton Brown, Jr., were traveling on a Greyhound bus en route from Ft. Lauderdale, Florida, to Detroit, Michigan. The bus made a scheduled stop in Tallahassee, Florida. The passengers were required to disembark so the bus could be refueled and cleaned. As the passengers reboarded, the driver checked their tickets and then left to complete paperwork inside the terminal. As he left, the driver allowed three members of the Tallahassee Police Department to board the bus as part of a routine drug and weapons interdiction effort. The officers were dressed in plain clothes and carried concealed weapons and visible badges.

> Once onboard Officer Hoover knelt on the driver's seat and faced the rear of the bus. He could observe the passengers and ensure the safety of the two other officers without blocking the aisle or otherwise obstructing the bus exit. Officers Lang and Blackburn went to the rear of the bus. Blackburn remained stationed there, facing forward. Lang worked his way toward the front of the bus, speaking with individual passengers as he went. He asked the passengers about their travel plans and sought to match passengers with luggage in the overhead racks. To avoid blocking the aisle, Lang stood next to or just behind each passenger with whom he spoke.

According to Lang's testimony, passengers who declined to cooperate with him or who chose to exit the bus at any time would have been allowed to do so without argument. * * * Lang sometimes informed passengers of their right to refuse to cooperate. On the day in question, however, he did not.

Respondents were seated next to each other on the bus. Drayton was in the aisle seat, Brown in the seat next to the window. Lang approached respondents from the rear and leaned over Drayton's shoulder. He held up his badge long enough for respondents to identify him as a police officer. With his face 12–to–18 inches away from Drayton's, Lang spoke in a voice just loud enough for respondents to hear:

> "I'm Investigator Lang with the Tallahassee Police Department. We're conducting bus interdiction [sic], attempting to deter drugs and illegal weapons being transported on the bus. Do you have any bags on the bus?"

Both respondents pointed to a single green bag in the overhead luggage rack. Lang asked, "Do you mind if I check it?," and Brown responded, "Go ahead." Lang handed the bag to Officer Blackburn to check. The bag contained no contraband.

Officer Lang noticed that both respondents were wearing heavy jackets and baggy pants despite the warm weather. In Lang's experience drug traffickers often use baggy clothing to conceal weapons or narcotics. The officer thus asked Brown if he had any weapons or drugs in his possession. And he asked Brown: "Do you mind if I check your person?" Brown answered, "Sure," and cooperated by leaning up in his seat, pulling a cell phone out of his pocket, and opening up his jacket. Lang reached across Drayton and patted down Brown's jacket and pockets, including his waist area, sides, and upper thighs. In both thigh areas, Lang detected hard objects similar to drug packages detected on other occasions. Lang arrested and handcuffed Brown. Officer Hoover escorted Brown from the bus.

Lang then asked Drayton, "Mind if I check you?" Drayton responded by lifting his hands about eight inches from his legs. Lang conducted a pat-down of Drayton's thighs and detected hard objects similar to those found on Brown. He arrested Drayton and escorted him from the bus. A further search revealed that respondents had duct-taped plastic bundles of powder cocaine between several pairs of their boxer shorts. Brown possessed three bundles containing 483 grams of cocaine. Drayton possessed two bundles containing 295 grams of cocaine.

In their prosecution for federal drug offenses, Drayton and Brown moved to suppress the cocaine. The trial court denied the motion but on appeal the Court of Appeals held the motion should have been granted. The Supreme Court reversed:

> [I]t appears that the Court of Appeals would suppress any evidence obtained during suspicionless drug interdiction efforts aboard buses in the absence of a warning that passengers may refuse to cooperate. The Court of Appeals erred in adopting this approach.

> Applying the *Bostick* framework to the facts of this particular case, we conclude that the police did not seize respondents when they boarded the bus and began questioning passengers. The officers gave the passengers no reason to believe that they were required to answer the officers' questions. When Officer Lang approached respondents, he did not brandish a weapon or make

any intimidating movements. He left the aisle free so that respondents could exit. He spoke to passengers one by one and in a polite, quiet voice. Nothing he said would suggest to a reasonable person that he or she was barred from leaving the bus or otherwise terminating the encounter.

There were ample grounds for the District Court to conclude that "everything that took place between Officer Lang and [respondents] suggests that it was cooperative" and that there "was nothing coercive [or] confrontational" about the encounter. There was no application of force, no intimidating movement, no overwhelming show of force, no brandishing of weapons, no blocking of exits, no threat, no command, not even an authoritative tone of voice. It is beyond question that had this encounter occurred on the street, it would be constitutional. The fact that an encounter takes place on a bus does not on its own transform standard police questioning of citizens into an illegal seizure. Indeed, because many fellow passengers are present to witness officers' conduct, a reasonable person may feel even more secure in his or her decision not to cooperate with police on a bus than in other circumstances.

Respondents make much of the fact that Officer Lang displayed his badge. [But wearing or displaying of a badge does not] * * * constitute a seizure. And while neither Lang nor his colleagues were in uniform or visibly armed, those factors should have little weight in the analysis. Officers are often required to wear uniforms and in many circumstances this is cause for assurance, not discomfort. Much the same can be said for wearing sidearms. That most law enforcement officers are armed is a fact well known to the public. The presence of a holstered firearm thus is unlikely to contribute to the coerciveness of the encounter absent active brandishing of the weapon.

Officer Hoover's position at the front of the bus also does not tip the scale in respondents' favor. Hoover did nothing to intimidate passengers, and he said nothing to suggest that people could not exit and indeed he left the aisle clear. * * *

536 U.S. at 205–06, 122 S.Ct. at 2111–12, 153 L.Ed.2d at 253–54. Even after Brown was arrested, Drayton's status did not change:

The arrest of one person does not mean that everyone around him has been seized by police. If anything, Brown's arrest should have put Drayton on notice of the consequences of continuing the encounter by answering the officers' questions. Even after arresting Brown, Lang addressed Drayton in a polite manner and provided him with no indication that he was required to answer Lang's questions.

536 U.S. at 206, 122 S.Ct. at 2113, 153 L.Ed.2d at 254.

Having concluded that neither Brown nor Drayton were seized, the majority turned to whether their consents were voluntary and hence effective:

In circumstances such as these, where the question of voluntariness pervades both the search and seizure inquiries, the respective analyses turn on very similar facts. And * * * respondents' consent to the search of their luggage and their persons was voluntary. Nothing Officer Lang said indicated a command to consent to the search. Rather, when respondents informed Lang that they had a bag on the bus, he asked for their permission to check it. And when Lang requested to search Brown and Drayton's persons, he asked first if they objected, thus indicating to a reasonable person that he or she was free to refuse. Even after arresting Brown, Lang provided Drayton with no indication that he was required to consent to a search. To the contrary, Lang asked for Drayton's permission to search him ("Mind if I check you?"), and Drayton agreed.

The Court has rejected in specific terms the suggestion that police officers must always inform citizens of their right to refuse when seeking permission to conduct a warrantless consent search. Nor do this Court's decisions suggest that even though there are no *per se* rules, a presumption of invalidity attaches if a citizen consented without explicit notification that he or she was free to refuse to cooperate. Instead, the Court has repeated that the totality of the circumstances must control, without giving extra weight to the absence of this type of warning. Although Officer Lang did not inform respondents of their right to refuse the search, he did request permission to search, and the totality of the circumstances indicates that their consent was voluntary, so the searches were reasonable.

In a society based on law, the concept of agreement and consent should be given a weight and dignity of its own. Police officers act in full accord with the law when they ask citizens for consent. It reinforces the rule of law for the citizen to advise the police of his or her wishes and for the police to act in reliance on that understanding. When this exchange takes place, it dispels inferences of coercion.

536 U.S. at 206–07, 122 S.Ct. at 2113, 153 L.Ed.2d at 254–55.

Three members of the Court concluded that Drayton and Brown had been seized:

[T]he driver with the tickets entitling the passengers to travel had yielded his custody of the bus and its seated travelers to three police officers, whose authority apparently superseded the driver's own. The officers took control of the entire passenger compartment, one stationed at the door keeping surveillance of all the occupants, the others working forward from the back. With one officer right behind him and the other one forward, a third officer accosted each passenger at quarters extremely close and so cramped that as many as half the passengers could not even have stood to face the speaker. None was asked whether he was willing to converse with the police or to take part in the enquiry. Instead the officer said the police were "conducting bus interdiction," in the course of which they "would like ... cooperation." The reasonable inference was that the "interdiction" was not a consensual exercise, but one the police would carry out whatever the circumstances; that they would prefer "cooperation" but would not let the lack of it stand in their way. There was no contrary indication that day, since no passenger had refused the cooperation requested, and there was no reason for any passenger to believe that the driver would return and the trip resume until the police were satisfied. The scene was set and an atmosphere of obligatory participation was established by this introduction. Later requests to search prefaced with "Do you mind ..." would naturally have been understood in the terms with which the encounter began.

It is very hard to imagine that either Brown or Drayton would have believed that he stood to lose nothing if he refused to cooperate with the police, or that he had any free choice to ignore the police altogether. No reasonable passenger could have believed that, only an uncomprehending one.

536 U.S. at 211–12, 122 S.Ct. at 2116, 153 L.Ed.2d at 258 (Souter, J., dissenting). The dissenters would not have reached the question of the voluntariness of the consent.

Bostick's analysis applies, the Court made clear in Brendlin v. California, 551 U.S. 249, 127 S.Ct. 2400, 168 L.Ed.2d 132 (2007), "[w]hen the actions of the police do not show an unambiguous intent to restrain or when an individual's submission to a show of governmental authority takes the form of passive acquiescence * * *." In *Brendlin*, a front seat passenger in an automobile was held to have been seized when the driver pulled over in response to a police officer's signal. The officer's show of force would be considered by a reasonable passenger as directed to all occupants of the vehicle, the Court explained, and once the vehicle came to a stop Brendlin submitted by staying inside.

A person in a vehicle that was required to stop to accommodate an officer's stop of another vehicle would not be seized, the Court commented, because that person "would not perceive a show of authority as directed at him or his car." It also added:

> California claims that, under today's rule, "all taxi cab and bus passengers would be 'seized' under the Fourth Amendment when the cab or bus driver is pulled over by the police for running a red light." But the relationship between driver and passenger is not the same in a common carrier as it is in a private vehicle, and the expectations of police officers and passengers differ accordingly. In those cases, as here, the crucial question would be whether a reasonable person in the passenger's position would feel free to take steps to terminate the encounter.

551 U.S. at 262 n. 6, 127 S.Ct. at 2410 n. 6.

B. ARRESTS AND ASSOCIATED SEARCHES

Page 181. Insert the following in the Editors' Introduction after the unit, *Warrant Requirements—Arrests*:

Warrant Requirements—State Law Demands and Fourth Amendment Reasonableness. State law sometimes requires arrest warrants for certain arrests. The relationship between these state law demands and Fourth Amendment reasonableness was at issue in Virginia v. Moore, 553 U.S. 164, 128 S.Ct. 1598, 170 L.Ed.2d 559 (2008).

Moore was arrested by Virginia officers for the misdemeanor of driving on a suspended license. Virginia law required the officers to issue a citation for this offense rather than make a custodial arrest, unless the perpetrator failed or refused to discontinue the violation of the law. In a search incident to that arrest, the officers found cocaine and cash. The Virginia courts ultimately held that because state law required a warrant for the arrest, the search was unreasonable as a matter of Fourth Amendment law and the cocaine and cash had to be suppressed. The Supreme Court reversed.

First, the majority concluded that despite the violation of state law, the arrest was reasonable in Fourth Amendment terms. Virginia is entitled to prohibit warrantless arrests permitted by Fourth Amendment law, but also to enforce that prohibition by means other than excluding evidence obtained by means of the prohibited arrests. Further, incorporating state-law arrest limits into Fourth Amendment law would produce a "vague and unpredictable" federal constitutional regime, because federal constitutional law would also require application of sometimes-problematic state law. Finally, reading reasonableness to require compliance with state law would also mean that Fourth Amendment protections would arbitrarily and inappropriately vary from place to place.

Second, the *Moore* majority rejected Moore's contention that even if his arrest was not constitutionally unreasonable, the search incident to the arrest was constitutionally invalid. An incidental search is constitutionally permissible if the arrest is constitutional. The arrest need not be "lawful" in the sense that it must also reflect compliance with state law. 553 U.S. at 176–78, 128 S.Ct. at 1607–08.

Page 184. Insert the following in the Editors' Introduction at the end of the unit, *Warrant Requirements—Search for Person to be Arrested*:

Payton and the case law following it were reaffirmed in Kirk v. Louisiana, 536 U.S. 635, 122 S.Ct. 2458, 153 L.Ed.2d 599 (2002) (per curiam). Officers conducting surveillance of Kirk's apartment observed several transactions in which persons approached the apartment door, Kirk came to the door, the person gave Kirk money and he gave the person "a small object" in return. The officers stopped the fourth person after left the apartment and apparently confirmed their suspicions that he had purchased drugs from Kirk at the apartment. The Court explained:

> The officers later testified that "[b]ecause the stop took place within a block of the apartment, [they] feared that evidence would be destroyed and ordered that the apartment be entered." Thus, "[t]hey immediately knocked on the door of the apartment, arrested the defendant, searched him thereto and discovered the cocaine and the money." Although the officers sought and obtained a search warrant while they detained petitioner in his home, they only obtained this warrant after they had entered his home, arrested him, frisked him, found a drug vial in his underwear, and observed contraband in plain view in the apartment.

Kirk unsuccessfully moved to suppress the evidence obtained by the police as the inadmissible result of an impermissible warrantless entry, arrest, and search. The state appellate court declined to address whether the officers had exigent circumstances sufficient to justify a warrantless entry of the apartment, because "the evidence required to prove that the defendant possessed cocaine with the intent to distribute, namely the cocaine and the money, was not found in the apartment, but on his person." Because "[t]he officers had probable cause to arrest and properly searched the defendant incident thereto ... [, t]he trial court properly denied the motion to suppress." The Supreme Court summarily reversed and remanded for further proceedings:

> As *Payton* makes plain, police officers need either a warrant or probable cause plus exigent circumstances in order to make a lawful entry into a home. The Court of Appeal's ruling to the contrary, and consequent failure to assess whether exigent circumstances were present in this case, violated *Payton*.

536 U.S. at 638, 122 S.Ct. at 2459, 153 L.Ed.2d at 603.

The complexity of warrant requirements related to arrests and the apparent difficulty of courts in arriving at proper analyses of such matters were illustrated by State v. Overton, 2000 WL 1232422 (Ohio App.2000) (unreported), cert. denied 534 U.S. 982, 122 S.Ct. 389, 151 L.Ed.2d 317 (2001). The state court set out the facts:

> Toledo Police Detective Daniel Navarre testified that on November 23, 1998, he had a warrant for the arrest of appellant on a charge of permitting drug abuse. In the early morning hours, Detective Navarre and other officers went to appellant's residence to serve the arrest warrant. Detective Navarre testified that he knocked on the door and watched through a glass window while appellant, whom he recognized from previous encounters, came down the stairs. Appellant did not open the door. Detective Navarre told her he had a warrant for her arrest. Navarre testified that appellant looked at him and signaled him to leave. Navarre then kicked the door in while appellant ran upstairs. Navarre chased appellant as she ran into a room. Navarre testified that appellant attempted to close a door to the room but he was able to push it open. Navarre testified that he watched as appellant fell on a couch and threw a rolled up twenty dollar bill into the air. When the bill landed, pieces of crack cocaine fell out of it. Navarre then arrested appellant on the warrant. She was later indicted for the cocaine.
>
> On cross-examination, Navarre testified that the reason he attempted to arrest appellant on November 23, 1998, for a warrant that was issued in August of 1998, was because he believed that appellant had been threatening witnesses in an unrelated murder case.

The arrest warrant issued for Overton's violation of the following Ohio statute:

> No person who is the owner, lessee, or occupant, or who has custody, control, or supervision, of premises or real estate, including vacant land, shall knowingly permit the premises or real estate, including vacant land, to be used for the commission of a felony drug abuse offense by another person.

The complaint on which the warrant issued was signed by Detective Andre Woodson and was certified by T.A. Hearst, a Toledo Municipal Court Clerk. It read:

Complainant being duly sworn states that Desarie Overton defendant at Toledo, Lucas County, Ohio on or about July 10, 1998 did violate ORC #2925.13 constituting a charge of permitting drug abuse in that the defendant, being the owner, lessee, or occupant of certain premises, did knowingly permit such premises to be used for the commission of a felony drug abuse offense, to wit: Desarie Overton being the lessee, owner, or occupant of 620 Belmont, Toledo, Ohio 43607 knowingly permitted Cocaine, a schedule two controlled substance to be sold and possessed by the occupants, there, both being in violation of the Ohio Revised code, a felony drug abuse offense. This offense occurred in Toledo, Lucas County, Ohio.

Overton sought suppression of the drug. The trial court denied the motion to suppress and a split court of appeals found no error. In explanation, the appellate court wrote:

The complaint in this case listed a specific code section and contained specific factual information sworn to by a fellow Toledo Police Detective. The complaint was certified by a clerk of court * * *. Detective Navarre testified that because he already knew appellant, he recognized her when she came to the door. Based on the foregoing we conclude that Detective Navarre had reasonable ground to believe that the offense was committed and reasonable ground to believe that the person alleged to have committed the offense is guilty of the violation. Therefore, the Court finds that Detective Navarre had probable cause to arrest appellant in this case. Appellant's * * * assignment of error is found not well taken.

Overton sought review from the United States Supreme Court, which refused to grant certiorari. Four justices joined a "statement" by Justice Breyer, in which he explained:

As far as the record before us reveals, the only evidence in this case offered to the Magistrate to show "probable cause" for issuing the warrant consisted of a "complaint" presented to the Magistrate, signed by Detective Andre Woodson. That complaint sets forth Overton's name, the date of the offense, the name of the offense ("permitting drug abuse"), and the statutory reference. It * * * sets forth the relevant crime in general terms, it refers to Overton, and it says she committed the crime. But nowhere does it indicate *how Detective Woodson knows, or why he believes, that Overton committed the crime.*

This Court has previously made clear that affidavits or complaints of this kind do not provide sufficient support for the issuance of an arrest warrant. * * * I [can] find [no] basis, on the papers before us, to conclude that the evidence was admissible *despite* the inadequacy of the arrest warrant.

I consequently conclude that the city of Toledo clearly violated the Fourth Amendment warrant requirement. Because the Court already has answered directly the basic legal question presented in this case, I would not grant certiorari for the purpose of hearing that question argued once again. I would, however, summarily reverse the decision below. I realize that we cannot act as a court of simple error correction and that the unpublished intermediate court decision below lacks significant value as precedent. Nonetheless, the matter has a general aspect. The * * * print on the complaint offers some support for Overton's claims that the "complaint" is a form that the police filled in with her name and address. And that fact, if true, helps to support her claim that her case is not unique. That possibility, along with the clarity of the constitutional error, convinces me that the appropriate disposition of this case is a summary reversal.

534 U.S. at 983–86, 122 S.Ct. at 390–91, 151 L.Ed.2d at 317–18 (statement of Breyer, J., respecting the denial of the petition for writ of certiorari).

Page 187.   Insert the following in the unit, *Excessive Force*, in the Editors' Introduction after the first paragraph beginning on this page:

The significance of the deadly/nondeadly force distinction was deemphasized in Scott v. Harris, 550 U.S. 372, 382–83, 127 S.Ct. 1769, 1777–78, 167 L.Ed.2d 686 (2007), in which the Court stressed that the ultimate question is whether the officer's actions—however labeled—"were reasonable." *Scott* held reasonable the actions of an officer (Scott) in ramming Harris's fleeing automobile in an effort to terminate a ten mile high speed chase. "[I]n judging whether Scott's actions were reasonable," the Court explained, "we must consider the risk of bodily harm that Scott's actions posed to [Harris] in light of the threat to the public that Scott was trying to eliminate." Harris, it continued, "posed an actual and imminent threat to the lives of any pedestrians who might have been present, to other civilian motorists, and to the officers involved in the chase." Further, "Scott's actions posed a high likelihood of serious injury or death to respondent— though not the near *certainty* of death posed by, say, shooting a fleeing felon in the back of the head, or pulling alongside a fleeing motorist's car and shooting the motorist."

Developing the process for considering the relevant factors, *Scott* added:

> We think it appropriate in this process to take into account not only the number of lives at risk, but also their relative culpability. It was [Harris], after all, who intentionally placed himself and the public in danger by unlawfully engaging in the reckless, high-speed flight that ultimately produced the choice between two evils that Scott confronted. * * * By contrast, those who might have been harmed had Scott not taken the action he did were entirely innocent. * * *
>
> But * * * [c]ouldn't the innocent public equally have been protected, and the tragic accident entirely avoided, if the police had simply ceased their pursuit? We think the police need not have taken that

chance and hoped for the best. Whereas Scott's action—ramming [Harris] off the road—was *certain* to eliminate the risk that [Harris] posed to the public, ceasing pursuit was not. First of all, there would have been no way to convey convincingly to [Harris] that the chase was off, and that he was free to go. * * *

Second, we are loath to lay down a rule requiring the police to allow fleeing suspects to get away whenever they drive *so recklessly* that they put other people's lives in danger. It is obvious the perverse incentives such a rule would create: Every fleeing motorist would know that escape is within his grasp, if only he accelerates to 90 miles per hour, crosses the double-yellow line a few times, and runs a few red lights. The Constitution assuredly does not impose this invitation to impunity-earned-by-recklessness. Instead, we lay down a more sensible rule: A police officer's attempt to terminate a dangerous high-speed car chase that threatens the lives of innocent bystanders does not violate the Fourth Amendment, even when it places the fleeing motorist at risk of serious injury or death.

550 U.S. at 384–86, 127 S.Ct. at 1778–79.

Page 187.   Insert the following in the Editors' Introduction at the end of the unit, *Excessive Force***:**

An aspect of the prohibition against excessive force was before the Supreme Court in Brosseau v. Haugen, 543 U.S. 194, 125 S.Ct. 596, 160 L.Ed.2d 583 (2004). Officer Rochelle Brosseau, a member of the Puyallup, Washington, Police Department, shot Kenneth Haugen in the back as Haugen attempted to flee from law enforcement authorities in his vehicle. Haugen, who was not killed, was subject to arrest for a variety of reasons, including "a felony no-bail warrant out for [his] arrest on drug and other offenses." He sued under Rev. Stat. § 1979, 42 U.S.C. § 1983, claiming that the shot fired by Brosseau constituted excessive force and violated his federal constitutional rights. The District Court granted summary judgment to Brosseau, finding she was entitled to qualified immunity. The Court of Appeals for the Ninth Circuit reversed.

The Supreme Court held that the court of appeals had erred in holding that Brosseau was not entitled to qualified immunity. She was entitled to such immunity unless it was clearly established that she was violating Haugen's Fourth Amendments rights under *Garner* and *Graham*. Specifically, the issue was whether it was clearly established that the Fourth Amendment was violated by "shoot[ing] a disturbed felon, set on avoiding capture through vehicular flight, when persons in the immediate area are at risk from that flight."

The Court indicated that "only a handful of cases" relevant to the specific situation existed at the time of the shooting. It concluded:

These * * * cases taken together undoubtedly show that this area is one in which the result depends very much on the facts of each case.

None of them squarely governs the case here; they do suggest that Brosseau's actions fell in the " 'hazy border between excessive and acceptable force.' " The cases by no means "clearly establish" that Brosseau's conduct violated the Fourth Amendment.

543 U.S. at 201, 125 S.Ct. at 600. It did not comment on the merits of the basic constitutional claim—that in fact the shooting constituted excessive force under Fourth Amendment law. In addition, it noted a number of decisions postdating Brosseau's conduct, which it found irrelevant to the qualified immunity question before it.

2. "INCIDENTAL" SEARCHES OF VEHICLES

Page 199. Add the following new case and note after New York v. Belton:

Thornton v. United States

Supreme Court of the United States, 2004.
541 U.S. 615, 124 S.Ct. 2127, 158 L.Ed.2d 905.

■ CHIEF JUSTICE REHNQUIST delivered the opinion of the Court except as to footnote 4.

In *New York v. Belton,* 453 U.S. 454, 101 S.Ct. 2860, 69 L.Ed.2d 768 (1981), we held that when a police officer has made a lawful custodial arrest of an occupant of an automobile, the Fourth Amendment allows the officer to search the passenger compartment of that vehicle as a contemporaneous incident of arrest. We * * * granted certiorari * * * to determine whether *Belton's* rule is limited to situations where the officer makes contact with the occupant while the occupant is inside the vehicle, or whether it applies as well when the officer first makes contact with the arrestee after the latter has stepped out of his vehicle. * * *

Officer Deion Nichols of the Norfolk, Virginia, Police Department, who was in uniform but driving an unmarked police car, first noticed petitioner Marcus Thornton when petitioner slowed down so as to avoid driving next to him. Nichols suspected that petitioner knew he was a police officer and for some reason did not want to pull next to him. His suspicions aroused, Nichols pulled off onto a side street and petitioner passed him. After petitioner passed him, Nichols ran a check on petitioner's license tags, which revealed that the tags had been issued to a 1982 Chevy two-door and not to a Lincoln Town Car, the model of car petitioner was driving. Before Nichols had an opportunity to pull him over, petitioner drove into a parking lot, parked, and got out of the vehicle. Nichols saw petitioner leave his vehicle as he pulled in behind him. He parked the patrol car, accosted petitioner, and asked him for his driver's license. He also told him that his license tags did not match the vehicle that he was driving.

Petitioner appeared nervous. He began rambling and licking his lips; he was sweating. Concerned for his safety, Nichols asked petitioner if he had any narcotics or weapons on him or in his vehicle. Petitioner said no. Nichols then asked petitioner if he could pat him down, to which petitioner agreed. Nichols felt a bulge in petitioner's left front pocket and again asked him if he had any illegal narcotics on him. This time petitioner stated that he did, and he reached into his pocket and pulled out two individual bags, one containing three bags of marijuana and the other containing a large amount of crack cocaine. Nichols handcuffed petitioner, informed him that he was under arrest, and placed him in the back seat of the patrol car. He then searched petitioner's vehicle and found a BryCo .9–millimeter handgun under the driver's seat.

A grand jury charged petitioner with possession with intent to distribute cocaine base * * *, possession of a firearm after having been previously convicted of a crime punishable by a term of imprisonment exceeding one year * * *, and possession of a firearm in furtherance of a drug trafficking crime * * *. Petitioner sought to suppress, *inter alia,* the firearm as the fruit of an unconstitutional search. After a hearing, the District Court denied petitioner's motion to suppress, holding that the automobile search was valid under *New York v. Belton, supra,* and alternatively that Nichols could have conducted an inventory search of the automobile. A jury convicted petitioner on all three counts; he was sentenced to 180 months' imprisonment and 8 years of supervised release.

Petitioner appealed, challenging only the District Court's denial of the suppression motion. * * * The United States Court of Appeals for the Fourth Circuit affirmed. * * * We granted certiorari * * *.

In *Belton,* an officer overtook a speeding vehicle on the New York Thruway and ordered its driver to pull over. Suspecting that the occupants possessed marijuana, the officer directed them to get out of the car and arrested them for unlawful possession. He searched them and then searched the passenger compartment of the car. We considered the constitutionally permissible scope of a search in these circumstances and sought to lay down a workable rule governing that situation.

We * * * held that "when a policeman has made a lawful custodial arrest of the occupant of an automobile, he may, as a contemporaneous incident of that arrest, search the passenger compartment of that automobile."

In so holding, we placed no reliance on the fact that the officer in *Belton* ordered the occupants out of the vehicle, or initiated contact with them while they remained within it. Nor do we find such a factor persuasive in distinguishing the current situation, as it bears no logical relationship to *Belton's* rationale. There is simply no basis to conclude that the span of the area generally within the arrestee's immediate control is determined by whether the arrestee exited the vehicle at the officer's direction, or whether the officer initiated contact with him while he remained in the car. * * *

In all relevant aspects, the arrest of a suspect who is next to a vehicle presents identical concerns regarding officer safety and the destruction of evidence as the arrest of one who is inside the vehicle. An officer may search a suspect's vehicle under *Belton* only if the suspect is arrested. A custodial arrest is fluid and "[t]he danger to the police officer flows from *the fact of the arrest,* and its attendant proximity, stress, and uncertainty." The stress is no less merely because the arrestee exited his car before the officer initiated contact, nor is an arrestee less likely to attempt to lunge for a weapon or to destroy evidence if he is outside of, but still in control of, the vehicle. In either case, the officer faces a highly volatile situation. It would make little sense to apply two different rules to what is, at bottom, the same situation.

In some circumstances it may be safer and more effective for officers to conceal their presence from a suspect until he has left his vehicle. Certainly that is a judgment officers should be free to make. But under the strictures of petitioner's proposed "contact initiation" rule, officers who do so would be unable to search the car's passenger compartment in the event of a custodial arrest, potentially compromising their safety and placing incriminating evidence at risk of concealment or destruction. The Fourth Amendment does not require such a gamble.

Petitioner argues, however, that *Belton* will fail to provide a "bright-line" rule if it applies to more than vehicle "occupants." But *Belton* allows police to search the passenger compartment of a vehicle incident to a lawful custodial arrest of both "occupants" and "recent occupants." Indeed, the respondent in *Belton* was not inside the car at the time of the arrest and search; he was standing on the highway. In any event, while an arrestee's status as a "recent occupant" may turn on his temporal or spatial relationship to the car at the time of the arrest and search,[2] it certainly does not turn on whether he was inside or outside the car at the moment that the officer first initiated contact with him.

To be sure, not all contraband in the passenger compartment is likely to be readily accessible to a "recent occupant." It is unlikely in this case that petitioner could have reached under the driver's seat for his gun once he was outside of his automobile. But the firearm and the passenger compartment in general were no more inaccessible than were the contraband and the passenger compartment in *Belton.* The need for a clear rule,

---

2. Petitioner argues that if we reject his proposed "contact initiation" rule, we should limit the scope of *Belton* to "recent occupants" who are within "reaching distance" of the car. We decline to address petitioner's argument, however, as it is outside the question on which we granted certiorari, and was not addressed by the Court of Appeals. We note that it is unlikely that petitioner would even meet his own standard as he apparently conceded in the Court of Appeals that he was in "close proximity, both temporally and spatially," to his vehicle when he was approached by Nichols.

readily understood by police officers and not depending on differing estimates of what items were or were not within reach of an arrestee at any particular moment, justifies the sort of generalization which *Belton* enunciated.[3] Once an officer determines that there is probable cause to make an arrest, it is reasonable to allow officers to ensure their safety and to preserve evidence by searching the entire passenger compartment.

Rather than clarifying the constitutional limits of a *Belton* search, petitioner's "contact initiation" rule would obfuscate them. Under petitioner's proposed rule, an officer approaching a suspect who has just alighted from his vehicle would have to determine whether he actually confronted or signaled confrontation with the suspect while he remained in the car, or whether the suspect exited his vehicle unaware of, and for reasons unrelated to, the officer's presence. This determination would be inherently subjective and highly fact specific, and would require precisely the sort of ad hoc determinations on the part of officers in the field and reviewing courts that *Belton* sought to avoid. Experience has shown that such a rule is impracticable, and we refuse to adopt it. So long as an arrestee is the sort of "recent occupant" of a vehicle such as petitioner was here, officers may search that vehicle incident to the arrest.[4]

The judgment of the Court of Appeals is affirmed.

It is so ordered.

■ JUSTICE O'CONNOR, concurring in part.

I join all but footnote 4 of the Court's opinion. Although the opinion is a logical extension of the holding of *New York v. Belton,* 453 U.S. 454, 101 S.Ct. 2860, 69 L.Ed.2d 768 (1981), I write separately to express my dissatisfaction with the state of the law in this area. As Justice SCALIA

3. Justice STEVENS contends that *Belton's* bright-line rule "is not needed for cases in which the arrestee is first accosted when he is a pedestrian, because *Chimel* [v. *California,* 395 U.S. 752, 89 S.Ct. 2034, 23 L.Ed.2d 685 (1969),] itself provides all the guidance that is necessary." Under Justice STEVENS' approach, however, even if the car itself was within the arrestee's reaching distance under *Chimel,* police officers and courts would still have to determine whether a particular object within the passenger compartment was also within an arrestee's reaching distance under *Chimel.* This is exactly the type of unworkable and fact-specific inquiry that *Belton* rejected by holding that the entire passenger compartment may be searched when " 'the area within the immediate control of the arrestee' ... arguably includes the interior of an automobile and the arrestee is its recent occupant."

4. Whatever the merits of Justice SCALIA's opinion concurring in the judgment, this is the wrong case in which to address them. Petitioner has never argued that *Belton* should be limited "to cases where it is reasonable to believe evidence relevant to the crime of arrest might be found in the vehicle," nor did any court below consider Justice SCALIA's reasoning. * * * And the United States has never had an opportunity to respond to such an approach. Under these circumstances, it would be imprudent to overrule, for all intents and purposes, our established constitutional precedent, which governs police authority in a common occurrence such as automobile searches pursuant to arrest, and we decline to do so at this time.

forcefully argues, lower court decisions seem now to treat the ability to search a vehicle incident to the arrest of a recent occupant as a police entitlement rather than as an exception justified by the twin rationales of *Chimel v. California*, 395 U.S. 752, 89 S.Ct. 2034, 23 L.Ed.2d 685 (1969). That erosion is a direct consequence of *Belton's* shaky foundation. While the approach Justice SCALIA proposes appears to be built on firmer ground, I am reluctant to adopt it in the context of a case in which neither the Government nor the petitioner has had a chance to speak to its merit.

■ JUSTICE SCALIA with whom JUSTICE GINSBURG joins, concurring in the judgment.

* * *

When petitioner's car was searched in this case, he was neither in, nor anywhere near, the passenger compartment of his vehicle. Rather, he was handcuffed and secured in the back of the officer's squad car. The risk that he would nevertheless "grab a weapon or evidentiary ite[m]" from his car was remote in the extreme. The Court's effort to apply our current doctrine to this search stretches it beyond its breaking point, and for that reason I cannot join the Court's opinion.

I

I see three reasons why the search in this case might have been justified to protect officer safety or prevent concealment or destruction of evidence. None ultimately persuades me.

The first is that, despite being handcuffed and secured in the back of a squad car, petitioner might have escaped and retrieved a weapon or evidence from his vehicle * * *. But the risk here is far from obvious, and in a context as frequently recurring as roadside arrests, the Government's inability to come up with even a single example of a handcuffed arrestee's retrieval of arms or evidence from his vehicle undermines its claims. The risk that a suspect handcuffed in the back of a squad car might escape and recover a weapon from his vehicle is surely no greater than the risk that a suspect handcuffed in his residence might escape and recover a weapon from the next room * * *.

The second defense of the search in this case is that, since the officer could have conducted the search at the time of arrest (when the suspect was still near the car), he should not be penalized for having taken the sensible precaution of securing the suspect in the squad car first. * * * The weakness of this argument is that it assumes that, one way or another, the search must take place. But conducting a * * * search [incident to arrest] is not the Government's right; it is an exception—justified by necessity—to a rule that would otherwise render the search unlawful. If "sensible police procedures" require that suspects be handcuffed and put in squad cars, then police should handcuff suspects, put them in squad cars, and not conduct the search. Indeed, if an officer leaves a suspect unrestrained nearby just to manufacture authority to search, one could argue that the search is unreasonable *precisely because* the dangerous conditions justifying it existed only by virtue of the officer's failure to follow sensible procedures.

The third defense of the search is that, even though the arrestee posed no risk here, *Belton* searches in general are reasonable, and the benefits of a bright-line rule justify upholding that small minority of searches that, on their particular facts, are not reasonable. The validity of this argument rests on the accuracy of *Belton*'s claim that the passenger compartment is "in fact generally, even if not inevitably," within the suspect's immediate control. By the United States' own admission, however, "[t]he practice of restraining an arrestee on the scene before searching a car that he just occupied is so prevalent that holding that *Belton* does not apply in that setting would ... 'largely render *Belton* a dead letter.' " Reported cases involving this precise factual scenario—a motorist handcuffed and secured in the back of a squad car when the search takes place—are legion. Some courts uphold such searches even when the squad car carrying the hand-cuffed arrestee has already left the scene.

The popularity of the practice is not hard to fathom. If *Belton entitles* an officer to search a vehicle upon arresting the driver despite having taken measures that eliminate any danger, what rational officer would not take those measures? If it was ever true that the passenger compartment is "in fact generally, even if not inevitably," within the arrestee's immediate control at the time of the search, it certainly is not true today. * * *

II

If *Belton* searches are justifiable, it is not because the arrestee might grab a weapon or evidentiary item from his car, but simply because the car might contain evidence relevant to the crime for which he was arrested. * * *

There is nothing irrational about broader police authority to search for evidence when and where the perpetrator of a crime is lawfully arrested. The fact of prior lawful arrest distinguishes the arrestee from society at large, and distinguishes a search for evidence of *his* crime from general rummaging. Moreover, it is not illogical to assume that evidence of a crime is most likely to be found where the suspect was apprehended.

* * *

[I]f we are going to continue to allow *Belton* searches * * *, we should at least be honest about why we are doing so. *Belton* cannot reasonably be explained as a mere application of *Chimel*. Rather, it is a return to the broader sort of search incident to arrest that we allowed before *Chimel*— limited, of course, to searches of motor vehicles, a category of "effects" which give rise to a reduced expectation of privacy and heightened law enforcement needs.

Recasting *Belton* in these terms would have at least one important practical consequence. In *United States v. Robinson*, 414 U.S. 218, 235, 94 S.Ct. 467, 38 L.Ed.2d 427 (1973), we held that authority to search an arrestee's person does not depend on the actual presence of one of *Chimel*'s two rationales in the particular case; rather, the fact of arrest alone justifies the search. That holding stands in contrast to *Rabinowitz*, where we did not treat the fact of arrest alone as sufficient, but upheld the search only after noting that it was "not general or exploratory for whatever might be turned up" but reflected a reasonable belief that evidence would be found. The two different rules make sense: When officer safety or imminent evidence concealment or destruction is at issue, officers should not have to make fine judgments in the heat of the moment. But in the context of a general evidence-gathering search, the state interests that might justify any overbreadth are far less compelling. A motorist may be arrested for a wide variety of offenses; in many cases, there is no reasonable basis to believe relevant evidence might be found in the car. I would therefore limit *Belton* searches to cases where it is reasonable to believe evidence relevant to the crime of arrest might be found in the vehicle.

In this case, as in *Belton,* petitioner was lawfully arrested for a drug offense. It was reasonable for Officer Nichols to believe that further contraband or similar evidence relevant to the crime for which he had been arrested might be found in the vehicle from which he had just alighted and which was still within his vicinity at the time of arrest. I would affirm the decision below on that ground.

■ JUSTICE STEVENS, with whom JUSTICE SOUTER joins, dissenting.

* * *

Belton's basic rationale * * * rested not on a concern for officer safety, but rather on an overriding desire to hew "to a straightforward rule, easily applied, and predictably enforced." * * * [T]he interest in certainty that supports *Belton's* bright-line rule surely does not justify an expansion of the rule that only blurs those clear lines. [*Belton*] would [not] have allowed the search of petitioner's car.

* * * *Belton* was demonstrably concerned only with the narrow but common circumstance of a search occasioned by the arrest of a suspect who was seated in or driving an automobile at the time the law enforcement official approached. Normally, after such an arrest has occurred, the officer's safety is no longer in jeopardy, but he must decide what, if any, search for incriminating evidence he should conduct. *Belton* provided previously unavailable and therefore necessary guidance for that category of cases.

The bright-line rule crafted in *Belton* is not needed for cases in which the arrestee is first accosted when he is a pedestrian, because *Chimel* itself provides all the guidance that is necessary. The only genuine justification for extending *Belton* to cover such circumstances is the interest in uncovering potentially valuable evidence. In my opinion, that goal must give way to the citizen's constitutionally protected interest in privacy when there is already in place a well-defined rule limiting the permissible scope of a search of an arrested pedestrian. The *Chimel* rule should provide the same protection to a "recent occupant" of a vehicle as to a recent occupant of a house.

Unwilling to confine the *Belton* rule to the narrow class of cases it was designed to address, the Court extends *Belton's* reach without supplying any guidance for the future application of its swollen rule. We are told that officers may search a vehicle incident to arrest "[s]o long as [the] arrestee is the sort of 'recent occupant' of a vehicle such as petitioner was here." But we are not told how recent is recent, or how close is close, perhaps because in this case "the record is not clear." As the Court cautioned in *Belton* itself, "[w]hen a person cannot know how a court will apply a settled principle to a recurring factual situation, that person cannot know the scope of his constitutional protection, nor can a policeman know the scope of his authority." Without some limiting principle, I fear that today's decision will contribute to "a massive broadening of the automobile exception," when officers have probable cause to arrest an individual but not to search his car.

Accordingly, I respectfully dissent.

Arizona v. Gant

Supreme Court of the United States, 2009.
556 U.S. 332, 129 S.Ct. 1710, 173 L.Ed.2d 485.

■ JUSTICE STEVENS delivered the opinion of the Court.

After Rodney Gant was arrested for driving with a suspended license, handcuffed, and locked in the back of a patrol car, police officers searched his car and discovered cocaine in the pocket of a jacket on the backseat. Because Gant could not have accessed his car to retrieve weapons or evidence at the time of the search, the Arizona Supreme Court held that the search-incident-to-arrest exception to the Fourth Amendment's warrant requirement, as defined in *Chimel v. California,* 395 U.S. 752, 89 S.Ct. 2034, 23 L.Ed.2d 685 (1969), and applied to vehicle searches in *New York v. Belton,* 453 U.S. 454, 101 S.Ct. 2860, 69 L.Ed.2d 768 (1981), did not justify the search in this case. We agree with that conclusion.

* * *

I

On August 25, 1999, acting on an anonymous tip that the residence at 2524 North Walnut Avenue was being used to sell drugs, Tucson police officers Griffith and Reed knocked on the front door and asked to speak to the owner. Gant answered the door and, after identifying himself, stated that he expected the owner to return later. The officers left the residence and conducted a records check, which revealed that Gant's driver's license had been suspended and there was an outstanding warrant for his arrest for driving with a suspended license.

When the officers returned to the house that evening, they found a man near the back of the house and a woman in a car parked in front of it. After a third officer arrived, they arrested the man for providing a false name and the woman for possessing drug paraphernalia. Both arrestees were handcuffed and secured in separate patrol cars when Gant arrived. The officers recognized his car as it entered the driveway, and Officer Griffith confirmed that Gant was the driver by shining a flashlight into the car as it drove by him. Gant parked at the end of the driveway, got out of his car, and shut the door. Griffith, who was about 30 feet away, called to Gant, and they approached each other, meeting 10–to–12 feet from Gant's car. Griffith immediately arrested Gant and handcuffed him.

Because the other arrestees were secured in the only patrol cars at the scene, Griffith called for backup. When two more officers arrived, they locked Gant in the backseat of their vehicle. After Gant had been hand-cuffed and placed in the back of a patrol car, two officers searched his car: One of them found a gun, and the other discovered a bag of cocaine in the pocket of a jacket on the backseat.

Gant was charged with two offenses—possession of a narcotic drug for sale and possession of drug paraphernalia (*i.e.*, the plastic bag in which the cocaine was found). He moved to suppress the evidence seized from his car on the ground that the warrantless search violated the Fourth Amendment. * * *

The trial court * * * denied the motion to suppress. Relying on the fact that the police saw Gant commit the crime of driving without a license and apprehended him only shortly after he exited his car, the court held that the search was permissible as a search incident to arrest. A jury found Gant guilty on both drug counts, and he was sentenced to a 3–year term of imprisonment.

After protracted state-court proceedings, the Arizona Supreme Court concluded that the search of Gant's car was unreasonable within the meaning of the Fourth Amendment. * * *

The chorus that has called for us to revisit *Belton* includes courts, scholars, and Members of this Court who have questioned that decision's clarity and its fidelity to Fourth Amendment principles. We therefore granted the State's petition for certiorari.

II

In *Chimel,* we held that a search incident to arrest may only include "the arrestee's person and the area 'within his immediate control'—

construing that phrase to mean the area from within which he might gain possession of a weapon or destructible evidence." That limitation, which continues to define the boundaries of the exception, ensures that the scope of a search incident to arrest is commensurate with its purposes of protecting arresting officers and safeguarding any evidence of the offense of arrest that an arrestee might conceal or destroy. If there is no possibility that an arrestee could reach into the area that law enforcement officers seek to search, both justifications for the search-incident-to-arrest exception are absent and the rule does not apply.

In *Belton,* * * * we held that when an officer lawfully arrests "the occupant of an automobile, he may, as a contemporaneous incident of that arrest, search the passenger compartment of the automobile" and any containers therein. That holding was based in large part on our assumption "that articles inside the relatively narrow compass of the passenger compartment of an automobile are in fact generally, even if not inevitably, within 'the area into which an arrestee might reach.' "

* * *

III

[O]ur [*Belton*] opinion has been widely understood to allow a vehicle search incident to the arrest of a recent occupant even if there is no possibility the arrestee could gain access to the vehicle at the time of the search. * * *

Under this broad reading of *Belton,* a vehicle search would be authorized incident to every arrest of a recent occupant notwithstanding that in most cases the vehicle's passenger compartment will not be within the arrestee's reach at the time of the search. To read *Belton* as authorizing a vehicle search incident to every recent occupant's arrest would thus untether the rule from the justifications underlying the *Chimel* exception—a result clearly incompatible with our statement in *Belton* that it "in no way alters the fundamental principles established in the *Chimel* case regarding the basic scope of searches incident to lawful custodial arrests." Accordingly, we reject this reading of *Belton* and hold that the *Chimel* rationale authorizes police to search a vehicle incident to a recent occupant's arrest only when the arrestee is unsecured and within reaching distance of the passenger compartment at the time of the search.[4]

Although it does not follow from *Chimel,* we also conclude that circumstances unique to the vehicle context justify a search incident to a lawful arrest when it is "reasonable to believe evidence relevant to the crime of arrest might be found in the vehicle." [*Thornton v. United States,*

---

4. Because officers have many means of ensuring the safe arrest of vehicle occupants, it will be the rare case in which an officer is unable to fully effectuate an arrest so that a real possibility of access to the arrestee's vehicle remains. But in such a case a search incident to arrest is reasonable under the Fourth Amendment.

541 U.S. 615, 632, 124 S.Ct. 2127, 158 L.Ed.2d 905 (2004)] (SCALIA, J., concurring in judgment). In many cases, as when a recent occupant is arrested for a traffic violation, there will be no reasonable basis to believe the vehicle contains relevant evidence. But in others, including *Belton* and *Thornton,* the offense of arrest will supply a basis for searching the passenger compartment of an arrestee's vehicle and any containers therein.

Neither the possibility of access nor the likelihood of discovering offense-related evidence authorized the search in this case. Unlike in *Belton,* which involved a single officer confronted with four unsecured arrestees, the five officers in this case outnumbered the three arrestees, all of whom had been handcuffed and secured in separate patrol cars before the officers searched Gant's car. Under those circumstances, Gant clearly was not within reaching distance of his car at the time of the search. An evidentiary basis for the search was also lacking in this case. Whereas Belton and Thornton were arrested for drug offenses, Gant was arrested for driving with a suspended license—an offense for which police could not expect to find evidence in the passenger compartment of Gant's car. Because police could not reasonably have believed either that Gant could have accessed his car at the time of the search or that evidence of the offense for which he was arrested might have been found therein, the search in this case was unreasonable.

IV

The State * * * argues that *Belton* searches are reasonable regardless of the possibility of access in a given case because that expansive rule correctly balances law enforcement interests, including the interest in a bright-line rule, with an arrestee's limited privacy interest in his vehicle.

For several reasons, we reject the State's argument. First, the State seriously undervalues the privacy interests at stake. Although we have recognized that a motorist's privacy interest in his vehicle is less substantial than in his home, the former interest is nevertheless important and deserving of constitutional protection. * * *

At the same time as it undervalues these privacy concerns, the State exaggerates the clarity that its reading of *Belton* provides. Courts that have read *Belton* expansively are at odds regarding how close in time to the arrest and how proximate to the arrestee's vehicle an officer's first contact with the arrestee must be to bring the encounter within *Belton*'s purview and whether a search is reasonable when it commences or continues after the arrestee has been removed from the scene. The rule has thus generated a great deal of uncertainty, particularly for a rule touted as providing a "bright line."

Contrary to the State's suggestion, a broad reading of *Belton* is also unnecessary to protect law enforcement safety and evidentiary interests. Under our view, *Belton* and *Thornton* permit an officer to conduct a vehicle search when an arrestee is within reaching distance of the vehicle or it is reasonable to believe the vehicle contains evidence of the offense of arrest. Other established exceptions to the warrant requirement authorize a vehicle search under additional circumstances when safety or evidentiary concerns demand. For instance, *Michigan v. Long,* 463 U.S. 1032, 103 S.Ct. 3469, 77 L.Ed.2d 1201 (1983), permits an officer to search a vehicle's passenger compartment when he has reasonable suspicion that an individual, whether or not the arrestee, is "dangerous" and might access the vehicle to "gain immediate control of weapons." If there is probable cause to believe a vehicle contains evidence of criminal activity, *United States v. Ross,* 456 U.S. 798, 820–821, 102 S.Ct. 2157, 72 L.Ed.2d 572 (1982), authorizes a search of any area of the vehicle in which the evidence might be found. * * * *Ross* allows searches for evidence relevant to offenses other than the offense of arrest, and the scope of the search authorized is broader. Finally, there may be still other circumstances in which safety or evidentiary interests would justify a search. Cf. *Maryland v. Buie,* 494 U.S. 325, 334, 110 S.Ct. 1093, 108 L.Ed.2d 276 (1990) (holding that, incident to arrest, an officer may conduct a limited protective sweep of those areas of a house in which he reasonably suspects a dangerous person may be hiding).

These exceptions together ensure that officers may search a vehicle when genuine safety or evidentiary concerns encountered during the arrest of a vehicle's recent occupant justify a search. Construing *Belton* broadly to allow vehicle searches incident to any arrest would serve no purpose except to provide a police entitlement, and it is anathema to the Fourth Amendment to permit a warrantless search on that basis. For these reasons, we are unpersuaded by the State's arguments that a broad reading of *Belton* would meaningfully further law enforcement interests and justify a substantial intrusion on individuals' privacy.

V

* * *

We do not agree * * * that consideration of police reliance interests requires a different result. Although it appears that the State's reading of *Belton* has been widely taught in police academies and that law enforcement officers have relied on the rule in conducting vehicle searches during the past 28 years, many of these searches were not justified by the reasons underlying the *Chimel* exception. Countless individuals guilty of nothing more serious than a traffic violation have had their constitutional right to the security of their private effects violated as a result. The fact that the law enforcement community may view the State's version of the *Belton* rule as an entitlement does not establish the sort of reliance interest that could outweigh the countervailing interest that all individuals share in having their constitutional rights fully protected. * * *

VI

Police may search a vehicle incident to a recent occupant's arrest only if the arrestee is within reaching distance of the passenger compartment at the time of the search or it is reasonable to believe the vehicle contains evidence of the offense of arrest. When these justifications are absent, a search of an arrestee's vehicle will be unreasonable unless police obtain a warrant or show that another exception to the warrant requirement applies. The Arizona Supreme Court correctly held that this case involved an unreasonable search. Accordingly, the judgment of the State Supreme Court is affirmed.

It is so ordered.

■ JUSTICE SCALIA, concurring.

* * * In my view we should simply abandon the *Belton-Thornton* charade of officer safety and overrule those cases. I would hold that a vehicle search incident to arrest is *ipso facto* "reasonable" only when the object of the search is evidence of the crime for which the arrest was made, or of another crime that the officer has probable cause to believe occurred. Because respondent was arrested for driving without a license (a crime for which no evidence could be expected to be found in the vehicle), I would hold in the present case that the search was unlawful.

* * *

No other Justice, however, shares my view that application of *Chimel* in this context should be entirely abandoned. It seems to me unacceptable for the Court to come forth with a 4–to–1–to–4 opinion that leaves the governing rule uncertain. I am therefore confronted with the choice of either leaving the current understanding of *Belton* and *Thornton* in effect, or acceding to what seems to me the artificial narrowing of those cases adopted by Justice STEVENS. The latter, as I have said, does not provide the degree of certainty I think desirable in this field; but the former opens the field to what I think are plainly unconstitutional searches-which is the greater evil. I therefore join the opinion of the Court.

■ JUSTICE BREYER, dissenting.

I agree with Justice ALITO that *New York v. Belton,* 453 U.S. 454, 101 S.Ct. 2860, 69 L.Ed.2d 768 (1981), is best read as setting forth a bright-line rule that permits a warrantless search of the passenger compartment of an automobile incident to the lawful arrest of an occupant—regardless of the danger the arrested individual in fact poses. I also agree with Justice STEVENS, however, that the rule can produce results divorced from its underlying Fourth Amendment rationale. For that reason I would look for a better rule—were the question before us one of first impression.

The matter, however, is not one of first impression, and that fact makes a substantial difference. The *Belton* rule has been followed not only by this Court * * *, but also by numerous other courts. Principles of *stare decisis* must apply, and those who wish this Court to change a well-established legal precedent—where, as here, there has been considerable reliance on the legal rule in question—bear a heavy burden. I have not found that burden met. Nor do I believe that the other considerations ordinarily relevant when determining whether to overrule a case are satisfied. I consequently join Justice ALITO's dissenting opinion with the exception of Part II–E.

■ JUSTICE ALITO, with whom THE CHIEF JUSTICE and JUSTICE KENNEDY join, and with whom JUSTICE BREYER joins except as to Part II–E, dissenting.

* * *

I

Although the Court refuses to acknowledge that it is overruling *Belton* and *Thornton,* there can be no doubt that it does so.

* * *

The precise holding in *Belton* could not be clearer. The Court stated unequivocally: "[W]e hold that when a policeman has made a lawful custodial arrest of the occupant of an automobile, he may, as a contemporaneous incident of that arrest, search the passenger compartment of that automobile." (footnote omitted).

* * *

II

* * *

C

* * * The *Belton* rule has not proved to be unworkable. On the contrary, the rule was adopted for the express purpose of providing a test that would be relatively easy for police officers and judges to apply. The Court correctly notes that even the *Belton* rule is not perfectly clear in all situations. Specifically, it is sometimes debatable whether a search is or is not contemporaneous with an arrest, but that problem is small in comparison with the problems that the Court's new two-part rule will produce.

The first part of the Court's new rule—which permits the search of a vehicle's passenger compartment if it is within an arrestee's reach at the time of the search—reintroduces the same sort of case-by-case, fact-specific decisionmaking that the *Belton* rule was adopted to avoid. As the situation in *Belton* illustrated, there are cases in which it is unclear whether an arrestee could retrieve a weapon or evidence in the passenger compartment of a car.

Even more serious problems will also result from the second part of the Court's new rule, which requires officers making roadside arrests to determine whether there is reason to believe that the vehicle contains evidence of the crime of arrest. What this rule permits in a variety of situations is entirely unclear.

* * *

E

* * * The Court is harshly critical of *Belton*'s reasoning, but the problem that the Court perceives cannot be remedied simply by overruling *Belton*. *Belton* represented only a modest—and quite defensible—extension of *Chimel,* as I understand that decision.

Prior to *Chimel,* the Court's precedents * * * sustained searches that extended far beyond an arrestee's grabbing area.

The *Chimel* Court, in an opinion written by Justice Stewart, overruled these cases. Concluding that there are only two justifications for a warrantless search incident to arrest—officer safety and the preservation of evidence—the Court stated that such a search must be confined to "the arrestee's person" and "the area from within which he might gain possession of a weapon or destructible evidence."

Unfortunately, *Chimel* did not say whether "the area from within which [an arrestee] might gain possession of a weapon or destructible evidence" is to be measured at the time of the arrest or at the time of the search, but unless the *Chimel* rule was meant to be a specialty rule, applicable to only a few unusual cases, the Court must have intended for this area to be measured at the time of arrest.

This is so because the Court can hardly have failed to appreciate the following two facts. First, in the great majority of cases, an officer making an arrest is able to handcuff the arrestee and remove him to a secure place before conducting a search incident to the arrest. Second, because it is safer for an arresting officer to secure an arrestee before searching, it is likely that this is what arresting officers do in the great majority of cases. (And it appears, not surprisingly, that this is in fact the prevailing practice.) Thus, if the area within an arrestee's reach were assessed, not at the time of arrest, but at the time of the search, the *Chimel* rule would rarely come into play.

Moreover, if the applicability of the *Chimel* rule turned on whether an arresting officer chooses to secure an arrestee prior to conducting a search, rather than searching first and securing the arrestee later, the rule would "create a perverse incentive for an arresting officer to prolong the period during which the arrestee is kept in an area where he could pose a danger to the officer." If this is the law, * * * "the law would truly be, as Mr. Bumble said, 'a ass.' "

I do not think that this is what the *Chimel* Court intended. Handcuffs were in use in 1969. The ability of arresting officers to secure arrestees before conducting a search—and their incentive to do so—are facts that can hardly have escaped the Court's attention. I therefore believe that the *Chimel* Court intended that its new rule apply in cases in which the arrestee is handcuffed before the search is conducted.

The *Belton* Court, in my view, proceeded on the basis of this interpretation of *Chimel*. Again speaking through Justice Stewart, the *Belton* Court reasoned that articles in the passenger compartment of a car are "generally, even if not inevitably" within an arrestee's reach. This is undoubtedly true at the time of the arrest of a person who is seated in a car but plainly not true when the person has been removed from the car and placed in handcuffs. Accordingly, the *Belton* Court must have proceeded on the assumption that the *Chimel* rule was to be applied at the time of arrest. And that is why the *Belton* Court was able to say that its decision "in no way alter[ed] the fundamental principles established in the *Chimel* case regarding the basic scope of searches incident to lawful custodial arrests." Viewing *Chimel* as having focused on the time of arrest, *Belton*'s only new step was to eliminate the need to decide on a case-by-case basis whether a particular person seated in a car actually could have reached the part of the passenger compartment where a weapon or evidence was hidden. For this reason, if we are going to reexamine *Belton,* we should also reexamine the reasoning in *Chimel* on which *Belton* rests.

F

The Court, however, does not reexamine *Chimel* and thus leaves the law relating to searches incident to arrest in a confused and unstable state. The first part of the Court's new two-part rule—which permits an arresting officer to search the area within an arrestee's reach at the time of the search—applies, at least for now, only to vehicle occupants and recent occupants, but there is no logical reason why the same rule should not apply to all arrestees.

The second part of the Court's new rule, which the Court takes uncritically from Justice SCALIA's separate opinion in *Thornton*, raises doctrinal and practical problems that the Court makes no effort to address. Why, for example, is the standard for this type of evidence-gathering search "reason to believe" rather than probable cause? And why is this type of search restricted to evidence of the offense of arrest? It is true that an arrestee's vehicle is probably more likely to contain evidence of the crime of arrest than of some other crime, but if reason-to-believe is the governing standard for an evidence-gathering search incident to arrest, it is not easy to see why an officer should not be able to search when the officer has reason to believe that the vehicle in question possesses evidence of a crime other than the crime of arrest.

Nor is it easy to see why an evidence-gathering search incident to arrest should be restricted to the passenger compartment. The *Belton* rule was limited in this way because the passenger compartment was considered to be the area that vehicle occupants can generally reach, but since the second part of the new rule is not based on officer safety or the preservation of evidence, the ground for this limitation is obscure.

III

Respondent in this case has not asked us to overrule *Belton,* much less *Chimel.* Respondent's argument rests entirely on an interpretation of *Belton* that is plainly incorrect, an interpretation that disregards *Belton*'s explicit delineation of its holding. I would therefore leave any reexamination of our prior precedents for another day, if such a reexamination is to be undertaken at all. In this case, I would simply apply *Belton* and reverse the judgment below.

Page 199.   Add the following new subchapter after New York v. Belton:

3.   PERMISSIBILITY OF CUSTODIAL ARRESTS

Whether the Fourth Amendment imposed any limitations upon those offenses for which custodial arrests may be made long troubled the courts. The issue was finally addressed by the United States Supreme Court in the following case.

This question is clearly related to traffic stops, the subject of subchapter D of this chapter.

Atwater v. City of Lago Vista

Supreme Court of the United States, 2001.
532 U.S. 318, 121 S.Ct. 1536, 149 L.Ed.2d 549.

■ JUSTICE SOUTER delivered the opinion of the Court.

The question is whether the Fourth Amendment forbids a warrantless arrest for a minor criminal offense, such as a misdemeanor seatbelt violation punishable only by a fine. We hold that it does not.

I

A

In Texas, if a car is equipped with safety belts, a front-seat passenger must wear one, Tex. Tran.Code Ann. § 545.413(a) (1999), and the driver must secure any small child riding in front, § 545.413(b). Violation of either provision is "a misdemeanor punishable by a fine not less than $25 or more than $50." § 545.413(d). Texas law expressly authorizes "[a]ny peace officer [to] arrest without warrant a person found committing a violation" of these seatbelt laws, § 543.001, although it permits police to issue citations in lieu of arrest, §§ 543.003–543.005.

In March 1997, Petitioner Gail Atwater was driving her pickup truck in Lago Vista, Texas, with her 3–year–old son and 5–year–old daughter in the front seat. None of them was wearing a seatbelt. Respondent Bart

Turek, a Lago Vista police officer at the time, observed the seatbelt violations and pulled Atwater over. According to Atwater's complaint (the allegations of which we assume to be true for present purposes), Turek approached the truck and "yell[ed]" something to the effect of "[w]e've met before" and "[y]ou're going to jail."[1] He then called for backup and asked to see Atwater's driver's license and insurance documentation, which state law required her to carry. When Atwater told Turek that she did not have the papers because her purse had been stolen the day before, Turek said that he had "heard that story two-hundred times."

Atwater asked to take her "frightened, upset, and crying" children to a friend's house nearby, but Turek told her, "[y]ou're not going anywhere." As it turned out, Atwater's friend learned what was going on and soon arrived to take charge of the children. Turek then handcuffed Atwater, placed her in his squad car, and drove her to the local police station, where booking officers had her remove her shoes, jewelry, and eyeglasses, and empty her pockets. Officers took Atwater's "mug shot" and placed her, alone, in a jail cell for about one hour, after which she was taken before a magistrate and released on $310 bond.

Atwater was charged with driving without her seatbelt fastened, failing to secure her children in seatbelts, driving without a license, and failing to provide proof of insurance. She ultimately pleaded no contest to the misdemeanor seatbelt offenses and paid a $50 fine; the other charges were dismissed.

B

Atwater and her husband, petitioner Michael Haas, filed suit in a Texas state court under 42 U.S.C. § 1983 against Turek and respondents City of Lago Vista and Chief of Police Frank Miller. So far as concerns us, petitioners (whom we will simply call Atwater) alleged that respondents (for simplicity, the City) had violated Atwater's Fourth Amendment "right to be free from unreasonable seizure," and sought compensatory and punitive damages.

The City removed the suit to the United States District Court for the Western District of Texas. Given Atwater's admission that she had "violated the law" and the absence of any allegation "that she was harmed or detained in any way inconsistent with the law," the District Court ruled the Fourth Amendment claim "meritless" and granted the City's summary judgment motion. A panel of the United States Court of Appeals for the Fifth Circuit reversed. It concluded that "an arrest for a first-time seat belt offense" was an unreasonable seizure within the meaning of the Fourth Amendment, and held that Turek was not entitled to qualified immunity.

---

1. Turek had previously stopped Atwater for what he had thought was a seatbelt violation, but had realized that Atwater's son, although seated on the vehicle's armrest, was in fact belted in. Atwater acknowledged that her son's seating position was unsafe, and Turek issued a verbal warning.

Sitting en banc, the Court of Appeals vacated the panel's decision and affirmed the District Court's summary judgment for the City. * * *

We granted certiorari to consider whether the Fourth Amendment, either by incorporating common-law restrictions on misdemeanor arrests or otherwise, limits police officers' authority to arrest without warrant for minor criminal offenses. We now affirm.

II

The Fourth Amendment safeguards "[t]he right of the people to be secure in their persons, houses, papers, and effects, against unreasonable searches and seizures." In reading the Amendment, we are guided by "the traditional protections against unreasonable searches and seizures afforded by the common law at the time of the framing," *Wilson v. Arkansas,* 514 U.S. 927, 931, 115 S.Ct. 1914, 131 L.Ed.2d 976 (1995), since "[a]n examination of the common-law understanding of an officer's authority to arrest sheds light on the obviously relevant, if not entirely dispositive, consideration of what the Framers of the Amendment might have thought to be reasonable," *Payton v. New York,* 445 U.S. 573, 591, 100 S.Ct. 1371, 63 L.Ed.2d 639 (1980) (footnote omitted). Thus, the first step here is to assess Atwater's claim that peace officers' authority to make warrantless arrests for misdemeanors was restricted at common law (whether "common law" is understood strictly as law judicially derived or, instead, as the whole body of law extant at the time of the framing). Atwater's specific contention is that "founding-era common-law rules" forbade peace officers to make warrantless misdemeanor arrests except in cases of "breach of the peace," a category she claims was then understood narrowly as covering only those nonfelony offenses "involving or tending toward violence." Although her historical argument is by no means insubstantial, it ultimately fails.

A

* * *

1

Atwater's historical argument begins with our quotation from Halsbury in *Carroll v. United States,* 267 U.S. 132, 45 S.Ct. 280, 69 L.Ed. 543 (1925), that

" '[i]n cases of misdemeanor, a peace officer like a private person has at common law no power of arresting without a warrant except when a breach of the peace has been committed in his presence or there is reasonable ground for supposing that a breach of peace is about to be committed or renewed in his presence.' " *Id.,* at 157, 45 S.Ct. 280 (quoting 9 Halsbury, Laws of England § 612, p. 299 (1909)).

But the isolated quotation tends to mislead. * * * [S]tatements about the common law of warrantless misdemeanor arrest simply are not uniform. Rather, "[a]t common law there is a difference of opinion among the authorities as to whether this right to arrest [without a warrant] extends to all misdemeanors." American Law Institute, Code of Criminal Procedure, Commentary to § 21, p. 231 (1930).

* * *

We * * * find disagreement, not unanimity, among both the common-law jurists and the text-writers who sought to pull the cases together and summarize accepted practice. Having reviewed the relevant English decisions, as well as English and colonial American legal treatises, legal dictionaries, and procedure manuals, we simply are not convinced that Atwater's is the correct, or even necessarily the better, reading of the common-law history.

2

A second, and equally serious, problem for Atwater's historical argument is posed by the "divers Statutes," M. Dalton, Country Justice ch. 170, § 4, p. 582 (1727), enacted by Parliament well before this Republic's founding that authorized warrantless misdemeanor arrests without reference to violence or turmoil. * * * The so-called "nightwalker" statutes are perhaps the most notable examples. From the enactment of the Statute of Winchester in 1285, through its various readoptions and until its repeal in 1827, night watchmen were authorized and charged "as . . . in Times past" to "watch the Town continually all Night, from the Sun-setting unto the Sun-rising" and were directed that "if any Stranger do pass by them, he shall be arrested until Morning. . . ." 13 Edw. I, ch. 4, §§ 5–6, 1 Statutes at Large 232–233 * * *. And according to Blackstone, these watchmen had virtually limitless warrantless nighttime arrest power: "Watchmen, either those appointed by the statute of Winchester . . . or such as are merely assistants to the constable, may *virtute officii* arrest all offenders, and particularly nightwalkers, and commit them to custody till the morning." 4 Blackstone 289 * * *.

Nor were the nightwalker statutes the only legislative sources of warrantless arrest authority absent real or threatened violence, as the parties and their *amici* here seem to have assumed. On the contrary, following the Edwardian legislation and throughout the period leading up to the framing, Parliament repeatedly extended warrantless arrest power to cover misdemeanor-level offenses not involving any breach of the peace. * * * The point is that the statutes riddle Atwater's supposed common-law rule with enough exceptions to unsettle any contention that the law of the mother country would have left the Fourth Amendment's Framers of a view that it would necessarily have been unreasonable to arrest without warrant for a misdemeanor unaccompanied by real or threatened violence.

B

An examination of specifically American evidence is to the same effect. Neither the history of the framing era nor subsequent legal development indicates that the Fourth Amendment was originally understood, or has traditionally been read, to embrace Atwater's position.

1

To begin with, Atwater has cited no particular evidence that those who framed and ratified the Fourth Amendment sought to limit peace officers' warrantless misdemeanor arrest authority to instances of actual breach of the peace, and our own review of the recent and respected compilations of framing-era documentary history has likewise failed to reveal any such design. Nor have we found in any of the modern historical accounts of the Fourth Amendment's adoption any substantial indication that the Framers intended such a restriction. Indeed, to the extent these modern histories address the issue, their conclusions are to the contrary.

The evidence of actual practice also counsels against Atwater's position. During the period leading up to and surrounding the framing of the Bill of Rights, colonial and state legislatures, like Parliament before them, regularly authorized local peace officers to make warrantless misdemeanor arrests without conditioning statutory authority on breach of the peace.

* * *

* * * We simply cannot conclude that the Fourth Amendment, as originally understood, forbade peace officers to arrest without a warrant for misdemeanors not amounting to or involving breach of the peace.

2

Nor does Atwater's argument from tradition pick up any steam from the historical record as it has unfolded since the framing, there being no indication that her claimed rule has ever become "woven . . . into the fabric" of American law. The story, on the contrary, is of two centuries of uninterrupted (and largely unchallenged) state and federal practice permitting warrantless arrests for misdemeanors not amounting to or involving breach of the peace.[2]

* * *

III

While it is true here that history, if not unequivocal, has expressed a decided, majority view that the police need not obtain an arrest warrant

---

2. We need not, and thus do not, speculate whether the Fourth Amendment entails an "in the presence" requirement for purposes of misdemeanor arrests. Cf. *Welsh v. Wisconsin,* 466 U.S. 740, 756, 104 S.Ct. 2091, 80 L.Ed.2d 732 (1984) (White, J., dissenting) ("[T]he requirement that a misdemeanor must have occurred in the officer's presence to justify a warrantless arrest is not grounded in the Fourth Amendment").

merely because a misdemeanor stopped short of violence or a threat of it, Atwater does not wager all on history. Instead, she asks us to mint a new rule of constitutional law on the understanding that when historical practice fails to speak conclusively to a claim grounded on the Fourth Amendment, courts are left to strike a current balance between individual and societal interests by subjecting particular contemporary circumstances to traditional standards of reasonableness. Atwater accordingly argues for a modern arrest rule, one not necessarily requiring violent breach of the peace, but nonetheless forbidding custodial arrest, even upon probable cause, when conviction could not ultimately carry any jail time and when the government shows no compelling need for immediate detention.[3]

If we were to derive a rule exclusively to address the uncontested facts of this case, Atwater might well prevail. She was a known and established resident of Lago Vista with no place to hide and no incentive to flee, and common sense says she would almost certainly have buckled up as a condition of driving off with a citation. In her case, the physical incidents of arrest were merely gratuitous humiliations imposed by a police officer who was (at best) exercising extremely poor judgment. Atwater's claim to live free of pointless indignity and confinement clearly outweighs anything the City can raise against it specific to her case.

But we have traditionally recognized that a responsible Fourth Amendment balance is not well served by standards requiring sensitive, case-by-case determinations of government need, lest every discretionary judgment in the field be converted into an occasion for constitutional review. Often enough, the Fourth Amendment has to be applied on the spur (and in the heat) of the moment, and the object in implementing its command of reasonableness is to draw standards sufficiently clear and simple to be applied with a fair prospect of surviving judicial second-guessing months and years after an arrest or search is made. Courts attempting to strike a reasonable Fourth Amendment balance thus credit the government's side with an essential interest in readily administrable rules.

At first glance, Atwater's argument may seem to respect the values of clarity and simplicity, so far as she claims that the Fourth Amendment generally forbids warrantless arrests for minor crimes not accompanied by violence or some demonstrable threat of it (whether "minor crime" be defined as a fine-only traffic offense, a fine-only offense more generally, or a misdemeanor.) But the claim is not ultimately so simple, nor could it be, for complications arise the moment we begin to think about the possible applications of the several criteria Atwater proposes for drawing a line between minor crimes with limited arrest authority and others not so restricted.

3. Although it is unclear from Atwater's briefs whether the rule she proposes would bar custodial arrests for fine-only offenses even when made pursuant to a warrant, at oral argument Atwater's counsel "concede[d] that if a warrant were obtained, this arrest ... would ... be reasonable."

One line, she suggests, might be between "jailable" and "fine-only" offenses, between those for which conviction could result in commitment and those for which it could not. The trouble with this distinction, of course, is that an officer on the street might not be able to tell. It is not merely that we cannot expect every police officer to know the details of frequently complex penalty schemes, but that penalties for ostensibly identical conduct can vary on account of facts difficult (if not impossible) to know at the scene of an arrest. Is this the first offense or is the suspect a repeat offender? Is the weight of the marijuana a gram above or a gram below the fine-only line? Where conduct could implicate more than one criminal prohibition, which one will the district attorney ultimately decide to charge? And so on.

But Atwater's refinements would not end there. She represents that if the line were drawn at nonjailable traffic offenses, her proposed limitation should be qualified by a proviso authorizing warrantless arrests where "necessary for enforcement of the traffic laws or when [an] offense would otherwise continue and pose a danger to others on the road." (Were the line drawn at misdemeanors generally, a comparable qualification would presumably apply.) The proviso only compounds the difficulties. Would, for instance, either exception apply to speeding? At oral argument, Atwater's counsel said that "it would not be reasonable to arrest a driver for speeding unless the speeding rose to the level of reckless driving." But is it not fair to expect that the chronic speeder will speed again despite a citation in his pocket, and should that not qualify as showing that the "offense would . . . continue" under Atwater's rule? And why, as a constitutional matter, should we assume that only reckless driving will "pose a danger to others on the road" while speeding will not?

There is no need for more examples to show that Atwater's general rule and limiting proviso promise very little in the way of administrability. It is no answer that the police routinely make judgments on grounds like risk of immediate repetition; they surely do and should. But there is a world of difference between making that judgment in choosing between the discretionary leniency of a summons in place of a clearly lawful arrest, and making the same judgment when the question is the lawfulness of the warrantless arrest itself. * * *

One may ask, of course, why these difficulties may not be answered by a simple tie breaker for the police to follow in the field: if in doubt, do not arrest. The first answer is that in practice the tie breaker would boil down to something akin to a least-restrictive-alternative limitation, which is itself one of those "ifs, ands, and buts" rules, generally thought inappropriate in working out Fourth Amendment protection. Beyond that, whatever help the tie breaker might give would come at the price of a systematic disincentive to arrest in situations where even Atwater concedes that arresting would serve an important societal interest. An officer not quite sure that the drugs weighed enough to warrant jail time or not quite certain about a suspect's risk of flight would not arrest, even though it could perfectly well turn out that, in fact, the offense called for incarceration and the defendant was long gone on the day of trial. Multiplied many times over, the costs to society of such underenforcement could easily outweigh the costs to defendants of being needlessly arrested and booked, as Atwater herself acknowledges.

Just how easily the costs could outweigh the benefits may be shown by asking, as one Member of this Court did at oral argument, "how bad the problem is out there." The very fact that the law has never jelled the way Atwater would have it leads one to wonder whether warrantless misdemeanor arrests need constitutional attention, and there is cause to think the answer is no. So far as such arrests might be thought to pose a threat to the probable-cause requirement, anyone arrested for a crime without formal process, whether for felony or misdemeanor, is entitled to a magistrate's review of probable cause within 48 hours, and there is no reason to think the procedure in this case atypical in giving the suspect a prompt opportunity to request release. Many jurisdictions, moreover, have chosen to impose more restrictive safeguards through statutes limiting warrantless arrests for minor offenses. It is of course easier to devise a minor-offense limitation by statute than to derive one through the Constitution, simply because the statute can let the arrest power turn on any sort of practical consideration without having to subsume it under a broader principle. It is, in fact, only natural that States should resort to this sort of legislative regulation, for, as Atwater's own *amici* emphasize, it is in the interest of the police to limit petty-offense arrests, which carry costs that are simply too great to incur without good reason. Finally, and significantly, under current doctrine the preference for categorical treatment of Fourth Amendment claims gives way to individualized review when a defendant makes a colorable argument that an arrest, with or without a warrant, was "conducted in an extraordinary manner, unusually harmful to [his] privacy or even physical interests." *Whren v. United States,* [517 U.S. 806, 818, 116 S.Ct. 1769, 135 L.Ed.2d 89 (1996)].

The upshot of all these influences, combined with the good sense (and, failing that, the political accountability) of most local lawmakers and law-enforcement officials, is a dearth of horribles demanding redress. Indeed, when Atwater's counsel was asked at oral argument for any indications of comparably foolish, warrantless misdemeanor arrests, he could offer only one. We are sure that there are others, but just as surely the country is not confronting anything like an epidemic of unnecessary minor-offense arrests.[4] That fact caps the reasons for rejecting Atwater's request for the development of a new and distinct body of constitutional law.

---

4. The dissent insists that a minor traffic infraction "may serve as an excuse" for harassment, and that fine-only misdemeanor prohibitions "may be enforced" in an arbitrary manner. Thus, the dissent warns, the rule that we recognize today "has potentially serious consequences for the everyday lives of Americans" and "carries with it grave poten-

Accordingly, we confirm today what our prior cases have intimated: * * * [I]f an officer has probable cause to believe that an individual has committed even a very minor criminal offense in his presence, he may, without violating the Fourth Amendment, arrest the offender.

IV

Atwater's arrest satisfied constitutional requirements. There is no dispute that Officer Turek had probable cause to believe that Atwater had committed a crime in his presence. She admits that neither she nor her children were wearing seat belts, as required by Tex. Tran.Code Ann. § 545.413 (1999). Turek was accordingly authorized (not required, but authorized) to make a custodial arrest without balancing costs and benefits or determining whether or not Atwater's arrest was in some sense necessary.

Nor was the arrest made in an "extraordinary manner, unusually harmful to [her] privacy or . . . physical interests." *Whren v. United States,* 517 U.S., at 818, 116 S.Ct. 1769. As our citations in *Whren* make clear, the question whether a search or seizure is "extraordinary" turns, above all else, on the manner in which the search or seizure is executed. Atwater's arrest was surely "humiliating," as she says in her brief, but it was no more "harmful to . . . privacy or . . . physical interests" than the normal custodial arrest. She was handcuffed, placed in a squad car, and taken to the local police station, where officers asked her to remove her shoes, jewelry, and glasses, and to empty her pockets. They then took her photograph and placed her in a cell, alone, for about an hour, after which she was taken before a magistrate, and released on $310 bond. The arrest and booking were inconvenient and embarrassing to Atwater, but not so extraordinary as to violate the Fourth Amendment.

The Court of Appeals's en banc judgment is affirmed.

It is so ordered.

■ JUSTICE O'CONNOR, with whom JUSTICE STEVENS, JUSTICE GINSBURG, and JUSTICE BREYER join, dissenting.

The Fourth Amendment guarantees the right to be free from "unreasonable searches and seizures." The Court recognizes that the arrest of Gail Atwater was a "pointless indignity" that served no discernible state interest, and yet holds that her arrest was constitutionally permissible. Because the Court's position is inconsistent with the explicit guarantee of the Fourth Amendment, I dissent.

tial for abuse." But the dissent's own language (*e.g.,* "may," "potentially") betrays the speculative nature of its claims. Noticeably absent from the parade of horribles is any indication that the "potential for abuse" has ever ripened into a reality. In fact, as we have pointed out in text, there simply is no evidence of widespread abuse of minor-offense arrest authority.

I

A full custodial arrest, such as the one to which Ms. Atwater was subjected, is the quintessential seizure. When a full custodial arrest is effected without a warrant, the plain language of the Fourth Amendment requires that the arrest be reasonable. It is beyond cavil that "[t]he touchstone of our analysis under the Fourth Amendment is always 'the reasonableness in all the circumstances of the particular governmental invasion of a citizen's personal security.'" *Pennsylvania v. Mimms*, 434 U.S. 106, 108–109, 98 S.Ct. 330, 54 L.Ed.2d 331 (1977) *(per curiam)* (quoting *Terry v. Ohio*, 392 U.S. 1, 19, 88 S.Ct. 1868, 20 L.Ed.2d 889 (1968)).

We have "often looked to the common law in evaluating the reasonableness, for Fourth Amendment purposes, of police activity." But history is just one of the tools we use in conducting the reasonableness inquiry. And when history is inconclusive, as the majority amply demonstrates it is in this case, we will "evaluate the search or seizure under traditional standards of reasonableness by assessing, on the one hand, the degree to which it intrudes upon an individual's privacy and, on the other, the degree to which it is needed for the promotion of legitimate governmental interests." * * *

The majority gives a brief nod to this bedrock principle of our Fourth Amendment jurisprudence, and even acknowledges that "Atwater's claim to live free of pointless indignity and confinement clearly outweighs anything the City can raise against it specific to her case." But instead of remedying this imbalance, the majority allows itself to be swayed by the worry that "every discretionary judgment in the field [will] be converted into an occasion for constitutional review." It therefore mints a new rule that "[i]f an officer has probable cause to believe that an individual has committed even a very minor criminal offense in his presence, he may, without violating the Fourth Amendment, arrest the offender." This rule is not only unsupported by our precedent, but runs contrary to the principles that lie at the core of the Fourth Amendment.

* * *

* * * The Court's thorough exegesis makes it abundantly clear that warrantless misdemeanor arrests were not the subject of a clear and consistently applied rule at common law. We therefore must engage in the balancing test required by the Fourth Amendment. While probable cause is surely a necessary condition for warrantless arrests for fine-only offenses, any realistic assessment of the interests implicated by such arrests demonstrates that probable cause alone is not a sufficient condition.

* * *

A custodial arrest exacts an obvious toll on an individual's liberty and privacy, even when the period of custody is relatively brief. The arrestee is subject to a full search of her person and confiscation of her possessions. If the arrestee is the occupant of a car, the entire passenger compartment of the car, including packages therein, is subject to search as well. The arrestee may be detained for up to 48 hours without having a magistrate determine whether there in fact was probable cause for the arrest. Because people arrested for all types of violent and nonviolent offenses may be housed together awaiting such review, this detention period is potentially dangerous. And once the period of custody is over, the fact of the arrest is a permanent part of the public record.

We have said that "the penalty that may attach to any particular offense seems to provide the clearest and most consistent indication of the State's interest in arresting individuals suspected of committing that offense." *Welsh v. Wisconsin,* 466 U.S. 740, 754, n. 14, 104 S.Ct. 2091, 80 L.Ed.2d 732 (1984). If the State has decided that a fine, and not imprisonment, is the appropriate punishment for an offense, the State's interest in taking a person suspected of committing that offense into custody is surely limited, at best. This is not to say that the State will never have such an interest. A full custodial arrest may on occasion vindicate legitimate state interests, even if the crime is punishable only by fine. Arrest is the surest way to abate criminal conduct. It may also allow the police to verify the offender's identity and, if the offender poses a flight risk, to ensure her appearance at trial. But when such considerations are not present, a citation or summons may serve the State's remaining law enforcement interests every bit as effectively as an arrest.

* * * I would require that when there is probable cause to believe that a fine-only offense has been committed, the police officer should issue a citation unless the officer is "able to point to specific and articulable facts which, taken together with rational inferences from those facts, reasonably warrant [the additional] intrusion" of a full custodial arrest. *Terry v. Ohio,* 392 U.S., at 21, 88 S.Ct. 1868.

* * *

II

The record in this case makes it abundantly clear that Ms. Atwater's arrest was constitutionally unreasonable. Atwater readily admits—as she did when Officer Turek pulled her over—that she violated Texas' seatbelt law. While Turek was justified in stopping Atwater, neither law nor reason supports his decision to arrest her instead of simply giving her a citation. The officer's actions cannot sensibly be viewed as a permissible means of balancing Atwater's Fourth Amendment interests with the State's own legitimate interests.

* * *

III

The Court's error * * * does not merely affect the disposition of this case. The *per se* rule that the Court creates has potentially serious consequences for the everyday lives of Americans. A broad range of conduct falls into the category of fine-only misdemeanors. In Texas alone, for example, disobeying any sort of traffic warning sign is a misdemeanor punishable only by fine, as is failing to pay a highway toll, and driving with expired license plates. Nor are fine-only crimes limited to the traffic context. In several States, for example, littering is a criminal offense punishable only by fine.

To be sure, such laws are valid and wise exercises of the States' power to protect the public health and welfare. My concern lies not with the decision to enact or enforce these laws, but rather with the manner in which they may be enforced. Under today's holding, when a police officer has probable cause to believe that a fine-only misdemeanor offense has occurred, that officer may stop the suspect, issue a citation, and let the person continue on her way. Or, if a traffic violation, the officer may stop the car, arrest the driver, search the driver, search the entire passenger compartment of the car including any purse or package inside, and impound the car and inventory all of its contents. Although the Fourth Amendment expressly requires that the latter course be a reasonable and proportional response to the circumstances of the offense, the majority gives officers unfettered discretion to choose that course without articulating a single reason why such action is appropriate.

Such unbounded discretion carries with it grave potential for abuse. The majority takes comfort in the lack of evidence of "an epidemic of unnecessary minor-offense arrests." But the relatively small number of published cases dealing with such arrests proves little and should provide little solace. Indeed, as the recent debate over racial profiling demonstrates all too clearly, a relatively minor traffic infraction may often serve as an excuse for stopping and harassing an individual. After today, the arsenal available to any officer extends to a full arrest and the searches permissible concomitant to that arrest. An officer's subjective motivations for making a traffic stop are not relevant considerations in determining the reasonableness of the stop. But it is precisely because these motivations are beyond our purview that we must vigilantly ensure that officers' poststop actions—which are properly within our reach—comport with the Fourth Amendment's guarantee of reasonableness.

* * *

The Court neglects the Fourth Amendment's express command in the name of administrative ease. In so doing, it cloaks the pointless indignity that Gail Atwater suffered with the mantle of reasonableness. I respectfully dissent.

C. FIELD DETENTIONS FOR INVESTIGATION AND RELATED SEARCHES

1. FIELD DETENTION

Page 207. Insert the following Editors' Introduction: Reasonable Suspicion at the end of that portion titled, "Reasonable Suspicion as Applied":

The Supreme Court elaborated on reasonable suspicion analysis in United States v. Arvizu, 534 U.S. 266, 122 S.Ct. 744, 151 L.Ed.2d 740 (2002). A border patrol agent—Stoddard—stopped Arvizu's minivan on a remote and unpaved road near Douglas, Arizona. After obtaining Arvizu's consent, Stoddard searched the vehicle and found marijuana. The District Court concluded that given all of the circumstances the agent had reasonable suspicion for the stop. Reversing, the Ninth Circuit took a restrictive approach to the issue:

> "What factors law enforcement officers may consider in deciding to stop and question citizens minding their own business should, if possible, be carefully circumscribed and clearly articulated. When courts invoke multi-factor tests, balancing of interests or fact-specific weighing of circumstances, this introduces a troubling degree of uncertainty and unpredictability into the process; no one can be sure whether a particular combination of factors will justify a stop until a court has ruled on it." [United States v. Montero–Camargo, 208 F.3d 1122, 1142 (9th Cir.2000) (en banc)] (Kozinski, J. concurring). Thus we attempt here to describe and clearly delimit the extent to which certain factors may be considered by law enforcement officers in making stops such as the stop involved here.

Dividing the factors considered by the District Court into two groups, the Court of Appeals first held that seven were entitled to little or no weight at all. These included Stoddard's testimony that the minivan slowed down when approaching him parked off the road; Stoddard's testimony that the driver failed to acknowledge the parked agent; Stoddard's observation that the children sitting in the back appeared to have their knees at a high level suggesting their feet were on something; and Stoddard's testimony that the children in the van waived at him in an odd manner. Three were properly considered: Stoddard's knowledge that the road was used by persons smuggling illegally entered aliens; observation of the minivan near the time of the border agents' shift chance, a time often chosen by smugglers; and the agent's experience that minivans of the sort driven by Arvizu were often used by smugglers. But these three together were insufficient to constitute reasonable suspicion.

A unanimous Supreme Court reversed, disapproving of the intermediate court's approach to the case:

When discussing how reviewing courts should make reasonable-suspicion determinations, we have said repeatedly that they must look at the "totality of the circumstances" of each case to see whether the detaining officer has a "particularized and objective basis" for suspecting legal wrongdoing. This process allows officers to draw on their own experience and specialized training to make inferences from and deductions about the cumulative information available to them that "might well elude an untrained person."

Our cases have recognized that the concept of reasonable suspicion is somewhat abstract. But we have deliberately avoided reducing it to " 'a neat set of legal rules.' " * * *

We think that the approach taken by the Court of Appeals here departs sharply from the teachings of these cases. The court's evaluation and rejection of seven of the listed factors in isolation from each other does not take into account the "totality of the circumstances," as our cases have understood that phrase.

The Court of Appeals' view that it was necessary to "clearly delimit" an officer's consideration of certain factors to reduce "troubling ... uncertainty," also runs counter to our cases and underestimates the usefulness of the reasonable-suspicion standard in guiding officers in the field. * * *

Having considered the totality of the circumstances and given due weight to the factual inferences drawn by the law enforcement officer and District Court Judge, we hold that Stoddard had reasonable suspicion to believe that [Arvizu] was engaged in illegal activity. It was reasonable for Stoddard to infer from his observations, his registration check, and his experience as a border patrol agent that [Arvizu] had set out from Douglas along a little-traveled route used by smugglers to avoid [a nearby] checkpoint. Stoddard's knowledge further supported a commonsense inference that [Arvizu] intended to pass through the area at a time when officers would be leaving their backroads patrols to change shifts. The likelihood that [Arvizu] and his family were on a picnic outing was diminished by the fact that the minivan had turned away from the known recreational areas accessible to the east on Rucker Canyon Road. Corroborating this inference was the fact that recreational areas farther to the north would have been easier to reach by taking [an alternative route passing through the checkpoint], as opposed to the 40–to–50–mile trip on unpaved and primitive roads. The children's elevated knees suggested the existence of concealed cargo in the passenger compartment. Finally, * * * Stoddard's assessment of [Arvizu]'s reactions upon seeing him and the children's mechanical-like waving, which continued for a full four to five minutes, were entitled to some weight.

[Arvizu] argues that we must rule in his favor because the facts suggested a family in a minivan on a holiday outing. A determination that reasonable suspicion exists, however, need not rule out the possibility of innocent conduct. Undoubtedly, each of these factors alone is susceptible to innocent explanation, and some factors are more probative than others. Taken together, we believe they sufficed to form a particularized and objective basis for Stoddard's stopping the vehicle, making the stop reasonable within the meaning of the Fourth Amendment.

534 U.S. at 273–78, 122 S.Ct. at 750–52, 151 L.Ed.2d at 749–52.

Page 212.   Insert the following in Editors' Introduction: Reasonable Suspicion before "Stop and Frisk in Practice":

Consideration of Race

The Ninth Circuit, sitting en banc, rejected Supreme Court dictum suggesting that in making a *Terry* stop of a person suspected of being an illegal alien the person's Hispanic appearance could be considered. United States v. Montero–Camargo, 208 F.3d 1122 (9th Cir.2000), cert. denied, 531 U.S. 889, 121 S.Ct. 211, 148 L.Ed.2d 148 (2000) (opinion on rehearing en banc). This aspect of the decision is addressed in the material supplementing page 348 of the text.

Montero–Camargo's concern clearly extended beyond the border-related law enforcement activity before it. The court observed, "A significant body of research shows that race is routinely and improperly used as a proxy for criminality, and is often the defining factor in police officers' decisions to arrest, stop or frisk potential suspects." It then commented more generally on the relevance of race to reasonable suspicion:

[W]e do not * * * preclude the use of racial or ethnic appearance as one factor relevant to reasonable suspicion or probable cause when a particular suspect has been identified as having a specific racial or ethnic appearance, be it Caucasian, African–American, Hispanic or other. We note, however, that a stop based solely on the fact that the racial or ethnic appearance of an individual matches the racial or ethnic description of a specific suspect would not be justified.

208 F.3d at 1134 n. 21. It continued:

Hispanic appearance, or any other racial or ethnic appearance, including Caucasian, may be considered when the suspected perpetrator of a specific offense has been identified as having such an appearance. Even in such circumstances, however, persons of a particular racial or ethnic group may not be stopped and questioned because of such appearance, unless there are other individualized or particularized factors which, together with the racial or ethnic appearance identified, rise to the level of reasonable suspicion or probable cause. To the extent that our prior cases have approved the use of Hispanic appearance as a factor where there was no particularized, individual suspicion, they are overruled.

208 F.3d at 1134 n. 22.

Page 219.   Insert the following in Note 2 after Florida v. Royer:

The issue was addressed again in Kaupp v. Texas, 538 U.S. 626, 123 S.Ct. 1843, 155 L.Ed.2d 814 (2003) (per curiam). The facts were as follows:

> After a 14–year–old girl disappeared in January 1999, the Harris County [Texas] Sheriff's Department learned she had had a sexual relationship with her 19–year–old half brother, who had been in the company of * * * Robert Kaupp, then 17 years old, on the day of the girl's disappearance. On January 26th, deputy sheriffs questioned the brother and Kaupp at headquarters; Kaupp was cooperative and was permitted to leave, but the brother failed a polygraph examination (his third such failure). Eventually he confessed that he had fatally stabbed his half sister and placed her body in a drainage ditch. He implicated Kaupp in the crime.

> * * * Detective Gregory Pinkins * * * decided (in his words) to "get [Kaupp] in and confront him with what [the brother] had said." In the company of two other plain clothes detectives and three uniformed officers, Pinkins went to Kaupp's house at approximately 3 a.m. on January 27th. After Kaupp's father let them in, Pinkins, with at least two other officers, went to Kaupp's bedroom, awakened him with a flashlight, identified himself, and said, " 'we need to go and talk.' " Kaupp said " 'Okay.' " The two officers then handcuffed Kaupp and led him, shoeless and dressed only in boxer shorts and a T-shirt, out of his house and into a patrol car. The state points to nothing in the record indicating Kaupp was told that he was free to decline to go with the officers.

> They stopped for 5 or 10 minutes where the victim's body had just been found, in anticipation of confronting Kaupp with the brother's confession, and then went on to the sheriff's headquarters. There, they took Kaupp to an interview room, removed his handcuffs, and advised him of his rights under *Miranda v. Arizona,* 384 U.S. 436, 86 S.Ct. 1602, 16 L.Ed.2d 694 (1966). Kaupp first denied any involvement in the victim's disappearance, but 10 or 15 minutes into the interrogation, told of the brother's confession, he admitted having some part in the crime. He did not, however, acknowledge causing the fatal wound or confess to murder, for which he was later indicted.

Summarily rejecting the state court's conclusion that no arrest occurred until after the confession, a unanimous Supreme Court explained:

> Although certain seizures may be justified on something less than probable cause we have never "sustained against Fourth Amendment challenge the involuntary removal of a suspect from his home to a police station and his detention there for investigative purposes ... absent probable cause or judicial authorization." Such involuntary transport to a police station for questioning is "sufficiently like arres[t] to invoke the traditional rule that arrests may constitutionally be made only on probable cause."

* * *

Contrary reasons mentioned by the state courts are no answer to the facts. Kaupp's " 'Okay' " in response to Pinkins's statement is no showing of consent under the circumstances. Pinkins offered Kaupp no choice, and a group of police officers rousing an adolescent out of bed in the middle of the night with the words "we need to go and talk" presents no option but "to go." * * * If reasonable doubt were possible on this point, the ensuing events would resolve it: removal from one's house in handcuffs on a January night with nothing on but underwear for a trip to a crime scene on the way to an interview room at law enforcement headquarters. * * * It cannot seriously be suggested that when the detectives began to question Kaupp, a reasonable person in his situation would have thought he was sitting in the interview room as a matter of choice, free to change his mind and go home to bed.

538 U.S. at 630–32, 123 S.Ct. at 1846–47, 155 L.Ed.2d at 820–21. The state, the Court noted, did not claim to have probable cause.

Page 221.   Insert the following after Florida v. Royer and accompanying notes:

Illinois v. Wardlow

Supreme Court of the United States, 2000.
528 U.S. 119, 120 S.Ct. 673, 145 L.Ed.2d 570.

■ Chief Justice Rehnquist delivered the opinion of the Court.

Respondent Wardlow fled upon seeing police officers patrolling an area known for heavy narcotics trafficking. Two of the officers caught up with him, stopped him and conducted a protective pat-down search for weapons. Discovering a .38–caliber handgun, the officers arrested Wardlow. We hold that the officers' stop did not violate the Fourth Amendment to the United States Constitution.

On September 9, 1995, Officers Nolan and Harvey were working as uniformed officers in the special operations section of the Chicago Police Department. The officers were driving the last car of a four car caravan converging on an area known for heavy narcotics trafficking in order to investigate drug transactions. The officers were traveling together because they expected to find a crowd of people in the area, including lookouts and customers.

As the caravan passed 4035 West Van Buren, Officer Nolan observed respondent Wardlow standing next to the building holding an opaque bag. Respondent looked in the direction of the officers and fled. Nolan and Harvey turned their car southbound, watched him as he ran through the gangway and an alley, and eventually cornered him on the street. Nolan then exited his car and stopped respondent. He immediately conducted a protective pat-down search for weapons because in his experience it was common for there to be weapons in the near vicinity of narcotics transactions. During the frisk, Officer Nolan squeezed the bag respondent was carrying and felt a heavy, hard object similar to the shape of a gun. The officer then opened the bag and discovered a .38–caliber handgun with five live rounds of ammunition. The officers arrested Wardlow.

The Illinois trial court denied respondent's motion to suppress, finding the gun was recovered during a lawful stop and frisk. Following a stipulated bench trial, Wardlow was convicted of unlawful use of a weapon by a felon. The Illinois Appellate Court reversed Wardlow's conviction, concluding that the gun should have been suppressed because Officer Nolan did not have reasonable suspicion sufficient to justify an investigative stop pursuant to Terry v. Ohio, 392 U.S. 1, 88 S.Ct. 1868, 20 L.Ed.2d 889 (1968).

The Illinois Supreme Court agreed. * * * Relying on Florida v. Royer, 460 U.S. 491, 103 S.Ct. 1319, 75 L.Ed.2d 229 (1983), the court explained that although police have the right to approach individuals and ask questions, the individual has no obligation to respond. The person may decline to answer and simply go on his or her way, and the refusal to respond, alone, does not provide a legitimate basis for an investigative stop. The court then determined that flight may simply be an exercise of this right to "go on one's way," and, thus, could not constitute reasonable suspicion justifying a *Terry* stop.

The Illinois Supreme Court also rejected the argument that flight combined with the fact that it occurred in a high crime area supported a finding of reasonable suspicion * * *. We granted certiorari, and now reverse.

This case, involving a brief encounter between a citizen and a police officer on a public street, is governed by the analysis we first applied in *Terry*. In *Terry*, we held that an officer may, consistent with the Fourth Amendment, conduct a brief, investigatory stop when the officer has a reasonable, articulable suspicion that criminal activity is afoot. While "reasonable suspicion" is a less demanding standard than probable cause and requires a showing considerably less than preponderance of the evidence, the Fourth Amendment requires at least a minimal level of objective justification for making the stop. The officer must be able to articulate more than an "inchoate and unparticularized suspicion or 'hunch'" of criminal activity.[1]

Nolan and Harvey were among eight officers in a four car caravan that was converging on an area known for heavy narcotics trafficking, and the officers anticipated encountering a large number of people in the area, including drug customers and individuals serving as lookouts. It was in this context that Officer Nolan decided to investigate Wardlow after observing him flee. An individual's presence in an area of expected criminal activity, standing alone, is not enough to support a reasonable, particularized

---

1. We granted certiorari solely on the question of whether the initial stop was supported by reasonable suspicion. Therefore, we express no opinion as to the lawfulness of the frisk independently of the stop.

suspicion that the person is committing a crime. But officers are not required to ignore the relevant characteristics of a location in determining whether the circumstances are sufficiently suspicious to warrant further investigation. Accordingly, we have previously noted the fact that the stop occurred in a "high crime area" among the relevant contextual considerations in a *Terry* analysis. Adams v. Williams, 407 U.S. 143, 144 and 147–148, 92 S.Ct. 1921, 32 L.Ed.2d 612 (1972).

In this case, moreover, it was not merely respondent's presence in an area of heavy narcotics trafficking that aroused the officers' suspicion but his unprovoked flight upon noticing the police. Our cases have also recognized that nervous, evasive behavior is a pertinent factor in determining reasonable suspicion. Headlong flight—wherever it occurs—is the consummate act of evasion: it is not necessarily indicative of wrongdoing, but it is certainly suggestive of such. In reviewing the propriety of an officer's conduct, courts do not have available empirical studies dealing with inferences drawn from suspicious behavior, and we cannot reasonably demand scientific certainty from judges or law enforcement officers where none exists. Thus, the determination of reasonable suspicion must be based on commonsense judgments and inferences about human behavior. We conclude Officer Nolan was justified in suspecting that Wardlow was involved in criminal activity, and, therefore, in investigating further.

Such a holding is entirely consistent with our decision in Florida v. Royer, 460 U.S. 491, 103 S.Ct. 1319, 75 L.Ed.2d 229 (1983), where we held that when an officer, without reasonable suspicion or probable cause, approaches an individual, the individual has a right to ignore the police and go about his business. And any "refusal to cooperate, without more, does not furnish the minimal level of objective justification needed for a detention or seizure." Florida v. Bostick, 501 U.S. 429, 437, 111 S.Ct. 2382, 115 L.Ed.2d 389 (1991). But unprovoked flight is simply not a mere refusal to cooperate. Flight, by its very nature, is not "going about one's business"; in fact, it is just the opposite. Allowing officers confronted with such flight to stop the fugitive and investigate further is quite consistent with the individual's right to go about his business or to stay put and remain silent in the face of police questioning.

Respondent and *amici* also argue that there are innocent reasons for flight from police and that, therefore, flight is not necessarily indicative of ongoing criminal activity. This fact is undoubtedly true, but does not establish a violation of the Fourth Amendment. Even in *Terry*, the conduct justifying the stop was ambiguous and susceptible of an innocent explanation. The officer observed two individuals pacing back and forth in front of a store, peering into the window and periodically conferring. All of this conduct was by itself lawful, but it also suggested that the individuals were casing the store for a planned robbery. *Terry* recognized that the officers could detain the individuals to resolve the ambiguity.

In allowing such detentions, *Terry* accepts the risk that officers may stop innocent people. Indeed, the Fourth Amendment accepts that risk in connection with more drastic police action; persons arrested and detained on probable cause to believe they have committed a crime may turn out to be innocent. The *Terry* stop is a far more minimal intrusion, simply allowing the officer to briefly investigate further. If the officer does not learn facts rising to the level of probable cause, the individual must be allowed to go on his way. But in this case the officers found respondent in possession of a handgun, and arrested him for violation of an Illinois firearms statute. No question of the propriety of the arrest itself is before us.

The judgment of the Supreme Court of Illinois is reversed, and the cause is remanded for further proceedings not inconsistent with this opinion.

It is so ordered.

■ JUSTICE STEVENS, with whom JUSTICE SOUTER, JUSTICE GINSBURG, and JUSTICE BREYER join, concurring in part and dissenting in part.

The State of Illinois asks this Court to announce a "bright-line rule" authorizing the temporary detention of anyone who flees at the mere sight of a police officer. Respondent counters by asking us to adopt the opposite *per se* rule—that the fact that a person flees upon seeing the police can never, by itself, be sufficient to justify a temporary investigative stop of the kind authorized by Terry v. Ohio, 392 U.S. 1, 88 S.Ct. 1868, 20 L.Ed.2d 889 (1968).

The Court today wisely endorses neither *per se* rule. Instead, it rejects the proposition that "flight is . . . necessarily indicative of ongoing criminal activity," adhering to the view that "[t]he concept of reasonable suspicion . . . is not readily, or even usefully, reduced to a neat set of legal rules," but must be determined by looking to "the totality of the circumstances—the whole picture." Abiding by this framework, the Court concludes that "Officer Nolan was justified in suspecting that Wardlow was involved in criminal activity."

Although I agree with the Court's rejection of the *per se* rules proffered by the parties, unlike the Court, I am persuaded that in this case the brief testimony of the officer who seized respondent does not justify the conclusion that he had reasonable suspicion to make the stop. Before discussing the specific facts of this case, I shall comment on the parties' requests for a *per se* rule.

I

* * *

The question in this case concerns "the degree of suspicion that attaches to" a person's flight—or, more precisely, what "commonsense conclusions" can be drawn respecting the motives behind that flight. A pedestrian may break into a run for a variety of reasons—to catch up with a friend a block or two away, to seek shelter from an impending storm, to arrive at a bus stop before the bus leaves, to get home in time for dinner, to resume jogging after a pause for rest, to avoid contact with a bore or a bully, or simply to answer the call of nature—any of which might coincide with the arrival of an officer in the vicinity. A pedestrian might also run because he or she has just sighted one or more police officers. In the latter instance, the State properly points out "that the fleeing person may be, inter alia, (1) an escapee from jail; (2) wanted on a warrant, (3) in possession of contraband, (i.e. drugs, weapons, stolen goods, etc.); or (4) someone who has just committed another type of crime."[2] In short, there are unquestionably circumstances in which a person's flight is suspicious, and undeniably instances in which a person runs for entirely innocent reasons.

Given the diversity and frequency of possible motivations for flight, it would be profoundly unwise to endorse either *per se* rule. The inference we can reasonably draw about the motivation for a person's flight, rather, will depend on a number of different circumstances. Factors such as the time of day, the number of people in the area, the character of the neighborhood, whether the officer was in uniform, the way the runner was dressed, the direction and speed of the flight, and whether the person's behavior was otherwise unusual might be relevant in specific cases. This number of variables is surely sufficient to preclude either a bright-line rule that always justifies, or that never justifies, an investigative stop based on the sole fact that flight began after a police officer appeared nearby.

Still, Illinois presses for a *per se* rule regarding "unprovoked flight upon seeing a clearly identifiable police officer." The phrase "upon seeing," as used by Illinois, apparently assumes that the flight is motivated by the presence of the police officer.[3] Illinois contends that unprovoked flight is "an extreme reaction," because innocent people simply do not "flee at the mere sight of the police." To be sure, Illinois concedes, an innocent person—even one distrustful of the police—might "avoid eye contact or even sneer at the sight of an officer," and that would not justify a *Terry* stop or any sort of *per se* inference. But, Illinois insists, unprovoked flight is

2. If the fleeing person exercises his or her right to remain silent after being stopped, only in the third of the State's four hypothetical categories is the stop likely to lead to probable cause to make an arrest. And even in the third category, flight does not necessarily indicate that the officer is "dealing with an armed and dangerous individual." Terry v. Ohio, 392 U.S. 1, 27, 88 S.Ct. 1868, 20 L.Ed.2d 889 (1968).

3. Nowhere in Illinois' briefs does it specify what it means by "unprovoked." At oral argument, Illinois explained that if officers precipitate a flight by threats of violence, that flight is "provoked." But if police officers in a patrol car—with lights flashing and siren sounding—descend upon an individual for the sole purpose of seeing if he or she will run, the ensuing flight is "unprovoked."

altogether different. Such behavior is so "aberrant" and "abnormal" that a *per se* inference is justified.

Even assuming we know that a person runs because he sees the police, the inference to be drawn may still vary from case to case. Flight to escape police detection, we have said, may have an entirely innocent motivation:

> "[I]t is a matter of common knowledge that men who are entirely innocent do sometimes fly from the scene of a crime through fear of being apprehended as the guilty parties, or from an unwillingness to appear as witnesses. Nor is it true as an accepted axiom of criminal law that 'the wicked flee when no man pursueth, but the righteous are as bold as a lion.' Innocent men sometimes hesitate to confront a jury— not necessarily because they fear that the jury will not protect them, but because they do not wish their names to appear in connection with criminal acts, are humiliated at being obliged to incur the popular odium of an arrest and trial, or because they do not wish to be put to the annoyance or expense of defending themselves." Alberty v. United States, 162 U.S. 499, 511, 16 S.Ct. 864, 40 L.Ed. 1051 (1896).

In addition to these concerns, a reasonable person may conclude that an officer's sudden appearance indicates nearby criminal activity. And where there is criminal activity there is also a substantial element of danger— either from the criminal or from a confrontation between the criminal and the police. These considerations can lead to an innocent and understandable desire to quit the vicinity with all speed.[4]

Among some citizens, particularly minorities and those residing in high crime areas, there is also the possibility that the fleeing person is entirely innocent, but, with or without justification, believes that contact with the police can itself be dangerous, apart from any criminal activity associated with the officer's sudden presence. For such a person, unprovoked flight is neither "aberrant" nor "abnormal."[5] Moreover, these concerns and fears

---

4. * * * One study [of bystander victimization,] * * * Sherman, Steele, Laufersweiler, Hooper & Julian, Stray Bullets and "Mushrooms": Random Shootings of Bystanders in Four Cities, 1977–1988, 5 Journal of Quantitative Criminology 297, 303 (1989)[,] * * * culling data from newspaper reports in four large cities over an 11–year period, found "substantial increases in reported bystander killings and woundings in all four cities." From 1986 to 1988, for example, the study identified 250 people who were killed or wounded in bystander shootings in the four survey cities. Most significantly for the purposes of the present case, the study found that such incidents "rank at the top of public outrage." The saliency of this phenom-

enon, in turn, "violate[s] the routine assumptions" of day-to-day affairs, and, "[w]ith enough frequency ... it shapes the conduct of daily life."

5. See, e.g., Kotlowitz, Hidden Casualties: Drug War's Emphasis on Law Enforcement Takes a Toll on Police, Wall Street Journal, Jan. 11, 1991, p. A2, col. 1 ("Black leaders complained that innocent people were picked up in the drug sweeps.... Some teenagers were so scared of the task force they ran even if they weren't selling drugs").

Many stops never lead to an arrest, which further exacerbates the perceptions of discrimination felt by racial minorities and people living in high crime areas. See Goldberg, The Color of Suspicion, N.Y. Times are known to the police officers themselves,[6] and are validated by law enforcement investigations into their own practices. Accordingly, the evidence supporting the reasonableness of these beliefs is too pervasive to be dismissed as random or rare, and too persuasive to be disparaged as inconclusive or insufficient.[7] In any event, just as we do not require "scientific certainty" for our commonsense conclusion that unprovoked flight can sometimes indicate suspicious motives, neither do we require scientific certainty to conclude that unprovoked flight can occur for other, innocent reasons.[8]

The probative force of the inferences to be drawn from flight is a function of the varied circumstances in which it occurs. Sometimes those inferences are entirely consistent with the presumption of innocence, sometimes they justify further investigation, and sometimes they justify an immediate stop and search for weapons. * * *

"Unprovoked flight," in short, describes a category of activity too broad and varied to permit a *per se* reasonable inference regarding the motivation for the activity. While the innocent explanations surely do not establish that the Fourth Amendment is always violated whenever someone is stopped solely on the basis of an unprovoked flight, neither do the suspicious motivations establish that the Fourth Amendment is never

Magazine, June 20, 1999, p. 85 (reporting that in 2-year period, New York City Police Department Street Crimes Unit made 45,000 stops, only 9,500, or 20%, of which resulted in arrest); Casimir, [Minority Men: We are Frisk Targets, N.Y. Daily News, March 26, 1999, p. 34] (reporting that in 1997, New York City's Street Crimes Unit conducted 27,061 stop-and-frisks, only 4,647 of which, 17%, resulted in arrest). Even if these data were race neutral, they would still indicate that society as a whole is paying a significant cost in infringement on liberty by these virtually random stops.

6. The Chief of the Washington, D.C., Metropolitan Police Department, for example, confirmed that "sizeable percentages of Americans today—especially Americans of color—still view policing in the United States to be discriminatory, if not by policy and definition, certainly in its day-to-day application." P. Verniero, Attorney General of New Jersey, Interim Report of the State Police Review Team Regarding Allegations of Racial Profiling 46 (Apr. 20, 1999) * * *.

7. Taking into account these and other innocent motivations for unprovoked flight leads me to reject Illinois' requested *per se* rule in favor of adhering to a totality-of-the-circumstances test. This conclusion does not,

as Illinois suggests, "establish a separate *Terry* analysis based on the individual characteristics of the person seized." My rejection of a *per se* rule, of course, applies to members of all races.

It is true, as Illinois points out, that *Terry* approved of the stop and frisk procedure notwithstanding "[t]he wholesale harassment by certain elements of the police community, of which minority groups, particularly Negroes, frequently complain." But in this passage, *Terry* simply held that such concerns would not preclude the use of the stop and frisk procedure altogether. Nowhere did *Terry* suggest that such concerns cannot inform a court's assessment of whether reasonable suspicion sufficient to justify a particular stop existed.

8. As a general matter, local courts often have a keener and more informed sense of local police practices and events that may heighten these concerns at particular times or locations. Thus, a reviewing court may accord substantial deference to a local court's determination that fear of the police is especially acute in a specific location or at a particular time.

violated when a *Terry* stop is predicated on that fact alone. For these reasons, the Court is surely correct in refusing to embrace either *per se* rule advocated by the parties. The totality of the circumstances, as always, must dictate the result.

II

Guided by that totality-of-the-circumstances test, the Court concludes that Officer Nolan had reasonable suspicion to stop respondent. In this respect, my view differs from the Court's. The entire justification for the stop is articulated in the brief testimony of Officer Nolan. Some facts are perfectly clear; others are not. This factual insufficiency leads me to conclude that the Court's judgment is mistaken.

Respondent Wardlow was arrested a few minutes after noon on September 9, 1995. Nolan was part of an eight-officer, four-car caravan patrol team. The officers were headed for "one of the areas in the 11th District [of Chicago] that's high [in] narcotics traffic." The reason why four cars were in the caravan was that "[n]ormally in these different areas there's an enormous amount of people, sometimes lookouts, customers." Officer Nolan testified that he was in uniform on that day, but he did not recall whether he was driving a marked or an unmarked car.

Officer Nolan and his partner were in the last of the four patrol cars that "were all caravaning eastbound down Van Buren." Nolan first observed respondent "in front of 4035 West Van Buren." Wardlow "looked in our direction and began fleeing." Nolan then "began driving southbound down the street observing [respondent] running through the gangway and the alley southbound," and observed that Wardlow was carrying a white, opaque bag under his arm. After the car turned south and intercepted respondent as he "ran right towards us," Officer Nolan stopped him and conducted a "protective search," which revealed that the bag under respondent's arm contained a loaded handgun.

This terse testimony is most noticeable for what it fails to reveal. Though asked whether he was in a marked or unmarked car, Officer Nolan could not recall the answer. He was not asked whether any of the other three cars in the caravan were marked, or whether any of the other seven officers were in uniform. Though he explained that the size of the caravan was because "[n]ormally in these different areas there's an enormous amount of people, sometimes lookouts, customers," Officer Nolan did not testify as to whether anyone besides Wardlow was nearby 4035 West Van Buren. Nor is it clear that that address was the intended destination of the caravan. As the Appellate Court of Illinois interpreted the record, "it appears that the officers were simply driving by, on their way to some unidentified location, when they noticed defendant standing at 4035 West Van Buren."[9] Officer Nolan's testimony also does not reveal how fast the

---

9. Of course, it would be a different case if the officers had credible information respecting that specific street address which reasonably led them to believe that criminal

officers were driving. It does not indicate whether he saw respondent notice the other patrol cars. And it does not say whether the caravan, or any part of it, had already passed Wardlow by before he began to run.

Indeed, the Appellate Court thought the record was even "too vague to support the inference that . . . defendant's flight was related to his expectation of police focus on him." Presumably, respondent did not react to the first three cars, and we cannot even be sure that he recognized the occupants of the fourth as police officers. The adverse inference is based entirely on the officer's statement: "He looked in our direction and began fleeing."[10]

No other factors sufficiently support a finding of reasonable suspicion. Though respondent was carrying a white, opaque bag under his arm, there is nothing at all suspicious about that. Certainly the time of day—shortly after noon—does not support Illinois' argument. Nor were the officers "responding to any call or report of suspicious activity in the area." Officer Nolan did testify that he expected to find "an enormous amount of people," including drug customers or lookouts, and the Court points out that "[i]t was in this context that Officer Nolan decided to investigate Wardlow after observing him flee." This observation, in my view, lends insufficient weight to the reasonable suspicion analysis; indeed, in light of the absence of testimony that anyone else was nearby when respondent began to run, this observation points in the opposite direction.

The State, along with the majority of the Court, relies as well on the assumption that this flight occurred in a high crime area. Even if that assumption is accurate, it is insufficient because even in a high crime neighborhood unprovoked flight does not invariably lead to reasonable suspicion. On the contrary, because many factors providing innocent motivations for unprovoked flight are concentrated in high crime areas, the character of the neighborhood arguably makes an inference of guilt less appropriate, rather than more so. Like unprovoked flight itself, presence in a high crime neighborhood is a fact too generic and susceptible to innocent explanation to satisfy the reasonable suspicion inquiry.

It is the State's burden to articulate facts sufficient to support reasonable suspicion. In my judgment, Illinois has failed to discharge that burden. I am not persuaded that the mere fact that someone standing on a sidewalk looked in the direction of a passing car before starting to run is sufficient to justify a forcible stop and frisk.

I therefore respectfully dissent from the Court's judgment to reverse the court below.

activity was afoot in that narrowly defined area.

10. Officer Nolan also testified that respondent "was looking *at* us," (emphasis added), though this minor clarification hardly seems sufficient to support the adverse inference.

Hiibel v. Sixth Judicial District Court of Nevada, Humboldt County, et al.

Supreme Court of the United States, 2004.
542 U.S. 177, 124 S.Ct. 2451, 159 L.Ed.2d 292.

■ JUSTICE KENNEDY delivered the opinion of the Court.

The petitioner was arrested and convicted for refusing to identify himself during a stop allowed by *Terry v. Ohio,* 392 U.S. 1, 88 S.Ct. 1868, 20 L.Ed.2d 889 (1968). He challenges his conviction under the Fourth and Fifth Amendments to the United States Constitution, applicable to the States through the Fourteenth Amendment.

I

The sheriff's department in Humboldt County, Nevada, received an afternoon telephone call reporting an assault. The caller reported seeing a man assault a woman in a red and silver GMC truck on Grass Valley Road. Deputy Sheriff Lee Dove was dispatched to investigate. When the officer arrived at the scene, he found the truck parked on the side of the road. A man was standing by the truck, and a young woman was sitting inside it. The officer observed skid marks in the gravel behind the vehicle, leading him to believe it had come to a sudden stop.

The officer approached the man and explained that he was investigating a report of a fight. The man appeared to be intoxicated. The officer asked him if he had "any identification on [him]," which we understand as a request to produce a driver's license or some other form of written identification. The man refused and asked why the officer wanted to see identification. The officer responded that he was conducting an investigation and needed to see some identification. The unidentified man became agitated and insisted he had done nothing wrong. The officer explained that he wanted to find out who the man was and what he was doing there. After continued refusals to comply with the officer's request for identification, the man began to taunt the officer by placing his hands behind his back and telling the officer to arrest him and take him to jail. This routine kept up for several minutes: the officer asked for identification 11 times and was refused each time. After warning the man that he would be arrested if he continued to refuse to comply, the officer placed him under arrest.

We now know that the man arrested on Grass Valley Road is Larry Dudley Hiibel. Hiibel was charged with "willfully resist[ing], delay[ing], or obstruct[ing] a public officer in discharging or attempting to discharge any legal duty of his office" in violation of Nev.Rev.Stat. (NRS) § 199.280 (2003). The government reasoned that Hiibel had obstructed the officer in carrying out his duties under § 171.123, a Nevada statute that defines the legal rights and duties of a police officer in the context of an investigative stop. Section 171.123 provides in relevant part:

"1. Any peace officer may detain any person whom the officer encounters under circumstances which reasonably indicate that the person has committed, is committing or is about to commit a crime.

. . .

"3. The officer may detain the person pursuant to this section only to ascertain his identity and the suspicious circumstances surrounding his presence abroad. Any person so detained shall identify himself, but may not be compelled to answer any other inquiry of any peace officer."

Hiibel was tried in the Justice Court of Union Township. The court agreed that Hiibel's refusal to identify himself as required by § 171.123 "obstructed and delayed Dove as a public officer in attempting to discharge his duty" in violation of § 199.280. Hiibel was convicted and fined $250. The Sixth Judicial District Court affirmed, rejecting Hiibel's argument that the application of § 171.123 to his case violated the Fourth and Fifth Amendments. On review the Supreme Court of Nevada rejected the Fourth Amendment challenge in a divided opinion. Hiibel petitioned for rehearing, seeking explicit resolution of his Fifth Amendment challenge. The petition was denied without opinion. We granted certiorari.

II

NRS § 171.123(3) is an enactment sometimes referred to as a "stop and identify" statute.

Stop and identify statutes often combine elements of traditional vagrancy laws with provisions intended to regulate police behavior in the course of investigatory stops. The statutes vary from State to State, but all permit an officer to ask or require a suspect to disclose his identity. * * * In some States, a suspect's refusal to identify himself is a misdemeanor offense or civil violation; in others, it is a factor to be considered in whether the suspect has violated loitering laws. In other States, a suspect may decline to identify himself without penalty.

* * *

The Court has recognized * * * constitutional limitations on the scope and operation of stop and identify statutes. In *Brown v. Texas,* 443 U.S. 47, 52, 99 S.Ct. 2637, 61 L.Ed.2d 357 (1979), the Court invalidated a conviction for violating a Texas stop and identify statute on Fourth Amendment grounds. The Court ruled that the initial stop was not based on specific, objective facts establishing reasonable suspicion to believe the suspect was involved in criminal activity. Absent that factual basis for detaining the defendant, the Court held, the risk of "arbitrary and abusive police practices" was too great and the stop was impermissible. Four Terms later, the Court invalidated a modified stop and identify statute on vagueness grounds. See *Kolender v. Lawson,* 461 U.S. 352, 103 S.Ct. 1855, 75 L.Ed.2d

903 (1983). The California law in *Kolender* required a suspect to give an officer " 'credible and reliable' " identification when asked to identify himself. The Court held that the statute was void because it provided no standard for determining what a suspect must do to comply with it, resulting in " 'virtually unrestrained power to arrest and charge persons with a violation.' "

The present case begins where our prior cases left off. Here there is no question that the initial stop was based on reasonable suspicion, satisfying the Fourth Amendment requirements noted in *Brown*. Further, the petitioner has not alleged that the statute is unconstitutionally vague, as in *Kolender*. Here the Nevada statute is narrower and more precise. The statute in *Kolender* had been interpreted to require a suspect to give the officer "credible and reliable" identification. In contrast, the Nevada Supreme Court has interpreted NRS § 171.123(3) to require only that a suspect disclose his name. As we understand it, the statute does not require a suspect to give the officer a driver's license or any other document. Provided that the suspect either states his name or communicates it to the officer by other means—a choice, we assume, that the suspect may make—the statute is satisfied and no violation occurs.

III

Hiibel argues that his conviction cannot stand because the officer's conduct violated his Fourth Amendment rights. We disagree.

* * *

Obtaining a suspect's name in the course of a *Terry* stop serves important government interests. Knowledge of identity may inform an officer that a suspect is wanted for another offense, or has a record of violence or mental disorder. On the other hand, knowing identity may help clear a suspect and allow the police to concentrate their efforts elsewhere. Identity may prove particularly important in cases such as this, where the police are investigating what appears to be a domestic assault. Officers called to investigate domestic disputes need to know whom they are dealing with in order to assess the situation, the threat to their own safety, and possible danger to the potential victim.

Although it is well established that an officer may ask a suspect to identify himself in the course of a *Terry* stop, it has been an open question whether the suspect can be arrested and prosecuted for refusal to answer. * * *

[T]he Fourth Amendment does not impose obligations on the citizen but instead provides rights against the government. As a result, the Fourth Amendment itself cannot require a suspect to answer questions. This case concerns a different issue, however. Here, the source of the legal obligation arises from Nevada state law, not the Fourth Amendment. Further, the statutory obligation does not go beyond answering an officer's request to disclose a name. * * *

The principles of *Terry* permit a State to require a suspect to disclose his name in the course of a *Terry* stop. The reasonableness of a seizure under the Fourth Amendment is determined "by balancing its intrusion on the individual's Fourth Amendment interests against its promotion of legitimate government interests." *Delaware v. Prouse,* 440 U.S. 648, 654, 99 S.Ct. 1391, 59 L.Ed.2d 660 (1979). The Nevada statute satisfies that standard. The request for identity has an immediate relation to the purpose, rationale, and practical demands of a *Terry* stop. The threat of criminal sanction helps ensure that the request for identity does not become a legal nullity. On the other hand, the Nevada statute does not alter the nature of the stop itself: it does not change its duration. A state law requiring a suspect to disclose his name in the course of a valid *Terry* stop is consistent with Fourth Amendment prohibitions against unreasonable searches and seizures.

Petitioner argues that the Nevada statute circumvents the probable cause requirement, in effect allowing an officer to arrest a person for being suspicious. According to petitioner, this creates a risk of arbitrary police conduct that the Fourth Amendment does not permit. * * * Petitioner's concerns are met by the requirement that a *Terry* stop must be justified at its inception and "reasonably related in scope to the circumstances which justified" the initial stop. Under these principles, an officer may not arrest a suspect for failure to identify himself if the request for identification is not reasonably related to the circumstances justifying the stop. * * * It is clear in this case that the request for identification was "reasonably related in scope to the circumstances which justified" the stop. The officer's request was a commonsense inquiry, not an effort to obtain an arrest for failure to identify after a *Terry* stop yielded insufficient evidence. The stop, the request, and the State's requirement of a response did not contravene the guarantees of the Fourth Amendment.

IV

Petitioner further contends that his conviction violates the Fifth Amendment's prohibition on compelled self-incrimination. The Fifth Amendment states that "[n]o person ... shall be compelled in any criminal case to be a witness against himself." To qualify for the Fifth Amendment privilege, a communication must be testimonial, incriminating, and compelled. See *United States v. Hubbell,* 530 U.S. 27, 34–38, 120 S.Ct. 2037, 147 L.Ed.2d 24 (2000).

Respondents urge us to hold that the statements NRS § 171.123(3) requires are nontestimonial, and so outside the Clause's scope. We decline to resolve the case on that basis. "[T]o be testimonial, an accused's communication must itself, explicitly or implicitly, relate a factual assertion or disclose information." *Doe v. United States,* 487 U.S. 201, 210, 108 S.Ct.

2341, 101 L.Ed.2d 184 (1988). Stating one's name may qualify as an assertion of fact relating to identity. Production of identity documents might meet the definition as well. As we noted in *Hubbell,* acts of production may yield testimony establishing "the existence, authenticity, and custody of items [the police seek]." Even if these required actions are testimonial, however, petitioner's challenge must fail because in this case disclosure of his name presented no reasonable danger of incrimination.

The Fifth Amendment * * * "protects against any disclosures that the witness reasonably believes could be used in a criminal prosecution or could lead to other evidence that might be so used." * * *

In this case petitioner's refusal to disclose his name was not based on any articulated real and appreciable fear that his name would be used to incriminate him, or that it "would furnish a link in the chain of evidence needed to prosecute" him. *Hoffman v. United States,* 341 U.S. 479, 486, 71 S.Ct. 814, 95 L.Ed. 1118 (1951). As best we can tell, petitioner refused to identify himself only because he thought his name was none of the officer's business. Even today, petitioner does not explain how the disclosure of his name could have been used against him in a criminal case. While we recognize petitioner's strong belief that he should not have to disclose his identity, the Fifth Amendment does not override the Nevada Legislature's judgment to the contrary absent a reasonable belief that the disclosure would tend to incriminate him.

The narrow scope of the disclosure requirement is also important. One's identity is, by definition, unique; yet it is, in another sense, a universal characteristic. Answering a request to disclose a name is likely to be so insignificant in the scheme of things as to be incriminating only in unusual circumstances. In every criminal case, it is known and must be known who has been arrested and who is being tried. Even witnesses who plan to invoke the Fifth Amendment privilege answer when their names are called to take the stand. Still, a case may arise where there is a substantial allegation that furnishing identity at the time of a stop would have given the police a link in the chain of evidence needed to convict the individual of a separate offense. In that case, the court can then consider whether the privilege applies, and, if the Fifth Amendment has been violated, what remedy must follow. We need not resolve those questions here.

The judgment of the Nevada Supreme Court is

Affirmed.

■ JUSTICE STEVENS, dissenting.

* * * [T]he broad constitutional right to remain silent, which derives from the Fifth Amendment's guarantee that "[n]o person ... shall be compelled in any criminal case to be a witness against himself," U.S. Const., Amdt. 5, is not as circumscribed as the Court suggests, and does not admit even of the narrow exception defined by the Nevada statute.

* * * The protections of the Fifth Amendment are directed squarely toward those who are the focus of the government's investigative and prosecutorial powers. In a criminal trial, the indicted defendant has an unqualified right to refuse to testify and may not be punished for invoking that right. The unindicted target of a grand jury investigation enjoys the same constitutional protection even if he has been served with a subpoena. So does an arrested suspect during custodial interrogation in a police station.

There is no reason why the subject of police interrogation based on mere suspicion, rather than probable cause, should have any lesser protection. * * *

The * * * compelled statement at issue in this case is clearly testimonial. * * *

[T]he Court * * * concludes that the State can compel the disclosure of one's identity because it is not "incriminating." But our cases have afforded Fifth Amendment protection to statements that are "incriminating" in a much broader sense than the Court suggests. It has "long been settled that [the Fifth Amendment's] protection encompasses compelled statements that lead to the discovery of incriminating evidence even though the statements themselves are not incriminating and are not introduced into evidence." *United States v. Hubbell,* 530 U.S. 27, 37, 120 S.Ct. 2037, 147 L.Ed.2d 24 (2000). By "incriminating" we have meant disclosures that "could be used in a criminal prosecution or could lead to other evidence that might be so used," *Kastigar v. United States,* 406 U.S. 441, 445, 92 S.Ct. 1653, 32 L.Ed.2d 212 (1972)—communications, in other words, that "would furnish a link in the chain of evidence needed to prosecute the claimant for a federal crime," *Hoffman v. United States,* 341 U.S. 479, 486, 71 S.Ct. 814, 95 L.Ed. 1118 (1951). Thus, "[c]ompelled testimony that communicates information that may 'lead to incriminating evidence' is privileged even if the information itself is not inculpatory." *Hubbell,* 530 U.S., at 38.

[I]t is clear that the disclosure of petitioner's identity is protected. The Court reasons that we should not assume that the disclosure of petitioner's name would be used to incriminate him or that it would furnish a link in a chain of evidence needed to prosecute him. But why else would an officer ask for it? And why else would the Nevada Legislature require its disclosure only when circumstances "reasonably indicate that the person has committed, is committing or is about to commit a crime"? If the Court is correct, then petitioner's refusal to cooperate did not impede the police investigation. Indeed, if we accept the predicate for the Court's holding, the statute requires nothing more than a useless invasion of privacy. I think that, on the contrary, the Nevada Legislature intended to provide its police officers with a useful law enforcement tool, and that the very existence of the statute demonstrates the value of the information it demands.

A person's identity obviously bears informational and incriminating worth, "even if the [name] itself is not inculpatory." A name can provide the key to a broad array of information about the person, particularly in the hands of a police officer with access to a range of law enforcement databases. And that information, in turn, can be tremendously useful in a criminal prosecution. It is therefore quite wrong to suggest that a person's identity provides a link in the chain to incriminating evidence "only in unusual circumstances."

The officer in this case told petitioner, in the Court's words, that "he was conducting an investigation and needed to see some identification." As the target of that investigation, petitioner, in my view, acted well within his rights when he opted to stand mute. Accordingly, I respectfully dissent.

■ JUSTICE BREYER, with whom JUSTICE SOUTER and JUSTICE GINSBURG join, dissenting.

[P]olice may conduct a *Terry* stop only within circumscribed limits. And one of those limits invalidates laws that compel responses to police questioning.

* * * [In 1984] the Court wrote that an "officer may ask the *[Terry]* detainee a moderate number of questions to determine his identity and to try to obtain information confirming or dispelling the officer's suspicions. *But the detainee is not obliged to respond.*" *Berkemer v. McCarty,* 468 U.S. 420, 439, 104 S.Ct. 3138, 82 L.Ed.2d 317 (1984) (emphasis added).

[T]he Court's statement in *Berkemer,* while technically dicta, is the kind of strong dicta that the legal community typically takes as a statement of the law. And that law has remained undisturbed for more than 20 years.

There is no good reason now to reject this generation-old statement of the law. There are sound reasons rooted in Fifth Amendment considerations for adhering to this Fourth Amendment legal condition circumscribing police authority to stop an individual against his will. Administrative considerations also militate against change. Can a State, in addition to requiring a stopped individual to answer "What's your name?" also require an answer to "What's your license number?" or "Where do you live?" Can a police officer, who must know how to make a *Terry* stop, keep track of the constitutional answers? After all, answers to any of these questions may, or may not, incriminate, depending upon the circumstances.

Indeed, as the majority points out, a name itself—even if it is not "Killer Bill" or "Rough 'em up Harry"—will sometimes provide the police with "a link in the chain of evidence needed to convict the individual of a separate offense." The majority reserves judgment about whether compulsion is permissible in such instances. How then is a police officer in the midst of a *Terry* stop to distinguish between the majority's ordinary case and this special case where the majority reserves judgment?

The majority presents no evidence that the rule enunciated by * * * the *Berkemer* Court, which for nearly a generation has set forth a settled

Terry stop condition, has significantly interfered with law enforcement. Nor has the majority presented any other convincing justification for change. I would not begin to erode a clear rule with special exceptions.

I consequently dissent.

Page 229. Insert the following new subsection after subsection 2. Weapons Searches:

3. STOP AND FRISK ON SUSPICION OF CARRYING A FIREARM

Where police concern is that a person on the street is carrying a handgun, the situation is arguably different from other field situations.

In these situations, is any legitimate investigatory purpose served by a stop? An officer may, of course, wish to search the person to determine whether the person in fact has a handgun. Arguably, however, the right to make a weapons frisk in field situations is not a legitimate objective in itself but only a way of assuring officers' safety as they conduct investigations supported on other grounds. If a stop is made only because it triggers the opportunity to frisk for weapons, perhaps the right to stop is being misused. As is discussed on pages 208–09 of the text, the Supreme Court appears to have ignored the argument that investigatory stops on reasonable suspicion that the persons are illegally in possession of weapons are unreasonable because those stops pose too high a risk of the power to search being abused.

Whatever the Fourth Amendment theory, it seems clear that the authority permitted officers under Terry v. Ohio, 392 U.S. 1, 88 S.Ct. 1868, 20 L.Ed.2d 889 (1968) and subsequent case law is in fact used to conduct searches as ends in themselves. The report on New York "stop & frisk" practices, quoted on pages 203–04 of the text, asserted that in practice stop and frisk often served not as a basis for protecting officers while they conduct investigations concerning other suspected crimes but rather as a means of determining by search whether in fact suspects are illegally carrying handguns.

Perhaps generally-applicable criteria for limiting law enforcement field practices should be relaxed where officers fear a person in a public place has a handgun. When the case reprinted in this subsection was in the Florida Supreme Court, two members of that tribunal urged that the officers' actions should be evaluated under a version of the Fourth Amendment reasonable suspicion requirement requiring less rigorous corroboration of an anonymous tip than is otherwise demanded:

> An anonymous tip concerning an individual with an illegally concealed firearm presents a unique situation. When confronted with this situation, police officers may not be able to verify more than the innocent details of the tip without substantially risking their safety or the safety of the general public. * * *

I would do what the majority of jurisdictions have done and recognize a "firearm exception" to the general rule that the corroboration of only the innocent details of an anonymous tip does not provide police officers with a reasonable suspicion of criminal activity. In my view, this holding is necessary because the great risk of harm to the public and police in such a situation substantially outweighs the limited privacy intrusion to the suspect. Such a holding is true to the dictates of *Terry*. "*The officer need not be absolutely certain that the individual is armed; the issue is whether a reasonably prudent [person] in the circumstances would be warranted in the belief that his safety or that of others was in danger.*" *Terry*, 392 U.S. at 27, 88 S.Ct. 1868 (emphasis added). Clearly, it is reasonable in today's society for law enforcement officers confronted with the circumstances presented in this case to conduct a stop and frisk.

I strongly emphasize that this holding should apply only to investigatory stop and frisks supported by reliable anonymous tips regarding individuals possessing illegally concealed firearms. As explained by the United States Court of Appeals, District of Columbia Circuit, the distinction between an anonymous tip involving a firearm and a tip involving possession of other contraband, such as illegal drugs, is significant:

> Th[e] element of imminent danger distinguishes a gun tip from one involving possession of drugs. If there is any doubt about the reliability of an anonymous tip in the latter case, the police can limit their response to surveillance or engage in "controlled buys." Where guns are involved, however, there is the risk that an attempt to "wait out" the suspect might have fatal consequences.

United States v. Clipper, [973 F.2d 944, 951 (D.C.Cir.1992)].

J.L. v. State, 727 So.2d 204, 214–15 (Fla.1998) (Overton, J., dissenting).

Florida v. J. L.

Supreme Court of the United States, 2000.
529 U.S. 266, 120 S.Ct. 1375, 146 L.Ed.2d 254.

■ JUSTICE GINSBURG delivered the opinion of the Court.

The question presented in this case is whether an anonymous tip that a person is carrying a gun is, without more, sufficient to justify a police officer's stop and frisk of that person. We hold that it is not.

I

On October 13, 1995, an anonymous caller reported to the Miami–Dade Police that a young black male standing at a particular bus stop and wearing a plaid shirt was carrying a gun. So far as the record reveals, there is no audio recording of the tip, and nothing is known about the informant.

Sometime after the police received the tip—the record does not say how long—two officers were instructed to respond. They arrived at the bus stop about six minutes later and saw three black males "just hanging out [there]." One of the three, respondent J. L., was wearing a plaid shirt. Apart from the tip, the officers had no reason to suspect any of the three of illegal conduct. The officers did not see a firearm, and J. L. made no threatening or otherwise unusual movements. One of the officers approached J. L., told him to put his hands up on the bus stop, frisked him, and seized a gun from J. L.'s pocket. The second officer frisked the other two individuals, against whom no allegations had been made, and found nothing.

J. L., who was at the time of the frisk "10 days shy of his 16th birth[day]," was charged under state law with carrying a concealed firearm without a license and possessing a firearm while under the age of 18. He moved to suppress the gun as the fruit of an unlawful search, and the trial court granted his motion. The intermediate appellate court reversed, but the Supreme Court of Florida quashed that decision and held the search invalid under the Fourth Amendment.

Anonymous tips, the Florida Supreme Court stated, are generally less reliable than tips from known informants and can form the basis for reasonable suspicion only if accompanied by specific indicia of reliability, for example, the correct forecast of a subject's " 'not easily predicted' " movements. (quoting Alabama v. White, 496 U. S. 325, 332, 110 S.Ct. 2412, 110 L.Ed.2d 301 (1990)). The tip leading to the frisk of J. L., the court observed, provided no such predictions, nor did it contain any other qualifying indicia of reliability. Two justices dissented. The safety of the police and the public, they maintained, justifies a "firearm exception" to the general rule barring investigatory stops and frisks on the basis of bare-boned anonymous tips.

Seeking review in this Court, the State of Florida noted that the decision of the State's Supreme Court conflicts with decisions of other courts declaring similar searches compatible with the Fourth Amendment. We granted certiorari, and now affirm the judgment of the Florida Supreme Court.

II

Our "stop and frisk" decisions begin with Terry v. Ohio, 392 U. S. 1, 88 S.Ct. 1868, 20 L.Ed.2d 889 (1968). This Court held in *Terry*

"[W]here a police officer observes unusual conduct which leads him reasonably to conclude in light of his experience that criminal activity may be afoot and that the persons with whom he is dealing may be armed and presently dangerous, where in the course of investigating this behavior he identifies himself as a policeman and makes reasonable inquiries, and where nothing in the initial stages of the encounter serves to dispel his reasonable fear for his own or others' safety, he is entitled for the protection of himself and others in the area to conduct a carefully limited search of the outer clothing of such persons in an attempt to discover weapons which might be used to assault him.''

In the instant case, the officers' suspicion that J. L. was carrying a weapon arose not from any observations of their own but solely from a call made from an unknown location by an unknown caller. Unlike a tip from a known informant whose reputation can be assessed and who can be held responsible if her allegations turn out to be fabricated, see Adams v. Williams, 407 U. S. 143, 146–147, 92 S.Ct. 1921, 32 L.Ed.2d 612 (1972), "an anonymous tip alone seldom demonstrates the informant's basis of knowledge or veracity," Alabama v. White, 496 U. S., at 329, 110 S.Ct. 2412. As we have recognized, however, there are situations in which an anonymous tip, suitably corroborated, exhibits "sufficient indicia of reliability to provide reasonable suspicion to make the investigatory stop." Id., at 327. The question we here confront is whether the tip pointing to J. L. had those indicia of reliability.

In *White*, the police received an anonymous tip asserting that a woman was carrying cocaine and predicting that she would leave an apartment building at a specified time, get into a car matching a particular description, and drive to a named motel. Standing alone, the tip would not have justified a *Terry* stop. Only after police observation showed that the informant had accurately predicted the woman's movements, we explained, did it become reasonable to think the tipster had inside knowledge about the suspect and therefore to credit his assertion about the cocaine. Although the Court held that the suspicion in *White* became reasonable after police surveillance, we regarded the case as borderline. Knowledge about a person's future movements indicates some familiarity with that person's affairs, but having such knowledge does not necessarily imply that the informant knows, in particular, whether that person is carrying hidden contraband. We accordingly classified *White* as a "close case."

The tip in the instant case lacked the moderate indicia of reliability present in *White* and essential to the Court's decision in that case. The anonymous call concerning J. L. provided no predictive information and therefore left the police without means to test the informant's knowledge or credibility. That the allegation about the gun turned out to be correct does not suggest that the officers, prior to the frisks, had a reasonable basis for suspecting J. L. of engaging in unlawful conduct: The reasonableness of official suspicion must be measured by what the officers knew before they conducted their search. All the police had to go on in this case was the bare report of an unknown, unaccountable informant who neither explained how he knew about the gun nor supplied any basis for believing he had inside information about J. L. If *White* was a close case on the reliability of anonymous tips, this one surely falls on the other side of the line.

Florida contends that the tip was reliable because its description of the suspect's visible attributes proved accurate: There really was a young black male wearing a plaid shirt at the bus stop. The United States as *amicus curiae* makes a similar argument, proposing that a stop and frisk should be permitted "when (1) an anonymous tip provides a description of a particular person at a particular location illegally carrying a concealed firearm, (2) police promptly verify the pertinent details of the tip except the existence of the firearm, and (3) there are no factors that cast doubt on the reliability of the tip...." Brief for United States 16. These contentions misapprehend the reliability needed for a tip to justify a *Terry* stop.

An accurate description of a subject's readily observable location and appearance is of course reliable in this limited sense: It will help the police correctly identify the person whom the tipster means to accuse. Such a tip, however, does not show that the tipster has knowledge of concealed criminal activity. The reasonable suspicion here at issue requires that a tip be reliable in its assertion of illegality, not just in its tendency to identify a determinate person. Cf. 4 W. LaFave, Search and Seizure § 9.4(h), p. 213 (3d ed. 1996) (distinguishing reliability as to identification, which is often important in other criminal law contexts, from reliability as to the likelihood of criminal activity, which is central in anonymous-tip cases).

A second major argument advanced by Florida and the United States as *amicus* is, in essence, that the standard *Terry* analysis should be modified to license a "firearm exception." Under such an exception, a tip alleging an illegal gun would justify a stop and frisk even if the accusation would fail standard pre-search reliability testing. We decline to adopt this position.

Firearms are dangerous, and extraordinary dangers sometimes justify unusual precautions. Our decisions recognize the serious threat that armed criminals pose to public safety; *Terry's* rule, which permits protective police searches on the basis of reasonable suspicion rather than demanding that officers meet the higher standard of probable cause, responds to this very concern. But an automatic firearm exception to our established reliability analysis would rove too far. Such an exception would enable any person seeking to harass another to set in motion an intrusive, embarrassing police search of the targeted person simply by placing an anonymous call falsely reporting the target's unlawful carriage of a gun. Nor could one securely confine such an exception to allegations involving firearms. Several Courts of Appeals have held it *per se* foreseeable for people carrying significant amounts of illegal drugs to be carrying guns as well. If police officers may properly conduct *Terry* frisks on the basis of bare-boned tips about guns, it would be reasonable to maintain under the above-cited decisions that the police should similarly have discretion to frisk based on bare-boned tips about narcotics. As we clarified when we made indicia of reliability critical in *Adams* and *White*, the Fourth Amendment is not so easily satisfied.*

The facts of this case do not require us to speculate about the circumstances under which the danger alleged in an anonymous tip might be so great as to justify a search even without a showing of reliability. We

---

* At oral argument, petitioner also advanced the position that J. L.'s youth made the stop and frisk valid, because it is a crime in Florida for persons under the age of 21 to

do not say, for example, that a report of a person carrying a bomb need bear the indicia of reliability we demand for a report of a person carrying a firearm before the police can constitutionally conduct a frisk. Nor do we hold that public safety officials in quarters where the reasonable expectation of Fourth Amendment privacy is diminished, such as airports, and schools, cannot conduct protective searches on the basis of information insufficient to justify searches elsewhere.

Finally, the requirement that an anonymous tip bear standard indicia of reliability in order to justify a stop in no way diminishes a police officer's prerogative, in accord with *Terry*, to conduct a protective search of a person who has already been legitimately stopped. We speak in today's decision only of cases in which the officer's authority to make the initial stop is at issue. In that context, we hold that an anonymous tip lacking indicia of reliability of the kind contemplated in *Adams* and *White* does not justify a stop and frisk whenever and however it alleges the illegal possession of a firearm.

The judgment of the Florida Supreme Court is affirmed.

It is so ordered.

■ JUSTICE KENNEDY, with whom THE CHIEF JUSTICE joins, concurring.

On the record created at the suppression hearing, the Court's decision is correct. The Court says all that is necessary to resolve this case, and I join the opinion in all respects. It might be noted, however, that there are many indicia of reliability respecting anonymous tips that we have yet to explore in our cases.

When a police officer testifies that a suspect aroused the officer's suspicion, and so justifies a stop and frisk, the courts can weigh the officer's credibility and admit evidence seized pursuant to the frisk even if no one, aside from the officer and defendant themselves, was present or observed the seizure. An anonymous telephone tip without more is different, however; for even if the officer's testimony about receipt of the tip is found credible, there is a second layer of inquiry respecting the reliability of the informant that cannot be pursued. If the telephone call is truly anonymous, the informant has not placed his credibility at risk and can lie with impunity. The reviewing court cannot judge the credibility of the informant and the risk of fabrication becomes unacceptable.

On this record, then, the Court is correct in holding that the telephone tip did not justify the arresting officer's immediate stop and frisk of

carry concealed firearms. This contention misses the mark. Even assuming that the arresting officers could be sure that J. L. was under 21, they would have had reasonable suspicion that J. L. was engaged in criminal activity only if they could be confident that he was carrying a gun in the first place. The mere fact that a tip, if true, would describe illegal activity does not mean that the police may make a *Terry* stop without meeting the reliability requirement, and the fact that J. L. was under 21 in no way made the gun tip more reliable than if he had been an adult.

respondent. There was testimony that an anonymous tip came in by a telephone call and nothing more. The record does not show whether some notation or other documentation of the call was made either by a voice recording or tracing the call to a telephone number. The prosecution recounted just the tip itself and the later verification of the presence of the three young men in the circumstances the Court describes.

It seems appropriate to observe that a tip might be anonymous in some sense yet have certain other features, either supporting reliability or narrowing the likely class of informants, so that the tip does provide the lawful basis for some police action. One such feature, as the Court recognizes, is that the tip predicts future conduct of the alleged criminal. There may be others. For example, if an unnamed caller with a voice which sounds the same each time tells police on two successive nights about criminal activity which in fact occurs each night, a similar call on the third night ought not be treated automatically like the tip in the case now before us. In the instance supposed, there would be a plausible argument that experience cures some of the uncertainty surrounding the anonymity, justifying a proportionate police response. In today's case, however, the State provides us with no data about the reliability of anonymous tips. Nor do we know whether the dispatcher or arresting officer had any objective reason to believe that this tip had some particular indicia of reliability.

If an informant places his anonymity at risk, a court can consider this factor in weighing the reliability of the tip. An instance where a tip might be considered anonymous but nevertheless sufficiently reliable to justify a proportionate police response may be when an unnamed person driving a car the police officer later describes stops for a moment and, face to face, informs the police that criminal activity is occurring. This too seems to be different from the tip in the present case.

Instant caller identification is widely available to police, and, if anonymous tips are proving unreliable and distracting to police, squad cars can be sent within seconds to the location of the telephone used by the informant. Voice recording of telephone tips might, in appropriate cases, be used by police to locate the caller. It is unlawful to make false reports to the police, and the ability of the police to trace the identity of anonymous telephone informants may be a factor which lends reliability to what, years earlier, might have been considered unreliable anonymous tips.

These matters, of course, must await discussion in other cases, where the issues are presented by the record.

D.   TRAFFIC STOPS

Page 231.   Add the following after the discussion in the Editors' Introduction of State v. Jones:

The intermediate appellate court's holding was affirmed on further review. State v. Jones, 88 Ohio St.3d 430, 727 N.E.2d 886 (Ohio 2000).

The permissibility of arrests as a matter of Fourth Amendment law is now addressed by Atwater v. City of Lago Vista, 532 U.S. 318, 121 S.Ct. 1536, 149 L.Ed.2d 549 (2001), reprinted in new subsection B(3) of this chapter, contained earlier in this supplement.

Page 232. Insert the following material in the Editors' Introduction before the unit on Definition and Requirements of Traffic Stops:

Frequency of Traffic Stops and Searches of Vehicles or Occupants

Information on the frequency of traffic stops and the public's perception of them was offered by Bureau of Justice Statistics, Contacts Between Police and the Public (2001), based on survey results. More than half (52.0%) of the reported contacts between the surveyed members of the public and the police were traffic stops. Further:

- In 1999 an estimated 10.3% of licensed drivers were pulled over by police one or more times in a traffic stop. The 10.3% represent 19.3 million stopped drivers. The 19.3 million includes 4 million pulled over more than once during the year. * * *

- Blacks (12.3%) were more likely than whites (10.4%) to be stopped at least once, and blacks (3.0%) were more likely than whites (2.1%) to be stopped more than once.

- Of the 19.3 million stopped drivers, police issued a ticket to 54.2%, carried out a search of some kind (either a physical search of the driver or a search of a vehicle) on 6.6%, handcuffed 3.1%, arrested 3.0%, and used or threatened force that the driver deemed excessive against 0.5%.

- During a traffic stop, police were more likely to carry out some type of search * * * on a black (11.0%) or Hispanic (11.3%) than a white (5.4%).

- Police searched the driver or the vehicle of an estimated 1.3 million drivers (6.6% of all stopped drivers). Two-thirds (66.4%) of the 1.3 million searches were without the driver's expressed consent. In nearly 90% (86.7%) of the 1.3 million searches, no drugs, alcohol, illegal weapons, or other evidence of criminal wrongdoing was found. * * *

- The vast majority of drivers stopped by police (84%) said they had been stopped for a legitimate reason, and an even larger majority (90%) felt police had behaved properly during the traffic stop.

Id., at 2.

Surveyed drivers who reported being stopped were asked what reason the officers gave for the stop. Most (51.2%) said "speeding." But 2.3% reported that the stop was because the police "suspected them of something," and 9.2% said the stop was a "record check" of some sort, as for example a check for driver's license, insurance coverage or vehicle registration. Id., at 16.

The results indicated considerable racial disparities in conducting searches. The report stressed, however, that the survey did not inquire regarding circumstances or conduct by drivers that might have explained the searches on racially neutral bases. As a result, it concluded, the survey data does not reveal wither the drivers' race, rather than other factors, explains these disparities. Id., at 22.

Approximately 427,000 drivers gave consent to search of their person and/or vehicle; most (55%) reported that the police lacked "legitimate reason" for these searches. About 845,000 drivers did not give consent but police nevertheless searched their persons or vehicles; more (71%) reported that officers lacked legitimate reason for the searches. Id., at 23.

The report explained that arrests of drivers occurred "for a variety of reasons," including assault on the officer, discovery of an outstanding arrest warrant, discovery of drugs or an illegal weapon, or the driver's performance on a sobriety test. Id., at 18. It did not mention arrest for the traffic offense on the basis of which the officer stopped the driver. 2.6% of white drivers were arrested; 5.2% of black drivers and 4.2% of hispanic drivers were arrested. Id.

Page 233. Insert the following in the Editors' Introduction after the second paragraph beginning on this page:

The Supreme Court has again described a traffic stop as a situation in which "[t]here is probable cause to believe that the driver has committed a minor vehicular offense." Arizona v. Johnson, 555 U.S. 323, ___, 129 S.Ct. 781, 787, 172 L.Ed.2d 694 (2009), quoting from Maryland v. Wilson, 519 U.S. 408, 413, 117 S.Ct. 882, 882, 137 L.Ed.2d 41 (1997). The Second Circuit, however, agreed with what it described as the position of majority of the federal circuits: probable cause is not required. "[N]o Fourth Amendment violation aris[es] from a traffic stop supported by a reasonable suspicion that a traffic violation has occurred." United States v. Stewart, 551 F.3d 187, 191 (2d Cir.2009).

The Supreme Court of Pennsylvania held that Fourth Amendment law (and Pennsylvania state constitutional law) *sometimes* permit a "traffic stop" on reasonable suspicion. This is permitted when the traffic offense is one for which "a post-stop investigation is normally feasible." This is the case if the offense is driving while impaired, and in this situation the stop is essentially a *Terry* stop for that investigation. It added:

> However, a vehicle stop based solely on offenses not "investigatable" cannot be justified by a mere reasonable suspicion, because the purposes of a *Terry* stop do not exist-maintaining the *status quo* while investigating is inapplicable where there is nothing further to investigate. An officer must have probable cause to make a constitutional vehicle stop for such offenses.

n v. Chase, 599 Pa. 80, 94, 960 A.2d 108, 116 (2008).

sert the following at the end of Note 4 after Knowles v. Iowa:

In Arizona v. Johnson, 555 U.S. 323, ___, 129 S.Ct. 781, 172 L.Ed.2d 694 (2009), however, the Court assumed that at least as a general rule, all passengers in a vehicle stopped as part of a routine traffic stop are seized and such seizures are reasonable. It stated:

> A lawful roadside stop begins when a vehicle is pulled over for investigation of a traffic violation. The temporary seizure of driver and passengers ordinarily continues, and remains reasonable, for the duration of the stop. Normally, the stop ends when the police have no further need to control the scene, and inform the driver and passengers they are free to leave.

555 U.S. at ___, 129 S.Ct. at 788.

Page 240.   Insert the following new note after Knowles v. Iowa:

5. **Weapon frisks of occupants.** Officers making a traffic stop may make patdown weapons frisks of any passengers as well as drivers, if the officers have reasonable suspicion that the person patted down may be armed and dangerous. Arizona v. Johnson, 555 U.S. 323, ___, 129 S.Ct. 781, 787–88, 172 L.Ed.2d 694 (2009).

Page 240.   Insert the following new case and note before State v. Soto:

Illinois v. Caballes

Supreme Court of the United States, 2005.
543 U.S. 405, 125 S.Ct. 834, 160 L.Ed.2d 842.

■ JUSTICE STEVENS delivered the opinion of the Court.

Illinois State Trooper Daniel Gillette stopped respondent for speeding on an interstate highway. When Gillette radioed the police dispatcher to report the stop, a second trooper, Craig Graham, a member of the Illinois State Police Drug Interdiction Team, overheard the transmission and immediately headed for the scene with his narcotics-detection dog. When they arrived, respondent's car was on the shoulder of the road and respondent was in Gillette's vehicle. While Gillette was in the process of writing a warning ticket, Graham walked his dog around respondent's car. The dog alerted at the trunk. Based on that alert, the officers searched the trunk, found marijuana, and arrested respondent. The entire incident lasted less than 10 minutes.

Respondent was convicted of a narcotics offense and sentenced to 12 years' imprisonment and a $256,136 fine. The trial judge denied his motion to suppress the seized evidence and to quash his arrest. He held that the officers had not unnecessarily prolonged the stop and that the dog alert was sufficiently reliable to provide probable cause to conduct the search. * * * [T]he Illinois Supreme Court reversed, concluding that because the canine sniff was performed without any " 'specific and articulable facts' " to suggest drug activity, the use of the dog "unjustifiably enlarg[ed] the scope of a routine traffic stop into a drug investigation."

The question on which we granted certiorari is narrow: "Whether the Fourth Amendment requires reasonable, articulable suspicion to justify using a drug-detection dog to sniff a vehicle during a legitimate traffic stop." Thus, we proceed on the assumption that the officer conducting the dog sniff had no information about respondent except that he had been stopped for speeding; accordingly, we have omitted any reference to facts about respondent that might have triggered a modicum of suspicion.

Here, the initial seizure of respondent when he was stopped on the highway was based on probable cause, and was concededly lawful. It is nevertheless clear that a seizure that is lawful at its inception can violate the Fourth Amendment if its manner of execution unreasonably infringes interests protected by the Constitution. *United States v. Jacobsen,* 466 U.S. 109, 124, 104 S.Ct. 1652, 80 L.Ed.2d 85 (1984). A seizure that is justified solely by the interest in issuing a warning ticket to the driver can become unlawful if it is prolonged beyond the time reasonably required to complete that mission. In an earlier case involving a dog sniff that occurred during an unreasonably prolonged traffic stop, the Illinois Supreme Court held that use of the dog and the subsequent discovery of contraband were the product of an unconstitutional seizure. *People v. Cox,* 202 Ill.2d 462, 270 Ill.Dec. 81, 782 N.E.2d 275 (2002). We may assume that a similar result would be warranted in this case if the dog sniff had been conducted while respondent was being unlawfully detained.

In the state-court proceedings, however, the judges carefully reviewed the details of Officer Gillette's conversations with respondent and the precise timing of his radio transmissions to the dispatcher to determine whether he had improperly extended the duration of the stop to enable the dog sniff to occur. We have not recounted those details because we accept the state court's conclusion that the duration of the stop in this case was entirely justified by the traffic offense and the ordinary inquiries incident to such a stop.

Despite this conclusion, the Illinois Supreme Court held that the initially lawful traffic stop became an unlawful seizure solely as a result of the canine sniff that occurred outside respondent's stopped car. That is, the court characterized the dog sniff as the cause rather than the consequence of a constitutional violation. In its view, the use of the dog converted the citizen police encounter from a lawful traffic stop into a drug investigation, and because the shift in purpose was not supported by any reasonable suspicion that respondent possessed narcotics, it was unlawful. In our view, conducting a dog sniff would not change the character of a traffic stop that is lawful at its inception and otherwise executed in a reasonable manner, unless the dog sniff itself infringed respondent's constitutionally protected interest in privacy. Our cases hold that it did not.

Official conduct that does not "compromise any legitimate interest in privacy" is not a search subject to the Fourth Amendment. We have held that any interest in possessing contraband cannot be deemed "legitimate," and thus, governmental conduct that *only* reveals the possession of contraband "compromises no legitimate privacy interest." This is because the expectation "that certain facts will not come to the attention of the authorities" is not the same as an interest in "privacy that society is prepared to consider reasonable." In *United States v. Place,* 462 U.S. 696, 103 S.Ct. 2637, 77 L.Ed.2d 110 (1983), we treated a canine sniff by a well-trained narcotics detection dog as *"sui generis"* because it "discloses only the presence or absence of narcotics, a contraband item." Respondent likewise concedes that "drug sniffs are designed, and if properly conducted are generally likely, to reveal only the presence of contraband." Brief for Respondent 17. Although respondent argues that the error rates, particularly the existence of false positives, call into question the premise that drug-detection dogs alert only to contraband, the record contains no evidence or findings that support his argument. Moreover, respondent does not suggest that an erroneous alert, in and of itself, reveals any legitimate private information, and, in this case, the trial judge found that the dog sniff was sufficiently reliable to establish probable cause to conduct a full-blown search of the trunk.

Accordingly, the use of a well-trained narcotics-detection dog—one that "does not expose noncontraband items that otherwise would remain hidden from public view," during a lawful traffic stop, generally does not implicate legitimate privacy interests. In this case, the dog sniff was performed on the exterior of respondent's car while he was lawfully seized for a traffic violation. Any intrusion on respondent's privacy expectations does not rise to the level of a constitutionally cognizable infringement.

This conclusion is entirely consistent with our recent decision that the use of a thermal-imaging device to detect the growth of marijuana in a home constituted an unlawful search. *Kyllo v. United States,* 533 U.S. 27, 121 S.Ct. 2038, 150 L.Ed.2d 94 (2001). Critical to that decision was the fact that the device was capable of detecting lawful activity—in that case, intimate details in a home, such as "at what hour each night the lady of the house takes her daily sauna and bath." The legitimate expectation that information about perfectly lawful activity will remain private is categorically distinguishable from respondent's hopes or expectations concerning the nondetection of contraband in the trunk of his car. A dog sniff conducted during a concededly lawful traffic stop that reveals no information other than the location of a substance that no individual has any right to possess does not violate the Fourth Amendment.

The judgment of the Illinois Supreme Court is vacated, and the case is remanded for further proceedings not inconsistent with this opinion.

It is so ordered.

■ THE CHIEF JUSTICE took no part in the decision of this case.

■ JUSTICE SOUTER, dissenting.

I would hold that using the dog for the purposes of determining the presence of marijuana in the car's trunk was a search unauthorized as an incident of the speeding stop and unjustified on any other ground. I would accordingly affirm the judgment of the Supreme Court of Illinois, and I respectfully dissent.

In *United States v. Place,* 462 U.S. 696, 103 S.Ct. 2637, 77 L.Ed.2d 110 (1983), we categorized the sniff of the narcotics-seeking dog as *"sui generis"* under the Fourth Amendment and held it was not a search. The classification rests not only upon the limited nature of the intrusion, but on a further premise that experience has shown to be untenable, the assumption that trained sniffing dogs do not err. * * *

At the heart both of *Place* and the Court's opinion today is the proposition that sniffs by a trained dog are *sui generis* because a reaction by the dog in going alert is a response to nothing but the presence of contraband. Hence, the argument goes, because the sniff can only reveal the presence of items devoid of any legal use, the sniff "does not implicate legitimate privacy interests" and is not to be treated as a search.

The infallible dog, however, is a creature of legal fiction. * * * [The] supposed infallibility [of drug sniffing dogs] is belied by judicial opinions describing well-trained animals sniffing and alerting with less than perfect accuracy, whether owing to errors by their handlers, the limitations of the dogs themselves, or even the pervasive contamination of currency by cocaine. Indeed, a study cited by Illinois in this case for the proposition that dog sniffs are "generally reliable" shows that dogs in artificial testing situations return false positives anywhere from 12.5 to 60% of the time, depending on the length of the search. See Reply Brief for Petitioner 13; K. Garner et al., Duty Cycle of the Detector Dog: A Baseline Study 12 (Apr.2001) (prepared under Federal Aviation Administration grant by the Institute for Biological Detection Systems of Auburn University). In practical terms, the evidence is clear that the dog that alerts hundreds of times will be wrong dozens of times.

Once the dog's fallibility is recognized, however, that ends the justification claimed in *Place* for treating the sniff as *sui generis* under the Fourth Amendment: the sniff alert does not necessarily signal hidden contraband, and opening the container or enclosed space whose emanations the dog has sensed will not necessarily reveal contraband or any other evidence of crime. * * * And when that aura of uniqueness disappears, there is no basis in *Place's* reasoning, and no good reason otherwise, to ignore the actual function that dog sniffs perform. They are conducted to obtain information about the contents of private spaces beyond anything that human senses could perceive, even when conventionally enhanced. * * * Thus in practice the government's use of a trained narcotics dog functions as a limited search to reveal undisclosed facts about private enclosures, to be used to justify a further and complete search of the enclosed area. And given the fallibility of the dog, the sniff is the first step in a process that may disclose "intimate details" without revealing contraband, just as a thermal-imaging device might do * * *.

It makes sense, then, to treat a sniff as the search that it amounts to in practice, and to rely on the body of our Fourth Amendment cases, including *Kyllo,* in deciding whether such a search is reasonable. As a general proposition, using a dog to sniff for drugs is subject to the rule that the object of enforcing criminal laws does not, without more, justify suspicionless Fourth Amendment intrusions. Since the police claim to have had no particular suspicion that Caballes was violating any drug law,[1] this sniff search must stand or fall on its being ancillary to the traffic stop that led up to it. It is true that the police had probable cause to stop the car for an offense committed in the officer's presence, which Caballes concedes could have justified his arrest. There is no occasion to consider authority incident to arrest, however, for the police did nothing more than detain Caballes long enough to check his record and write a ticket. As a consequence, the reasonableness of the search must be assessed in relation to the actual delay the police chose to impose, and * * * the Fourth Amendment consequences of stopping for a traffic citation are settled law.

In *Berkemer v. McCarty,* 468 U.S. 420, 439–440, 104 S.Ct. 3138, 82 L.Ed.2d 317 (1984), we held that the analogue of the common traffic stop was the limited detention for investigation authorized by *Terry v. Ohio,* 392 U.S. 1, 88 S.Ct. 1868, 20 L.Ed.2d 889 (1968). While *Terry* authorized a restricted incidental search for weapons when reasonable suspicion warrants such a safety measure, the Court took care to keep a *Terry* stop from automatically becoming a foot in the door for all investigatory purposes; the permissible intrusion was bounded by the justification for the detention, Although facts disclosed by enquiry within this limit might give grounds to go further, the government could not otherwise take advantage of a suspect's immobility to search for evidence unrelated to the reason for the detention. That has to be the rule unless *Terry* is going to become an opensesame for general searches, and that rule requires holding that the police do not have reasonable grounds to conduct sniff searches for drugs simply because they have stopped someone to receive a ticket for a highway offense. Since the police had no indication of illegal activity beyond the speed of the car in this case, the sniff search should be held unreasonable under the Fourth Amendment and its fruits should be suppressed.

Nothing in the case relied upon by the Court, *United States v. Jacobsen,* 466 U.S. 109, 104 S.Ct. 1652, 80 L.Ed.2d 85 (1984), unsettled the limit of reasonable enquiry adopted in *Terry.* In *Jacobsen,* the Court found that no Fourth Amendment search occurred when federal agents analyzed powder they had already lawfully obtained. The Court noted that because

---

1. Despite the remarkable fact that the police pulled over a car for going 71 miles an hour on I80, the State maintains that excessive speed was the only reason for the stop, and the case comes to us on that assumption.

the test could only reveal whether the powder was cocaine, the owner had no legitimate privacy interest at stake. As already explained, however, the use of a sniffing dog in cases like this is significantly different and properly treated as a search that does indeed implicate Fourth Amendment protection.

In *Jacobsen*, once the powder was analyzed, that was effectively the end of the matter: either the powder was cocaine, a fact the owner had no legitimate interest in concealing, or it was not cocaine, in which case the test revealed nothing about the powder or anything else that was not already legitimately obvious to the police. But in the case of the dog sniff, the dog does not smell the disclosed contraband; it smells a closed container. An affirmative reaction therefore does not identify a substance the police already legitimately possess, but informs the police instead merely of a reasonable chance of finding contraband they have yet to put their hands on. The police will then open the container and discover whatever lies within, be it marijuana or the owner's private papers. Thus, while *Jacobsen* could rely on the assumption that the enquiry in question would either show with certainty that a known substance was contraband or would reveal nothing more, both the certainty and the limit on disclosure that may follow are missing when the dog sniffs the car.[2]

The Court today does not go so far as to say explicitly that sniff searches by dogs trained to sense contraband always get a free pass under the Fourth Amendment, since it reserves judgment on the constitutional significance of sniffs assumed to be more intrusive than a dog's walk around a stopped car. For this reason, I do not take the Court's reliance on *Jacobsen* as actually signaling recognition of a broad authority to conduct suspicionless sniffs for drugs in any parked car, about which Justice GINSBURG is rightly concerned, or on the person of any pedestrian minding his own business on a sidewalk. But the Court's stated reasoning provides no apparent stopping point short of such excesses. For the sake of providing a workable framework to analyze cases on facts like these, which

---

2. It would also be error to claim that some variant of the plainview doctrine excuses the lack of justification for the dog sniff in this case. When an officer observes an object left by its owner in plain view, no search occurs because the owner has exhibited "no intention to keep [the object] to himself." In contrast, when an individual conceals his possessions from the world, he has grounds to expect some degree of privacy. While plain view may be enhanced somewhat by technology, there are limits. As *Kyllo v. United States,* 533 U.S. 27, 33, 121 S.Ct. 2038, 150 L.Ed.2d 94 (2001), explained in treating the thermal-imaging device as outside the plain-view doctrine, "[w]e have previously reserved judgment as to how much technological enhancement of ordinary perception" turns mere observation into a Fourth Amendment search. While *Kyllo* laid special emphasis on the heightened privacy expectations that surround the home, closed car trunks are accorded some level of privacy protection. As a result, if Fourth Amendment protections are to have meaning in the face of superhuman, yet fallible, techniques like the use of trained dogs, those techniques must be justified on the basis of their reasonableness, lest everything be deemed in plain view.

are certain to come along, I would treat the dog sniff as the familiar search it is in fact, subject to scrutiny under the Fourth Amendment.

■ JUSTICE GINSBURG, with whom JUSTICE SOUTER joins, dissenting.

* * *

In *Terry v. Ohio,* [392 U.S. 1, 88 S.Ct. 1868, 20 L.Ed.2d 889 (1968)], the Court upheld the stop and subsequent frisk of an individual based on an officer's observation of suspicious behavior and his reasonable belief that the suspect was armed. In a *Terry*-type investigatory stop, "the officer's action [must be] justified at its inception, and ... reasonably related in scope to the circumstances which justified the interference in the first place." In applying *Terry,* the Court has several times indicated that the limitation on "scope" is not confined to the duration of the seizure; it also encompasses the manner in which the seizure is conducted.

"A routine traffic stop," the Court has observed, "is a relatively brief encounter and 'is more analogous to a so-called *Terry* stop ... than to a formal arrest.' " * * * I would apply *Terry's* reasonable-relation test * * * to determine whether the canine sniff impermissibly expanded the scope of the initially valid seizure of Caballes.

It is hardly dispositive that the dog sniff in this case may not have lengthened the duration of the stop. *Terry,* it merits repetition, instructs that any investigation must be "reasonably related in *scope* to the circumstances which justified the interference in the first place." (emphasis added). The unwarranted and nonconsensual expansion of the seizure here from a routine traffic stop to a drug investigation broadened the scope of the investigation in a manner that, in my judgment, runs afoul of the Fourth Amendment.[3]

* * * Dog sniffs that detect only the possession of contraband may be employed without offense to the Fourth Amendment, the Court reasons, because they reveal no lawful activity and hence disturb no legitimate expectation of privacy.

In my view, the Court diminishes the Fourth Amendment's force by abandoning the second *Terry* inquiry (was the police action "reasonably related in scope to the circumstances [justifiying] the [initial] interference"). A drug-detection dog is an intimidating animal. Injecting such an animal into a routine traffic stop changes the character of the encounter between the police and the motorist. The stop becomes broader, more adversarial, and (in at least some cases) longer. Caballes—who, as far as Troopers Gillette and Graham knew, was guilty solely of driving six miles per hour over the speed limit—was exposed to the embarrassment and intimidation of being investigated, on a public thoroughfare, for drugs. Even if the drug sniff is not characterized as a Fourth Amendment

---

3. The question whether a police officer inquiring about drugs without reasonable suspicion unconstitutionally broadens a traffic investigation is not before the Court.

"search," the sniff surely broadened the scope of the traffic-violation-related seizure.

The Court has never removed police action from Fourth Amendment control on the ground that the action is well calculated to apprehend the guilty. Under today's decision, every traffic stop could become an occasion to call in the dogs, to the distress and embarrassment of the lawabiding population.

* * *

The dog sniff in this case, it bears emphasis, was for drug detection only. A dog sniff for explosives, involving security interests not presented here, would be an entirely different matter. * * * Even if the Court were to change course and characterize a dog sniff as an independent Fourth Amendment search, the immediate, present danger of explosives would likely justify a bomb sniff under the special needs doctrine.

* * *

For the reasons stated, I would hold that the police violated Caballes' Fourth Amendment rights when, without cause to suspect wrongdoing, they conducted a dog sniff of his vehicle. I would therefore affirm the judgment of the Illinois Supreme Court.

NOTE

In People v. Harris, 207 Ill.2d 515, 280 Ill.Dec. 294, 802 N.E.2d 219 (2003), the fact were as follows:

> Officer Vernard Reed of the Will County sheriff's department, observed a vehicle, driven by Keith Weathersby, make an illegal left turn * * *. Officer Reed initiated a traffic stop. During the course of the traffic stop, Officer Reed requested identification from defendant, a passenger in the vehicle. Officer Reed performed a check on defendant's identification card and discovered that defendant had an outstanding warrant for failure to appear in court. Officer Reed placed defendant under arrest. In an ensuing search, officer Reed recovered a peasized rock of cocaine * * *.

A split Illinois Supreme Court held the officer's actions impermissible:

> [W]e must consider whether the check was related to the initial justification for the stop. If the check was reasonably related to the purpose of the stop, no fourth amendment violation occurred. If the check was not reasonably related to the purpose of the stop, we must consider whether the law enforcement officer had a reasonable, articulable suspicion that would justify the check. If the check was so justified, no fourth amendment violation occurred. In the absence of a reasonable connection to the purpose of the stop or a reasonable, articulable suspicion, we must consider whether, in light of all the circumstances and common sense, the check impermissibly prolonged the detention or changed the fundamental nature of the stop.

* * *

> [R]egardless of the duration of the detention, the warrant check was impermissible because it changed the fundamental nature of the traffic stop. The warrant check converted the stop from a routine traffic stop into an investigation of past wrongdoing by defendant.

A mere request for identification, it stressed, would not have the same effect.

The Supreme Court summarily vacated the judgment and remanded the case for further consideration in light of *Caballes*. Illinois v. Harris, 543 U.S. 1135, 125 S.Ct. 1292, 161 L.Ed.2d 94 (2005).

The Illinois Supreme Court eventually held that in light of *Caballes*, Officer Reed's actions were reasonable and hence permissible. People v. Harris, 228 Ill.2d 222, 886 N.E.2d 947, 319 Ill.Dec. 823 (2008). Harris was properly detained because of the traffic stop and the request that he produce identification was permissible. His production of the identification was voluntary, because a reasonable person in Harris's situation would feel free to decline to provide the identification. Further, *Caballes* and other Supreme Court decisions make clear that officers' actions in questioning a person properly detained as part of a traffic stop do not alter the nature of the detention in a constitutionally-significant manner.

This is consistent with the Supreme Court's comment in Arizona v. Johnson, 555 U.S. 323, ___, 129 S.Ct. 781, 172 L.Ed.2d 694 (2009):

> An officer's inquiries into matters unrelated to the justification for the traffic stop, this Court has made plain, do not convert the encounter into something other than a lawful seizure, so long as those inquiries do not measurably extend the duration of the stop.

555 U.S. at ___, 129 S.Ct. at 788.

Page 245. Insert the following note after State v. Soto:

NOTE

The proof necessary to show a traffic stop was racially motive was considered at length in Commonwealth v. Lora, 451 Mass. 425, 886 N.E.2d 688 (2008). Lora was driving the vehicle stopped; he is Hispanic. He was stopped by a state police officer on an interstate highway passing through Auburn, Massachusetts. An analysis of 51 citations issued by the trooper on the stretch of the highway going through Auburn disclosed that 22 (or 43%) were issued to Hispanic or African American drivers. Auburn's population, according to census is 97.5 white, 1% Hispanic, and 0.6% African American. The trial judge suppressed the drugs found as a result of the stop.

On appeal, the order suppressing the drugs was reversed. The court explained:

> [S]tatistical evidence may be used to meet a defendant's initial burden of producing sufficient evidence to raise a reasonable inference of impermissible discrimination. At a minimum, that evidence must establish that the racial composition of motorists stopped for motor vehicle violations varied significantly from the racial composition of the population of motorists making use of the relevant roadways, and who therefore could have encountered the officer or officers whose actions have been called into question.

451 Mass. at 442, 886 N.E.2d at 701. Lora's evidence relied on census data and thus did not provide an adequate basis for determining the race of drivers encountered by the officer on the highway. Further, Auburn is a small city (population 15,901) and the racial composition of drivers on the interstate may not reflect the community through which the interstate travels at that point. Regarding the problem generally, the court added:

> Justices of this court have expressed considerable concern about the practice of racial profiling in prior decisions. These concerns would not be alleviated by a standard that nominally allows a defendant to make claim of selective enforcement of traffic laws, but forecloses such a claim in practice.

> On the other hand, the standard must be sufficiently rigorous that its imposition does not unnecessarily intrude on the exercise of powers constitutionally delegated to other branches of government. Balance is therefore important. While racial profiling evidence is relevant to assessing the constitutionality of a traffic stop, * * * the initial burden rests on the defendant to produce evidence that similarly situated persons were treated differently because of their race. The practical weight of this burden is admittedly daunting in some cases, but not impossible. It was done, and done well, in New Jersey. Data now being collected in Massachusetts, and the work of academic and other institutions to develop more sophisticated analytic tools with which to identify and measure the use of race in the context of traffic stops may be of assistance in meeting this burden.

451 Mass. at 445–46, 886 N.E.2d at 703–04.

E.   SOBRIETY CHECKPOINTS AND RELATED DETENTIONS

Page 252.   Insert the following case and note after Michigan v. Sitz and its note:

City of Indianapolis v. Edmond

Supreme Court of the United States, 2000.
531 U.S. 32, 121 S.Ct. 447, 148 L.Ed.2d 333.

■ JUSTICE O'CONNOR delivered the opinion of the Court.

In *Michigan Dept. of State Police v. Sitz,* 496 U.S. 444, 110 S.Ct. 2481, 110 L.Ed.2d 412 (1990), and *United States v. Martinez–Fuerte,* 428 U.S. 543, 96 S.Ct. 3074, 49 L.Ed.2d 1116 (1976), we held that brief, suspicionless seizures at highway checkpoints for the purposes of combating drunk driving and intercepting illegal immigrants were constitutional. We now consider the constitutionality of a highway checkpoint program whose primary purpose is the discovery and interdiction of illegal narcotics.

I

In August 1998, the city of Indianapolis began to operate vehicle checkpoints on Indianapolis roads in an effort to interdict unlawful drugs.

The city conducted six such roadblocks between August and November that year, stopping 1,161 vehicles and arresting 104 motorists. Fifty-five arrests were for drug-related crimes, while 49 were for offenses unrelated to drugs. The overall "hit rate" of the program was thus approximately nine percent.

The parties stipulated to the facts concerning the operation of the checkpoints by the Indianapolis Police Department (IPD) for purposes of the preliminary injunction proceedings instituted below. At each checkpoint location, the police stop a predetermined number of vehicles. Approximately 30 officers are stationed at the checkpoint. Pursuant to written directives issued by the chief of police, at least one officer approaches the vehicle, advises the driver that he or she is being stopped briefly at a drug checkpoint, and asks the driver to produce a license and registration. The officer also looks for signs of impairment and conducts an open-view examination of the vehicle from the outside. A narcotics-detection dog walks around the outside of each stopped vehicle.

The directives instruct the officers that they may conduct a search only by consent or based on the appropriate quantum of particularized suspicion. The officers must conduct each stop in the same manner until particularized suspicion develops, and the officers have no discretion to stop any vehicle out of sequence. The city agreed in the stipulation to operate the checkpoints in such a way as to ensure that the total duration of each stop, absent reasonable suspicion or probable cause, would be five minutes or less.

[C]heckpoint locations are selected weeks in advance based on such considerations as area crime statistics and traffic flow. The checkpoints are generally operated during daylight hours and are identified with lighted signs reading, "NARCOTICS CHECKPOINT __ MILE AHEAD, NARCOTICS K–9 IN USE, BE PREPARED TO STOP." Once a group of cars has been stopped, other traffic proceeds without interruption until all the stopped cars have been processed or diverted for further processing. * * * [T]he average stop for a vehicle not subject to further processing lasts two to three minutes or less.

Respondents James Edmond and Joell Palmer were each stopped at a narcotics checkpoint in late September 1998. Respondents then filed a lawsuit on behalf of themselves and the class of all motorists who had been stopped or were subject to being stopped in the future at the Indianapolis drug checkpoints. Respondents claimed that the roadblocks violated the Fourth Amendment of the United States Constitution and the search and seizure provision of the Indiana Constitution. Respondents requested declaratory and injunctive relief for the class, as well as damages and attorney's fees for themselves.

Respondents then moved for a preliminary injunction. * * * The United States District Court for the Southern District of Indiana * * * denied the motion for a preliminary injunction, holding that the checkpoint program did not violate the Fourth Amendment. A divided panel of the

United States Court of Appeals for the Seventh Circuit reversed, holding that the checkpoints contravened the Fourth Amendment. The panel denied rehearing. We granted certiorari, and now affirm.

* * *

III

It is well established that a vehicle stop at a highway checkpoint effectuates a seizure within the meaning of the Fourth Amendment. The fact that officers walk a narcotics-detection dog around the exterior of each car at the Indianapolis checkpoints does not transform the seizure into a search. See *United States v. Place,* 462 U.S. 696, 707, 103 S.Ct. 2637, 77 L.Ed.2d 110 (1983). Just as in *Place,* an exterior sniff of an automobile does not require entry into the car and is not designed to disclose any information other than the presence or absence of narcotics. Like the dog sniff in *Place,* a sniff by a dog that simply walks around a car is "much less intrusive than a typical search." Rather, what principally distinguishes these checkpoints from those we have previously approved is their primary purpose.

As petitioners concede, the Indianapolis checkpoint program unquestionably has the primary purpose of interdicting illegal narcotics. * * *

We have never approved a checkpoint program whose primary purpose was to detect evidence of ordinary criminal wrongdoing. Rather, our checkpoint cases have recognized only limited exceptions to the general rule that a seizure must be accompanied by some measure of individualized suspicion. We suggested in [*Delaware v. Prouse,* 440 U.S. 648, 663, 99 S.Ct. 1391, 59 L.Ed.2d 660 (1979)] that we would not credit the "general interest in crime control" as justification for a regime of suspicionless stops. Consistent with this suggestion, each of the checkpoint programs that we have approved was designed primarily to serve purposes closely related to the problems of policing the border or the necessity of ensuring roadway safety. Because the primary purpose of the Indianapolis narcotics checkpoint program is to uncover evidence of ordinary criminal wrongdoing, the program contravenes the Fourth Amendment.

Petitioners propose several ways in which the narcotics-detection purpose of the instant checkpoint program may instead resemble the primary purposes of the checkpoints in *Sitz* and *Martinez–Fuerte.* Petitioners state that the checkpoints in those cases had the same ultimate purpose of arresting those suspected of committing crimes. Securing the border and apprehending drunk drivers are, of course, law enforcement activities, and law enforcement officers employ arrests and criminal prosecutions in pursuit of these goals. If we were to rest the case at this high level of generality, there would be little check on the ability of the authorities to construct roadblocks for almost any conceivable law enforcement purpose. Without drawing the line at roadblocks designed primarily to serve the general interest in crime control, the Fourth Amendment would do little to prevent such intrusions from becoming a routine part of American life.

Petitioners also emphasize the severe and intractable nature of the drug problem as justification for the checkpoint program. There is no doubt that traffic in illegal narcotics creates social harms of the first magnitude. The law enforcement problems that the drug trade creates likewise remain daunting and complex, particularly in light of the myriad forms of spin-off crime that it spawns. The same can be said of various other illegal activities, if only to a lesser degree. But the gravity of the threat alone cannot be dispositive of questions concerning what means law enforcement officers may employ to pursue a given purpose. Rather, in determining whether individualized suspicion is required, we must consider the nature of the interests threatened and their connection to the particular law enforcement practices at issue. We are particularly reluctant to recognize exceptions to the general rule of individualized suspicion where governmental authorities primarily pursue their general crime control ends.

Nor can the narcotics-interdiction purpose of the checkpoints be rationalized in terms of a highway safety concern similar to that present in *Sitz*. The detection and punishment of almost any criminal offense serves broadly the safety of the community, and our streets would no doubt be safer but for the scourge of illegal drugs. Only with respect to a smaller class of offenses, however, is society confronted with the type of immediate, vehicle-bound threat to life and limb that the sobriety checkpoint in *Sitz* was designed to eliminate.

Petitioners also liken the anticontraband agenda of the Indianapolis checkpoints to the antismuggling purpose of the checkpoints in *Martinez–Fuerte*. Petitioners cite this Court's conclusion in *Martinez–Fuerte* that the flow of traffic was too heavy to permit "particularized study of a given car that would enable it to be identified as a possible carrier of illegal aliens," and claim that this logic has even more force here. The problem with this argument is that the same logic prevails any time a vehicle is employed to conceal contraband or other evidence of a crime. This type of connection to the roadway is very different from the close connection to roadway safety that was present in *Sitz* * * *. Further, the Indianapolis checkpoints are far removed from the border context that was crucial in *Martinez–Fuerte*. While the difficulty of examining each passing car was an important factor in validating the law enforcement technique employed in *Martinez–Fuerte,* this factor alone cannot justify a regime of suspicionless searches or seizures. Rather, we must look more closely at the nature of the public interests that such a regime is designed principally to serve.

The primary purpose of the Indianapolis narcotics checkpoints is in the end to advance "the general interest in crime control." We decline to suspend the usual requirement of individualized suspicion where the police seek to employ a checkpoint primarily for the ordinary enterprise of investigating crimes. We cannot sanction stops justified only by the generalized and ever-present possibility that interrogation and inspection may reveal that any given motorist has committed some crime.

Of course, there are circumstances that may justify a law enforcement checkpoint where the primary purpose would otherwise, but for some emergency, relate to ordinary crime control. For example, as the Court of Appeals noted, the Fourth Amendment would almost certainly permit an appropriately tailored roadblock set up to thwart an imminent terrorist attack or to catch a dangerous criminal who is likely to flee by way of a particular route. The exigencies created by these scenarios are far removed from the circumstances under which authorities might simply stop cars as a matter of course to see if there just happens to be a felon leaving the jurisdiction. While we do not limit the purposes that may justify a checkpoint program to any rigid set of categories, we decline to approve a program whose primary purpose is ultimately indistinguishable from the general interest in crime control.

Petitioners argue that our prior cases preclude an inquiry into the purposes of the checkpoint program. For example, they cite *Whren v. United States,* 517 U.S. 806, 116 S.Ct. 1769, 135 L.Ed.2d 89 (1996) * * * to support the proposition that "where the government articulates and pursues a legitimate interest for a suspicionless stop, courts should not look behind that interest to determine whether the government's 'primary purpose' is valid." [*Whren,* however, does] not control the instant situation.

In *Whren,* we held that an individual officer's subjective intentions are irrelevant to the Fourth Amendment validity of a traffic stop that is justified objectively by probable cause to believe that a traffic violation has occurred. We observed that our prior cases "foreclose any argument that the constitutional reasonableness of traffic stops depends on the actual motivations of the individual officers involved." In so holding, we expressly distinguished cases where we had addressed the validity of searches conducted in the absence of probable cause.

Whren therefore reinforces the principle that, while "[s]ubjective intentions play no role in ordinary, probable-cause Fourth Amendment analysis," programmatic purposes may be relevant to the validity of Fourth Amendment intrusions undertaken pursuant to a general scheme without individualized suspicion. Accordingly, *Whren* does not preclude an inquiry into programmatic purpose in such contexts. It likewise does not preclude an inquiry into programmatic purpose here.

* * *

Petitioners argue that the Indianapolis checkpoint program is justified by its lawful secondary purposes of keeping impaired motorists off the road and verifying licenses and registrations. If this were the case, however, law enforcement authorities would be able to establish checkpoints for virtually any purpose so long as they also included a license or sobriety check. For this reason, we examine the available evidence to determine the primary purpose of the checkpoint program. While we recognize the challenges inherent in a purpose inquiry, courts routinely engage in this enterprise in many areas of constitutional jurisprudence as a means of sifting abusive governmental conduct from that which is lawful. As a result, a program driven by an impermissible purpose may be proscribed while a program impelled by licit purposes is permitted, even though the challenged conduct may be outwardly similar. While reasonableness under the Fourth Amendment is predominantly an objective inquiry, our special needs and administrative search cases demonstrate that purpose is often relevant when suspicionless intrusions pursuant to a general scheme are at issue.[5]

It goes without saying that our holding today does nothing to alter the constitutional status of the sobriety and border checkpoints that we approved in *Sitz* and *Martinez–Fuerte,* or of the type of traffic checkpoint that we suggested would be lawful in *Prouse.* The constitutionality of such checkpoint programs still depends on a balancing of the competing interests at stake and the effectiveness of the program. When law enforcement authorities pursue primarily general crime control purposes at checkpoints such as here, however, stops can only be justified by some quantum of individualized suspicion.

Our holding also does not affect the validity of border searches or searches at places like airports and government buildings, where the need for such measures to ensure public safety can be particularly acute. Nor does our opinion speak to other intrusions aimed primarily at purposes beyond the general interest in crime control. Our holding also does not impair the ability of police officers to act appropriately upon information that they properly learn during a checkpoint stop justified by a lawful primary purpose, even where such action may result in the arrest of a motorist for an offense unrelated to that purpose. Finally, we caution that the purpose inquiry in this context is to be conducted only at the programmatic level and is not an invitation to probe the minds of individual officers acting at the scene.

Because the primary purpose of the Indianapolis checkpoint program is ultimately indistinguishable from the general interest in crime control, the checkpoints violate the Fourth Amendment. The judgment of the Court of Appeals is accordingly affirmed.

It is so ordered.

■ CHIEF JUSTICE REHNQUIST, with whom JUSTICE THOMAS joins, and with whom JUSTICE SCALIA joins as to Part I, dissenting.

---

5. Because petitioners concede that the primary purpose of the Indianapolis checkpoints is narcotics detection, we need not decide whether the State may establish a checkpoint program with the primary purpose of checking licenses or driver sobriety and a secondary purpose of interdicting narcotics. Specifically, we express no view on the question whether police may expand the scope of a license or sobriety checkpoint seizure in order to detect the presence of drugs in a stopped car.

The State's use of a drug-sniffing dog, according to the Court's holding, annuls what is otherwise plainly constitutional under our Fourth Amendment jurisprudence: brief, standardized, discretionless, roadblock seizures of automobiles, seizures which effectively serve a weighty state interest with only minimal intrusion on the privacy of their occupants. Because these seizures serve the State's accepted and significant interests of preventing drunken driving and checking for driver's licenses and vehicle registrations, and because there is nothing in the record to indicate that the addition of the dog sniff lengthens these otherwise legitimate seizures, I dissent.

I

* * * Petitioners acknowledge that the "primary purpose" of these roadblocks is to interdict illegal drugs, but this fact should not be controlling. Even accepting the Court's conclusion that the checkpoints at issue in [*Michigan Dept. of State Police v. Sitz,* 496 U.S. 444, 110 S.Ct. 2481, 110 L.Ed.2d 412 (1990), and *United States v. Martinez–Fuerte,* 428 U.S. 543, 96 S.Ct. 3074, 49 L.Ed.2d 1116 (1976),] were not primarily related to criminal law enforcement, the question whether a law enforcement purpose could support a roadblock seizure is not presented in this case. The District Court found that another "purpose of the checkpoints is to check driver's licenses and vehicle registrations," and the written directives state that the police officers are to "[l]ook for signs of impairment." The use of roadblocks to look for signs of impairment was validated by *Sitz,* and the use of roadblocks to check for driver's licenses and vehicle registrations was expressly recognized in *Delaware v. Prouse,* 440 U.S. 648, 663, 99 S.Ct. 1391, 59 L.Ed.2d 660 (1979). That the roadblocks serve these legitimate state interests cannot be seriously disputed, as the 49 people arrested for offenses unrelated to drugs can attest. And it would be speculative to conclude—given the District Court's findings, the written directives, and the actual arrests—that petitioners would not have operated these roadblocks but for the State's interest in interdicting drugs.

Because of the valid reasons for conducting these roadblock seizures, it is constitutionally irrelevant that petitioners also hoped to interdict drugs. In *Whren v. United States,* 517 U.S. 806, 116 S.Ct. 1769, 135 L.Ed.2d 89 (1996), we held that an officer's subjective intent would not invalidate an otherwise objectively justifiable stop of an automobile. The reasonableness of an officer's discretionary decision to stop an automobile, at issue in *Whren,* turns on whether there is probable cause to believe that a traffic violation has occurred. The reasonableness of highway checkpoints, at issue here, turns on whether they effectively serve a significant state interest with minimal intrusion on motorists. The stop in *Whren* was objectively reasonable because the police officers had witnessed traffic violations; so too the roadblocks here are objectively reasonable because they serve the substantial interests of preventing drunken driving and checking for driver's licenses and vehicle registrations with minimal intrusion on motorists.

Once the constitutional requirements for a particular seizure are satisfied, the subjective expectations of those responsible for it, be it police officers or members of a city council, are irrelevant. It is the objective effect of the State's actions on the privacy of the individual that animates the Fourth Amendment. Because the objective intrusion of a valid seizure does not turn upon anyone's subjective thoughts, neither should our constitutional analysis.

* * *

These stops effectively serve the State's legitimate interests; they are executed in a regularized and neutral manner; and they only minimally intrude upon the privacy of the motorists. They should therefore be constitutional.

II

The Court, unwilling to adopt the straightforward analysis that these precedents dictate, adds a new non-law-enforcement primary purpose test lifted from a distinct area of Fourth Amendment jurisprudence relating to the *searches* of homes and businesses. * * * [W]hatever sense a non-law-enforcement primary purpose test may make in the search setting, it is ill suited to brief roadblock seizures, where we have consistently looked at "the scope of the stop" in assessing a program's constitutionality.

We have already rejected [in *Sitz*] an invitation to apply the non-law-enforcement primary purpose test that the Court now finds so indispensable. * * * [T]he "perfectly plain" reason for not incorporating the "special needs" test in our roadblock seizure cases is that seizures of automobiles "deal neither with searches nor with the sanctity of private dwellings, ordinarily afforded the most stringent Fourth Amendment protection." *Martinez–Fuerte, supra,* at 561, 96 S.Ct. 3074.

The "special needs" doctrine, which has been used to uphold certain suspicionless searches performed for reasons unrelated to law enforcement, is an exception to the general rule that a search must be based on individualized suspicion of wrongdoing. See, *e.g., Camara v. Municipal Court of City and County of San Francisco,* 387 U.S. 523, 87 S.Ct. 1727, 18 L.Ed.2d 930 (1967) (home administrative search). The doctrine permits intrusions into a person's body and home, areas afforded the greatest Fourth Amendment protection. But there were no such intrusions here.

* * * The brief seizure of an automobile can hardly be compared to the intrusive search of the body or the home. * * *

Because of these extrinsic limitations upon roadblock seizures, the Court's newfound non-law-enforcement primary purpose test is both unnecessary to secure Fourth Amendment rights and bound to produce wide-ranging litigation over the "purpose" of any given seizure. Police designing highway roadblocks can never be sure of their validity, since a jury might later determine that a forbidden purpose exists. Roadblock stops identical to the one that we upheld in *Sitz* 10 years ago, or to the one that we upheld 24 years ago in *Martinez–Fuerte,* may now be challenged on the grounds that they have some concealed forbidden purpose.

* * *

■ JUSTICE THOMAS, dissenting.

Taken together, our decisions in *Michigan Dept. of State Police v. Sitz,* 496 U.S. 444, 110 S.Ct. 2481, 110 L.Ed.2d 412 (1990), and *United States v. Martinez–Fuerte,* 428 U.S. 543, 96 S.Ct. 3074, 49 L.Ed.2d 1116 (1976), stand for the proposition that suspicionless roadblock seizures are constitutionally permissible if conducted according to a plan that limits the discretion of the officers conducting the stops. I am not convinced that *Sitz* and *Martinez–Fuerte* were correctly decided. Indeed, I rather doubt that the Framers of the Fourth Amendment would have considered "reasonable" a program of indiscriminate stops of individuals not suspected of wrongdoing.

Respondents did not, however, advocate the overruling of *Sitz* and *Martinez–Fuerte,* and I am reluctant to consider such a step without the benefit of briefing and argument. For the reasons given by THE CHIEF JUSTICE, I believe that those cases compel upholding the program at issue here. I, therefore, join his opinion.

NOTE: "INFORMATIONAL" CHECKPOINT STOPS

The *Edmond*-type approach—a rule of automatic unconstitutionality—does not apply to checkpoint stops of an "information-seeking kind," the Supreme Court held in Illinois v. Lidster, 540 U.S. 419, 124 S.Ct. 885, 157 L.Ed.2d 843 (2004).

In *Lidster,* officers were investigating a hit-and-run incident in which a 70–year–old bicyclist was killed. The officers set up a checkpoint about a week after the incident at the same place and time of night the incident had occurred. Traffic going one way on the highway was stopped, an officer asked the occupants of each car whether they had seen anything happened there the night of the incident, and each driver was given an flyer describing the incident and asking help identifying the vehicle and driver involved. Lidster approached the checkpoint and swerved, nearly striking one of the officers. Officers conducted a sobriety test and Lidster was charged with driving under the influence of alcohol.

The Court rejected Lidster's contention that the evidence of his intoxication was obtained through an unconstitutional checkpoint stop. All of the justices agreed that the standard to be applied was not that applied in *Edmond*:

> The checkpoint stop here differs significantly from that in *Edmond.* The stop's primary law enforcement purpose was *not* to determine whether a vehicle's occupants were committing a crime, but to ask vehicle occupants, as members of the public, for their help in providing information about a crime in all likelihood committed by others. The police expected the information elicited to help them apprehend, not the vehicle's occupants, but other individuals.

* * *

[U]nlike *Edmond,* the context here (seeking information from the public) is one in which, by definition, the concept of individualized suspicion has little role to play. Like certain other forms of police activity, say, crowd control or public safety, an information-seeking stop is not the kind of event that involves suspicion, or lack of suspicion, of the relevant individual.

For another thing, information-seeking highway stops are less likely to provoke anxiety or to prove intrusive. The stops are likely brief. The police are not likely to ask questions designed to elicit self-incriminating information. And citizens will often react positively when police simply ask for their help as "responsible citizen[s]" to "give whatever information they may have to aid in law enforcement."

* * *

[W]e do not believe that an *Edmond*-type rule is needed to prevent an unreasonable proliferation of police checkpoints. Practical considerations—namely, limited police resources and community hostility to related traffic tie-ups—seem likely to inhibit any such proliferation. And, of course, the Fourth Amendment's normal insistence that the stop be reasonable in context will still provide an important legal limitation on police use of this kind of information-seeking checkpoint.

These considerations, taken together, convince us that an *Edmond*-type presumptive rule of unconstitutionality does not apply here. That does not mean the stop is automatically, or even presumptively, constitutional. It simply means that we must judge its reasonableness, hence, its constitutionality, on the basis of the individual circumstances. And * * * in judging reasonableness, we look to "the gravity of the public concerns served by the seizure, the degree to which the seizure advances the public interest, and the severity of the interference with individual liberty."

540 U.S. at 423–28, 124 S.Ct. at 889–90. Three members of the Court thought the case should be remanded for the State court to apply this analysis to the facts.

The majority, however, applied the analysis itself:

The relevant public concern was grave. Police were investigating a crime that had resulted in a human death. No one denies the police's need to obtain more information at that time. And the stop's objective was to help find the perpetrator of a specific and known crime, not of unknown crimes of a general sort.

The stop advanced this grave public concern to a significant degree. The police appropriately tailored their checkpoint stops to fit important criminal investigatory needs. The stops took place about one week after the hit-and-run accident, on the same highway near the location of the accident, and at about the same time of night. And police used the stops to obtain information from drivers, some of whom might well have been in the vicinity of the crime at the time it occurred.

Most importantly, the stops interfered only minimally with liberty of the sort the Fourth Amendment seeks to protect. Viewed objectively, each stop required only a brief wait in line—a very few minutes at most. Contact with the police lasted only a few seconds. Police contact consisted simply of a request for information and the distribution of a flyer. Viewed subjectively, the contact provided little reason for anxiety or alarm. The police stopped all vehicles systematically. And there is no allegation here that the police acted in a discriminatory or otherwise unlawful manner while questioning motorists during stops.

For these reasons we conclude that the checkpoint stop was constitutional.

540 U.S. at 427–28, 124 S.Ct. at 891.

F. PRETEXT MOTIVATION

Page 257. Add the following at the end of Note: Pretext Motivation Under State Law:

A pretext doctrine was adopted as a matter of state constitutional law in State v. Sullivan, 348 Ark. 647, 74 S.W.3d 215 (2002). But the next year the court made clear the doctrine applied only to arrests and not to traffic stops. It based the distinction "on the heightened intrusiveness associated with an arrest," and the absence of state case law applying the pretext approach to otherwise valid traffic stops. State v. Harmon, 353 Ark. 568, 113 S.W.3d 75 (2003). An intermediate New Mexico court held that pretext stops violate the state constitution. State v. Ochoa, 146 N.M. 32, 206 P.3d 143, 155–56 (2008), cert. granted 145 N.M. 572, 203 P.3d 103 (2008), cert. quashed 147 N.M. 464, 225 P.3d 794 (2009).

By a 4–3 vote, the New York Court of Appeals refused to adopt as a matter of state constitutional law the position rejected in *Whren*. See People v. Robinson, 97 N.Y.2d 341, 767 N.E.2d 638, 741 N.Y.S.2d 147 (2001). All seven judges agreed that a purely subjective approach was not appropriate.

Page 257. Add the following Notes after Whren v. United States:

NOTES

1. **Pretext Arrests.** *Whren* was reaffirmed and applied to an arrest in Arkansas v. Sullivan, 532 U.S. 769, 121 S.Ct. 1876, 149 L.Ed.2d 994 (2001) (per curiam). *Sullivan's* facts were as follows:

Officer Joe Taylor of the Conway, Arkansas, Police Department stopped respondent Sullivan for speeding and for having an improperly tinted windshield. Taylor approached Sullivan's vehicle, explained the reason for the stop, and requested Sullivan's license, registration, and insurance documentation. Upon seeing Sullivan's license, Taylor realized that he was aware of " 'intelligence on [Sullivan] regarding narcotics.' " When Sullivan opened his car door in an (unsuccessful) attempt to locate his registration and insurance papers, Taylor noticed a rusted roofing hatchet on the car's floorboard. Taylor then arrested Sullivan for speeding, driving without his registration and insurance documentation, carrying a weapon (the roofing hatchet), and improper window tinting.

After another officer arrived and placed Sullivan in his squad car, Officer Taylor conducted an inventory search of Sullivan's vehicle pursuant to the Conway Police Department's Vehicle Inventory Policy. Under the vehicle's armrest, Taylor discovered a bag containing a substance that appeared to him to be methamphetamine as well as numerous items of suspected drug parapher-nalia.

The trial court suppressed the items seized from the vehicle and on appeal by the State the Arkansas Supreme Court affirmed. On motion for rehearing, the state court explicitly refused to treat *Whren* as controlling, in part because "much of it is dicta." The trial judge acceptably concluded that "the arrest was pretextual and made for the purpose of searching Sullivan's vehicle for evidence of a crime," and, the appellate court concluded, "we do not believe that *Whren* disallows" suppres-sion on such a basis. Summarily reversing, the Supreme Court held that the Arkansas court's analysis could not be squared with *Whren*. "That *Whren* involved a traffic stop, rather than a custodial arrest," the majority observed, "is of no particular moment * * *." 532 U.S. at 771, 121 S.Ct. at 1879, 149 L.Ed.2d at 998.

2. **Relationship to Arrests for Traffic Offenses.** How, if at all, does *Whren* relate to Atwater v. City of Lago Vista, 532 U.S. 318, 121 S.Ct. 1536, 149 L.Ed.2d 549 (2001), reprinted in new subsection B(3) of this chapter, contained earlier in this supplement? In *Sullivan*, Justice Ginsburg, joined by Justices Stevens, O'Connor, and Breyer, commented:

> In *Atwater*, which recognized no constitutional limitation on arrest for a fine-only misdemeanor offense, this Court relied in part on a perceived "dearth of horribles demanding redress." Although I joined a dissenting opinion ques-tioning the relevance of the Court's conclusion on that score, I hope the Court's perception proves correct. But if it does not, if experience demonstrates "anything like an epidemic of unnecessary minor-offense arrests," I hope the Court will reconsider its recent precedent. See Vasquez v. Hillery, 474 U.S. 254, 266, 106 S.Ct. 617, 88 L.Ed.2d 598 (1986) (observing that Court has departed from stare decisis when necessary "to bring its opinions into agreement with experience and with facts newly ascertained") (quoting Burnet v. Coronado Oil & Gas Co., 285 U.S. 393, 412, 52 S.Ct. 443, 76 L.Ed. 815 (1932) (Brandeis, J., dissenting)).

532 U.S. at 773, 121 S.Ct. at 1879, 149 L.Ed.2d at 999 (Ginsburg, J., concurring). Justice Ginsburg seemed to regard a traffic offense arrest made for purposes of pursuing suspicions of drug trafficking as a horrible demanding redress. Was she correct?

3. **Searches Based on Reasonable Suspicion.** Does or should *Whren* apply to law enforcement action not requiring probable cause? In United States v. Knights, 534 U.S. 112, 122 S.Ct. 587, 151 L.Ed.2d 497 (2001), discussed in the material supplementing page 279 of the text, the Court seemed to apply *Whren* to the search of a probationer's residence which is reasonable if supported by reason-able suspicion. It explained only that the case presented no basis for examining "official purpose" because—citing *Whren*—"our holding rests on ordinary Fourth Amendment analysis that considers all of the circumstances of a search * * *." *Whren* applies, it suggested, except in "some special needs and administrative search cases" such as suspicionless stops of motorist at highway checkpoints. 534 U.S. at 122, 122 S.Ct. at 593, 151 L.Ed.2d at 507. Justice Souter alone indicated he would "reserve the question whether *Whren's* holding * * * should apply to searches based only upon reasonable suspicion." 534 U.S. at 123, 122 S.Ct. at 593, 151 L.Ed.2d at 507 (Souter, J., concurring).

4. **Effect of Announcement of Basis for Law Enforcement Action.**
What if any consequences flow from officers' announcement at the time of an arrest
or other action some legal basis for that action? This was addressed in Devenpeck v.
Alford, 543 U.S. 146, 125 S.Ct. 588, 160 L.Ed.2d 537 (2004).

After being told that Jerome Alford had activated "wig-wag" headlights (which
flash the left and right lights alternately) on his vehicle, Washington State Police
officers stopped him to investigate their concerns that he was impersonating a
police officer. When they observed that he had an operating tape recorder on the
seat, they told him he was being arrested for a violation of Washington's Privacy
Act, which prohibits recording certain conversations without the permission of the
participants. After the charge was dismissed, Alford sued the officers asserting a
federal cause of action under Rev. Stat. § 1979, 42 U.S.C. § 1983, and a state cause
of action for unlawful arrest and imprisonment. Both claims rested upon the
allegation that the defendant officers arrested him without probable cause in
violation of the Fourth and Fourteenth Amendments. A jury returned a verdict for
the defendants.

On appeal, this was reversed. The court of appeals rejected the officers'
contention that the arrest could be justified as one on probable cause to believe
Alford committed the offenses of impersonating a law-enforcement officer and
obstructing a law-enforcement officer. It applied a rule that when an arrest is
announced by an officer as resting on a particular offense, it can be later upheld as
one for a different offense only if that different offense is a crime involving the same
conduct as that relied upon by the officer and is "closely related" to that offense.
Since the defendants had stated that the arrest was for violation of the Privacy Act,
they could not later defend it as an arrest for impersonating an officer or obstructing an officer because these were not closely related to the possible Privacy Act
violation.

A unanimous Supreme Court (with the Chief Justice not participating) reversed, holding the defendants were not, as a matter of Fourth Amendment law,
limited to defending the arrest as one for an offense closely related to that the
officers announced at the time of the arrest.

> Our cases make clear that an arresting officer's state of mind (except for
> the facts that he knows) is irrelevant to the existence of probable cause. That is
> to say, his subjective reason for making the arrest need not be the criminal
> offense as to which the known facts provide probable cause. * * *

> The rule that the offense establishing probable cause must be "closely
> related" to, and based on the same conduct as, the offense identified by the
> arresting officer at the time of arrest is inconsistent with this precedent. Such a
> rule makes the lawfulness of an arrest turn upon the motivation of the
> arresting officer—eliminating, as validating probable cause, facts that played no
> part in the officer's expressed subjective reason for making the arrest, and
> offenses that are not "closely related" to that subjective reason.

543 U.S. at 153–54, 125 S.Ct. at 593–94. It continued:

> [T]he "closely related offense" rule is condemned by its perverse conse-
> quences. While it is assuredly good police practice to inform a person of the
> reason for his arrest at the time he is taken into custody, we have never held
> that to be constitutionally required. Hence, the predictable consequence of a
> rule limiting the probable cause inquiry to offenses closely related to (and

supported by the same facts as) those identified by the arresting officer is not, as respondent contends, that officers will cease making sham arrests on the hope that such arrests will later be validated, but rather that officers will cease providing reasons for arrest. And even if this option were to be foreclosed by adoption of a statutory or constitutional requirement, officers would simply give every reason for which probable cause could conceivably exist.

Even absent a requirement that an individual be informed of the reason for arrest when he is taken into custody, he will not be left to wonder for long. "[P]ersons arrested without a warrant must promptly be brought before a neutral magistrate for a judicial determination of probable cause." *County of Riverside v. McLaughlin,* 500 U.S. 44, 53, 111 S.Ct. 1661, 114 L.Ed.2d 49 (1991).

543 U.S. at 155, 125 S.Ct. at 595 (incorporating footnote into text).

During oral argument, Justice Souter observed that he thought Alford could prevail only if the Court held that the basis for an arrest must be stated by the officer when the arrest is made. He added, "I'll be candid with you. I think it is necessary."

The United States, appearing as amicus curiae in support of the officers, argued that the Fourth Amendment validity of an arrest turns on whether after the fact the courts determine there was probable cause for any offense based on the facts known to the officer at the time of the arrest. Counsel for the United States explained:

The * * * Government's position * * * is that * * * the analysis is simply did the facts known to the officer, viewed through the prism of an objectively reasonable officer, establish probable cause. And that to make an evaluation of the arrest turn upon the officer's subjective assessment of those facts—in other words, the working of his brain, the crunching of those facts that results in the spitting out of a legal conclusion—is contrary to this Court's precedent and guts the objective reasonable test[. It] would make * * * the validity of a Fourth Amendment action turn upon whether the officer is particularly smart, whether he's new, whether he's nervous, whether he says nothing at all or whether he decides to say, you're under arrest for everything listed in the Washington code book.

Justice Scalia elicited agreement from counsel for the officers that even if Alford's vehicle had an expired inspection sticker, his arrest could not be defended as one for failing to exhibit a valid inspection sticker if the officers had not noticed the expired sticker.

CHAPTER 5

"WARRANTLESS" SEARCHES

A. THE EMERGENCY DOCTRINE

Page 266. Insert the following new note after note 2 after Vale v. Louisiana:

2a. **Police-Created Exigent Circumstances.** In Kentucky v. King, 563 U.S. ___, 131 S.Ct. 1849, 179 L.Ed.2d 865 (2011), the Court addressed whether exigent circumstances permit a warrantless search where police themselves have some responsibility for the exigency.

Several Lexington, Kentucky uniformed police officers, including Officer Steven Cobb, were in pursuit of a suspect from whom a controlled buy of cocaine had been made. They believed he had entered one of two apartments and smelled marijuana smoke emanating from one of the apartments. Then they approached the door of that apartment:

> [T]he officers banged on the left apartment door "as loud as [they] could" and announced, " 'This is the police' " or " 'Police, police, police.' " Cobb said that "[a]s soon as [the officers] started banging on the door," they "could hear people inside moving," and "[i]t sounded as [though] things were being moved inside the apartment." These noises, Cobb testified, led the officers to believe that drug-related evidence was about to be destroyed.

> At that point, the officers announced that they "were going to make entry inside the apartment." Cobb then kicked in the door, the officers entered the apartment, and they found three people in the front room: respondent Hollis King, respondent's girlfriend, and a guest who was smoking marijuana. The officers performed a protective sweep of the apartment during which they saw marijuana and powder cocaine in plain view. In a subsequent search, they also discovered crack cocaine, cash, and drug paraphernalia.

Later, the suspected drug dealer who was the initial target of the investigation was found in the other apartment.

Justice Ginsburg concluded that the trial court erred in admitting the evidence obtained as a result of the entry. The officers had an opportunity to apply for a warrant, she reasoned. Any exigent circumstances were created by the choice of the officers to knock on the apartment door rather than seek a warrant. "The urgency [required to support an exigent circumstances search] must exist," she explained, "when the police come on the scene, not subsequent to their arrival, prompted by their own conduct." 563 U.S. at ___, 131 S.Ct. at 1864 (Ginsburg, J., dissenting).

An eight-justice majority, in an opinion by Justice Alito, concluded otherwise. If exigent circumstances exist and "the police did not create the exigency by engaging or threatening to engage in conduct that violates the Fourth Amendment, warrantless entry to prevent the destruction of evidence is reasonable and thus allowed."

The majority rejected a number of offered limitations on that rule, including ones that would deny officers the right to enter if it was reasonably foreseeable that the investigative tactics employed by the police would create exigent circumstances, if they acted in "bad faith," or if the officers engage in conduct that would cause a reasonable person to believe that entry is imminent and inevitable. With regard to the last proposed limitation, the Court explained:

> If [this] test were adopted, it would be extremely difficult for police officers to know how loudly they may announce their presence or how forcefully they may knock on a door without running afoul of the police-created exigency rule. And in most cases, it would be nearly impossible for a court to determine whether that threshold had been passed.

563 U.S. at ___, 131 S.Ct. at 1861.

Applying the adopted approach, the majority assumed—without deciding—that exigent circumstances existed. Nothing in the conduct of the officers prevented the prosecution from relying on those exigent circumstances. Contrary to King's argument, the evidence did not show the officers made a "demand" to be let into the apartment, "much less a demand that amounts to a threat to violate the Fourth Amendment." 563 U.S. at ___, 131 S.Ct. at 1863.

Justice Ginsburg was distressed by the implications of the majority's approach:

> The Court today arms the police with a way routinely to dishonor the Fourth Amendment's warrant requirement in drug cases. In lieu of presenting their evidence to a neutral magistrate, police officers may now knock, listen, then break the door down, nevermind that they had ample time to obtain a warrant.

563 U.S. at ___, 131 S.Ct. at 1864.

Page 266. Insert the following new cases after Vale v. Louisiana and its notes:

Illinois v. McArthur

Supreme Court of the United States, 2001.
531 U.S. 326, 121 S.Ct. 946, 148 L.Ed.2d 838.

■ JUSTICE BREYER delivered the opinion of the Court.

Police officers, with probable cause to believe that a man had hidden marijuana in his home, prevented that man from entering the home for about two hours while they obtained a search warrant. We must decide whether those officers violated the Fourth Amendment. * * *

I

A

On April 2, 1997, Tera McArthur asked two police officers to accompany her to the trailer where she lived with her husband, Charles, so that they could keep the peace while she removed her belongings. The two officers, Assistant Chief John Love and Officer Richard Skidis, arrived with Tera at the trailer at about 3:15 p.m. Tera went inside, where Charles was present. The officers remained outside.

When Tera emerged after collecting her possessions, she spoke to Chief Love, who was then on the porch. She suggested he check the trailer because "Chuck had dope in there." She added (in Love's words) that she had seen Chuck "slid[e] some dope underneath the couch."

Love knocked on the trailer door, told Charles what Tera had said, and asked for permission to search the trailer, which Charles denied. Love then sent Officer Skidis with Tera to get a search warrant.

Love told Charles, who by this time was also on the porch, that he could not reenter the trailer unless a police officer accompanied him. Charles subsequently reentered the trailer two or three times (to get cigarettes and to make phone calls), and each time Love stood just inside the door to observe what Charles did.

Officer Skidis obtained the warrant by about 5 p.m. He returned to the trailer and, along with other officers, searched it. The officers found under the sofa a marijuana pipe, a box for marijuana (called a "one-hitter" box), and a small amount of marijuana. They then arrested Charles.

B

Illinois subsequently charged Charles McArthur with unlawfully possessing drug paraphernalia and marijuana (less than 2.5 grams), both misdemeanors. McArthur moved to suppress the pipe, box, and marijuana on the ground that they were the "fruit" of an unlawful police seizure, namely, the refusal to let him reenter the trailer unaccompanied, which would have permitted him, he said, to "have destroyed the marijuana."

The trial court granted McArthur's suppression motion. The Appellate Court of Illinois affirmed, and the Illinois Supreme Court denied the State's petition for leave to appeal. We granted certiorari to determine whether the Fourth Amendment prohibits the kind of temporary seizure at issue here.

II

A

The Fourth Amendment says that the "right of the people to be secure in their persons, houses, papers, and effects, against unreasonable searches and seizures, shall not be violated." U.S. Const., Amdt. 4. Its "central requirement" is one of reasonableness. In order to enforce that requirement, this Court has interpreted the Amendment as establishing rules and presumptions designed to control conduct of law enforcement officers that may significantly intrude upon privacy interests. Sometimes those rules require warrants. We have said, for example, that in "the ordinary case," seizures of personal property are "unreasonable within the meaning of the

Fourth Amendment," without more, "unless . . . accomplished pursuant to a judicial warrant," issued by a neutral magistrate after finding probable cause. *United States v. Place,* 462 U.S. 696, 701, 103 S.Ct. 2637, 77 L.Ed.2d 110 (1983).

We nonetheless have made it clear that there are exceptions to the warrant requirement. When faced with special law enforcement needs, diminished expectations of privacy, minimal intrusions, or the like, the Court has found that certain general, or individual, circumstances may render a warrantless search or seizure reasonable.

In the circumstances of the case before us, we cannot say that the warrantless seizure was *per se* unreasonable. It involves a plausible claim of specially pressing or urgent law enforcement need, *i.e.,* "exigent circumstances." Moreover, the restraint at issue was tailored to that need, being limited in time and scope, and avoiding significant intrusion into the home itself, Consequently, rather than employing a *per se* rule of unreasonableness, we balance the privacy-related and law enforcement-related concerns to determine if the intrusion was reasonable.

We conclude that the restriction at issue was reasonable, and hence lawful, in light of the following circumstances, which we consider in combination. First, the police had probable cause to believe that McArthur's trailer home contained evidence of a crime and contraband, namely, unlawful drugs. The police had had an opportunity to speak with Tera McArthur and make at least a very rough assessment of her reliability. They knew she had had a firsthand opportunity to observe her husband's behavior, in particular with respect to the drugs at issue. And they thought, with good reason, that her report to them reflected that opportunity. Cf. *Massachusetts v. Upton,* 466 U.S. 727, 732–734, 104 S.Ct. 2085, 80 L.Ed.2d 721 (1984) *(per curiam)* (upholding search warrant issued in similar circumstances).

Second, the police had good reason to fear that, unless restrained, McArthur would destroy the drugs before they could return with a warrant. They reasonably might have thought that McArthur realized that his wife knew about his marijuana stash; observed that she was angry or frightened enough to ask the police to accompany her; saw that after leaving the trailer she had spoken with the police; and noticed that she had walked off with one policeman while leaving the other outside to observe the trailer. They reasonably could have concluded that McArthur, consequently suspecting an imminent search, would, if given the chance, get rid of the drugs fast.

Third, the police made reasonable efforts to reconcile their law enforcement needs with the demands of personal privacy. They neither searched the trailer nor arrested McArthur before obtaining a warrant. Rather, they imposed a significantly less restrictive restraint, preventing McArthur only from entering the trailer unaccompanied. They left his home and his belongings intact—until a neutral Magistrate, finding probable cause, issued a warrant.

Fourth, the police imposed the restraint for a limited period of time, namely, two hours. As far as the record reveals, this time period was no longer than reasonably necessary for the police, acting with diligence, to obtain the warrant. Compare *United States v. Place, supra,* at 709–710, 103 S.Ct. 2637 (holding 90–minute detention of luggage unreasonable based on nature of interference with person's travels and lack of diligence of police), with *United States v. Van Leeuwen,* 397 U.S. 249, 253, 90 S.Ct. 1029, 25 L.Ed.2d 282 (1970) (holding 29–hour detention of mailed package reasonable given unavoidable delay in obtaining warrant and minimal nature of intrusion). Given the nature of the intrusion and the law enforcement interest at stake, this brief seizure of the premises was permissible.

B

Our conclusion that the restriction was lawful finds significant support in this Court's case law. In *Segura v. United States,* 468 U.S. 796, 104 S.Ct. 3380, 82 L.Ed.2d 599 (1984), the Court considered the admissibility of drugs which the police had found in a lawful, warrant-based search of an apartment, but only after unlawfully entering the apartment and occupying it for 19 hours. The majority held that the drugs were admissible because, had the police acted lawfully throughout, they could have discovered and seized the drugs pursuant to the validly issued warrant. The minority disagreed. However, when describing alternative lawful search and seizure methods, both majority and minority assumed, at least for argument's sake, that the police, armed with reliable information that the apartment contained drugs, might lawfully have sealed the apartment from the outside, restricting entry into the apartment while waiting for the warrant.

In various other circumstances, this Court has upheld temporary restraints where needed to preserve evidence until police could obtain a warrant. See, *e.g., United States v. Place,* 462 U.S., at 706, 103 S.Ct. 2637 (reasonable suspicion justifies brief detention of luggage pending further investigation); *United States v. Van Leeuwen, supra,* at 253, 90 S.Ct. 1029 (reasonable suspicion justifies detaining package delivered for mailing).

We have found no case in which this Court has held unlawful a temporary seizure that was supported by probable cause and was designed to prevent the loss of evidence while the police diligently obtained a warrant in a reasonable period of time. But cf. *Welsh v. Wisconsin,* 466 U.S. 740, 754, 104 S.Ct. 2091, 80 L.Ed.2d 732 (1984) (holding warrantless entry into and arrest in home unreasonable despite possibility that evidence of noncriminal offense would be lost while warrant was being obtained).

C

Nor are we persuaded by the countervailing considerations that the parties or lower courts have raised. McArthur argues that the police proceeded without probable cause. But McArthur has waived this argument. And, in any event, it is without merit.

The Appellate Court of Illinois concluded that the police could not order McArthur to stay outside his home because McArthur's porch, where he stood at the time, was part of his home; hence the order "amounted to a constructive eviction" of McArthur from his residence. This Court has held, however, that a person standing in the doorway of a house is "in a 'public' place," and hence subject to arrest without a warrant permitting entry of the home. *United States v. Santana,* 427 U.S. 38, 42, 96 S.Ct. 2406, 49 L.Ed.2d 300 (1976). Regardless, we do not believe the difference to which the Appellate Court points—porch versus, *e.g.,* front walk—could make a significant difference here as to the reasonableness of the police restraint; and that, from the Fourth Amendment's perspective, is what matters.

The Appellate Court also found negatively significant the fact that Chief Love, with McArthur's consent, stepped inside the trailer's doorway to observe McArthur when McArthur reentered the trailer on two or three occasions. McArthur, however, reentered simply for his own convenience, to make phone calls and to obtain cigarettes. Under these circumstances, the reasonableness of the greater restriction (preventing reentry) implies the reasonableness of the lesser (permitting reentry conditioned on observation).

Finally, McArthur points to a case (and we believe it is the only case) that he believes offers direct support, namely, *Welsh v. Wisconsin, supra.* In *Welsh,* this Court held that police could not enter a home without a warrant in order to prevent the loss of evidence (namely, the defendant's blood alcohol level) of the "nonjailable traffic offense" of driving while intoxicated. McArthur notes that his two convictions are for misdemeanors, which, he says, are as minor, and he adds that the restraint, keeping him out of his home, was nearly as serious.

We nonetheless find significant distinctions. The evidence at issue here was of crimes that were "jailable," not "nonjailable." See Ill. Comp. Stat., ch. 720, § 550/4(a) (1998); ch. 730, § 5/5–8–3(3) (possession of less than 2.5 grams of marijuana punishable by up to 30 days in jail); ch. 720, § 600/3.5; ch. 730, § 5/5–8–3(1) (possession of drug paraphernalia punishable by up to one year in jail). In *Welsh,* we noted that, "[g]iven that the classification of state crimes differs widely among the States, the penalty that may attach to any particular offense seems to provide the clearest and most consistent indication of the State's interest in arresting individuals suspected of committing that offense." The same reasoning applies here, where class C misdemeanors include such widely diverse offenses as drag racing, drinking alcohol in a railroad car or on a railroad platform, bribery by a candidate for public office, and assault.

And the restriction at issue here is less serious. Temporarily keeping a person from entering his home, a consequence whenever police stop a person on the street, is considerably less intrusive than police entry into the home itself in order to make a warrantless arrest or conduct a search.

We have explained above why we believe that the need to preserve evidence of a "jailable" offense was sufficiently urgent or pressing to justify the restriction upon entry that the police imposed. We need not decide whether the circumstances before us would have justified a greater restriction for this type of offense or the same restriction were only a "nonjailable" offense at issue.

III

In sum, the police officers in this case had probable cause to believe that a home contained contraband, which was evidence of a crime. They reasonably believed that the home's resident, if left free of any restraint, would destroy that evidence. And they imposed a restraint that was both limited and tailored reasonably to secure law enforcement needs while protecting privacy interests. In our view, the restraint met the Fourth Amendment's demands.

The judgment of the Illinois Appellate Court is reversed, and the case is remanded for further proceedings not inconsistent with this opinion.

It is so ordered.

■ JUSTICE SOUTER, concurring.

I join the Court's opinion subject to this afterword on two points: the constitutionality of a greater intrusion than the one here and the permissibility of choosing impoundment over immediate search. Respondent McArthur's location made the difference between the exigency that justified temporarily barring him from his own dwelling and circumstances that would have supported a greater interference with his privacy and property. As long as he was inside his trailer, the police had probable cause to believe that he had illegal drugs stashed as his wife had reported and that with any sense he would flush them down the drain before the police could get a warrant to enter and search. This probability of destruction in anticipation of a warrant exemplifies the kind of present risk that undergirds the accepted exigent circumstances exception to the general warrant requirement. That risk would have justified the police in entering McArthur's trailer promptly to make a lawful, warrantless search. When McArthur stepped outside and left the trailer uninhabited, the risk abated and so did the reasonableness of entry by the police for as long as he was outside. This is so because the only justification claimed for warrantless action here is the immediate risk, and the limit of reasonable response by the police is set by the scope of the risk.

Since, however, McArthur wished to go back in, why was it reasonable to keep him out when the police could perfectly well have let him do as he chose, and then enjoyed the ensuing opportunity to follow him and make a warrantless search justified by the renewed danger of destruction? The answer is not that the law officiously insists on safeguarding a suspect's privacy from search, in preference to respecting the suspect's liberty to enter his own dwelling. Instead, the legitimacy of the decision to impound the dwelling follows from the law's strong preference for warrants, which underlies the rule that a search with a warrant has a stronger claim to justification on later, judicial review than a search without one. The law can hardly raise incentives to obtain a warrant without giving the police a fair chance to take their probable cause to a magistrate and get one.

■ JUSTICE STEVENS, dissenting.

The Illinois General Assembly has decided that the possession of less than 2.5 grams of marijuana is a class C misdemeanor. In so classifying the offense, the legislature made a concerted policy judgment that the possession of small amounts of marijuana for personal use does not constitute a particularly significant public policy concern. While it is true that this offense—like feeding livestock on a public highway or offering a movie for rent without clearly displaying its rating—may warrant a jail sentence of up to 30 days, the detection and prosecution of possessors of small quantities of this substance is by no means a law enforcement priority in the State of Illinois.

Because the governmental interest implicated by the particular criminal prohibition at issue in this case is so slight, this is a poor vehicle for probing the boundaries of the government's power to limit an individual's possessory interest in his or her home pending the arrival of a search warrant. Given my preference, I would, therefore, dismiss the writ of certiorari as improvidently granted.

Compelled by the vote of my colleagues to reach the merits, I would affirm. As the majority explains, the essential inquiry in this case involves a balancing of the "privacy-related and law enforcement-related concerns to determine if the intrusion was reasonable." Under the specific facts of this case, I believe the majority gets the balance wrong. Each of the Illinois jurists who participated in the decision of this case placed a higher value on the sanctity of the ordinary citizen's home than on the prosecution of this petty offense. They correctly viewed that interest—whether the home be a humble cottage, a secondhand trailer, or a stately mansion—as one meriting the most serious constitutional protection. Following their analysis and the reasoning in our decision in *Welsh v. Wisconsin*, 466 U.S. 740, 104 S.Ct. 2091, 80 L.Ed.2d 732 (1984) (holding that some offenses may be so minor as to make it unreasonable for police to undertake searches that would be constitutionally permissible if graver offenses were suspected), I would affirm.

Brigham City, Utah v. Stuart

Supreme Court of the United States, 2006.
547 U.S. 398, 126 S.Ct. 1943, 164 L.Ed.2d 650.

■ CHIEF JUSTICE ROBERTS delivered the opinion of the Court.

In this case we consider whether police may enter a home without a warrant when they have an objectively reasonable basis for believing that an occupant is seriously injured or imminently threatened with such injury. We conclude that they may.

I

This case arises out of a melee that occurred in a Brigham City, Utah, home in the early morning hours of July 23, 2000. At about 3 a.m., four police officers responded to a call regarding a loud party at a residence. Upon arriving at the house, they heard shouting from inside, and proceeded down the driveway to investigate. There, they observed two juveniles drinking beer in the backyard. They entered the backyard, and saw—through a screen door and windows—an altercation taking place in the kitchen of the home. According to the testimony of one of the officers, four adults were attempting, with some difficulty, to restrain a juvenile. The juvenile eventually "broke free, swung a fist and struck one of the adults in the face." The officer testified that he observed the victim of the blow spitting blood into a nearby sink. The other adults continued to try to restrain the juvenile, pressing him up against a refrigerator with such force that the refrigerator began moving across the floor. At this point, an officer opened the screen door and announced the officers' presence. Amid the tumult, nobody noticed. The officer entered the kitchen and again cried out, and as the occupants slowly became aware that the police were on the scene, the altercation ceased.

The officers subsequently arrested respondents and charged them with contributing to the delinquency of a minor, disorderly conduct, and intoxication. In the trial court, respondents filed a motion to suppress all evidence obtained after the officers entered the home, arguing that the warrantless entry violated the Fourth Amendment. The court granted the motion, and the Utah Court of Appeals affirmed.

Before the Supreme Court of Utah, Brigham City argued that although the officers lacked a warrant, their entry was nevertheless reasonable on either of two grounds. The court rejected both contentions and, over two dissenters, affirmed. First, the court held that the injury caused by the juvenile's punch was insufficient to trigger the so-called "emergency aid doctrine" because it did not give rise to an "objectively reasonable belief that an unconscious, semi-conscious, or missing person feared injured or dead [was] in the home." Furthermore, the court suggested that the doctrine was inapplicable because the officers had not sought to assist the injured adult, but instead had acted "exclusively in their law enforcement capacity."

The court also held that the entry did not fall within the exigent circumstances exception to the warrant requirement. This exception applies, the court explained, where police have probable cause and where "a reasonable person [would] believe that the entry was necessary to prevent physical harm to the officers or other persons." Under this standard, the court stated, the potential harm need not be as serious as that required to invoke the emergency aid exception. Although it found the case "a close and difficult call," the court nevertheless concluded that the officers' entry was not justified by exigent circumstances.

We granted certiorari in light of differences among state courts and the Courts of Appeals concerning the appropriate Fourth Amendment standard governing warrantless entry by law enforcement in an emergency situation.

II

It is a " 'basic principle of Fourth Amendment law that searches and seizures inside a home without a warrant are presumptively unreasonable.' " "[W]arrants are generally required to search a person's home or his person unless 'the exigencies of the situation' make the needs of law enforcement so compelling that the warrantless search is objectively reasonable under the Fourth Amendment." Mincey v. Arizona, 437 U.S. 385, 393–394, 98 S.Ct. 2408, 57 L.Ed.2d 290 (1978).

One exigency obviating the requirement of a warrant is the need to assist persons who are seriously injured or threatened with such injury. " 'The need to protect or preserve life or avoid serious injury is justification for what would be otherwise illegal absent an exigency or emergency.' " Id., at 392, 98 S.Ct. 2408. Accordingly, law enforcement officers may enter a home without a warrant to render emergency assistance to an injured occupant or to protect an occupant from imminent injury.

Respondents do not take issue with these principles, but instead advance two reasons why the officers' entry here was unreasonable. First, they argue that the officers were more interested in making arrests than quelling violence. They urge us to consider, in assessing the reasonableness of the entry, whether the officers were "indeed motivated primarily by a desire to save lives and property."

Our cases have repeatedly rejected this approach. An action is "reasonable" under the Fourth Amendment, regardless of the individual officer's state of mind, "as long as the circumstances, viewed *objectively*, justify [the] action." Scott v. United States, 436 U.S. 128, 138, 98 S.Ct. 1717, 56 L.Ed.2d 168 (1978) (emphasis added). The officer's subjective motivation is irrelevant. It therefore does not matter here—even if their subjective motives could be so neatly unraveled—whether the officers entered the kitchen to arrest respondents and gather evidence against them or to assist the injured and prevent further violence.

As respondents note, we have held in the context of programmatic searches conducted without individualized suspicion—such as checkpoints to combat drunk driving or drug trafficking—that "an inquiry into programmatic purpose" is sometimes appropriate. Indianapolis v. Edmond, 531 U.S. 32, 46, 121 S.Ct. 447, 148 L.Ed.2d 333 (2000) (emphasis added);

see also Florida v. Wells, 495 U.S. 1, 4, 110 S.Ct. 1632, 109 L.Ed.2d 1 (1990) (an inventory search must be regulated by "standardized criteria" or "established routine" so as not to "be a ruse for a general rummaging in order to discover incriminating evidence"). But this inquiry is directed at ensuring that the purpose behind the program is not "ultimately indistinguishable from the general interest in crime control." It has nothing to do with discerning what is in the mind of the individual officer conducting the search.

Respondents further contend that their conduct was not serious enough to justify the officers' intrusion into the home. They rely on Welsh v. Wisconsin, 466 U.S. 740, 753, 104 S.Ct. 2091, 80 L.Ed.2d 732 (1984), in which we held that "an important factor to be considered when determining whether any exigency exists is the gravity of the underlying offense for which the arrest is being made." This contention, too, is misplaced. *Welsh* involved a warrantless entry by officers to arrest a suspect for driving while intoxicated. There, the "only potential emergency" confronting the officers was the need to preserve evidence (i.e., the suspect's blood-alcohol level)—an exigency that we held insufficient under the circumstances to justify entry into the suspect's home. Here, the officers were confronted with ongoing violence occurring within the home. *Welsh* did not address such a situation.

We think the officers' entry here was plainly reasonable under the circumstances. The officers were responding, at 3 o'clock in the morning, to complaints about a loud party. As they approached the house, they could hear from within "an altercation occurring, some kind of a fight." "It was loud and it was tumultuous." The officers heard "thumping and crashing" and people yelling "stop, stop" and "get off me." As the trial court found, "it was obvious that . . . knocking on the front door" would have been futile. The noise seemed to be coming from the back of the house; after looking in the front window and seeing nothing, the officers proceeded around back to investigate further. They found two juveniles drinking beer in the backyard. From there, they could see that a fracas was taking place inside the kitchen. A juvenile, fists clenched, was being held back by several adults. As the officers watch, he breaks free and strikes one of the adults in the face, sending the adult to the sink spitting blood.

In these circumstances, the officers had an objectively reasonable basis for believing both that the injured adult might need help and that the violence in the kitchen was just beginning. Nothing in the Fourth Amendment required them to wait until another blow rendered someone "unconscious" or "semi-conscious" or worse before entering. The role of a peace officer includes preventing violence and restoring order, not simply rendering first aid to casualties; an officer is not like a boxing (or hockey) referee, poised to stop a bout only if it becomes too one-sided.

The manner of the officers' entry was also reasonable. After witnessing the punch, one of the officers opened the screen door and "yelled in police."

When nobody heard him, he stepped into the kitchen and announced himself again. Only then did the tumult subside. The officer's announcement of his presence was at least equivalent to a knock on the screen door. Indeed, it was probably the only option that had even a chance of rising above the din. Under these circumstances, there was no violation of the Fourth Amendment's knock-and-announce rule. Furthermore, once the announcement was made, the officers were free to enter; it would serve no purpose to require them to stand dumbly at the door awaiting a response while those within brawled on, oblivious to their presence.

Accordingly, we reverse the judgment of the Supreme Court of Utah, and remand the case for further proceedings not inconsistent with this opinion.

It is so ordered.

B. ADMINISTRATIVE INSPECTIONS AND SEARCHES OF LICENSED PREMISES

Page 279. Add the following to Note 2 after New York v. Burger:

The Court returned to searches of probationers in United States v. Knights, 534 U.S. 112, 122 S.Ct. 587, 151 L.Ed.2d 497 (2001). A California court placed Knights on probation for a drug offense. One term of the probation was that he submit his person, property, residence and vehicle to search by any probation officer or any law enforcement officer at any time. Knights signed an order stating that he understood and agreed to abide by the terms of probation. Several days later, a sheriff's department detective developed facts suggesting Knights was involved in vandalism of a power company's equipment. The detective was aware of the probation condition. He conducted a search of Knight's apartment and found a number of items suggesting Knight was involved in the vandalism. Charged with several federal crimes, Knights successfully sought suppression of the items found in his house. The lower federal courts—relying on *Griffin*—held that the probation condition authorized only probationary searches and did not make reasonable an investigatory search of the sort made in this case. The Government argued that Knights' acceptance of the probationary condition constituted effective consent for the search.

A unanimous Supreme Court reversed and held the search reasonable. Fourth Amendment reasonableness of the search, it explained, depends on the totality of the circumstances, and the probation search condition was one "salient circumstance" but no more. It continued:

> The touchstone of the Fourth Amendment is reasonableness, and the reasonableness of a search is determined "by assessing, on the one hand, the degree to which it intrudes upon an individual's privacy and, on the other, the degree to which it is needed for the promotion of legitimate governmental interests." Wyoming v. Houghton, 526 U.S. 295, 300, 119 S.Ct. 1297, 143 L.Ed.2d 408 (1999). Knights's status as a probationer subject to a search condition informs both sides of that balance. * * * Inherent in the very nature

of probation is that probationers "do not enjoy 'the absolute liberty to which every citizen is entitled.' " Just as other punishments for criminal convictions curtail an offender's freedoms, a court granting probation may impose reasonable conditions that deprive the offender of some freedoms enjoyed by law-abiding citizens.

The judge who sentenced Knights to probation determined that it was necessary to condition the probation on Knights's acceptance of the search provision. It was reasonable to conclude that the search condition would further the two primary goals of probation—rehabilitation and protecting society from future criminal violations. The probation order clearly expressed the search condition and Knights was unambiguously informed of it. The probation condition thus significantly diminished Knights's reasonable expectation of privacy.

In assessing the governmental interest side of the balance, it must be remembered that "the very assumption of the institution of probation" is that the probationer "is more likely than the ordinary citizen to violate the law." * * * And probationers have even more of an incentive to conceal their criminal activities and quickly dispose of incriminating evidence than the ordinary criminal because probationers are aware that they may be subject to supervision and face revocation of probation, and possible incarceration, in proceedings in which the trial rights of a jury and proof beyond a reasonable doubt, among other things, do not apply.

The State has a dual concern with a probationer. On the one hand is the hope that he will successfully complete probation and be integrated back into the community. On the other is the concern, quite justified, that he will be more likely to engage in criminal conduct than an ordinary member of the community. The view of the Court of Appeals in this case would require the State to shut its eyes to the latter concern and concentrate only on the former. But we hold that the Fourth Amendment does not put the State to such a choice. Its interest in apprehending violators of the criminal law, thereby protecting potential victims of criminal enterprise, may therefore justifiably focus on probationers in a way that it does not on the ordinary citizen.

We hold that the balance of these considerations requires no more than reasonable suspicion to conduct a search of this probationer's house. The degree of individualized suspicion required of a search is a determination of when there is a sufficiently high probability that criminal conduct is occurring to make the intrusion on the individual's privacy interest reasonable. Although the Fourth Amendment ordinarily requires the degree of probability embodied in the term "probable cause," a lesser degree satisfies the Constitution when the balance of governmental and private interests makes such a standard reasonable. Those interests warrant a lesser than probable-cause standard here. When an officer has reasonable suspicion that a probationer subject to a search condition is engaged in criminal activity, there is enough likelihood that criminal conduct is occurring that an intrusion on the probationer's significantly diminished privacy interests is reasonable.

The same circumstances that lead us to conclude that reasonable suspicion is constitutionally sufficient also render a warrant requirement unnecessary. See Illinois v. McArthur, 531 U.S. 326, 330, 121 S.Ct. 946, 148 L.Ed.2d 838

(2001) (noting that general or individual circumstances, including "diminished expectations of privacy," may justify an exception to the warrant requirement).

534 U.S. at 118–22, 122 S.Ct. at 591–93, 151 L.Ed.2d at 505–07. The Court added:

> We do not decide whether the probation condition so diminished, or completely eliminated, Knights's reasonable expectation of privacy (or constituted consent) that a search by a law enforcement officer without any individualized suspicion would have satisfied the reasonableness requirement of the Fourth Amendment. The terms of the probation condition permit such a search, but we need not address the constitutionality of a suspicionless search because the search in this case was supported by reasonable suspicion.

534 U.S. at 120 n. 6, 122 S.Ct. at 592 n. 6, 151 L.Ed.2d at 505 n. 6. The opinion also observed:

> Because our holding rests on ordinary Fourth Amendment analysis that considers all the circumstances of a search, there is no basis for examining official purpose. With the limited exception of some special needs and administrative search cases, "we have been unwilling to entertain Fourth Amendment challenges based on the actual motivations of individual officers." Whren v. United States, 517 U.S. 806, 813, 116 S.Ct. 1769, 135 L.Ed.2d 89 (1996).

534 U.S. at 122, 122 S.Ct. at 593, 151 L.Ed.2d at 507.

Justice Souter joined the Court's analysis but wrote separately to indicate "I would * * * reserve the question whether *Whren's* holding, that '[s]ubjective intentions play no role in ordinary, probable-cause Fourth Amendment analysis,' should extend to searches based only upon reasonable suspicion." 534 U.S. at 122–23, 122 S.Ct. at 593, 151 L.Ed.2d at 507 (Souter, J., concurring).

In Samson v. California, 547 U.S. 843, 126 S.Ct. 2193, 165 L.Ed.2d 250 (2006),—in the context of searches of parolees—the Court granted review "to answer a variation of the question this Court left open in [*Knights*]— whether a condition of release can so diminish or eliminate a released prisoner's reasonable expectation of privacy that a suspicionless search by a law enforcement officer would not offend the Fourth Amendment."

Samson had agreed—as required by statute—to be subject to search or seizure at any time as a condition of his parole. The Court did not reach whether the search could be held reasonable based on his "consent" alone or based on case law exempting certain "special needs" searches from Fourth Amendment requirements. Applying a totality of the circumstances analysis, the *Samson* majority held the search reasonable:

> [P]arolees are on the "continuum" of state-imposed punishments. On this continuum, parolees have fewer expectations of privacy than probationers, because parole is more akin to imprisonment than probation is to imprisonment.

* * *

Additionally * * * the parole search condition under California law—requiring inmates who opt for parole to submit to suspicionless searches by a parole officer or other peace officer "at any time,"—was "clearly expressed" to petitioner. He signed an order submitting to the condition and thus was "unambiguously" aware of it. In *Knights,* we found that acceptance of a clear and unambiguous search condition "significantly diminished Knights' reasonable expectation of privacy." Examining the totality of the circumstances pertaining to petitioner's status as a parolee, "an established variation on imprisonment," including the plain terms of the parole search condition, we conclude that petitioner did not have an expectation of privacy that society would recognize as legitimate.

The State's interests, by contrast, are substantial. * * * [A] State has an "overwhelming interest" in supervising parolees because "parolees . . . are more likely to commit future criminal offenses." Similarly, * * * a State's interests in reducing recidivism and thereby promoting reintegration and positive citizenship among probationers and parolees warrant privacy intrusions that would not otherwise be tolerated under the Fourth Amendment.

547 U.S. at 849–53, 126 S.Ct. at 2198–2200.

Page 279.   Add the following new notes after New York v. Burger:

3. **Cell Phones of Public Employees.** In City of Ontario, California v. Quon, ___ U.S. ___, 130 S.Ct. 2619, 177 L.Ed.2d 216 (2010), the city of Ontario issued a pager capable of sending and receiving text messages to Quon, a police officer and member of the Special Weapons and Tactics (SWAT) Team. A city employee investigating use of pages exceeding allotments obtained and reviewed a transcript of messages sent to and from Quon's pager during his work hours. Quon unsuccessfully sued the city, claiming violation of his Fourth Amendment rights. The Supreme Court upheld the district court's judgment for the city. It observed that in O'Connor v. Ortega, noted in note 2 above, the members of the Court disagreed "on the proper analytical framework for Fourth Amendment claims against government employers." *Quon* did not resolve that disagreement. Rather, it assumed Quon had a reasonable expectation of privacy in the messages but concluded the search of those messages—on the facts of the case—was reasonable under a special needs analysis. Justifying its cautious approach, the majority explained:

The Court must proceed with care when considering the whole concept of privacy expectations in communications made on electronic equipment owned by a government employer. The judiciary risks error by elaborating too fully on the Fourth Amendment implications of emerging technology before its role in society has become clear. * * * Prudence counsels caution before the facts in the instant case are used to establish far-reaching premises that define the existence, and extent, of privacy expectations enjoyed by employees when using employer-provided communication devices.

Rapid changes in the dynamics of communication and information transmission are evident not just in the technology itself but in what society accepts as proper behavior.

___ U.S. at ___, 130 S.Ct. at 2629.

4. **Drug Tests With Law Enforcement Purposes.** Drug test cases have similarly involved consideration of the appropriate effect to give to non-prosecution objectives of official activity infringing interests protected by the Fourth Amendment.

In Ferguson v. City of Charleston, 532 U.S. 67, 121 S.Ct. 1281, 149 L.Ed.2d 205 (2001), the Supreme Court noted:

> [In] four previous cases * * * we have considered whether comparable drug tests "fit within the closely guarded category of constitutionally permissible suspicionless searches." Chandler v. Miller, 520 U.S. 305, 309, 117 S.Ct. 1295, 137 L.Ed.2d 513 (1997). In three of those cases, we sustained drug tests for railway employees involved in train accidents, Skinner v. Railway Labor Executives' Ass'n, 489 U.S. 602, 109 S.Ct. 1402, 103 L.Ed.2d 639 (1989), for United States Customs Service employees seeking promotion to certain sensitive positions, National Treasury Employees v. Von Raab, 489 U.S. 656, 109 S.Ct. 1384, 103 L.Ed.2d 685 (1989), and for high school students participating in interscholastic sports, Vernonia School Dist. 47J v. Acton, 515 U.S. 646, 115 S.Ct. 2386, 132 L.Ed.2d 564 (1995). In the fourth case, we struck down such testing for candidates for designated state offices as unreasonable. Chandler v. Miller, 520 U.S. 305, 117 S.Ct. 1295, 137 L.Ed.2d 513 (1997).
>
> In each of those cases, we employed a balancing test that weighed the intrusion on the individual's interest in privacy against the "special needs" that supported the program. * * *

532 U.S. at 77–78, 121 S.Ct. at 1288, 149 L.Ed.2d at 216. Explaining the terminology, the Court continued:

> The term "special needs" first appeared in Justice Blackmun's opinion concurring in the judgment in New Jersey v. T.L.O., 469 U.S. 325, 351, 105 S.Ct. 733, 83 L.Ed.2d 720 (1985). In his concurrence, Justice Blackmun agreed with the Court that there are limited exceptions to the probable-cause requirement, in which reasonableness is determined by "a careful balancing of governmental and private interests," but concluded that such a test should only be applied "in those exceptional circumstances in which special needs, beyond the normal need for law enforcement, make the warrant and probable-cause requirement impracticable. . . ." This Court subsequently adopted the "special needs" terminology * * *, concluding that, in limited circumstances, a search unsupported by either warrant or probable cause can be constitutional when "special needs" other than the normal need for law enforcement provide sufficient justification.

532 U.S. at 74 n. 7, 121 S.Ct. at 1286 n. 7, 149 L.Ed.2d at 214 n. 7.

In *Ferguson*, the Court applied this special needs balancing test to a Charleston, North Carolina program in which pregnant women seeking medical care were—if they were suspected of cocaine use—given urine tests for cocaine. If they tested positive, the threat of criminal prosecution was used to compel them to accept treatment. Some who failed to cooperate were in fact prosecuted. Those who conducted the tests were staff members of a state hospital, and "the urine tests * * * were indisputably searches within the meaning of the Fourth Amendment."

Assuming that effective consent to the tests was not shown, the court held that the warrantless and suspicionless searches could not be upheld on the basis of the special needs analysis:

[T]he invasion of privacy in this case is far more substantial than in those cases. In the previous four cases, there was no misunderstanding about the purpose of the test or the potential use of the test results, and there were protections against the dissemination of the results to third parties. The use of an adverse test result to disqualify one from eligibility for a particular benefit, such as a promotion or an opportunity to participate in an extracurricular activity, involves a less serious intrusion on privacy than the unauthorized dissemination of such results to third parties. The reasonable expectation of privacy enjoyed by the typical patient undergoing diagnostic tests in a hospital is that the results of those tests will not be shared with nonmedical personnel without her consent. * * *

The critical difference between those four drug-testing cases and this one, however, lies in the nature of the "special need" asserted as justification for the warrantless searches. In each of those earlier cases, the "special need" that was advanced as a justification for the absence of a warrant or individualized suspicion was one divorced from the State's general interest in law enforcement. * * * In this case, however, the central and indispensable feature of the policy from its inception was the use of law enforcement to coerce the patients into substance abuse treatment. This fact distinguishes this case from circumstances in which physicians or psychologists, in the course of ordinary medical procedures aimed at helping the patient herself, come across information that under rules of law or ethics is subject to reporting requirements, which no one has challenged here.

532 U.S. at 78–79, 121 S.Ct. at 1288–90, 149 L.Ed.2d at 216–18. The Court rejected the argument that the programmatic purpose of the testing was the protection of the health of mothers and children and therefore sufficiently special to make the program reasonable. A purpose or interest indistinguishable from the general interest in crime control is not special. "[W]e examine all the available evidence," it explained, "to determine relevant primary purpose." Further:

[T]hroughout the development and application of the policy, the Charleston prosecutors and police were extensively involved in the day-to-day administration of the policy. * * *

While the ultimate goal of the program may well have been to get the women in question into substance abuse treatment and off of drugs, the immediate objective of the searches was to generate evidence for law enforcement purposes in order to reach that goal. The threat of law enforcement may ultimately have been intended as a means to an end, but the direct and primary purpose of [the] policy was to ensure the use of those means. In our opinion, this distinction is critical. Because law enforcement involvement always serves some broader social purpose or objective, under respondents' view, virtually any nonconsensual suspicionless search could be immunized under the special needs doctrine by defining the search solely in terms of its ultimate, rather than immediate, purpose. Such an approach is inconsistent with the Fourth Amendment. Given the primary purpose of the Charleston program, which was to use the threat of arrest and prosecution in order to force women into treatment, and given the extensive involvement of law enforcement officials at every stage of the policy, this case simply does not fit within the closely guarded category of "special needs."

532 U.S. at 82–84, 121 S.Ct. at 1290–92, 149 L.Ed.2d at 219–20.

Remanding the case for further proceedings consistent with its opinion, the Court clearly contemplated that the Court of Appeals would address whether the program assured "informed consent" that would render the tests reasonable.

Justice Kennedy concurred in the result, adopting a slightly different analysis. Justice Scalia, joined by the Chief Justice and Justice Thomas, dissented. The majority, he contended, had failed to identify the major contention:

> The first step in Fourth Amendment analysis is to identify the search or seizure at issue. What petitioners, the Court, and to a lesser extent the concurrence really object to is not the urine testing, but the hospital's reporting of positive drug-test results to police. But the latter is obviously not a search. At most it may be a "derivative use of the product of a past unlawful search," which, of course, "work[s] no new Fourth Amendment wrong" and "presents a question, not of rights, but of remedies." United States v. Calandra, 414 U.S. 338, 354, 94 S.Ct. 613, 38 L.Ed.2d 561 (1974). There is only one act that could conceivably be regarded as a search of petitioners in the present case: the taking of the urine sample. I suppose the testing of that urine for traces of unlawful drugs could be considered a search of sorts, but the Fourth Amendment protects only against searches of citizens' "persons, houses, papers, and effects"; and it is entirely unrealistic to regard urine as one of the "effects" (i.e., part of the property) of the person who has passed and abandoned it. Some would argue, I suppose, that testing of the urine is prohibited by some generalized privacy right "emanating" from the "penumbras" of the Constitution (a question that is not before us); but it is not even arguable that the testing of urine that has been lawfully obtained is a Fourth Amendment search.
> * * *

532 U.S. at 92–93, 121 S.Ct. at 1296, 149 L.Ed.2d at 225–26 (Scalia, J., dissenting). The mothers, he argued, were clearly shown to have given effective consent to the search at issue. Alternatively, he continued, the majority's refusal to apply the special needs doctrine was improper:

> The conclusion of the Court that the special-needs doctrine is inapplicable rests upon its contention that respondents "undert[ook] to obtain [drug] evidence from their patients" not for any medical purpose, but *"for the specific purpose of incriminating those patients."* (emphasis in original). In other words, the purported medical rationale was merely a pretext; there was no special need. This contention contradicts the District Court's finding of fact that the goal of the testing policy "was not to arrest patients but to facilitate their treatment and protect both the mother and unborn child." This finding is binding upon us unless clearly erroneous.

532 U.S. at 98, 121 S.Ct. at 1299–3000, 149 L.Ed.2d at 229.

5. **Drug Tests Without Law Enforcement Purposes.** Drug testing programs without law enforcement objectives are subject to even more relaxed Fourth Amendment standards. Mandatory drug testing of all middle and high school students participating in extracurricular activities was upheld in Board of Education v. Earls, 536 U.S. 822, 122 S.Ct. 2559, 153 L.Ed.2d 735 (2002). The Court stressed that the program "is not in any way related to the conduct of criminal investigations," and that the results of tests are not turned over to any law enforcement agency. These characteristics of the testing program, in the Court's view, assisting in reducing the invasion of the students' privacy to insignificance.

C.   CONSENT SEARCHES

1.   THE EFFECTIVENESS OF CONSENT

Page 291.   Add the following new notes to the Notes after Schneckloth v. Bustamonte:

4. **Consent Given During Bus Drug Interdiction Efforts.** In United States v. Drayton, 536 U.S. 194, 122 S.Ct. 2105, 153 L.Ed.2d 242 (2002), the Supreme Court addressed the voluntariness of consent given without warnings of a right to refuse and during drug interdiction efforts aboard a bus. *Drayton* is discussed earlier in the material supplementing page 179 of the text.

5. **Consent Given As Condition of Probation.** In United States v. Knights, 534 U.S. 112, 122 S.Ct. 587, 151 L.Ed.2d 497 (2001), the Court did not reach whether consent required as a condition of probation would be voluntary and thus itself support a search of a probationer. *Knights* is discussed in the material supplementing page 279 of the text.

2.   AUTHORITY TO CONSENT: "THIRD PARTY" CONSENTS

Page 299.   Insert the following Note after Illinois v. Rodriguez:

NOTE ON PRESENT AND OBJECTING OCCUPANTS

If the target of law enforcement interest is present and actively objects to a search, is third party consent nevertheless fully effective? The issue was addressed in Georgia v. Randolph, 547 U.S. 103, 126 S.Ct. 1515, 164 L.Ed.2d 208 (2006).

Scott Randolph and his wife of Americus, Georgia were having marital problems. They separated in late May 2001, and Mrs. Randolph took a great deal of her clothing and went with their son to her parents' home in Canada. Mr. Randolph remained at the residence in Americus. About July 4, 2001, Mrs. Randolph and the child returned to their house in Americus.

On July 6, 2001, Mrs. Randolph called police to report a domestic disturbance. Officers responded at around 9:00 a.m. When the officers arrived, Mrs. Randolph appeared very upset and complained that her husband had taken their child away from the house. She also accused Mr. Randolph of using large amounts of cocaine, thereby causing martial discord and financial problems for the family. Shortly thereafter, Mr. Randolph returned to the house without the child. He explained that he had taken the child to a neighbor's house because he was concerned that his wife was going to leave the country with the child again. He also accused his wife of being highly inebriated and an alcoholic. Sergeant Brett Murray accompanied Mrs. Randolph to the neighbor's house to retrieve the child.

After they returned to the Randolph residence, Murray confronted Mr. Randolph about his wife's allegations concerning his cocaine use and asked for consent to search the residence. Mr. Randolph responded with an unequivocal "no." Murray then turned to Mrs. Randolph and asked for her consent. Readily agreeing to the search, Mrs. Randolph took Murray to an upstairs bedroom. Peering in the doorway, the officer observed a "piece of cut straw" on a dresser in the room. Upon closer examination, the officer observed some white residue on the straw, which he believed had been used for ingesting cocaine.

Murray left the residence to retrieve an evidence bag from his vehicle. When he returned, Mrs. Randolph, after a discussion with her husband, announced she was withdrawing her consent to the search. The police officer called the district attorney's office. He then collected the straw and escorted the Randolphs to the police station.

Officers subsequently obtained a warrant to search the house. During the search pursuant to the warrant, a number of drug-related items were seized. An indictment was returned charging Mr. Randolph with possession of cocaine. He moved to suppress evidence of the drugs, arguing that the search of his residence over his express objection violated his Fourth Amendment rights. The trial court denied the motion, but the Georgia appellate courts reversed.

The Supreme Court affirmed by a 5-to-3 vote, holding that the consent was not effective. Justice Souter's opinion for the Court explained:

> *Matlock* * * * not only holds that a solitary co-inhabitant may sometimes consent to a search of shared premises, but stands for the proposition that the reasonableness of such a search is in significant part a function of commonly held understanding about the authority that co-inhabitants may exercise in ways that affect each other's interests.

* * *

> [I]t is fair to say that a caller standing at the door of shared premises would have no confidence that one occupant's invitation was a sufficiently good reason to enter when a fellow tenant stood there saying, "stay out." Without some very good reason, no sensible person would go inside under those conditions. Fear for the safety of the occupant issuing the invitation, or of someone else inside, would be thought to justify entry, but the justification then would be the personal risk, the threats to life or limb, not the disputed invitation.

> The visitor's reticence without some such good reason would show not timidity but a realization that when people living together disagree over the use of their common quarters, a resolution must come through voluntary accommodation, not by appeals to authority. Unless the people living together fall within some recognized hierarchy, like a household of parent and child or barracks housing military personnel of different grades, there is no societal understanding of superior and inferior, a fact reflected in a standard formulation of domestic property law, that "[e]ach cotenant . . . has the right to use and enjoy the entire property as if he or she were the sole owner, limited only by the same right in the other cotenants." 7 R. Powell, Powell on Real Property § 50.03[1], p. 50–14 (M. Wolf gen. ed.2005). The want of any recognized superior authority among disagreeing tenants is also reflected in the law's response when the disagreements cannot be resolved. The law does not ask who has the better side of the conflict; it simply provides a right to any co-tenant, even the most unreasonable, to obtain a decree partitioning the property (when the relationship is one of co-ownership) and terminating the relationship. And while a decree of partition is not the answer to disagreement among rental tenants,

this situation resembles co-ownership in lacking the benefit of any understanding that one or the other rental co-tenant has a superior claim to control the use of the quarters they occupy together. In sum, there is no common understanding that one co-tenant generally has a right or authority to prevail over the express wishes of another, whether the issue is the color of the curtains or invitations to outsiders.

* * *

Since the co-tenant wishing to open the door to a third party has no recognized authority in law or social practice to prevail over a present and objecting co-tenant, his disputed invitation, without more, gives a police officer no better claim to reasonableness in entering than the officer would have in the absence of any consent at all.

547 U.S. at 111–14, 126 S.Ct. at 1521–23. It continued:

[W]e have to admit that we are drawing a fine line; if a potential defendant with self-interest in objecting is in fact at the door and objects, the co-tenant's permission does not suffice for a reasonable search, whereas the potential objector, nearby but not invited to take part in the threshold colloquy, loses out.

This is the line we draw, and we think the formalism is justified. So long as there is no evidence that the police have removed the potentially objecting tenant from the entrance for the sake of avoiding a possible objection, there is practical value in the simple clarity of complementary rules, one recognizing the co-tenant's permission when there is no fellow occupant on hand, the other according dispositive weight to the fellow occupant's contrary indication when he expresses it. * * * [W]e think it would needlessly limit the capacity of the police to respond to ostensibly legitimate opportunities in the field if we were to hold that reasonableness required the police to take affirmative steps to find a potentially objecting co-tenant before acting on the permission they had already received. There is no ready reason to believe that efforts to invite a refusal would make a difference in many cases, whereas every co-tenant consent case would turn into a test about the adequacy of the police's efforts to consult with a potential objector.

547 U.S. at 121–22, 126 S.Ct. at 1527–28.

In some situations, the Court stressed, searches may be permissible without consent:

The co-tenant acting on his own initiative may be able to deliver evidence to the police, and can tell the police what he knows, for use before a magistrate in getting a warrant.

Sometimes, of course, the very exchange of information like this in front of the objecting inhabitant may render consent irrelevant by creating an exigency that justifies immediate action on the police's part; if the objecting tenant cannot be incapacitated from destroying easily disposable evidence during the time required to get a warrant.

547 U.S. at 116, 126 S.Ct. at 1524 (incorporating footnote into text).

Responding to a dissent, the majority added:

[T]his case has no bearing on the capacity of the police to protect domestic victims. The dissent's argument rests on the failure to distinguish two different issues: when the police may enter without committing a trespass, and when the police may enter to search for evidence. No question has been raised, or reasonably could be, about the authority of the police to enter a dwelling to protect a resident from domestic violence; so long as they have good reason to believe such a threat exists, it would be silly to suggest that the police would commit a tort by entering, say, to give a complaining tenant the opportunity to collect belongings and get out safely, or to determine whether violence (or threat of violence) has just occurred or is about to (or soon will) occur, however much a spouse or other co-tenant objected. (And since the police would then be lawfully in the premises, there is no question that they could seize any evidence in plain view or take further action supported by any consequent probable cause.) Thus, the question whether the police might lawfully enter over objection in order to provide any protection that might be reasonable is easily answered yes. The undoubted right of the police to enter in order to protect a victim, however, has nothing to do with the question in this case, whether a search with the consent of one co-tenant is good against another, standing at the door and expressly refusing consent.

547 U.S. at 118–19, 126 S.Ct. at 1525–26.

E.   SEARCH AND SEIZURES AT OR NEAR INTERNATIONAL BORDERS

1.   ENFORCEMENT ACTIVITY AT THE INTERNATIONAL BORDER

Page 337.   Insert the following new note after Montoya de Hernandez:

NOTE: "ROUTINE" SEARCHES OF VEHICLES AT THE BORDER

"[T]he Government's authority to conduct suspicionless inspections at the border includes the authority to remove, disassemble, and reassemble a vehicle's fuel tank", the Supreme Court held in United States v. Flores–Montano, 541 U.S. 149, 124 S.Ct. 1582, 158 L.Ed.2d 311 (2004).

The court below had held that the removal and disassembly of the gas tank of Flores–Montano's automobile went beyond a "routine" border search and under *Montoya de Hernandez* required reasonable suspicion. The Supreme Court responded:

[T]he reasons that might support a requirement of some level of suspicion in the case of highly intrusive searches of the person—dignity and privacy interests of the person being searched—simply do not carry over to vehicles. Complex balancing tests to determine what is a "routine" search of a vehicle, as opposed to a more "intrusive" search of a person, have no place in border searches of vehicles.

541 U.S. at 152, 124 S.Ct. at 1585. Some searches of property might be "so destructive" as to be barred as part of routine suspicionless border searches, the

Court noted. But "this was not one of them." Search of an automobile's gas tank, "which should be solely a repository for fuel," is not more of an invasion of privacy than a search of the passenger compartment. Removal and disassembly of the tank involved no serious damage to or destruction of the property.

The Court also rejected Flores–Montano's argument that the actual and potential delay of property owners necessitated by such searches demanded at least reasonable suspicion. It noted that in the case before it the actual delay was about an hour and generally disassembly and reassembly of a vehicle gas tank takes one to two hours. Then:

> Respondent points to no cases indicating the Fourth Amendment shields entrants from inconvenience or delay at the international border.
>
> * * * We think it clear that delays of one to two hours at international borders are to be expected.

541 U.S. at 155 n. 3, 124 S.Ct. at 1587 n. 3.

2. BORDER–RELATED ENFORCEMENT ACTIVITY

Page 348.   Add the following to Note 2:

The Ninth Circuit, sitting en banc in United States v. Montero–Camargo, 208 F.3d 1122 (9th Cir.2000), cert. denied, 531 U.S. 889, 121 S.Ct. 211, 148 L.Ed.2d 148 (2000) (opinion on rehearing en banc), reconsidered *Brignoni–Ponce's* indication that Hispanic appearance is a "relevant factor" in determining whether an officer has reasonable suspicion that a person is an illegal alien.

A passing motorist told border patrol agents at the Highway 86 permanent stationary checkpoint in El Centro, California, that two cars heading north, with Mexicali license plates, had just made U-turns on the highway shortly before the checkpoint. Two agents, Johnson and Fisher, drove south to investigate. About a mile from the checkpoint they saw a blue Chevrolet Blazer and a red Nissan sedan, both with Mexicali plates, pull off the shoulder and re-enter the highway heading south. The place where the agents saw that the vehicles had stopped following the U-turn was a deserted area on the side of the southbound highway located opposite the large sign on the northbound side advising drivers that the checkpoint was open.

Johnson pulled behind the Blazer and noticed that both occupants appeared to be Hispanic. He stopped the vehicle and determined that the occupants were Mexican citizens with I–586 cards authorizing them to travel up to 25 miles inside the United States. As the stop was made 50 miles from the border, he took them both into custody. Fisher followed the Nissan. When he caught up with the vehicle, he could see that the second driver also appeared to be Hispanic. Fisher ultimately pulled the Nissan over after following it for approximately four miles. When Johnson arrived, Fisher and Johnson searched the Nissan's trunk and found two large bags of marijuana. A subsequent search of the Blazer back at the checkpoint turned up a loaded .32 caliber pistol in the glove compartment and an ammunition clip that fit the pistol in the passenger's purse.

The occupants were charged with federal crimes and unsuccessfully moved to suppress the items found in the vehicles. In denying the motion, the district judge relied in part upon the agents' observations that the occupants of the vehicles were of Hispanic appearance. Affirming, the majority of the panel of the Ninth Circuit also cited that factor.

The en banc court, however, concluded that this reliance on Hispanic appearance was impermissible:

In [*Brignoni–Ponce*], the Court held that "[e]ven if [Border Patrol officers] saw enough to think that the occupants were of Mexican descent, this factor alone would justify neither a reasonable belief that they were aliens, nor a reasonable belief that the car concealed other aliens who were illegally in the country." In a brief dictum consisting of only half a sentence, the Court went on to state, however, that ethnic appearance could be a factor in a reasonable suspicion calculus.

In arriving at the dictum suggesting that ethnic appearance could be relevant, the Court relied heavily on now-outdated demographic information. In a footnote, the Court noted that:

The 1970 census and the INS figures for alien registration in 1970 provide the following information about the Mexican–American population in the border States. There were 1,619,064 persons of Mexican origin in Texas, and 200,004 (or 12.4%) of them registered as aliens from Mexico. In New Mexico there were 119,049 persons of Mexican origin, and 10,171 (or 8.5%) registered as aliens. In Arizona there were 239,811 persons of Mexican origin, and 34,075 (or 14.2%) registered as aliens. In California there were 1,857,267 persons of Mexican origin, and 379,951 (or 20.4%) registered as aliens.

Brignoni–Ponce was handed down in 1975, some twenty-five years ago. Current demographic data demonstrate that the statistical premises on which its dictum relies are no longer applicable. The Hispanic population of this nation, and of the Southwest and Far West in particular, has grown enormously—at least five-fold in the four states referred to in the Supreme Court's decision. According to the U.S. Census Bureau, as of January 1, 2000, that population group stands at nearly 34 million. Furthermore, Hispanics are heavily concentrated in certain states in which minorities are becoming if not the majority, then at least the single largest group, either in the state as a whole or in a significant number of counties. According to the same data, California has the largest Hispanic population of any state—estimated at 10,112,986 in 1998, while Texas has approximately 6 million. As of this year, minorities—Hispanics, Asians, blacks and Native Americans—comprise half of California's residents; by 2021, Hispanics are expected to be the Golden State's largest group, making up about 40% of the state's population. Today, in Los Angeles County, which is by far the state's biggest population center, Hispanics already constitute the largest single group.

One area where Hispanics are heavily in the majority is El Centro, the site of the vehicle stop. * * * [T]he majority of the people who pass through the El Centro checkpoint are Hispanic. * * * The population of Imperial County, in which El Centro is located, is 73% Hispanic. In Imperial County, as of 1998, Hispanics accounted for 105,355 of the total population of 144,051. More broadly, according to census data, five Southern California counties are home to more than a fifth of the nation's Hispanic population. During the current decade, Hispanics will become the single largest population group in Southern

California, and by 2040, will make up 59% of Southern California's population. Accordingly, Hispanic appearance is of little or no use in determining which particular individuals among the vast Hispanic populace should be stopped by law enforcement officials on the lookout for illegal aliens. Reasonable suspicion requires particularized suspicion, and in an area in which a large number of people share a specific characteristic, that characteristic casts too wide a net to play any part in a particularized reasonable suspicion determination.

Moreover, the demographic changes we describe have been accompanied by significant changes in the law restricting the use of race as a criterion in government decision-making. The use of race and ethnicity for such purposes has been severely limited. See Adarand Constructors v. Pena, 515 U.S. 200, 115 S.Ct. 2097, 132 L.Ed.2d 158 (1995); City of Richmond v. J.A. Croson Co., 488 U.S. 469, 109 S.Ct. 706, 102 L.Ed.2d 854 (1989). Relying on the principle that " '[o]ur Constitution is color-blind, and neither knows nor tolerates classes among citizens,' " the Supreme Court has repeatedly held that reliance "on racial or ethnic criteria must necessarily receive a most searching examination to make sure that it does not conflict with constitutional guarantees." Wygant v. Jackson Bd. of Ed., 476 U.S. 267, 273, 106 S.Ct. 1842, 90 L.Ed.2d 260 (1986). In invalidating the use of racial classifications used to remedy past discrimination in *Croson*, the Court applied strict scrutiny, stating that its rigorousness would ensure that:

> the means chosen "fit" this compelling goal so closely that there is little or no possibility that the motive for the classification was illegitimate racial prejudice or stereotype. Classifications based on race carry a danger of stigmatic harm. Unless they are strictly reserved for remedial settings, they may in fact promote notions of racial inferiority and lead to a politics of racial hostility.

The danger of stigmatic harm of the type that the Court feared overbroad affirmative action programs would pose is far more pronounced in the context of police stops in which race or ethnic appearance is a factor. So, too, are the consequences of "notions of racial inferiority" and the "politics of racial hostility" that the Court pointed to. Stops based on race or ethnic appearance send the underlying message to all our citizens that those who are not white are judged by the color of their skin alone. Such stops also send a clear message that those who are not white enjoy a lesser degree of constitutional protection—that they are in effect assumed to be potential criminals first and individuals second. It would be an anomalous result to hold that race may be considered when it harms people, but not when it helps them.

We decide no broad constitutional questions here. Rather, we are confronted with the narrow question of how to square the Fourth Amendment's requirement of individualized reasonable suspicion with the fact that the majority of the people who pass through the checkpoint in question are Hispanic. In order to answer that question, we conclude that, at this point in our nation's history, and given the continuing changes in our ethnic and racial composition, Hispanic appearance is, in general, of such little probative value that it may not be considered as a relevant factor where particularized or individualized suspicion is required. Moreover, we conclude, for the reasons we have indicated, that it is also not an appropriate factor.

208 F.3d at 1132–35. The court added:

In *Brignoni–Ponce*, the Supreme Court also noted that "[t]he Government also points out that trained officers can recognize the characteristic appearance of persons who live in Mexico, relying on such factors as the mode of dress and haircut." Those factors, however, have been largely ignored by lower courts, in favor of a broader reading of Mexican or Hispanic appearance. In reaching our holding, we do not reject the use of factors such as dress or haircut when they are relevant. Nor do we preclude the use of racial or ethnic appearance as one factor relevant to reasonable suspicion or probable cause when a particular suspect has been identified as having a specific racial or ethnic appearance, be it Caucasian, African–American, Hispanic or other. We note, however, that a stop based solely on the fact that the racial or ethnic appearance of an individual matches the racial or ethnic description of a specific suspect would not be justified.

208 F.3d at 1134 n. 21.

Despite its conclusion that Hispanic appearance could not be considered, the court affirmed the district court's denial of the motion to suppress:

We conclude that [other] factors, although not overwhelming, are sufficient to constitute reasonable suspicion for the stop. In reaching that result, however, we firmly reject any reliance upon the Hispanic appearance or ethnicity of the defendants. * * *

In affirming the district court's ruling, we note that the agents' initial decision to investigate the tip and to pursue the two vehicles was made without any knowledge on their part of the defendants' ethnicity or Hispanic appearance. Agents Johnson and Fisher observed that appearance only when the officers subsequently caught up with the defendants' cars. Moreover, the agents had enough information to justify the stop before they became aware of the defendants' likely ethnicity. Under these circumstances, there is no need to remand the matter to the district court for reconsideration of its decision. * * *

208 F.3d at 1139–40.

CHAPTER 6

ELECTRONIC SURVEILLANCE

B. THE FEDERAL STATUTE AND ITS APPLICATION

Page 369. Insert the following Note after the Notes to the Editors' Introduction:

EDITORS' NOTE: THE 2001 FEDERAL ANTI–TERRORISM LEGISLATION

In 2001, Congress passed and the president signed a response to increased concern with terrorism. This was the "Uniting and Strengthening America by Providing Appropriate Tools Required to Intercept and Obstruct Terrorism (USA PATRIOT ACT) Act of 2001," Public Law 107–56.

One commentator noted what he regarded as two misunderstandings concerning the legislation: "that there was not adequate authority in existing law to investigate and prosecute international or domestic terrorism and that ordinary citizens were unaffected by the changes." After analyzing the legislation, he concluded:

> [N]o "broad new authority" to conduct government surveillance was created after the terrorist attacks. Instead, there was fine tuning of existing authorities, much of it regarded as necessary by law enforcement, intelligence agencies, most civil libertarians, and technologists. But, it should also be clear, that a lot of the fine tuning will have significant consequences for ordinary Americans. We cannot anticipate right now exactly what those consequences will be, until we learn how courts will interpret the changes and how the Department of Justice will use them when it conducts investigations in the future.

Robert Ellis Smith, The Impact of the Federal Anti–Terrorism Legislation Upon Government Surveillance and Ordinary Americans, 50 R.I.Bar J. 11, 32 (2002).

Some of the provisions of the 2001 legislation dealt with the Foreign Intelligence Surveillance Act of 1978, 50 U.S.C. § 1801, which is beyond the scope of these materials. Under this statute, certain federal judges are authorized to issue orders permitting electronic surveillance for foreign intelligence information. 50 U.S.C. § 1805.

Before the legislation, an application for such electronic surveillance had to include a certification of one of specified federal officials regarding several things, including that "the purpose of the surveillance is to obtain foreign intelligence information * * *." The USA PATRIOT Act changed this to require only a certification that "a significant purpose of the surveillance is to obtain foreign intelligence information * * *."

A few provisions of the Act apply to regular federal warrants and are addressed in the material supplementing Chapter 3.

CHAPTER 7

INTERROGATION AND CONFESSIONS

Page 380. Insert the following in the portion of the Editors' Introduction titled, *Basic Issues and Policy Considerations:*

Statements made to law enforcement officers often seem in retrospect to have been so unwise as to suggest that they must have been the product of improper inducement. But a New York Times article, recounting in detail the color of many of these statements, offered the following as to why so many arrested persons make such admissions:

> "Everybody talks," said Daniel J. Castleman, chief of investigations for the Manhattan district attorney. "Almost nobody doesn't talk. And the reason for that is that people think they can either talk their way out of it or mitigate the crime. It's human nature."

Anemona Hartocollis, Remain Silent? Some in Custody Spell It All Out, New York Times, Jan. 5, 2007.

Page 382. Insert the following in the Editors' Introduction: Confessions and Confession Law in the Context of Modern Law Enforcement, after the material on *Reliability of Confessions:*

The Science of Interrogation and its Effects and Expert Testimony Based On This Science

Empirical studies of interrogation and its effects have given rise to considerable discussion as to whether those engaged in or using the studies can reach useful conclusions about the impact of various interrogation techniques on suspects' decisions to confess. Such experts might also, of course, be able to offer useful conclusions as to the voluntariness and reliability of various categories of confessions or perhaps even specific confessions. In litigation, these issues often arise in response to defendants' efforts to introduce expert testimony. Such testimony might be used at hearings before trial judges on issues concerning the admissibility of confessions. In addition, such testimony is sometimes offered at trial in support of defendants' contentions that juries should not credit prosecution evidence that the defendants confessed.

The courts are split on the admissibility of this testimony. To some extent, the differences among courts can be attributed to different standards for determining the admissibility of expert and opinion testimony. A number of the decisions involve offers of testimony by the authors of the study described in the material above.

A Kansas court held that the trial judge in a murder trial erred in permitting Dr. Richard Leo to testify that some of the techniques used by police interrogating the defendant have contributed to false confessions. The trial judge incorrectly refused to apply a traditional expert testimony standard limiting expert testimony to opinions based on techniques generally accepted in the scientific community. The defense is sufficiently able to challenge the credibility of confession evidence by cross-examination and argument, the appellate tribunal reasoned, and expert testimony admitted in the case impermissibly invaded the province of the jury. State v. Cobb, 30 Kan.App.2d 544, 43 P.3d 855 (2002), review denied.

Similarly, in a New Jersey murder prosecution the trial judge ruled in advance of trial that a defense expert would be permitted to testify that the interrogation of the defendant involved "risk factors" leading the expert to recommend caution regarding the reliability of the resulting confession. On pretrial appeal by the prosecution this was held error. The trial judge had improperly applied a flexible standard under which opinion testimony based on specialized knowledge—but not "hard science" accepted by the scientific community—is admissible. State v. Free, 351 N.J.Super. 203, 798 A.2d 83 (2002).

In contrast, an Indiana trial judge erred in excluding the testimony of Dr. Richard Ofshe, offered by the defense as an expert in the field of the "social psychology of police interrogation and false confessions." Police interrogators had falsely told the mentally retarded suspect his fingerprints had been found at the scene of the charged murder and the victim may have died from natural causes. Dr. Ofshe would have testified these techniques tend to persuade even innocent suspects that convictions are inevitable and ease the difficulty of admitting to involvement by persuading suspects that authorities may believe the actions involved were not criminal. He would also have testified that mentally impaired suspects are less able than other suspects to appreciate the long-range consequences of confessions, easier than other suspects to persuade to see the facts as asserted by interrogators, and generally more suggestible and more likely to give false confessions than other suspects. Dr. Ofshe's testimony, the defense claimed, was necessary to enable jurors to understand why the mentally retarded defendant "would succumb to the lies" although innocent of the crime. The Indiana Supreme Court agreed and explained:

> [T]he general substance of Dr. Ofshe's testimony would have assisted the jury regarding the psychology of relevant aspects of police interrogation and the interrogation of mentally retarded persons, topics outside common knowledge and experience. In the event that some of Dr. Ofshe's testimony to the jury would have [constituted prohibited] opinion testimony as to the truth or falsity of the defendant's statements, the trial court could have sustained individualized objections at trial. We hold that excluding the proffered expert testimony in its

entirety deprived the defendant of the opportunity to present a defense.

Miller v. State, 770 N.E.2d 763, 773–74 (Ind.2002).

The issues raised in these cases is similar to those raised by offers of expert testimony on the reliability of eyewitness identification testimony. Expert testimony on eyewitness identification is addressed in Chapter 10.

A.   THE REQUIREMENT OF "VOLUNTARINESS"

Page 391.   Add the following to Editors' Introduction: Development, Content, and Current Substance of the Voluntariness Requirement, after the material on *Harmless Error*:

Civil Liability for Coercive Questioning

Federal constitutional requirements applicable to police interrogation were addressed at length in Chavez v. Martinez, 538 U.S. 760, 123 S.Ct. 1994, 155 L.Ed.2d 984 (2003). At issue was not the admissibility of self-incriminating statements, however, but rather the possibility of civil liability for questioning conducted in violation of what the original plaintiff claimed were Fifth Amendment requirements.

The *Chavez* facts were set out in Justice Thomas' opinion:

> On November 28, 1997, police officers Maria Pea and Andrew Salinas were near a vacant lot in a residential area of Oxnard, California, investigating suspected narcotics activity. While Pea and Salinas were questioning an individual, they heard a bicycle approaching on a darkened path that crossed the lot. They ordered the rider, * * * Martinez, to dismount, spread his legs, and place his hands behind his head. Martinez complied. Salinas then conducted a patdown frisk and discovered a knife in Martinez's waistband. An altercation ensued. The parties disagree over what triggered the altercation. The officers maintain that Martinez ran away from them and that they tackled him while in pursuit; Martinez asserts that he never attempted to flee and Salinas tackled him without warning.
>
> There is some dispute about what occurred during the altercation. The officers claim that Martinez drew Salinas' gun from its holster and pointed it at them; Martinez denies this. Both sides agree, however, that Salinas yelled, " 'He's got my gun!' " Pea then drew her gun and shot Martinez several times, causing severe injuries that left Martinez permanently blinded and paralyzed from the waist down. The officers then placed Martinez under arrest.
>
> * * * Chavez, a patrol supervisor, arrived on the scene minutes later with paramedics. Chavez accompanied Martinez to the hospital and then questioned Martinez there while he was receiving treatment

from medical personnel. The interview lasted a total of about 10 minutes, over a 45–minute period, with Chavez leaving the emergency room for periods of time to permit medical personnel to attend to Martinez.

At first, most of Martinez's answers consisted of "I don't know," "I am dying," and "I am choking." Later in the interview, Martinez admitted that he took the gun from the officer's holster and pointed it at the police. He also admitted that he used heroin regularly. At one point, Martinez said "I am not telling you anything until they treat me," yet Chavez continued the interview. At no point during the interview was Martinez given *Miranda* warnings under *Miranda v. Arizona*, 384 U.S. 436, 86 S.Ct. 1602, 16 L.Ed.2d 694 (1966).

Authorities never charged Martinez with a crime and his answers were never used against him in any criminal prosecution. He filed a federal civil lawsuit seeking damages under 42 U.S.C. § 1983, arguing that Chavez's questioning violated his Fifth Amendment right not to be compelled to incriminate himself and his Fourteenth Amendment substantive due process right to be free from compulsive questioning. The district court granted summary judgment, holding that Chavez was entitled to qualified immunity. On appeal the court of appeals reversed and the Supreme Court granted review.

The justices produced six opinions. A majority agreed to reverse the judgment of the court of appeals below and remand for further proceedings.

A majority of six justices concluded that Martinez had not alleged conduct violating the Fifth Amendment and thus the Court did not need to address qualified immunity. That majority consisted of two groups.

Justice Thomas, joined by three other justices, reasoned that "the mere use of compulsive questioning [does not] violate the Constitution" and, specifically, the Fifth Amendment. Thus the Fifth Amendment could not be read as applying to the questioning in Chavez. The Fifth Amendment prohibits only compelling a person to be a witness in a "criminal case," Justice Thomas elaborated. Police questioning of the sort involved in *Chavez* does not constitute a criminal case. If coercive police questioning results in a suspect making incriminatory statements to the interrogating officers, "it is not until their use in a criminal case that a violation of the Self–Incrimination Clause occurs * * *." 538 U.S. at 767, 123 S.Ct. at 2001, 155 L.Ed.2d at 993 (Thomas, J., announcing the judgment of the Court).

Justice Souter, joined by Justice Bryer, assumed in a separate opinion that the Court *could* read the Fifth Amendment as applicable to questioning like that in *Chavez*. It *should* not, he concluded, at least in the case before it. He explained:

I do not * * * believe that Martinez can make the "powerful showing," subject to a realistic assessment of costs and risks, necessary to expand protection of the privilege against compelled self-incrimination to the point of the civil liability he asks us to recognize here. The most obvious drawback inherent in Martinez's purely Fifth Amendment claim to damages is its risk of global application in every instance of interrogation producing a statement inadmissible under Fifth and Fourteenth Amendment principles, or violating one of the complementary rules we have accepted in aid of the privilege against evidentiary use. If obtaining Martinez's statement is to be treated as a stand-alone violation of the privilege subject to compensation, why should the same not be true whenever the police obtain any involuntary self-incriminating statement, or whenever the government so much as threatens a penalty in derogation of the right to immunity, or whenever the police fail to honor *Miranda*? Martinez offers no limiting principle or reason to foresee a stopping place short of liability in all such cases.

Recognizing an action for damages in every such instance not only would revolutionize Fifth and Fourteenth Amendment law, but would beg the question that must inform every extension or recognition of a complementary rule in service of the core privilege: why is this new rule necessary in aid of the basic guarantee? Martinez has offered no reason to believe that the guarantee has been ineffective in all or many of those circumstances in which its vindication has depended on excluding testimonial admissions or barring penalties. And I have no reason to believe the law has been systemically defective in this respect.

538 U.S. at 778–79, 123 S.Ct. at 2007, 155 L.Ed.2d at 1001 (Souter, J., concurring in the judgment).

The justices all assumed that coercive questioning *could* violate the Fourteenth Amendment's Due Process Clause as construed in Rochin v. California, 342 U.S. 165, 72 S.Ct. 205, 96 L.Ed. 183 (1952) [discussed in the decision reprinted on pp. 58–59 of the text]. Justice Kennedy, joined by Justices Stevens and Ginsburg, developed this:

There is no rule against interrogating suspects who are in anguish and pain. * * * The Constitution does not forbid the police from offering a person an opportunity to volunteer evidence he wishes to reveal.

There are, however, actions police may not take if the prohibition against the use of coercion to elicit a statement is to be respected. The police may not prolong or increase a suspect's suffering against the suspect's will. That conduct would render government officials accountable for the increased pain. The officers must not give the impression that severe pain will be alleviated only if the declarant cooperates, for that, too, uses pain to extract a statement. In a case like this one, recovery should be available under § 1983 if a complainant can demonstrate that an officer exploited his pain and suffering with the purpose and intent of securing an incriminating statement. * * *

538 U.S. at 796–97, 123 S.Ct. at 2017 155 L.Ed.2d at 1012–13 (Kennedy, J., concurring in part and dissenting in part). These three justices believed that Martinez made the showing of a due process violation necessary to avoid summary judgment and thus that the court of appeals' judgment should be affirmed.

Justices Kennedy, Stevens and Ginsburg, in the opinion by Justice Kennedy, had also concluded—contrary to a majority of the Court—that the Self–Incrimination Clause applies even where, as in *Chavez*, the results of coercive questioning are not used in evidence. Consequently, they concluded, the court of appeals should be affirmed on that basis. But, Justice Kennedy noted, if those three justices adhered to their position that the court of appeals should simply be affirmed, there would be no majority of the Court for any specific disposition of the case before it. He added that "a ruling on substantive due process could provide much of the essential protection the Self–Incrimination Clause secures * * *," and a remand for further consideration would leave open the possibility that Martinez might get a favorable ruling on substantive due process grounds.

Justices Souter and Bryer, in Justice Souter's opinion, apparently concluded that the substantive due process issue had not been resolved by the court of appeals below. Therefore, they reasoned, a remand for consideration of that issue was appropriate. Justices Kennedy, Sevens and Ginsburg, despite their conclusion (described above) that the court of appeals would best be simply affirmed, decided to vote for the disposition of the case favored by Justices Souter and Bryer. Thus they joined the short portion of Justice Souter's opinion in which Justice Souter explained the basis for the disposition he and Justice Bryer favored. As a bottom line, the opinion *of the Court* in *Chavez* consisted of a single paragraph of the opinion written by Justice Souter:

> Whether Martinez may pursue a claim of liability for a substantive due process violation is thus an issue that should be addressed on remand, along with the scope and merits of any such action that may be found open to him.

538 U.S. at 779, 123 S.Ct. at 2008, 155 L.Ed.2d at 1001–02. The Supreme Court's judgment—reversal of the judgment of the court of appeals and remand to that court "for further proceedings"—was announced at the end of the opinion of Justice Thomas. This was despite the fact that Justice Thomas's opinion (in a unit joined by only two other justices) reasoned that Martinez failed to allege a substantive due process violation.

The split among the justices left somewhat unclear the potential effect of failure to comply with *Miranda*. Compare 538 U.S. at 771, 123 S.Ct. at 2004, 155 L.Ed.2d at 996 (Thomas, J., announcing the judgment of the court) ("Chavez's failure to read *Miranda* warnings to Martinez did not violate Martinez's constitutional rights and cannot be grounds for a § 1983 action.") with 538 U.S. at 779 n.*, 123 U.S. at 2007 n. *, 155 L.Ed.2d at 1001 n * (Souter, J., concurring in the judgment) ("The question whether the absence of *Miranda* warnings may be a basis for a § 1983 action under any circumstances is not before the Court.").

Page 399. Add the following to Note 2 after Colorado v. Connelly:

The Supreme Court resolved the matter in Corley v. United States, 556 U.S. 303, 129 S.Ct. 1558, 173 L.Ed.2d 443 (2009). The federal statute, *Corley* held by a 5–to–4 vote, did not completely nullify the *McNabb-Mallory* rule.

> We hold that § 3501 modified *McNabb-Mallory* without supplanting it. Under the rule as revised by § 3501(c), a district court with a suppression claim must find whether the defendant confessed within six hours of arrest (unless a longer delay was "reasonable considering the means of transportation and the distance to be traveled to the nearest available [magistrate]"). If the confession came within that period, it is admissible, subject to the other Rules of Evidence, so long as it was "made voluntarily and . . . the weight to be given [it] is left to the jury." If the confession occurred before presentment and beyond six hours, however, the court must decide whether delaying that long was unreasonable or unnecessary under the *McNabb-Mallory* cases, and if it was, the confession is to be suppressed.

556 U.S. at ___, 129 S.Ct. at 1571. The *Corley* majority was clearly influenced by its perception of the significance of the prompt presentation requirement:

> It * * * counts heavily against the position of the United States that it would leave the Rule 5 presentment requirement without any teeth, for as the Government again is forced to admit, if there is no *McNabb-Mallory* there is no apparent remedy for delay in presentment. One might not care if the prompt presentment requirement were just some administrative nicety, but in fact the rule has always mattered in very practical ways and still does. As we said, it stretches back to the common law, when it was "one of the most important" protections "against unlawful arrest." Today presentment is the point at which the judge is required to take several key steps to foreclose Government overreaching: informing the defendant of the charges against him, his right to remain silent, his right to counsel, the availability of bail, and any right to a preliminary hearing; giving the defendant a chance to consult with counsel; and deciding between detention or release.

> In a world without *McNabb-Mallory,* federal agents would be free to question suspects for extended periods before bringing them out in the open, and we have always known what custodial secrecy leads to. * * * "[C]ustodial police interrogation, by its very nature, isolates and pressures the individual," and there is mounting empirical evidence that these pressures can induce a frighteningly high percentage of people to confess to crimes they never committed.

556 U.S. at ___, 129 S.Ct. at 1571.

Page 400. Add the following new note after the Notes following Colorado v. Connelly:

5. **Overbearing Of the Will in Aggressive Interrogation Situations.** In State v. Petitjean, 140 Ohio App.3d 517, 748 N.E.2d 133 (2000), appeal not allowed 91 Ohio St.3d 1480, 744 N.E.2d 1194 (Ohio 2001), an appellate court took the

unusual action of finding error in a trial judge's conclusion that a confession was voluntary.

Shawn Petitjean was one of five or six persons police suspected in the murder of Tara Latimer. Latimer was stabbed to death in her apartment. She suffered eight stab wounds, which were inflicted with a knife. She was also beaten about the head and face. Her two young children were in the apartment but were not harmed. Two detectives, Steve Cruea and Joe Stutz, went to Petitjean's apartment and asked him to come to the stationhouse for a second interview. Four days later, Petitjean went to police headquarters. The detectives gave him a Non–Custodial Interview Form; Petitjean signed and dated the form. During the subsequent videotaped interview, Petitjean admitted to killing Latimer when he went to her apartment to complain about Latimer's interference in Petitjean's relationship with another woman. The detectives then for the first time read Petitjean his *Miranda* warnings.

A transcript of the interview included the following:

Cruea   And the whole truth of the matter is, Tara interfered with your relationship. * * * That's what it comes down to, okay. It's that or possible one other thing, and only one other thing, cause we know that she wasn't a god damn angel either okay. Maybe you went to her house to talk to her about the problem. Tara's.

Shawn   Mmhmm.

Cruea   And maybe she attacked you. The problem is Shawn, you're not telling us what the fuck happened. Without your help, you're going to be looking at a murder charge. If she attacked you and you had to defend yourself, let me know it. We're tired of fucking around with you on this. It ain't fun and games no more. Take the smile off your fucking face.

Shawn   It's not a game to me.

Cruea   Yeah, it is a game to you. And I'll tell you what's gonna happen, your game is gonna get you up for murder. When you possibly could have fucking self-defense. It's gonna get you murder. It's gonna get you the fucking chair. Do you understand what that means?

Shawn   I understand what you are saying.

* * *

Cruea   * * * Now let us know what the hell happened in there. If you had to defend yourself, you had to defend yourself. Cause I'm gonna tell you right, now. I don't think you're a god damn cold blooded killer because those two kids were kept safe, okay.

Shawn   I know.

Cruea   If you were a cold blooded killer, those kids would have been killed. They sure as hell wouldn't have been kept out of that mess. Shawn, you are involved in this and you know god damn good and well you are. Now you need to clear it up. You are the one that needs to clear it up. If we have to clear it up through evidence, you go bye-bye for a big long god damn time—for life or you lose your life.

Stutz   No choice.

Cruea   There is no choices. No jokes about it. There'll be no fucking deals. Now, the prosecutor has already promised us that. He has guaranteed it. Now if you had to defend yourself, get it out. Let us know it. We can work with that. We know she would attack you. We're not stupid. We know she's not a perfect little angel. In fact, she could be a downright nasty bitch. But if you're gonna let . . .

Shawn   What am I—what am I looking at if I do? Either way, I'm screwed.

Cruea   No, you're not. No, you're not if you had to defend yourself, Shawn, if you had to defend yourself and she happened to die out of it and you had to make it look like something else because you wanted to get the hell out of there, we can work with that. The prosecutor will be glad to work that.

Shawn   Yeah, but still what am I looking at?

Cruea   What do you mean, what are you looking at? Charge wise?

Shawn   Yes.

Cruea   If you got self-defense, you're not looking at much of anything. At the most, okay, at the most, an involuntary manslaughter. Jesus Criminy, you're lucky if you get 6 months out of something like that. If you're a good boy, which you obviously ain't been a major problem in the past . . .

Shawn   Right.

Cruea   . . . if you want to work with us and work with yourself, god damn you'd probably get two years of probation.

Shawn   _____ I'll work with you guys.

Petitjean then told the officers that Latimer had attacked him with a knife and that in the ensuing struggle she was stabbed once in the stomach. He later added that he stabbed her three times in the chest. He also stated that he "punched" her in the head "a couple of times." According to the prosecutor's statement to the court when Petitjean entered his guilty plea, Latimer was stabbed eight times and beaten about the head and face with a blunt instrument.

The officers admitted that they never believed that self-defense was a possibility, and said so only to induce Petitjean to confess.

The trial judge held that Petitjean was not in custody (and therefore *Miranda* did not apply) and his confession was voluntary. The appellate court agreed regarding custody but reversed on the voluntariness issue:

> [T]he officers told Petitjean that "you'd probably get two years of probation" if "you want to work with us." This specifically conditioned the availability of probation on Petitjean's waiver of his Fifth Amendment privilege. That assurance of leniency was a misstatement of the law that so undermined Petitjean's calculus that it critically affected his capacity for self-determination.
>
> In reaching a contrary conclusion, the trial court reasoned that the probation alternative was possible in the event that Petitjean was charged with a manslaughter offense. That view assumes that Petitjean would be charged with involuntary manslaughter, as the officers had suggested. Where, as here, the likely underlying offense, felonious assault, is a felony, involuntary man-

slaughter is a felony of the first degree, for which definite terms of imprisonment from three to ten years, not six months, must be imposed. Community control sanctions for involuntary manslaughter may technically be possible. However, given the violent nature of this homicide and the number and nature of the wounds inflicted upon the victim, that form of release was not a realistic possibility.

It was almost inevitable that should he confess to killing Latimer, Petitjean would be charged with voluntary manslaughter, if not murder. Voluntary manslaughter is a first degree felony which carries a presumption that a term of imprisonment is necessary. The penalty for murder is an indefinite term of fifteen years to life. In the event, and upon his confession, Petitjean was charged with aggravated murder, for which the penalty is death or imprisonment for life.

The probation alternative that the officers presented Petitjean was so remote from reality as to be illusory. Pitted against the alternative they gave him, which confronted him with the prospect of the death penalty should he remain silent, that false hope critically affected Petitjean's capacity for self-determination, * * * because it fatally undermined his capacity for rational calculation. Because of that, his will was overborne and his resulting decision to waive his Fifth Amendment rights to obtain the benefit to be derived from a waiver was involuntary.

Applying the totality-of-the-circumstances standard, * * * the trial court nevertheless found that Petitjean's decision to waive his rights was not impaired by the officers' statements. The court based its finding on two factors * * *.

First, the court found that the interrogation was not coercive because promises of leniency that the officers made were conditional and tentative, presented in the form of possibilities or probabilities. Read carefully, they may be. However, the suspect's capacity to understand those matters is affected by his prior experience, by the duration and tone of the interrogation, by the threats of punishment should he not accede, and by the source of the promises. Equivocal language alone is, therefore, insufficient to save police misrepresentations of leniency when those other factors weigh heavily in favor of a finding of involuntariness, as they do here.

Second, based on the record of his interrogation and his testimony at the suppression hearing, the trial court found as a matter of fact that Petitjean's will was not overborne. * * *

We have very carefully reviewed the videotaped interrogation as well as the transcript of the suppression hearing. We can find from those sources no credible evidence to support the trial court's finding that Petitjean's will was not overborne by the interrogation that caused him to waive his Fifth Amendment privilege. That record demonstrates, unequivocally, that Petitjean was "scared as hell," as he put it, by the officers' threats, and that he waived his privilege only after and because of their assurances. Indeed, nothing occurred at the suppression hearing to support a contrary finding. * * *

140 Ohio App.3d at 531–34, 748 N.E.2d at 144–45.

B. SELF-INCRIMINATION AND *MIRANDA*'S RIGHT TO COUNSEL

1. THE *MIRANDA* DECISION

Page 414.   Add the following to Note 1 after Miranda v. Arizona:

In Florida v. Powell, ___ U.S. ___, 130 S.Ct. 1195, 175 L.Ed.2d 1009 (2010), the written warnings were as follows:

> You have the right to remain silent. If you give up the right to remain silent, anything you say can be used against you in court. You have the right to talk to a lawyer before answering any of our questions. If you cannot afford to hire a lawyer, one will be appointed for you without cost and before any questioning. You have the right to use any of these rights at any time you want during this interview.

Two members of the Court regard the warning as inadequate because "[t]he more natural reading of the warning * * *, which (1) contained a temporal limit and (2) failed to mention his right to the presence of counsel in the interrogation room, is that Powell only had the right to consult with an attorney before the interrogation began, not that he had the right to have an attorney with him during questioning." ___ U.S. at ___, 130 S.Ct. at 1211 (Stevens, J., dissenting). The Court, however, held the warning sufficient:

> The [warning] informed Powell that he had "the right to talk to a lawyer before answering any of [their] questions" and "the right to use any of [his] rights at any time [he] want[ed] during th[e] interview." The first statement communicated that Powell could consult with a lawyer before answering any particular question, and the second statement confirmed that he could exercise that right while the interrogation was underway. In combination, the two warnings reasonably conveyed Powell's right to have an attorney present, not only at the outset of interrogation, but at all times.

___ U.S. at ___, 130 S.Ct. at 1204–05.

Page 414.   Add the following new Note 2a to the notes after Miranda v. Arizona:

2a. **Warning Efforts Frustrated by the Suspect.** Suppose the suspect frustrates efforts by officers to comply with *Miranda*?

In United States v. Patane, 542 U.S. 630, 124 S.Ct. 2620, 159 L.Ed.2d 667 (2004), a federal officer arrested Patane and began advising him of his *Miranda* rights. When the officer finished admonishing Patane that he had the right to remain silent, Patane interrupted by asserting that he new his rights. Without further efforts to comply with *Miranda*, the officer began questioning Patane. The Supreme Court analyzed the case on the assumption that *Miranda* had been violated. Justice Thomas's plurality opinion noted that the Government conceded the officer's conduct rendered Patane's statements in response to the questioning inadmissible. 542 U.S. at 635 n. 1, 124 S.Ct. at 2625 n. 1. Justice Souter commented that "the facts give off the scent of a made-up case." 542 U.S. at 645 n. 1, 124 S.Ct. at 2631 n. 1 (Souter, J., dissenting).

2. APPLICABILITY OF *MIRANDA*

b. THE REQUIREMENT OF "CUSTODY"

Page 428: Insert the following in the Editors' Introduction before the last paragraph of the Introduction:

The nature of the custody determination was again addressed in J.D.B. v. North Carolina, 564 U.S. ___, 131 S.Ct. 2394, ___ L.Ed.2d ___ (2011). J.D.B. was a 13–year-old seventh grade middle school student. A uniformed school resource police officer interrupted his class, removed him from the classroom, and escorted him to a conference room. In that room were—in addition to the resource officer—an assistant principal, an administrative intern, and a police juvenile investigator. J.D.B. was questioned for 30–45 minutes about a break-in and a larceny, and he made oral admissions and wrote out an incriminating statement. Failure to comply with the *Miranda* requirements did not affect the admissibility of the admissions and statements, the state courts held, because J.D.B. was not in custody. J.D.B.'s age, the North Carolina Supreme Court reasoned, was not relevant to whether he was in custody.

By a 5–to–4 vote, the Supreme Court held the state tribunal erred in its analysis. Generally, Justice Sotomayor explained for the majority, whether a suspect is "in custody" is an objective question:

> The benefit of the objective custody analysis is that it is "designed to give clear guidance to the police." Police must make in-the-moment judgments as to when to administer *Miranda* warnings. By limiting analysis to the objective circumstances of the interrogation, and asking how a reasonable person in the suspect's position would understand his freedom to terminate questioning and leave, the objective test avoids burdening police with the task of anticipating the idiosyncrasies of every individual suspect and divining how those particular traits affect each person's subjective state of mind.

564 U.S. at ___, 131 S.Ct. at 2402.

Nevertheless, the age of a child-suspect must be considered in determining whether the suspect was in custody, "[s]o long as the child's age was known to the officer at the time of the interview, or would have been objectively apparent to any reasonable officer * * *." The *J.D.B.* majority explained:

> [A] reasonable child subjected to police questioning will sometimes feel pressured to submit when a reasonable adult would feel free to go. We think it clear that courts can account for that reality without doing any damage to the objective nature of the custody analysis.

564 U.S. at ___, 131 S.Ct. at 2403.

This, the majority continued, is not inconsistent with the discussion in Yarborough v. Alvarado, 541 U.S. 652, 124 S.Ct. 2140, 158 L.Ed.2d 938 (2004):

> [A] child's age differs from other personal characteristics that, even when known to police, have no objectively discernible relationship to a reasonable person's understanding of his freedom of action. *Alvarado,* holds, for instance, that a suspect's prior interrogation history with law enforcement has no role to play in the custody analysis because such experience could just as easily lead a reasonable person to feel free to walk away as to feel compelled to stay in place. Because the effect in any given case would be "contingent [on the] psycholog[y]" of the individual suspect, the Court explained, such experience cannot be considered without compromising the objective nature of the custody analysis. A child's age, however, is different. Precisely because childhood yields objective conclusions * * * considering age in the custody analysis in no way involves a determination of how youth "subjectively affect[s] the mindset" of any particular child.

564 U.S. at ___, 131 S.Ct. at 2404–05.

Justice Alito, writing for the four dissenters, found the majority's result "fundamentally inconsistent" with the need for clarity in *Miranda* law:

> Age * * * is in no way the only personal characteristic that may correlate with pliability, and in future cases the Court will be forced to choose between two unpalatable alternatives. It may choose to limit today's decision by arbitrarily distinguishing a suspect's age from other personal characteristics—such as intelligence, education, occupation, or prior experience with law enforcement—that may also correlate with susceptibility to coercive pressures. Or, if the Court is unwilling to draw these arbitrary lines, it will be forced to effect a fundamental transformation of the *Miranda* custody test—from a clear, easily applied prophylactic rule into a highly fact-intensive standard resembling the voluntariness test that the *Miranda* Court found to be unsatisfactory.

564 U.S. at ___, 131 S.Ct. at 2409 (Alito, J., dissenting). Further, the dissenters argued that suspects unusually sensitive to law enforcement pressure because of their age or other characteristics could be adequately protected by those suspects' ability to challenge the voluntariness of their statements:

> The voluntariness inquiry is flexible and accommodating by nature, and the Court's precedents already make clear that "special care" must be exercised in applying the voluntariness test where the confession of a "mere child" is at issue. If *Miranda* 's rigid, one-size-fits-all standards fail to account for the unique needs of juveniles, the response should be to rigorously apply the constitutional rule against

coercion to ensure that the rights of minors are protected. There is no need to run *Miranda* off the rails.

564 U.S. at ___, 131 S.Ct. at 2417.

Page 434. Add the following new note to the notes after Berkemer v. McCarty:

3. **Post-conviction incarceration as "custody."** Prison incarceration after conviction does not constitute custody for *Miranda* purposes, the Supreme Court held in Maryland v. Shatzer, ___ U.S. ___, 130 S.Ct. 1213, 175 L.Ed.2d 1045 (2010). The majority explained this as applied to the question of whether a prison inmate returned to the general prison population after invoking his *Miranda* rights remains in custody:

> Without minimizing the harsh realities of incarceration, we think lawful imprisonment imposed upon conviction of a crime does not create the coercive pressures identified in Miranda.
>
> Interrogated suspects who have previously been convicted of crime live in prison. When they are released back into the general prison population, they return to their accustomed surroundings and daily routine—they regain the degree of control they had over their lives prior to the interrogation. Sentenced prisoners, in contrast to the *Miranda* paradigm, are not isolated with their accusers. They live among other inmates, guards, and workers, and often can receive visitors and communicate with people on the outside by mail or telephone.
>
> Their detention, moreover, is relatively disconnected from their prior unwillingness to cooperate in an investigation. The former interrogator has no power to increase the duration of incarceration, which was determined at sentencing. And even where the possibility of parole exists, the former interrogator has no apparent power to decrease the time served. * * *

___ U.S. at ___, 130 S.Ct. at 1224–25. "[W]hat might be termed interrogative custody"—"[w]hen a prisoner is removed from the general prison population and taken to a separate location for questioning"—is, however, custody for *Miranda* purposes. ___ U.S. at ___ n. 8, 130 S.Ct. at 1225 n. 8.

3.   THE RIGHT TO PREVENT QUESTIONING

Page 435. Insert the following in the Editors' Introduction before the material on Edwards Rule Not "Offense Specific":

Duration of the Edwards Bar to Interrogation

The duration of the bar to interrogation was addressed in Maryland v. Shatzer, ___ U.S. ___, 130 S.Ct. 1213, 175 L.Ed.2d 1045 (2010). On August 7, 2003, officers questioned Shatzer about a child sexual abuse offense. Shatzer was at the time of the questioning imprisoned after conviction for an unrelated child molestation offense. When Shatzer invoked his right to counsel, the interrogation stopped and Shatzer was returned to the general prison population. On March 2, 2006 officers approached Shatzer—still imprisoned on the same conviction but in a different institution—and sought to question him about the sexual abuse matter. He was warned, waived his rights, and was questioned. Five days later, on March 7, officers returned, warned him and obtained waivers, and administered a polygraph test Shatzer had agreed on March 2 to take. After the test, he admitted the offense. The state court held that Shatzer's actions in 2003 triggered *Edwards*, and the bar to reapproaching Shatzer was still applicable in March of 2006. Thus his statement was inadmissible.

The Supreme Court reversed. It reasoned that the rationale for the *Edwards* presumption of involuntariness does not apply in situations such as *Shatzer*:

> It is easy to believe that a suspect may be coerced or badgered into abandoning his earlier refusal to be questioned without counsel in the paradigm *Edwards* case. That is a case in which the suspect has been arrested for a particular crime and is held in uninterrupted pretrial custody while that crime is being actively investigated. After the initial interrogation, and up to and including the second one, he remains cut off from his normal life and companions, "thrust into" and isolated in an "unfamiliar," "police-dominated atmosphere," where his captors "appear to control [his] fate." * * *

> When * * * a suspect has been released from his pretrial custody and has returned to his normal life for some time before the later attempted interrogation, there is little reason to think that his change of heart regarding interrogation without counsel has been coerced. He has no longer been isolated. He has likely been able to seek advice from an attorney, family members, and friends. And he knows from his earlier experience that he need only demand counsel to bring the interrogation to a halt; and that investigative custody does not last indefinitely. In these circumstances, it is far fetched to think that a police officer's asking the suspect whether he would like to waive his *Miranda* rights will any more "wear down the accused," than did the first such request at the original attempted interrogation—which is of course not deemed coercive. * * * Uncritical extension of *Edwards* to this situation would not significantly increase the number of genuinely coerced confessions excluded.

___ U.S. at ___, 130 S.Ct. at 1220–21. As a result, it continued:

> The protections offered by *Miranda*, which we have deemed sufficient to ensure that the police respect the suspect's desire to have an attorney present the first time police interrogate him, adequately ensure that result when a suspect who initially requested counsel is reinterrogated after a break in custody that is of sufficient duration to dissipate its coercive effects. * * * We think it appropriate to specify a period of time to avoid the consequence that continuation of the *Edwards* presumption "will not reach the correct result most of the time." It seems to us that period is 14 days. That provides plenty of time for the suspect to get reacclimated to his normal life, to consult with friends and counsel, and to shake off any residual coercive effects of his prior custody.

___ U.S. at ___, 130 S.Ct. at 1222–23.

Shatzer, of course, was not literally released from custody. But as is explained in the material supplementing page 434 of the text, *Shatzer* also held that incarceration in the general prison population after conviction is not "custody" for purposes of *Miranda*. Consequently, "[b]ecause Shatzer experienced a break in *Miranda* custody lasting more than two weeks between the first and second attempts at interrogation, *Edwards* does not mandate suppression of his March 2006 statements." ___ U.S. at ___, 130 S.Ct. at 1227.

Page 447. Add the following new note to the Notes following Davis v. United States:

1b. **Invoking the Right to Remain Silent.** May a suspect raise a barrier to further questioning by invoking the right to remain silent rather than the right to counsel? If so, what is necessary to raise that barrier? Is simply remaining silent enough?

In State v. Hodges, 118 Wash.App. 668, 77 P.3d 375 (2003), the court reported that Hodges, after being arrested for burglary, "responded at first to police questioning * * *." Specifically:

> Officer Hughey, the first officer to interact with Hodges, testified that he read Hodges his Miranda rights, and that Hodges stated that he understood his rights. Hodges then admitted to knocking on al-Sadoon's door, and upon hearing no response, entered the home. But when Hughey asked Hodges, "what happened next?" Hodges did not answer. Believing that Hodges would no longer cooperate, Officer Hughey left to run Hodges' information through the police database, leaving Hodges with Officer Diamond. Diamond placed Hodges in his patrol car and proceeded to question him, eliciting an admission that Hodges had entered the house and did not have permission to do so.

Hodges argued that his refusal to answer Hughey's question, "what happened next," was an assertion of his right to remain silent, all subsequent questioning should have ceased and since it did not his admission to Diamond was the product of impermissible interrogation. The prosecution responded that under the rationale of *Davis*, a suspect must unequivocally invoke the right to silence and silence alone can never constitute such an invocation of the right. Rejecting authority supporting the prosecution's view, the court explained:

> Silence in the face of repeated questioning over a period of time may constitute an invocation of the right to remain silent. The right to remain silent need not be articulated so long as it is clear and unequivocal. Nevertheless, Hodges' failure to respond to Hughey's question was not a clear and unequivocal invocation of his right to remain silent. He did not answer the question, "what happened next," but shortly thereafter answered a different officer's question without hesitation. Hodges therefore failed to invoke his *Miranda* rights, and Diamond was free to continue to question him.

77 P.2d at 377–78. Another court had appropriately reached the opposite result where "the defendant maintained her silence for several minutes and, perhaps, as many as ten minutes in the face of repeated questioning by the police."

Page 448.   Add the following at the end of Note 2:

In Montejo v. Louisiana, ___ U.S. ___, ___, 129 S.Ct. 2079, 2091, 173 L.Ed.2d 955 (2009), the majority appeared to embrace the view that a person cannot invoke the *Miranda* rights anticipatorily. *Montejo* is discussed in the material supplementing the Editors' Introduction on page 494 of the text.

Page 448. Add the following case after Davis v. United States:

Berghuis v. Thompkins

Supreme Court of the United States, 2010.
___ U.S. ___, 130 S.Ct. 2250, 176 L.Ed.2d 1098.

■ JUSTICE KENNEDY delivered the opinion of the Court.

* * *

I

A

On January 10, 2000, a shooting occurred outside a mall in Southfield, Michigan. Among the victims was Samuel Morris, who died from multiple gunshot wounds. The other victim, Frederick France, recovered from his injuries and later testified. Thompkins, who was a suspect, fled. About one year later he was found in Ohio and arrested there.

Two Southfield police officers traveled to Ohio to interrogate Thompkins, then awaiting transfer to Michigan. The interrogation began around 1:30 p.m. and lasted about three hours. The interrogation was conducted in a room that was 8 by 10 feet, and Thompkins sat in a chair that resembled a school desk (it had an arm on it that swings around to provide a surface to write on). At the beginning of the interrogation, one of the officers, Detective Helgert, presented Thompkins with a form derived from the *Miranda* rule. It stated:

"NOTIFICATION OF CONSTITUTIONAL RIGHTS AND STATEMENT

"1.   You have the right to remain silent.

"2.   Anything you say can and will be used against you in a court of law.

"3.   You have a right to talk to a lawyer before answering any questions and you have the right to have a lawyer present with you while you are answering any questions.

"4.   If you cannot afford to hire a lawyer, one will be appointed to represent you before any questioning, if you wish one.

"5.   You have the right to decide at any time before or during questioning to use your right to remain silent and your right to talk with a lawyer while you are being questioned."

Helgert asked Thompkins to read the fifth warning out loud. Thompkins complied. Helgert later said this was to ensure that Thompkins could read, and Helgert concluded that Thompkins understood English. Helgert then read the other four *Miranda* warnings out loud and asked Thompkins to sign the form to demonstrate that he understood his rights. Thompkins declined to sign the form. The record contains conflicting evidence about whether Thompkins then verbally confirmed that he understood the rights listed on the form.

Officers began an interrogation. At no point during the interrogation did Thompkins say that he wanted to remain silent, that he did not want to talk with the police, or that he wanted an attorney. Thompkins was "[l]argely" silent during the interrogation, which lasted about three hours. He did give a few limited verbal responses, however, such as "yeah," "no," or "I don't know." And on occasion he communicated by nodding his head.

Thompkins also said that he "didn't want a peppermint" that was offered to him by the police and that the chair he was "sitting in was hard."

About 2 hours and 45 minutes into the interrogation, Helgert asked Thompkins, "Do you believe in God?" Thompkins made eye contact with Helgert and said "Yes," as his eyes "well[ed] up with tears." Helgert asked, "Do you pray to God?" Thompkins said "Yes." Helgert asked, "Do you pray to God to forgive you for shooting that boy down?" Thompkins answered "Yes" and looked away. Thompkins refused to make a written confession, and the interrogation ended about 15 minutes later.

Thompkins was charged with first-degree murder, assault with intent to commit murder, and certain firearms-related offenses. He moved to suppress the statements made during the interrogation. He argued that he had invoked his Fifth Amendment right to remain silent, requiring police to end the interrogation at once, see *Michigan v. Mosley*, 423 U.S. 96, 103, 96 S.Ct. 321, 46 L.Ed.2d 313 (1975). The trial court denied the motion.

* * *

The jury found Thompkins guilty on all counts. He was sentenced to life in prison without parole.

B

* * *

Thompkins appealed * * * the trial court's refusal to suppress his pretrial statements under *Miranda*. The Michigan Court of Appeals rejected the *Miranda* claim, ruling that Thompkins had not invoked his right to remain silent * * *. The Michigan Supreme Court denied discretionary review.

Thompkins filed a petition for a writ of habeas corpus in the United States District Court for the Eastern District of Michigan. The District Court rejected Thompkins's *Miranda* * * * claim[ ]. It noted that, under the Antiterrorism and Effective Death Penalty Act of 1996 (AEPA), a federal court cannot grant a petition for a writ of habeas corpus unless the state court's adjudication of the merits was "contrary to, or involved an unreasonable application of, clearly established Federal law." 28 U.S.C. § 2254(d)(1). The District Court reasoned that Thompkins did not invoke his right to remain silent * * *.

The United States Court of Appeals for the Sixth Circuit reversed * * *.

We granted certiorari.

II

Under AEDPA, a federal court may not grant a habeas corpus application "with respect to any claim that was adjudicated on the merits in State court proceedings," unless the state court's decision "was contrary to, or involved an unreasonable application of, clearly established Federal law, as determined by the Supreme Court of the United States," or "was based on an unreasonable determination of the facts in light of the evidence presented in the State court proceeding." The relevant state-court decision here is the Michigan Court of Appeals' decision affirming Thompkins's conviction and rejecting his *Miranda* * * * claim[ ] on the merits.

III

The *Miranda* Court formulated a warning that must be given to suspects before they can be subjected to custodial interrogation. * * *

All concede that the warning given in this case was in full compliance with these requirements. The dispute centers on the response—or nonresponse—from the suspect.

A

Thompkins * * * contends that he "invoke[d] his privilege" to remain silent by not saying anything for a sufficient period of time, so the interrogation should have "cease[d]" before he made his inculpatory statements. [S]ee *Mosley,* 423 U.S., at 103, 96 S.Ct. 321 (police must " 'scrupulously hono[r]' " this "critical safeguard" when the accused invokes his or her " 'right to cut off questioning' ").

This argument is unpersuasive. In the context of invoking the *Miranda* right to counsel, the Court in *Davis v. United States,* 512 U.S. 452, 459, 114 S.Ct. 2350, 129 L.Ed.2d 362 (1994), held that a suspect must do so "unambiguously." If an accused makes a statement concerning the right to counsel "that is ambiguous or equivocal" or makes no statement, the police are not required to end the interrogation, or ask questions to clarify whether the accused wants to invoke his or her *Miranda* rights.

The Court has not yet stated whether an invocation of the right to remain silent can be ambiguous or equivocal, but there is no principled reason to adopt different standards for determining when an accused has invoked the *Miranda* right to remain silent and the *Miranda* right to counsel at issue in *Davis.* Both protect the privilege against compulsory self-incrimination by requiring an interrogation to cease when either right is invoked.

There is good reason to require an accused who wants to invoke his or her right to remain silent to do so unambiguously. A requirement of an unambiguous invocation of *Miranda* rights results in an objective inquiry that "avoid[s] difficulties of proof and . . . provide[s] guidance to officers" on how to proceed in the face of ambiguity. If an ambiguous act, omission, or statement could require police to end the interrogation, police would be required to make difficult decisions about an accused's unclear intent and face the consequence of suppression "if they guess wrong." Suppression of a voluntary confession in these circumstances would place a significant burden on society's interest in prosecuting criminal activity. Treating an ambiguous or equivocal act, omission, or statement as an invocation of *Miranda* rights "might add marginally to *Miranda's* goal of dispelling the compulsion inherent in custodial interrogation." But "as *Miranda* holds, full comprehension of the rights to remain silent and request an attorney are sufficient to dispel whatever coercion is inherent in the interrogation process."

Thompkins did not say that he wanted to remain silent or that he did not want to talk with the police. Had he made either of these simple, unambiguous statements, he would have invoked his " 'right to cut off questioning.' " Here he did neither, so he did not invoke his right to remain silent.

* * *

C

Thompkins next argues that * * * the police were not allowed to question him until they obtained a waiver first. [*North Carolina v. Butler*, 441 U.S. 369, 373, 99 S.Ct. 1755, 60 L.Ed.2d 286 (1979)] forecloses this argument. The *Butler* Court held that courts can infer a waiver of *Miranda* rights "from the actions and words of the person interrogated." This principle would be inconsistent with a rule that requires a waiver at the outset. The *Butler* Court thus rejected the rule proposed by the *Butler* dissent, which would have "requir[ed] the police to obtain an express waiver of [*Miranda* rights] before proceeding with interrogation." This holding also makes sense given that "the primary protection afforded suspects subject[ed] to custodial interrogation is the *Miranda* warnings themselves." The *Miranda* rule and its requirements are met if a suspect receives adequate *Miranda* warnings, understands them, and has an opportunity to invoke the rights before giving any answers or admissions. Any waiver, express or implied, may be contradicted by an invocation at any time. If the right to counsel or the right to remain silent is invoked at any point during questioning, further interrogation must cease.

Interrogation provides the suspect with additional information that can put his or her decision to waive, or not to invoke, into perspective. As questioning commences and then continues, the suspect has the opportunity to consider the choices he or she faces and to make a more informed decision, either to insist on silence or to cooperate. When the suspect knows that *Miranda* rights can be invoked at any time, he or she has the opportunity to reassess his or her immediate and long-term interests. Cooperation with the police may result in more favorable treatment for the suspect; the apprehension of accomplices; the prevention of continuing injury and fear; beginning steps towards relief or solace for the victims; and the beginning of the suspect's own return to the law and the social order it seeks to protect.

In order for an accused's statement to be admissible at trial, police must have given the accused a *Miranda* warning. If that condition is established, the court can proceed to consider whether there has been an express or implied waiver of *Miranda* rights. In making its ruling on the admissibility of a statement made during custodial questioning, the trial court, of course, considers whether there is evidence to support the conclusion that, from the whole course of questioning, an express or implied waiver has been established. Thus, after giving a *Miranda* warning, police may interrogate a suspect who has neither invoked nor waived his or her *Miranda* rights. On these premises, it follows the police were not required to obtain a waiver of Thompkins's *Miranda* rights before commencing the interrogation.

D

In sum, * * * Thompkins did not invoke his right to remain silent and stop the questioning. * * * The state court's decision rejecting Thompkins's *Miranda* claim was thus correct under *de novo* review and therefore necessarily reasonable under the more deferential AEDPA standard of review.

* * *

The judgment of the Court of Appeals is reversed, and the case is remanded with instructions to deny the petition.

It is so ordered.

■ JUSTICE SOTOMAYOR, with whom JUSTICE STEVENS, JUSTICE GINSBURG, and JUSTICE BREYER join, dissenting.

* * *

I

* * * Because I believe Thompkins is entitled to relief * * * on the ground that his statements were admitted at trial without the prosecution having carried its burden to show that he waived his right to remain silent; because longstanding principles of judicial restraint counsel leaving for another day the questions of law the Court reaches out to decide; and because the Court's answers to those questions do not result from a faithful application of our prior decisions, I respectfully dissent.

* * *

The strength of Thompkins' *Miranda* claims depends in large part on the circumstances of the 3–hour interrogation, at the end of which he made inculpatory statements later introduced at trial. The Court's opinion downplays record evidence that Thompkins remained almost completely silent and unresponsive throughout that session. * * *

Thompkins' nonresponsiveness is particularly striking in the context of the officers' interview strategy, later explained as conveying to Thompkins "that this was his opportunity to explain his side [of the story]" because "[e]verybody else, including [his] co-[d]efendants, had given their version," and asking him "[w]ho is going to speak up for you if you don't speak up for yourself?" Yet, Helgert confirmed that the *"only* thing [Thompkins said] relative to his involvement [in the shooting]" occurred near the end of the interview—*i.e.,* in response to the questions about God. (emphasis added). The only other responses Helgert could remember Thompkins giving were that " '[h]e didn't want a peppermint' " and " 'the chair that he was sitting in was hard.' "* * *

Thompkins contends * * * that his conduct during the interrogation invoked his right to remain silent, requiring police to terminate questioning. * * * I would not reach this question * * *. But * * * I cannot agree with the Court's much broader ruling that a suspect must clearly invoke his right to silence by speaking. * * *

A

Thompkins' claim * * * rests on the clearly established federal law of *Miranda* and *Mosley.* In *Miranda,* the Court concluded that "[i]f [an] individual indicates in any manner, at any time prior to or during questioning, that he wishes to remain silent, the interrogation must cease.... [A]ny statement taken after the person invokes his privilege cannot be other than the product of compulsion, subtle or otherwise." In *Mosley,* the Court said that a "critical safeguard" of the right to remain silent is a suspect's " 'right to cut off questioning.' " Thus, "the admissibility of statements obtained after the person in custody has decided to remain silent depends under *Miranda* on whether his 'right to cut off questioning' was 'scrupulously honored.' "

* * * Thompkins did not remain absolutely silent, and this Court has not previously addressed whether a suspect can invoke the right to silence by remaining uncooperative and nearly silent for 2 hours and 45 minutes.

B

The Court * * * extend[s] *Davis* to hold that police may continue questioning a suspect until he unambiguously invokes his right to remain silent. Because Thompkins neither said "he wanted to remain silent" nor said "he did not want to talk with the police," the Court concludes, he did not clearly invoke his right to silence.

I disagree with this novel application of *Davis.* Neither the rationale nor holding of that case compels today's result. *Davis* involved the right to counsel, not the right to silence. The Court in *Davis* reasoned that extending *Edwards'* "rigid" prophylactic rule to ambiguous requests for a lawyer would transform *Miranda* into a " 'wholly irrational obstacl[e] to legitimate police investigative activity' " by "needlessly prevent[ing] the police from questioning a suspect in the absence of counsel even if [he] did not wish to have a lawyer present." But *Miranda* itself "distinguished between the procedural safeguards triggered by a request to remain silent and a request for an attorney." *Mosley* upheld the admission of statements when police immediately stopped interrogating a suspect who invoked his right to silence, but reapproached him after a 2–hour delay and obtained inculpatory responses relating to a different crime after administering fresh *Miranda* warnings. The different effects of invoking the rights are consistent with distinct standards for invocation. To the extent *Mosley* contemplates a more flexible form of prophylaxis than *Edwards*—and, in particular, does not categorically bar police from reapproaching a suspect who has invoked his right to remain silent—*Davis'* concern about " 'wholly irrational obstacles' " to police investigation applies with less force.

In addition, the suspect's equivocal reference to a lawyer in *Davis* occurred only *after* he had given express oral and written waivers of his rights. *Davis'* holding is explicitly predicated on that fact. The Court ignores this aspect of *Davis,* as well as the decisions of numerous federal and state courts declining to apply a clear-statement rule when a suspect has not previously given an express waiver of rights.

In my mind, a more appropriate standard for addressing a suspect's ambiguous invocation of the right to remain silent is the constraint *Mosley* places on questioning a suspect who has invoked that right: The suspect's " 'right to cut off questioning' " must be " 'scrupulously honored.' " Such a standard is necessarily precautionary and fact specific. The rule would acknowledge that some statements or conduct are so equivocal that police may scrupulously honor a suspect's rights without terminating questioning—for instance, if a suspect's actions are reasonably understood to indicate a willingness to listen before deciding whether to respond. But other statements or actions—in particular, when a suspect sits silent throughout prolonged interrogation, long past the point when he could be deciding whether to respond-cannot reasonably be understood other than as an invocation of the right to remain silent. Under such circumstances, "scrupulous" respect for the suspect's rights will require police to terminate questioning under *Mosley*.

To be sure, such a standard does not provide police with a bright-line rule. But, as we have previously recognized, *Mosley* itself does not offer clear guidance to police about when and how interrogation may continue after a suspect invokes his rights. Given that police have for nearly 35 years applied *Mosley's* fact-specific standard in questioning suspects who have invoked their right to remain silent; that our cases did not during that time resolve what statements or actions suffice to invoke that right; and that neither Michigan nor the Solicitor General have provided evidence in this case that the status quo has proved unworkable, I see little reason to believe today's clear-statement rule is necessary to ensure effective law enforcement.

Davis' clear-statement rule is also a poor fit for the right to silence. Advising a suspect that he has a "right to remain silent" is unlikely to convey that he must speak (and must do so in some particular fashion) to ensure the right will be protected. By contrast, telling a suspect "he has the right to the presence of an attorney, and that if he cannot afford an attorney one will be appointed for him prior to any questioning if he so desires," implies the need for speech to exercise that right. *Davis'* requirement that a suspect must "clearly reques[t] an attorney" to terminate questioning thus aligns with a suspect's likely understanding of the *Miranda* warnings in a way today's rule does not. The Court suggests Thompkins could have employed the "simple, unambiguous" means of saying "he wanted to remain silent" or "did not want to talk with the police." But the *Miranda* warnings give no hint that a suspect should use those magic words, and there is little reason to believe police—who have ample incentives to avoid invocation—will provide such guidance.

Conversely, the Court's concern that police will face difficult decisions about an accused's unclear intent and suffer the consequences of " 'guess[ing] wrong,' " is misplaced. If a suspect makes an ambiguous statement or engages in conduct that creates uncertainty about his intent to invoke his right, police can simply ask for clarification. * * * Given this straightfoward mechanism by which police can "scrupulously hono[r]" a suspect's right to silence, today's clear-statement rule can only be seen as accepting "as tolerable the certainty that some poorly expressed requests [to remain silent] will be disregarded," without any countervailing benefit. Police may well prefer not to seek clarification of an ambiguous statement out of fear that a suspect will invoke his rights. But "our system of justice is not founded on a fear that a suspect will exercise his rights." * * *

The Court asserts in passing that treating ambiguous statements or acts as an invocation of the right to silence will only " 'marginally' " serve *Miranda's* goals. Experience suggests the contrary. In the 16 years since *Davis* was decided, ample evidence has accrued that criminal suspects often use equivocal or colloquial language in attempting to invoke their right to silence. A number of lower courts that have (erroneously, in my view) imposed a clear-statement requirement for invocation of the right to silence have rejected as ambiguous an array of statements whose meaning might otherwise be thought plain. At a minimum, these decisions suggest that differentiating "clear" from "ambiguous" statements is often a subjective inquiry. Even if some of the cited decisions are themselves in tension with *Davis'* admonition that a suspect need not " 'speak with the discrimination of an Oxford don' " to invoke his rights, they demonstrate that today's decision will significantly burden the exercise of the right to silence. Notably, when a suspect "understands his (expressed) wishes to have been ignored … in contravention of the 'rights' just read to him by his interrogator, he may well see further objection as futile and confession (true or not) as the only way to end his interrogation."

For these reasons, I believe a precautionary requirement that police "scrupulously hono[r]" a suspect's right to cut off questioning is a more faithful application of our precedents than the Court's awkward and needless extension of *Davis*.

* * *

Today's decision turns *Miranda* upside down. Criminal suspects must now unambiguously invoke their right to remain silent—which, counterintuitively, requires them to speak. * * * I respectfully dissent.

NOTE

Thompkins appeared to involve only the *Miranda* right to remain silent and not the right to counsel. But does the decision—particularly part III(C) of the Court's opinion—reflect a determination or assumption by the Court that the prosecution need not prove that the defendant made at least an "implied" waiver of the right to counsel before interrogation begins?

The United States, in an amicus curiae brief, took the position that *Davis* applies to a suspect who is considering in the first instance whether to invoke his rights following warnings as well as one who initially waived his rights and then reconsidered. Using different standards in the two situations, it reasoned, "would create uncertainties in an area in which the Court has stressed the need for clear 'guidance to police officers conducting interrogations.' *Davis*, 412 U.S. at 458–459." Brief for the United States as Amicus Curiae Supporting Petitioner, at 15–16. The brief continued:

> After a suspect receives his *Miranda* warnings, he may invoke them, thereby ending the interview, or he may waive them and make statements to the police. But he may also take no action to invoke or waive his right, instead waiting to see how the interview unfolds. In those circumstances, the police may conduct interrogation—*i.e.*, may make statements reasonably likely to elicit an incriminating response.

Brief for the United States, at 19–20. Perhaps the *Thompkins* majority accepted the United States' contention that this reflected the state of the law.

4. WAIVER OF THE *MIRANDA* RIGHTS

Page 466. Add the following case after Moran v. Burbine:

Berghuis v. Thompkins

Supreme Court of the United States, 2010.
___ U.S. ___, 130 S.Ct. 2250, 176 L.Ed.2d 1098.

■ JUSTICE KENNEDY delivered the opinion of the Court.

[Other portions of the opinions of the Court and the dissenters discuss the facts and procedural history of the case and Thompkins's contentions that he was questioned by officers before they first obtained a waiver and that he invoked his right to remain silent. These are reprinted in the material supplementing page 448 of the text.]

I

* * *

B

* * * The Michigan Court of Appeals rejected the *Miranda* claim, ruling that Thompkins had * * * had waived [his right to remain silent]. * * * The Michigan Supreme Court denied discretionary review.

Thompkins filed a petition for a writ of habeas corpus in the United States District Court for the Eastern District of Michigan. The District Court rejected Thompkins's *Miranda* * * * claim[ ]. It noted that, under the Antiterrorism and Effective Death Penalty Act of 1996 (AEDPA), a federal court cannot grant a petition for a writ of habeas corpus unless the state court's adjudication of the merits was "contrary to, or involved an unreasonable application of, clearly established Federal law." The District Court * * * held * * * that the Michigan Court of Appeals was not unreasonable in determining that Thompkins had waived his right to remain silent.

The United States Court of Appeals for the Sixth Circuit reversed * * *. The Court of Appeals ruled that the state court, in rejecting Thompkins's *Miranda* claim, unreasonably applied clearly established federal law and based its decision on an unreasonable determination of the facts. The Court of Appeals acknowledged that a waiver of the right to remain silent need not be express, as it can be " 'inferred from the actions and words of the person interrogated.' " The panel held, nevertheless, that the state court was unreasonable in finding an implied waiver in the circumstances here. The Court of Appeals found that the state court unreasonably determined the facts because "the evidence demonstrates that Thompkins was silent for two hours and forty-five minutes." According to the Court of Appeals, Thompkins's "persistent silence for nearly three hours in response to questioning and repeated invitations to tell his side of the story offered a clear and unequivocal message to the officers: Thompkins did not wish to waive his rights."

* * *

III

* * *

B

We * * * consider whether Thompkins waived his right to remain silent. * * * [T]he accused's statement during a custodial interrogation is inadmissible at trial unless the prosecution can establish that the accused "in fact knowingly and voluntarily waived [*Miranda*] rights" when making the statement. The waiver inquiry "has two distinct dimensions": waiver must be "voluntary in the sense that it was the product of a free and deliberate choice rather than intimidation, coercion, or deception," and "made with a full awareness of both the nature of the right being abandoned and the consequences of the decision to abandon it."

Some language in *Miranda* could be read to indicate that waivers are difficult to establish absent an explicit written waiver or a formal, express oral statement. * * *

The course of decisions since *Miranda,* informed by the application of *Miranda* warnings in the whole course of law enforcement, demonstrates that waivers can be established even absent formal or express statements of waiver that would be expected in, say, a judicial hearing to determine if a guilty plea has been properly entered. * * *

The prosecution * * * does not need to show that a waiver of *Miranda* rights was express. An implicit waiver of the "right to remain silent" is sufficient to admit a suspect's statement into evidence. [North Carolina v. Butler, 441 U.S. 369, 99 S.Ct. 1755, 60 L.Ed.2d 286 (1979)] made clear that a waiver of *Miranda* rights may be implied through "the defendant's silence, coupled with an understanding of his rights and a course of conduct indicating waiver." The Court in *Butler* therefore "retreated" from the "language and tenor of the *Miranda* opinion," which "suggested that the Court would require that a waiver . . . be 'specifically made.' "

If the State establishes that a *Miranda* warning was given and the accused made an uncoerced statement, this showing, standing alone, is insufficient to demonstrate "a valid waiver" of *Miranda* rights. The prosecution must make the additional showing that the accused understood these rights. Where the prosecution shows that a *Miranda* warning was given and that it was understood by the accused, an accused's uncoerced statement establishes an implied waiver of the right to remain silent.

Although *Miranda* imposes on the police a rule that is both formalistic and practical when it prevents them from interrogating suspects without first providing them with a *Miranda* warning, it does not impose a formalistic waiver procedure that a suspect must follow to relinquish those rights. As a general proposition, the law can presume that an individual who, with a full understanding of his or her rights, acts in a manner inconsistent with their exercise has made a deliberate choice to relinquish the protection those rights afford. The Court's cases have recognized that a waiver of *Miranda* rights need only meet the standard of *Johnson v. Zerbst,* 304 U.S. 458, 464, 58 S.Ct. 1019, 82 L.Ed. 1461 (1938). As *Butler* recognized, *Miranda* rights can therefore be waived through means less formal than a typical waiver on the record in a courtroom, given the practical constraints and necessities of interrogation and the fact that *Miranda* 's main protection lies in advising defendants of their rights.

The record in this case shows that Thompkins waived his right to remain silent. There is no basis in this case to conclude that he did not understand his rights; and on these facts it follows that he chose not to invoke or rely on those rights when he did speak. First, there is no contention that Thompkins did not understand his rights; and from this it follows that he knew what he gave up when he spoke. There was more than enough evidence in the record to conclude that Thompkins understood his *Miranda* rights. Thompkins received a written copy of the *Miranda* warnings; Detective Helgert determined that Thompkins could read and understand English; and Thompkins was given time to read the warnings. Thompkins, furthermore, read aloud the fifth warning, which stated that "you have the right to decide at any time before or during questioning to use your right to remain silent and your right to talk with a lawyer while you are being questioned." (capitalization omitted). He was thus aware that his right to remain silent would not dissipate after a certain amount of time and that police would have to honor his right to be silent and his right to counsel during the whole course of interrogation. Those rights, the warning made clear, could be asserted at any time. Helgert, moreover, read the warnings aloud.

Second, Thompkins's answer to Detective Helgert's question about whether Thompkins prayed to God for forgiveness for shooting the victim is a "course of conduct indicating waiver" of the right to remain silent. If Thompkins wanted to remain silent, he could have said nothing in response to Helgert's questions, or he could have unambiguously invoked his *Miranda* rights and ended the interrogation. The fact that Thompkins made a statement about three hours after receiving a *Miranda* warning does not overcome the fact that he engaged in a course of conduct indicating waiver. Police are not required to rewarn suspects from time to time. Thompkins's answer to Helgert's question about praying to God for forgiveness for shooting the victim was sufficient to show a course of conduct indicating waiver. This is confirmed by the fact that before then Thompkins had given sporadic answers to questions throughout the interrogation.

Third, there is no evidence that Thompkins's statement was coerced. Thompkins does not claim that police threatened or injured him during the interrogation or that he was in any way fearful. The interrogation was conducted in a standard-sized room in the middle of the afternoon. It is true that apparently he was in a straight-backed chair for three hours, but there is no authority for the proposition that an interrogation of this length is inherently coercive. Indeed, even where interrogations of greater duration were held to be improper, they were accompanied, as this one was not, by other facts indicating coercion, such as an incapacitated and sedated suspect, sleep and food deprivation, and threats. The fact that Helgert's question referred to Thompkins's religious beliefs also did not render Thompkins's statement involuntary. "[T]he Fifth Amendment privilege is not concerned 'with moral and psychological pressures to confess emanating from sources other than official coercion.'" In these circumstances,

Thompkins knowingly and voluntarily made a statement to police, so he waived his right to remain silent.

* * *

The judgment of the Court of Appeals is reversed, and the case is remanded with instructions to deny the petition.

It is so ordered.

■ JUSTICE SOTOMAYOR, with whom JUSTICE STEVENS, JUSTICE GINSBURG, and JUSTICE BREYER join, dissenting.

The Court concludes today that a criminal suspect waives his right to remain silent if, after sitting tacit and uncommunicative through nearly three hours of police interrogation, he utters a few one-word responses. * * * [This, and the other proposition announced today,] mark a substantial retreat from the protection against compelled self-incrimination that *Miranda v. Arizona,* 384 U.S. 436, 86 S.Ct. 1602, 16 L.Ed.2d 694 (1966), has long provided during custodial interrogation. The broad rules the Court announces today are also troubling because they are unnecessary to decide this case, which is governed by the deferential standard of review set forth in the Antiterrorism and Effective Death Penalty Act of 1996 (AEDPA). * * * I believe Thompkins is entitled to relief under AEDPA on the ground that his statements were admitted at trial without the prosecution having carried its burden to show that he waived his right to remain silent * * *.

I

* * *

Thompkins' federal habeas petition is governed by AEDPA, under which a federal court may not grant the writ unless the state court's adjudication of the merits of the claim at issue "was contrary to, or involved an unreasonable application of, clearly established Federal law, as determined by the Supreme Court of the United States," or "was based on an unreasonable determination of the facts in light of the evidence presented in the State court proceeding." §§ 2254(d)(1), (2).

The relevant clearly established federal law for purposes of § 2254(d)(1) begins with our landmark *Miranda* decision * * *.

Even when warnings have been administered and a suspect has not affirmatively invoked his rights, statements made in custodial interrogation may not be admitted as part of the prosecution's case in chief "unless and until" the prosecution demonstrates that an individual "knowingly and intelligently waive[d] [his] rights." "[A] heavy burden rests on the government to demonstrate that the defendant knowingly and intelligently waived his privilege against self-incrimination and his right to retained or appointed counsel." The government must satisfy the "high standar[d] of proof for the waiver of constitutional rights [set forth in] *Johnson v. Zerbst,* 304 U.S. 458, 58 S.Ct. 1019, 82 L.Ed. 1461 (1938)."

The question whether a suspect has validly waived his right is "entirely distinct" as a matter of law from whether he invoked that right. The questions are related, however, in terms of the practical effect on the exercise of a suspect's rights. A suspect may at any time revoke his prior waiver of rights—or, closer to the facts of this case, guard against the possibility of a future finding that he implicitly waived his rights—by invoking the rights and thereby requiring the police to cease questioning.

II

A

* * *

Rarely do this Court's precedents provide clearly established law so closely on point with the facts of a particular case. Together, *Miranda* and *Butler* establish that a court "must presume that a defendant did not waive his right[s]"; the prosecution bears a "heavy burden" in attempting to demonstrate waiver; the fact of a "lengthy interrogation" prior to obtaining statements is "strong evidence" against a finding of valid waiver; "mere silence" in response to questioning is "not enough"; and waiver may not be presumed "simply from the fact that a confession was in fact eventually obtained."

It is undisputed here that Thompkins never expressly waived his right to remain silent. His refusal to sign even an acknowledgment that he understood his *Miranda* rights evinces, if anything, an intent not to waive those rights. That Thompkins did not make the inculpatory statements at issue until after approximately 2 hours and 45 minutes of interrogation serves as "strong evidence" against waiver. *Miranda* and *Butler* expressly preclude the possibility that the inculpatory statements themselves are sufficient to establish waiver.

In these circumstances, Thompkins' "actions and words" preceding the inculpatory statements simply do not evidence a "course of conduct indicating waiver" sufficient to carry the prosecution's burden. Although the Michigan court stated that Thompkins "sporadically" participated in the interview, that court's opinion and the record before us are silent as to the subject matter or context of even a single question to which Thompkins purportedly responded, other than the exchange about God and the statements respecting the peppermint and the chair. Unlike in *Butler*, Thompkins made no initial declaration akin to "I will talk to you." Indeed, Michigan and the United States concede that no waiver occurred in this case until Thompkins responded "yes" to the questions about God. I believe it is objectively unreasonable under our clearly established precedents to conclude the prosecution met its "heavy burden" of proof on a record consisting of three one-word answers, following 2 hours and 45 minutes of silence punctuated by a few largely nonverbal responses to unidentified questions.

B

Perhaps because our prior *Miranda* precedents so clearly favor Thompkins, the Court today goes beyond AEDPA's deferential standard of review and announces a new general principle of law. Any new rule, it must be emphasized, is unnecessary to the disposition of this case. * * *

The Court concludes that when *Miranda* warnings have been given and understood, "an accused's uncoerced statement establishes an implied waiver of the right to remain silent." More broadly still, the Court states that, "[a]s a general proposition, the law can presume that an individual who, with a full understanding of his or her rights, acts in a manner inconsistent with their exercise has made a deliberate choice to relinquish the protection those rights afford."

These principles flatly contradict our longstanding views that "a valid waiver will not be presumed ... simply from the fact that a confession was in fact eventually obtained," and that "[t]he courts must presume that a defendant did not waive his rights." * * * At best, the Court today creates an unworkable and conflicting set of presumptions that will undermine *Miranda's* goal of providing "concrete constitutional guidelines for law enforcement agencies and courts to follow." At worst, it overrules *sub silentio* an essential aspect of the protections *Miranda* has long provided for the constitutional guarantee against self-incrimination.

* * *

Today's dilution of the prosecution's burden of proof to the bare fact that a suspect made inculpatory statements after *Miranda* warnings were given and understood takes an unprecedented step away from the "high standards of proof for the waiver of constitutional rights" this Court has long demanded. When waiver is to be inferred during a custodial interrogation, there are sound reasons to require evidence beyond inculpatory statements themselves. *Miranda* and our subsequent cases are premised on the idea that custodial interrogation is inherently coercive. Requiring proof of a course of conduct beyond the inculpatory statements themselves is critical to ensuring that those statements are voluntary admissions and not the dubious product of an overborne will.

Today's decision thus ignores the important interests *Miranda* safeguards. The underlying constitutional guarantee against self-incrimination reflects "many of our fundamental values and most noble aspirations," our society's "preference for an accusatorial rather than an inquisitorial system of criminal justice"; a "fear that self-incriminating statements will be elicited by inhumane treatment and abuses" and a resulting "distrust of self-deprecatory statements"; and a realization that while the privilege is "sometimes a shelter to the guilty, [it] is often a protection to the innocent." For these reasons, we have observed, a criminal law system "which comes to depend on the 'confession' will, in the long run, be less reliable and more subject to abuses than a system relying on independent investigation." "By bracing against 'the possibility of unreliable statements in every instance of in-custody interrogation,'" *Miranda's* prophylactic rules serve to " 'protect the fairness of the trial itself.' " Today's decision bodes poorly for the fundamental principles that *Miranda* protects.

Today's decision turns *Miranda* upside down. Criminal suspects must now unambiguously invoke their right to remain silent—which, counterintuitively, requires them to speak. At the same time, suspects will be legally presumed to have waived their rights even if they have given no clear expression of their intent to do so. Those results, in my view, find no basis in *Miranda* or our subsequent cases and are inconsistent with the fair-trial principles on which those precedents are grounded. Today's broad new rules are all the more unfortunate because they are unnecessary to the disposition of the case before us. I respectfully dissent.

5. "FRUITS" OF AN INADMISSIBLE CONFESSION

Page 476.   Insert the following Note and case after Oregon v. Elstad:

NOTE: PHYSICAL EVIDENCE OBTAINED AS A RESULT OF A MIRANDA VIOLATION

Whether the Fifth Amendment requires suppression of physical evidence obtained by using statements of a suspect themselves inadmissible because they were elicited in violation of *Miranda* was addressed in United States v. Patane, 542 U.S. 630, 124 S.Ct. 2620, 159 L.Ed.2d 667 (2004).

Officers arrested Patane and without complying with *Miranda* asked him about a .40 Glock pistol the officers had been told Patane possessed. Patane informed the officers the gun was in his bedroom and gave them permission to retrieve it. They did. The lower federal courts held the gun inadmissible. They discounted *Elstad's* indication to the contrary on the basis of Dickerson v. United States, 530 U.S. 428, 120 S.Ct. 2326, 147 L.Ed.2d 405 (2000), reprinted later in this supplement.

A split five-to-four majority of the Supreme Court reversed. Justice Thomas, joined by the Chief Justice and Justice Scalia, explained in a plurality opinion that the "fruit of the poisonous tree" rule of Fourth Amendment jurisprudence did not apply because *Miranda*, properly read, made clear there was no poisonous tree in this situation. A *Miranda* violation occurs only if police fail to comply with *Miranda's* directives *and* a resulting statement is admitted into evidence. Failure to give the *Miranda* warnings itself does not violate a suspect's constitutional rights or the *Miranda* rule. "The *Miranda* rule is not a code of police conduct * * *." 542 U.S. at 637, 124 S.Ct. at 2626 (plurality opinion of Thomas, J., announcing the judgment of the court).

An analysis considering a possible need to deter police conduct, the plurality asserted, would be improper here, because in these situations there is nothing the Court can properly consider as needing to be deterred. Mere unwarned questionings of suspects, when not accompanied by actual use of resulting self-incriminating statements, are not actions the Court can properly act to discourage or deter.

The five-justice majority was made up of those joining Justice Thomas's opinion and Justice Kennedy, joined by Justice O'Connor. Justice Kennedy explained for these justices:

> [I]t is sufficient to note that the Government presents an even stronger case for admitting the evidence obtained as the result of Patane's unwarned statement [than was presented in prior cases permitting use of evidence obtained following an unwarned interrogation]. Admission of nontestimonial physical fruits (the Glock in this case), even more so than the postwarning statements to the police in *Elstad* and *Michigan v. Tucker,* 417 U.S. 433, 94 S.Ct. 2357, 41 L.Ed.2d 182 (1974), does not run the risk of admitting into trial an accused's coerced incriminating statements against himself. In light of the important probative value of reliable physical evidence, it is doubtful that exclusion can be justified by a deterrence rationale sensitive to both law enforcement interests and a suspect's rights during an in-custody interrogation. Unlike the plurality, however, I find it unnecessary to decide whether the detective's failure to give Patane the full *Miranda* warnings should be characterized as a violation of the *Miranda* rule itself, or whether there is "[any]thing to deter" so long as the unwarned statements are not later introduced at trial.

542 U.S. at 645, 124 S.Ct. at 2631 (Kennedy, J., concurring in the judgment).

Three dissenters argued that the majority mischaracterized the issue:

> * * * The issue actually presented today is whether courts should apply the fruit of the poisonous tree doctrine lest we create an incentive for the police to omit *Miranda* warnings, before custodial interrogation. In closing their eyes to the consequences of giving an evidentiary advantage to those who ignore *Miranda,* the majority adds an important inducement for interrogators to ignore the rule in that case.

> * * *

> There is no way to read this case except as an unjustifiable invitation to law enforcement officers to flout *Miranda* when there may be physical evidence to be gained. The incentive is an odd one, coming from the Court on the same day it decides *Missouri v. Seibert,* [reprinted later in this supplement]. I respectfully dissent.

542 U.S. at 645–47, 124 S.Ct. at 2631–32 (Souter, J., dissenting). Justice Breyer, dissenting separately, would have applied the approach he took in *Seibert*. Since the lower courts made no explicit finding that the officers acted in good faith, he would have applied a rule requiring exclusion of physical evidence obtained from unwarned questioning. 542 U.S. at 647–48, 124 S.Ct. at 2632 (Breyer, J., dissenting).

The Supreme Judicial Court of Massachusetts concluded in Commonwealth v. Martin, 444 Mass. 213, 827 N.E.2d 198 (2005), that the state constitutional privilege against self-incrimination required a common-law rule of evidence excluding physical evidence obtained as a result of unwarned statements where state constitutional law required the *Miranda* warnings for those statements to be admissible. It explained:

> To apply the *Patane* analysis to the broader rights embodied in [the state constitutional provision] would have a corrosive effect on them, undermine the respect we have accorded them, and demean their importance to a system of justice chosen by the citizens of Massachusetts in 1780.

444 Mass. at 219, 827 N.E.2d at 203. A similar result was reached in State v. Peterson, 181 Vt. 436, 923 A.2d 585 (2007).

Missouri v. Seibert

Supreme Court of the United States, 2004.
542 U.S. 600, 124 S.Ct. 2601, 159 L.Ed.2d 643.

■ JUSTICE SOUTER announced the judgment of the Court and delivered an opinion, in which JUSTICE STEVENS, JUSTICE GINSBURG, and JUSTICE BREYER join.

This case tests a police protocol for custodial interrogation that calls for giving no warnings of the rights to silence and counsel until interrogation has produced a confession. Although such a statement is generally inadmissible, since taken in violation of *Miranda v. Arizona,* 384 U.S. 436, 86 S.Ct. 1602, 16 L.Ed.2d 694 (1966), the interrogating officer follows it with *Miranda* warnings and then leads the suspect to cover the same ground a second time. The question here is the admissibility of the repeated statement. * * *

I

Respondent Patrice Seibert's 12–year–old son Jonathan had cerebral palsy, and when he died in his sleep she feared charges of neglect because of bedsores on his body. In her presence, two of her teenage sons and two of their friends devised a plan to conceal the facts surrounding Jonathan's death by incinerating his body in the course of burning the family's mobile home, in which they planned to leave Donald Rector, a mentally ill teenager living with the family, to avoid any appearance that Jonathan had been unattended. Seibert's son Darian and a friend set the fire, and Donald died.

Five days later, the police awakened Seibert at 3 a.m. at a hospital where Darian was being treated for burns. In arresting her, Officer Kevin Clinton followed instructions from Rolla, Missouri, officer Richard Hanrahan that he refrain from giving *Miranda* warnings. After Seibert had been taken to the police station and left alone in an interview room for 15 to 20 minutes, Hanrahan questioned her without *Miranda* warnings for 30 to 40 minutes, squeezing her arm and repeating "Donald was also to die in his sleep." After Seibert finally admitted she knew Donald was meant to die in the fire, she was given a 20–minute coffee and cigarette break. Officer Hanrahan then turned on a tape recorder, gave Seibert the *Miranda* warnings, and obtained a signed waiver of rights from her. He resumed the questioning with "Ok, 'trice, we've been talking for a little while about what happened on Wednesday the twelfth, haven't we?," and confronted her with her prewarning statements:

> Hanrahan: "Now, in discussion you told us, you told us that there was a[n] understanding about Donald."

Seibert: "Yes."

Hanrahan: "Did that take place earlier that morning?"

Seibert: "Yes."

Hanrahan: "And what was the understanding about Donald?"

Seibert: "If they could get him out of the trailer, to take him out of the trailer."

Hanrahan: "And if they couldn't?"

Seibert: "I, I never even thought about it. I just figured they would."

Hanrahan: " 'Trice, didn't you tell me that he was supposed to die in his sleep?"

Seibert: "If that would happen, 'cause he was on that new medicine,' you know . . . ."

Hanrahan: "The Prozac? And it makes him sleepy. So he was supposed to die in his sleep?"

Seibert: "Yes."

After being charged with first-degree murder for her role in Donald's death, Seibert sought to exclude both her prewarning and postwarning statements. At the suppression hearing, Officer Hanrahan testified that he made a "conscious decision" to withhold *Miranda* warnings, thus resorting to an interrogation technique he had been taught: question first, then give the warnings, and then repeat the question "until I get the answer that she's already provided once." He acknowledged that Seibert's ultimate statement was "largely a repeat of information . . . obtained" prior to the warning.

The trial court suppressed the prewarning statement but admitted the responses given after the *Miranda* recitation. A jury convicted Seibert of second-degree murder. On appeal, the Missouri Court of Appeals affirmed, treating this case as indistinguishable from *Oregon v. Elstad,* 470 U.S. 298, 105 S.Ct. 1285, 84 L.Ed.2d 222 (1985).

The Supreme Court of Missouri reversed, holding that "[i]n the circumstances here, where the interrogation was nearly continuous, . . . the second statement, clearly the product of the invalid first statement, should have been suppressed." The court distinguished *Elstad* on the ground that warnings had not intentionally been withheld there * * *.

We granted certiorari * * *.

II

* * *

In *Miranda,* * * * "to reduce the risk of a coerced confession and to implement the Self–Incrimination Clause," this Court * * * concluded that "the accused must be adequately and effectively apprised of his rights and the exercise of those rights must be fully honored." *Miranda* conditioned the admissibility at trial of any custodial confession on warning a suspect of his rights: failure to give the prescribed warnings and obtain a waiver of rights before custodial questioning generally requires exclusion of any statements obtained. Conversely, giving the warnings and getting a waiver has generally produced a virtual ticket of admissibility; maintaining that a statement is involuntary even though given after warnings and voluntary waiver of rights requires unusual stamina, and litigation over voluntariness tends to end with the finding of a valid waiver. To point out the obvious, this common consequence would not be common at all were it not that *Miranda* warnings are customarily given under circumstances allowing for a real choice between talking and remaining silent.

III

* * *

The technique of interrogating in successive, unwarned and warned phases raises a new challenge to *Miranda*. Although we have no statistics on the frequency of this practice, it is not confined to Rolla, Missouri. An officer of that police department testified that the strategy of withholding *Miranda* warnings until after interrogating and drawing out a confession was promoted not only by his own department, but by a national police training organization and other departments in which he had worked. Consistently with the officer's testimony, the Police Law Institute, for example, instructs that "officers may conduct a two-stage interrogation.... At any point during the pre-*Miranda* interrogation, usually after arrestees have confessed, officers may then read the *Miranda* warnings and ask for a waiver. If the arrestees waive their *Miranda* rights, officers will be able to repeat any *subsequent* incriminating statements later in court." Police Law Institute, Illinois Police Law Manual 83 (Jan.2001–Dec.2003), http:// www. illinoispolicelaw.org/training/lessons/ILPLMIR.pdf (as visited Dec. 31, 2003, and available in the Clerk of Court's case file) (hereinafter Police Law Manual) (emphasis in original).[2] The upshot of all this advice is a question-first practice of some popularity, * * * sometimes in obedience to departmental policy.

IV

When a confession so obtained is offered and challenged, attention must be paid to the conflicting objects of *Miranda* and question-first.

---

2. Emphasizing the impeachment exception to the *Miranda* rule * * *, some training programs advise officers to omit *Miranda* warnings altogether or to continue questioning after the suspect invokes his rights. * * *

It is not the case, of course, that law enforcement educators en masse are urging that *Miranda* be honored only in the breach. Most police manuals do not advocate the question-first tactic, because they understand that *Oregon v. Elstad,* 470 U.S. 298, 105 S.Ct. 1285, 84 L.Ed.2d 222 (1985), involved an officer's good-faith failure to warn.

Miranda addressed "interrogation practices ... likely ... to disable [an individual] from making a free and rational choice" about speaking, and held that a suspect must be "adequately and effectively" advised of the choice the Constitution guarantees. The object of question-first is to render *Miranda* warnings ineffective by waiting for a particularly opportune time to give them, after the suspect has already confessed.

Just as "no talismanic incantation [is] required to satisfy [*Miranda*'s] strictures," *California v. Prysock,* 453 U.S. 355, 359, 101 S.Ct. 2806, 69 L.Ed.2d 696 (1981) *(per curiam),* it would be absurd to think that mere recitation of the litany suffices to satisfy *Miranda* in every conceivable circumstance. "The inquiry is simply whether the warnings reasonably 'conve[y] to [a suspect] his rights as required by *Miranda.*'" *Duckworth v. Eagan,* 492 U.S. 195, 203, 109 S.Ct. 2875, 106 L.Ed.2d 166 (1989) (quoting *Prysock, supra,* at 361). The threshold issue when interrogators question first and warn later is thus whether it would be reasonable to find that in these circumstances the warnings could function "effectively" as *Miranda* requires. Could the warnings effectively advise the suspect that he had a real choice about giving an admissible statement at that juncture? Could they reasonably convey that he could choose to stop talking even if he had talked earlier? For unless the warnings could place a suspect who has just been interrogated in a position to make such an informed choice, there is no practical justification for accepting the formal warnings as compliance with *Miranda,* or for treating the second stage of interrogation as distinct from the first, unwarned and inadmissible segment.[4]

There is no doubt about the answer that proponents of question-first give to this question about the effectiveness of warnings given only after successful interrogation, and we think their answer is correct. By any objective measure, applied to circumstances exemplified here, it is likely that if the interrogators employ the technique of withholding warnings until after interrogation succeeds in eliciting a confession, the warnings will be ineffective in preparing the suspect for successive interrogation, close in time and similar in content. After all, the reason that question-first is catching on is as obvious as its manifest purpose, which is to get a confession the suspect would not make if he understood his rights at the

---

4. Respondent Seibert argues that her second confession should be excluded from evidence under the doctrine known by the metaphor of the "fruit of the poisonous tree," developed in the Fourth Amendment context * * *: evidence otherwise admissible but discovered as a result of an earlier violation is excluded as tainted, lest the law encourage future violations. But the Court in *Elstad* rejected the * * * fruits doctrine for analyzing the admissibility of a subsequent warned confession following "an initial failure ... to administer the warnings required by *Miranda.*" * * * In a sequential confession case, clarity is served if the later confession is approached by asking whether in the circumstances the *Miranda* warnings given could reasonably be found effective. If yes, a court can take up the standard issues of voluntary waiver and voluntary statement; if no, the subsequent statement is inadmissible for want of adequate *Miranda* warnings, because the earlier and later statements are realistically seen as parts of a single, unwarned sequence of questioning.

outset; the sensible underlying assumption is that with one confession in hand before the warnings, the interrogator can count on getting its duplicate, with trifling additional trouble. Upon hearing warnings only in the aftermath of interrogation and just after making a confession, a suspect would hardly think he had a genuine right to remain silent, let alone persist in so believing once the police began to lead him over the same ground again.[5] A more likely reaction on a suspect's part would be perplexity about the reason for discussing rights at that point, bewilderment being an unpromising frame of mind for knowledgeable decision. What is worse, telling a suspect that "anything you say can and will be used against you," without expressly excepting the statement just given, could lead to an entirely reasonable inference that what he has just said will be used, with subsequent silence being of no avail. Thus, when *Miranda* warnings are inserted in the midst of coordinated and continuing interrogation, they are likely to mislead and "depriv[e] a defendant of knowledge essential to his ability to understand the nature of his rights and the consequences of abandoning them." *Moran v. Burbine,* 475 U.S. 412, 424, 106 S.Ct. 1135, 89 L.Ed.2d 410 (1986). By the same token, it would ordinarily be unrealistic to treat two spates of integrated and proximately conducted questioning as independent interrogations subject to independent evaluation simply because *Miranda* warnings formally punctuate them in the middle.

V

Missouri argues that a confession repeated at the end of an interrogation sequence envisioned in a question-first strategy is admissible on the authority of *Oregon v. Elstad,* 470 U.S. 298, 105 S.Ct. 1285, 84 L.Ed.2d 222 (1985), but the argument disfigures that case. * * * This Court noted that the pause in the living room "was not to interrogate the suspect but to notify his mother of the reason for his arrest," and described the incident as having "none of the earmarks of coercion." The Court, indeed, took care to mention that the officer's initial failure to warn was an "oversight" that "may have been the result of confusion as to whether the brief exchange qualified as 'custodial interrogation' or . . . may simply have reflected . . . reluctance to initiate an alarming police procedure before [an officer] had spoken with respondent's mother." * * * Although the *Elstad* Court expressed no explicit conclusion about either officer's state of mind, it is fair to read *Elstad* as treating the living room conversation as a good-faith *Miranda* mistake, not only open to correction by careful warnings before

---

5. It bears emphasizing that the effectiveness *Miranda* assumes the warnings can have must potentially extend through the repeated interrogation, since a suspect has a right to stop at any time. It seems highly unlikely that a suspect could retain any such understanding when the interrogator leads him a second time through a line of questioning the suspect has already answered fully. The point is not that a later unknowing or involuntary confession cancels out an earlier, adequate warning; the point is that the warning is unlikely to be effective in the question-first sequence we have described.

systematic questioning in that particular case, but posing no threat to warn-first practice generally.

The contrast between *Elstad* and this case reveals a series of relevant facts that bear on whether *Miranda* warnings delivered midstream could be effective enough to accomplish their object: the completeness and detail of the questions and answers in the first round of interrogation, the overlapping content of the two statements, the timing and setting of the first and the second, the continuity of police personnel, and the degree to which the interrogator's questions treated the second round as continuous with the first. In *Elstad,* it was not unreasonable to see the occasion for questioning at the station house as presenting a markedly different experience from the short conversation at home; since a reasonable person in the suspect's shoes could have seen the station house questioning as a new and distinct experience, the *Miranda* warnings could have made sense as presenting a genuine choice whether to follow up on the earlier admission.

At the opposite extreme are the facts here, which by any objective measure reveal a police strategy adapted to undermine the *Miranda* warnings.[6] The unwarned interrogation was conducted in the station house, and the questioning was systematic, exhaustive, and managed with psychological skill. When the police were finished there was little, if anything, of incriminating potential left unsaid. The warned phase of questioning proceeded after a pause of only 15 to 20 minutes, in the same place as the unwarned segment. When the same officer who had conducted the first phase recited the *Miranda* warnings, he said nothing to counter the probable misimpression that the advice that anything Seibert said could be used against her also applied to the details of the inculpatory statement previously elicited. In particular, the police did not advise that her prior statement could not be used.[7] Nothing was said or done to dispel the oddity of warning about legal rights to silence and counsel right after the police had led her through a systematic interrogation, and any uncertainty on her part about a right to stop talking about matters previously discussed would only have been aggravated by the way Officer Hanrahan set the scene by saying "we've been talking for a little while about what happened on Wednesday the twelfth, haven't we?" The impression that the further questioning was a mere continuation of the earlier questions and responses was fostered by references back to the confession already given. It would have been reasonable to regard the two sessions as parts of a continuum, in which it would have been unnatural to refuse to repeat at the second stage

---

6. Because the intent of the officer will rarely be as candidly admitted as it was here (even as it is likely to determine the conduct of the interrogation), the focus is on facts apart from intent that show the question-first tactic at work.

7. We do not hold that a formal addendum warning that a previous statement could not be used would be sufficient to change the character of the question-first procedure to the point of rendering an ensuing statement admissible, but its absence is clearly a factor that blunts the efficacy of the warnings and points to a continuing, not a new, interrogation.

what had been said before. These circumstances must be seen as challenging the comprehensibility and efficacy of the *Miranda* warnings to the point that a reasonable person in the suspect's shoes would not have understood them to convey a message that she retained a choice about continuing to talk.[8]

VI

Strategists dedicated to draining the substance out of *Miranda* cannot accomplish [this] by training instructions * * *. Because the question-first tactic effectively threatens to thwart *Miranda*'s purpose of reducing the risk that a coerced confession would be admitted, and because the facts here do not reasonably support a conclusion that the warnings given could have served their purpose, Seibert's postwarning statements are inadmissible. The judgment of the Supreme Court of Missouri is affirmed.

It is so ordered.

■ JUSTICE BREYER, concurring.

In my view, the following simple rule should apply to the two-stage interrogation technique: Courts should exclude the "fruits" of the initial unwarned questioning unless the failure to warn was in good faith. Cf. *Oregon v. Elstad,* 470 U.S. 298, 309, 318, n. 5, 105 S.Ct. 1285, 84 L.Ed.2d 222 (1985); *United States v. Leon,* 468 U.S. 897, 104 S.Ct. 3405, 82 L.Ed.2d 677 (1984). I believe this is a sound and workable approach to the problem this case presents. Prosecutors and judges have long understood how to apply the "fruits" approach, which they use in other areas of law. And in the workaday world of criminal law enforcement the administrative simplicity of the familiar has significant advantages over a more complex exclusionary rule.

I believe the plurality's approach in practice will function as a "fruits" test. The truly "effective" *Miranda* warnings on which the plurality insists, will occur only when certain circumstances—a lapse in time, a change in location or interrogating officer, or a shift in the focus of the questioning—intervene between the unwarned questioning and any postwarning statement.

I consequently join the plurality's opinion in full. I also agree with JUSTICE KENNEDY's opinion insofar as it is consistent with this approach and makes clear that a good-faith exception applies.

■ JUSTICE KENNEDY, concurring in the judgment.

* * * Although I agree with much in the careful and convincing opinion for the plurality, my approach does differ in some respects, requiring this separate statement.

---

8. Because we find that the warnings were inadequate, there is no need to assess the actual voluntariness of the statement.

The *Miranda* rule has become an important and accepted element of the criminal justice system. At the same time, not every violation of the rule requires suppression of the evidence obtained. Evidence is admissible when the central concerns of *Miranda* are not likely to be implicated and when other objectives of the criminal justice system are best served by its introduction. Thus, we have held that statements obtained in violation of the rule can be used for impeachment, so that the truth finding function of the trial is not distorted by the defense, that there is an exception to protect countervailing concerns of public safety, and that physical evidence obtained in reliance on statements taken in violation of the rule is admissible. These cases, in my view, are correct. They recognize that admission of evidence is proper when it would further important objectives without compromising *Miranda*'s central concerns. Under these precedents, the scope of the *Miranda* suppression remedy depends on a consideration of those legitimate interests and on whether admission of the evidence under the circumstances would frustrate *Miranda's* central concerns and objectives.

Oregon v. Elstad, 470 U.S. 298, 105 S.Ct. 1285, 84 L.Ed.2d 222 (1985), reflects this approach. * * * The Court held that, although a *Miranda* violation made the first statement inadmissible, the postwarning statements could be introduced against the accused because "neither the general goal of deterring improper police conduct nor the Fifth Amendment goal of assuring trustworthy evidence would be served by suppression" given the facts of that case.

In my view, *Elstad* was correct in its reasoning and its result. *Elstad* reflects a balanced and pragmatic approach to enforcement of the *Miranda* warning. An officer may not realize that a suspect is in custody and warnings are required. The officer may not plan to question the suspect or may be waiting for a more appropriate time. Skilled investigators often interview suspects multiple times, and good police work may involve referring to prior statements to test their veracity or to refresh recollection. In light of these realities it would be extravagant to treat the presence of one statement that cannot be admitted under *Miranda* as sufficient reason to prohibit subsequent statements preceded by a proper warning. * * *

This case presents different considerations. The police used a two-step questioning technique based on a deliberate violation of *Miranda*. The *Miranda* warning was withheld to obscure both the practical and legal significance of the admonition when finally given. As JUSTICE SOUTER points out, the two-step technique permits the accused to conclude that the right not to respond did not exist when the earlier incriminating statements were made. The strategy is based on the assumption that *Miranda* warnings will tend to mean less when recited midinterrogation, after inculpatory statements have already been obtained. This tactic relies on an intentional misrepresentation of the protection that *Miranda* offers and does not serve any legitimate objectives that might otherwise justify its use.

Further, the interrogating officer here relied on the defendant's pre-warning statement to obtain the postwarning statement used against her at trial. The postwarning interview resembled a cross-examination. The officer confronted the defendant with her inadmissible prewarning statements and pushed her to acknowledge them. (" 'Trice, didn't you tell me that he was supposed to die in his sleep?'"). This shows the temptations for abuse inherent in the two-step technique. Reference to the prewarning statement was an implicit suggestion that the mere repetition of the earlier statement was not independently incriminating. The implicit suggestion was false.

The technique used in this case distorts the meaning of *Miranda* and furthers no legitimate countervailing interest. * * * When an interrogator uses this deliberate, two-step strategy, predicated upon violating *Miranda* during an extended interview, postwarning statements that are related to the substance of prewarning statements must be excluded absent specific, curative steps.

The plurality concludes that whenever a two-stage interview occurs, admissibility of the postwarning statement should depend on "whether the *Miranda* warnings delivered midstream could have been effective enough to accomplish their object" given the specific facts of the case. This test envisions an objective inquiry from the perspective of the suspect, and applies in the case of both intentional and unintentional two-stage interrogations. In my view, this test cuts too broadly. *Miranda'* s clarity is one of its strengths, and a multifactor test that applies to every two-stage interrogation may serve to undermine that clarity. I would apply a narrower test applicable only in the infrequent case, such as we have here, in which the two-step interrogation technique was used in a calculated way to undermine the *Miranda* warning.

The admissibility of postwarning statements should continue to be governed by the principles of *Elstad* unless the deliberate two-step strategy was employed. If the deliberate two-step strategy has been used, postwarning statements that are related to the substance of prewarning statements must be excluded unless curative measures are taken before the postwarning statement is made. Curative measures should be designed to ensure that a reasonable person in the suspect's situation would understand the import and effect of the *Miranda* warning and of the *Miranda* waiver. For example, a substantial break in time and circumstances between the prewarning statement and the *Miranda* warning may suffice in most circumstances, as it allows the accused to distinguish the two contexts and appreciate that the interrogation has taken a new turn. Alternatively, an additional warning that explains the likely inadmissibility of the prewarning custodial statement may be sufficient. No curative steps were taken in this case, however, so the postwarning statements are inadmissible and the conviction cannot stand.

For these reasons, I concur in the judgment of the Court.

■ JUSTICE O'CONNOR, with whom THE CHIEF JUSTICE, JUSTICE SCALIA, and JUSTICE THOMAS join, dissenting.

The plurality devours *Oregon v. Elstad,* 470 U.S. 298, 105 S.Ct. 1285, 84 L.Ed.2d 222 (1985), even as it accuses petitioner's argument of "disfigur[ing]" that decision. I believe that we are bound by *Elstad* to reach a different result, and I would vacate the judgment of the Supreme Court of Missouri.

I

On two preliminary questions I am in full agreement with the plurality. First, the plurality appropriately follows *Elstad* in concluding that Seibert's statement cannot be held inadmissible under a "fruit of the poisonous tree" theory. Second, the plurality correctly declines to focus its analysis on the subjective intent of the interrogating officer.

* * *

* * * I [also] believe that the approach espoused by Justice KENNEDY is ill advised. Justice KENNEDY would extend *Miranda's* exclusionary rule to any case in which the use of the "two-step interrogation technique" was "deliberate" or "calculated." This approach untethers the analysis from facts knowable to, and therefore having any potential directly to affect, the suspect. Far from promoting "clarity," the approach will add a third step to the suppression inquiry. In virtually every two-stage interrogation case, in addition to addressing the standard *Miranda* and voluntariness questions, courts will be forced to conduct the kind of difficult, state-of-mind inquiry that we normally take pains to avoid.

II

The plurality's adherence to *Elstad,* and mine to the plurality, end there. Our decision in *Elstad* rejected * * * the argument that the "lingering compulsion" inherent in a defendant's having let the "cat out of the bag" required suppression. * * * [T]oday's plurality [reasons]: "[T]he coercive impact of the unconstitutionally obtained statement remains, because in a defendant's mind it has sealed his fate. It is this impact that must be dissipated in order to make a subsequent confession admissible."

We rejected this theory outright. We did so not because we refused to recognize the "psychological impact of the suspect's conviction that he has let the cat out of the bag," but because we refused to "endo[w]" those "psychological effects" with "constitutional implications." To do so, we said, would "effectively immuniz[e] a suspect who responds to pre-*Miranda* warning questions from the consequences of his subsequent informed waiver," an immunity that "comes at a high cost to legitimate law enforcement activity, while adding little desirable protection to the individual's interest in not being *compelled* to testify against himself." The plurality might very well think that we struck the balance between Fifth

Amendment rights and law enforcement interests incorrectly in *Elstad;* but that is not normally a sufficient reason for ignoring the dictates of *stare decisis.*

I would analyze the two-step interrogation procedure under the voluntariness standards central to the Fifth Amendment and reiterated in *Elstad. Elstad* commands that if Seibert's first statement is shown to have been involuntary, the court must examine whether the taint dissipated through the passing of time or a change in circumstances: "When a prior statement is actually coerced, the time that passes between confessions, the change in place of interrogations, and the change in identity of the interrogators all bear on whether that coercion has carried over into the second confession." In addition, Seibert's second statement should be suppressed if she showed that it was involuntary despite the *Miranda* warnings. Although I would leave this analysis for the Missouri courts to conduct on remand, I note that, unlike the officers in *Elstad,* Officer Hanrahan referred to Seibert's unwarned statement during the second part of the interrogation when she made a statement at odds with her unwarned confession. ("'Trice, didn't you tell me that he was supposed to die in his sleep?"). Such a tactic may bear on the voluntariness inquiry.

* * *

Because I believe that the plurality gives insufficient deference to *Elstad* and that Justice KENNEDY places improper weight on subjective intent, I respectfully dissent.

6. Legislative "Modification" of *Miranda*

Page 488. Insert the following case after United States v. Dickerson:

Dickerson v. United States

Supreme Court of the United States, 2000.
530 U.S. 428, 120 S.Ct. 2326, 147 L.Ed.2d 405.

■ Chief Justice Rehnquist delivered the opinion of the Court.

In Miranda v. Arizona, 384 U.S. 436, 86 S.Ct. 1602, 16 L.Ed.2d 694 (1966), we held that certain warnings must be given before a suspect's statement made during custodial interrogation could be admitted in evidence. In the wake of that decision, Congress enacted 18 U.S.C. § 3501, which in essence laid down a rule that the admissibility of such statements should turn only on whether or not they were voluntarily made. We hold that *Miranda*, being a constitutional decision of this Court, may not be in effect overruled by an Act of Congress, and we decline to overrule *Miranda* ourselves. We therefore hold that *Miranda* and its progeny in this Court govern the admissibility of statements made during custodial interrogation in both state and federal courts.

Petitioner Dickerson was indicted for bank robbery, conspiracy to commit bank robbery, and using a firearm in the course of committing a crime of violence, all in violation of the applicable provisions of Title 18 of the United States Code. Before trial, Dickerson moved to suppress a statement he had made at a Federal Bureau of Investigation field office, on the grounds that he had not received *"Miranda* warnings" before being interrogated. The District Court granted his motion to suppress, and the Government took an interlocutory appeal to the United States Court of Appeals for the Fourth Circuit. That court, by a divided vote, reversed the District Court's suppression order. * * *

Because of the importance of the questions raised by the Court of Appeals' decision, we granted certiorari, and now reverse.

We begin with a brief historical account of the law governing the admission of confessions. Prior to *Miranda*, we evaluated the admissibility of a suspect's confession under a voluntariness test. The roots of this test developed in the common law, as the courts of England and then the United States recognized that coerced confessions are inherently untrustworthy. * * * Over time, our cases recognized two constitutional bases for the requirement that a confession be voluntary to be admitted into evidence: the Fifth Amendment right against self-incrimination and the Due Process Clause of the Fourteenth Amendment.

[F]or the middle third of the 20th century our cases based the rule against admitting coerced confessions primarily, if not exclusively, on notions of due process. * * * Those cases refined the test into an inquiry that examines "whether a defendant's will was overborne" by the circumstances surrounding the giving of a confession. The due process test takes into consideration "the totality of all the surrounding circumstances—both the characteristics of the accused and the details of the interrogation." * * *

We have never abandoned this due process jurisprudence, and thus continue to exclude confessions that were obtained involuntarily. But our decisions in Malloy v. Hogan, 378 U.S. 1, 84 S.Ct. 1489, 12 L.Ed.2d 653 (1964), and *Miranda* changed the focus of much of the inquiry in determining the admissibility of suspects' incriminating statements. In *Malloy*, we held that the Fifth Amendment's Self–Incrimination Clause is incorporated in the Due Process Clause of the Fourteenth Amendment and thus applies to the States. We decided *Miranda* on the heels of *Malloy*.

* * *

Two years after *Miranda* was decided, Congress enacted § 3501. * * *

Given § 3501's express designation of voluntariness as the touchstone of admissibility, its omission of any warning requirement, and the instruction for trial courts to consider a nonexclusive list of factors relevant to the circumstances of a confession, we agree with the Court of Appeals that Congress intended by its enactment to overrule *Miranda*. Because of the obvious conflict between our decision in *Miranda* and § 3501, we must address whether Congress has constitutional authority to thus supersede *Miranda*. If Congress has such authority, § 3501's totality-of-the-circumstances approach must prevail over *Miranda's* requirement of warnings; if not, that section must yield to *Miranda's* more specific requirements.

The law in this area is clear. This Court has supervisory authority over the federal courts, and we may use that authority to prescribe rules of evidence and procedure that are binding in those tribunals. However, the power to judicially create and enforce nonconstitutional "rules of procedure and evidence for the federal courts exists only in the absence of a relevant Act of Congress." Congress retains the ultimate authority to modify or set aside any judicially created rules of evidence and procedure that are not required by the Constitution.

But Congress may not legislatively supersede our decisions interpreting and applying the Constitution. This case therefore turns on whether the *Miranda* Court announced a constitutional rule or merely exercised its supervisory authority to regulate evidence in the absence of congressional direction. * * * [T]he Court of Appeals concluded that the protections announced in *Miranda* are not constitutionally required.

We disagree with the Court of Appeals' conclusion, although we concede that there is language in some of our opinions that supports the view taken by that court. But first and foremost of the factors on the other side—that *Miranda* is a constitutional decision—is that both *Miranda* and two of its companion cases applied the rule to proceedings in state courts—to wit, Arizona, California, and New York. Since that time, we have consistently applied *Miranda's* rule to prosecutions arising in state courts. With respect to proceedings in state courts, our "authority is limited to enforcing the commands of the United States Constitution."

The *Miranda* opinion itself begins by stating that the Court granted certiorari "to explore some facets of the problems ... of applying the privilege against self-incrimination to in-custody interrogation, *and to give concrete constitutional guidelines for law enforcement agencies and courts to follow*." (emphasis added). In fact, the majority opinion is replete with statements indicating that the majority thought it was announcing a constitutional rule. * * *

Additional support for our conclusion that *Miranda* is constitutionally based is found in the *Miranda* Court's invitation for legislative action to protect the constitutional right against coerced self-incrimination. After discussing the "compelling pressures" inherent in custodial police interrogation, the *Miranda* Court concluded that, "[i]n order to combat these pressures and to permit a full opportunity to exercise the privilege against self-incrimination, the accused must be adequately and effectively appraised of his rights and the exercise of those rights must be fully honored." However, the Court emphasized that it could not foresee "the potential alternatives for protecting the privilege which might be devised by

Congress or the States," and it accordingly opined that the Constitution would not preclude legislative solutions that differed from the prescribed *Miranda* warnings but which were "at least as effective in apprising accused persons of their right of silence and in assuring a continuous opportunity to exercise it."[11]

The Court of Appeals also relied on the fact that we have, after our *Miranda* decision, made exceptions from its rule * * *. But we have also broadened the application of the *Miranda* doctrine * * *. These decisions illustrate the principle—not that *Miranda* is not a constitutional rule—but that no constitutional rule is immutable. No court laying down a general rule can possibly foresee the various circumstances in which counsel will seek to apply it, and the sort of modifications represented by these cases are as much a normal part of constitutional law as the original decision.

The Court of Appeals also noted that in Oregon v. Elstad, 470 U.S. 298, 105 S.Ct. 1285, 84 L.Ed.2d 222 (1985), we stated that " '[t]he *Miranda* exclusionary rule . . . serves the Fifth Amendment and sweeps more broadly than the Fifth Amendment itself.' " Our decision in that case—refusing to apply the traditional "fruits" doctrine developed in Fourth Amendment cases—does not prove that *Miranda* is a nonconstitutional decision, but simply recognizes the fact that unreasonable searches under the Fourth Amendment are different from unwarned interrogation under the Fifth Amendment.

As an alternative argument for sustaining the Court of Appeals' decision, the court-invited *amicus curiae*[12] contends that the section complies with the requirement that a legislative alternative to *Miranda* be equally as effective in preventing coerced confessions. See Brief for Paul G. Cassell as Amicus Curiae 28–39. We agree with the *amicus'* contention that there are more remedies available for abusive police conduct than there were at the time *Miranda* was decided. But we do not agree that these additional measures supplement § 3501's protections sufficiently to meet the constitutional minimum. *Miranda* requires procedures that will warn a suspect in custody of his right to remain silent and which will assure the suspect that the exercise of that right will be honored. * * * § 3501 explicitly eschews a requirement of pre-interrogation warnings in favor of an approach that looks to the administration of such warnings as only one factor in determining the voluntariness of a suspect's confession. The additional remedies cited by *amicus* do not, in our view, render them,

---

11. The Court of Appeals relied in part on our statement that the *Miranda* decision in no way "creates a 'constitutional straight-jacket.' " However, a review of our opinion in *Miranda* clarifies that this disclaimer was intended to indicate that the Constitution does not require police to administer the particular *Miranda* warnings, not that the Constitution does not require a procedure that is effective in securing Fifth Amendment rights.

12. Because no party to the underlying litigation argued in favor of § 3501's constitutionality in this Court, we invited Professor Paul Cassell to assist our deliberations by arguing in support of the judgment below.

together with § 3501 an adequate substitute for the warnings required by *Miranda*.

The dissent argues that it is judicial overreaching for this Court to hold § 3501 unconstitutional unless we hold that the *Miranda* warnings are required by the Constitution, in the sense that nothing else will suffice to satisfy constitutional requirements. But we need not go farther than *Miranda* to decide this case. In *Miranda*, the Court noted that reliance on the traditional totality-of-the-circumstances test raised a risk of overlooking an involuntary custodial confession, a risk that the Court found unacceptably great when the confession is offered in the case in chief to prove guilt. The Court therefore concluded that something more than the totality test was necessary. As discussed above, § 3501 reinstates the totality test as sufficient. Section 3501 therefore cannot be sustained if *Miranda* is to remain the law.

Whether or not we would agree with *Miranda's* reasoning and its resulting rule, were we addressing the issue in the first instance, the principles of *stare decisis* weigh heavily against overruling it now. While " 'stare decisis is not an inexorable command,' " particularly when we are interpreting the Constitution, "even in constitutional cases, the doctrine carries such persuasive force that we have always required a departure from precedent to be supported by some 'special justification.' "

We do not think there is such justification for overruling *Miranda*. *Miranda* has become embedded in routine police practice to the point where the warnings have become part of our national culture. While we have overruled our precedents when subsequent cases have undermined their doctrinal underpinnings, we do not believe that this has happened to the *Miranda* decision. If anything, our subsequent cases have reduced the impact of the *Miranda* rule on legitimate law enforcement while reaffirming the decision's core ruling that unwarned statements may not be used as evidence in the prosecution's case in chief.

The disadvantage of the *Miranda* rule is that statements which may be by no means involuntary, made by a defendant who is aware of his "rights," may nonetheless be excluded and a guilty defendant go free as a result. But experience suggests that the totality-of-the-circumstances test which § 3501 seeks to revive is more difficult than *Miranda* for law enforcement officers to conform to, and for courts to apply in a consistent manner. The requirement that *Miranda* warnings be given does not, of course, dispense with the voluntariness inquiry. But as we said in Berkemer v. McCarty, 468 U.S. 420, 104 S.Ct. 3138, 82 L.Ed.2d 317 (1984), "[c]ases in which a defendant can make a colorable argument that a self-incriminating statement was 'compelled' despite the fact that the law enforcement authorities adhered to the dictates of *Miranda* are rare."

In sum, we conclude that *Miranda* announced a constitutional rule that Congress may not supersede legislatively. Following the rule of *stare decisis*, we decline to overrule *Miranda* ourselves. The judgment of the Court of Appeals is therefore

Reversed.

■ JUSTICE SCALIA, with whom JUSTICE THOMAS joins, dissenting.

Those to whom judicial decisions are an unconnected series of judgments that produce either favored or disfavored results will doubtless greet today's decision as a paragon of moderation, since it declines to overrule Miranda v. Arizona, 384 U.S. 436, 86 S.Ct. 1602, 16 L.Ed.2d 694 (1966). Those who understand the judicial process will appreciate that today's decision is not a reaffirmation of *Miranda*, but a radical revision of the most significant element of *Miranda* (as of all cases): the rationale that gives it a permanent place in our jurisprudence.

Marbury v. Madison, 1 Cranch 137, 2 L.Ed. 60 (1803), held that an Act of Congress will not be enforced by the courts if what it prescribes violates the Constitution of the United States. That was the basis on which *Miranda* was decided. One will search today's opinion in vain, however, for a statement (surely simple enough to make) that what 18 U.S.C. § 3501 prescribes—the use at trial of a voluntary confession, even when a *Miranda* warning or its equivalent has failed to be given—violates the Constitution. The reason the statement does not appear is not only (and perhaps not so much) that it would be absurd, inasmuch as § 3501 excludes from trial precisely what the Constitution excludes from trial, viz., compelled confessions; but also that Justices whose votes are needed to compose today's majority are on record as believing that a violation of *Miranda* is not a violation of the Constitution. And so, to justify today's agreed-upon result, the Court must adopt a significant new, if not entirely comprehensible, principle of constitutional law. As the Court chooses to describe that principle, statutes of Congress can be disregarded, not only when what they prescribe violates the Constitution, but when what they prescribe contradicts a decision of this Court that "announced a constitutional rule." As I shall discuss in some detail, the only thing that can possibly mean in the context of this case is that this Court has the power, not merely to apply the Constitution but to expand it, imposing what it regards as useful "prophylactic" restrictions upon Congress and the States. That is an immense and frightening antidemocratic power, and it does not exist.

It takes only a small step to bring today's opinion out of the realm of power-judging and into the mainstream of legal reasoning: The Court need only go beyond its carefully couched iterations that "*Miranda* is a constitutional decision," that "*Miranda* is constitutionally based," that *Miranda* has "constitutional underpinnings," and come out and say quite clearly: "We reaffirm today that custodial interrogation that is not preceded by *Miranda* warnings or their equivalent violates the Constitution of the United States." It cannot say that, because a majority of the Court does not believe it. The Court therefore acts in plain violation of the Constitution when it denies effect to this Act of Congress.

I

Early in this Nation's history, this Court established the sound proposition that constitutional government in a system of separated powers requires judges to regard as inoperative any legislative act, even of Congress itself, that is "repugnant to the Constitution." * * * The power we recognized in *Marbury* will thus permit us, indeed require us, to "disregar[d]" § 3501, a duly enacted statute governing the admissibility of evidence in the federal courts, only if it "be in opposition to the constitution"—here, assertedly, the dictates of the Fifth Amendment.

It was once possible to characterize the so-called *Miranda* rule as resting (however implausibly) upon the proposition that what the statute here before us permits—the admission at trial of un-*Mirandized* confessions—violates the Constitution. That is the fairest reading of the *Miranda* case itself. The Court began by announcing that the Fifth Amendment privilege against self-incrimination applied in the context of extrajudicial custodial interrogation—itself a doubtful proposition as a matter both of history and precedent. Having extended the privilege into the confines of the station house, the Court liberally sprinkled throughout its sprawling 60–page opinion suggestions that, because of the compulsion inherent in custodial interrogation, the privilege was violated by any statement thus obtained that did not conform to the rules set forth in *Miranda*, or some functional equivalent. * * *

So understood, *Miranda* was objectionable for innumerable reasons, not least the fact that cases spanning more than 70 years had rejected its core premise that, absent the warnings and an effective waiver of the right to remain silent and of the (thitherto unknown) right to have an attorney present, a statement obtained pursuant to custodial interrogation was necessarily the product of compulsion. Moreover, history and precedent aside, the decision in *Miranda*, if read as an explication of what the Constitution requires, is preposterous. There is, for example, simply no basis in reason for concluding that a response to the very first question asked, by a suspect who already knows all of the rights described in the *Miranda* warning, is anything other than a volitional act. And even if one assumes that the elimination of compulsion absolutely requires informing even the most knowledgeable suspect of his right to remain silent, it cannot conceivably require the right to have counsel present. There is a world of difference, which the Court recognized under the traditional voluntariness test but ignored in *Miranda*, between compelling a suspect to incriminate himself and preventing him from foolishly doing so of his own accord. Only the latter (which is not required by the Constitution) could explain the Court's inclusion of a right to counsel and the requirement that it, too, be knowingly and intelligently waived. Counsel's presence is not required to tell the suspect that he need not speak; the interrogators can do that. The only good reason for having counsel there is that he can be counted on to advise the suspect that he should not speak.

Preventing foolish (rather than compelled) confessions is likewise the only conceivable basis for the rules * * * that courts must exclude any confession elicited by questioning conducted, without interruption, after the suspect has indicated a desire to stand on his right to remain silent, or initiated by police after the suspect has expressed a desire to have counsel present. Nonthreatening attempts to persuade the suspect to reconsider that initial decision are not, without more, enough to render a change of heart the product of anything other than the suspect's free will. Thus, what is most remarkable about the *Miranda* decision—and what made it unacceptable as a matter of straightforward constitutional interpretation in the *Marbury* tradition—is its palpable hostility toward the act of confession *per se*, rather than toward what the Constitution abhors, compelled confession. The Constitution is not, unlike the *Miranda* majority, offended by a criminal's commendable qualm of conscience or fortunate fit of stupidity.

For these reasons, and others more than adequately developed in the *Miranda* dissents and in the subsequent works of the decision's many critics, any conclusion that a violation of the *Miranda* rules necessarily amounts to a violation of the privilege against compelled self-incrimination can claim no support in history, precedent, or common sense, and as a result would at least presumptively be worth reconsidering even at this late date. But that is unnecessary, since the Court has (thankfully) long since abandoned the notion that failure to comply with *Miranda's* rules is itself a violation of the Constitution.

II

As the Court today acknowledges, since *Miranda* we have explicitly, and repeatedly, interpreted that decision as having announced, not the circumstances in which custodial interrogation runs afoul of the Fifth or Fourteenth Amendment, but rather only "prophylactic" rules that go beyond the right against compelled self-incrimination. * * *

In light of these cases, and our statements to the same effect in others, it is simply no longer possible for the Court to conclude, even if it wanted to, that a violation of *Miranda's* rules is a violation of the Constitution. But * * * that is what is required before the Court may disregard a law of Congress governing the admissibility of evidence in federal court. The Court today insists that the decision in *Miranda* is a "constitutional" one; that it has "constitutional underpinnings"; a "constitutional basis" and a "constitutional origin"; that it was "constitutionally based"; and that it announced a "constitutional rule." It is fine to play these word games; but what makes a decision "constitutional" in the only sense relevant here—in the sense that renders it impervious to supersession by congressional legislation such as § 3501—is the determination that the Constitution requires the result that the decision announces and the statute ignores. By disregarding congressional action that concededly does not violate the Constitution, the Court flagrantly offends fundamental principles of separation of powers, and arrogates to itself prerogatives reserved to the representatives of the people.

The Court seeks to avoid this conclusion in two ways: First, by misdescribing these post-*Miranda* cases as mere dicta. The Court concedes only "that there is language in some of our opinions that supports the view" that *Miranda's* protections are not "constitutionally required." It is not a matter of *language*; it is a matter of *holdings*. The proposition that failure to comply with *Miranda's* rules does not establish a constitutional violation was central to the holdings of [Michigan v. Tucker, 417 U.S. 433, 94 S.Ct. 2357, 41 L.Ed.2d 182 (1974), Oregon v. Hass, 420 U.S. 714, 95 S.Ct. 1215, 43 L.Ed.2d 570 (1975), New York v. Quarles, 467 U.S. 649, 104 S.Ct. 2626, 81 L.Ed.2d 550 (1984) and Oregon v. Elstad, 470 U.S. 298, 105 S.Ct. 1285, 84 L.Ed.2d 222 (1985)].

The second way the Court seeks to avoid the impact of these cases is simply to disclaim responsibility for reasoned decisionmaking. It says:

"These decisions illustrate the principle—not that *Miranda* is not a constitutional rule—but that no constitutional rule is immutable. No court laying down a general rule can possibly foresee the various circumstances in which counsel will seek to apply it, and the sort of modifications represented by these cases are as much a normal part of constitutional law as the original decision."

The issue, however, is not whether court rules are "mutable"; they assuredly are. It is not whether, in the light of "various circumstances," they can be "modifi[ed]"; they assuredly can. The issue is whether, *as mutated and modified*, they must *make sense*. The requirement that they do so is the only thing that prevents this Court from being some sort of nine-headed Caesar, giving thumbs-up or thumbs-down to whatever outcome, case by case, suits or offends its collective fancy. And if confessions procured in violation of *Miranda* are confessions "compelled" in violation of the Constitution, [many] post-*Miranda* decisions [permitting the use of such confessions] * * * do not make sense. The only reasoned basis for their outcome was that a violation of *Miranda* is not a violation of the Constitution. * * *

Finally, the Court asserts that *Miranda* must be a "constitutional decision" announcing a "constitutional rule," and thus immune to congressional modification, because we have since its inception applied it to the States. If this argument is meant as an invocation of *stare decisis*, it fails because, though it is true that our cases applying *Miranda* against the States must be reconsidered if *Miranda* is not required by the Constitution, it is likewise true that our cases * * * based on the principle that *Miranda* is *not* required by the Constitution will have to be reconsidered if it *is*. So the *stare decisis* argument is a wash. If, on the other hand, the argument is meant as an appeal to logic rather than *stare decisis*, it is a classic example of begging the question: Congress's attempt to set aside *Miranda*, since it represents an assertion that violation of *Miranda* is not a violation of the

Constitution, also represents an assertion that the Court has no power to impose *Miranda* on the States. To answer this assertion—not by showing why violation of *Miranda* is a violation of the Constitution—but by asserting that *Miranda* does apply against the States, is to assume precisely the point at issue. In my view, our continued application of the *Miranda* code to the States despite our consistent statements that running afoul of its dictates does not necessarily—or even usually—result in an actual constitutional violation, represents not the source of *Miranda's* salvation but rather evidence of its ultimate illegitimacy. * * *

III

There was available to the Court a means of reconciling the established proposition that a violation of *Miranda* does not itself offend the Fifth Amendment with the Court's assertion of a right to ignore the present statute. That means of reconciliation was argued strenuously by both petitioner and the United States, who were evidently more concerned than the Court is with maintaining the coherence of our jurisprudence. It is not mentioned in the Court's opinion because, I assume, a majority of the Justices intent on reversing believes that incoherence is the lesser evil. They may be right.

Petitioner and the United States contend that there is nothing at all exceptional, much less unconstitutional, about the Court's adopting prophylactic rules to buttress constitutional rights, and enforcing them against Congress and the States. Indeed, the United States argues that "[p]rophylactic rules are now and have been for many years a feature of this Court's constitutional adjudication." That statement is not wholly inaccurate, if by "many years" one means since the mid–1960's. However, in their zeal to validate what is in my view a lawless practice, the United States and petitioner greatly overstate the frequency with which we have engaged in it. * * *

[P]etitioner's and the United States' suggestions to the contrary notwithstanding, what the Court did in *Miranda* (assuming, as later cases hold, that *Miranda* went beyond what the Constitution actually requires) is in fact extraordinary. That the Court has, on rare and recent occasion, repeated the mistake does not transform error into truth, but illustrates the potential for future mischief that the error entails. Where the Constitution has wished to lodge in one of the branches of the Federal Government some limited power to supplement its guarantees, it has said so. See Amdt. 14, § 5 ("The Congress shall have power to enforce, by appropriate legislation, the provisions of this article"). The power with which the Court would endow itself under a "prophylactic" justification for *Miranda* goes far beyond what it has permitted Congress to do under authority of that text. Whereas we have insisted that congressional action under § 5 of the Fourteenth Amendment must be "congruent" with, and "proportional" to, a constitutional violation, the *Miranda* nontextual power to embellish confers authority to prescribe preventive measures against not only constitutionally prohibited compelled confessions, but also * * * foolhardy ones.

I applaud, therefore, the refusal of the Justices in the majority to enunciate this boundless doctrine of judicial empowerment as a means of rendering today's decision rational. In nonetheless joining the Court's judgment, however, they overlook two truisms: that actions speak louder than silence, and that (in judge-made law at least) logic will out. Since there is in fact no other principle that can reconcile today's judgment with the post-*Miranda* cases that the Court refuses to abandon, what today's decision will stand for, whether the Justices can bring themselves to say it or not, is the power of the Supreme Court to write a prophylactic, extraconstitutional Constitution, binding on Congress and the States.

IV

Thus, while I agree with the Court that § 3501 cannot be upheld without also concluding that *Miranda* represents an illegitimate exercise of our authority to review state-court judgments, I do not share the Court's hesitation in reaching that conclusion. * * *

Neither am I persuaded by the argument for retaining *Miranda* that touts its supposed workability as compared with the totality-of-the-circumstances test it purported to replace. *Miranda's* proponents cite *ad nauseam* the fact that the Court was called upon to make difficult and subtle distinctions in applying the "voluntariness" test in some 30–odd due process "coerced confessions" cases in the 30 years between Brown v. Mississippi, 297 U.S. 278, 56 S.Ct. 461, 80 L.Ed. 682 (1936), and *Miranda*. It is not immediately apparent, however, that the judicial burden has been eased by the "bright-line" rules adopted in *Miranda*. In fact, in the 34 years since *Miranda* was decided, this Court has been called upon to decide nearly 60 cases involving a host of *Miranda* issues * * *.

Moreover, it is not clear why the Court thinks that the "totality-of-the-circumstances test ... is more difficult than *Miranda* for law enforcement officers to conform to, and for courts to apply in a consistent manner." Indeed, I find myself persuaded by Justice O'Connor's rejection of this same argument in her opinion in [Withrow v. Williams, 507 U.S. 680, 711, 113 S.Ct. 1745, 123 L.Ed.2d 407 (1993)] (O'Connor, J., joined by Rehnquist, C. J., concurring in part and dissenting in part):

> "*Miranda*, for all its alleged brightness, is not without its difficulties; and voluntariness is not without its strengths.... *Miranda* creates as many close questions as it resolves. The task of determining whether a defendant is in 'custody' has proved to be 'a slippery one.' And the supposedly 'bright' lines that separate interrogation from spontaneous declaration, the exercise of a right from waiver, and the adequate warning from the inadequate, likewise have turned out to be rather dim and ill defined. The totality-of-the-circumstances approach, on the other hand, permits each fact to be taken into account without resort

to formal and dispositive labels. By dispensing with the difficulty of producing a yes-or-no answer to questions that are often better answered in shades and degrees, *the voluntariness inquiry often can make judicial decisionmaking easier rather than more onerous.*" (Emphasis added; citations omitted.)

But even were I to agree that the old totality-of-the-circumstances test was more cumbersome, it is simply not true that *Miranda* has banished it from the law and replaced it with a new test. Under the current regime, which the Court today retains in its entirety, courts are frequently called upon to undertake *both* inquiries. That is because, as explained earlier, voluntariness remains the *constitutional* standard, and as such continues to govern the admissibility for impeachment purposes of statements taken in violation of *Miranda*, the admissibility of the "fruits" of such statements, and the admissibility of statements challenged as unconstitutionally obtained despite the interrogator's compliance with *Miranda*.

Finally, I am not convinced by petitioner's argument that *Miranda* should be preserved because the decision occupies a special place in the "public's consciousness." As far as I am aware, the public is not under the illusion that we are infallible. I see little harm in admitting that we made a mistake in taking away from the people the ability to decide for themselves what protections (beyond those required by the Constitution) are reasonably affordable in the criminal investigatory process. And I see much to be gained by reaffirming for the people the wonderful reality that they govern themselves—which means that "[t]he powers not delegated to the United States by the Constitution" that the people adopted, "nor prohibited . . . to the States" by that Constitution, "are reserved to the States respectively, or to the people," U.S. Const., Amdt. 10.

* * *

Today's judgment converts *Miranda* from a milestone of judicial overreaching into the very Cheops' Pyramid (or perhaps the Sphinx would be a better analogue) of judicial arrogance. In imposing its Court-made code upon the States, the original opinion at least asserted that it was demanded by the Constitution. Today's decision does not pretend that it is—and yet still asserts the right to impose it against the will of the people's representatives in Congress. Far from believing that *stare decisis* compels this result, I believe we cannot allow to remain on the books even a celebrated decision—especially a celebrated decision—that has come to stand for the proposition that the Supreme Court has power to impose extraconstitutional constraints upon Congress and the States. This is not the system that was established by the Framers, or that would be established by any sane supporter of government by the people.

I dissent from today's decision, and, until § 3501 is repealed, will continue to apply it in all cases where there has been a sustainable finding that the defendant's confession was voluntary.

Page 490. Add the following to Note 3 after *Dickerson*:

After extensive discussion, the Supreme Court of New Jersey refused to hold that recording was required by constitutional considerations. State v. Cook, 179 N.J. 533, 847 A.2d 530 (2004). It did, however, state:

> The judiciary bears the "responsibility to guarantee the proper administration of justice . . . and, particularly, the administration of criminal justice." Our courts thus have the "independent obligation . . . to take all appropriate measures to ensure the fair and proper administration of a criminal trial." Where such appropriate measures are available, they should be employed to the fullest extent feasible to enhance the fairness of proceedings.
>
> The proverbial "time has arrived" for this Court to evaluate fully the protections that electronic recordation affords to both the State and to criminal defendants. That inquiry should include whether to encourage electronic recordation through the use of a presumption against admissibility of a non-recorded statement, or other means. Those considerations are important and nuanced, and should be addressed in a context broader than that permitted in any one criminal appeal. The balancing of interests will require careful and deliberate study if we are to be successful in securing to the judicial system, law enforcement, and defendants the benefits of recordation without unduly hampering the legitimate needs of law enforcement. We believe that the criminal justice system will be well served if our supervisory authority is brought to bear on this issue and we will exercise that authority mindful of the various interests involved. Accordingly, we will establish a committee to study and make recommendations on the use of electronic recordation of custodial interrogations.

179 N.J. at 546–47, 847 A.2d at 561–62. See also, Clark v. State, 374 Ark. 292, 287 S.W.3d 567 (2008) (exercising supervisory authority, court refers the "practicability" of adopting rule concerning electronic recording of statements to Committee on Criminal Practice for study and consideration).

The Dallas, Texas police department decided to begin videotaping statements by homicide suspects, but only after training sessions for the detectives conducted by prosecutors. "[V]ideotapes, particularly of hours of interrogation leading up to a confession, can backfire on a detective who isn't trained to understand fully how their behavior will appear to jurors." Another person interviewed explained the need for training by commenting, "Some interrogators are more professional than others." Jason Trehan, Police to videotape confessions, *Dallas Morning News*, May 30, 2005, p. 9A.

Page 490. Add the following new Note after *Dickerson*:

4. **Recording Statute.** Illinois has enacted a statute, effective in 2005, providing as follows:

> § 103–2.1. When statements by accused may be used.
>
> * * *
>
> (b) An oral, written, or sign language statement of an accused made as a result of a custodial interrogation at a police station or other place of detention shall be presumed to be inadmissible as evidence against the accused in any criminal proceeding * * * unless:

(1) an electronic recording is made of the custodial interrogation; and

(2) the recording is substantially accurate and not intentionally altered.

* * *

(d) If the court finds, by a preponderance of the evidence, that the defendant was subjected to a custodial interrogation in violation of this Section, then any statements made by the defendant during or following that non-recorded custodial interrogation, even if otherwise in compliance with this Section, are presumed to be inadmissible in any criminal proceeding against the defendant except for the purposes of impeachment.

(e) Nothing in this Section precludes the admission * * * of a statement made during a custodial interrogation by a suspect who requests, prior to making the statement, to respond to the interrogator's questions only if an electronic recording is not made of the statement, provided that an electronic recording is made of the statement of agreeing to respond to the interrogator's question, only if a recording is not made of the statement * * *. Nothing in this Section precludes the admission of a statement, otherwise inadmissible under this Section, that is used only for impeachment and not as substantive evidence.

(f) The presumption of inadmissibility of a statement made by a suspect at a custodial interrogation at a police station or other place of detention may be overcome by a preponderance of the evidence that the statement was voluntarily given and is reliable, based on the totality of the circumstances.

* * *

In response to *Cook*, discussed in note 3, the New Jersey Supreme Court adopted New Jersey Court Rule 3:17 requiring recording. State v. Delgado, 188 N.J. 48, 62–63, 902 A.2d 888, 896 (2006). Regarding the effect of law enforcement's failure to record a statement, the rule provides:

(d) The failure to electronically record a defendant's custodial interrogation in a place of detention shall be a factor for consideration by the trial court in determining the admissibility of a statement, and by the jury in determining whether the statement was made, and if so, what weight, if any, to give to the statement.

(e) In the absence of an electronic recordation required under [this rule], the court shall, upon request of the defendant, provide the jury with a cautionary instruction.

C.   SIXTH AMENDMENT RIGHT TO COUNSEL

Page 492.   Insert the following in the Editors' Introduction after the first paragraph beginning on this page:

In Rothgery v. Gillespie County, 554 U.S. 191, 128 S.Ct. 2578, 71 L.Ed.2d 366 (2008), the Court held that the Sixth Amendment attached when: (1) the defendant had been arrested; (2) a peace officer filed with a magistrate a sworn document that recited that the defendant was charged with a specified felony; (3) the defendant appeared before the magistrate; (4) the magistrate informed the defendant of the charge against him and set bail; and (5) the defendant was jailed until he posted the bail set. In this situation, the appearance before the magistrate reflected the initiation of adversary judicial proceedings. The Court explicitly rejected that the Sixth Amendment attached only if a prosecutor was involved in, or at least aware of, the proceedings.

Does the Sixth Amendment attach if no document referring to a charge offense has been filed? *Rothgery* purported to simply apply what the Court described as its holdings that "the right to counsel guaranteed by the Sixth Amendment applies in the first appearance before a judicial officer at which a defendant is told of the formal accusation against him and restrictions are imposed on his liberty." Later, the Court observed that "an accusation filed with a judicial officer is sufficiently formal," at least "when the accusation prompts arraignment and restrictions on the accused's liberty to facilitate the prosecution."

Page 494. Insert the following in the Editors' Introduction after the third paragraph beginning on this page:

Sixth Amendment Edwards *Rule and Intertwined Offenses.* The offense for which officers approached McNeil was apparently unrelated to that on which his Sixth Amendment right to counsel had attached. Texas v. Cobb, 532 U.S. 162, 121 S.Ct. 1335, 149 L.Ed.2d 321 (2001), addressed the effect of *McNeil* where the offenses as to which the Sixth Amendment right to counsel has attached and that for which officers reapproach the suspect are related or "intertwined." In *Cobb*, a mother and her young daughter were reported missing after their residence was burglarized. Cobb was indicted for the burglary and accepted appointed counsel. Officers approached him and questioned him about the murders of the mother and her daughter; he admitted the killings. His confession was used in his prosecution for the capital murder of more than one person in a single transaction. Cobb's Sixth Amendment right to counsel had attached on the burglary charge, the state court reasoned. Because the murders were closely related factually to—or "factually interwoven with"—the burglary, the Sixth Amendment attached regarding those offenses as well. Since the police had not obtained counsel's permission to approach Cobb without counsel's presence, the state tribunal concluded, the confession was obtained in violation of the Sixth Amendment, and its use required reversal of the conviction.

The Supreme Court reversed, holding Cobb's confession admissible. *McNeil* "meant what it said"—"that the Sixth Amendment is 'offense specific.' " But the Court added:

> Although it is clear that the Sixth Amendment right to counsel attaches only to charged offenses, we have recognized in other contexts that the definition of an "offense" is not necessarily limited to the four

corners of a charging instrument. In *Blockburger v. United States,* 284 U.S. 299, 52 S.Ct. 180, 76 L.Ed. 306 (1932), we explained that "where the same act or transaction constitutes a violation of two distinct statutory provisions, the test to be applied to determine whether there are two offenses or only one, is whether each provision requires proof of a fact which the other does not." We have since applied the *Blockburger* test to delineate the scope of the Fifth Amendment's Double Jeopardy Clause, which prevents multiple or successive prosecutions for the "same offence." We see no constitutional difference between the meaning of the term "offense" in the contexts of double jeopardy and of the right to counsel. Accordingly, we hold that when the Sixth Amendment right to counsel attaches, it does encompass offenses that, even if not formally charged, would be considered the same offense under the *Blockburger* test.

532 U.S. at 172–73, 121 S.Ct. at 1343, 149 L.Ed.2d at 331–32. Burglary requires proof of entry into or remaining in premises and capital murder does not; capital murder requires proof of killing more than one person and burglary does not. Therefore, the murders were not the same offense as the burglary and the fact that Cobb's Sixth Amendment right to counsel had attached to the burglary charge did not mean it also attached on the murder charge. Consequently, Cobb had no Sixth Amendment right implicated by the officers' approach concerning the murders.

Four members of the Court dissented:

We can, and should, define "offense" in terms of the conduct that constitutes the crime that the offender committed on a particular occasion, including criminal acts that are "closely related to" or "inextricably intertwined with" the particular crime set forth in the charging instrument.

532 U.S. at 186, 121 S.Ct. at 1350, 149 L.Ed.2d at 340 (BREYER, J., dissenting). The Texas court, he added, properly determined that the murders were closely related to the burglary. Continuing, the dissenters criticized the majority's approach:

The majority's rule permits law enforcement officials to question those charged with a crime without first approaching counsel, through the simple device of asking questions about any other related crime not actually charged in the indictment. Thus, the police could ask the individual charged with robbery about, say, the assault of the cashier not yet charged, or about any other uncharged offense (unless under *Blockburger's* definition it counts as the "same crime"), all *without notifying counsel.* Indeed, the majority's rule would permit law enforcement officials to question anyone charged with any crime in any one of the examples just given about his or her conduct on the single relevant occasion without notifying counsel unless the prosecutor has charged every possible crime arising out of that same brief course of conduct.

532 U.S. at 182–83, 121 S.Ct. at 1348, 149 L.Ed.2d at 338. The majority responded:

> The dissent seems to presuppose that officers will possess complete knowledge of the circumstances surrounding an incident, such that the officers will be able to tailor their investigation to avoid addressing factually related offenses. Such an assumption, however, ignores the reality that police often are not yet aware of the exact sequence and scope of events they are investigating—indeed, that is why police must investigate in the first place. Deterred by the possibility of violating the Sixth Amendment, police likely would refrain from questioning certain defendants altogether.

532 U.S. at 173–74, 121 S.Ct. at 1343–44, 149 L.Ed.2d at 332.

Justice Kennedy, joined by Justices Scalia and Thomas, wrote separately to observe that the underlying theory of *Jackson* "seems questionable" and the majority neither reaffirmed nor gave approval of *Jackson*. *Jackson*, these justices reasoned, bars officers from approaching a defendant who has accepted appointed counsel even if the defendant wishes to speak to the officers. If *Jackson* is to remain authoritative, they added, it should apply only where a suspect has made a clear and unambiguous assertion of the right not to speak outside the presence of counsel. 532 U.S. at 175–76, 121 S.Ct. at 1344–45, 149 L.Ed.2d at 333–34 (Kennedy, J., concurring).

Page 494. Insert the following in the Editors' Introduction after the paragraph carrying over onto the page:

Jackson's application of the *Edwards* rule in the Sixth Amendment context was dramatically modified by a 5-to-4 in Montejo v. Louisiana, ___ U.S. ___, 129 S.Ct. 2079, 173 L.Ed.2d 955 (2009). At issue in *Montejo* was the effect of the Sixth Amendment on a defendant who had apparently made no request for counsel but nevertheless was appointed an attorney at a preliminary appearance before the trial court.

The *Jackson* rule, Justice Scalia's *Montejo* majority opinion reasoned, must be that after the Sixth Amendment attaches and a defendant is actually represented by counsel, police cannot initiate interrogation without the lawyer being present. This "would prevent police-initiated interrogation entirely once the Sixth Amendment right attaches, at least in those States that appoint counsel promptly without request from the defendant." Addressing the merits of *Jackson* so construed, the Court continued:

> What does the *Jackson* rule actually achieve by way of preventing unconstitutional conduct? * * * [T]he purpose of the rule is to preclude the State from badgering defendants into waiving their previously asserted rights. The effect of this badgering might be to coerce a waiver, which would render the subsequent interrogation a violation of the Sixth Amendment. Even though involuntary waivers are invalid even apart from *Jackson*, mistakes are of course possible when courts

conduct case-by-case voluntariness review. A bright-line rule like that adopted in *Jackson* ensures that no fruits of interrogations made possible by badgering-induced involuntary waivers are ever erroneously admitted at trial.

But without *Jackson*, how many would be? The answer is few if any. The principal reason is that the Court has already taken substantial other, overlapping measures toward the same end. Under *Miranda*'s prophylactic protection of the right against compelled self-incrimination, any suspect subject to custodial interrogation has the right to have a lawyer present if he so requests, and to be advised of that right. Under *Edwards'* prophylactic protection of the *Miranda* right, once such a defendant "has invoked his right to have counsel present," interrogation must stop. And * * * no subsequent interrogation may take place until counsel is present, "whether or not the accused has consulted with his attorney."

These three layers of prophylaxis are sufficient. Under the *Miranda-Edwards* * * * line of cases (which is not in doubt), a defendant who does not want to speak to the police without counsel present need only say as much when he is first approached and given the *Miranda* warnings.

___ U.S. at ___, 129 S.Ct. at 2089–90. The *Jackson* rule, consequently was overruled.

This means that although the Sixth Amendment is applicable, officers are not barred from reapproaching a defendant who for whom counsel has been appointed or who has retained counsel.

The majority also addressed concern that under its approach courts will have to resolve difficult issues posed by defendants' claims that statements made during preliminary court appearances (perhaps in response to questions whether they desired appointment of counsel) constitute *Edwards* invocations of the right to counsel:

That concern is misguided. "We have in fact never held that a person can invoke his *Miranda* rights anticipatorily, in a context other than 'custodial interrogation'. . . ." What matters for *Miranda* and *Edwards* is what happens when the defendant is approached for interrogation, and (if he consents) what happens during the interrogation—not what happened at any preliminary hearing.

___ U.S. at ___, 129 S.Ct. at 2091. While perhaps *Montejo* did not technically *hold* that a person cannot invoke the *Miranda* rights anticipatorily (see the discussion in the text at pages 447–48 note 2), the opinion thus appears to announce the majority's view that this cannot be done.

Page 503:   Change Note to Notes, number existing material Note 1, and add the following new notes:

2.   In Fellers v. United States, 540 U.S. 519, 124 S.Ct. 1019, 157 L.Ed.2d 1016 (2004), the facts were as follows:

On February 24, 2000, after a grand jury indicted petitioner for conspiracy to distribute methamphetamine, Lincoln Police Sergeant Michael Garnett and Lancaster County Deputy Sheriff Jeff Bliemeister went to petitioner's home in Lincoln, Nebraska, to arrest him. The officers knocked on petitioner's door and, when petitioner answered, identified themselves and asked if they could come in. Petitioner invited the officers into his living room.

The officers advised petitioner they had come to discuss his involvement in methamphetamine distribution. They informed petitioner that they had a federal warrant for his arrest and that a grand jury had indicted him for conspiracy to distribute methamphetamine. The officers told petitioner that the indictment referred to his involvement with certain individuals, four of whom they named. Petitioner then told the officers that he knew the four people and had used methamphetamine during his association with them.

After spending about 15 minutes in petitioner's home, the officers transported petitioner to the Lancaster County jail. There, the officers advised petitioner for the first time of his rights under *Miranda* * * *. Petitioner and the two officers signed a *Miranda* waiver form, and petitioner then reiterated the inculpatory statements he had made earlier, admitted to having associated with other individuals implicated in the charged conspiracy, and admitted to having loaned money to one of them even though he suspected that she was involved in drug transactions.

The district court suppressed the statements Fellers made at his home but admitted those made at the jail. On appeal, the Court of Appeals affirmed. It held that no Sixth Amendment violation occurred at Fellers' home because "the officers did not interrogate" Fellers there.

Before the Supreme Court, the Government defended the result below on the ground that the officers were simply informing Fellers of the basis for his arrest:

[T]he government did not deliberately elicit statements from petitioner at the time of his arrest so as to raise any Sixth Amendment issue. The officers did not ask petitioner questions, or encourage him to reveal incriminating information. Rather, the officers simply informed petitioner, in a single continuous statement, that they were there "to discuss" his involvement in methamphetamine distribution, that he had been indicted for conspiring to distribute methamphetamine, that the officers had an arrest warrant, and that the charges concerned petitioner's involvement with certain individuals. Courts have long held that informing a person of the charges that support his arrest is not an interrogation tactic or its equivalent, but is routine police practice that is consistent with the Federal Rules of Criminal Procedure. * * *

[P]etitioner contends that the officer's use of the word "discuss" to introduce his brief description of the indictment constituted an "invitation * * * to discuss pending charges." Taken in context, the record indicates that Bliemeister merely used colloquial language to inform petitioner that he wished to tell petitioner about the charges that he faced. Although one meaning of the word "discuss" denotes speaking about a topic with another person, another common use of the word denotes speaking about a topic to another person, as a lecture or speech would "discuss" a topic.

Brief for the United States, at 8, 18.

A unanimous Supreme Court rejected this and reversed:

The Court of Appeals erred in holding that the absence of an "interrogation" foreclosed petitioner's claim that the jailhouse statements should have been suppressed as fruits of the statements taken from petitioner at his home. First, there is no question that the officers in this case "deliberately elicited" information from petitioner. Indeed, the officers, upon arriving at petitioner's house, informed him that their purpose in coming was to discuss his involvement in the distribution of methamphetamine and his association with certain charged co-conspirators. Because the ensuing discussion took place after petitioner had been indicted, outside the presence of counsel, and in the absence of any waiver of petitioner's Sixth Amendment rights, the Court of Appeals erred in holding that the officers' actions did not violate the Sixth Amendment standards established in *Massiah* and its progeny.

540 U.S. at 524–25, 124 S.Ct. at 1023.

The specific issue in *Fellers*, of course, was the admissibility of the statements made at the jail. Regarding that, the Court held:

The Court of Appeals did not reach the question whether the Sixth Amendment requires suppression of petitioner's jailhouse statements on the ground that they were the fruits of previous questioning conducted in violation of the Sixth Amendment deliberate-elicitation standard. We have not had occasion to decide whether the rationale of *Elstad* applies when a suspect makes incriminating statements after a knowing and voluntary waiver of his right to counsel notwithstanding earlier police questioning in violation of Sixth Amendment standards. We therefore remand to the Court of Appeals to address this issue in the first instance.

540 U.S. at 525, 124 S.Ct. at 1023.

3. **Impeachment use.** A statement elicited in violation of a defendant's Sixth Amendment right to counsel, the Court held in Kansas v. Ventris, ___ U.S. ___, 129 S.Ct. 1841, 173 L.Ed.2d 801 (2009), can be used to impeach a defendant who testifies at trial. The Court found the analysis it had used in recognizing impeachment exceptions to other constitutional rules (see text. Pp. 39–40) applicable here:

[P]reventing impeachment use of statements taken in violation of [the Sixth Amendment] would add little appreciable deterrence. Officers have significant incentive to ensure that they and their informants comply with the Constitution's demands, since statements lawfully obtained can be used for all purposes rather than simply for impeachment. And the *ex ante* probability that evidence gained in violation of [the Sixth Amendment] would be of use for impeachment is exceedingly small. An investigator would have to anticipate both that the defendant would choose to testify at trial (an unusual occurrence to begin with) *and* that he would testify inconsistently despite the admissibility of his prior statement for impeachment. Not likely to happen—or at least not likely enough to risk squandering the opportunity of using a properly obtained statement for the prosecution's case in chief.

___ U.S. at ___, 129 S.Ct. at 1847.

CHAPTER 8

UNDERCOVER INVESTIGATIONS

B. ELICITATION OF SELF-INCRIMINATING STATEMENTS

Page 529.   Add the following new Note to the Notes after United States v. Henry:

3. **Prohibition against use of uncorroborated testimony of "jailhouse snitches."** In Kansas v. Ventris, ___ U.S. ___, 129 S.Ct. 1841, 173 L.Ed.2d 801 (2009), the Court addressed the argument "that jailhouse snitches are so inherently unreliable that this Court should craft a broader exclusionary rule for uncorroborated statements obtained by that means. Brief for National Association of Criminal Defense Lawyers 25–26."

Ventris was tried for a number of crimes, including murder, robbery, burglary and theft. He took the witness stand at trial and testified that the robbery and murder were committed by his companion. The prosecution then offered the testimony of an informant it had planted in Ventris's cell that Ventris admitted to the informant that "[h]e'd shot this man in his head and in his chest" and taken "his keys, his wallet, about $350.00, and . . . a vehicle." The trial court allowed the informant's testimony, but instructed the jury to "consider with caution" all testimony given in exchange for benefits from the State. The jury ultimately acquitted Ventris of felony murder and theft but returned a guilty verdict on the burglary and robbery counts. Rejecting the broad exclusionary proposal, the Court explained:

> Our legal system * * * is built on the premise that it is the province of the jury to weigh the credibility of competing witnesses, and we have long purported to avoid "establish[ing] this Court as a rule-making organ for the promulgation of state rules of criminal procedure." It would be especially inappropriate to fabricate such a rule in this case, where it appears the jury took to heart the trial judge's cautionary instruction on the unreliability of rewarded informant testimony by acquitting Ventris of felony murder.

___ U.S. at ___ n. *, 129 S.Ct. at 1847n. *.

CHAPTER 9

GRAND JURY INVESTIGATIVE FUNCTIONS

A. THE SUBPOENA POWER

Page 555. Add the following to Note 5 on "Self–Incrimination Privilege to Resist Production of Documents":

The application of the privilege against compelled self-incrimination in this context and its relationship to immunity extended to one from whom documents are sought are explored further in the material supplementing Note 5 on page 564 of the text.

B. QUESTIONING AND THE PRIVILEGE AGAINST COMPELLED SELF–INCRIMINATION

Page 564. Add the following to Note 5 on "Immunity":

The relationship between a grant of use immunity and a witness's Fifth Amendment privilege to resist a grand jury subpoena *duces tecum* for the production of documents (discussed in Note 5 on page 554 of the text) was explored in United States v. Hubbell, 530 U.S. 27, 120 S.Ct. 2037, 147 L.Ed.2d 24 (2000).

Independent Counsel appointed to consider matters related to the Whitewater Development Corporation was investigating whether Webster Hubbell had kept a plea bargaining promise to provide full information about matter relating to Whitewater. Counsel secured a grand jury subpoena *duces tecum* directing Hubbell to produce in federal court documents of 11 sorts. Hubbell refused in reliance upon his self-incrimination privilege. In response, Independent Counsel secured a court order granting him use immunity "to the extent allowed by law" and directing him to produce the documents. Hubbell then produced more than 13,000 pages of material. Using information in those documents, Independent Counsel obtained an indictment against Hubbell for various tax-related crimes and mail and wire fraud. Hubbell sought dismissal of the indictment on the ground that the prosecution was the result of his production of the documents and the grant of immunity therefore entitled him to relief from that prosecution.

The Government responded that the only Fifth Amendment protection Hubbell had was from the testimonial aspects of his act of producing the documents. The grant of immunity, it acknowledged, prohibited use against him of evidence derived from those testimonial aspects of his act of production. But, it continued, the challenged prosecution resulted not from his act of production but rather from the incriminating contents of the documents produced. Those contents were not protected by the privilege and the grant of immunity therefore did not protect him from the Government's use of the contents of the produced documents or evidence derived from those contents. At trial, the Government argued, it would not use the produced documents themselves or any evidence regarding Hubbell's production of them. The prosecution, the Government continued more specifically, was the product not of the *testimonial aspects* of the act of production but only of the *physical*—and *nontestimonial*—aspects of that act. Hubbell had no Fifth Amendment protection against being compelled to engage in the nontestimonial physical act of production, and thus the grant of immunity did not entitled him to be free of the Government's use of the physical act itself or evidence derived from it. Under *Kastigar*, it argued, Hubbell's physical act of production was the independent source of its prosecution.

The Supreme Court, however, agreed with Hubbell. He was entitled to protection from his "compelled testimony"—which was the testimonial aspect of his act of production—and evidence derived from that. The Government "made 'derivative use' of the testimonial aspect of [Hubbell's act of production] in obtaining the indictment against [him] and preparing its case for trial."

Hubbell had a right to refuse to produce the documents, since the Government introduced no evidence that it had—prior to Hubbell's production of the documents—prior knowledge of either the existence or whereabouts of those documents. The Government contended that the documents consisted of business and tax records and common knowledge suggested a businessman such as Hubbell would have them. Thus their existence and possession by him were "foregone conclusion[s]." Under the case law discussed on pages 554–55 of the text, the Government's argument continued, Hubbell's testimonial acknowledgment that the documents existed and were in his possession would not sufficiently add to the Government's information to trigger Fifth Amendment protection. Rejecting this, the Court held the Government had not made a sufficient showing, which apparently requires a showing that the prosecutors had more specific knowledge regarding the documents it sought.

The Court explained further:

It is apparent from the text of the subpoena itself that the prosecutor needed [Hubbell's] assistance both to identify potential sources of information and to produce those sources. Given the breadth of the description of the 11 categories of documents called for by the subpoena, the collection and production of the materials demanded was tantamount to answering a series of interrogatories asking a witness to disclose the existence and location of particular documents fitting certain broad descriptions. * * *

[W]e cannot accept the Government's submission that [Hubbell's] immunity did not preclude its derivative use of the produced documents because its "possession of the documents [was] the fruit *only* of a simple physical act—the act of producing the documents." It was unquestionably necessary for [Hubbell] to make extensive use of "the contents of his own mind" in identifying the hundreds of documents responsive to the requests in the subpoena. The assembly of those documents was like telling an inquisitor the combination to a wall safe, not like being forced to surrender the key to a strongbox. The Government's anemic view of [Hubbell's] act of production as a mere physical act that is principally non-testimonial in character and can be entirely divorced from its "implicit" testimonial aspect so as to constitute a "legitimate, wholly independent source" (as required by *Kastigar*) for the documents produced simply fails to account for these realities.

530 U.S. at 42–43, 120 S.Ct. at 2046–47, 147 L.Ed.2d at 39–40 (emphasis in original). It continued:

> *Kastigar* requires that [Hubbell's] motion to dismiss the indictment on immunity grounds be granted unless the Government proves that the evidence it used in obtaining the indictment and proposed to use at trial was derived from legitimate sources "wholly independent" of the testimonial aspect of [his] immunized conduct in assembling and producing the documents described in the subpoena. The Government, however, does not claim that it could make such a showing. Rather, it contends that its prosecution of respondent must be considered proper unless someone—presumably [Hubbell]—shows that "there is some substantial relation between the compelled testimonial communications implicit in the act of production (as opposed to the act of production standing alone) and some aspect of the information used in the investigation or the evidence presented at trial." We could not accept this submission without repudiating the basis for our conclusion in *Kastigar* that the statutory guarantee of use and derivative-use immunity is as broad as the constitutional privilege itself. This we are not prepared to do.

530 U.S. at 45–46, 120 S.Ct. at 2048, 147 L.Ed.2d at 41–42. Generalizing, it commented:

> In sum, we have no doubt that the constitutional privilege against self-incrimination protects the target of a grand jury investigation from being compelled to answer questions designed to elicit information about the existence of sources of potentially incriminating evidence. That constitutional privilege has the same application to the testimonial aspect of a response to a subpoena seeking discovery of those sources. * * *

530 U.S. at 43, 120 S.Ct. at 2047, 147 L.Ed.2d at 40.

CHAPTER 10

EYEWITNESS IDENTIFICATION

Page 570. Add the following to the Editors' Introduction before the first paragraph beginning on this page:

2003 Illinois legislation mandated that the Illinois State Police conduct a study of the field use of sequential identification procedures, in which persons or photographs are presented to witnesses one at a time rather than all at once. Research suggested that this sequential approach produced less false identifications than the traditional simultaneous procedures. In 2006, a report of the study was issued. Sheri H. Mecklenberg, Report to the Legislature of the State of Illinois: The Illinois Pilot Program on Sequential Double–Blind Identification Procedures (March 17, 2006).

The report evaluated 548 procedures; 319 of these were conducted by sequential presentation of the persons or photos and 229 were conducted by simultaneous presentation. It looked, first, to those cases in which the witness identified a "filler" subject or photo—one included with no reason to believe it was or depicted the perpetrator. These were assumed to reflect erroneous identifications. Second, it looked to those cases in which the witness identified a non-filler. Although no conclusive evidence established that these were of the actual perpetrator, they were assumed to be accurate. The results were as follows:

	Simultaneous Presentations	Sequential Presentations
Number of Procedures	319	229
"Inaccurate" Identification of Fillers	2.8%	9.2%
"Accurate" Identification	59.9%	45.0%
No Identification	37.6%	47.2%

Id. at 38. Earlier research had indicated that inaccurate identifications would be made in about 15% of procedures, so the low rates of inaccurate identifications of fillers was unexpected.

Perhaps the most significant result was the better performance of the traditional simultaneous presentation method. This resulted in less inaccurate identifications and more apparently accurate ones than the sequential procedures.

The study also compared live lineups with photo showings. This showed no statistical difference with regard to sequential procedures. Regarding simultaneous procedures, live lineups resulted in fewer filler identifications (although this was not statistically significant), more apparently accurate identifications and fewer "no picks." Id. at 40.

Where the race of the witness and the suspect were different, the false filler identifications were statistically the same in both simultaneous and sequential procedures. Id. at 39. False filler identifications were made in 8 of the 203 cross-race situations, or in 3.9% of them. Such false identifications were made in 21 of the 334 same-race situations, or 6.3% of these.

B. EVIDENTIARY AND PROCEDURAL SAFEGUARDS AGAINST UNREASONABLE EYEWITNESS TESTIMONY

Page 594. Insert the following in the Editors' Introduction after the quotation from United States v. Hall:

The Supreme Court of New Jersey concluded, "In light of the social science research noting the fallibility of eyewitness identifications, we direct that the charge should underscore, for jurors in all eyewitness identification cases, that eyewitness identification testimony requires close scrutiny and should not be accepted uncritically." It therefore specified that before the enumeration of factors to be considered by the jury in gauging the reliability and believability of an eyewitness's identification, the following language must appear:

> Although nothing may appear more convincing than a witness's categorical identification of a perpetrator, you must critically analyze such testimony. Such identifications, although made in good faith, may be mistaken. Therefore, when analyzing such testimony, be advised that a witness's level of confidence, standing alone, may not be an indication of the reliability of the identification.

State v. Romero, 191 N.J. 59, 76, 922 A.2d 693, 703 (2007).

The Connecticut Supreme Court was persuaded by the scientific literature that it should exercise its supervisory power to address the risk that those viewing an identification procedure will be told, or may assume, that the perpetrator or at least a suspect will be among those in the procedure. State v. Ledbetter, 275 Conn. 534, 881 A.2d 290 (2005). The scientific literature, it concluded, supports concern that witnesses may use the "relative judgment process":

> Without * * * a warning [from the administrator of the identification procedure that the perpetrator may not be present in a photographic array, lineup or show-up], * * * the witness feels obligated to select one of the photographs or participants in the procedure, which may result in the witness choosing the individual who is the most similar to

or least dissimilar from the actual perpetrator, regardless of whether the perpetrator is one of the choices in the identification procedure.

Consequently:

[U]nless there is no significant risk of misidentification, we direct the trial courts of this state to incorporate an instruction in the charge to the jury, warning the jury of the risk of misidentification, in those cases where: (1) the state has offered eyewitness identification evidence; (2) that evidence resulted from an identification procedure; and (3) the administrator of that procedure failed to instruct the witness that the perpetrator may or may not be present in the procedure. We adopt the following language for use by our trial courts in such cases in the future:

In this case, the state has presented evidence that an eyewitness identified the defendant in connection with the crime charged. That identification was the result of an identification procedure in which the individual conducting the procedure either indicated to the witness that a suspect was present in the procedure or failed to warn the witness that the perpetrator may or may not be in the procedure.

Psychological studies have shown that indicating to a witness that a suspect is present in an identification procedure or failing to warn the witness that the perpetrator may or may not be in the procedure increases the likelihood that the witness will select one of the individuals in the procedure, even when the perpetrator is not present. Thus, such behavior on the part of the procedure administrator tends to increase the probability of a misidentification.

This information is not intended to direct you to give more or less weight to the eyewitness identification evidence offered by the state. It is your duty to determine whether that evidence is to be believed. You may, however, take into account the results of the psychological studies, as just explained to you, in making that determination.

275 Conn. at 587–80, 881 A.2d at 318–19 (italics in original).

Page 601. Change Note to Notes, number the existing note as 1 and add the following notes:

2. **Cromedy Exonerated.** On remand in *Cromedy*, the prosecution prepared to retry Cromedy and in that process did DNA analysis that had not previously been done. The results indicated that the semen found in the victim did not come from Cromedy. Nevertheless, the prosecutor opposed Cromedy's release until the prosecution had an opportunity to talk with the victim. If the victim stood by her trial testimony that she had not had sex with anyone else around the time of the rape, the trial prosecutor commented, the charges would probably be dropped. Several days later, the prosecutor announced that the victim's mother reported that the victim did not wish to pursue the case and therefore the prosecution asked for dismissal of the case. The trial judge complied and dismissed the charges. Kathy Carter, No apology offered as rape charge is dropped, *Newark Star–Ledger*, Dec. 31,

1999; Kathy Carter, Man jailed for six years tastes freedom after DNA test clears him in rape, *Newark Star–Ledger*, Dec. 15, 1999.

Would the jury have been affected by the charge the Supreme Court held should have been given? Trial counsel for Cromedy said it certainly would have helped. He stressed that it would have been possible for him to have intertwined the instruction and the argument by telling the jury that "you'll hear the judge tell you …" He believed that often juries try to follow such instructions, but he acknowledged that his extensive appellate work may have made him more inclined to believe this. He did emphasize that expert testimony would have helped more than the jury charge. Interview with Anderson D. Harkov, May 6, 2002. The trial prosecutor did not respond to requests to discuss the case on remand.

3. **"Cross–Ethnic" Identifications.** Where the defendant is Hispanic and the witness Caucasian, should any special precautions developed in the cross-racial identification context apply? In State v. Romero, 191 N.J. 59, 922 A.2d 693 (2007), the Supreme Court of New Jersey held that despite *Cromedy*, no specific instruction tailored to the cross-ethnic nature of the identification is required. "Social science research," it explained, "does not tie identification unreliability directly to ethnic differences in the same way that racial differences can affect identification reliability." 191 N.J. at 71–72, 922 A.2d at 700.

PART TWO

Prosecution and Adjudication

CHAPTER 11

The Initial Appearance and Detention

Page 615. Add the following note after Note 3:

4. **Does a Fourth Amendment probable-cause hearing trigger the attachment of the Sixth Amendment right to counsel?** In *Rothgery v. Gillespie County, Texas,* 554 U.S. 191, 128 S.Ct. 2578, 171 L.Ed.2d 366 (2008), the defendant was arrested as a felon in possession of a firearm based upon erroneous information that he had a previous felony conviction, and brought before a magistrate for an "article 15.17 hearing." This hearing combines the Fourth Amendment's required probable-cause determination with the setting of bail and the point at which the arrested is formally apprised of the accusation against him. Mr. Rothgery's numerous oral and written requests for an attorney were ignored, and he was subsequently indicted, rearrested, and jailed for three weeks when he could not post bail. Sixth months after the article 15.17 hearing Mr. Rothgery was finally assigned a lawyer, who obtained a bail reduction and assembled the paperwork that prompted the indictment's dismissal. Mr. Rothgery then brought a civil rights action under 42 U.S.C. § 1983 alleging that had the state provided counsel within a reasonable time after his hearing, he would not have been jailed.

The Supreme Court reversed the Fifth Circuit's summary judgment in favor of the government, holding that the article 15.17 hearing marked the initiation of adversarial judicial criminal proceedings, which triggered the attachment of the right to counsel and the consequent state obligation to appoint counsel within a reasonable time once the defendant makes such a request. Relying on *Michigan v. Jackson*, 475 U.S. 625, 106 S.Ct. 1404, 89 L.Ed.2d 631 (1986) and *Brewer v. Williams*, 430 U.S. 387, 97 S.Ct. 1232, 51 L.Ed.2d 424 (1977), and noting that the overwhelming consensus of jurisdictions (the Federal government, the District of Columbia, and 43 States) take "the first step of appointing counsel before, at, or just after initial appearance," the Court rejected the County's argument that the Sixth Amendment does not attach until a prosecutor (as opposed to a police officer) is aware of or involved in that initial proceeding.

The majority made clear that its narrow holding did not speak to whether the article 15.17 hearing, though it plainly triggers attachment, "is a critical stage requiring the presence of counsel" at the hearing itself. Further, it agreed with the dissent that its holding did not address the issue of "whether the 6-month delay in appointment of counsel resulted in prejudice to Rothgery's Sixth Amendment rights." 554 U.S. at 212 n.17, 128 S.Ct. at 2592 n.17.

CHAPTER 13

DISCRETION TO PROSECUTE

B. LIMITS ON PROSECUTORIAL DISCRETION

Page 666.   Insert the following at the end of the untitled introduction:

Prosecutors' charging decisions and the decisions as to how to proceed with prosecutions may be limited by a federal constitutional due process prohibition against inconsistent positions in different cases. The issue was presented in Bradshaw v. Stumpf, 545 U.S. 175, 125 S.Ct. 2398, 162 L.Ed.2d 143 (2005).

Stumpf, Wesley and Edmonds were involved in the robbery of Norman and Mary Jane Stout and the murder of Mrs. Stout. Stumpf pled guilty to aggravated murder before a three judge panel, which held a hearing and satisfied itself as to the "factual basis" for the plea. A penalty hearing was then held before the panel. The State argued that Stumpf was the triggerperson in the killing. The panel found Stumpf was the "principal offender" in the murder and that the aggravating factors outweighed the any mitigating considerations. It sentenced him to death.

Later, Wesley was put on trial. At this trial, the State produced the testimony of one Eastman whom it had located since Stumpf's sentencing. On the basis of Eastman's testimony, the State argued that the evidence showed Wesley was the principal offender in Mrs. Stout's death. Wesley was convicted but sentenced to life imprisonment. Stumpf challenged his conviction and death sentence in federal habeas corpus, and was denied relief in the District Court. The Court of Appeals for the Sixth Circuit reversed:

[W]e * * * find[ ] that the use of inconsistent, irreconcilable theories to convict two defendants for the same crime is a due process violation. * * * [T]he due process challenge to the use of inconsistent theories is based on the notion of fundamental fairness. Because inconsistent theories render convictions unreliable, they constitute a violation of the due process rights of any defendant in whose trial they are used. * * *

[T]he state's due process violation mandates that both Stumpf's plea and his sentence be set aside. * * * [I]t was necessary for the three-judge panel to find Stumpf specifically intended the death of Mary Jane Stout in order to accept his plea to aggravated murder. The prosecution offered virtually no evidence regarding intent other than its contention that Stumpf shot Mrs. Stout. Had the prosecution's alternate theory been heard by the three judge panel, there is a reasonable probability that it would have found Stumpf guilty of something less than aggravated murder.

Moreover, there is more than a reasonable probability that the three judge panel would not have sentenced Stumpf to death had the prosecution not employed inconsistent and irreconcilable theories. In explaining its reasoning for finding that the aggravating factors in Stumpf's case outweighed the mitigating factors (and therefore that Stumpf deserved the death penalty), the court's first pronouncement was that it had "f[oun]d beyond a reasonable doubt that the Defendant was the principal offender in count one of the indictment," *i.e.*, the aggravated murder charge. In turn, this finding prevented the panel from concluding that Stumpf was *not* the principal offender, which would have been "a powerful mitigating factor."

Stumpf v. Mitchell, 367 F.3d 594, 611, 613, 616–17 (6th Cir. 2004).

The Supreme Court reversed, explaining in part:

> The Court of Appeals was * * * wrong to hold that prosecutorial inconsistencies between the Stumpf and Wesley cases required voiding Stumpf's guilty plea. Stumpf's assertions of inconsistency relate entirely to the prosecutor's arguments about which of the two men, Wesley or Stumpf, shot Mrs. Stout. * * * [T]he precise identity of the triggerman was immaterial to Stumpf's conviction for aggravated murder. Moreover, Stumpf has never provided an explanation of how the prosecution's postplea use of inconsistent arguments could have affected the knowing, voluntary, and intelligent nature of his plea.

> The prosecutor's use of allegedly inconsistent theories may have a more direct effect on Stumpf's sentence, however, for it is at least arguable that the sentencing panel's conclusion about Stumpf's principal role in the offense was material to its sentencing determination. The opinion below leaves some ambiguity as to the overlap between how the lower court resolved Stumpf's due process challenge to his conviction, and how it resolved Stumpf' challenge to his sentence. It is not clear whether the Court of Appeals would have concluded that Stumpf was entitled to resentencing had the court not also considered the conviction invalid. Likewise, the parties' briefing to this Court, and the question on which we granted certiorari, largely focused on the lower court's determination about Stumpf's conviction. In these circumstances, it would be premature for this Court to resolve the merits of Stumpf's sentencing claim, and we therefore express no opinion on whether the prosecutor's actions amounted to a due process violation, or whether any such violation would have been prejudicial. The Court of Appeals should have the opportunity to consider, in the first instance, the question of how Eastman's testimony and the prosecutor's conduct in the Stumpf and Wesley cases relate to Stumpf's death sentence in particular. Accordingly, we vacate the portion of the judgment below relating to Stumpf's prosecutorial inconsistency claim, and we remand the case for further proceedings consistent with this opinion.

545 U.S. at 186–88, 125 S.Ct. at 2407.

Page 674.   Add the following to Note 3:

The respondent in United States v. Bass, 536 U.S. 862, 122 S.Ct. 2389, 153 L.Ed.2d 769 (2002) moved for discovery from the Government of its capital charging policies when notice was filed of intent to seek the death penalty against him. He claimed discrimination because he is an African–American and attempted to make a prima facie showing by statistics from the U.S. Justice Department showing that nationwide African–Americans are charged with capital offenses more than twice as often as whites and that in capital cases the Government enters into plea bargains more frequently with whites. Based on this showing, the District Court ordered the Government to respond to the discovery requests. When it refused, the court dismissed the notice of intent to seek the death penalty. This action was upheld on appeal.

The Supreme Court, in a *per curiam* opinion, reversed. Under *Armstrong*, both discriminatory effect and intent must be shown. Respondent's efforts to show discriminatory effect have failed:

> Even assuming that the Armstrong requirement can be satisfied by a nation-wide showing (as opposed to a showing regarding the record of the decision-makers in respondent's case), raw statistics regarding overall charges say nothing about charges brought against similarly situated defendants. And the statistics regarding plea bargains are even less relevant, since respondent was offered a plea bargain but declined it. * * * Under Armstrong, therefore, because respondent failed to submit relevant evidence that similarly situated persons were treated differently, he was not entitled to discovery.

536 U.S. at 863–64, 122 S.Ct. at 2389, 153 L.Ed.2d at 772.

Page 678. Add the following new section at the end of the chapter:

C. EMBODYING THE CHARGING DECISION IN A PLEADING

The decision to charge a person with a criminal offense must, of course, be formalized in a pleading. Precisely how this must be done is often determined by jurisdiction-specific pleading requirements. As the Supreme Court made clear in the case that follows, there are nevertheless minimal federal constitutional requirements.

United States v. Resendiz–Ponce

Supreme Court of the United States, 2007.
549 U.S. 102, 127 S.Ct. 782, 166 L.Ed.2d 591.

■ JUSTICE STEVENS delivered the opinion of the Court.

A jury convicted respondent Juan Resendiz–Ponce, a Mexican citizen, of illegally attempting to reenter the United States. Because the indictment failed to allege a specific overt act that he committed in seeking reentry, the Court of Appeals set aside his conviction and remanded for dismissal of the indictment. We granted the Government's petition for certiorari * * *.

* * *

I

Respondent was deported twice, once in 1988 and again in 2002, before his attempted reentry on June 1, 2003. On that day, respondent walked up to a port of entry and displayed a photo identification of his cousin to the border agent. Respondent told the agent that he was a legal resident and that he was traveling to Calexico, California. Because he did not resemble his cousin, respondent was questioned, taken into custody, and ultimately charged with a violation of 8 U.S.C. § 1326(a). The indictment [was as follows]:

UNITED STATES DISTRICT COURT
FOR THE DISTRICT OF ARIZONA
No. CR 03–810–PHX EHC
United States of America, plaintiff
v.

Juan Resendiz–Ponce, aka: Juan Ponce Resendiz, defendant
[Filed: July 30, 2003]

INDICTMENT

VIO: 8 U.S.C. §§ 1326(a) and enhanced by (b)(2)

(Attempted Reentry After Deportation)

On or about June 1, 2003, JUAN RESENDIZ–PONCE, an alien, knowingly and intentionally attempted to enter the United States of America at or near San Luis in the District of Arizona, after having been previously denied admission, excluded, deported, and removed from the United States at or near Nogales, Arizona, on or about October 15, 2002, and not having obtained the express consent of the Secretary of the Department of Homeland Security to reapply for admission.

In violation of Title 8, United States Code, Sections 1326(a) and enhanced by (b)(2).

A TRUE BILL

/s/ JOHN T. ZIEGHER
John T. Ziegher
Foreperson of the grand jury

Date: July 30, 2003

PAUL K. CHARLTON
United States Attorney
District of Arizona

/s/ [ILLEGIBLE]
Mary Beth Phillips
Assistant U.S. Attorney

[Eds.]

Respondent moved to dismiss the indictment, contending that it "fail[ed] to allege an essential element, an overt act, or to state the essential facts of such overt act." The District Court denied the motion and, after the jury found him guilty, sentenced respondent to a 63–month term of imprisonment.

The Ninth Circuit reversed, reasoning that an indictment's omission of "an essential element of the offense is a fatal flaw not subject to mere harmless error analysis." * * *

II

* * *

The Government does not disagree with respondent's submission that he cannot be guilty of attempted reentry in violation of 8 U.S.C. § 1326(a) unless he committed an overt act qualifying as a substantial step toward completion of his goal. Nor does it dispute that "[a]n indictment must set forth each element of the crime that it charges." *Almendarez–Torres v. United States,* 523 U.S. 224, 228, 118 S.Ct. 1219, 140 L.Ed.2d 350 (1998). It instead contends that the indictment at bar implicitly alleged that respondent engaged in the necessary overt act "simply by alleging that he 'attempted to enter the United States.'" We agree.

Not only does the word "attempt" as used in common parlance connote action rather than mere intent, but more importantly, as used in the law for centuries, it encompasses both the overt act and intent elements. Consequently, an indictment alleging attempted illegal reentry under § 1326(a) need not specifically allege a particular overt act or any other "component par[t]" of the offense. See *Hamling v. United States,* 418 U.S. 87, 119, 94 S.Ct. 2887, 41 L.Ed.2d 590 (1974). Just as it was enough for the indictment in *Hamling* to allege that the defendant mailed "obscene" material in violation of 18 U.S.C. § 1461, it was enough for the indictment in this case to point to the relevant criminal statute and allege that "[o]n or about June 1, 2003," respondent "attempted to enter the United States of America at or near San Luis in the District of Arizona."

In *Hamling,* we identified two constitutional requirements for an indictment: "first, [that it] contains the elements of the offense charged and fairly informs a defendant of the charge against which he must defend, and, second, [that it] enables him to plead an acquittal or conviction in bar of future prosecutions for the same offense." In this case, the use of the word "attempt," coupled with the specification of the time and place of respondent's attempted illegal reentry, satisfied both. Indeed, the time-and-place information provided respondent with more adequate notice than would an indictment describing particular overt acts. After all, a given defendant may have approached the border or lied to a border-patrol agent in the course of countless attempts on innumerable occasions. For the same reason, the time-and-date specification in respondent's indictment provided ample protection against the risk of multiple prosecutions for the same crime.

* * *

Respondent is of course correct that while an indictment parroting the language of a federal criminal statute is often sufficient, there are crimes that must be charged with greater specificity. A clear example is the statute making it a crime for a witness summoned before a congressional committee to refuse to answer any question "pertinent to the question under inquiry." 2 U.S.C. § 192. As we explained at length in our opinion in *Russell v. United States,* 369 U.S. 749, 82 S.Ct. 1038, 8 L.Ed.2d 240 (1962), a valid indictment for such a refusal to testify must go beyond the words of § 192 and allege the subject of the congressional hearing in order to determine whether the defendant's refusal was "pertinent." Based on a number of cases arising out of congressional investigations, we recognized that the relevant hearing's subject was frequently uncertain but invariably "central to every prosecution under the statute." Both to provide fair notice to defendants and to assure that any conviction would arise out of the theory of guilt presented to the grand jury, we held that indictments under § 192 must do more than restate the language of the statute.

Our reasoning in *Russell* suggests that there was no infirmity in the present indictment. First, unlike the statute at issue in *Russell,* guilt under 8 U.S.C. § 1326(a) does not "depen[d] so crucially upon such a specific identification of fact." Second, before explaining the special need for particularity in charges brought under 2 U.S.C. § 192, Justice Stewart noted that, in 1872, Congress had enacted a statute reflecting "the drift of the law away from the rules of technical and formalized pleading which had characterized an earlier era." After the repeal of that statute, there was no other legislation dealing generally with the subject of indictments until the promulgation of Federal Rule of Criminal Procedure 7(c)(1). As we have said, the Federal Rules "were designed to eliminate technicalities in criminal pleadings and are to be construed to secure simplicity in procedure." *United States v. Debrow,* 346 U.S. 374, 376, 74 S.Ct. 113, 98 L.Ed. 92 (1953). While detailed allegations might well have been required under common-law pleading rules, they surely are not contemplated by Rule 7(c)(1), which provides that an indictment "shall be a plain, concise, and definite written statement of the essential facts constituting the offense charged."

Because we are satisfied that respondent's indictment fully complied with that Rule and did not deprive him of any significant protection that the constitutional guarantee of a grand jury was intended to confer, we reverse the judgment of the Court of Appeals and remand the case for further proceedings consistent with this opinion.

It is so ordered.

■ Justice Scalia, dissenting.

It is well established that an indictment must allege all the elements of the charged crime. As the Court acknowledges, it is likewise well established that "attempt" contains two substantive elements: the *intent* to commit the underlying crime, and the undertaking of *some action* toward commission of that crime. It should follow, then, that when the Government indicts for attempt to commit a crime, it must allege both that the defendant had the intent to commit the crime, *and* that he took some action toward its commission. Any rule to the contrary would be an exception to the standard practice.

* * *

My dissenting view that the indictment was faulty (a point on which we requested supplemental briefing) puts me in the odd position of being the sole Justice who must decide the question on which we granted certiorari: whether a constitutionally deficient indictment is structural error, as the Ninth Circuit held, or rather is amenable to harmless-error analysis. I cannot vote to affirm or to reverse the judgment without resolving that issue. Since the full Court will undoubtedly have to speak to the point on another day (it dodged the bullet today by inviting and deciding a *different* constitutional issue—albeit, to be fair, a narrower one) there is little use in my setting forth my views in detail. * * * I would find the error to be structural. I would therefore affirm the judgment of the Ninth Circuit.

NOTE

The Court of Appeals explained its holding that harmless error did not apply as follows:

> Failure to allege an essential element of the offense is a fatal flaw not subject to mere harmless error analysis. The purpose of this rule is to secure the basic institutional purpose of the grand jury, by ensuring that a defendant is not "convicted on the basis of facts not found by, and perhaps not even presented to, the grand jury that indicted him." As the Supreme Court has explained, this purpose has its constitutional roots in the Fifth and Sixth Amendments and historical roots in the English common-law tradition. *Russell v. United States,* 369 U.S. 749, 770, 82 S.Ct. 1038, 8 L.Ed.2d 240 (1962). While this protection may not extend to incidentals and details unnecessary to a conviction, an overt act that is a substantial step toward underlying offense is at the very core of an attempt charge. The defendant has a right to be apprised of what overt act the government will try to prove at trial, and he has a right to have a grand jury consider whether to charge that specific overt act. * * * A grand jury never passed on a specific overt act, and Resendiz was never given notice of what specific overt act would be proved at trial.

United States v. Resendiz–Ponce, 425 F.3d 729, 732–733 (9th Cir. 2005).

CHAPTER 15

RIGHT TO A SPEEDY TRIAL

A. SIXTH AMENDMENT SPEEDY TRIAL GUARANTEE

Page 718. Add the following new Note after Note 4:

4a. Delay attributable to the defendant and defense counsel. Allocation of responsibility or blame for delay was addressed in Vermont v. Brillon, ____ U.S. ____, 129 S.Ct. 1283, 173 L.Ed.2d 231 (2009). First the Court held the court below had erred in attributing to the state responsibility for the delays sought by counsel appointed to represent defendant Brillon:

> An assigned counsel's failure "to move the case forward" does not warrant attribution of delay to the State. * * * [A]ssigned counsel generally are not state actors for purposes of a speedy-trial claim. * * *
>
> A contrary conclusion could encourage appointed counsel to delay proceedings by seeking unreasonable continuances, hoping thereby to obtain a dismissal of the indictment on speedy-trial grounds. Trial courts might well respond by viewing continuance requests made by appointed counsel with skepticism, concerned that even an apparently genuine need for more time is in reality a delay tactic. Yet the same considerations would not attend a privately retained counsel's requests for time extensions. We see no justification for treating defendants' speedy-trial claims differently based on whether their counsel is privately retained or publicly assigned.

____ U.S., at ____, 129 S.Ct., at 1291–92.

Second, the Court held, the state tribunal erred by failing to consider the actions of defendant Brillon himself. The lawyer who represented Brillon at trial was the sixth attorney to represent him. Three days before trial was scheduled, Brillon purported to "fire" his first appointed attorney, Richard Ammons, who was subsequently taken off the case by the judge. Another appointed attorney, Gerard Altieri, moved to withdraw on among other grounds that Brillon had threatened his life during a break. The Court explained:

> Brillon sought to dismiss Ammons on the eve of trial. His strident, aggressive behavior with regard to Altieri, whom he threatened, further impeded prompt trial and likely made it more difficult for the Defender General's office to find replacement counsel. Even after the trial court's warning regarding delay, Brillon sought dismissal of yet another attorney, Donaldson. Just as a State's "deliberate attempt to delay the trial in order to hamper the defense should be weighted heavily against the [State]," so too should a defendant's deliberate attempt to disrupt proceedings be weighted heavily against the defendant. Absent Brillon's deliberate efforts to force the withdrawal of Ammons and Altieri, no speedy-trial issue would have arisen. The effect of these earlier events should have been factored into the court's analysis of subsequent delay.

___ U.S., at ___, 129 S.Ct., at 1292.

Page 720.   Add the following to Note 6:

What constitutes a waiver of the requirement of trial within 180 days? In New York v. Hill, 528 U.S. 110, 120 S.Ct. 659, 145 L.Ed.2d 560 (2000), respondent's attorney agreed to a trial setting on a murder charge at a time beyond the 180 day time period. The New York Court of Appeals reversed respondent's murder conviction on the ground counsel's agreement was not a waiver under the Interstate Agreement on Detainers of respondent's right to be tried within 180 days. The Supreme Court, in an opinion for a unanimous Court by Justice Scalia, reversed. Undoubtedly, rights can be waived under the Interstate Agreement as in other legal proceedings. The question, then, is whether the right to trial within 180 days is one that can be waived only by personal action of the client, or whether the attorney can waive for the client. The Court concluded that the attorney can waive for the client:

> Scheduling matters are plainly among those for which agreement by counsel generally controls. This case does not involve a purported prospective waiver of all protection of the IAD's [Interstate Agreement on Detainers] time limits or of the IAD generally, but merely agreement to a specified delay in trial. When that subject is under consideration, only counsel is in a position to assess the benefit or detriment of the delay to the defendant's case. Likewise, only counsel is in a position to assess whether the defense would even be prepared to proceed any earlier. Requiring express assent from the defendant himself for such routine and often repetitive scheduling determinations would consume time to no apparent purpose. The text of the IAD, moreover, confirms what the reason of the matter suggests: in allowing the court to grant "good-cause continuances" when either "prisoner or his counsel" is present, it contemplates that scheduling questions may be left to counsel. Art. III(a)

528 U.S. at 115, 120 S.Ct. at 664, 145 L.Ed.2d at 567.

The Interstate Agreement on Detainers contains a provision that prohibits a receiving state from returning an inmate to the sending state prior to trial. Return under those circumstances requires "an order dismissing the [case] with prejudice." The respondent in Alabama v. Bozeman, 533 U.S. 146, 121 S.Ct. 2079, 150 L.Ed.2d 188 (2001), incarcerated in a federal prison in Florida, was brought to Alabama for arraignment and appointment of counsel on pending state charges. After arraignment, he was returned to federal prison until once again brought to Alabama for trial. On appeal from his conviction, the Alabama Supreme Court held that the prohibiting of "shuttling" a prisoner between the sending and receiving states was absolute and required dismissing the charge with prejudice.

The United States Supreme Court, in a unanimous opinion authored by Justice Breyer, agreed. While it is not clear why this provision is part of the Interstate Agreement, it is clear that it was violated. The language is absolute, which argues against the application of a concept of harmlessness or *de minimis* violation. It is not clear why Alabama chose to act as it did, except perhaps to reduce for the county the costs of pretrial incarceration. While the Court refuses to recognize a softening gloss to the text, it does note that under New York v. Hill the inmate could waive his or her right to continuous presence in the receiving state to enable temporary return to the sending state.

B. FEDERAL SPEEDY TRIAL ACT

Page 731.   Add the following to the Notes after United States v. Taylor:

1b.   **Time granted for preparation of pre-trial motions.** When a district court grants a defendant additional time to prepare pre-trial motions, is this time automatically excludable or is it only excludable if certain case-specific findings are made? In Bloate v. United States, ___ U.S. ___, 130 S.Ct. 1345, 176 L.Ed.2d 54 (2010), a split Supreme Court held that such time periods are not automatically excludable. The majority reasoned in part that this interpretation of the statute was most consistent with its basic purpose:

> [T]he Act serves not only to protect defendants, but also to vindicate the public interest in the swift administration of justice. * * * [R]eading [the statute] to exclude *all* time for preparing pretrial motions would undermine the guarantee of a speedy trial, and thus harm the public interest we have recognized * * *.

___ U.S. at ___, 130 S.Ct. at 1356.

1c.   **Exclusion of times pretrial motions are pending**. One portion of the statute provides that "[a]ny period of * * * delay resulting from any pretrial motion, from the filing of the motion through the conclusion of the hearing on, or other prompt disposition of, such motion" "shall be excluded in computing * * * the time within which the trial must commence." 18 U.S.C.A. § 3161(h)(1)(D). This is automatic, in the sense that the period between the filing and disposition of such a motion is to be excluded regardless of whether the filing or consideration of the motion actually caused postponement of the start of the trial. Requring trial judges to decide whether particular motions caused postponements of trial would make the exclusion "significantly more difficult to administer. And [this] would significantly hinder the Speedy Trial Act's efforts to secure fair and efficient criminal trial proceedings." United States v. Tinklenberg, 563 U.S. ___, ___, 131 S.Ct. 2007, 2014, ___ L.Ed.2d ___ (2011).

3.   **Prospective waivers under the federal statute.** In Zedner v. United States, 547 U.S. 489, 126 S.Ct. 1976, 164 L.Ed.2d 749 (2006), the Supreme Court held that a defendant may not prospectively waive the application of the Speedy Trial Act. When Zedner sought a delay in proceedings—an "adjournment"—the trial judge successfully asked that he sign a written waiver of his rights under the Act to a speedy trial and to move for dismissal for lack of a speedy trial. Several months later, the judge granted another request by Zedner for a 91-day delay. The judge did not make the findings required under section 3161(h)(8) of the statute (set out in Note 1 above) that would exclude the period of delay from the calculations necessary to determine whether the later trial was timely as required by the statute. Apparently, the judge believed that the waiver had render the Act inapplicable. The Supreme Court held that the waiver was invalid:

> The purposes of the Act * * * cut against exclusion on the grounds of mere consent or waiver. If the Act were designed solely to protect a defendant's right to a speedy trial, it would make sense to allow a defendant to waive the application of the Act. But the Act was designed with the public interest firmly

in mind. That public interest cannot be served, the Act recognizes, if defendants may opt out of the Act entirely.

547 U.S. at 500–01, 126 S.Ct. at 1985.

18 U.S.C. § 3162(a)(2) provides that a defendant's failure to move for dismissal prior to trial or a plea of guilty constitutes a waiver of the right to dismissal. But, *Zedner* concluded, this does not suggest Congress intended to authorize prospective dismissals:

> [T]here is no reason to think that Congress wanted to treat prospective and retrospective waivers similarly. Allowing prospective waivers would seriously undermine the Act because there are many cases—like the case at hand—in which the prosecution, the defense, and the court would all be happy to opt out of the Act, to the detriment of the public interest. The sort of retrospective waiver allowed by § 3161(a)(2) does not pose a comparable danger because the prosecution and the court cannot know until the trial actually starts or the guilty plea is actually entered whether the defendant will forgo moving to dismiss. As a consequence, the prosecution and the court retain a strong incentive to make sure that the trial begins on time.

547 U.S. at 502, 126 S.Ct. at 1986.

4. **Estoppel as barring relief under the statute.** A defendant might sometimes be barred by estoppel from seeking relief under the Speedy Trial Act, the Supreme Court acknowledged in Zedner v. United States, 547 U.S. 489, 126 S.Ct. 1976, 164 L.Ed.2d 749 (2006). But it made clear that a substantial showing would be required and in light of the invalidity of prospective waivers courts should be reluctant to find estoppel applicable.

In *Zedner*, Court considered whether Zedner was estoped from arguing that the 91 day delay as a result of his second request should be counted in determining whether his trial was held on time because the judge did not make the specific findings required by section 3161(h)(8) for exclusion of the period of delay from the Act. The Government argued that Zedner's seeking the continuance and enjoyment of the benefits of that continuance estopped him from contending he was entitled to dismissal because of the precise procedural manner in which the continuance was granted. The Court rejected the Government's contention. It reasoned that estoppel might apply if the defendant's position in seeking dismissal was "clearly inconsistent" with the position the defendant took in seeking delay for which the defendant sought dismissal. But in *Zedner*, all parties approached the request for a continuance on the mistaken assumption that defendant Zedner had effectively waived application of the Act. Zedner thus simply took the position that granting the continuance would be a sound exercise of the judge's discretion to manage its calendar. This position was not clearly inconsistent with its later position that the continuance was not permissible under the Act, and thus did not estop Zedner from making that contention in his efforts to obtain dismissal. 547 U.S. 505–06, 126 S.Ct. at 1988.

CHAPTER 16

COMPETENCY TO STAND TRIAL

Page 734. Add the following at the end of the untitled introduction to the Chapter:

The interplay between the standards for competency to stand trial, competency waive counsel and plead guilty, and competency to represent oneself at trial was explored in *Indiana v. Edwards*, 554 U.S. 164, 128 S.Ct. 2379, 171 L.Ed.2d 345 (2008), discussed more fully in your 2008 Supplement on p. 290, the section covering self-representation. In the *Edwards* case, the trial court found that the mentally ill defendant was competent to stand trial under the *Dusky* standard, but he was not sufficiently competent to represent himself at his trial. The Supreme Court agreed that the Constitution does not forbid States from insisting upon representation by counsel for those competent enough to stand trial but who suffer from severe mental illness to the point where they are not competent to conduct trial proceedings by themselves. The Court distinguished *Godinez* on multiple grounds.

> In *Godinez*, the higher standard sought to measure the defendant's ability to proceed on his own to enter a guilty plea; here the higher standard seeks to measure the defendant's ability to conduct trial proceedings. To put the matter more specifically, the *Godinez* defendant sought only to change his pleas to guilty, he did not seek to conduct trial proceedings, and his ability to conduct a defense at trial was expressly not an issue.

554 U.S. at 173, 128 S.Ct. at 2385. The Court concluded that precedent such as *Dusky, Godinez,* and *Faretta v. California*, 422 U.S. 806, 95 S.Ct. 2525, 45 L.Ed.2d 562 (1975) (reproduced on page 1132 the casebook), combined with the nature of mental illness cautioned against a single competency standard to decide both whether a defendant who is represented can proceed to trial and whether a defendant who goes to trial must be permitted to represent himself.

B. PROCESSING OF INCOMPETENT DEFENDANTS

Page 752. Add the following at the end of the page, as part of Note 3:

The Court re-visited the question of forced medication in Sell v. United States, 539 U.S. 166, 123 S.Ct. 2174, 156 L.Ed.2d 197 (2003). Sell, a dentist, was charged with various counts of Medicaid fraud and mail fraud.

He had a history of mental illness and was confined in the United States Medical Center as incompetent to stand trial. Staff at the center wished to administer medication that would assist Sell in becoming competent. In addition, staff believed Sell to be dangerous to himself and others and wished to administer medication to address that circumstance. Sell refused medication and sought a court order prohibiting forced administration. Ultimately, the Eighth Circuit held that although Sell was not a danger to himself or others, he could be forced to take medication solely to assist him in attaining competency to stand trial.

The Supreme Court, in an opinion by Justice Breyer, reversed. The Constitution permits forced medication but requires more complicated findings than merely a desire to assist the patient to attain trial competency. Building on *Harper* and *Riggins*, the Court prescribed the circumstances under which a court order of forced medication for one charged with non-violent offenses is permissible constitutionally:

> These two cases, Harper and Riggins, indicate that the Constitution permits the Government involuntarily to administer antipsychotic drugs to a mentally ill defendant facing serious criminal charges in order to render that defendant competent to stand trial, but only if the treatment is medically appropriate, is substantially unlikely to have side effects that may undermine the fairness of the trial, and, taking account of less intrusive alternatives, is necessary significantly to further important governmental trial-related interests.

539 U.S. at 179, 123 S.Ct. at 2184. The Court elaborated on that standard:

> First, a court must find that important governmental interests are at stake. The Government's interest in bringing to trial an individual accused of a serious crime is important. That is so whether the offense is a serious crime against the person or a serious crime against property. In both instances the Government seeks to protect through application of the criminal law the basic human need for security.
> * * *
> Courts, however, must consider the facts of the individual case in evaluating the Government's interest in prosecution. Special circumstances may lessen the importance of that interest. The defendant's failure to take drugs voluntarily, for example, may mean lengthy confinement in an institution for the mentally ill—and that would diminish the risks that ordinarily attach to freeing without punishment one who has committed a serious crime. We do not mean to suggest that civil commitment is a substitute for a criminal trial. The Government has a substantial interest in timely prosecution. And it may be difficult or impossible to try a defendant who regains competence after years of commitment during which memories may fade and evidence may be lost. The potential for future confinement affects, but does not totally undermine, the strength of the need for prosecution. The same is true of the possibility that the defendant has already been

confined for a significant amount of time (for which he would receive credit toward any sentence ultimately imposed, see 18 U.S.C. § 3585(b)). Moreover, the Government has a concomitant, constitutionally essential interest in assuring that the defendant's trial is a fair one.

Second, the court must conclude that involuntary medication will significantly further those concomitant state interests. It must find that administration of the drugs is substantially likely to render the defendant competent to stand trial. At the same time, it must find that administration of the drugs is substantially unlikely to have side effects that will interfere significantly with the defendant's ability to assist counsel in conducting a trial defense, thereby rendering the trial unfair. * * *

Third, the court must conclude that involuntary medication is necessary to further those interests. The court must find that any alternative, less intrusive treatments are unlikely to achieve substantially the same results. * * * And the court must consider less intrusive means for administering the drugs, e.g., a court order to the defendant backed by the contempt power, before considering more intrusive methods.

Fourth, as we have said, the court must conclude that administration of the drugs is medically appropriate, i.e., in the patient's best medical interest in light of his medical condition. The specific kinds of drugs at issue may matter here as elsewhere. Different kinds of antipsychotic drugs may produce different side effects and enjoy different levels of success.

539 U.S. at 180–81, 123 S.Ct. at 2184–85. The Court then suggested that forced administration upon a showing of dangerousness might be a preferable course of action when it is available:

We emphasize that the court applying these standards is seeking to determine whether involuntary administration of drugs is necessary significantly to further a particular governmental interest, namely, the interest in rendering the defendant competent to stand trial. A court need not consider whether to allow forced medication for that kind of purpose, if forced medication is warranted for a different purpose, such as the purposes set out in *Harper* related to the individual's dangerousness, or purposes related to the individual's own interests where refusal to take drugs puts his health gravely at risk. * * * There are often strong reasons for a court to determine whether forced administration of drugs can be justified on these alternative grounds before turning to the trial competence question.

For one thing, the inquiry into whether medication is permissible, say, to render an individual nondangerous is usually more "objective and manageable" than the inquiry into whether medication is permissible to render a defendant competent. * * * The medical experts may find it easier to provide an informed opinion about whether, given the risk of side effects, particular drugs are medically appropriate and necessary to control a patient's potentially dangerous behavior (or to avoid serious harm to the patient himself) than to try to balance harms and benefits related to the more quintessentially legal questions of trial fairness and competence.

For another thing, courts typically address involuntary medical treatment as a civil matter, and justify it on these alternative, *Harper*-type grounds. Every State provides avenues through which, for example, a doctor or institution can seek appointment of a guardian with the power to make a decision authorizing medication—when in the best interests of a patient who lacks the mental competence to make such a decision. * * * And courts, in civil proceedings, may authorize involuntary medication where the patient's failure to accept treatment threatens injury to the patient or others. * * *

If a court authorizes medication on these alternative grounds, the need to consider authorization on trial competence grounds will likely disappear. Even if a court decides medication cannot be authorized on the alternative grounds, the findings underlying such a decision will help to inform expert opinion and judicial decisionmaking in respect to a request to administer drugs for trial competence purposes. At the least, they will facilitate direct medical and legal focus upon such questions as: Why is it medically appropriate forcibly to administer antipsychotic drugs to an individual who (1) is not dangerous and (2) is competent to make up his own mind about treatment? Can bringing such an individual to trial alone justify in whole (or at least in significant part) administration of a drug that may have adverse side effects, including side effects that may to some extent impair a defense at trial? We consequently believe that a court, asked to approve forced administration of drugs for purposes of rendering a defendant compe-tent to stand trial, should ordinarily determine whether the Govern-ment seeks, or has first sought, permission for forced administration of drugs on these other *Harper*-type grounds; and, if not, why not.

539 U.S. at 181–83, 123 S.Ct. at 2185–86. Justice Scalia, joined by Justices O'Connor and Thomas, dissented on the ground that the Eighth Circuit, and consequently the Supreme Court, lacked jurisdiction over the case because it did not come under the collateral order rule properly understood.

Page 752. Add the following new note:

4. **Effect of Incompetency on Execution.** An impaired defendant may be—or become—incompetent for purposes other than continuing trial. In Ford v. Wainwright, 477 U.S. 399, 106 S.Ct. 2595, 91 L.Ed.2d 335 (1986), a split Court made clear that the Eighth Amendment's prohibition of cruel and unusual punish-ment may bar the carrying out of a sentence of death upon a convicted but impaired defendant. As a matter of federal constitutional law, then, a convicted defendant

may be incompetent to be executed. No opinion in *Ford* attracted a majority of the members of the Court, however. The Eighth Amendment's requirements were developed by a five justice majority opinion in Panetti v. Quarterman, 551 U.S. 930, 127 S.Ct. 2842, 168 L.Ed.2d 662 (2007).

Panetti found the Eighth Amendment's procedural requirements set out in Justice Powell's concurring opinion in *Ford*:

> Once a prisoner seeking a stay of execution has made "a substantial threshold showing of insanity," the protection afforded by procedural due process includes a "fair hearing" in accord with fundamental fairness. This protection means a prisoner must be accorded an "opportunity to be heard," though "a constitutionally acceptable procedure may be far less formal than a trial."

551 U.S. at 949, 127 S.Ct. at 2856, quoting from *Ford*, 477 U.S. at 426, 424, 106 S.Ct. at 2609-10 (Powell, J., concurring in part and concurring in the judgment).

On the substantive criterion to be applied, *Panetti* found less guidance in the *Ford* opinions:

> Writing for four Justices, Justice Marshall concluded by indicating that the Eighth Amendment prohibits execution of "one whose mental illness prevents him from comprehending the reasons for the penalty or its implications." Justice Powell, in his separate opinion, asserted that the Eighth Amendment "forbids the execution only of those who are unaware of the punishment they are about to suffer and why they are to suffer it."

551 U.S. at 957, 127 S.Ct. at 2861. The lower courts in *Panetti* had applied a standard that required only that Panetti know that he is to be executed and that the reason the State gives for that execution is his commission of the crimes of which he was convicted. Panetti argued that even if he met these criterion, he nevertheless was incompetent to be executed. A psychotic mental disorder, he asserted, caused him to have a delusional beliefs that the State's given reason for the execution is a "sham" and in truth the State is executing him to stop him from preaching. The lower courts held evidence of such beliefs irrelevant because under *Ford* a defendant cannot establish incompetency to be executed by showing he lacks a rational understanding of the State's reasons for executing him.

The Supreme Court held that the standard applied by the lower federal courts was improper because it failed to implement the rationales relied upon in *Ford*:

> The principles set forth in *Ford* are put at risk by a rule that deems delusions relevant only with respect to the State's announced reason for a punishment or the fact of an imminent execution, as opposed to the real interests the State seeks to vindicate. We likewise find no support elsewhere in *Ford*, * * * for the proposition that a prisoner is automatically foreclosed from demonstrating incompetency once a court has found he can identify the stated reason for his execution. A prisoner's awareness of the State's rationale for an execution is not the same as a rational understanding of it. *Ford* does not foreclose inquiry into the latter.

* * *

> [Panetti's] submission is that he suffers from a severe, documented mental illness that is the source of gross delusions preventing him from comprehending

the meaning and purpose of the punishment to which he has been sentenced. This argument, we hold, should have been considered.

551 U.S. at 959–60, 127 S.Ct. at 2861–62. Particularly since the record before it was developed under a standard found to be improper, the Court declined to articulate a rule governing all competency to be executed situations. It therefore remanded the case for further proceedings, clearly anticipating that more fully developed expert testimony "may clarify the extent to which severe delusions may render a subject's perception of reality so distorted that he should be deemed incompetent [to be executed]." 551 U.S. at 962, 127 S.Ct. at 2863.

CHAPTER 17

DISCOVERY AND DISCLOSURE

A. PROSECUTORIAL DISCLOSURE

1. CONSTITUTIONAL OBLIGATIONS

Page 771. Add the following at the end of Note 1:

The respondent in Illinois v. Fisher, 540 U.S. 544, 124 S.Ct. 1200, 157 L.Ed.2d 1060 (2004) was arrested for possession of cocaine. His attorney moved for discovery of the substance upon which the arrest was based, but respondent absconded, not to be found for ten years. In the meantime police had destroyed the substance after it had tested positive for cocaine. The Illinois Appellate Court held that the destruction violated due process because of the discovery motion that had been pending. The United States Supreme Court, in a per curiam opinion, reversed. The *Youngblood* rule, requiring a showing of bad faith, applies here:

> We have never held or suggested that the existence of a pending discovery request eliminates the necessity of showing bad faith on the part of police. Indeed, the result reached in this case demonstrates why such a per se rule would negate the very reason we adopted the bad-faith requirement in the first place: to "limi[t] the extent of the police's obligation to preserve evidence to reasonable grounds and confin[e] it to that class of cases where the interests of justice most clearly require it." 488 U.S., at 58, 109 S.Ct. 333.

540 U.S. at 548, 124 S.Ct. at 1202.

Page 775. Add the following before 2. Statutory Considerations:

United States v. Ruiz

Supreme Court of the United States, 2002.
536 U.S. 622, 122 S.Ct. 2450, 153 L.Ed.2d 586.

■ JUSTICE BREYER delivered the opinion of the Court.

In this case we primarily consider whether the Fifth and Sixth Amendments require federal prosecutors, before entering into a binding plea agreement with a criminal defendant, to disclose "impeachment information relating to any informants or other witnesses." App. to Pet. for Cert. 46a. We hold that the Constitution does not require that disclosure.

I

After immigration agents found 30 kilograms of marijuana in Angela Ruiz's luggage, federal prosecutors offered her what is known in the

Southern District of California as a "fast track" plea bargain. That bargain—standard in that district—asks a defendant to waive indictment, trial, and an appeal. In return, the Government agrees to recommend to the sentencing judge a two-level departure downward from the otherwise applicable United States Sentencing Guidelines sentence. In Ruiz's case, a two level departure downward would have shortened the ordinary Guidelines-specified 18–to–24–month sentencing range by 6 months, to 12–to–18 months. 241 F.3d 1157, 1161 (C.A.9 2001).

The prosecutors' proposed plea agreement contains a set of detailed terms. Among other things, it specifies that "any [known] information establishing the factual innocence of the defendant" "has been turned over to the defendant," and it acknowledges the Government's "continuing duty to provide such information." App. to Pet. for Cert. 45a–46a. At the same time it requires that the defendant "waiv[e] the right" to receive "impeachment information relating to any informants or other witnesses" as well as the right to receive information supporting any affirmative defense the defendant raises if the case goes to trial. Id., at 46a. Because Ruiz would not agree to this last-mentioned waiver, the prosecutors withdrew their bargaining offer. The Government then indicted Ruiz for unlawful drug possession. And despite the absence of any agreement, Ruiz ultimately pleaded guilty.

At sentencing, Ruiz asked the judge to grant her the same two-level downward departure that the Government would have recommended had she accepted the "fast track" agreement. The Government opposed her request, and the District Court denied it, imposing a standard Guideline sentence instead. 241 F.3d, at 1161.

Relying on 18 U.S.C. § 3742, * * *, Ruiz appealed her sentence to the United States Court of Appeals for the Ninth Circuit. The Ninth Circuit vacated the District Court's sentencing determination. The Ninth Circuit pointed out that the Constitution requires prosecutors to make certain impeachment information available to a defendant before trial. 241 F.3d, at 1166. It decided that this obligation entitles defendants to receive that same information before they enter into a plea agreement. Id., at 1164. The Ninth Circuit also decided that the Constitution prohibits defendants from waiving their right to that information. Id., at 1165–1166. And it held that the prosecutors' standard "fast track" plea agreement was unlawful because it insisted upon that waiver. Id., at 1167. The Ninth Circuit remanded the case so that the District Court could decide any related factual disputes and determine an appropriate remedy. Id., at 1169.

The Government sought certiorari. It stressed what it considered serious adverse practical implications of the Ninth Circuit's constitutional holding. And it added that the holding is unique among courts of appeals. Pet. for Cert. 8. We granted the Government's petition. 534 U.S. 1074, 122 S.Ct. 803, 151 L.Ed.2d 689 (1992).

II [jurisdiction discussion omitted]

III

The constitutional question concerns a federal criminal defendant's waiver of the right to receive from prosecutors exculpatory impeachment material—a right that the Constitution provides as part of its basic "fair trial" guarantee. See U.S. Const., Amdts. 5, 6. See also Brady v. Maryland, 373 U.S. 83, 87, 83 S.Ct. 1194, 10 L.Ed.2d 215 (1963) (Due process requires prosecutors to "avoi[d] . . . an unfair trial" by making available "upon request" evidence "favorable to an accused . . . where the evidence is material either to guilt or to punishment"); United States v. Agurs, 427 U.S. 97, 112–113, 96 S.Ct. 2392, 49 L.Ed.2d 342 (1976) (defense request unnecessary); Kyles v. Whitley, 514 U.S. 419, 435, 115 S.Ct. 1555, 131 L.Ed.2d 490 (1995) (exculpatory evidence is evidence the suppression of which would "undermin[e] confidence in the verdict"); Giglio v. United States, 405 U.S. 150, 154, 92 S.Ct. 763, 31 L.Ed.2d 104 (1972) (exculpatory evidence includes "evidence affecting" witness "credibility," where the witness' "reliability" is likely "determinative of guilt or innocence").

When a defendant pleads guilty he or she, of course, forgoes not only a fair trial, but also other accompanying constitutional guarantees. Boykin v. Alabama, 395 U.S. 238, 243, 89 S.Ct. 1709, 23 L.Ed.2d 274 (1969) (pleading guilty implicates the Fifth Amendment privilege against self-incrimination, the Sixth Amendment right to confront one's accusers, and the Sixth Amendment right to trial by jury). Given the seriousness of the matter, the Constitution insists, among other things, that the defendant enter a guilty plea that is "voluntary" and that the defendant must make related waivers "knowing[ly], intelligent[ly], [and] with sufficient awareness of the relevant circumstances and likely consequences." Brady v. United States, 397 U.S. 742, 748, 90 S.Ct. 1463, 25 L.Ed.2d 747 (1970); see also Boykin, supra, at 242, 89 S.Ct. 1709.

In this case, the Ninth Circuit in effect held that a guilty plea is not "voluntary" (and that the defendant could not, by pleading guilty, waive his right to a fair trial) unless the prosecutors first made the same disclosure of material impeachment information that the prosecutors would have had to make had the defendant insisted upon a trial. We must decide whether the Constitution requires that preguilty plea disclosure of impeachment information. We conclude that it does not.

First, impeachment information is special in relation to the fairness of a trial, not in respect to whether a plea is voluntary ("knowing," "intelligent," and "sufficient[ly] aware"). Of course, the more information the defendant has, the more aware he is of the likely consequences of a plea, waiver, or decision, and the wiser that decision will likely be. But the Constitution does not require the prosecutor to share all useful information with the defendant. Weatherford v. Bursey, 429 U.S. 545, 559, 97 S.Ct. 837, 51 L.Ed.2d 30 (1977) ("There is no general constitutional right to discovery in a criminal case"). And the law ordinarily considers a waiver knowing, intelligent, and sufficiently aware if the defendant fully understands the nature of the right and how it would likely apply in general in the circumstances—even though the defendant may not know the specific detailed consequences of invoking it. A defendant, for example, may waive his right to remain silent, his right to a jury trial, or his right to counsel even if the defendant does not know the specific questions the authorities intend to ask, who will likely serve on the jury, or the particular lawyer the State might otherwise provide. Cf. Colorado v. Spring, 479 U.S. 564, 573–575, 107 S.Ct. 851, 93 L.Ed.2d 954 (1987) (Fifth Amendment privilege against self-incrimination waived when defendant received standard Miranda warnings regarding the nature of the right but not told the specific interrogation questions to be asked).

It is particularly difficult to characterize impeachment information as critical information of which the defendant must always be aware prior to pleading guilty given the random way in which such information may, or may not, help a particular defendant. The degree of help that impeachment information can provide will depend upon the defendant's own independent knowledge of the prosecution's potential case—a matter that the Constitution does not require prosecutors to disclose.

Second, we have found no legal authority embodied either in this Court's past cases or in cases from other circuits that provide significant support for the Ninth Circuit's decision. To the contrary, this Court has found that the Constitution, in respect to a defendant's awareness of relevant circumstances, does not require complete knowledge of the relevant circumstances, but permits a court to accept a guilty plea, with its accompanying waiver of various constitutional rights, despite various forms of misapprehension under which a defendant might labor. See Brady v. United States, 397 U.S., at 757, 90 S.Ct. 1463 (defendant "misapprehended the quality of the State's case"); ibid. (defendant misapprehended "the likely penalties"); ibid. (defendant failed to "anticipate a change in the law regarding" relevant "punishments"); McMann v. Richardson, 397 U.S. 759, 770, 90 S.Ct. 1441, 25 L.Ed.2d 763 (1970) (counsel "misjudged the admissibility" of a "confession"); United States v. Broce, 488 U.S. 563, 573, 109 S.Ct. 757, 102 L.Ed.2d 927 (1989) (counsel failed to point out a potential defense); Tollett v. Henderson, 411 U.S. 258, 267, 93 S.Ct. 1602, 36 L.Ed.2d 235 (1973) (counsel failed to find a potential constitutional infirmity in grand jury proceedings). It is difficult to distinguish, in terms of importance, (1) a defendant's ignorance of grounds for impeachment of potential witnesses at a possible future trial from (2) the varying forms of ignorance at issue in these cases.

Third, due process considerations, the very considerations that led this Court to find trial-related rights to exculpatory and impeachment information in Brady and Giglio, argue against the existence of the "right" that the Ninth Circuit found here. This Court has said that due process considerations include not only (1) the nature of the private interest at stake, but also (2) the value of the additional safeguard, and (3) the adverse impact of the requirement upon the Government's interests. Ake v. Oklahoma, 470 U.S. 68, 77, 105 S.Ct. 1087, 84 L.Ed.2d 53 (1985). Here, as we have just pointed out, the added value of the Ninth Circuit's "right" to a defendant is often limited, for it depends upon the defendant's independent awareness of the details of the Government's case. And in any case, as the proposed plea agreement at issue here specifies, the Government will provide "any information establishing the factual innocence of the defendant" regardless. That fact, along with other guilty-plea safeguards, see Fed. Rule Crim. Proc. 11, diminishes the force of Ruiz's concern that, in the absence of impeachment information, innocent individuals, accused of crimes, will plead guilty. Cf. McCarthy v. United States, 394 U.S. 459, 465–467, 89 S.Ct. 1166, 22 L.Ed.2d 418 (1969) (discussing Rule 11's role in protecting a defendant's constitutional rights).

At the same time, a constitutional obligation to provide impeachment information during plea bargaining, prior to entry of a guilty plea, could seriously interfere with the Government's interest in securing those guilty pleas that are factually justified, desired by defendants, and help to secure the efficient administration of justice. The Ninth Circuit's rule risks premature disclosure of Government witness information, which, the Government tells us, could "disrupt ongoing investigations" and expose prospective witnesses to serious harm. Brief for United States 25. Cf. Amendments to Federal Rules of Criminal Procedure: Hearings before the Subcommittee on Criminal Justice of the House Committee on the Judiciary, 94th Cong., 1st Sess., 92 (1975) (statement of John C. Keney, Acting Assistant Attorney General, Criminal Div., Dept. of Justice) (opposing mandated witness disclosure three days before trial because of documented instances of witness intimidation). And the careful tailoring that characterizes most legal Government witness disclosure requirements suggests recognition by both Congress and the Federal Rules Committees that such concerns are valid. See, e.g., 18 U.S.C. § 3432 (witness list disclosure required in capital cases three days before trial with exceptions); § 3500 (Government witness statements ordinarily subject to discovery only after testimony given); Fed. Rule Crim. Proc. 16(a)(2) (embodies limitations of 18 U.S.C. § 3500). Compare 156 F.R.D. 460, 461–462 (1994) (congressional proposal to significantly broaden § 3500) with 167 F.R.D. 221, 223, n. (judicial conference opposing congressional proposal).

Consequently, the Ninth Circuit's requirement could force the Government to abandon its "general practice" of not "disclos[ing] to a defendant pleading guilty information that would reveal the identities of cooperating informants, undercover investigators, or other prospective witnesses." Brief for United States 25. It could require the Government to devote substantially more resources to trial preparation prior to plea bargaining, thereby depriving the plea-bargaining process of its main resource-saving advantages. Or it could lead the Government instead to abandon its heavy reliance upon plea bargaining in a vast number—90% or more—of federal criminal cases. We cannot say that the Constitution's due process require-ment demands so radical a change in the criminal justice process in order to achieve so comparatively small a constitutional benefit.

These considerations, taken together, lead us to conclude that the Constitution does not require the Government to disclose material im-peachment evidence prior to entering a plea agreement with a criminal defendant.

In addition, we note that the "fast track" plea agreement requires a defendant to waive her right to receive information the Government has regarding any "affirmative defense" she raises at trial. Pet. for Cert. 46a. We do not believe the Constitution here requires provision of this informa-tion to the defendant prior to plea bargaining—for most (though not all) of the reasons previously stated. That is to say, in the context of this agreement, the need for this information is more closely related to the fairness of a trial than to the voluntariness of the plea; the value in terms of the defendant's added awareness of relevant circumstances is ordinarily limited; yet the added burden imposed upon the Government by requiring its provision well in advance of trial (often before trial preparation begins) can be serious, thereby significantly interfering with the administration of the plea bargaining process.

For these reasons the decision of the Court of Appeals for the Ninth Circuit is

Reversed.

■ JUSTICE THOMAS, concurring in the judgment.

I agree with the Court that the Constitution does not require the Government to disclose either affirmative defense information or impeach-ment information relating to informants or other witnesses before entering into a binding plea agreement with a criminal defendant. The Court, however, suggests that the constitutional analysis turns in some part on the "degree of help" such information would provide to the defendant at the plea stage, * * *, a distinction that is neither necessary nor accurate. To the extent that the Court is implicitly drawing a line based on a flawed characterization about the usefulness of certain types of information, I can only concur in the judgment. The principle supporting Brady was "avoid-ance of an unfair trial to the accused." Brady v. Maryland, 373 U.S. 83, 87, 83 S.Ct. 1194, 10 L.Ed.2d 215 (1963). That concern is not implicated at the plea stage regardless.

CHAPTER 20

DOUBLE JEOPARDY

A. FORMER ACQUITTAL

Page 839.   Add the following before Note 2:

1a. **Trial Court's Ability to Reconsider Ruling that Evidence is Insufficient.** If a trial judge during trial holds that the evidence is insufficient, does double jeopardy bar the judge from later reconsidering that ruling? The issue was addressed in Smith v. Massachusetts, 543 U.S. 462, 125 S.Ct. 1129, 160 L.Ed.2d 914 (2005).

Smith and his girlfriend were tried together. Smith was charged with three counts: assault with intent to murder, assault with a dangerous weapon, and unlawful possession of a firearm with a barrel less than 16 inches in length. When the prosecution rested, Smith moved for a required finding of not guilty on the firearms charge because no evidence had directly shown that the length of the barrel was less than 16 inches. Out of the jury's presence, the trial court granted the motion. The judge marked "Allowed" on Smith's written motion and caused the allowance of the motion to be reflected on the docket.

Trial proceeded and Smith's co-defendant presented one witness. Both defendants rested, and a short recess was taken. At the end of the recess and before final arguments to the jury, the prosecutor showed the judge case law authority indicating that the jury could infer the length of the firearm's barrel from testimony such as that produced by the prosecution. The judge announced orally that she was "reversing" her previous ruling and would permit the firearm count to go to the jury. Notations to this effect were made on Smith's motion and the docket. The jury convicted Smith on all three counts submitted to it.

A 5–to–4 majority of the Supreme Court held this violated double jeopardy. The judge's ruling was a judgment of acquittal on that count, apparently on its face final. The majority explained:

> The Double Jeopardy Clause's guarantee cannot be allowed to become a potential snare for those who reasonably rely upon it. If, after a facially unqualified midtrial dismissal of one count, the trial has proceeded to the defendant's introduction of evidence, the acquittal must be treated as final, unless the availability of reconsideration has been plainly established by pre-existing rule or case authority expressly applicable to midtrial rulings on the sufficiency of the evidence. That requirement was not met here.

543 U.S. at 473, 125 S.Ct. at 1137. Massachusetts law gave Smith no reason to doubt the finality of the trial court's ruling.

The dissenters would have found no serious double jeopardy problem presented. The real question, they asserted, was whether on the facts there was a violation of

Smith's due process right to "a timely, fully informed opportunity to meet the State's charges." Here, Smith suffered no prejudice from what occurred. 543 U.S. at 476, 125 S.Ct. at 1139 (Ginsburg, J., dissenting). The majority responded:

> The dissent goes to great lengths to establish that there was no prejudice here, since the acquittal was legally wrong, and the defendant was deprived of no available defense. But the Double Jeopardy Clause has never required prejudice beyond the very exposure to a second jeopardy. To put it differently: requiring someone to defend against a charge of which he has already been acquitted is prejudice *per se* for purposes of the Double Jeopardy Clause—even when the acquittal was erroneous because the evidence was sufficient. Of course it is not even clear that the dissent's due-process analysis would acknowledge prejudice when a midtrial acquittal was correct when rendered, so long as evidence sufficient to sustain the charge was eventually introduced (after the acquittal and during the defendant's case). Our double=-jeopardy cases make clear that an acquittal bars the prosecution from seeking "another opportunity to supply evidence which it failed to muster" before jeopardy terminated.

543 U.S. at 473 n. 7, 125 S.Ct. at 1137 n. 7.

Page 847.   Add the following before Note 10:

9a. **When the jury hangs on the death penalty.** The Supreme Court addressed the double jeopardy implications of a hung jury at the penalty phase of a capital murder trial in Sattazahn v. Pennsylvania, 537 U.S. 101, 123 S.Ct. 732, 154 L.Ed.2d 588 (2003). Petitioner was convicted of first degree murder and other offenses, but the jury hung 9 to 3 in favor of life imprisonment at the penalty phase. The trial court discharged the jury and sentenced the petitioner to life. The Pennsylvania Supreme court reversed the conviction for first degree murder and the state announced its intention to seek the death penalty. The Pennsylvania Supreme Court rejected petitioner's pre-trial claim that double jeopardy would preclude the imposition of the death penalty.

The Supreme Court, in a 5 to 4 opinion by Justice Scalia, affirmed. Justice Scalia distinguished *Bullington*:

> Under the Bullington line of cases just discussed, the touchstone for double-jeopardy protection in capital-sentencing proceedings is whether there has been an "acquittal." Petitioner here cannot establish that the jury or the court "acquitted" him during his first capital-sentencing proceeding. As to the jury: The verdict form returned by the foreman stated that the jury deadlocked 9-to-3 on whether to impose the death penalty; it made no findings with respect to the alleged aggravating circumstance. That result—or more appropriately, that non-result—cannot fairly be called an acquittal "based on findings sufficient to establish legal entitlement to the life sentence." * * *
>
> The entry of a life sentence by the judge was not "acquittal," either. As the Pennsylvania Supreme Court explained:
>
>> " 'Under Pennsylvania's sentencing scheme, the judge has no discretion to fashion sentence once he finds that the jury is deadlocked. The statute directs him to enter a life sentence. 42 Pa.C.S. § 9711(c)(1)(v) (... if ... further deliberation will not result in a unanimous agreement as to the sentence, ... the court *shall* sentence the defendant to life imprisonment.) (emphasis added). The judge makes no findings and resolves no factual

matter. Since judgment is not based on findings which resolve some factual matter, it is not sufficient to establish legal entitlement to a life sentence. A default judgment does not trigger a double jeopardy bar to the death penalty upon retrial.' " 563 Pa., at 548, 763 A.2d, at 367 (quoting Martorano, 535 Pa., at 194, 634 A.2d, at 1070).

It could be argued, perhaps, that the statutorily required entry of a life sentence creates an "entitlement" even without an "acquittal," because that is what the Pennsylvania Legislature intended—i.e., it intended that the life sentence should survive vacation of the underlying conviction. The Pennsylvania Supreme Court, however, did not find such intent in the statute—and there was eminently good cause not to do so. A State's simple interest in closure might make it willing to accept the default penalty of life imprisonment when the conviction is affirmed and the case is, except for that issue, at an end—but unwilling to do so when the case must be retried anyway. And its interest in conservation of resources might make it willing to leave the sentencing issue unresolved (and the default life sentence in place) where the cost of resolving it is the empaneling of a new jury and, in all likelihood, a repetition of much of the guilt phase of the first trial—though it is eager to attend to that unfinished business if there is to be a new jury and a new trial anyway.

537 U.S. at 109–10, 123 S.Ct. at 738–39. Justice Scalia, writing only for himself, The Chief Justice and Justice Thomas, would have gone further. He opined that the definition of "offense" under Apprendi v. New Jersey [Chapter 23 of this Supplement] should also apply to double jeopardy issues. Under that analysis, had the jury decided to impose life, that would have acquitted the defendant of the offense of first degree murder plus aggravating circumstances and would have precluded re-prosecution for any version of first degree murder. That is not what happened in this case, however. Justice O'Connor concurred to explicitly reject the notion that *Apprendi* could apply in this situation. Justice Ginsburg, joined by Justices Stevens, Souter and Breyer, dissented.

Page 855.   Add the following to the Notes after Ashe v. Swenson:

5.   **Different verdicts on several counts.** What analysis is appropriate if a jury acquits on some counts but is unable to reach a verdict on others so that mistrials are declared on those counts? In Yeager v. United States, ___ U.S. ___, 129 S.Ct. 2360, 174 L.Ed.2d 78 (2009), a majority—over vigorous dissent—held that under *Ashe* reprosecution on the mistried counts would be barred if the defendant showed that the acquittals demonstrated that the jury necessarily resolved in the defendant's favor an issue of ultimate fact that the prosecution must prove to convict him on the mistried counts.

In *Yeager*, the Court of Appeals had held that the inability of the jury to reach verdicts on the mistried counts should be considered in determining whether the defendant has proved that the acquittals reflected that the jury necessarily resolved the fact at issue in the defendant's favor. It concluded that the inability to reach a verdict on the mistried counts was inconsistent with the acquittals. On this basis, it reasoned the defendant had failed to prove the acquittals necessarily resolved the controlling factual question in the defendant's favor. This, the *Yeager* majority held, was error. Under *Ashe*, the "record of [the] prior proceeding" is to be considered in determining the significance of an acquittal in that proceeding. But "a jury speaks only through its verdict." Therefore, a jury's failure to reach a verdict is not a relevant part of the record entitled to consideration. ____ U.S. at ____, 129 S.Ct. at 2367–68.

C. TERMINATION WITHOUT ACQUITTAL OR CONVICTION

1. MISTRIALS

Page 891. Add the following before Note 5 after Illinois v. Somerville:

4a. **Assessing whether a jury is unable to reach a verdict.** The federal constitutional duties of a trial judge considering whether to grant a mistrial because of a hung jury were addressed—somewhat—in Renico v. Lett, ____ U.S. ____, 130 S.Ct. 1855, 176 L.Ed.2d 678 (2010). A mistrial is appropriate only when there is "a high degree of necessity." But the trial judge must be afforded broad discretion in deciding whether requiring the jury to further deliberate may enable the jury to reach a unanimous and just verdict. Denying trial judges such discretion might lead them to employ coercive means to break deadlocks and thus result in improper verdicts. In the case before it, the Court decided only that the state courts' ultimate holding that the trial judge acted acceptably in declaring a mistrial was not an unreasonable application of clearly established federal law justifying federal habeas corpus relief. The majority carefully withheld judgment on whether the trial judge acted as she should have and on whether the state appellate courts should have found her actions an abuse of discretion. ____ U.S. at ____, 130 S.Ct. at 1862.

CHAPTER 22

ADJUDICATION OF GUILT BY PLEA

A. ENTRY OF THE PLEA OF GUILTY

Page 938. Add the following Note:

2a. **Harmless and plain errors under Rule 11.** The respondent in United States v. Vonn, 535 U.S. 55, 122 S.Ct. 1043, 152 L.Ed.2d 90 (2002) entered a plea of guilty in a ceremony in which the District Court judge failed to admonish him about his right to counsel at trial in violation of Rule 11(c)(3). [Casebook p. 937] There was no trial objection to this omission. On appeal from the District Court's refusal to permit withdrawal of the plea, the government argued that the burden was upon the respondent under the plain error provision in Federal Rules of Criminal Procedure Rule 52(b) ("Plain errors or defects affecting substantial rights may be noticed although they were not brought to the attention of the trial court.") to show that substantial rights were violated by the error. The Court of Appeals rejected that argument in favor of the position that the promulgation of Rule 11(h), [Casebook p. 937] which was closely modeled after Rule 52(a), meant that all errors under Rule 11, whether objected to or not, should be analyzed under a harmless error rule that requires reversal unless the government can show the error did not affect substantial rights. Failure to incorporate Rule 52(b) into Rule 11, while incorporating Rule 52(a) signaled a rejection of the plain error rule. The Court of Appeals also held that only the record of the plea ceremony could be considered in deciding whether substantial rights had been affected—not other parts of the trial record nor evidence produced by a post-trial evidentiary hearing. The Court of Appeals vacated the conviction.

The Supreme Court, in an opinion by Justice Souter, vacated the judgment of the Court of Appeals. Respondent had relied heavily upon the Supreme Court's opinion in McCarthy v. United States that applied an automatic reversal consequence to Rule 11 deficiencies. However appropriate the *McCarthy* rule may have been when announced, all of that changed in 1975 when Rule 11 was transformed from a brief statement of principles to a detailed system for regulating the acceptance of guilty pleas. Further, when the harmless error language of Rule 11(h) was added in 1983, it was for the express purpose of abrogating *McCarthy* in view of the 1975 changes. There was no occasion in 1983 to address the plain error branch of Rule 52, so no implication should be drawn that the promulgation of Rule 11(h) reflects a rejection of plain error. To hold otherwise would be to ignore Rule 52(b). If the respondent's position were adopted a criminal defendant would have no incentive to object to Rule 11 deficiencies at the earliest possible opportunity—there would be no punishment for delaying until it is strategically advantageous to raise the issue.

As to the second branch of the Court of Appeals' opinion—that determining whether substantial rights were affected is confined to examining the record of the plea ceremony—the Supreme Court held that other parts of the record of the District Court proceedings should also be consulted in making the harmless/plain error determination. In this case the correct Rule 11(c)(3) admonition had been provided by the magistrate upon respondent's first appearance in court, which suggests that the later omission may not have affected substantial rights.

C. Plea Bargaining

2. "Voluntariness" of Pleas and Related Matters

a. BASIC VOLUNTARINESS CONSIDERATIONS

Page 969. Add the following to the notes after Brady v. United States:

3. **Challenging whether a plea was informed and voluntary**. The constitutional requirements for guilty pleas were applied in Bradshaw v. Stumpf, 545 U.S. 175, 125 S.Ct. 2398, 162 L.Ed.2d 143 (2005).

During a robbery perpetrated by three persons, Mary Jane Stout was killed and Norman Stout was shot but survived. Stumpf was charged with a number of crimes based on these events, including attempted aggravated murder of Norman Stout, aggravated robbery and two counts of grand theft. He was also charged with the aggravated murder of Mary Jane Stout. The murder indictment listed four statutory "specifications," three of which each made Stumpf eligible for the death penalty. A three judge panel was assigned the case. In return for Stumpf's agreement to plead guilty to the murder and attempted murder charges and one of the alleged capital specifications, the State agreed to drop most of the other charges and the remaining capital specifications. The presiding judge held a plea hearing and engaged in a colloquy with Stumpf and defense counsel. He then accepted the plea. The next day the panel held a "factual basis" hearing at which the State introduced evidence indicating that Stumpf himself had shot Mary Jane Stout. The defense challenged that Stumpf was the triggerperson and unsuccessfully moved for acquittal. The panel overruled the motion to acquit, satisfied itself that the plea had a factual basis, found Stumpf guilty of the attempted murder, the aggravated murder and the capital specification, and entered a verdict reflecting this. A penalty hearing was next held before the panel, after which the panel sentenced Stumpf to death.

In a federal habeas corpus proceeding, the Sixth Circuit Court of Appeals held that the records of the plea and evidentiary hearing demonstrated that the plea was constitutionally invalid. Stumpf and perhaps his attorneys, it reasoned, were unaware that the murder to which he was pleading required the intent to kill. The defense attempted to challenge the State's version of the offense at the factual hearing and contested whether Stumpf himself had shot Mary Jane Stout. The court of appeals added that the State could show that despite the record the plea was constitutionally adequate, but it had produced no extrinsic evidence to do so. Stumpf v. Mitchell, 367 F.3d 594 (6th Cir. 2004). The Court of Appeals' position was that for all practical purposes, all parties agreed that whether Stumpf had the required specific intent to kill turned on whether he was the actual shooter. When he entered his plea, Stumpf did not understand that although he retained the right at the factual basis hearing to challenge the State's contention that he was the shooter, by his plea he admitted that he acted with the necessary specific intent to kill. This prevented the plea from being voluntary, knowingly and intelligent as federal constitutional law requires.

The Supreme Court reversed:

> Stumpf's guilty plea would indeed be invalid if he had not been aware of the nature of the charges against him, including the elements of the aggravated murder charge to which he pleaded guilty. * * *

> But the Court of Appeals erred in finding that Stumpf had not been properly informed before pleading guilty. In Stumpf's plea hearing, his attorneys represented on the record that they had explained to their client the elements of the aggravated murder charge; Stumpf himself then confirmed that this representation was true. While the court taking a defendant's plea is responsible for ensuring "a record adequate for any review that may be later sought," we have never held that the judge must himself explain the elements of each charge to the defendant on the record. Rather, the constitutional prerequisites of a valid plea may be satisfied where the record accurately reflects that the nature of the charge and the elements of the crime were explained to the defendant by his own, competent counsel. Where a defendant is represented by competent counsel, the court usually may rely on that counsel's assurance that the defendant has been properly informed of the nature and elements of the charge to which he is pleading guilty.

> Seeking to counter this natural inference, Stumpf argues, in essence, that his choice to plead guilty to the aggravated murder charge was so inconsistent with his denial of having shot the victim that he could only have pleaded guilty out of ignorance of the charge's specific intent requirement. But Stumpf's asserted inconsistency is illusory. The aggravated murder charge's intent element did not require any showing that Stumpf had himself shot Mrs. Stout. Rather, Ohio law considers aiders and abettors equally in violation of the aggravated murder statute, so long as the aiding and abetting is done with the specific intent to cause death. As a result, Stumpf's steadfast assertion that he had not shot Mrs. Stout would not necessarily have precluded him from admitting his specific intent under the statute.

545 U.S. at 182–84, 125 S.Ct. at 2405–06.

It then added:

> Finally, Stumpf, like the Court of Appeals, relies on the perception that he obtained a bad bargain by his plea—that the State's dropping several non-murder charges and two of the three capital murder specifications was a bad tradeoff for Stumpf's guilty plea. But a plea's validity may not be collaterally attacked merely because the defendant made what turned out, in retrospect, to be a poor deal. Rather, the shortcomings of the deal Stumpf obtained cast doubt on the validity of his plea only if they show either that he made the unfavorable plea on the constitutionally defective advice of counsel, or that he could not have understood the terms of the bargain he and Ohio agreed to. Though Stumpf did bring an independent claim asserting ineffective assistance of counsel, that claim is not before us in this case. And in evaluating the validity of Stumpf's plea, we are reluctant to accord much weight to his *post hoc* reevaluation of the wisdom of the bargain. Stumpf pleaded guilty knowing that the State had copious evidence against him, including the testimony of Mr.

Stout; the plea eliminated two of the three capital specifications the State could rely on in seeking the death penalty; and the plea allowed Stumpf to assert his acceptance of responsibility as an argument in mitigation. Under these circumstances, the plea may well have been a knowing, voluntary, and intelligent reaction to a litigation situation that was difficult, to say the least. * * *

545 U.S. at 185, 125 S.Ct. at 2407.

CHAPTER 23

ADJUDICATION OF GUILT OR INNOCENCE BY TRIAL

A. PROOF BEYOND A REASONABLE DOUBT

Page 1010. Replace Note 2 with the following principal case and notes:

Apprendi v. New Jersey

Supreme Court of the United States, 2000.
530 U.S. 466, 120 S.Ct. 2348, 147 L.Ed.2d 435.

■ JUSTICE STEVENS delivered the opinion of the Court.

A New Jersey statute classifies the possession of a firearm for an unlawful purpose as a "second-degree" offense. N.J. Stat. Ann. § 2C:39–4(a) (West 1995). Such an offense is punishable by imprisonment for "between five years and 10 years." § 2C:43–6(a)(2). A separate statute, described by that State's Supreme Court as a "hate crime" law, provides for an "extended term" of imprisonment if the trial judge finds, by a preponderance of the evidence, that "[t]he defendant in committing the crime acted with a purpose to intimidate an individual or group of individuals because of race, color, gender, handicap, religion, sexual orientation or ethnicity." N.J. Stat. Ann. § 2C:44–3(e) (West Supp.2000). The extended term authorized by the hate crime law for second-degree offenses is imprisonment for "between 10 and 20 years." § 2C:43–7(a)(3).

The question presented is whether the Due Process Clause of the Fourteenth Amendment requires that a factual determination authorizing an increase in the maximum prison sentence for an offense from 10 to 20 years be made by a jury on the basis of proof beyond a reasonable doubt.

I

At 2:04 a.m. on December 22, 1994, petitioner Charles C. Apprendi, Jr., fired several .22–caliber bullets into the home of an African–American family that had recently moved into a previously all-white neighborhood in Vineland, New Jersey. Apprendi was promptly arrested and, at 3:05 a.m., admitted that he was the shooter. After further questioning, at 6:04 a.m., he made a statement—which he later retracted—that even though he did not know the occupants of the house personally, "because they are black in color he does not want them in the neighborhood." 159 N.J. 7, 10, 731 A.2d 485, 486 (1999).

A New Jersey grand jury returned a 23–count indictment charging Apprendi with four first-degree, eight second-degree, six third-degree, and five fourth-degree offenses. The charges alleged shootings on four different dates, as well as the unlawful possession of various weapons. None of the counts referred to the hate crime statute, and none alleged that Apprendi acted with a racially biased purpose.

The parties entered into a plea agreement, pursuant to which Apprendi pleaded guilty to two counts (3 and 18) of second-degree possession of a firearm for an unlawful purpose, N.J. Stat. Ann. § 2C:39–4a (West 1995), and one count (22) of the third-degree offense of unlawful possession of an antipersonnel bomb, § 2C:39–3a; the prosecutor dismissed the other 20 counts. Under state law, a second-degree offense carries a penalty range of 5 to 10 years, § 2C:43–6(a)(2); a third-degree offense carries a penalty range of between 3 and 5 years, § 2C:43–6(a)(3). As part of the plea agreement, however, the State reserved the right to request the court to impose a higher "enhanced" sentence on count 18 (which was based on the December 22 shooting) on the ground that that offense was committed with a biased purpose, as described in § 2C:44–3(e). Apprendi, correspondingly, reserved the right to challenge the hate crime sentence enhancement on the ground that it violates the United States Constitution.

At the plea hearing, the trial judge heard sufficient evidence to establish Apprendi's guilt on counts 3, 18, and 22; the judge then confirmed that Apprendi understood the maximum sentences that could be imposed on those counts. Because the plea agreement provided that the sentence on the sole third-degree offense (count 22) would run concurrently with the other sentences, the potential sentences on the two second-degree counts were critical. If the judge found no basis for the biased purpose enhancement, the maximum consecutive sentences on those counts would amount to 20 years in aggregate; if, however, the judge enhanced the sentence on count 18, the maximum on that count alone would be 20 years and the maximum for the two counts in aggregate would be 30 years, with a 15–year period of parole ineligibility.

After the trial judge accepted the three guilty pleas, the prosecutor filed a formal motion for an extended term. The trial judge thereafter held an evidentiary hearing on the issue of Apprendi's "purpose" for the shooting on December 22. Apprendi adduced evidence from a psychologist and from seven character witnesses who testified that he did not have a reputation for racial bias. He also took the stand himself, explaining that the incident was an unintended consequence of overindulgence in alcohol, denying that he was in any way biased against African–Americans, and denying that his statement to the police had been accurately described. The judge, however, found the police officer's testimony credible, and concluded that the evidence supported a finding "that the crime was motivated by racial bias." App. to Pet. for Cert. 143a. Having found "by a preponderance of the evidence" that Apprendi's actions were taken "with a purpose to intimidate" as provided by the statute, id., at 138a, 139a, 144, 731 A.2d 485a, the trial judge held that the hate crime enhancement applied. Rejecting Apprendi's constitutional challenge to the statute, the judge sentenced him to a 12–year term of imprisonment on count 18, and to shorter concurrent sentences on the other two counts.

Apprendi appealed, arguing, inter alia, that the Due Process Clause of the United States Constitution requires that the finding of bias upon which his hate crime sentence was based must be proved to a jury beyond a reasonable doubt, In re Winship, 397 U.S. 358, 90 S.Ct. 1068, 25 L.Ed.2d 368 (1970). Over dissent, the Appellate Division of the Superior Court of New Jersey upheld the enhanced sentence. 304 N.J.Super. 147, 698 A.2d 1265 (1997). Relying on our decision in McMillan v. Pennsylvania, 477 U.S. 79, 106 S.Ct. 2411, 91 L.Ed.2d 67 (1986), the appeals court found that the state legislature decided to make the hate crime enhancement a "sentencing factor," rather than an element of an underlying offense—and that decision was within the State's established power to define the elements of its crimes. The hate crime statute did not create a presumption of guilt, the court determined, and did not appear "tailored to permit the . . . finding to be a tail which wags the dog of the substantive offense." 304 N.J.Super., at 154, 698 A.2d, at 1269 (quoting McMillan, 477 U.S., at 88, 106 S.Ct. 2411). Characterizing the required finding as one of "motive," the court described it as a traditional "sentencing factor," one not considered an "essential element" of any crime unless the legislature so provides. 304 N.J.Super., at 158, 698 A.2d, at 1270. While recognizing that the hate crime law did expose defendants to "greater and additional punishment," id., at 156, 698 A.2d, at 1269 (quoting McMillan, 477 U.S., at 88, 106 S.Ct. 2411), the court held that that "one factor standing alone" was not sufficient to render the statute unconstitutional, Ibid.

A divided New Jersey Supreme Court affirmed. 159 N.J. 7, 731 A.2d 485 (1999). The court began by explaining that while due process only requires the State to prove the "elements" of an offense beyond a reasonable doubt, the mere fact that a state legislature has placed a criminal component "within the sentencing provisions" of the criminal code "does not mean that the finding of a biased purpose to intimidate is not an essential element of the offense." Id., at 20, 731 A.2d, at 492. "Were that the case," the court continued, "the Legislature could just as easily allow judges, not juries, to determine if a kidnapping victim has been released unharmed." Ibid. (citing state precedent requiring such a finding to be submitted to a jury and proved beyond a reasonable doubt). Neither could the constitutional question be settled simply by defining the hate crime statute's "purpose to intimidate" as "motive" and thereby excluding the provision from any traditional conception of an "element" of a crime. Even if one could characterize the language this way—and the court doubted that such a characterization was accurate—proof of motive did not ordinarily "increase the penal consequences to an actor." Ibid. Such "[l]abels," the court concluded, would not yield an answer to Apprendi's constitutional question. Ibid.

While noting that we had just last year expressed serious doubt concerning the constitutionality of allowing penalty-enhancing findings to be determined by a judge by a preponderance of the evidence, Jones v. United States, 526 U.S. 227, 119 S.Ct. 1215, 143 L.Ed.2d 311 (1999), the court concluded that those doubts were not essential to our holding. Turning then, as the appeals court had, to McMillan, as well as to Almendarez–Torres v. United States, 523 U.S. 224, 118 S.Ct. 1219, 140 L.Ed.2d 350 (1998), the court undertook a multifactor inquiry and then held that the hate crime provision was valid. In the majority's view, the statute did not allow impermissible burden shifting, and did not "create a separate offense calling for a separate penalty." 159 N.J., at 24, 731 A.2d, at 494. Rather, "the Legislature simply took one factor that has always been considered by sentencing courts to bear on punishment and dictated the weight to be given that factor." Ibid., 731 A.2d, at 494–495. As had the appeals court, the majority recognized that the state statute was unlike that in McMillan inasmuch as it increased the maximum penalty to which a defendant could be subject. But it was not clear that this difference alone would "change the constitutional calculus," especially where, as here, "there is rarely any doubt whether the defendants committed the crimes with the purpose of intimidating the victim on the basis of race or ethnicity." 159 N.J., at 24–25, 731 A.2d, at 495. Moreover, in light of concerns "idiosyncratic" to hate crime statutes drawn carefully to avoid "punishing thought itself," the enhancement served as an appropriate balance between those concerns and the State's compelling interest in vindicating the right "to be free of invidious discrimination." Id., at 25–26, 731 A.2d, at 495.

The dissent rejected this conclusion, believing instead that the case turned on two critical characteristics: (1) "a defendant's mental state in committing the subject offense . . . necessarily involves a finding so integral to the charged offense that it must be characterized as an element thereof"; and (2) "the significantly increased sentencing range triggered by . . . the finding of a purpose to intimidate" means that the purpose "must be treated as a material element [that] must be found by a jury beyond a reasonable doubt." Id., at 30, 731 A.2d, at 498. In the dissent's view, the facts increasing sentences in both Almendarez–Torres (recidivism) and Jones (serious bodily injury) were quite distinct from New Jersey's required finding of purpose here; the latter finding turns directly on the conduct of the defendant during the crime and defines a level of culpability necessary to form the hate crime offense. While acknowledging "analytical tensions" in this Court's post-Winship jurisprudence, the dissenters concluded that "there can be little doubt that the sentencing factor applied to this defendant—the purpose to intimidate a victim because of race—must fairly be regarded as an element of the crime requiring inclusion in the indictment and proof beyond a reasonable doubt." 159 N.J., at 51, 731 A.2d, at 512.

We granted certiorari, 528 U.S. 1018, 120 S.Ct. 525, 145 L.Ed.2d 407 (1999), and now reverse.

II

It is appropriate to begin by explaining why certain aspects of the case are not relevant to the narrow issue that we must resolve. First, the State has argued that even without the trial judge's finding of racial bias, the judge could have imposed consecutive sentences on counts 3 and 18 that would have produced the 12–year term of imprisonment that Apprendi received; Apprendi's actual sentence was thus within the range authorized by statute for the three offenses to which he pleaded guilty. Brief for Respondent 4. The constitutional question, however, is whether the 12–year sentence imposed on count 18 was permissible, given that it was above the 10–year maximum for the offense charged in that count. The finding is legally significant because it increased—indeed, it doubled—the maximum range within which the judge could exercise his discretion, converting what otherwise was a maximum 10–year sentence on that count into a minimum sentence. The sentences on counts 3 and 22 have no more relevance to our disposition than the dismissal of the remaining 18 counts.

Second, although the constitutionality of basing an enhanced sentence on racial bias was argued in the New Jersey courts, that issue was not raised here. The substantive basis for New Jersey's enhancement is thus not at issue; the adequacy of New Jersey's procedure is. The strength of the state interests that are served by the hate crime legislation has no more bearing on this procedural question than the strength of the interests served by other provisions of the criminal code.

Third, we reject the suggestion by the State Supreme Court that "there is rarely any doubt" concerning the existence of the biased purpose that will support an enhanced sentence, 159 N.J., at 25, 731 A.2d, at 495. In this very case, that issue was the subject of the full evidentiary hearing we described. We assume that both the purpose of the offender, and even the known identity of the victim, will sometimes be hotly disputed, and that the outcome may well depend in some cases on the standard of proof and the identity of the factfinder.

Fourth, because there is no ambiguity in New Jersey's statutory scheme, this case does not raise any question concerning the State's power to manipulate the prosecutor's burden of proof by, for example, relying on a presumption rather than evidence to establish an element of an offense, cf. Mullaney v. Wilbur, 421 U.S. 684, 95 S.Ct. 1881, 44 L.Ed.2d 508 (1975); Sandstrom v. Montana, 442 U.S. 510, 99 S.Ct. 2450, 61 L.Ed.2d 39 (1979), or by placing the affirmative defense label on "at least some elements" of traditional crimes, Patterson v. New York, 432 U.S. 197, 210, 97 S.Ct. 2319, 53 L.Ed.2d 281 (1977). The prosecutor did not invoke any presumption to buttress the evidence of racial bias and did not claim that Apprendi had the burden of disproving an improper motive. The question whether Apprendi had a constitutional right to have a jury find such bias on the basis of proof beyond a reasonable doubt is starkly presented.

Our answer to that question was foreshadowed by our opinion in Jones v. United States, 526 U.S. 227, 119 S.Ct. 1215, 143 L.Ed.2d 311 (1999), construing a federal statute. We there noted that "under the Due Process Clause of the Fifth Amendment and the notice and jury trial guarantees of the Sixth Amendment, any fact (other than prior conviction) that increases the maximum penalty for a crime must be charged in an indictment, submitted to a jury, and proven beyond a reasonable doubt." Id., at 243, n. 6, 119 S.Ct. 1215. The Fourteenth Amendment commands the same answer in this case involving a state statute.

III

In his 1881 lecture on the criminal law, Oliver Wendell Holmes, Jr., observed: "The law threatens certain pains if you do certain things, intending thereby to give you a new motive for not doing them. If you persist in doing them, it has to inflict the pains in order that its threats may continue to be believed." New Jersey threatened Apprendi with certain pains if he unlawfully possessed a weapon and with additional pains if he selected his victims with a purpose to intimidate them because of their race. As a matter of simple justice, it seems obvious that the procedural safeguards designed to protect Apprendi from unwarranted pains should apply equally to the two acts that New Jersey has singled out for punishment. Merely using the label "sentence enhancement" to describe the latter surely does not provide a principled basis for treating them differently.

At stake in this case are constitutional protections of surpassing importance: the proscription of any deprivation of liberty without "due process of law," Amdt. 14, and the guarantee that "[i]n all criminal prosecutions, the accused shall enjoy the right to a speedy and public trial, by an impartial jury," Amdt. 6.[1] Taken together, these rights indisputably entitle a criminal defendant to "a jury determination that [he] is guilty of every element of the crime with which he is charged, beyond a reasonable

---

1. Apprendi has not here asserted a constitutional claim based on the omission of any reference to sentence enhancement or racial bias in the indictment. He relies entirely on the fact that the "due process of law" that the Fourteenth Amendment requires the States to provide to persons accused of crime encompasses the right to a trial by jury, Duncan v. Louisiana, 391 U.S. 145, 88 S.Ct. 1444, 20 L.Ed.2d 491 (1968), and the right to have every element of the offense proved beyond a reasonable doubt, In re Winship, 397 U.S. 358, 90 S.Ct. 1068, 25 L.Ed.2d 368 (1970). That Amendment has not, however, been construed to include the Fifth Amendment right to "presentment or indictment of a Grand Jury" that was implicated in our recent decision in Almendarez–Torres v. United States, 523 U.S. 224, 118 S.Ct. 1219, 140 L.Ed.2d 350 (1998). We thus do not address the indictment question separately today.

doubt." United States v. Gaudin, 515 U.S. 506, 510, 115 S.Ct. 2310, 132 L.Ed.2d 444 (1995); see also Sullivan v. Louisiana, 508 U.S. 275, 278, 113 S.Ct. 2078, 124 L.Ed.2d 182 (1993); Winship, 397 U.S., at 364, 90 S.Ct. 1068 ("[T]he Due Process Clause protects the accused against conviction except upon proof beyond a reasonable doubt of every fact necessary to constitute the crime with which he is charged").

As we have, unanimously, explained, Gaudin, 515 U.S., at 510–511, 115 S.Ct. 2310, the historical foundation for our recognition of these principles extends down centuries into the common law. "[T]o guard against a spirit of oppression and tyranny on the part of rulers," and "as the great bulwark of [our] civil and political liberties," 2 J. Story, Commentaries on the Constitution of the United States 540–541 (4th ed. 1873), trial by jury has been understood to require that "the truth of every accusation, whether preferred in the shape of indictment, information, or appeal, should afterwards be confirmed by the unanimous suffrage of twelve of [the defendant's] equals and neighbours. . . ." 4 W. Blackstone, Commentaries on the Laws of England 343 (1769) (hereinafter Blackstone) (emphasis added). See also Duncan v. Louisiana, 391 U.S. 145, 151–154, 88 S.Ct. 1444, 20 L.Ed.2d 491 (1968).

Equally well founded is the companion right to have the jury verdict based on proof beyond a reasonable doubt. "The 'demand for a higher degree of persuasion in criminal cases was recurrently expressed from ancient times, [though] its crystallization into the formula "beyond a reasonable doubt" seems to have occurred as late as 1798. It is now accepted in common law jurisdictions as the measure of persuasion by which the prosecution must convince the trier of all the essential elements of guilt.' C. McCormick, Evidence § 321, pp. 681–682 (1954); see also 9 J. Wigmore, Evidence § 2497 (3d ed.1940)." Winship, 397 U.S., at 361, 90 S.Ct. 1068. We went on to explain that the reliance on the "reasonable doubt" standard among common-law jurisdictions " 'reflect[s] a profound judgment about the way in which law should be enforced and justice administered.' " Id., at 361–362, 90 S.Ct. 1068 (quoting Duncan, 391 U.S., at 155, 88 S.Ct. 1444).

* * *

Since Winship, we have made clear beyond peradventure that Winship's due process and associated jury protections extend, to some degree, "to determinations that [go] not to a defendant's guilt or innocence, but simply to the length of his sentence." Almendarez–Torres, 523 U.S., at 251, 118 S.Ct. 1219 (SCALIA, J., dissenting). This was a primary lesson of Mullaney v. Wilbur, 421 U.S. 684, 95 S.Ct. 1881, 44 L.Ed.2d 508 (1975), in which we invalidated a Maine statute that presumed that a defendant who acted with an intent to kill possessed the "malice aforethought" necessary to constitute the State's murder offense (and therefore, was subject to that crime's associated punishment of life imprisonment). The statute placed the burden on the defendant of proving, in rebutting the statutory presumption, that he acted with a lesser degree of culpability, such as in the heat of passion, to win a reduction in the offense from murder to manslaughter (and thus a reduction of the maximum punishment of 20 years).

The State had posited in Mullaney that requiring a defendant to prove heat-of-passion intent to overcome a presumption of murderous intent did not implicate Winship protections because, upon conviction of either offense, the defendant would lose his liberty and face societal stigma just the same. Rejecting this argument, we acknowledged that criminal law "is concerned not only with guilt or innocence in the abstract, but also with the degree of criminal culpability" assessed. 421 U.S., at 697–698, 95 S.Ct. 1881. Because the "consequences" of a guilty verdict for murder and for manslaughter differed substantially, we dismissed the possibility that a State could circumvent the protections of Winship merely by "redefin[ing] the elements that constitute different crimes, characterizing them as factors that bear solely on the extent of punishment." 421 U.S., at 698, 95 S.Ct. 1881.

IV

It was in McMillan v. Pennsylvania, 477 U.S. 79, 106 S.Ct. 2411, 91 L.Ed.2d 67 (1986), that this Court, for the first time, coined the term "sentencing factor" to refer to a fact that was not found by a jury but that could affect the sentence imposed by the judge. That case involved a challenge to the State's Mandatory Minimum Sentencing Act, 42 Pa. Cons.Stat. § 9712 (1982). According to its provisions, anyone convicted of certain felonies would be subject to a mandatory minimum penalty of five years imprisonment if the judge found, by a preponderance of the evidence, that the person "visibly possessed a firearm" in the course of committing one of the specified felonies. 477 U.S., at 81–82, 106 S.Ct. 2411. Articulating for the first time, and then applying, a multifactor set of criteria for determining whether the Winship protections applied to bar such a system, we concluded that the Pennsylvania statute did not run afoul of our previous admonitions against relieving the State of its burden of proving guilt, or tailoring the mere form of a criminal statute solely to avoid Winship's strictures. 477 U.S., at 86–88, 106 S.Ct. 2411.

We did not, however, there budge from the position that (1) constitutional limits exist to States' authority to define away facts necessary to constitute a criminal offense, id., at 85–88, 106 S.Ct. 2411, and (2) that a state scheme that keeps from the jury facts that "expos[e] [defendants] to greater or additional punishment," id., at 88, 106 S.Ct. 2411, may raise serious constitutional concern. As we explained:

> "Section 9712 neither alters the maximum penalty for the crime committed nor creates a separate offense calling for a separate penalty; it operates solely to limit the sentencing court's discretion in selecting a penalty within the range already available to it without the special finding of visible possession of a firearm.... The statute gives no

impression of having been tailored to permit the visible possession finding to be a tail which wags the dog of the substantive offense. Petitioners' claim that visible possession under the Pennsylvania statute is 'really' an element of the offenses for which they are being punished—that Pennsylvania has in effect defined a new set of upgraded felonies—would have at least more superficial appeal if a finding of visible possession exposed them to greater or additional punishment, cf. 18 U.S.C. § 2113(d) (providing separate and greater punishment for bank robberies accomplished through 'use of a dangerous weapon or device'), but it does not." Id., at 87–88, 106 S.Ct. 2411.

Finally, as we made plain in Jones last Term, Almendarez–Torres v. United States, 523 U.S. 224, 118 S.Ct. 1219, 140 L.Ed.2d 350 (1998), represents at best an exceptional departure from the historic practice that we have described. In that case, we considered a federal grand jury indictment, which charged the petitioner with "having been 'found in the United States ... after being deported,'" in violation of 8 U.S.C. § 1326(a)—an offense carrying a maximum sentence of two years. 523 U.S., at 227, 118 S.Ct. 1219. Almendarez–Torres pleaded guilty to the indictment, admitting at the plea hearing that he had been deported, that he had unlawfully reentered this country, and that "the earlier deportation had taken place 'pursuant to' three earlier 'convictions' for aggravated felonies." Ibid. The Government then filed a presentence report indicating that Almendarez–Torres' offense fell within the bounds of § 1326(b) because, as specified in that provision, his original deportation had been subsequent to an aggravated felony conviction; accordingly, Almendarez–Torres could be subject to a sentence of up to 20 years. Almendarez–Torres objected, contending that because the indictment "had not mentioned his earlier aggravated felony convictions," he could be sentenced to no more than two years in prison. Ibid.

Rejecting Almendarez–Torres' objection, we concluded that sentencing him to a term higher than that attached to the offense alleged in the indictment did not violate the strictures of Winship in that case. Because Almendarez–Torres had admitted the three earlier convictions for aggravated felonies—all of which had been entered pursuant to proceedings with substantial procedural safeguards of their own—no question concerning the right to a jury trial or the standard of proof that would apply to a contested issue of fact was before the Court. Although our conclusion in that case was based in part on our application of the criteria we had invoked in McMillan, the specific question decided concerned the sufficiency of the indictment. More important, as Jones made crystal clear, 526 U.S., at 248–249, 119 S.Ct. 1215, our conclusion in Almendarez–Torres turned heavily upon the fact that the additional sentence to which the defendant was subject was "the prior commission of a serious crime." 523 U.S., at 230, 118 S.Ct. 1219; see also id., at 243, 118 S.Ct. 1219 (explaining that "recidivism ... is a traditional, if not the most traditional, basis for a sentencing court's increasing an offender's sentence"); id., at 244, 118 S.Ct. 1219 (emphasizing "the fact that recidivism 'does not relate to the commission of the offense ...'"); Jones, 526 U.S., at 249–250, n. 10, 119 S.Ct. 1215 ("The majority and the dissenters in Almendarez–Torres disagreed over the legitimacy of the Court's decision to restrict its holding to recidivism, but both sides agreed that the Court had done just that"). Both the certainty that procedural safeguards attached to any "fact" of prior conviction, and the reality that Almendarez–Torres did not challenge the accuracy of that "fact" in his case, mitigated the due process and Sixth Amendment concerns otherwise implicated in allowing a judge to determine a "fact" increasing punishment beyond the maximum of the statutory range.

Even though it is arguable that Almendarez–Torres was incorrectly decided, and that a logical application of our reasoning today should apply if the recidivist issue were contested, Apprendi does not contest the decision's validity and we need not revisit it for purposes of our decision today to treat the case as a narrow exception to the general rule we recalled at the outset. Given its unique facts, it surely does not warrant rejection of the otherwise uniform course of decision during the entire history of our jurisprudence.

In sum, our reexamination of our cases in this area, and of the history upon which they rely, confirms the opinion that we expressed in Jones. Other than the fact of a prior conviction, any fact that increases the penalty for a crime beyond the prescribed statutory maximum must be submitted to a jury, and proved beyond a reasonable doubt. With that exception, we endorse the statement of the rule set forth in the concurring opinions in that case: "[I]t is unconstitutional for a legislature to remove from the jury the assessment of facts that increase the prescribed range of penalties to which a criminal defendant is exposed. It is equally clear that such facts must be established by proof beyond a reasonable doubt." 526 U.S., at 252–253, 119 S.Ct. 1215 (opinion of Stevens, J.); see also id., at 253, 119 S.Ct. 1215 (opinion of Scalia, J.).

V

The New Jersey statutory scheme that Apprendi asks us to invalidate allows a jury to convict a defendant of a second-degree offense based on its finding beyond a reasonable doubt that he unlawfully possessed a prohibited weapon; after a subsequent and separate proceeding, it then allows a judge to impose punishment identical to that New Jersey provides for crimes of the first degree, N.J. Stat. Ann. § 2C:43–6(a)(1) (West 1999), based upon the judge's finding, by a preponderance of the evidence, that the defendant's "purpose" for unlawfully possessing the weapon was "to intimidate" his victim on the basis of a particular characteristic the victim possessed. In light of the constitutional rule explained above, and all of the cases supporting it, this practice cannot stand.

New Jersey's defense of its hate crime enhancement statute has three primary components: (1) the required finding of biased purpose is not an "element" of a distinct hate crime offense, but rather the traditional "sentencing factor" of motive; (2) McMillan holds that the legislature can authorize a judge to find a traditional sentencing factor on the basis of a preponderance of the evidence; and (3) Almendarez–Torres extended McMillan's holding to encompass factors that authorize a judge to impose a sentence beyond the maximum provided by the substantive statute under which a defendant is charged. None of these persuades us that the constitutional rule that emerges from our history and case law should incorporate an exception for this New Jersey statute.

New Jersey's first point is nothing more than a disagreement with the rule we apply today. Beyond this, we do not see how the argument can succeed on its own terms. The state high court evinced substantial skepticism at the suggestion that the hate crime statute's "purpose to intimidate" was simply an inquiry into "motive." We share that skepticism. The text of the statute requires the factfinder to determine whether the defendant possessed, at the time he committed the subject act, a "purpose to intimidate" on account of, inter alia, race. By its very terms, this statute mandates an examination of the defendant's state of mind—a concept known well to the criminal law as the defendant's mens rea. It makes no difference in identifying the nature of this finding that Apprendi was also required, in order to receive the sentence he did for weapons possession, to have possessed the weapon with a "purpose to use [the weapon] unlawfully against the person or property of another," § 2C:39–4(a). A second mens rea requirement hardly defeats the reality that the enhancement statute imposes of its own force an intent requirement necessary for the imposition of sentence. On the contrary, the fact that the language and structure of the "purpose to use" criminal offense is identical in relevant respects to the language and structure of the "purpose to intimidate" provision demonstrates to us that it is precisely a particular criminal mens rea that the hate crime enhancement statute seeks to target. The defendant's intent in committing a crime is perhaps as close as one might hope to come to a core criminal offense "element."

The foregoing notwithstanding, however, the New Jersey Supreme Court correctly recognized that it does not matter whether the required finding is characterized as one of intent or of motive, because "[l]abels do not afford an acceptable answer." 159 N.J., at 20, 731 A.2d, at 492. That point applies as well to the constitutionally novel and elusive distinction between "elements" and "sentencing factors." McMillan, 477 U.S., at 86, 106 S.Ct. 2411 (noting that the sentencing factor—visible possession of a firearm—"might well have been included as an element of the enumerated offenses"). Despite what appears to us the clear "elemental" nature of the factor here, the relevant inquiry is one not of form, but of effect—does the required finding expose the defendant to a greater punishment than that authorized by the jury's guilty verdict?

As the New Jersey Supreme Court itself understood in rejecting the argument that the required "motive" finding was simply a "traditional" sentencing factor, proof of motive did not ordinarily "increase the penal consequences to an actor." 159 N.J., at 20, 731 A.2d, at 492. Indeed, the effect of New Jersey's sentencing "enhancement" here is unquestionably to turn a second-degree offense into a first degree offense, under the State's own criminal code. The law thus runs directly into our warning in Mullaney that Winship is concerned as much with the category of substantive offense as "with the degree of criminal culpability" assessed. 421 U.S., at 698, 95 S.Ct. 1881. This concern flows not only from the historical pedigree of the jury and burden rights, but also from the powerful interests those rights serve. The degree of criminal culpability the legislature chooses to associate with particular, factually distinct conduct has significant implications both for a defendant's very liberty, and for the heightened stigma associated with an offense the legislature has selected as worthy of greater punishment.

The preceding discussion should make clear why the State's reliance on McMillan is likewise misplaced. The differential in sentence between what Apprendi would have received without the finding of biased purpose and what he could receive with it is not, it is true, as extreme as the difference between a small fine and mandatory life imprisonment. Mullaney, 421 U.S., at 700, 95 S.Ct. 1881. But it can hardly be said that the potential doubling of one's sentence—from 10 years to 20—has no more than a nominal effect. Both in terms of absolute years behind bars, and because of the more severe stigma attached, the differential here is unquestionably of constitutional significance. When a judge's finding based on a mere preponderance of the evidence authorizes an increase in the maximum punishment, it is appropriately characterized as "a tail which wags the dog of the substantive offense." McMillan, 477 U.S., at 88, 106 S.Ct. 2411.

New Jersey would also point to the fact that the State did not, in placing the required biased purpose finding in a sentencing enhancement provision, create a "separate offense calling for a separate penalty." Ibid. As for this, we agree wholeheartedly with the New Jersey Supreme Court that merely because the state legislature placed its hate crime sentence "enhancer" "within the sentencing provisions" of the criminal code "does not mean that the finding of a biased purpose to intimidate is not an essential element of the offense." 159 N.J., at 20, 731 A.2d, at 492. Indeed, the fact that New Jersey, along with numerous other States, has also made precisely the same conduct the subject of an independent substantive offense makes it clear that the mere presence of this "enhancement" in a sentencing statute does not define its character.

New Jersey's reliance on Almendarez–Torres is also unavailing. The reasons supporting an exception from the general rule for the statute construed in that case do not apply to the New Jersey statute. Whereas recidivism "does not relate to the commission of the offense" itself, 523

U.S., at 230, 244, 118 S.Ct. 1219, New Jersey's biased purpose inquiry goes precisely to what happened in the "commission of the offense." Moreover, there is a vast difference between accepting the validity of a prior judgment of conviction entered in a proceeding in which the defendant had the right to a jury trial and the right to require the prosecutor to prove guilt beyond a reasonable doubt, and allowing the judge to find the required fact under a lesser standard of proof.

Finally, this Court has previously considered and rejected the argument that the principles guiding our decision today render invalid state capital sentencing schemes requiring judges, after a jury verdict holding a defendant guilty of a capital crime, to find specific aggravating factors before imposing a sentence of death. Walton v. Arizona, 497 U.S. 639, 647–649, 110 S.Ct. 3047, 111 L.Ed.2d 511 (1990); id., at 709–714, 110 S.Ct. 3047 (Stevens, J., dissenting). For reasons we have explained, the capital cases are not controlling:

> "Neither the cases cited, nor any other case, permits a judge to determine the existence of a factor which makes a crime a capital offense. What the cited cases hold is that, once a jury has found the defendant guilty of all the elements of an offense which carries as its maximum penalty the sentence of death, it may be left to the judge to decide whether that maximum penalty, rather than a lesser one, ought to be imposed.... The person who is charged with actions that expose him to the death penalty has an absolute entitlement to jury trial on all the elements of the charge." Almendarez–Torres, 523 U.S., at 257, n. 2, 118 S.Ct. 1219 (Scalia, J., dissenting) (emphasis deleted).

See also Jones, 526 U.S., at 250–251, 119 S.Ct. 1215.

* * *

The New Jersey procedure challenged in this case is an unacceptable departure from the jury tradition that is an indispensable part of our criminal justice system. Accordingly, the judgment of the Supreme Court of New Jersey is reversed, and the case is remanded for further proceedings not inconsistent with this opinion.

It is so ORDERED.

■ JUSTICE SCALIA, concurring [omitted].

■ JUSTICE THOMAS, with whom JUSTICE SCALIA joins as to Parts I and II, concurring.

I join the opinion of the Court in full. I write separately to explain my view that the Constitution requires a broader rule than the Court adopts.

I

This case turns on the seemingly simple question of what constitutes a "crime." Under the Federal Constitution, "the accused" has the right (1) "to be informed of the nature and cause of the accusation" (that is, the basis on which he is accused of a crime), (2) to be "held to answer for a capital, or otherwise infamous crime" only on an indictment or presentment of a grand jury, and (3) to be tried by "an impartial jury of the State and district wherein the crime shall have been committed." Amdts. 5 and 6. See also Art. III, § 2, cl. 3 ("The Trial of all Crimes ... shall be by Jury"). With the exception of the Grand Jury Clause, see Hurtado v. California, 110 U.S. 516, 538, 4 S.Ct. 111, 28 L.Ed. 232 (1884), the Court has held that these protections apply in state prosecutions, Herring v. New York, 422 U.S. 853, 857, and n. 7, 95 S.Ct. 2550, 45 L.Ed.2d 593 (1975). Further, the Court has held that due process requires that the jury find beyond a reasonable doubt every fact necessary to constitute the crime. In re Winship, 397 U.S. 358, 364, 90 S.Ct. 1068, 25 L.Ed.2d 368 (1970).

All of these constitutional protections turn on determining which facts constitute the "crime"—that is, which facts are the "elements" or "ingredients" of a crime. In order for an accusation of a crime (whether by indictment or some other form) to be proper under the common law, and thus proper under the codification of the common-law rights in the Fifth and Sixth Amendments, it must allege all elements of that crime; likewise, in order for a jury trial of a crime to be proper, all elements of the crime must be proved to the jury (and, under Winship, proved beyond a reasonable doubt). See J. Story, Commentaries on the Constitution §§ 928–929, pp. 660–662, § 934, p. 664 (1833); J. Archbold, Pleading and Evidence in Criminal Cases *41, *99–* 100 (5th Am. ed. 1846) (hereinafter Archbold).

Thus, it is critical to know which facts are elements. This question became more complicated following the Court's decision in McMillan v. Pennsylvania, 477 U.S. 79, 106 S.Ct. 2411, 91 L.Ed.2d 67 (1986), which spawned a special sort of fact known as a sentencing enhancement. Such a fact increases a defendant's punishment but is not subject to the constitutional protections to which elements are subject. JUSTICE O'CONNOR'S dissent, in agreement with McMillan and Almendarez–Torres v. United States, 523 U.S. 224, 118 S.Ct. 1219, 140 L.Ed.2d 350 (1998), takes the view that a legislature is free (within unspecified outer limits) to decree which facts are elements and which are sentencing enhancements.

Sentencing enhancements may be new creatures, but the question that they create for courts is not. Courts have long had to consider which facts are elements in order to determine the sufficiency of an accusation (usually an indictment). The answer that courts have provided regarding the accusation tells us what an element is, and it is then a simple matter to apply that answer to whatever constitutional right may be at issue in a case—here, Winship and the right to trial by jury. A long line of essentially uniform authority addressing accusations, and stretching from the earliest reported cases after the founding until well into the 20th century, establishes that the original understanding of which facts are elements was even broader than the rule that the Court adopts today.

This authority establishes that a "crime" includes every fact that is by law a basis for imposing or increasing punishment (in contrast with a fact that mitigates punishment). Thus, if the legislature defines some core crime and then provides for increasing the punishment of that crime upon a finding of some aggravating fact—of whatever sort, including the fact of a prior conviction—the core crime and the aggravating fact together constitute an aggravated crime, just as much as grand larceny is an aggravated form of petit larceny. The aggravating fact is an element of the aggravated crime. Similarly, if the legislature, rather than creating grades of crimes, has provided for setting the punishment of a crime based on some fact—such as a fine that is proportional to the value of stolen goods—that fact is also an element. No multi-factor parsing of statutes, of the sort that we have attempted since McMillan, is necessary. One need only look to the kind, degree, or range of punishment to which the prosecution is by law entitled for a given set of facts. Each fact necessary for that entitlement is an element.

II

[omitted]

III

The consequence of the above discussion for our decisions in Almendarez–Torres and McMillan should be plain enough, but a few points merit special mention.

First, it is irrelevant to the question of which facts are elements that legislatures have allowed sentencing judges discretion in determining punishment (often within extremely broad ranges). Bishop, immediately after setting out the traditional rule on elements, explained why: "The reader should distinguish between the foregoing doctrine, and the doctrine ... that, within the limits of any discretion as to the punishment which the law may have allowed, the judge, when he pronounces sentence, may suffer his discretion to be influenced by matter shown in aggravation or mitigation, not covered by the allegations of the indictment.... The aggravating circumstances spoken of cannot swell the penalty above what the law has provided for the acts charged against the prisoner, and they are interposed merely to check the judicial discretion in the exercise of the permitted mercy [in finding mitigating circumstances]. This is an entirely different thing from punishing one for what is not alleged against him." 1 Bishop, Criminal Procedure § 85, at 54.

See also 1 J. Bishop, New Commentaries on the Criminal Law §§ 600–601, pp. 370–371, § 948, p. 572 (8th ed. 1892) (similar). In other words, establishing what punishment is available by law and setting a specific punishment within the bounds that the law has prescribed are two different things. Cf. 4 W. Blackstone, Commentaries on the Law of England 371–372 (1769) (noting judges' broad discretion in setting amount of fine and length of imprisonment for misdemeanors, but praising determinate punishment and "discretion ... regulated by law"); Perley, 86 Me., at 429, 432, 30 A., at 74, 75–76 (favorably discussing Bishop's rule on elements without mentioning, aside from quotation of statute in statement of facts, that defendant's conviction for robbery exposed him to imprisonment for life or any term of years). Thus, it is one thing to consider what the Constitution requires the prosecution to do in order to entitle itself to a particular kind, degree, or range of punishment of the accused, see Woodruff, 68 F., at 538, and quite another to consider what constitutional constraints apply either to the imposition of punishment within the limits of that entitlement or to a legislature's ability to set broad ranges of punishment. In answering the former constitutional question, I need not, and do not, address the latter.

Second, and related, one of the chief errors of Almendarez–Torres—an error to which I succumbed—was to attempt to discern whether a particular fact is traditionally (or typically) a basis for a sentencing court to increase an offender's sentence. 523 U.S., at 243–244, 118 S.Ct. 1219; see id., at 230, 241, 118 S.Ct. 1219. For the reasons I have given, it should be clear that this approach just defines away the real issue. What matters is the way by which a fact enters into the sentence. If a fact is by law the basis for imposing or increasing punishment—for establishing or increasing the prosecution's entitlement—it is an element. (To put the point differently, I am aware of no historical basis for treating as a nonelement a fact that by law sets or increases punishment.) When one considers the question from this perspective, it is evident why the fact of a prior conviction is an element under a recidivism statute. Indeed, cases addressing such statutes provide some of the best discussions of what constitutes an element of a crime. One reason frequently offered for treating recidivism differently, a reason on which we relied in Almendarez–Torres, supra, at 235, 118 S.Ct. 1219, is a concern for prejudicing the jury by informing it of the prior conviction. But this concern, of which earlier courts were well aware, does not make the traditional understanding of what an element is any less applicable to the fact of a prior conviction. See, e.g., Maguire, 47 Md., at 498; Sickles, 156 N.Y., at 547, 51 N.E., at 290.

Third, I think it clear that the common-law rule would cover the McMillan situation of a mandatory minimum sentence (in that case, for visible possession of a firearm during the commission of certain crimes). No doubt a defendant could, under such a scheme, find himself sentenced to the same term to which he could have been sentenced absent the mandatory minimum. The range for his underlying crime could be 0 to 10 years, with the mandatory minimum of 5 years, and he could be sentenced to 7. (Of course, a similar scenario is possible with an increased maximum.) But it is equally true that his expected punishment has increased as a result of the narrowed range and that the prosecution is empowered, by invoking the mandatory minimum, to require the judge to impose a higher punishment than he might wish. The mandatory minimum "entitl[es] the government," Woodruff, 68 F., at 538, to more than it would otherwise be entitled

(5 to 10 years, rather than 0 to 10 and the risk of a sentence below 5). Thus, the fact triggering the mandatory minimum is part of "the punishment sought to be inflicted," Bishop, Criminal Procedure, at 50; it undoubtedly "enters into the punishment" so as to aggravate it, id., § 540, at 330, and is an "ac[t] to which the law affixes . . . punishment," id., § 80, at 51. Further, just as in Hobbs and Searcy, it is likely that the change in the range available to the judge affects his choice of sentence. Finally, in numerous cases, such as Lacy, Garcia, and Jones, the aggravating fact raised the whole range—both the top and bottom. Those courts, in holding that such a fact was an element, did not bother with any distinction between changes in the maximum and the minimum. What mattered was simply the overall increase in the punishment provided by law. And in several cases, such as Smith and Woodruff, the very concept of maximums and minimums had no applicability, yet the same rule for elements applied.

Finally, I need not in this case address the implications of the rule that I have stated for the Court's decision in Walton v. Arizona, 497 U.S. 639, 647–649, 110 S.Ct. 3047, 111 L.Ed.2d 511 (1990). Walton did approve a scheme by which a judge, rather than a jury, determines an aggravating fact that makes a convict eligible for the death penalty, and thus eligible for a greater punishment. In this sense, that fact is an element. But that scheme exists in a unique context, for in the area of capital punishment, unlike any other area, we have imposed special constraints on a legislature's ability to determine what facts shall lead to what punishment—we have restricted the legislature's ability to define crimes. Under our recent capital-punishment jurisprudence, neither Arizona nor any other jurisdiction could provide—as, previously, it freely could and did—that a person shall be death eligible automatically upon conviction for certain crimes. We have interposed a barrier between a jury finding of a capital crime and a court's ability to impose capital punishment. Whether this distinction between capital crimes and all others, or some other distinction, is sufficient to put the former outside the rule that I have stated is a question for another day.[2]

For the foregoing reasons, as well as those given in the Court's opinion, I agree that the New Jersey procedure at issue is unconstitutional.

■ JUSTICE O'CONNOR, with whom THE CHIEF JUSTICE, JUSTICE KENNEDY, and JUSTICE BREYER join, dissenting.

Last Term, in Jones v. United States, 526 U.S. 227, 119 S.Ct. 1215, 143 L.Ed.2d 311 (1999), this Court found that our prior cases suggested the following principle: "[U]nder the Due Process Clause of the Fifth Amendment and the notice and jury trial guarantees of the Sixth Amendment, any

---

2. It is likewise unnecessary to consider whether (and, if so, how) the rule regarding elements applies to the Sentencing Guidelines, given the unique status that they have under Mistretta v. United States, 488 U.S. 361, 109 S.Ct. 647, 102 L.Ed.2d 714 (1989). But it may be that this special status is irrelevant, because the Guidelines "have the force and effect of laws." Id., at 413, 109 S.Ct. 647 (SCALIA, J., dissenting).

fact (other than prior conviction) that increases the maximum penalty for a crime must be charged in an indictment, submitted to a jury, and proven beyond a reasonable doubt." Id., at 243, n. 6, 119 S.Ct. 1215. At the time, Justice KENNEDY rightly criticized the Court for its failure to explain the origins, contours, or consequences of its purported constitutional principle; for the inconsistency of that principle with our prior cases; and for the serious doubt that the holding cast on sentencing systems employed by the Federal Government and States alike. Id., at 254, 264–272, 119 S.Ct. 1215 (dissenting opinion). Today, in what will surely be remembered as a watershed change in constitutional law, the Court imposes as a constitutional rule the principle it first identified in Jones.

I

Our Court has long recognized that not every fact that bears on a defendant's punishment need be charged in an indictment, submitted to a jury, and proved by the government beyond a reasonable doubt. Rather, we have held that the "legislature's definition of the elements of the offense is usually dispositive." McMillan v. Pennsylvania, 477 U.S. 79, 85, 106 S.Ct. 2411, 91 L.Ed.2d 67 (1986); see also Almendarez–Torres v. United States, 523 U.S. 224, 228, 118 S.Ct. 1219, 140 L.Ed.2d 350 (1998); Patterson v. New York, 432 U.S. 197, 210, 211, n. 12, 97 S.Ct. 2319, 53 L.Ed.2d 281 (1977). Although we have recognized that "there are obviously constitutional limits beyond which the States may not go in this regard," id., at 210, 97 S.Ct. 2319, and that "in certain limited circumstances Winship's reasonable-doubt requirement applies to facts not formally identified as elements of the offense charged," McMillan, supra, at 86, 106 S.Ct. 2411, we have proceeded with caution before deciding that a certain fact must be treated as an offense element despite the legislature's choice not to characterize it as such. We have therefore declined to establish any bright-line rule for making such judgments and have instead approached each case individually, sifting through the considerations most relevant to determining whether the legislature has acted properly within its broad power to define crimes and their punishments or instead has sought to evade the constitutional requirements associated with the characterization of a fact as an offense element. See, e.g., Monge v. California, 524 U.S. 721, 728–729, 118 S.Ct. 2246, 141 L.Ed.2d 615 (1998); McMillan, supra, at 86, 106 S.Ct. 2411.

* * *

II

That the Court's rule is unsupported by the history and case law it cites is reason enough to reject such a substantial departure from our settled jurisprudence. Significantly, the Court also fails to explain adequately why the Due Process Clauses of the Fifth and Fourteenth Amendments and the jury trial guarantee of the Sixth Amendment require application of its rule. Upon closer examination, it is possible that the Court's "increase in the maximum penalty" rule rests on a meaningless formalism that accords, at best, marginal protection for the constitutional rights that it seeks to effectuate.

Any discussion of either the constitutional necessity or the likely effect of the Court's rule must begin, of course, with an understanding of what exactly that rule is. As was the case in Jones, however, that discussion is complicated here by the Court's failure to clarify the contours of the constitutional principle underlying its decision. See Jones, 526 U.S., at 267, 119 S.Ct. 1215 (Kennedy, J., dissenting). In fact, there appear to be several plausible interpretations of the constitutional principle on which the Court's decision rests.

For example, under one reading, the Court appears to hold that the Constitution requires that a fact be submitted to a jury and proved beyond a reasonable doubt only if that fact, as a formal matter, extends the range of punishment beyond the prescribed statutory maximum. A State could, however, remove from the jury (and subject to a standard of proof below "beyond a reasonable doubt") the assessment of those facts that define narrower ranges of punishment, within the overall statutory range, to which the defendant may be sentenced. Thus, apparently New Jersey could cure its sentencing scheme, and achieve virtually the same results, by drafting its weapons possession statute in the following manner: First, New Jersey could prescribe, in the weapons possession statute itself, a range of 5 to 20 years' imprisonment for one who commits that criminal offense. Second, New Jersey could provide that only those defendants convicted under the statute who are found by a judge, by a preponderance of the evidence, to have acted with a purpose to intimidate an individual on the basis of race may receive a sentence greater than 10 years' imprisonment.

The Court's proffered distinction of Walton v. Arizona suggests that it means to announce a rule of only this limited effect. The Court claims the Arizona capital sentencing scheme is consistent with the constitutional principle underlying today's decision because Arizona's first-degree murder statute itself authorizes both life imprisonment and the death penalty. See Ariz.Rev.Stat. Ann. § 13–1105(C) (1989). " '[O]nce a jury has found the defendant guilty of all the elements of an offense which carries as its maximum penalty the sentence of death, it may be left to the judge to decide whether that maximum penalty, rather than a lesser one, ought to be imposed.' " (quoting Almendarez–Torres, 523 U.S., at 257, n. 2, 118 S.Ct. 1219 (Scalia, J., dissenting)). Of course, as explained above, an Arizona sentencing judge can impose the maximum penalty of death only if the judge first makes a statutorily required finding that at least one aggravating factor exists in the defendant's case. Thus, the Arizona first-degree murder statute authorizes a maximum penalty of death only in a formal sense. In real terms, however, the Arizona sentencing scheme removes from the jury the assessment of a fact that determines whether the defendant can receive that maximum punishment. The only difference, then, between the Arizona scheme and the New Jersey scheme we consider here—apart from the magnitude of punishment at stake—is that New Jersey has not prescribed the 20–year maximum penalty in the same statute that it defines the crime to be punished. It is difficult to understand, and the Court does not explain, why the Constitution would require a state legislature to follow such a meaningless and formalistic difference in drafting its criminal statutes.

Under another reading of the Court's decision, it may mean only that the Constitution requires that a fact be submitted to a jury and proved beyond a reasonable doubt if it, as a formal matter, increases the range of punishment beyond that which could legally be imposed absent that fact. A State could, however, remove from the jury (and subject to a standard of proof below "beyond a reasonable doubt") the assessment of those facts that, as a formal matter, decrease the range of punishment below that which could legally be imposed absent that fact. Thus, consistent with our decision in Patterson, New Jersey could cure its sentencing scheme, and achieve virtually the same results, by drafting its weapons possession statute in the following manner: First, New Jersey could prescribe, in the weapons possession statute itself, a range of 5 to 20 years' imprisonment for one who commits that criminal offense. Second, New Jersey could provide that a defendant convicted under the statute whom a judge finds, by a preponderance of the evidence, not to have acted with a purpose to intimidate an individual on the basis of race may receive a sentence no greater than 10 years' imprisonment.

The rule that Justice Thomas advocates in his concurring opinion embraces this precise distinction between a fact that increases punishment and a fact that decreases punishment. ("'[A] 'crime' includes every fact that is by law a basis for imposing or increasing punishment (in contrast with a fact that mitigates punishment)'"). The historical evidence on which Justice Thomas relies, however, demonstrates both the difficulty and the pure formalism of making a constitutional "elements" rule turn on such a difference. For example, the Wisconsin statute considered in Lacy v. State, 15 Wis. *13 (1862), could plausibly qualify as either increasing or mitigating punishment on the basis of the same specified fact. There, Wisconsin provided that the willful and malicious burning of a dwelling house in which "the life of no person shall have been destroyed" was punishable by 7 to 14 years in prison, but that the same burning at a time in which "there was no person lawfully in the dwelling house" was punishable by only 3 to 10 years in prison. Wis.Rev.Stat., ch. 165, § 1 (1858). Although the statute appeared to make the absence of persons from the affected dwelling house a fact that mitigated punishment, the Wisconsin Supreme Court found that the presence of a person in the affected house constituted an aggravating circumstance. Lacy, supra, at *15–*16. As both this example and the above hypothetical redrafted New Jersey statute demonstrate, whether a fact is responsible for an increase or a decrease in punishment rests in the eye of the beholder. Again, it is difficult to understand, and neither the Court nor Justice Thomas explains, why the Constitution would require a state legislature to follow such a meaningless and formalistic difference in drafting its criminal statutes.

If either of the above readings is all that the Court's decision means, "the Court's principle amounts to nothing more than chastising [the New Jersey Legislature] for failing to use the approved phrasing in expressing its intent as to how [unlawful weapons possession] should be punished." Jones, 526 U.S., at 267, 119 S.Ct. 1215 (Kennedy, J., dissenting). If New Jersey can, consistent with the Constitution, make precisely the same differences in punishment turn on precisely the same facts, and can remove the assessment of those facts from the jury and subject them to a standard of proof below "beyond a reasonable doubt," it is impossible to say that the Fifth, Sixth, and Fourteenth Amendments require the Court's rule. For the same reason, the "structural democratic constraints" that might discourage a legislature from enacting either of the above hypothetical statutes would be no more significant than those that would discourage the enactment of New Jersey's present sentence-enhancement statute. In all three cases, the legislature is able to calibrate punishment perfectly, and subject to a maximum penalty only those defendants whose cases satisfy the sentence-enhancement criterion. As Justice Kennedy explained in Jones, "[n]o constitutional values are served by so formalistic an approach, while its constitutional costs in statutes struck down ... are real." 526 U.S., at 267, 119 S.Ct. 1215.

Given the pure formalism of the above readings of the Court's opinion, one suspects that the constitutional principle underlying its decision is more far reaching. The actual principle underlying the Court's decision may be that any fact (other than prior conviction) that has the effect, in real terms, of increasing the maximum punishment beyond an otherwise applicable range must be submitted to a jury and proved beyond a reasonable doubt. ("[T]he relevant inquiry is one not of form, but of effect—does the required finding expose the defendant to a greater punishment than that authorized by the jury's guilty verdict?"). The principle thus would apply not only to schemes like New Jersey's, under which a factual determination exposes the defendant to a sentence beyond the prescribed statutory maximum, but also to all determinate-sentencing schemes in which the length of a defendant's sentence within the statutory range turns on specific factual determinations (e.g., the federal Sentencing Guidelines). Justice THOMAS essentially concedes that the rule outlined in his concurring opinion would require the invalidation of the Sentencing Guidelines.

I would reject any such principle. As explained above, it is inconsistent with our precedent and would require the Court to overrule, at a minimum, decisions like Patterson and Walton. More importantly, given our approval of—and the significant history in this country of—discretionary sentencing by judges, it is difficult to understand how the Fifth, Sixth, and Fourteenth Amendments could possibly require the Court's or Justice THOMAS' rule. Finally, in light of the adoption of determinate-sentencing schemes by many States and the Federal Government, the consequences of the Court's and Justice THOMAS' rules in terms of sentencing schemes invalidated by today's decision will likely be severe.

As the Court acknowledges, we have never doubted that the Constitution permits Congress and the state legislatures to define criminal offenses, to prescribe broad ranges of punishment for those offenses, and to give judges discretion to decide where within those ranges a particular defendant's punishment should be set. That view accords with historical practice under the Constitution. "From the beginning of the Republic, federal judges were entrusted with wide sentencing discretion. The great majority of federal criminal statutes have stated only a maximum term of years and a maximum monetary fine, permitting the sentencing judge to impose any term of imprisonment and any fine up to the statutory maximum." K. Stith & J. Cabranes, Fear of Judging: Sentencing Guidelines in the Federal Courts 9 (1998) (footnote omitted). Under discretionary-sentencing schemes, a judge bases the defendant's sentence on any number of facts neither presented at trial nor found by a jury beyond a reasonable doubt. As one commentator has explained:

> "During the age of broad judicial sentencing discretion, judges frequently made sentencing decisions on the basis of facts that they determined for themselves, on less than proof beyond a reasonable doubt, without eliciting very much concern from civil libertarians. ... The sentence in any number of traditional discretionary situations depended quite directly on judicial findings of specific contested facts. ... Whether because such facts were directly relevant to the judge's retributionist assessment of how serious the particular offense was (within the spectrum of conduct covered by the statute of conviction), or because they bore on a determination of how much rehabilitation the offender's character was likely to need, the sentence would be higher or lower, in some specific degree determined by the judge, based on the judge's factual conclusions." Lynch, Towards A Model Penal Code, Second (Federal?), 2 Buffalo Crim. L.Rev. 297, 320 (1998) (footnote omitted).

Accordingly, under the discretionary-sentencing schemes, a factual determination made by a judge on a standard of proof below "beyond a reasonable doubt" often made the difference between a lesser and a greater punishment.

For example, in Williams v. New York, a jury found the defendant guilty of first-degree murder and recommended life imprisonment. The judge, however, rejected the jury's recommendation and sentenced Williams to death on the basis of additional facts that he learned through a presentence investigation report and that had neither been charged in an indictment nor presented to the jury. 337 U.S., at 242–245, 69 S.Ct. 1079. In rejecting Williams' due process challenge to his death sentence, we explained that there was a long history of sentencing judges exercising "wide discretion in the sources and types of evidence used to assist [them] in determining the kind and extent of punishment to be imposed within limits fixed by law." Id., at 246, 69 S.Ct. 1079. Specifically, we held that the Constitution does not restrict a judge's sentencing decision to information that is charged in an indictment and subject to cross-examination in open court. "The due process clause should not be treated as a device for freezing the evidential procedure of sentencing in the mold of trial procedure." Id., at 251, 69 S.Ct. 1079.

Under our precedent, then, a State may leave the determination of a defendant's sentence to a judge's discretionary decision within a prescribed range of penalties. When a judge, pursuant to that sentencing scheme, decides to increase a defendant's sentence on the basis of certain contested facts, those facts need not be proved to a jury beyond a reasonable doubt. The judge's findings, whether by proof beyond a reasonable doubt or less, suffice for purposes of the Constitution. Under the Court's decision today, however, it appears that once a legislature constrains judges' sentencing discretion by prescribing certain sentences that may only be imposed (or must be imposed) in connection with the same determinations of the same contested facts, the Constitution requires that the facts instead be proved to a jury beyond a reasonable doubt. I see no reason to treat the two schemes differently. See, e.g., McMillan, 477 U.S., at 92, 106 S.Ct. 2411 ("We have some difficulty fathoming why the due process calculus would change simply because the legislature has seen fit to provide sentencing courts with additional guidance"). In this respect, I agree with the Solicitor General that "[a] sentence that is constitutionally permissible when selected by a court on the basis of whatever factors it deems appropriate does not become impermissible simply because the court is permitted to select that sentence only after making a finding prescribed by the legislature." Brief for United States as Amicus Curiae 7. Although the Court acknowledges the legitimacy of discretionary sentencing by judges, it never provides a sound reason for treating judicial factfinding under determinate-sentencing schemes differently under the Constitution.

Justice Thomas' attempt to explain this distinction is similarly unsatisfying. His explanation consists primarily of a quotation, in turn, of a 19th-century treatise writer, who contended that the aggravation of punishment within a statutory range on the basis of facts found by a judge " 'is an entirely different thing from punishing one for what is not alleged against him.' " (quoting 1 J. Bishop, Commentaries on Law of Criminal Procedure § 85, p. 54 (rev.2d ed. 1872)). As our decision in Williams v. New York demonstrates, however, that statement does not accurately describe the reality of discretionary sentencing conducted by judges. A defendant's actual punishment can be affected in a very real way by facts never alleged in an indictment, never presented to a jury, and never proved beyond a reasonable doubt. In Williams' case, facts presented for the first time to the judge, for purposes of sentencing alone, made the difference between life imprisonment and a death sentence.

Consideration of the purposes underlying the Sixth Amendment's jury trial guarantee further demonstrates why our acceptance of judge-made findings in the context of discretionary sentencing suggests the approval of the same judge-made findings in the context of determinate sentencing as well. One important purpose of the Sixth Amendment's jury trial guarantee is to protect the criminal defendant against potentially arbitrary judges. It effectuates this promise by preserving, as a constitutional matter, certain fundamental decisions for a jury of one's peers, as opposed to a judge. For example, the Court has recognized that the Sixth Amendment's guarantee was motivated by the English experience of "competition . . . between judge and jury over the real significance of their respective roles," Jones, 526 U.S., at 245, 119 S.Ct. 1215, and "measures [that were taken] to diminish the juries' power," ibid. We have also explained that the jury trial guarantee was understood to provide "an inestimable safeguard against the corrupt or overzealous prosecutor and against the compliant, biased, or eccentric judge. If the defendant preferred the common-sense judgment of a jury to the more tutored but perhaps less sympathetic reaction of the single judge, he was to have it." Duncan v. Louisiana, 391 U.S. 145, 156, 88 S.Ct. 1444, 20 L.Ed.2d 491 (1968). Blackstone explained that the right to trial by jury was critically important in criminal cases because of "the violence and partiality of judges appointed by the crown, . . . who might then, as in France or Turkey, imprison, dispatch, or exile any man that was obnoxious to the government, by an instant declaration, that such is their will and pleasure." 4 Blackstone, Commentaries, at 343. Clearly, the concerns animating the Sixth Amendment's jury trial guarantee, if they were to extend to the sentencing context at all, would apply with greater strength to a discretionary-sentencing scheme than to determinate sentencing. In the former scheme, the potential for mischief by an arbitrary judge is much greater, given that the judge's decision of where to set the defendant's sentence within the prescribed statutory range is left almost entirely to discretion. In contrast, under a determinate-sentencing system, the discretion the judge wields within the statutory range is tightly constrained. Accordingly, our approval of discretionary-sentencing schemes, in which a defendant is not entitled to have a jury make factual findings relevant to sentencing despite the effect those findings have on the severity of the defendant's sentence, demonstrates that the defendant should have no right to demand that a jury make the equivalent factual determinations under a determinate-sentencing scheme.

The Court appears to hold today, however, that a defendant is entitled to have a jury decide, by proof beyond a reasonable doubt, every fact relevant to the determination of sentence under a determinate-sentencing scheme. If this is an accurate description of the constitutional principle underlying the Court's opinion, its decision will have the effect of invalidating significant sentencing reform accomplished at the federal and state levels over the past three decades. Justice Thomas' rule, as he essentially concedes, would have the same effect.

Prior to the most recent wave of sentencing reform, the Federal Government and the States employed indeterminate-sentencing schemes in which judges and executive branch officials (e.g., parole board officials) had substantial discretion to determine the actual length of a defendant's sentence. See, e.g., U.S. Dept. of Justice, S. Shane–DuBow, A. Brown, & E. Olsen, Sentencing Reform in the United States: History, Content, and Effect 6–7 (Aug.1985) (hereinafter Shane–DuBow); Report of Twentieth Century Fund Task Force on Criminal Sentencing, Fair and Certain Punishment 11–13 (1976) (hereinafter Task Force Report); A. Dershowitz, Criminal Sentencing in the United States: An Historical and Conceptual Overview, 423 Annals Am. Acad. Pol. & Soc. Sci. 117, 128–129 (1976). Studies of indeterminate-sentencing schemes found that similarly situated defendants often received widely disparate sentences. See, e.g., Shane–Dubow 7; Task Force Report 14. Although indeterminate sentencing was intended to soften the harsh and uniform sentences formerly imposed under mandatory-sentencing systems, some studies revealed that indeterminate sentencing actually had the opposite effect. See, e.g., A. Campbell, Law of Sentencing 13 (1978) ("Paradoxically the humanitarian impulse sparking the adoption of indeterminate sentencing systems in this country has resulted in an actual increase of the average criminal's incarceration term"); Task Force Report 13 ("[T]he data seem to indicate that in those jurisdictions where the sentencing structure is more indeterminate, judicially imposed sentences tend to be longer").

In response, Congress and the state legislatures shifted to determinate-sentencing schemes that aimed to limit judges' sentencing discretion and, thereby, afford similarly situated offenders equivalent treatment. See, e.g., Cal.Penal Code Ann. § 1170 (West Supp.2000). The most well known of these reforms was the federal Sentencing Reform Act of 1984, 18 U.S.C. § 3551 et seq. In the Act, Congress created the United States Sentencing Commission, which in turn promulgated the Sentencing Guidelines that now govern sentencing by federal judges. See, e.g., United States Sentencing Commission, Guidelines Manual (Nov.1998). Whether one believes the determinate-sentencing reforms have proved successful or not—and the subject is one of extensive debate among commentators—the apparent effect of the Court's opinion today is to halt the current debate on sentencing reform in its tracks and to invalidate with the stroke of a pen three decades' worth of nationwide reform, all in the name of a principle with a questionable constitutional pedigree. Indeed, it is ironic that the Court, in the name of constitutional rights meant to protect criminal defendants from the potentially arbitrary exercise of power by prosecutors and judges, appears to rest its decision on a principle that would render unconstitutional efforts by Congress and the state legislatures to place constraints on that very power in the sentencing context.

Finally, perhaps the most significant impact of the Court's decision will be a practical one—its unsettling effect on sentencing conducted under current federal and state determinate-sentencing schemes. As I have explained, the Court does not say whether these schemes are constitutional, but its reasoning strongly suggests that they are not. Thus, with respect to past sentences handed down by judges under determinate-sentencing schemes, the Court's decision threatens to unleash a flood of petitions by convicted defendants seeking to invalidate their sentences in whole or in part on the authority of the Court's decision today. Statistics compiled by the United States Sentencing Commission reveal that almost a half-million cases have been sentenced under the Sentencing Guidelines since 1989. See Memorandum from U.S. Sentencing Commission to Supreme Court Library, dated June 8, 2000 (total number of cases sentenced under federal Sentencing Guidelines since 1989) (available in Clerk of Court's case file). Federal cases constitute only the tip of the iceberg. In 1998, for example, federal criminal prosecutions represented only about 0.4% of the total number of criminal prosecutions in federal and state courts. See National Center for State Courts, A National Perspective: Court Statistics Project (federal and state court filings, 1998), http:// www.ncsc.dni.us/divisions/ research/csp/csp98–fscf.html (showing that, in 1998, 57,691 criminal cases were filed in federal court compared to 14,623,330 in state courts). Because many States, like New Jersey, have determinate-sentencing schemes, the number of individual sentences drawn into question by the Court's decision could be colossal.

The decision will likely have an even more damaging effect on sentencing conducted in the immediate future under current determinate-sentencing schemes. Because the Court fails to clarify the precise contours of the constitutional principle underlying its decision, federal and state judges are left in a state of limbo. Should they continue to assume the constitutionality of the determinate-sentencing schemes under which they have operated for so long, and proceed to sentence convicted defendants in accord with those governing statutes and guidelines? The Court provides no answer, yet its reasoning suggests that each new sentence will rest on shaky ground. The most unfortunate aspect of today's decision is that our precedents did not foreordain this disruption in the world of sentencing. Rather, our cases traditionally took a cautious approach to questions like the one presented in this case. The Court throws that caution to the wind and, in the process, threatens to cast sentencing in the United States into what will likely prove to be a lengthy period of considerable confusion.

III

* * *

■ JUSTICE BREYER, with whom CHIEF JUSTICE REHNQUIST joins, dissenting [omitted].

NOTES

1. About two weeks before its decision in *Apprendi*, the Court decided Castillo v. United States, 530 U.S. 120, 120 S.Ct. 2090, 147 L.Ed.2d 94 (2000), which was a prosecution of members of the Branch–Davidian religious sect for using machineguns in commission of crimes of violence. The federal statute provides that "Whoever, during and in relation to any crime of violence ... uses or carries a firearm, shall, in addition to the punishment provided for such crime of violence ..., be sentenced to imprisonment for five years, and if the firearm is ... a machinegun ... to imprisonment for thirty years." The Fifth Circuit upheld a conviction and 30 year sentence arising from a trial in which the District Court judge found after the jury had returned verdicts of guilty of use of firearms during crimes of violence that the firearms were machineguns. The Supreme Court, in an opinion by Justice Breyer for a virtually unanimous Court, held that Congress intended to create a separate offense of use of a machinegun to commit a crime of violence and did not intend that use of a machinegun should be a "sentence enhancer." Therefore, the jury should have been given the question whether the firearms were machineguns during the guilt/innocence phase of the trial rather than permitting the judge to decide that question during the sentencing phase.

2. **Mandatory minimum sentences.** In Harris v. United States, 536 U.S. 545, 122 S.Ct. 2406, 153 L.Ed.2d 524 (2002), the defendant was convicted of carrying a firearm in relation to a drug trafficking offense. At sentencing, the district court found that he had "brandished" the firearm and consequently sentenced him to a mandatory minimum sentence of seven years in prison instead of the five year minimum that would otherwise have applied. The Court, in an opinion by Justice Kennedy, held that brandishing a firearm was intended by Congress to be a sentencing factor rather than an element of the offense. Then for a plurality of the Court (joined in by The Chief Justice, Justice O'Connor, and Justice Scalia) Justice Kennedy said that McMillan v. Pennsylvania [discussed at length in the *Apprendi* opinion] survived *Apprendi*. There is a fundamental difference between a fact finding that increases the maximum sentence and one that increases a minimum sentence. A sentencing judge may increase a minimum in the absence of finding the fact in question so long as the sentence does not exceed the maximum but may never increase the maximum sentence except as authorized by a finding of fact. Facts that inform sentencing discretion do not become elements of the offense merely because a legislature mandates a specified minimum sentence when a defined sentencing fact is found. Justice Kennedy concluded,

> Read together, *McMillan* and *Apprendi* mean that those facts setting the outer limits of a sentence, and of the judicial power to impose it, are the elements of the crime for the purposes of the constitutional analysis. Within the range authorized by the jury's verdict, however, the political system may channel judicial discretion—and rely upon judicial expertise—by requiring defendants to serve minimum terms after judges make certain factual findings. It is critical not to abandon that understanding at this late date. Legislatures and their constituents have relied upon *McMillan* to exercise control over sentencing through dozens of statutes like the one the Court approved in that case. Congress and the States have conditioned mandatory minimum sentences upon judicial findings that, as here, a firearm was possessed, brandished, or discharged, * * * or among other examples, that the victim was over 60 years of age, * * * that the defendant possessed a certain quantity of drugs, * * *

that the victim was related to the defendant, * * * and that the defendant was a repeat offender * * *. We see no reason to overturn those statutes or cast uncertainty upon the sentences imposed under them.

536 U.S. at 547, 122 S.Ct. at 2409, 153 L.Ed.2d at 544–45. Justice Breyer, who dissented in *Apprendi*, made the fifth vote. He would not favor subjecting an increase the maximum sentence, let alone the minimum, to the Fifth and Sixth Amendment requirements imposed by *Apprendi*. Justice Thomas, joined by Justices Stevens, Souter and Ginsburg, dissented.

3. **Capital sentencing.** The Supreme Court applied *Apprendi* to capital murder penalty proceedings in Ring v. Arizona, 536 U.S. 584, 122 S.Ct. 2428, 153 L.Ed.2d 556 (2002). Under Arizona's procedure in death penalty cases, the trial judge—not the jury—determines the presence or absence of aggravating factors upon which depend the availability of the death penalty. This procedure had previously been upheld by the Court in Walton v. Arizona, 497 U.S. 639, 110 S.Ct. 3047, 111 L.Ed.2d 511 (1990) on the ground that the additional facts to be found by the judge are sentencing considerations, not elements of the offense. Writing for the Court, Justice Ginsburg overruled *Walton* because the Arizona procedure violates the jury trial right recognized in *Apprendi*. The trial judge in *Ring* imposed the death penalty after finding that of the three participants in the robbery-murder, Ring fired the fatal shot. This finding was based largely on the testimony of one of the robbers at the sentencing phase of the trial. Under Arizona law, the "normal" penalty for conviction of capital murder is life imprisonment. Only if the trial judge makes specified additional fact findings is the death penalty authorized. Under *Apprendi*, such a scheme requires jury fact finding.

The Supreme Court in Schriro v. Summerlin, 542 U.S. 348, 124 S.Ct. 2519, 159 L.Ed.2d 442 (2004) held that *Ring* is not to be applied retroactively to cases that became final before the date of its decision. Justice Scalia summarized the Court's position:

> The right to jury trial is fundamental to our system of criminal procedure, and States are bound to enforce the Sixth Amendment's guarantees as we interpret them. But it does not follow that, when a criminal defendant has had a full trial and one round of appeals in which the State faithfully applied the Constitution as we understood it at the time, he may nevertheless continue to litigate his claims indefinitely in hopes that we will one day have a change of heart. *Ring* announced a new procedural rule that does not apply retroactively to cases already final on direct review.

542 U.S. at 358, 124 S.Ct. at 2526.

4. **Determinate sentencing.** What are the implications of *Apprendi* for systems of determinate sentencing, such as the federal sentencing guidelines? See *United States v. Booker* in Chapter 25 of this Supplement.

Page 1018.   Insert new note after Mullaney v. Wilbur:

10. **Shackling and other courtroom practices.** The Supreme Court has announced:

> [T]he Fifth and Fourteenth Amendments prohibit the use of physical restraints visible to the jury absent a trial court determination, in the exercise of its discretion, that they are justified by a state interest specific to a particular trial. Such a determination may of course take into account the factors that courts have traditionally relied on in gauging potential security problems and the risk of escape at trial.

Deck v. Missouri, 544 U.S. 622, 629, 125 S.Ct. 2007, 2012, 161 L.Ed.2d 953 (2005). Explaining, the Court continued:

> Visible shackling undermines the presumption of innocence and the related fairness of the factfinding process. It suggests to the jury that the justice system itself sees a "need to separate a defendant from the community at large."

544 U.S. at 630, 125 S.Ct. at 2013. In addition, shackling interferes with a defendant's ability to interact with his attorney and thus diminishes the right to counsel. Further, it undermines the dignity of the judicial process. 544 U.S. at 631–32, 125 S.Ct. at 2013.

In *Deck*, the Court held that the federal constitution also limits the ability of trial courts to shackle criminal defendants during the penalty of a capital proceeding.

In contrast to the established limits on "state-sponsored courtroom practices," the Court concluded in Carey v. Musladin, 549 U.S. 70, 127 S.Ct. 649, 166 L.Ed.2d 482 (2006), "the effect on a defendant's fair-trial rights of [private-actor] spectator conduct * * * is an open question in our jurisprudence." The California court had held that Musladin's federal constitutional right to a fair trial was not denied because some spectators at his murder trial wore buttons with a photo of the victim on them. *Carey* held that this holding by the state court was not contrary to, or an unreasonable application of, clearly established federal constitutional as is required for certain state defendants to obtain federal habeas corpus relief.

B.   Right to Trial by Jury

2.   Composition of the Jury

Page 1038.   Add the following to Note 4:

4a.   **Step 1—The prima facie case.** The standard for determining whether a prima facie case has been made under the first step of the *Batson* analysis was addressed in Johnson v. California, 545 U.S. 162, 125 S.Ct. 2410, 162 L.Ed.2d 129 (2005). California case law established that the prima facie case is made only if the party challenging the strikes shows that it is more likely than not that the other party's peremptory challenges, if unexplained, were based on impermissible considerations. The Court evaluated this in light of *Batson's* purposes:

> The constitutional interests *Batson* sought to vindicate are not limited to the rights possessed by the defendant on trial, nor to those citizens who desire to participate "in the administration of the law, as jurors." Undoubtedly, the overriding interest in eradicating discrimination from our civic institutions suffers whenever an individual is excluded from making a significant contribution to governance on account of his race. Yet the "harm from discriminatory jury selection extends beyond that inflicted on the defendant and the excluded juror to touch the entire community. Selection procedures that purposefully exclude black persons from juries undermine public confidence in the fairness of our system of justice." *Batson*, 476 U.S., at 87, 106 S.Ct. 1712.

> The *Batson* framework is designed to produce actual answers to suspicions and inferences that discrimination may have infected the jury selection process. The inherent uncertainty present in inquiries of discriminatory purpose coun-

sels against engaging in needless and imperfect speculation when a direct answer can be obtained by asking a simple question. * * *

545 U.S. at 171–72, 125 S.Ct. at 2418. The California courts' standard is inconsistent with Batson, the *Johnson* majority held. "[A] defendant satisfies the requirements of *Batson's* first step by producing evidence sufficient to permit the trial judge to draw an inference that discrimination has occurred." 545 U.S. at 170, 125 S.Ct. at 2417.

4b. Steps 2 and 3—Neutral explanation or purposeful discrimination? In Miller–El v. Dretke, 545 U.S. 231, 125 S.Ct. 2317, 162 L.Ed.2d 196 (2005), the Supreme Court applied *Batson* and made clear that the lower state and federal courts reviewing the Texas conviction and death penalty had failed to apply *Batson* with sufficient rigor. Two years earlier the Court has considered the case and held that the court of appeals erred in denying a certificate of appealability. Miller–El v. Cockrell, 537 U.S. 322, 123 S.Ct. 1029, 154 L.Ed.2d 931 (2003). In 2005, the Court addressed the merits of Miller–El's *Batson* claim.

At Miller–El's 1985 trial, he had unsuccessfully challenged the prosecution's use of peremptory challenges under the pre-*Batson* decision in *Swain*. After *Batson*, his claim was reevaluated under the new standard and he was denied relief in the state courts, federal district court and the Fifth Circuit Court of Appeals. The trial judge had accepted the prosecution's offered race-neutral reasons for the strikes and courts subsequently reviewing the matter held that this was supported by the record.

A majority of the Supreme Court disagreed.

Batson's individualized focus came with a weakness of its own owing to its very emphasis on the particular reasons a prosecutor might give. If any facially neutral reason sufficed to answer a *Batson* challenge, then *Batson* would not amount to much more than *Swain*. Some stated reasons are false, and although some false reasons are shown up within the four corners of a given case, sometimes a court may not be sure unless it looks beyond the case at hand. Hence *Batson's* explanation that a defendant may rely on "all relevant circumstances" to raise an inference of purposeful discrimination.

545 U.S. at 239–40, 125 S.Ct. at 2325. It then held that the lower courts' conclusions that the strikes in Miller–El's case were made on race-neutral grounds "was shown up as wrong to a clear and convincing degree." First, the majority relied on the statistics:

> The numbers describing the prosecution's use of peremptories are remarkable. Out of 20 black members of the 108–person venire panel for Miller–El's trial, only 1 served. Although 9 were excused for cause or by agreement, 10 were peremptorily struck by the prosecution. "The prosecutors used their peremptory strikes to exclude 91% of the eligible African-American venire members.... Happenstance is unlikely to produce this disparity."

545 U.S. at 240–41, 125 S.Ct. at 2325.

The Court continued:

> More powerful than these bare statistics, however, are side-by-side comparisons of some black venire panelists who were struck and white panelists allowed to serve. If a prosecutor's proffered reason for striking a black panelist applies just as well to an otherwise-similar nonblack who is permitted to serve, that is evidence tending to prove purposeful discrimination to be considered at *Batson's* third step.

545 U.S. at 241, 125 S.Ct. at 2325. Looking in great detail at the voir dire questioning of two black panelists, the Court concluded that Miller–El's claim that the racially-neutral explanations given were pretext was supported by the record's demonstration that those explanations also applied to other panel members, most of them white, who were not struck.

Next, the Court observed that on the record before it, "[t]he case for discrimination goes beyond these comparisons to include broader patterns of practice during the jury selection." It noted that the prosecution had exercised its right to rearrange randomly the order in which the panel members were seated and reached for questioning—to "shuffle" the jurors—when a predominant number of black panel members were seated at the front of the panel. It had delayed formal objection to the defense's shuffle until the new racial composition of the seating order was clear. It also more often asked black panel members for thoughts on capital punishment using questions describing the method of execution in rhetorical and graphic detail. This enabled the prosecution to elicit expressions of hesitation to consider death from black panel members and thus to create grounds to strike the members for cause or at least "to elicit a plausibly neutral grounds for a peremptory strike." The record also suggested the prosecution used misleading questions designed to artificially create grounds to strike for cause disproportionately when questioning black panel members.

Finally, the Court went beyond the record made in the case at hand:

There is a final body of evidence that confirms [our] conclusion. We know that for decades leading up to the time this case was tried prosecutors in the Dallas County office had followed a specific policy of systematically excluding blacks from juries, as we explained the last time the case was here [on whether the Court of Appeals had erred in denying a certificate of appealability].

"Although most of the witnesses [presented at the *Swain* hearing in 1986] denied the existence of a systematic policy to exclude African-Americans, others disagreed. A Dallas County district judge testified that, when he had served in the District Attorney's Office from the late-1950's to early-1960's, his superior warned him that he would be fired if he permitted any African-Americans to serve on a jury. Similarly, another Dallas County district judge and former assistant district attorney from 1976 to 1978 testified that he believed the office had a systematic policy of excluding African-Americans from juries."

"Of more importance, the defense presented evidence that the District Attorney's Office had adopted a formal policy to exclude minorities from jury service.... A manual entitled 'Jury Selection in a Criminal Case' [sometimes known as the Sparling Manual] was distributed to prosecutors. It contained an article authored by a former prosecutor (and later a judge) under the direction of his superiors in the District Attorney's Office, outlining the reasoning for excluding minorities from jury service. Although the manual was written in 1968, it remained in circulation until 1976, if not later, and was available at least to one of the prosecutors in Miller-El's trial." *Miller-El v. Cockrell,* [537 U.S. 322, 334–335, 123 S.Ct. 1029, 154 L.Ed.2d 931 (2003)].

545 U.S. at 263–64, 125 S.Ct. at 2338–39.

In *Snyder v. Louisiana,* 552 U.S. 472, 128 S.Ct. 1203, 170 L.Ed.2d 175 (2008), the Supreme Court found that the trial and appellate courts in Louisiana had committed clear error in accepting a "neutral explanation" for the prosecutor's use of a peremptory challenge, and therefore reversed the defendant's first-degree murder conviction and death penalty. Three years earlier the Court granted certiorari, vacated the judgment, and remanded this defendant's conviction in light of *Miller–El*. *Snyder v. Louisiana*, 545 U.S. 1137, 125 S.Ct. 2956, 162 L.Ed.2d 884 (2005). During voir dire, the prosecutor had used peremptory strikes against all five of the black prospective jurors who survived challenges for cause. While the issue of discriminatory intent relies on the credibility of the prosecutor and the demeanor of jurors, and thus is a determination peculiarly within the province of the trial judge, the Court rejected both race–neutral reasons offered by the government for striking juror Jeffrey Brooks. The first reason, Mr. Brooks' "nervousness," was rejected because the record did not show that the trial judge actually made a determination concerning the juror's demeanor. The second reason proffered for the strike, Mr. Brooks' student-teaching obligations, failed because there were "more than 50 members of the venire who expressed concern that the jury service or sequestration would interfere with work, school, family, or other obligations." The prosecutor had accepted white jurors who disclosed equally serious conflicting obligations.

The *Snyder* Court again declined to address the issue of whether, in *Batson* cases (as in other circumstances), once a discriminatory intent is shown to be a motivating factor, the burden shifts to the prosecution to show that the discriminatory factor was not determinative. Given the facts of this case, nothing the prosecutor could have done, or might do on remand, would demonstrate a non-pretextual motivation for the strike.

Page 1041.   Add the following to Note 9 after Powers v. Ohio:

The Michigan Supreme Court's determination that a state defendant (Smith) failed to show systematic exclusion of African–Americans was held not to be an unreasonable application of clearly established federal law in Berghuis v. Smith, ___ U.S. ___, 130 S.Ct. 1382, 176 L.Ed.2d 249 (2010). African–Americans constituted 7.28% of the county's jury-eligible population and 6% of the pool from which potential jurors were drawn. The Court noted various methods of measuring fair and reasonable representation and indicated that its case law mandates no specific method. The Michigan court's use of a combined method therefore was acceptable. Smith relied in part on "the County's practice of excusing people who merely alleged hardship or simply failed to show up for jury service, its reliance on mail notices, its failure to follow up on nonresponses, its use of residential addresses at least 15 months old, and the refusal of * * * police to enforce court orders for the appearance of prospective jurors." The evidence, however, showed only that these practices *might* contribute to underrepresentation, not that they in fact did do so. Supreme Court case law, moreover, "has never 'clearly established' that jury-selection-process features of the kind on Smith's list can give rise to a fair-cross-section claim." The Court added, "We have also never 'clearly' decided, and have no need to consider here, whether the impact of social and economic factors can support a fair-cross-section claim." ___ U.S. at ___ n. 6, 130 S.Ct. at 1395 n. 6.

Page 1042.   Add the following after Note 10:

10a.   **Relationship of peremptories to challenges for cause.** The respondent in United States v. Martinez–Salazar, 528 U.S. 304, 120 S.Ct. 774, 145 L.Ed.2d 792 (2000) challenged a member of a jury panel for bias. The United States District Court judge denied that challenge and respondent then used one of his 10 peremptory challenges to prevent the panel member from serving on the jury. Following conviction, the Ninth Circuit reversed on the ground the trial judge should have granted the challenge for cause and by its failure to do so compelled defendant to use one of his allotment of peremptories on that panelist. While the challenged panelist did not sit on the jury, the defendant was deprived of one of his peremptories in the process and that is a reversible event. The Supreme Court, in an opinion by Justice Ginsburg, reversed.

The Government argued that a criminal defendant should be required to use a peremptory challenge on a panelist to preserve error when a trial court erroneously denies a challenge for cause directed to that panelist. While the Court rejected that argument, it did hold that if a defendant chooses to use a peremptory on a panelist whom he or she believes should have been excused for cause that action cures the error:

> The Court of Appeals erred in concluding that the District Court's for-cause mistake compelled Martinez–Salazar to challenge [the panel member] peremptorily, thereby reducing his allotment of peremptory challenges by one. A hard choice is not the same as no choice. Martinez–Salazar, together with his codefendant, received and exercised 11 peremptory challenges (10 for the petit jury, one in selecting an alternate juror). That is all he is entitled to under the Rule.
>
> After objecting to the District Court's denial of his for-cause challenge, Martinez–Salazar had the option of letting [the panel member] sit on the petit jury and, upon conviction, pursuing a Sixth Amendment challenge on appeal. Instead, Martinez–Salazar elected to use a challenge to remove [the panel member] because he did not want [him] to sit on his jury. This was Martinez–Salazar's choice. The District Court did not demand—and Rule 24(b) did not require—that Martinez–Salazar use a peremptory challenge curatively.
>
> In choosing to remove [the panel member] rather than taking his chances on appeal, Martinez–Salazar did not lose a peremptory challenge. Rather, he used the challenge in line with a principal reason for peremptories: to help secure the constitutional guarantee of trial by an impartial jury.

528 U.S. at 315–16, 120 S.Ct. at 781–982, 145 L.Ed.2d at 803. Justice Scalia, joined by Justice Kennedy, dissented from the Court's position that a criminal defendant is not required to exercise a peremptory challenge to preserve error in denial of a challenge for cause.

C.   CONFRONTATION, CROSS-EXAMINATION AND COMPULSORY PROCESS TO OBTAIN WITNESSES

1.   CONFRONTATION

Page 1068.   Add the following case before Notes:

Crawford v. Washington

Supreme Court of the United States, 2004.
541 U.S. 36, 124 S.Ct. 1354, 158 L.Ed.2d 177.

■ JUSTICE SCALIA delivered the opinion of the Court.

Petitioner Michael Crawford stabbed a man who allegedly tried to rape his wife, Sylvia. At his trial, the State played for the jury Sylvia's tape-recorded statement to the police describing the stabbing, even though he had no opportunity for cross-examination. The Washington Supreme Court upheld petitioner's conviction after determining that Sylvia's statement was reliable. The question presented is whether this procedure complied with the Sixth Amendment's guarantee that, "[i]n all criminal prosecutions, the accused shall enjoy the right ... to be confronted with the witnesses against him."

I

On August 5, 1999, Kenneth Lee was stabbed at his apartment. Police arrested petitioner later that night. After giving petitioner and his wife *Miranda* warnings, detectives interrogated each of them twice. Petitioner eventually confessed that he and Sylvia had gone in search of Lee because he was upset over an earlier incident in which Lee had tried to rape her. The two had found Lee at his apartment, and a fight ensued in which Lee was stabbed in the torso and petitioner's hand was cut.

Petitioner gave the following account of the fight:

"Q. Okay. Did you ever see anything in [Lee's] hands?

"A. I think so, but I'm not positive.

"Q. Okay, when you think so, what do you mean by that?

"A. I coulda swore I seen him goin' for somethin' before, right before everything happened. He was like reachin', fiddlin' around down here and stuff ... and I just ... I don't know, I think, this is just a possibility, but I think, I think that he pulled somethin' out and I grabbed for it and that's how I got cut ... but I'm not positive. I, I, my mind goes blank when things like this happen. I mean, I just, I remember things wrong, I remember things that just doesn't, don't make sense to me later." App. 155 (punctuation added).

Sylvia generally corroborated petitioner's story about the events leading up to the fight, but her account of the fight itself was arguably different—particularly with respect to whether Lee had drawn a weapon before petitioner assaulted him:

"Q. Did Kenny do anything to fight back from this assault?

"A. (pausing) I know he reached into his pocket ... or somethin' ... I don't know what.

"Q. After he was stabbed?

"A. He saw Michael coming up. He lifted his hand ... his chest open, he might [have] went to go strike his hand out or something and then (inaudible).

"Q. Okay, you, you gotta speak up.

"A. Okay, he lifted his hand over his head maybe to strike Michael's hand down or something and then he put his hands in his . . . put his right hand in his right pocket . . . took a step back . . . Michael proceeded to stab him . . . then his hands were like . . . how do you explain this . . . open arms . . . with his hands open and he fell down . . . and we ran (describing subject holding hands open, palms toward assailant).

"Q. Okay, when he's standing there with his open hands, you're talking about Kenny, correct?

"A. Yeah, after, after the fact, yes.

"Q. Did you see anything in his hands at that point?

"A. (pausing) um um (no)." *Id.,* at 137 (punctuation added).

The State charged petitioner with assault and attempted murder. At trial, he claimed self-defense. Sylvia did not testify because of the state marital privilege, which generally bars a spouse from testifying without the other spouse's consent. See Wash. Rev.Code § 5.60.060(1) (1994). In Washington, this privilege does not extend to a spouse's out-of-court statements admissible under a hearsay exception, see *State v. Burden,* 120 Wash.2d 371, 377, 841 P.2d 758, 761 (1992), so the State sought to introduce Sylvia's tape-recorded statements to the police as evidence that the stabbing was not in self-defense. Noting that Sylvia had admitted she led petitioner to Lee's apartment and thus had facilitated the assault, the State invoked the hearsay exception for statements against penal interest, Wash. Rule Evid. 804(b)(3) (2003).

Petitioner countered that, state law notwithstanding, admitting the evidence would violate his federal constitutional right to be "confronted with the witnesses against him." Amdt. 6. According to our description of that right in *Ohio v. Roberts,* 448 U.S. 56, 100 S.Ct. 2531, 65 L.Ed.2d 597 (1980), it does not bar admission of an unavailable witness's statement against a criminal defendant if the statement bears "adequate 'indicia of reliability.' " *Id.,* at 66, 100 S.Ct. 2531. To meet that test, evidence must either fall within a "firmly rooted hearsay exception" or bear "particularized guarantees of trustworthiness." *Ibid.* The trial court here admitted the statement on the latter ground, offering several reasons why it was trustworthy: Sylvia was not shifting blame but rather corroborating her husband's story that he acted in self-defense or "justified reprisal"; she had direct knowledge as an eyewitness; she was describing recent events; and she was being questioned by a "neutral" law enforcement officer. App. 76–77. The prosecution played the tape for the jury and relied on it in closing, arguing that it was "damning evidence" that "completely refutes [petitioner's] claim of self-defense." Tr. 468 (Oct. 21, 1999). The jury convicted petitioner of assault.

The Washington Court of Appeals reversed. It applied a nine-factor test to determine whether Sylvia's statement bore particularized guarantees of trustworthiness, and noted several reasons why it did not: The statement contradicted one she had previously given; it was made in response to specific questions; and at one point she admitted she had shut her eyes during the stabbing. The court considered and rejected the State's argument that Sylvia's statement was reliable because it coincided with petitioner's to such a degree that the two "interlocked." The court determined that, although the two statements agreed about the events leading up to the stabbing, they differed on the issue crucial to petitioner's self-defense claim: "[Petitioner's] version asserts that Lee may have had something in his hand when he stabbed him; but Sylvia's version has Lee grabbing for something only after he has been stabbed." App. 32.

The Washington Supreme Court reinstated the conviction, unanimously concluding that, although Sylvia's statement did not fall under a firmly rooted hearsay exception, it bore guarantees of trustworthiness: " '[W]hen a codefendant's confession is virtually identical [to, *i.e.,* interlocks with,] that of a defendant, it may be deemed reliable.' " 147 Wash.2d 424, 437, 54 P.3d 656, 663 (2002) (quoting *State v. Rice,* 120 Wash.2d 549, 570, 844 P.2d 416, 427 (1993)). The court explained:

> "Although the Court of Appeals concluded that the statements were contradictory, upon closer inspection they appear to overlap . . . .
>
> "[B]oth of the Crawfords' statements indicate that Lee was possibly grabbing for a weapon, but they are equally unsure when this event may have taken place. They are also equally unsure how Michael received the cut on his hand, leading the court to question when, if ever, Lee possessed a weapon. In this respect they overlap.
>
> "[N]either Michael nor Sylvia clearly stated that Lee had a weapon in hand from which Michael was simply defending himself. And it is this omission by both that interlocks the statements and makes Sylvia's statement reliable." 147 Wash.2d, at 438–439, 54 P.3d, at 664 (internal quotation marks omitted).

We granted certiorari to determine whether the State's use of Sylvia's statement violated the Confrontation Clause. 539 U.S. 914, 123 S.Ct. 2275, 156 L.Ed.2d 129 (2003).

II

The Sixth Amendment's Confrontation Clause provides that, "[i]n all criminal prosecutions, the accused shall enjoy the right . . . to be confronted with the witnesses against him." We have held that this bedrock procedural guarantee applies to both federal and state prosecutions. *Pointer v. Texas,* 380 U.S. 400, 406, 85 S.Ct. 1065, 13 L.Ed.2d 923 (1965). As noted above, *Roberts* says that an unavailable witness's out-of-court statement may be admitted so long as it has adequate indicia of reliability—*i.e.,* falls within a "firmly rooted hearsay exception" or bears "particularized guarantees of trustworthiness." 448 U.S., at 66, 100 S.Ct. 2531. Petitioner argues that this test strays from the original meaning of the Confrontation Clause and urges us to reconsider it.

A

The Constitution's text does not alone resolve this case. One could plausibly read "witnesses against" a defendant to mean those who actually testify at trial, cf. *Woodsides v. State,* 3 Miss. 655, 664–665 (1837), those whose statements are offered at trial, see 3 J. Wigmore, Evidence § 1397, p. 104 (2d ed.1923) (hereinafter Wigmore), or something in-between, see *infra,* at 1364. We must therefore turn to the historical background of the Clause to understand its meaning.

* * *

III

This history supports two inferences about the meaning of the Sixth Amendment.

A

First, the principal evil at which the Confrontation Clause was directed was the civil-law mode of criminal procedure, and particularly its use of *ex parte* examinations as evidence against the accused. It was these practices that the Crown deployed in notorious treason cases like Raleigh's; that the Marian statutes invited; that English law's assertion of a right to confrontation was meant to prohibit; and that the founding-era rhetoric decried. The Sixth Amendment must be interpreted with this focus in mind.

Accordingly, we once again reject the view that the Confrontation Clause applies of its own force only to in-court testimony, and that its application to out-of-court statements introduced at trial depends upon "the law of Evidence for the time being." 3 Wigmore § 1397, at 101; accord, *Dutton v. Evans,* 400 U.S. 74, 94, 91 S.Ct. 210, 27 L.Ed.2d 213 (1970) (Harlan, J., concurring in result). Leaving the regulation of out-of-court statements to the law of evidence would render the Confrontation Clause powerless to prevent even the most flagrant inquisitorial practices. Raleigh was, after all, perfectly free to confront those who read Cobham's confession in court.

This focus also suggests that not all hearsay implicates the Sixth Amendment's core concerns. An off-hand, overheard remark might be unreliable evidence and thus a good candidate for exclusion under hearsay rules, but it bears little resemblance to the civil-law abuses the Confrontation Clause targeted. On the other hand, *ex parte* examinations might sometimes be admissible under modern hearsay rules, but the Framers certainly would not have condoned them.

The text of the Confrontation Clause reflects this focus. It applies to "witnesses" against the accused—in other words, those who "bear testimony." 1 N. Webster, An American Dictionary of the English Language (1828). "Testimony," in turn, is typically "[a] solemn declaration or affirmation made for the purpose of establishing or proving some fact." *Ibid.* An accuser who makes a formal statement to government officers bears testimony in a sense that a person who makes a casual remark to an acquaintance does not. The constitutional text, like the history underlying the common-law right of confrontation, thus reflects an especially acute concern with a specific type of out-of-court statement.

Various formulations of this core class of "testimonial" statements exist: "*ex parte* in-court testimony or its functional equivalent—that is, material such as affidavits, custodial examinations, prior testimony that the defendant was unable to cross-examine, or similar pretrial statements that declarants would reasonably expect to be used prosecutorially," Brief for Petitioner 23; "extrajudicial statements . . . contained in formalized testimonial materials, such as affidavits, depositions, prior testimony, or confessions," *White v. Illinois,* 502 U.S. 346, 365, 112 S.Ct. 736, 116 L.Ed.2d 848 (1992) (THOMAS, J., joined by SCALIA, J., concurring in part and concurring in judgment); "statements that were made under circumstances which would lead an objective witness reasonably to believe that the statement would be available for use at a later trial," Brief for National Association of Criminal Defense Lawyers et al. as *Amici Curiae* 3. These formulations all share a common nucleus and then define the Clause's coverage at various levels of abstraction around it. Regardless of the precise articulation, some statements qualify under any definition—for example, *ex parte* testimony at a preliminary hearing.

Statements taken by police officers in the course of interrogations are also testimonial under even a narrow standard. Police interrogations bear a striking resemblance to examinations by justices of the peace in England. The statements are not *sworn* testimony, but the absence of oath was not dispositive. Cobham's examination was unsworn, see 1 Jardine, Criminal Trials, at 430, yet Raleigh's trial has long been thought a paradigmatic confrontation violation, see, *e.g., Campbell,* 1 Rich., at 130. Under the Marian statutes, witnesses were typically put on oath, but suspects were not. See 2 Hale, Pleas of the Crown, at 52. Yet Hawkins and others went out of their way to caution that such unsworn confessions were not admissible against anyone but the confessor. See *supra,* at 1360.

That interrogators are police officers rather than magistrates does not change the picture either. Justices of the peace conducting examinations under the Marian statutes were not magistrates as we understand that office today, but had an essentially investigative and prosecutorial function. See 1 Stephen, Criminal Law of England, at 221; Langbein, Prosecuting Crime in the Renaissance, at 34–45. England did not have a professional police force until the 19th century, see 1 Stephen, *supra,* at 194–200, so it is not surprising that other government officers performed the investigative functions now associated primarily with the police. The involvement of government officers in the production of testimonial evidence presents the same risk, whether the officers are police or justices of the peace.

In sum, even if the Sixth Amendment is not solely concerned with testimonial hearsay, that is its primary object, and interrogations by law enforcement officers fall squarely within that class.[1]

B

The historical record also supports a second proposition: that the Framers would not have allowed admission of testimonial statements of a witness who did not appear at trial unless he was unavailable to testify, and the defendant had had a prior opportunity for cross-examination. The text of the Sixth Amendment does not suggest any open-ended exceptions from the confrontation requirement to be developed by the courts. Rather, the "right . . . to be confronted with the witnesses against him," Amdt. 6, is most naturally read as a reference to the right of confrontation at common law, admitting only those exceptions established at the time of the founding. See *Mattox v. United States,* 156 U.S. 237, 243, 15 S.Ct. 337, 39 L.Ed. 409 (1895); cf. *Houser,* 26 Mo., at 433–435. As the English authorities above reveal, the common law in 1791 conditioned admissibility of an absent witness's examination on unavailability and a prior opportunity to cross-examine. The Sixth Amendment therefore incorporates those limitations. The numerous early state decisions applying the same test confirm that these principles were received as part of the common law in this country.

We do not read the historical sources to say that a prior opportunity to cross-examine was merely a sufficient, rather than a necessary, condition for admissibility of testimonial statements. They suggest that this requirement was dispositive, and not merely one of several ways to establish reliability. This is not to deny, as THE CHIEF JUSTICE notes, that "[t]here were always exceptions to the general rule of exclusion" of hearsay evidence. *Post,* at 1377. Several had become well established by 1791. See 3 Wigmore § 1397, at 101; Brief for United States as *Amicus Curiae* 13, n. 5. But there is scant evidence that exceptions were invoked to admit *testimonial* statements against the accused in a *criminal* case.[2] Most of the hearsay

---

1. We use the term "interrogation" in its colloquial, rather than any technical legal, sense. Cf. *Rhode Island v. Innis,* 446 U.S. 291, 300–301, 100 S.Ct. 1682, 64 L.Ed.2d 297 (1980). Just as various definitions of "testimonial" exist, one can imagine various definitions of "interrogation," and we need not select among them in this case. Sylvia's recorded statement, knowingly given in response to structured police questioning, qualifies under any conceivable definition

2. The one deviation we have found involves dying declarations. The existence of that exception as a general rule of criminal hearsay law cannot be disputed. See, *e.g., Mattox v. United States,* 156 U.S. 237, 243–244, 15 S.Ct. 337, 39 L.Ed. 409 (1895); *King v. Reason,* 16 How. St. Tr. 1, 24–38 (K.B. 1722); 1 D. Jardine, Criminal Trials 435 (1832); Cooley, Constitutional Limitations, at *318; 1 G. Gilbert, Evidence 211 (C. Lofft ed. 1791); see also F. Heller, The Sixth Amendment 105 (1951) (asserting that this was the

exceptions covered statements that by their nature were not testimonial—
for example, business records or statements in furtherance of a conspiracy.
We do not infer from these that the Framers thought exceptions would
apply even to prior testimony. Cf. *Lilly v. Virginia,* 527 U.S. 116, 134, 119
S.Ct. 1887, 144 L.Ed.2d 117 (1999) (plurality opinion) ("[A]ccomplices'
confessions that inculpate a criminal defendant are not within a firmly
rooted exception to the hearsay rule")

IV

Our case law has been largely consistent with these two principles. Our
leading early decision, for example, involved a deceased witness's prior trial
testimony. *Mattox v. United States,* 156 U.S. 237, 15 S.Ct. 337, 39 L.Ed. 409
(1895). In allowing the statement to be admitted, we relied on the fact that
the defendant had had, at the first trial, an adequate opportunity to
confront the witness: "The substance of the constitutional protection is
preserved to the prisoner in the advantage he has once had of seeing the
witness face to face, and of subjecting him to the ordeal of a cross-
examination. This, the law says, he shall under no circumstances be
deprived of. . . ." *Id.,* at 244, 15 S.Ct. 337.

Our later cases conform to *Mattox's* holding that prior trial or preliminary hearing testimony is admissible only if the defendant had an adequate
opportunity to cross-examine. See *Mancusi v. Stubbs,* 408 U.S. 204, 213–
216, 92 S.Ct. 2308, 33 L.Ed.2d 293 (1972); *California v. Green,* 399 U.S.
149, 165–168, 90 S.Ct. 1930, 26 L.Ed.2d 489 (1970); *Pointer v. Texas,* 380
U.S., at 406–408, 85 S.Ct. 1065; cf. *Kirby v. United States,* 174 U.S. 47, 55–
61, 19 S.Ct. 574, 43 L.Ed. 890 (1899). Even where the defendant had such
an opportunity, we excluded the testimony where the government had not
established unavailability of the witness. See *Barber v. Page,* 390 U.S. 719,
722–725, 88 S.Ct. 1318, 20 L.Ed.2d 255 (1968); cf. *Motes v. United States,*
178 U.S. 458, 470–471, 20 S.Ct. 993, 44 L.Ed. 1150 (1900). We similarly
excluded accomplice confessions where the defendant had no opportunity to
cross-examine. See *Roberts v. Russell,* 392 U.S. 293, 294–295, 88 S.Ct. 1921,
20 L.Ed.2d 1100 (1968) *(per curiam); Bruton v. United States,* 391 U.S. 123,
126–128, 88 S.Ct. 1620, 20 L.Ed.2d 476 (1968); *Douglas v. Alabama,* 380
U.S. 415, 418–420, 85 S.Ct. 1074, 13 L.Ed.2d 934 (1965). In contrast, we
considered reliability factors beyond prior opportunity for cross-examination when the hearsay statement at issue was not testimonial. See *Dutton
v. Evans,* 400 U.S., at 87–89, 91 S.Ct. 210 (plurality opinion).

only recognized criminal hearsay exception at
common law). Although many dying declarations may not be testimonial, there is authority for admitting even those that clearly are.
See *Woodcock, supra,* at 501–504, 168 Eng.
Rep., at 353–354; *Reason, supra,* at 24–38;
Peake, Evidence, at 64; cf. *Radbourne, supra,*
at 460–462, 168 Eng. Rep., at 332–333. We
need not decide in this case whether the
Sixth Amendment incorporates an exception
for testimonial dying declarations. If this exception must be accepted on historical
grounds, it is *sui generis.*

Even our recent cases, in their outcomes, hew closely to the traditional line. *Ohio v. Roberts*, 448 U.S., at 67–70, 100 S.Ct. 2531, admitted testimony from a preliminary hearing at which the defendant had examined the witness. *Lilly v. Virginia, supra,* excluded testimonial statements that the defendant had had no opportunity to test by cross-examination. And *Bourjaily v. United States*, 483 U.S. 171, 181–184, 107 S.Ct. 2775, 97 L.Ed.2d 144 (1987), admitted statements made unwittingly to an FBI informant after applying a more general test that did *not* make prior cross-examination an indispensable requirement.[3]

Lee v. Illinois, 476 U.S. 530, 106 S.Ct. 2056, 90 L.Ed.2d 514 (1986), on which the State relies, is not to the contrary. There, we *rejected* the State's attempt to admit an accomplice confession. The State had argued that the confession was admissible because it "interlocked" with the defendant's. We dealt with the argument by rejecting its premise, holding that "when the discrepancies between the statements are not insignificant, the codefendant's confession may not be admitted." *Id.,* at 545, 106 S.Ct. 2056. Respondent argues that "[t]he logical inference of this statement is that when the discrepancies between the statements *are* insignificant, then the codefendant's statement *may* be admitted." Brief for Respondent 6. But this is merely a possible inference, not an inevitable one, and we do not draw it here. If *Lee* had meant authoritatively to announce an exception—previously unknown to this Court's jurisprudence—for interlocking confessions, it would not have done so in such an oblique manner. Our only precedent on interlocking confessions had addressed the entirely different question whether a limiting instruction cured prejudice to codefendants from admitting a defendant's *own* confession against him in a joint trial. See *Parker v. Randolph*, 442 U.S. 62, 69–76, 99 S.Ct. 2132, 60 L.Ed.2d 713 (1979) (plurality opinion), abrogated by *Cruz v. New York*, 481 U.S. 186, 107 S.Ct. 1714, 95 L.Ed.2d 162 (1987).

Our cases have thus remained faithful to the Framers' understanding: Testimonial statements of witnesses absent from trial have been admitted

---

3. One case arguably in tension with the rule requiring a prior opportunity for cross-examination when the proffered statement is testimonial is *White v. Illinois*, 502 U.S. 346, 112 S.Ct. 736, 116 L.Ed.2d 848 (1992), which involved, *inter alia,* statements of a child victim to an investigating police officer admitted as spontaneous declarations. *Id.,* at 349–351, 112 S.Ct. 736. It is questionable whether testimonial statements would ever have been admissible on that ground in 1791; to the extent the hearsay exception for spontaneous declarations existed at all, it required that the statements be made "immediat[ely] upon the hurt received, and before [the declarant] had time to devise or contrive any thing for her own advantage." *Thompson v. Trevanion*, Skin. 402, 90 Eng. Rep. 179 (K.B.1694). In any case, the only question presented in *White* was whether the Confrontation Clause imposed an unavailability requirement on the types of hearsay at issue. See 502 U.S., at 348–349, 112 S.Ct. 736. The holding did not address the question whether certain of the statements, because they were testimonial, had to be excluded *even if* the witness was unavailable. We "[took] as a given ... that the testimony properly falls within the relevant hearsay exceptions." *Id.,* at 351, n. 4, 112 S.Ct. 736.

only where the declarant is unavailable, and only where the defendant has had a prior opportunity to cross-examine.

V

Although the results of our decisions have generally been faithful to the original meaning of the Confrontation Clause, the same cannot be said of our rationales. *Roberts* conditions the admissibility of all hearsay evidence on whether it falls under a "firmly rooted hearsay exception" or bears "particularized guarantees of trustworthiness." 448 U.S., at 66, 100 S.Ct. 2531. This test departs from the historical principles identified above in two respects. First, it is too broad: It applies the same mode of analysis whether or not the hearsay consists of *ex parte* testimony. This often results in close constitutional scrutiny in cases that are far removed from the core concerns of the Clause. At the same time, however, the test is too narrow: It admits statements that *do* consist of *ex parte* testimony upon a mere finding of reliability. This malleable standard often fails to protect against paradigmatic confrontation violations.

Members of this Court and academics have suggested that we revise our doctrine to reflect more accurately the original understanding of the Clause. See, *e.g., Lilly,* 527 U.S., at 140–143, 119 S.Ct. 1887 (BREYER, J., concurring); *White,* 502 U.S., at 366, 112 S.Ct. 736 (THOMAS, J., joined by SCALIA, J., concurring in part and concurring in judgment); A. Amar, The Constitution and Criminal Procedure 125–131 (1997); Friedman, Confrontation: The Search for Basic Principles, 86 Geo. L.J. 1011 (1998). They offer two proposals: First, that we apply the Confrontation Clause only to testimonial statements, leaving the remainder to regulation by hearsay law—thus eliminating the overbreadth referred to above. Second, that we impose an absolute bar to statements that are testimonial, absent a prior opportunity to cross-examine—thus eliminating the excessive narrowness referred to above.

In *White,* we considered the first proposal and rejected it. 502 U.S., at 352–353, 112 S.Ct. 736. Although our analysis in this case casts doubt on that holding, we need not definitively resolve whether it survives our decision today, because Sylvia Crawford's statement is testimonial under any definition. This case does, however, squarely implicate the second proposal.

A

Where testimonial statements are involved, we do not think the Framers meant to leave the Sixth Amendment's protection to the vagaries of the rules of evidence, much less to amorphous notions of "reliability." Certainly none of the authorities discussed above acknowledges any general reliability exception to the common-law rule. Admitting statements deemed reliable by a judge is fundamentally at odds with the right of confrontation. To be sure, the Clause's ultimate goal is to ensure reliability of evidence, but it is a procedural rather than a substantive guarantee. It commands, not that evidence be reliable, but that reliability be assessed in a particular manner: by testing in the crucible of cross-examination. The Clause thus reflects a judgment, not only about the desirability of reliable evidence (a point on which there could be little dissent), but about how reliability can best be determined. Cf. 3 Blackstone, Commentaries, at 373 ("This open examination of witnesses ... is much more conducive to the clearing up of truth"); M. Hale, History and Analysis of the Common Law of England 258 (1713) (adversarial testing "beats and bolts out the Truth much better").

The *Roberts* test allows a jury to hear evidence, untested by the adversary process, based on a mere judicial determination of reliability. It thus replaces the constitutionally prescribed method of assessing reliability with a wholly foreign one. In this respect, it is very different from exceptions to the Confrontation Clause that make no claim to be a surrogate means of assessing reliability. For example, the rule of forfeiture by wrongdoing (which we accept) extinguishes confrontation claims on essentially equitable grounds; it does not purport to be an alternative means of determining reliability. See *Reynolds v. United States,* 98 U.S. 145, 158–159, 25 L.Ed. 244 (1879).

The Raleigh trial itself involved the very sorts of reliability determinations that *Roberts* authorizes. In the face of Raleigh's repeated demands for confrontation, the prosecution responded with many of the arguments a court applying *Roberts* might invoke today: that Cobham's statements were self-inculpatory, 2 How. St. Tr., at 19, that they were not made in the heat of passion, *id.,* at 14, and that they were not "extracted from [him] upon any hopes or promise of Pardon," *id.,* at 29. It is not plausible that the Framers' only objection to the trial was that Raleigh's judges did not properly weigh these factors before sentencing him to death. Rather, the problem was that the judges refused to allow Raleigh to confront Cobham in court, where he could cross-examine him and try to expose his accusation as a lie.

Dispensing with confrontation because testimony is obviously reliable is akin to dispensing with jury trial because a defendant is obviously guilty. This is not what the Sixth Amendment prescribes.

B

The legacy of *Roberts* in other courts vindicates the Framers' wisdom in rejecting a general reliability exception. The framework is so unpredictable that it fails to provide meaningful protection from even core confrontation violations.

Reliability is an amorphous, if not entirely subjective, concept. There are countless factors bearing on whether a statement is reliable; the nine-factor balancing test applied by the Court of Appeals below is representative. See, *e.g., People v. Farrell,* 34 P.3d 401, 406–407 (Colo.2001) (eight-factor test). Whether a statement is deemed reliable depends heavily on which factors the judge considers and how much weight he accords each of them. Some courts wind up attaching the same significance to opposite facts. For example, the Colorado Supreme Court held a statement more reliable because its inculpation of the defendant was "detailed," *id.,* at 407, while the Fourth Circuit found a statement more reliable because the portion implicating another was "fleeting," *United States v. Photogrammetric Data Servs., Inc.,* 259 F.3d 229, 245 (C.A.4 2001). The Virginia Court of Appeals found a statement more reliable because the witness was in custody and charged with a crime (thus making the statement more obviously against her penal interest), see *Nowlin v. Commonwealth,* 40 Va.App. 327, 335–338, 579 S.E.2d 367, 371–372 (2003), while the Wisconsin Court of Appeals found a statement more reliable because the witness was *not* in custody and *not* a suspect, see *State v. Bintz,* 2002 WI App. 204, ¶ 13, 257 Wis.2d 177, 187, 650 N.W.2d 913, 918. Finally, the Colorado Supreme Court in one case found a statement more reliable because it was given "immediately after" the events at issue, *Farrell, supra,* at 407, while that same court, in another case, found a statement more reliable because two years had elapsed, *Stevens v. People,* 29 P.3d 305, 316 (Colo.2001).

The unpardonable vice of the *Roberts* test, however, is not its unpredictability, but its demonstrated capacity to admit core testimonial statements that the Confrontation Clause plainly meant to exclude. Despite the plurality's speculation in *Lilly,* 527 U.S., at 137, 119 S.Ct. 1887, that it was "highly unlikely" that accomplice confessions implicating the accused could survive *Roberts,* courts continue routinely to admit them. * * *

To add insult to injury, some of the courts that admit untested testimonial statements find reliability in the very factors that *make* the statements testimonial. As noted earlier, one court relied on the fact that the witness's statement was made to police while in custody on pending charges—the theory being that this made the statement more clearly against penal interest and thus more reliable. *Nowlin, supra,* at 335–338, 579 S.E.2d, at 371–372. Other courts routinely rely on the fact that a prior statement is given under oath in judicial proceedings. *E.g., Gallego, supra,* at 168, 579 S.E.2d 367 (plea allocution); *Papajohn, supra,* at 1120 (grand jury testimony). That inculpating statements are given in a testimonial setting is not an antidote to the confrontation problem, but rather the trigger that makes the Clause's demands most urgent. It is not enough to point out that most of the usual safeguards of the adversary process attend the statement, when the single safeguard missing is the one the Confrontation Clause demands.

C

Roberts' failings were on full display in the proceedings below. Sylvia Crawford made her statement while in police custody, herself a potential suspect in the case. Indeed, she had been told that whether she would be released "depend[ed] on how the investigation continues." App. 81. In response to often leading questions from police detectives, she implicated her husband in Lee's stabbing and at least arguably undermined his self-defense claim. Despite all this, the trial court admitted her statement, listing several reasons why it was reliable. In its opinion reversing, the Court of Appeals listed several *other* reasons why the statement was *not* reliable. Finally, the State Supreme Court relied exclusively on the interlocking character of the statement and disregarded every other factor the lower courts had considered. The case is thus a self-contained demonstration of *Roberts'* unpredictable and inconsistent application.

Each of the courts also made assumptions that cross-examination might well have undermined. The trial court, for example, stated that Sylvia Crawford's statement was reliable because she was an eyewitness with direct knowledge of the events. But Sylvia at one point told the police that she had "shut [her] eyes and . . . didn't really watch" part of the fight, and that she was "in shock." App. 134. The trial court also buttressed its reliability finding by claiming that Sylvia was "being questioned by law enforcement, and, thus, the [questioner] is . . . neutral to her and not someone who would be inclined to advance her interests and shade her version of the truth unfavorably toward the defendant." *Id.,* at 77. The Framers would be astounded to learn that *ex parte* testimony could be admitted against a criminal defendant because it was elicited by "neutral" government officers. But even if the court's assessment of the officer's motives was accurate, it says nothing about Sylvia's perception of her situation. Only cross-examination could reveal that.

The State Supreme Court gave dispositive weight to the interlocking nature of the two statements—that they were both ambiguous as to when and whether Lee had a weapon. The court's claim that the two statements were *equally* ambiguous is hard to accept. Petitioner's statement is ambiguous only in the sense that he had lingering doubts about his recollection: "A. I coulda swore I seen him goin' for somethin' before, right before everything happened. . . . [B]ut I'm not positive." *Id.,* at 155. Sylvia's statement, on the other hand, is truly inscrutable, since the key timing detail was simply assumed in the leading question she was asked: "Q. Did Kenny do anything to fight back from this assault?" *Id.,* at 137. Moreover, Sylvia specifically said Lee had nothing in his hands after he was stabbed, while petitioner was not asked about that.

The prosecutor obviously did not share the court's view that Sylvia's statement was ambiguous—he called it "damning evidence" that "completely refutes [petitioner's] claim of self-defense." Tr. 468 (Oct. 21, 1999). We have no way of knowing whether the jury agreed with the prosecutor or the court. Far from obviating the need for cross-examination, the "interlocking" ambiguity of the two statements made it all the more imperative that they be tested to tease out the truth.

We readily concede that we could resolve this case by simply reweighing the "reliability factors" under *Roberts* and finding that Sylvia Crawford's statement falls short. But we view this as one of those rare cases in which the result below is so improbable that it reveals a fundamental failure on our part to interpret the Constitution in a way that secures its intended constraint on judicial discretion. Moreover, to reverse the Washington Supreme Court's decision after conducting our own reliability analysis would perpetuate, not avoid, what the Sixth Amendment condemns. The Constitution prescribes a procedure for determining the reliability of testimony in criminal trials, and we, no less than the state courts, lack authority to replace it with one of our own devising.

We have no doubt that the courts below were acting in utmost good faith when they found reliability. The Framers, however, would not have been content to indulge this assumption. They knew that judges, like other government officers, could not always be trusted to safeguard the rights of the people; the likes of the dread Lord Jeffreys were not yet too distant a memory. They were loath to leave too much discretion in judicial hands. Cf. U.S. Const., Amdt. 6 (criminal jury trial); Amdt. 7 (civil jury trial); *Ring v. Arizona,* 536 U.S. 584, 611–612, 122 S.Ct. 2428, 153 L.Ed.2d 556 (2002) (SCALIA, J., concurring). By replacing categorical constitutional guarantees with open-ended balancing tests, we do violence to their design. Vague standards are manipulable, and, while that might be a small concern in run-of-the-mill assault prosecutions like this one, the Framers had an eye toward politically charged cases like Raleigh's—great state trials where the impartiality of even those at the highest levels of the judiciary might not be so clear. It is difficult to imagine *Roberts'* providing any meaningful protection in those circumstances.

* * *

Where nontestimonial hearsay is at issue, it is wholly consistent with the Framers' design to afford the States flexibility in their development of hearsay law—as does *Roberts,* and as would an approach that exempted such statements from Confrontation Clause scrutiny altogether. Where testimonial evidence is at issue, however, the Sixth Amendment demands what the common law required: unavailability and a prior opportunity for cross-examination. We leave for another day any effort to spell out a comprehensive definition of "testimonial."[4] Whatever else the term covers, it applies at a minimum to prior testimony at a preliminary hearing, before a grand jury, or at a former trial; and to police interrogations. These are the modern practices with closest kinship to the abuses at which the Confrontation Clause was directed.

In this case, the State admitted Sylvia's testimonial statement against petitioner, despite the fact that he had no opportunity to cross-examine

---

4. We acknowledge THE CHIEF JUSTICE's objection, that our refusal to articulate a comprehensive definition in this case will cause interim uncertainty. But it can hardly be any worse than the status quo. The difference is that the *Roberts* test is *inherently,* and therefore *permanently,* unpredictable.

her. That alone is sufficient to make out a violation of the Sixth Amendment. *Roberts* notwithstanding, we decline to mine the record in search of indicia of reliability. Where testimonial statements are at issue, the only indicium of reliability sufficient to satisfy constitutional demands is the one the Constitution actually prescribes: confrontation.

The judgment of the Washington Supreme Court is reversed, and the case is remanded for further proceedings not inconsistent with this opinion.

It is so ordered.

■ CHIEF JUSTICE REHNQUIST, with whom JUSTICE O'CONNOR joins, concurring in the judgment.

I dissent from the Court's decision to overrule *Ohio v. Roberts,* 448 U.S. 56, 100 S.Ct. 2531, 65 L.Ed.2d 597 (1980). I believe that the Court's adoption of a new interpretation of the Confrontation Clause is not backed by sufficiently persuasive reasoning to overrule long-established precedent. Its decision casts a mantle of uncertainty over future criminal trials in both federal and state courts, and is by no means necessary to decide the present case.

* * *

In choosing the path it does, the Court of course overrules *Ohio v. Roberts,* 448 U.S. 56, 100 S.Ct. 2531, 65 L.Ed.2d 597 (1980), a case decided nearly a quarter of a century ago. *Stare decisis* is not an inexorable command in the area of constitutional law, see *Payne v. Tennessee,* 501 U.S. 808, 828, 111 S.Ct. 2597, 115 L.Ed.2d 720 (1991), but by and large, it "is the preferred course because it promotes the evenhanded, predictable, and consistent development of legal principles, fosters reliance on judicial decisions, and contributes to the actual and perceived integrity of the judicial process," *id.,* at 827, 111 S.Ct. 2597. And in making this appraisal, doubt that the new rule is indeed the "right" one should surely be weighed in the balance. Though there are no vested interests involved, unresolved questions for the future of everyday criminal trials throughout the country surely counsel the same sort of caution. The Court grandly declares that "[w]e leave for another day any effort to spell out a comprehensive definition of 'testimonial,' " *ante,* at 1374. But the thousands of federal prosecutors and the tens of thousands of state prosecutors need answers as to what beyond the specific kinds of "testimony" the Court lists, see *ibid.,* is covered by the new rule. They need them now, not months or years from now. Rules of criminal evidence are applied every day in courts throughout the country, and parties should not be left in the dark in this manner.

To its credit, the Court's analysis of "testimony" excludes at least some hearsay exceptions, such as business records and official records. See *ante,* at 1367. To hold otherwise would require numerous additional witnesses without any apparent gain in the truth-seeking process. Likewise to the Court's credit is its implicit recognition that the mistaken application of its new rule by courts which guess wrong as to the scope of the rule is subject to harmless-error analysis. * * *

* * *

NOTES: FLESHING OUT OF *CRAWFORD*

1. **When are responses to police interrogation "testimonial"?** The Supreme Court somewhat fleshed out *Crawford* in Davis v. Washington, 547 U.S. 813, 126 S.Ct. 2266, 165 L.Ed.2d 224 (2006), involving two consolidated cases. It explained:

> These cases require us to determine when statements made to law enforcement personnel during a 911 call or at a crime scene are "testimonial" and thus subject to the requirements of the Sixth Amendment's Confrontation Clause.

* * *

> Without attempting to produce an exhaustive classification of all conceivable statements—or even all conceivable statements in response to police interrogation—as either testimonial or nontestimonial, it suffices to decide the present cases to hold as follows: Statements are nontestimonial when made in the course of police interrogation under circumstances objectively indicating that the primary purpose of the interrogation is to enable police assistance to meet an ongoing emergency. They are testimonial when the circumstances objectively indicate that there is no such ongoing emergency, and that the primary purpose of the interrogation is to establish or prove past events potentially relevant to later criminal prosecution.

547 U.S. at 817, 822, 126 S.Ct. at 2270, 2273–74. It added:

> Our holding refers to interrogations because, as explained below, the statements in the cases presently before us are the products of interrogations—which in some circumstances tend to generate testimonial responses. This is not to imply, however, that statements made in the absence of any interrogation are necessarily nontestimonial. * * * And of course even when interrogation exists, it is in the final analysis the declarant's statements, not the interrogator's questions, that the Confrontation Clause requires us to evaluate.

547 U.S. at 822 n.1, 126 S.Ct. at 2274 n 1.

One case—*Davis*—involved a statement to an officer and the other statements to a 911 operator. The Court observed:

> If 911 operators are not themselves law enforcement officers, they may at least be agents of law enforcement when they conduct interrogations of 911 callers. For purposes of this opinion (and without deciding the point), we consider their acts to be acts of the police. * * * [T]herefore, our holding today makes it unnecessary to consider whether and when statements made to someone other than law enforcement personnel are "testimonial."

547 U.S. at 822 n.2, 126 S.Ct. at 2274 n. 2.

In *Davis*, the witness—McCottry—had called 911 to seek help and was in part responding to questions by the 911 operator. The Court ruled:

The difference between the interrogation in *Davis* and the one in *Crawford* is apparent on the face of things. In *Davis*, McCottry was speaking about events *as they were actually happening,* rather than "describ[ing] past events." Sylvia Crawford's interrogation, on the other hand, took place hours after the events she described had occurred. Moreover, any reasonable listener would recognize that McCottry (unlike Sylvia Crawford) was facing an ongoing emergency. Although one *might* call 911 to provide a narrative report of a crime absent any imminent danger, McCottry's call was plainly a call for help against bona fide physical threat. Third, the nature of what was asked and answered in *Davis*, again viewed objectively, was such that the elicited statements were necessary to be able to *resolve* the present emergency, rather than simply to learn (as in *Crawford*) what had happened in the past. That is true even of the operator's effort to establish the identity of the assailant, so that the dispatched officers might know whether they would be encountering a violent felon. And finally, the difference in the level of formality between the two interviews is striking. Crawford was responding calmly, at the station house, to a series of questions, with the officer-interrogator taping and making notes of her answers; McCottry's frantic answers were provided over the phone, in an environment that was not tranquil, or even (as far as any reasonable 911 operator could make out) safe.

We conclude from all this that the circumstances of McCottry's interrogation objectively indicate its primary purpose was to enable police assistance to meet an ongoing emergency. She simply was not acting as a *witness;* she was not *testifying.* What she said was not "a weaker substitute for live testimony" at trial, like * * * Sylvia Crawford's statement in *Crawford.* In [*Crawford*], the *ex parte* actor[ ] and the evidentiary product[ ] of the *ex parte* communication aligned perfectly with their courtroom analogues. McCottry's emergency statement does not. No "witness" goes into court to proclaim an emergency and seek help.

547 U.S. at 827–28, 126 S.Ct. at 2277.

In the other case, *Hammon*, officers responded to a domestic disturbance at the home of Hershel and Amy Hammon. The officers found Ms. Hammon on the porch and Mr. Hammon in the house. Both occupants maintained at first that there was no problem. Once officer talked more extensively with Ms. Hammon, who reported that Mr. Hammon had been violent towards her. The officer's testimony about Ms. Hammon's statements was admitted at Mr. Hammon's later trial. Finding this impermissible, the Court explained:

[T]he interrogation was part of an investigation into possibly criminal past conduct * * *. There was no emergency in progress; the interrogating officer testified that he had heard no arguments or crashing and saw no one throw or break anything. * * * When the officer questioned Amy for the second time, and elicited the challenged statements, he was not seeking to determine (as in *Davis*) "what is happening," but rather "what happened." Objectively viewed, the primary, if not indeed the sole, purpose of the interrogation was to investigate a possible crime—which is, of course, precisely what the officer *should* have done.

It is true that the *Crawford* interrogation was more formal. It followed a *Miranda* warning, was tape-recorded, and took place at the station house. While these features certainly strengthened the statements' testimonial aspect—made it more objectively apparent, that is, that the purpose of the exercise was to nail down the truth about past criminal events—none was essential to the point. It was formal enough that Amy's interrogation was conducted in a separate room, away from her husband (who tried to intervene), with the officer receiving her replies for use in his "investigat[ion]." What we called the "striking resemblance" of the *Crawford* statement to civil-law *ex parte* examinations, is shared by Amy's statement here. Both declarants were actively separated from the defendant—officers forcibly prevented Hershel from participating in the interrogation. Both statements deliberately recounted, in response to police questioning, how potentially criminal past events began and progressed. And both took place some time after the events described were over. Such statements under official interrogation are an obvious substitute for live testimony, because they do precisely *what a witness does* on direct examination; they are inherently testimonial.

547 U.S. at 829–30, 126 S.Ct. at 2279.

The Court also supplemented another aspect of *Crawford's* discussion:

[W]hen defendants seek to undermine the judicial process by procuring or coercing silence from witnesses and victims, the Sixth Amendment does not require courts to acquiesce. While defendants have no duty to assist the State in proving their guilt, they *do* have the duty to refrain from acting in ways that destroy the integrity of the criminal-trial system. We reiterate what we said in *Crawford:* that "the rule of forfeiture by wrongdoing ... extinguishes confrontation claims on essentially equitable grounds." That is, one who obtains the absence of a witness by wrongdoing forfeits the constitutional right to confrontation.

We take no position on the standards necessary to demonstrate such forfeiture, but federal courts using Federal Rule of Evidence 804(b)(6), which codifies the forfeiture doctrine, have generally held the Government to the preponderance-of-the-evidence standard. State courts tend to follow the same practice. Moreover, if a hearing on forfeiture is required, * * * "hearsay evidence, including the unavailable witness's out-of-court statements, may be considered." * * * *Crawford,* * * * did not destroy the ability of courts to protect the integrity of their proceedings.

547 U.S. at 833, 126 S.Ct. at 2280.

2. *Davis* involved domestic dispute situations. In Michigan v. Bryant, 562 U.S. ___, 131 S.Ct. 1143, 179 L.Ed.2d 93 (2011), the Court applied *Crawford* to a "new context * * * involving a victim found in a public location, suffering from a fatal gunshot wound, and a perpetrator whose location was unknown at the time the police located the victim." The facts were as follows:

Around 3:25 a.m. on April 29, 2001, Detroit, Michigan police officers responded to a radio dispatch indicating that a man had been shot. At the scene, they found the victim, Anthony Covington, lying on the ground next to his car in a gas station parking lot. Covington had a gunshot wound to his abdomen, appeared to be in great pain, and spoke with difficulty.

The police asked him "what had happened, who had shot him, and where the shooting had occurred." Covington stated that "Rick" shot him at around 3 a.m. He also indicated that he had a conversation with Bryant, whom he recognized based on his voice, through the back door of Bryant's house.

Covington explained that when he turned to leave, he was shot through the door and then drove to the gas station, where police found him.

Covington's conversation with the police ended within 5 to 10 minutes when emergency medical services arrived. Covington was transported to a hospital and died within hours.

At Bryant's trial for murder and other offenses, the prosecution was permitted to introduce the officers' testimony as to what Covington told them. By a vote of 6 to 2, the Supreme Court held that this was permissible under *Crawford* and *Davis*.

"[W]hether an emergency exists and is ongoing" Justice Sotomayor stressed for the majority, "is a highly context-dependent inquiry." Situations involving non-domestic violence and guns may indicate a greater and broader threat than those involved in *Davis*. Further:

> [W]hether an ongoing emergency exists is simply one factor—albeit an important factor—that informs the ultimate inquiry regarding the "primary purpose" of an interrogation. Another factor * * * is the importance of *informality* in an encounter between a victim and police. Formality is not the sole touchstone of our primary purpose inquiry because, although formality suggests the absence of an emergency and therefore an increased likelihood that the purpose of the interrogation is to "establish or prove past events potentially relevant to later criminal prosecution," informality does not necessarily indicate the presence of an emergency or the lack of testimonial intent.

562 U.S. at ___, 131 S.Ct. at 1160 (emphasis in original). The majority continued:

> In addition to the circumstances in which an encounter occurs, the statements and actions of both the declarant and interrogators provide objective evidence of the primary purpose of the interrogation. * * *
>
> * * * *Davis* requires a combined inquiry that accounts for both the declarant and the interrogator. In many instances, the primary purpose of the interrogation will be most accurately ascertained by looking to the contents of both the questions and the answers. To give an extreme example, if the police say to a victim, "Tell us who did this to you so that we can arrest and prosecute them," the victim's response that "Rick did it," appears purely accusatory because by virtue of the phrasing of the question, the victim necessarily has prosecution in mind when she answers.

562 U.S. at ___, 131 S.Ct. at 1160–61. Addressing the facts of the case before it, the majority explained:

> [T]here was an ongoing emergency here where an armed shooter, whose motive for and location after the shooting were unknown, had mortally wounded Covington within a few blocks and a few minutes of the location where the police found Covington.

*   *   *

We turn * * * to [the ultimate inquiry whether the primary purpose of the interrogation was to enable police assistance to meet the ongoing emergency], as informed by the circumstances of the ongoing emergency * * *. The circumstances of the encounter provide important context for understanding Covington's statements to the police. When the police arrived at Covington's side, their first question to him was "What happened?" Covington's response was either "Rick shot me" or "I was shot," followed very quickly by an identification of "Rick" as the shooter. In response to further questions, Covington explained that the shooting occurred through the back door of Bryant's house and provided a physical description of the shooter. When he made the statements, Covington was lying in a gas station parking lot bleeding from a mortal gunshot wound to his abdomen. His answers to the police officers' questions were punctuated with questions about when emergency medical services would arrive. He was obviously in considerable pain and had difficulty breathing and talking. From this description of his condition and report of his statements, we cannot say that a person in Covington's situation would have had a "primary purpose" "to establish or prove past events potentially relevant to later criminal prosecution."

For their part, the police responded to a call that a man had been shot. * * * [T]hey did not know why, where, or when the shooting had occurred. Nor did they know the location of the shooter or anything else about the circumstances in which the crime occurred. The questions they asked—"what had happened, who had shot him, and where the shooting occurred"—were the exact type of questions necessary to allow the police to " 'assess the situation, the threat to their own safety, and possible danger to the potential victim' "and to the public, including to allow them to ascertain "whether they would be encountering a violent felon," In other words, they solicited the information necessary to enable them "to meet an ongoing emergency."

Nothing in Covington's responses indicated to the police that, contrary to their expectation upon responding to a call reporting a shooting, there was no emergency or that a prior emergency had ended. Covington did indicate that he had been shot at another location about 25 minutes earlier, but he did not know the location of the shooter at the time the police arrived and, as far as we can tell from the record, he gave no indication that the shooter, having shot at him twice, would be satisfied that Covington was only wounded. In fact, Covington did not indicate any possible motive for the shooting, and thereby gave no reason to think that the shooter would not shoot again if he arrived on the scene. As we noted in *Davis,* "initial inquiries" may "*often* ... produce nontestimonial statements." The initial inquiries in this case resulted in the type of nontestimonial statements we contemplated in *Davis.*

562 U.S. at ___, 131 S.Ct. at 1164–66. Justice Thomas reached the same result but on other grounds. Justices Scalia and Ginsburg concluded, for different reasons, that Covington's statements were testimonial.

3. **Forfeiture by wrongdoing.** The Court elaborated on the requirements of the forfeiture by wrongdoing exception to the Confrontation Clause in *Giles v. California*, 554 U.S. 353, 128 S.Ct. 2678, 171 L.Ed.2d 488 (2008). As described in Note 1 above, the Court in *Crawford v. Washington*, 541 U.S. 36, 53–54, 124 S.Ct. 1354, 158 L.Ed.2d 177 (2004) held that the Sixth Amendment's Confrontation Clause gives defendants the right to cross–examine witnesses who give testimony against them, except in cases where an exception to the confrontation right was recognized at the founding. In *Giles*, a trial judge in a California court had permitted prosecutors to introduce statements that the murder victim, the defendant's girlfriend, made to a police officer responding to a domestic violence call about three weeks before her murder. These statements, describing violent acts committed against the victim and death threats made against her by the defendant,

were admitted to rebut the defendant's trial testimony that the shooting was in self–defense. The California Supreme Court affirmed the first–degree murder conviction after concluding that Giles had forfeited his right to confront the victim's testimony because it found Giles had committed the murder for which he was on trial—an intentional criminal act that made the victim unavailable to testify.

The Supreme Court reversed after reviewing precedent and treatises indicating that the exception applied "only when the defendant engaged in conduct *designed* to prevent the witness from testifying." 554 U.S. at 359, 128 S.Ct. at 2683 (emphasis in original). This intent requirement is presently codified in Fed. Rule of Evid. 804(6)(b). In cases where the evidence suggested that the defendant wrongfully caused the absence of the witness but had not done so to prevent the witness from testifying, unconfronted testimony was excluded unless it fell under the separate common law dying–declaration exception to confrontation for statements made by speakers who were on the brink of death and aware that they were dying. Upon remand, the state court may consider the defendant's prior acts of domestic abuse culminating in murder as evidence "that may support a finding that the crime expressed the intent to isolate the victim and to stop her from reporting abuse to the authorities or cooperating with a criminal prosecution—rendering her prior statements admissible under the forfeiture doctrine." 554 U.S. at 377, 128 S.Ct. at 2693.

4. **Analysts' certificates.** In Melendez–Diaz v. Massachusetts, ___ U.S. ___, 129 S.Ct. 2527, 174 L.Ed.2d 314 (2009), a prosecution for drug offenses, the prosecution was permitted over objection to introduce into evidence three "certificates of analysis" showing the results of a forensic analysis performed on a substance seized from the defendants and contended by the prosecution to be cocaine. The certificates were sworn to before a notary public by analysts at the State Laboratory Institute of the Massachusetts Department of Public Health and reported the weight of the seized bags. They also stated that the bags "[h]a[ve] been examined with the following results: The substance was found to contain: Cocaine."

By a 5–to–4 vote, the Supreme Court held this violated the defendant's rights under Crawford. "Absent a showing that the analysts were unavailable to testify at trial *and* that [Melendez–Diaz] had a prior opportunity to cross-examine them, [Melendez–Diaz] was entitled to 'be confronted with' the analysts at trial." ___ U.S. at ___, 129 S.Ct. at 2532.

The *Melendez-Diaz* majority indicated there would be no constitutional impediment to at least some so-called "notice-and-demand statutes." These provisions permit the prosecution to provide pretrial notice to a defendant of the prosecution's intent to offer an analyst's report at trial. A defendant wishing to object to the admission of the report without the analyst's personal presence in court must object before trial. "There is no conceivable reason," the Court noted, "why [a defendant] cannot * * * be compelled to exercise his Confrontation Clause rights before trial."

The dissenters predicted dire results from the *Melendez-Diaz* decision:

[T]he Court threatens to disrupt forensic investigations across the country and to put prosecutions nationwide at risk of dismissal based on erratic, all-too-frequent instances when a particular laboratory technician, now invested by the Court's new constitutional designation as the analyst, simply does not or cannot appear.

___ U.S. at ___, 129 S.Ct. at 2549 (Kennedy, J., dissenting). They pointed out the uncertainty in the Court's opinion as to the analyst (or analysts) that must appear in person in cases such as the one before the Court: the person who calibrated the machine to be used to test the suspected drug, the person who prepared the sample, placed it in the machine and removed the machine's printout, the person who interpreted the machine's print out, and/or the supervisory person who vouched that the others followed established procedures.

The dissenters would apparently limit *Crawford* by holding it applicable only to out-of-court statements of witnesses who are in some sense "conventional" ones. Such witnesses might be defined as those who have personal knowledge of some aspect of the defendant's guilt. This would render *Crawford* inapplicable to the "analysts" brought under it by the majority.

Under *Melendez-Diaz*, an analyst's report is not rendered admissible by the prosecution's use of a so-called "surrogate" witness, an expert who did not sign the report or observe any of the testing resulting in the report. Bullcoming v. New Mexico, 564 U.S. ___, 131 S.Ct. 62, 177 L.Ed.2d 1152 (2011). Justice Sotomayor wrote separately, in part to note that the majority was not addressing whether a report would be admissible if supported by the in-court testimony of a surrogate witness who is "a supervisor, reviewer, or someone else with a personal, albeit limited, connection to the scientific test at issue." In *Bullcoming* itself, the witness conceded that he did not observe any of the underlying testing and played no role in producing the offered report. Therefore, the Court did not need to address what kind and degree of involvement might make a surrogate witness sufficiency to meet confrontation requirements. 564 U.S. at ___, 131 S.Ct. at ___ (Sotomayor, J., concurring in part).

5. ***Crawford* is not retroactive.** *Crawford* does not apply retroactively to cases that became final before the date of the decision in *Crawford*—March 8, 2004. Whorton v. Bockting, 549 U.S. 406, 127 S.Ct. 1173, 167 L.Ed.2d 1 (2007).

Page 1070.   Add the following note after Note 3:

3a. ***Roberts* test overruled in *Crawford*.** Though the *Roberts* test was overruled, the *Crawford* majority makes clear that the results in that and most other cases remain the same. Where there has been prior opportunity by a defendant to cross-examine a declarant, the admission of her testimony does not violate the Confrontation Clause if she is unavailable at trial. Most of the prior cases admitting hearsay evidence despite a Confrontation Clause claim involved statements that were not testimonial, such as business records or statements in furtherance of a conspiracy. In the absence of prior confrontation or a hearsay exception firmly established at the founding, testimony is now inadmissible even if it otherwise bears "indicia of reliability." In terms of hearsay exceptions, the Court in *Giles* noted only "two forms of testimonial statements that were admitted at common law even though they were unconfronted"—dying declarations and forfeiture by wrongdoing. *Giles v. California*, 554 U.S. 353, 358–60, 128 S.Ct. 2678, 2682–83, 171 L.Ed.2d 488 (2008).

Note also that the *Crawford* test applies only to testimony (whether given in or out of court), not to non-testimonial hearsay statements (such as business records). "Testimony" is a "solemn declaration or affirmation made for the purpose of establishing or proving some fact." *Crawford v. Washington*, 541 U.S. 36, 51, 124 S.Ct. 1354, 1364, 158 L.Ed.2d 177 (2004). While the *Crawford* Court does not attempt to fully define "testimony," it appears to include in the class of statements prohibited by the confrontation clause affidavits, custodial examinations, prior testimony that the defendant was unable to cross-examine, grand jury statements, ex parte testimony at a preliminary hearing, and police custodial interrogations.

Page 1073. Add the following note after Note 6:

6a. *Crawford* **casts doubt on** *White.* In Footnote 3 of its opinion, the Crawford Court noted that the admission of the child's statement to police admitted as a spontaneous declaration is "arguably in tension with the rule requiring a prior opportunity for cross-examination when the proffered statement is testimonial." *Crawford v. Washington,* 541 U.S. 36, 124 S.Ct. 1354, 158 L.Ed.2d 177 (2004), on page 264 of your supplement. However, the Court in *White* addressed only the issue of whether the Confrontation Clause imposed an unavailability requirement. Justice Scalia's majority opinion in *Crawford* also expressed doubt as to whether the *White* Court's rejection of the proposal that the Confrontation Clause applies *only* to testimonial statements (leaving all others to regulation by hearsay rules) survives *Crawford. Id.,* on page 265 of your supplement.

Page 1075. Add the following before Note 8:

7a. **Comment on ability of defendant to tailor his or her testimony.** The prosecutor in Portuondo v. Agard, 529 U.S. 61, 120 S.Ct. 1119, 146 L.Ed.2d 47 (2000) asked the jury in her closing argument to take into account in assessing the credibility of the witnesses that defendant had the advantage in his testimony of hearing the testimony of the State's witnesses and thus of tailoring his testimony to answer theirs. The Second Circuit held this argument violated respondent's Fifth and Sixth Amendment rights. The Supreme Court, in an opinion by Justice Scalia, reversed. It rejected the argument that Griffin v. California [discussed in Carter v. Kentucky beginning on Casebook p. 1087], which prohibited comment upon a defendant's failure to testify at trial, is a basis for the rule urged here:

> What we prohibited the prosecutor from urging the jury to do in *Griffin* was something *the jury is not permitted to do.* The defendant's right to hold the prosecution to proving its case without his assistance is not to be impaired by the jury's counting the defendant's silence at trial against him—and upon request the court must instruct the jury to that effect.... It is reasonable enough to expect a jury to comply with that instruction since, as we observed in *Griffin,* the inference of guilt from silence is not always "natural or irresistible." A defendant might refuse to testify simply out of fear that he will be made to look bad by clever counsel, or fear " 'that his prior convictions will prejudice the jury.' " By contrast, it is natural and irresistible for a jury, in evaluating the relative credibility of a defendant who testifies last, to have in mind and weigh in the balance the fact that he heard the testimony of all those who preceded him. It is one thing (as *Griffin* requires) for the jury to evaluate all the other evidence in the case without giving any effect to the defendant's refusal to testify; it is something else (and quite impossible) for the jury to evaluate the credibility of the defendant's testimony while blotting out from its mind the fact that before giving the testimony the defendant had been sitting there listening to the other witnesses. Thus, the principle respondent asks us to adopt here differs from what we adopted in *Griffin* in one or the other of the following respects: It either prohibits inviting the jury to do what the jury is perfectly entitled to do; or it requires the jury to do what is practically impossible.

529 U.S. at 67–68, 120 S.Ct. at 1124, 146 L.Ed.2d at 55. Nor is a prohibition on this mode of comment justified by Brooks v. Tennessee, [discussed in Casebook p. 783]

in which the Court had declared unconstitutional a statute requiring a testifying defendant to testify at the beginning of the presentation of the defense case-in-chief:

> Indeed, in *Brooks v. Tennessee*, 406 U.S. 605, 92 S.Ct. 1891, 32 L.Ed.2d 358 (1972), the Court suggested that arguing credibility to the jury—which would include the prosecutor's comments here—is the preferred means of counteracting tailoring of the defendant's testimony. In that case, the Court found unconstitutional Tennessee's attempt to defeat tailoring by requiring defendants to testify at the outset of the defense or not at all. This requirement, it said, impermissibly burdened the defendant's right to testify because it forced him to decide whether to do so before he could determine that it was in his best interest.... The Court expressed its awareness, however, of the danger that tailoring presented. The antidote, it said, was not Tennessee's heavy-handed rule, but the more nuanced "adversary system[, which] reposes judgment of the credibility of all witnesses in the jury." The adversary system surely envisions—indeed, it requires—that the prosecutor be allowed to bring to the jury's attention the danger that the Court was aware of.

529 U.S. at 70, 120 S.Ct. at 1125–26, 146 L.Ed.2d at 57. Justice Ginsburg, joined by Justice Souter, dissented.

2.   CROSS-EXAMINATION AND COMPULSORY PROCESS TO OBTAIN WITNESSES

Page 1086.   Add the following before Section D:

   5.   **Challenging prior convictions disclosed on direct examination.** Petitioner in Ohler v. United States, 529 U.S. 753, 120 S.Ct. 1851, 146 L.Ed.2d 826 (2000) was being tried for importing and possessing about 80 pounds of marijuana. The trial court ruled that if she testified the government would be permitted to impeach her testimony with a prior felony conviction for possession of methamphetamine. She testified and her counsel brought out her prior conviction on direct examination. On appeal from her conviction, she sought to challenge the admissibility of the prior conviction, but the Ninth Circuit held that she had waived that right by testifying about it on direct examination. The Supreme Court, in an opinion by The Chief Justice, affirmed. The Court said that waiver of ability to challenge admissibility by testifying about the prior conviction is merely one of many choices that litigants must make:

> [B]oth the Government and the defendant in a criminal trial must make choices as the trial progresses. For example, the defendant must decide whether or not to take the stand in her own behalf. If she has an innocent or mitigating explanation for evidence that might otherwise incriminate, acquittal may be more likely if she takes the stand. Here, for example, petitioner testified that she had no knowledge of the marijuana discovered in the van, that the van had been taken to Mexico without her permission, and that she had gone there simply to retrieve the van. But once the defendant testifies, she is subject to cross-examination, including impeachment by prior convictions, and the decision to take the stand may prove damaging instead of helpful. A defendant has a further choice to make if she decides to testify, notwithstanding a prior conviction. The defendant must choose whether to introduce the conviction on direct examination and remove the sting or to take her chances with the prosecutor's possible elicitation of the conviction on cross-examination.

The Government, too, in a case such as this, must make a choice. If the defendant testifies, it must choose whether or not to impeach her by use of her prior conviction. Here the trial judge had indicated he would allow its use, but the Government still had to consider whether its use might be deemed reversible error on appeal. This choice is often based on the Government's appraisal of the apparent effect of the defendant's testimony. If she has offered a plausible, innocent explanation of the evidence against her, it will be inclined to use the prior conviction; if not, it may decide not to risk possible reversal on appeal from its use.

529 U.S. at 757–58, 120 S.Ct. at 1854, 146 L.Ed.2d at 831. Justice Souter, joined by Justices Stevens, Ginsburg and Breyer, dissented. He found that the choice outlined by the Court should not be required of a criminal defendant:

Previously convicted witnesses may testify honestly, but some convictions raise more than the ordinary question about the witness's readiness to speak truthfully. A factfinder who appreciates a heightened possibility of perjury will respond with heightened scrutiny, and when a defendant discloses prior convictions at the outset of her testimony, the jury will bear those convictions in mind as she testifies, and will scrutinize what she says more carefully. The purpose of Rule 609, in making some convictions admissible to impeach a witness's credibility, is thus fully served by a defendant's own testimony that the convictions occurred.

It is true that when convictions are revealed only on cross-examination, the revelation also warns the factfinder, but the timing of their disclosure may do more. The jury may feel that in testifying without saying anything about the convictions the defendant has meant to conceal them. The jury's assessment of the defendant's testimony may be affected not only by knowing that she has committed crimes in the past, but by blaming her for not being forthcoming when she seemingly could have been. Creating such an impression of current deceit by concealment is very much at odds with any purpose behind Rule 609, being obviously antithetical to dispassionate factfinding in support of a sound conclusion. The chance to create that impression is a tactical advantage for the Government, but only in the majority's dismissive sense of the term; it may affect the outcome of the trial, but only if it disserves the search for truth.

Allowing the defendant to introduce the convictions on direct examination thus tends to promote fairness of trial without depriving the Government of anything to which it is entitled. There is no reason to discourage the defendant from introducing the conviction herself, as the majority's waiver rule necessarily does.

529 U.S. at 764, 120 S.Ct. at 1857–58, 146 L.Ed.2d at 835.

D.   EXERCISE AT TRIAL OF THE PRIVILEGE AGAINST COMPELLED SELF-INCRIMINATION

2.   WAIVER

Page 1099.   Add the following after Note 1:

2. **May a witness claim innocence and the Fifth Amendment?** The respondent in Ohio v. Reiner, 532 U.S. 17, 121 S.Ct. 1252, 149 L.Ed.2d 158 (2001)

was on trial for the death of his two-month-old son. The defense theory was that the babysitter did it. The sitter claimed she was innocent but also claimed the privilege against compelled self-incrimination. At the State's request, the trial court granted her transactional immunity. She testified, telling the jury she was doing so because of the immunity. The Ohio Supreme Court found the granting of immunity to be error because in its view a person cannot both claim innocence and the Fifth Amendment. Because the sitter told the jury she had been given a grant of immunity by the trial court, the jury might have inferred that the trial court believed in her innocence, which was prejudicial to the defendant under the circumstances. The United States Supreme Court, in a *per curiam* opinion, reversed the Ohio Supreme Court:

> We have held that the privilege's protection extends only to witnesses who have "reasonable cause to apprehend danger from a direct answer." * * * That inquiry is for the court; the witness' assertion does not by itself establish the risk of incrimination. * * * A danger of "imaginary and unsubstantial character" will not suffice. * * * But we have never held, as the Supreme Court of Ohio did, that the privilege is unavailable to those who claim innocence. To the contrary, we have emphasized that one of the Fifth Amendment's "basic functions . . . is to protect innocent men . . . 'who otherwise might be ensnared by ambiguous circumstances.' " Grunewald v. United States, 353 U.S. 391, 421, 77 S.Ct. 963, 1 L.Ed.2d 931 (1957) * * *. In *Grunewald*, we recognized that truthful responses of an innocent witness, as well as those of a wrongdoer, may provide the government with incriminating evidence from the speaker's own mouth. * * *

532 U.S. at 21, 121 S.Ct. at 1254, 149 L.Ed.2d at 162.

CHAPTER 24

EFFECTIVE ASSISTANCE OF COUNSEL

Page 1102. Add the following after the first paragraph:

In Alabama v. Shelton, 535 U.S. 654, 122 S.Ct. 1764, 152 L.Ed.2d 888 (2002), the Supreme Court addressed an issue that had been raised in *Scott*: the right to counsel when a misdemeanor jail sentence is assessed but its imposition or execution is suspended. Shelton was convicted of a misdemeanor and sentenced to 30 days incarceration, which was suspended in favor of two years' probation. On appeal, the Alabama Supreme Court vacated the probation sentence because although Shelton was indigent, he was not offered counsel to assist him. The Supreme Court, in a five-to-four decision authored by Justice Ginsburg, affirmed.

Three positions were argued: (1) that the Sixth Amendment applies fully when a sentence is assessed but suspended, (2) that the Sixth Amendment applies only if and when the suspended sentence is revoked and incarceration ordered, and (3) that the Sixth Amendment has no applicability in a misdemeanor case that terminates in a suspended sentence. The Court rejected the third position on the ground that if probation is revoked the defendant is then incarcerated as punishment for the original offense, not the probation violation. It is therefore the uncounseled conviction that results in incarceration, which is a result prohibited by the Sixth Amendment. While such a defendant would probably be entitled to counsel if brought back to court in a revocation hearing, that is not a substitute for counsel during proceedings leading up to conviction:

> [T]he sole issue at the [probation revocation] hearing—apart from determinations about the necessity of confinement, * * *—is whether the defendant breached the terms of probation. * * * The validity or reliability of the underlying conviction is beyond attack. * * *

We think it plain that a hearing so timed and structured cannot compensate for the absence of trial counsel, for it does not even address the key Sixth Amendment inquiry: whether the adjudication of guilt corresponding to the prison sentence is sufficiently reliable to permit incarceration. Deprived of counsel when tried, convicted, and sentenced, and unable to challenge the original judgment at a subsequent probation revocation hearing, a defendant in Shelton's circumstances faces incarceration on a conviction that has never been subjected to "the crucible of meaningful adversarial testing," United States v.

Cronic, 466 U.S. 648, 656, 104 S.Ct. 2039, 80 L.Ed.2d 657 (1984). The Sixth Amendment does not countenance this result.

535 U.S. at 666–67, 122 S.Ct. at 1772, 152 L.Ed.2d at 901. The Court answered the argument that imposition of a right to counsel in such cases would impose an undue burden on the States:

> Most jurisdictions already provide a state-law right to appointed counsel more generous than that afforded by the Federal Constitution. * * * All but 16 States, for example, would provide counsel to a defendant in Shelton's circumstances, either because he received a substantial fine or because state law authorized incarceration for the charged offense or provided for a maximum prison term of one year. * * * There is thus scant reason to believe that a rule conditioning imposition of a suspended sentence on provision of appointed counsel would affect existing practice in the large majority of the States. And given the current commitment of most jurisdictions to affording court-appointed counsel to indigent misdemeanants while simultaneously preserving the option of probationary punishment, we do not share amicus' concern that other States may lack the capacity and resources to do the same.

535 U.S. at 668–70, 122 S.Ct. at 1773–74, 152 L.Ed.2d at 902–03.

Alabama argued that there can be no constitutional impediment to the assessment and suspension of a sentence if under state law that sentence cannot ever be executed. The suspended sentence would be enforced by contempt proceedings, not by execution of the original sentence. The Court rejected this position in part because it was presented late in the litigation so had not been subjected to lower court scrutiny. The Court adverted to the possibility that the Alabama Supreme Court might find that position attractive.

Justice Scalia, joined by The Chief Justice, Justice Kennedy, and Justice Thomas, dissented. He suggested there could be no constitutional objection to a state-law system in which at proceedings to revoke probation, a defendant is provided counsel and given the opportunity to retry all issues related to guilt or innocence of the original charge. He also took issue with the Court's characterization of the practical consequences of its decision on the States:

> Our prior opinions placed considerable weight on the practical consequences of expanding the right to appointed counsel beyond cases of actual imprisonment. * * * Today, the Court gives this consideration the back of its hand. Its observation that "[a]ll but 16 States" already appoint counsel for defendants like respondent * * * is interesting but quite irrelevant, since today's holding is not confined to defendants like respondent. Appointed counsel must henceforth be offered before any defendant can be awarded a suspended sentence, no matter how short. Only 24 States have announced a rule of this scope.

Thus, the Court's decision imposes a large, new burden on a majority of the States, including some of the poorest (e.g., Alabama, Arkansas, and Mississippi, see U.S. Census Bureau, Statistical Abstract of the United States 426 (2001)). That burden consists not only of the cost of providing state-paid counsel in cases of such insignificance that even financially prosperous defendants sometimes forgo the expense of hired counsel; but also the cost of enabling courts and prosecutors to respond to the "over-lawyering" of minor cases. * * * Nor should we discount the burden placed on the minority 24 States that currently provide counsel: that they keep their current disposition forever in place, however imprudent experience proves it to be.

535 U.S. at 679–81, 122 S.Ct. at 1778–80, 152 L.Ed.2d at 908–10.

The Sixth Amendment right to counsel is "offense specific," that is, it applies only to the offense with which the defendant was charged at the time counsel was appointed. If the defendant is later arrested for a different offense, he or she is not automatically represented for that offense by the attorney appointed previously. What constitutes a "different offense?" In Texas v. Cobb, 532 U.S. 162, 121 S.Ct. 1335, 149 L.Ed.2d 321 (2001), the Supreme Court in an opinion by Chief Justice Rehnquist, announced the rule that offenses are different if they would be the different for double jeopardy purposes under the *Blockburger* [Casebook p. 857] rule—each offense requires proof of a fact that the other does not. In this case, Cobb had been charged with burglary and counsel had been appointed for him. Over a year later, he was questioned about the fate of two persons who had disappeared from the scene of the burglary and he confessed to killing them. The capital murder charge arising from that confession was under *Blockburger* different from the burglary charge filed earlier—the burglary requires proof of entry into a building or habitation which capital murder did not and capital murder on the theory charged required proof of the killing of two persons during the same criminal transaction, which burglary does not. Therefore, it was sufficient that the police complied with Miranda v. Arizona in the murder interrogation since for the capital murder case Cobb was unrepresented.

A. THE RIGHT TO HAVE COUNSEL BE "EFFECTIVE"

Page 1124. Add the following before Note 1:

0.5. **Inadequate investigation of mitigating circumstances.** The habeas petitioner in Wiggins v. Smith, Warden, 539 U.S. 510, 123 S.Ct. 2527, 156 L.Ed.2d 471 (2003) claimed his public defenders rendered ineffective assistance at the sentencing phase of his capital murder trial because they failed to investigate mitigating evidence that could have been presented to the jury. Counsel learned from a presentence investigation report that their client had a difficult life and from social service files of his years in foster care that those difficulties extended throughout his childhood. They conducted no further investigation into his background although funds were available to do so. They planned to present a defense to the death penalty that their client could not be given death because he did not personally perpetrate the murder. Focusing on that defense, they did not pursue the mitigation route beyond pointing out he had no prior convictions for crimes of violence. After the jury gave the death penalty, a federal district court granted habeas relief on the ground counsel were ineffective in failing to investigate the mitigating circumstances of their client's early life hardships. The Fourth Circuit reversed, but in a 7 to 2 opinion by Justice O'Connor, the Supreme Court reversed the Fourth Circuit.

Justice O'Connor concluded that counsel's performance fell well below the professional standards required by *Strickland*. In habeas proceedings conducted by new counsel, a forensic social worker filed a social history report showing a devastating childhood for the defendant:

> [P]etitioner's mother, a chronic alcoholic, frequently left Wiggins and his siblings home alone for days, forcing them to beg for food and to eat paint chips and garbage. * * * Mrs. Wiggins' abusive behavior included beating the children for breaking into the kitchen, which she often kept locked. She had sex with men while her children slept in the same bed and, on one occasion, forced petitioner's hand against a hot stove burner—an incident that led to petitioner's hospitalization. * * * At the age of six, the State placed Wiggins in foster care. Petitioner's first and second foster mothers abused him physically, * * * and, as petitioner explained to [social worker] Selvog, the father in his second foster home repeatedly molested and raped him. * * * At age 16, petitioner ran away from his foster home and began living on the streets. He returned intermittently to additional foster homes, including one in which the foster mother's sons allegedly gang-raped him on more than one occasion. * * * After leaving the foster care system, Wiggins entered a Job Corps program and was allegedly sexually abused by his supervisor. * * *

539 U.S. at 516–17, 123 S.Ct. at 2532. The presentence report and the foster home records, which were in the possession of trial counsel, hinted at such deprivations, but counsel made no effort to investigate the matters further. Justice O'Connor emphasized that the question is not whether a mitigation case should have been presented by counsel, a matter that will often involve complex professional judgments, but whether the failure to investigate to determine whether a mitigation claim existed was ineffective assistance.

The failure to investigate fell below applicable standards:

> Counsel's decision not to expand their investigation beyond the PSI and the DSS [foster home] records fell short of the professional standards that prevailed in Maryland in 1989. As [trial lawyer] Schlaich acknowledged, standard practice in Maryland in capital cases at the time of Wiggins' trial included the preparation of a social history report. * * * Despite the fact that the Public Defender's office made funds available for the retention of a forensic social worker, counsel chose not to commission such a report. * * * Counsel's conduct similarly fell short of the standards for capital defense work articulated by the American Bar Association (ABA)—standards to which we long have referred as "guides to determining what is reasonable." Strickland, supra, at 688, 104 S.Ct. 2052; Williams v. Taylor, supra, at 396, 120 S.Ct. 1495. The ABA Guidelines provide that investigations into mitigating evidence "should comprise efforts to discover *all reasonably available* mitigating evidence and evidence to rebut any

aggravating evidence that may be introduced by the prosecutor." ABA Guidelines for the Appointment and Performance of Counsel in Death Penalty Cases 11.4.1(C), p. 93 (1989) (emphasis added). Despite these well-defined norms, however, counsel abandoned their investigation of petitioner's background after having acquired only rudimentary knowledge of his history from a narrow set of sources. Cf. id., 11.8.6, p. 133 (noting that among the topics counsel should consider presenting are medical history, educational history, employment and training history, family and social history, prior adult and juvenile correctional experience, and religious and cultural influences) (emphasis added); 1 ABA Standards for Criminal Justice 4–4.1, commentary, p. 4–55 ("The lawyer also has a substantial and important role to perform in raising mitigating factors both to the prosecutor initially and to the court at sentencing.... Investigation is essential to fulfillment of these functions").

The scope of their investigation was also unreasonable in light of what counsel actually discovered in the DSS records. The records revealed several facts: Petitioner's mother was a chronic alcoholic; Wiggins was shuttled from foster home to foster home and displayed some emotional difficulties while there; he had frequent, lengthy absences from school; and, on at least one occasion, his mother left him and his siblings alone for days without food. * * * As the Federal District Court emphasized, any reasonably competent attorney would have realized that pursuing these leads was necessary to making an informed choice among possible defenses, particularly given the apparent absence of any aggravating factors in petitioner's background. 164 F.Supp.2d, at 559. Indeed, counsel uncovered no evidence in their investigation to suggest that a mitigation case, in its own right, would have been counterproductive, or that further investigation would have been fruitless; this case is therefore distinguishable from our precedents in which we have found limited investigations into mitigating evidence to be reasonable. See, e.g., Strickland, 466 U.S., at 699, 104 S.Ct. 2052 (concluding that counsel could "reasonably surmise ... that character and psychological evidence would be of little help"); Burger v. Kemp, 483 U.S. 776, 794, 107 S.Ct. 3114, 97 L.Ed.2d 638 (1987) (concluding counsel's limited investigation was reasonable because he interviewed all witnesses brought to his attention, discovering little that was helpful and much that was harmful); Darden v. Wainwright, 477 U.S. 168, 186, 106 S.Ct. 2464, 91 L.Ed.2d 144 (1986) (concluding that counsel engaged in extensive preparation and that the decision to present a mitigation case would have resulted in the jury hearing evidence that petitioner had been convicted of violent crimes and spent much of his life in jail). Had counsel investigated further, they may well have discovered the sexual abuse later revealed during state postconviction proceedings.

539 U.S. at 524–25, 123 S.Ct. at 2536–37. Justice O'Connor then concluded that counsel's failures were prejudicial to petitioner:

Wiggins' sentencing jury heard only one significant mitigating factor—that Wiggins had no prior convictions. Had the jury been able to place petitioner's excruciating life history on the mitigating side of the scale, there is a reasonable probability that at least one juror would have struck a different balance. Cf. Borchardt v. Maryland, 367 Md. 91, 139–140, 786 A.2d 631, 660 (2001) (noting that as long as a single juror concludes that mitigating evidence outweighs aggravating evidence, the death penalty cannot be imposed); App. 369 (instructing the jury: "If you unanimously find that the State has proven by a preponderance of the evidence that the aggravating circumstance does outweigh the mitigating circumstances, then consider whether death is the appropriate sentence").

Moreover, in contrast to the petitioner in Williams v. Taylor, supra, Wiggins does not have a record of violent conduct that could have been introduced by the State to offset this powerful mitigating narrative. * * * As the Federal District Court found, the mitigating evidence in this case is stronger, and the State's evidence in support of the death penalty far weaker, than in Williams, where we found prejudice as the result of counsel's failure to investigate and present mitigating evidence. * * * We thus conclude that the available mitigating evidence, taken as a whole, "might well have influenced the jury's appraisal" of Wiggins' moral culpability. * * *

539 U.S. at 537–38, 123 S.Ct. at 2543–44. Justice Scalia, joined by Justice Thomas, dissented.

Counsel was also found to have inadequately investigated in Rompilla v. Beard, 545 U.S. 374, 125 S.Ct. 2456, 162 L.Ed.2d 360 (2005), because in preparing for Rompilla's capital murder trial for a 1988 killing they failed to examine the record of his 1974 convictions for rape, burglary and theft. The prosecution had informed the defense it would introduce a transcript of the victim's testimony in support of its request for the death penalty. One defense lawyer did review that testimony but neither defense lawyer examined the remainder of the file. Had counsel examined the file, the Court concluded, counsel would have learned that the defense tactic of arguing doubt at to Rompilla's guilt was flawed. Counsel would also have obtained leads to information on Rompilla's childhood and mental health that would have permitted them to present a case for mitigation. 545 U.S. at 390–91, 125 S.Ct. at 2468.

The four dissenters accused the *Rompilla* majority of creating a *per se* rule that defense counsel must review all documents in a "case file" of any prior conviction the prosecution might rely on at trial. This rule, they argued, will cause defense lawyers to divert limited resources from more important tasks to reviews of such files. 545 U.S. at 396, 125 S.Ct. at 2471 (Kennedy, J., dissenting). The majority denied creating such a rule.

Page 1125. Add the following before Note 2:

1a. How should prejudice be defined when counsel's deficiency occurred at the sentencing phase of the proceedings? In Glover v. United States, 531 U.S. 198, 121 S.Ct. 696, 148 L.Ed.2d 604 (2001), the District Court imposed a sentence of 84 months in prison for several offenses. At sentencing, the defense attorney failed to argue that a money laundering and tax evasion count should be regarded as a single count for sentencing purposes. Later cases said that those counts should be grouped together for sentencing. The Seventh Circuit denied an ineffective assistance claim on the ground that the deficiency in performance, if it occurred, resulted in an increase of only 6 to 21 months in the prison sentence, which does not qualify as prejudice under *Strickland*. The Supreme Court in an opinion by Justice Kennedy for a unanimous court reversed. There is no precedent for imposing a quantitative requirement on sentence prejudice and there is no principle for determining if such a requirement were to be imposed where a line should be drawn.

Page 1126.   Add the following before Note 3:

2a.   **Failing to give timely notice of appeal.** Under what circumstances is the failure of defense counsel to give notice of appeal ineffective assistance of counsel? The respondent in Roe v. Flores–Ortega, 528 U.S. 470, 120 S.Ct. 1029, 145 L.Ed.2d 985 (2000) was convicted in California on his plea of no contest to state charges of murder. The trial judge informed him that he could appeal that conviction by giving a notice of appeal within 60 days. The public defender representing him conferred with him following conviction and sentencing but did not file a notice of appeal within the prescribed time. There was disagreement about whether the post-conviction conference included the possibility of an appeal. Respondent recalled that the public defender indicated she would file an appeal, while the public defender had no recollection of that part of the conversation. Under California law, failure to file a notice of appeal in a timely manner forfeits the right to take an appeal unless the failure was due to ineffective assistance of counsel.

The Ninth Circuit on federal habeas held respondent was entitled to an out-of-time appeal. Under its precedent, there is ineffective assistance of counsel in failing to file a timely notice of appeal unless there is a showing the client consented to that course of inaction. The Supreme Court, in an opinion by Justice O'Connor, vacated the Ninth Circuit's decision. The Court framed the question in these terms:

> We have long held that a lawyer who disregards specific instructions from the defendant to file a notice of appeal acts in a manner that is professionally unreasonable.... This is so because a defendant who instructs counsel to initiate an appeal reasonably relies upon counsel to file the necessary notice. Counsel's failure to do so cannot be considered a strategic decision; filing a notice of appeal is a purely ministerial task, and the failure to file reflects inattention to the defendant's wishes. At the other end of the spectrum, a defendant who explicitly tells his attorney not to file an appeal plainly cannot later complain that, by following his instructions, his counsel performed deficiently. The question presented in this case lies between those poles: Is counsel deficient for not filing a notice of appeal when the defendant has not clearly conveyed his wishes one way or the other?

528 U.S. at 477, 120 S.Ct. at 1035, 145 L.Ed.2d at 995. The Court further refined the inquiry into counsel's duties in this context:

> In those cases where the defendant neither instructs counsel to file an appeal nor asks that an appeal not be taken, we believe the question whether counsel has performed deficiently by not filing a notice of appeal is best answered by first asking a separate, but antecedent, question: whether counsel in fact consulted with the defendant about an appeal. We employ the term "consult" to convey a specific meaning—advising the defendant about the advantages and disadvantages of taking an appeal, and making a reasonable effort to discover the defendant's wishes. If counsel has consulted with the defendant, the question of deficient performance is easily answered: Counsel performs in a professionally unreasonable manner only by failing to follow the defendant's express instructions with respect to an appeal.... If counsel has not consulted with the defendant, the court must in turn ask a second, and subsidiary, question: whether counsel's failure to consult with the defendant itself constitutes deficient performance. That question lies at the heart of this case: Under what circumstances does counsel have an obligation to consult with the defendant about an appeal?

528 U.S. at 478, 120 S.Ct. at 1035, 145 L.Ed.2d at 995–96. The Court then applied the first branch of *Strickland* to determine in what circumstances counsel's failure to consult would be deficient. It concluded:

> that counsel has a constitutionally-imposed duty to consult with the defendant about an appeal when there is reason to think either (1) that a rational defendant would want to appeal (for example, because there are nonfrivolous grounds for appeal), or (2) that this particular defendant reasonably demonstrated to counsel that he was interested in appealing. In making this determination, courts must take into account all the information counsel knew or should have known.... Although not determinative, a highly relevant factor in this inquiry will be whether the conviction follows a trial or a guilty plea, both because a guilty plea reduces the scope of potentially appealable issues and because such a plea may indicate that the defendant seeks an end to judicial proceedings. Even in cases when the defendant pleads guilty, the court must consider such factors as whether the defendant received the sentence bargained for as part of the plea and whether the plea expressly reserved or waived some or all appeal rights. Only by considering all relevant factors in a given case can a court properly determine whether a rational defendant would have desired an appeal or that the particular defendant sufficiently demonstrated to counsel an interest in an appeal.

528 U.S. at 479, 120 S.Ct. at 1036, 145 L.Ed.2d at 997. The Court then predicted that "courts evaluating the reasonableness of counsel's performance using the inquiry we have described will find, in the vast majority of cases, that counsel had a duty to consult with the defendant about an appeal." 528 U.S. at 481, 120 S.Ct. at 1037, 145 L.Ed.2d at 997.

The Court then applied the prejudice branch of *Strickland* to this case. The question is not whether the client would prevail on an appeal but whether he or she can "demonstrate that there is a reasonable probability that, but for counsel's deficient failure to consult with him about an appeal, he would have timely appealed." 528 U.S. at 484, 120 S.Ct. at 1038, 145 L.Ed.2d at 999. If there is a showing that counsel was deficient in not consulting with the client about an appeal and that had such consultation occurred the client would have desired to appeal, then a claim of ineffective assistance is shown. The remedy is to order an out-of-time appeal of the case.

Justice Souter, joined by Justices Stevens and Ginsburg, dissented from that portion of the Court's opinion in which the standards for requiring consultation were articulated. Instead of the Court's standard, Justice Souter would require consultation "almost always in those cases in which a plea of guilty has not obviously waived any claims of error." 528 U.S. at 488, 120 S.Ct. at 1040–41, 145 L.Ed.2d at 1002.

Page 1127.   Add the following before Note 4:

3a. **Duty to defer to or consult client.** When does a defense lawyer's failure to obtain the defendant's consent to particular actions by the lawyer, or at least to consult with the defendant before taking such action, have constitutional ramifications? The matter was addressed in Florida v. Nixon, 543 U.S. 175, 125 S.Ct. 551, 160 L.Ed.2d 565 (2004).

Nixon, charged with capital murder, was disruptive at his trial and uncooperative in some dealings with defense counsel, Corin. Counsel explained to Nixon that
in counsel's view, the best approach was to concede guilt and focus on persuading
the jury to recommend life rather than death. Nixon simply did not respond with
approval or disapproval. Counsel then proceeded to admit Nixon's guilt to the jury
and unsuccessfully attempted to persuade the jury not to recommend the death
sentence. The Florida Supreme Court held Nixon was denied effective representation. Counsel can concede a defendant's guilt, it reasoned, only with the defendant's
affirmative and explicit authorization, and Nixon's counsel did not get this.

A unanimous Supreme Court (with the Chief Justice not participating) reversed. It began:

> An attorney undoubtedly has a duty to consult with the client regarding
> "important decisions," including questions of overarching defense strategy.
> That obligation, however, does not require counsel to obtain the defendant's
> consent to "every tactical decision." *Taylor v. Illinois,* 484 U.S. 400, 417–418,
> 108 S.Ct. 646, 98 L.Ed.2d 798 (1988) (an attorney has authority to manage
> most aspects of the defense without obtaining his client's approval). But certain
> decisions regarding the exercise or waiver of basic trial rights are of such
> moment that they cannot be made for the defendant by a surrogate. A
> defendant, this Court affirmed, has "the ultimate authority" to determine
> "whether to plead guilty, waive a jury, testify in his or her own behalf, or take
> an appeal." *Jones v. Barnes,* 463 U.S. 745, 751, 103 S.Ct. 3308, 77 L.Ed.2d 987
> (1983). Concerning those decisions, an attorney must both consult with the
> defendant and obtain consent to the recommended course of action.

545 U.S. at 186, 125 S.Ct. at 560. But a concession of guilt is neither a guilty plea
nor the functional equivalent of one.

> Corin was obliged to, and in fact several times did, explain his proposed trial
> strategy to Nixon. Given Nixon's constant resistance to answering inquiries put
> to him by counsel and court, Corin was not additionally required to gain
> express consent before conceding Nixon's guilt. The two evidentiary hearings
> conducted by the Florida trial court demonstrate beyond doubt that Corin
> fulfilled his duty of consultation by informing Nixon of counsel's proposed
> strategy and its potential benefits. Nixon's characteristic silence each time
> information was conveyed to him, in sum, did not suffice to render unreason-
> able Corin's decision to concede guilt and to home in, instead, on the life or
> death penalty issue.

545 U.S. at 189, 125 S.Ct. at 561.

Cronic did not apply, the Court stressed, because Corin's concession of his
client's guilt was not a failure to function in any meaningful sense. It added that
"such a concession in a run-of-the-mine trial might present a closer question."
Finally:

> To summarize, in a capital case, counsel must consider in conjunction both the
> guilt and penalty phases in determining how best to proceed. When counsel
> informs the defendant of the strategy counsel believes to be in the defendant's
> best interest and the defendant is unresponsive, counsel's strategic choice is not
> impeded by any blanket rule demanding the defendant's explicit consent.
> Instead, if counsel's strategy, given the evidence bearing on the defendant's

guilt, satisfies the *Strickland* standard, that is the end of the matter; no tenable claim of ineffective assistance would remain.

545 U.S. at 192, 125 S.Ct. at 563.

Page 1128. Add the following after Note 5:

5a. **Judicial failure to inquire into a known conflict.** The petitioner in Mickens v. Taylor, Warden, 535 U.S. 162, 122 S.Ct. 1237, 152 L.Ed.2d 291 (2002) discovered after his conviction and death sentence for capital murder that his appointed attorney had been the attorney in juvenile court for the victim of his offense. The same judge appointed the lawyer in the victim's case and in petitioner's case. Petitioner argued that because the judge knew or should have known of the conflict, a rule of automatic reversal should apply. But the Supreme Court, in a five to four opinion by Justice Scalia, rejected that argument. The rule of Cuyler v. Sullivan—that requires a showing of an actual conflict that adversely affected representation, but does not require proof of the prejudice to the outcome required by *Strickland*—is a sufficient standard. That is not changed by the fact that the trial judge knew or should have know of the conflict. Justice Scalia went further to suggest that in cases of conflict by successive representation the prejudice requirement of *Strickland* might be appropriate, but that taking such a position would go beyond what was required to decide this case.

What are possible conflicts in successive representation in a case such as this?

Page 1130. Insert the following after the Notes:

EDITORS' NOTE: THE RIGHT TO RETAINED COUNSEL OF CHOICE

The Sixth Amendment right to counsel, of course, applies to a defendant who does not require appointed counsel. In this context, the Supreme Court reaffirmed in United States v. Gonzalez–Lopez, 548 U.S. 140, 126 S.Ct. 2557, 165 L.Ed.2d 409 (2006), the right includes the right to choose who will provide the representation. This right is, of course, subject to qualification. In *Gonzalez–Lopez*, however, it was clear that the federal District Judge "erroneously deprived [Gonzalez–Lopez] of his counsel of choice."

A split Court held that a defendant shows a complete Sixth Amendment violation by demonstrating a wrongful deprivation of counsel of choice. The defendant need not show that actual counsel was ineffective under *Strickland* or—as the dissenters argued—that there was "an identifiable difference in the quality of the representation" that the defendant received as a result of the deprivation of counsel of choice. Justice Scalia explained for the 5 to 4 majority that the right to effective representation as applied in *Strickland* is derived from the right to a fair trial. He continued:

> The right to select counsel of one's choice, by contrast, has never been derived from the Sixth Amendment's purpose of ensuring a fair trial. It has been regarded as the root meaning of the constitutional guarantee. Where the right to be assisted by counsel of one's choice is wrongly denied, therefore, it is unnecessary to conduct an ineffectiveness or prejudice inquiry to establish a Sixth Amendment violation. Deprivation of the right is "complete" when the

defendant is erroneously prevented from being represented by the lawyer he wants, regardless of the quality of the representation he received. To argue otherwise is to confuse the right to counsel of choice—which is the right to a particular lawyer regardless of comparative effectiveness—with the right to effective counsel—which imposes a baseline requirement of competence on whatever lawyer is chosen or appointed.

548 U.S. at 147–48, 126 S.Ct. at 2563.

Finally, *Gonzalez–Lopez* held that a violation of a defendant's Sixth Amendment right to representation by counsel of choice "bears directly on the 'framework within which the trial proceeds,' or indeed on whether it proceeds at all." Thus it is not subject to harmless error analysis. 548 U.S. at 150, 126 S.Ct. at 2564–65.

B. SELF-REPRESENTATION AND WAIVER OF SIXTH AMENDMENT RIGHTS

Page 1142.   Add the following new note at the bottom of the page:

1.   **Waiving counsel to plead guilty.** Does a *Faretta*-like procedure apply to proceedings in which the defendant waives the right to counsel while pleading guilty? The respondent in Iowa v. Tovar, 541 U.S. 77, 124 S.Ct. 1379, 158 L.Ed.2d 209 (2004) waived counsel and plead guilty to driving while intoxicated. He was later convicted a second time of the same offense and still later charged with third offense driving while intoxicated—a felony. In defense of that charge, he contended that the first conviction was invalid because he had not been warned by the trial judge of the dangers and disadvantages of waiving counsel when he waived counsel to plead guilty. The Iowa Supreme Court agreed, holding that the Sixth Amendment requires two admonitions to be given in such a circumstance:

> "[T]he trial judge [must] advise the defendant generally that there are defenses to criminal charges that may not be known by laypersons and that the danger in waiving the assistance of counsel in deciding whether to plead guilty is the risk that a viable defense will be overlooked," * * * in addition, "[t]he defendant should be admonished that by waiving his right to an attorney he will lose the opportunity to obtain an independent opinion on whether, under the facts and applicable law, it is wise to plead guilty,"

541 U.S. at 91, 124 S.Ct. at 1389. The United States Supreme Court, in an opinion for a unanimous Court by Justice Ginsburg, held that the Sixth Amendment does not require those admonitions. The Court noted that a waiver of a constitutional right must be voluntary, knowing and intelligent. There is no claim in this case that Tovar did not understand his rights or the consequences of waiving them. No particular set of admonitions is required to effectuate a valid waiver:

> We hold that neither warning [required by the Iowa Supreme Court] is mandated by the Sixth Amendment. The constitutional requirement is satisfied when the trial court informs the accused of the nature of the charges against him, of his right to be counseled regarding his plea, and of the range of allowable punishments attendant upon the entry of a guilty plea.

541 U.S. at 81, 124 S.Ct. at 1383.

Page 1142.   Add the following note at the end of the Chapter:

2.   **Does a mentally ill defendant deemed competent to stand trial have a Sixth Amendment right to represent himself under _Faretta_?** In _Indiana v. Edwards_, 554 U.S. 164, 128 S.Ct. 2379, 171 L.Ed.2d 345 (2008), the Court answered "not necessarily." Mr. Edwards, who suffered from schizophrenia, tried to steal a pair of shoes from a department store, and fired at a store security officer when he was caught. After a few years in a mental hospital and three competency hearings, defendant was found competent to stand trial. His first trial resulted in a jury verdict of guilt on criminal recklessness and theft, but no decision on the attempted murder and battery charges. Mr. Edwards moved to represent himself on the retrial of the remaining charges, his request was denied, and he was found guilty. The Indiana Supreme Court reversed the convictions on the ground that _Faretta_ (supra Casebook p. 1132) and _Godinez_ (supra Casebook p. 733) required the State to allow Edwards to represent himself. The Supreme Court reversed, concluding that

> _Faretta_ does not answer the question before us both because it did not consider the problem of mental competency (cf. 422 U.S. at 835 (Faretta was "literate, competent, and understanding")), and because _Faretta_ itself and later cases have made clear that the right of self-representation is not absolute.

554 U.S. at 171, 128 S.Ct. at 2384.

Resolving the matter, the Court explained:

> We * * * conclude that the Constitution permits judges to take realistic account of the particular defendant's mental capacities by asking whether a defendant who seeks to conduct his own defense at trial is mentally competent to do so. That is to say, the Constitution permits States to insist upon representation by counsel for those competent enough to stand trial * * * but who still suffer from severe mental illness to the point where they are not competent to conduct trial proceedings by themselves.

554 U.S. at 177–78, 128 S.Ct. at 2387–88.

Such a conclusion is consistent with precedent and buttressed by an amicus brief from the American Psychiatric Association, explaining that mental illness varies in degree and over time, such that an individual may well be able to satisfy _Dusky's_ mental competence standard (able to work with counsel), yet be unable to carry out the basic tasks needed to present his own defense. Self-representation will not affirm the dignity and autonomy of an individual in that instance, and may undercut the possibility of a fair trial.

CHAPTER 25

SENTENCING

B. STRUCTURING THE SENTENCING SYSTEM

2. CONTROLLING SENTENCING DISCRETION BY APPELLATE REVIEW

b. APPELLATE REVIEW OF SENTENCES IMPOSED

Page 1170. Add the following before Note 2:

1a. **Constitutionality of three strikes laws.** The Supreme Court reviewed two California three strikes law cases and upheld the applicability of the law in each. The petitioner in Ewing v. California, 538 U.S. 11, 123 S.Ct. 1179, 155 L.Ed.2d 108 (2003) was given a prison sentence of 25 years to life under the three strikes law for grand theft of three golf clubs, which had a total value of just under $1200. Ewing had numerous prior misdemeanor and felony convictions, including three burglaries and one robbery committed in close proximity to each other, which qualified under the law as serious or violent felonies. The offense of grand theft is a "wobbler" offense—one that can be charged by the prosecutor as either a misdemeanor or a felony and if charged as a felony can be reduced by the trial judge to a misdemeanor. The trial judge refused to reduce Ewing's grand theft felony conviction. Under California law, the judge also had discretion to dismiss prior convictions alleged to invoke the three strikes law, but the trial judge in this case refused to do so.

The Supreme Court, in a three-judge opinion for the Court by Justice O'Connor upheld the sentence under the Eighth Amendment. Justice O'Connor discussed the history of three strikes laws:

> For many years, most States have had laws providing for enhanced sentencing of repeat offenders. * * * Yet between 1993 and 1995, three strikes laws effected a sea change in criminal sentencing throughout the Nation. These laws responded to widespread public concerns about crime by targeting the class of offenders who pose the greatest threat to public safety: career criminals. As one of the chief architects of California's three strikes law has explained: "Three Strikes was intended to go beyond simply making sentences tougher. It was intended to be a focused effort to create a sentencing policy that would use the judicial system to reduce serious and violent crime." Ardaiz, California's Three Strikes Law: History, Expectations, Consequences 32 McGeorge L.Rev. 1, 12 (2000) (hereinafter Ardaiz).

> Throughout the States, legislatures enacting three strikes laws made a deliberate policy choice that individuals who have repeatedly engaged in serious or violent criminal behavior, and whose conduct has not been deterred by more conventional approaches to punishment, must be isolated from society in order

to protect the public safety. Though three strikes laws may be relatively new, our tradition of deferring to state legislatures in making and implementing such important policy decisions is longstanding. * * *

Our traditional deference to legislative policy choices finds a corollary in the principle that the Constitution "does not mandate adoption of any one penological theory." * * * A sentence can have a variety of justifications, such as incapacitation, deterrence, retribution, or rehabilitation. * * * Some or all of these justifications may play a role in a State's sentencing scheme. Selecting the sentencing rationales is generally a policy choice to be made by state legislatures, not federal courts.

When the California Legislature enacted the three strikes law, it made a judgment that protecting the public safety requires incapacitating criminals who have already been convicted of at least one serious or violent crime. Nothing in the Eighth Amendment prohibits California from making that choice.

To the contrary, our cases establish that "States have a valid interest in deterring and segregating habitual criminals." * * * Recidivism has long been recognized as a legitimate basis for increased punishment. * * *

California's justification is no pretext. Recidivism is a serious public safety concern in California and throughout the Nation. According to a recent report, approximately 67 percent of former inmates released from state prisons were charged with at least one "serious" new crime within three years of their release. * * * In particular, released property offenders like Ewing had higher recidivism rates than those released after committing violent, drug, or public-order offenses. * * * Approximately 73 percent of the property offenders released in 1994 were arrested again within three years, compared to approximately 61 percent of the violent offenders, 62 percent of the public-order offenders, and 66 percent of the drug offenders. * * *

538 U.S. at 24–26, 123 S.Ct. at 1187–88. Ewing will eventually become eligible for parole. His sentence does not violate the Eighth Amendment. Justice Scalia concurred in the judgment on the ground that it is not possible to apply an Eighth Amendment proportionality principle intelligently. Justice Thomas, also concurring in the judgment, agreed with Justice Scalia but added that he believes that the Eighth Amendment contains no proportionality principle. Justice Stevens, joined by Justices Souter, Ginsburg and Breyer, dissented.

On the same day it decided *Ewing*, the Court decided Lockyer v. Andrade, 538 U.S. 63, 123 S.Ct. 1166, 155 L.Ed.2d 144 (2003). Andrade on two separate occasions stole videotapes from convenience stores. Since Andrade had prior misdemeanor convictions, the prosecutor exercised discretion to charge the two current offenses as felonies. A jury found him guilty of both offenses and that he had previously been convicted of three first-degree residential burglaries, which qualified as serious or violent felony convictions under the three strikes law. He was sentenced to 25 years to life on each count, to run consecutively, for an effective sentence of 50 years to life. The California Court of Appeals rejected Andrade's Eighth Amendment claim. A federal district court denied habeas relief, but the Ninth Circuit reversed on Eighth Amendment grounds.

The Supreme Court in a five to four decision reversed the Ninth Circuit. Writing for the Court, Justice O'Connor identified the issue as whether under 28

U.S.C. § 2254(d)(1) the California Court of Appeals' proceeding "resulted in a decision that was contrary to, or involved an unreasonable application of, clearly established Federal law, as determined by the Supreme Court of the United States." Justice O'Connor concluded that the California court's decision did not meet that standard:

> First, a state court decision is "contrary to our clearly established precedent if the state court applies a rule that contradicts the governing law set forth in our cases" or "if the state court confronts a set of facts that are materially indistinguishable from a decision of this Court and nevertheless arrives at a result different from our precedent." Williams v. Taylor, supra, at 405–406, 120 S.Ct. 1495 * * *. In terms of length of sentence and availability of parole, severity of the underlying offense, and the impact of recidivism, Andrade's sentence implicates factors relevant in both *Rummel* and *Solem*. Because *Harmelin* and *Solem* specifically stated that they did not overrule *Rummel*, it was not contrary to our clearly established law for the California Court of Appeal to turn to *Rummel* in deciding whether a sentence is grossly disproportionate. * * * Indeed, Harmelin allows a state court to reasonably rely on Rummel in determining whether a sentence is grossly disproportionate. The California Court of Appeal's decision was therefore not "contrary to" the governing legal principles set forth in our cases.
>
> Andrade's sentence also was not materially indistinguishable from the facts in *Solem*. The facts here fall in between the facts in *Rummel* and the facts in *Solem*. *Solem* involved a sentence of life in prison without the possibility of parole. * * * The defendant in *Rummel* was sentenced to life in prison with the possibility of parole. * * * Here, Andrade retains the possibility of parole. *Solem* acknowledged that *Rummel* would apply in a "similar factual situation." * * * And while this case resembles to some degree both *Rummel* and *Solem*, it is not materially indistinguishable from either. * * * Consequently, the state court did not "confron[t] a set of facts that are materially indistinguishable from a decision of this Court and nevertheless arriv[e] at a result different from our precedent." Williams v. Taylor, 529 U.S., at 406, 120 S.Ct. 1495.

538 U.S. at 73, 123 S.Ct. at 1173–74. Justice Souter, joined by Justices Stevens, Ginsburg and Breyer, dissented.

1b. **Life without parole for juvenile offenders.** The constitutionality of life sentences without parole imposed on juvenile offenders was addressed in Graham v. Florida, ___ U.S. ___, 130 S.Ct. 2011, 176 L.Ed.2d 825 (2010). Graham was convicted of armed burglary and attempted armed robbery committed when he was 16. His probation for those offenses was revoked on the basis of a home invasion robbery committed when he was 17, and he was sentenced to life without parole. Six justices agreed that the sentence violated the Eighth Amendment prohibition against cruel and unusual punishments applied to the States by the Fourteenth Amendment.

Chief Justice Roberts reached this result by comparing the penalty to the gravity of Graham's conduct. ___ U.S. at ___, 130 S.Ct. at 2039–42 (Roberts, C.J., concurring). The six-justice majority, however, adopted a categorical rule analysis that does not include consideration of the defendant's conduct:

> The Constitution prohibits the imposition of a life without parole sentence on a juvenile offender who did not commit homicide. A State need not

guarantee the offender eventual release, but if it imposes a sentence of life it must provide him or her with some realistic opportunity to obtain release before the end of that term.

___ U.S. at ___, 130 S.Ct. at 2034.

To determine whether life without parole is unconstitutional in these situations, the majority looked first to actual sentencing practices. It concluded that "in proportion to the opportunities for its imposition, life without parole sentences for juveniles convicted of nonhomicide crimes is as rare as other sentencing practices found to be cruel and unusual." Second, and in light of reduced culpability of juvenile offenders, the majority decided such sentences do not adequately serve legitimate penological goals. It reasoned specifically, for example, that "any limited deterrent effect provided by life without parole is not enough to justify the sentence." The majority rejected Chief Justice Roberts' approach in favor of its categorical rule in large part because courts could not, with "sufficient accuracy," distinguish the "few" nonhomicide juvenile offenders who could constitutionally be sentenced to life without parole from the "many" who could not. ___ U.S. at ___, 130 S.Ct. at 2032.

Page 1171. Add the following at the end of Note 3:

Appellate review of sentences imposed under state and federal advisory sentencing systems may be affected by the Supreme Court's application of the Sixth Amendment right to jury determinations to certain sentencing systems. This is addressed in the notes following United States v. Booker, reprinted in this supplement for insertion at page 1189 of the text. The effectiveness of appellate review in both mandatory and voluntary guideline regimes was evaluated in Bibas and Klein, The Sixth Amendment and Criminal Sentencing, 30 Cardozo L.Rev. 775, 783–89 (2008).

3. REDUCING DISCRETION BY "DETERMINATE" SENTENCING

a. STATE REFORMS

Page 1177. Add the following after Note 3:

4. **State sentencing reforms after *Blakely*.** In *Apprendi v. New Jersey* (on page 224 of your 2008 Supplement, which replaced Note 2 of your casebook on p. 1010), a bare five-member majority held that juries, not judges, must find beyond a reasonable doubt any facts that increases a defendant's statutory maximum sentence, except for recidivism. In *Blakely v. Washington*, 542 U.S. 296, 303–04, 124 S.Ct. 2531, 159 L.Ed.2d 403 (2004), the same five justice majority extended *Apprendi*'s rule to facts that raise maximum sentences under a state presumptive sentencing system. While a slight majority of states were unaffected because they did not employ mandatory guidelines or presumptive sentencing based upon judicial fact-finding, a number of other jurisdictions reacted by transforming their mandatory guidelines systems into advisory ones rather than sending facts formerly found by judges to juries. Appendices listing which states had mandatory sentencing regimes and how each state responded to the Supreme Court's new requirements can be found in Bibas and Klein, "The Sixth Amendment and Criminal Sentencing," 30 Cardozo Law Rev. 775 (2008), Appendix A, Tables I–IV and Appendix B.

b. FEDERAL REFORM: THE SENTENCING REFORM ACT OF 1984

Page 1186. Add the following new note to the notes after Mistretta v. United States:

2a. **Imprisonment to achieve rehabilitation.** 18 U.S.C. § 3553(a) provides that a federal judge in deciding whether to impose a prison sentence and the term of any such sentence to consider the factors set out in section 3553(a) (reprinted in note 2) "recognizing that imprisonment is not an appropriate means of promoting correction and rehabilitation." By this last language, the Supreme Court held in Tapia v. United States, 564 U.S. ___, 131 S.Ct. 2382, ___ L.Ed.2d ___ (2011), Congress has directed sentencing judges to assume that imprisonment is not an appropriate means of pursuing the objective of rehabilitating the offender. Thus a sentencing judge erred if he increased the length of the term of imprisonment imposed on Tapia to assure that she would be eligible for, and able to complete, a program of institutional drug treatment available in the federal prison system.

Page 1186. Add the following new note to the notes after Mistretta v. United States:

5a. **Retroactive amendment of the guidelines.** Retroactive amendments to the Guidelines are permitted. If a retroactive Guideline amendment is adopted, defendants previously sentenced based on a sentencing range that has been modified can move for a reduced sentence. 18 U.S.C.A. § 3582(c)(2). The Sentencing Commission retroactively amended the Guidelines to remedy the significant disparity between sentences for cocaine base and powder cocaine offenses. See United States Sentencing Commission, Guidelines Manual Supp.App. C, Amdt. 706 (Nov. 2010) (USSG) (effective Nov. 1, 2007) (adjusting Guidelines); *id.,* Amdt. 713 (effective Mar. 3, 2008) (making Amendment 706 retroactive). Can a defendant sentenced pursuant to a plea agreement providing for a particular sentence move for a reduced sentence after such a retroactive amendment? This caused a 4–1–4 split among the Justices in Freeman v. United States, 564 U.S. ___, 131 S.Ct. ___, ___ L.Ed.2d ___ (2011). Under *Freeman,* such a defendant can move for a reduced sentence if, but only if, the plea agreement "expressly uses a Guidelines sentencing range to establish the term of imprisonment, and that range is subsequently lowered by the Commission * * *." 564 U.S. at ___, 131 S.Ct. at ___ (Sotomayor, J., concurring in the judgment).

Page 1187.   Add the following after the first paragraph:

The Bureau of Prisons is authorized to reduce a federal determinate sentence by a much as one year for an inmate who successfully completes a prison substance abuse treatment program. In Lopez v. Davis, 531 U.S. 230, 121 S.Ct. 714, 148 L.Ed.2d 635 (2001), the Supreme Court upheld the Bureau's rule excluding inmates convicted of a felony that involves the "carrying, possession, or use of a firearm or other dangerous weapon" from eligibility for this sentence reduction.

Page 1188.   Add the following to Note 4:

The issue in Buford v. United States, 532 U.S. 59, 121 S.Ct. 1276, 149 L.Ed.2d 197 (2001) was the standard of appellate review of a trial court finding that prior convictions had not been functionally consolidated in earlier proceedings; under the Guidelines this finding requires a more severe sentence than if the prior convictions had been consolidated. The Seventh Circuit affirmed, in part on the ground that the standard of review is not *de novo*, as appellant had contended for, but deferential to the trial court's decision. The Supreme Court, in an opinion authored by Justice Breyer for a unanimous Court, agreed with the Seventh Circuit. Following its lead in *Koon*, the Court found special competence in the trial court regarding this decision that must be respected on appeal:

> We concluded there [in *Koon*] that the special competence of the district court helped to make deferential review appropriate. And that is true here as well. That is to say, the district court is in a better position than the appellate court to decide whether a particular set of individual circumstances demonstrates "functional consolidation."
>
> That is so because a district judge sees many more "consolidations" than does an appellate judge. As a trial judge, a district judge is likely to be more familiar with trial and sentencing practices in general, including consolidation procedures. And as a sentencing judge who must regularly review and classify defendants' criminal histories, a district judge is more likely to be aware of which procedures the relevant state or federal courts typically follow. Experience with trials, sentencing, and consolidations will help that judge draw the proper inferences from the procedural descriptions provided.

532 U.S. at 64–65, 121 S.Ct. at 1280, 149 L.Ed.2d at 203.

Page 1189. Insert the following new case and notes after *Mistretta* and the notes after it:

United States v. Booker

Supreme Court of the United States, 2005.
543 U.S. 220, 125 S.Ct. 738, 160 L.Ed.2d 621.

■ JUSTICE STEVENS delivered the opinion of the Court in part.***

The question presented * * * is whether an application of the Federal Sentencing Guidelines violated the Sixth Amendment. * * * We hold that * * * the Sixth Amendment * * * does apply to the Sentencing Guidelines. In a separate opinion authored by Justice BREYER, the Court concludes that in light of this holding, two provisions of the Sentencing Reform Act of 1984 (SRA) that have the effect of making the Guidelines mandatory must be invalidated in order to allow the statute to operate in a manner consistent with congressional intent.

I

Respondent Booker was charged with possession with intent to distribute at least 50 grams of cocaine base (crack). Having heard evidence that he had 92.5 grams in his duffel bag, the jury found him guilty of violating 21 U.S.C. § 841(a)(1). That statute prescribes a minimum sentence of 10 years in prison and a maximum sentence of life for that offense.

*** Justice SCALIA, Justice SOUTER,   join this opinion.
Justice THOMAS, and Justice GINSBURG

Based upon Booker's criminal history and the quantity of drugs found by the jury, the Sentencing Guidelines required the District Court Judge to select a "base" sentence of not less than 210 nor more than 262 months in prison. The judge, however, held a post-trial sentencing proceeding and concluded by a preponderance of the evidence that Booker had possessed an additional 566 grams of crack and that he was guilty of obstructing justice. Those findings mandated that the judge select a sentence between 360 months and life imprisonment; the judge imposed a sentence at the low end of the range. Thus, instead of the sentence of 21 years and 10 months that the judge could have imposed on the basis of the facts proved to the jury beyond a reasonable doubt, Booker received a 30–year sentence.

[T]he Court of Appeals for the Seventh Circuit held that this application of the Sentencing Guidelines conflicted with our holding in *Apprendi v. New Jersey,* 530 U.S. 466, 490, 120 S.Ct. 2348, 147 L.Ed.2d 435 (2000) [reprinted earlier in this Supplement], that "[o]ther than the fact of a prior conviction, any fact that increases the penalty for a crime beyond the prescribed statutory maximum must be submitted to a jury, and proved beyond a reasonable doubt." * * *

In [its petition for a writ of certiorari] the Government asks us to determine whether our *Apprendi* line of cases applies to the Sentencing Guidelines, and if so, what portions of the Guidelines remain in effect.

In this opinion, we explain why we agree with the lower courts' answer to the first question. In a separate opinion for the Court, Justice BREYER explains the Court's answer to the second question.

II

It has been settled throughout our history that the Constitution protects every criminal defendant "against conviction except upon proof beyond a reasonable doubt of every fact necessary to constitute the crime with which he is charged." *In re Winship,* 397 U.S. 358, 364, 90 S.Ct. 1068, 25 L.Ed.2d 368 (1970). It is equally clear that the "Constitution gives a criminal defendant the right to demand that a jury find him guilty of all the elements of the crime with which he is charged." *United States v. Gaudin,* 515 U.S. 506, 511, 115 S.Ct. 2310, 132 L.Ed.2d 444 (1995). These basic precepts, firmly rooted in the common law, have provided the basis for recent decisions interpreting modern criminal statutes and sentencing procedures.

* * *

In *Blakely v. Washington,* 542 U.S. 296, 124 S.Ct. 2531, 159 L.Ed.2d 403 (2004), we dealt with a determinate sentencing scheme similar to the Federal Sentencing Guidelines. There the defendant pleaded guilty to kidnaping, a class B felony punishable by a term of not more than 10 years. Other provisions of Washington law, comparable to the Federal Sentencing Guidelines, mandated a "standard" sentence of 49-to-53 months, unless the judge found aggravating facts justifying an exceptional sentence. Although the prosecutor recommended a sentence in the standard range, the judge found that the defendant had acted with " 'deliberate cruelty' " and sentenced him to 90 months.

[T]he requirements of the Sixth Amendment were clear. The application of Washington's sentencing scheme violated the defendant's right to have the jury find the existence of " 'any particular fact' " that the law makes essential to his punishment. That right is implicated whenever a judge seeks to impose a sentence that is not solely based on "facts reflected in the jury verdict or admitted by the defendant." (emphasis deleted). We rejected the State's argument that the jury verdict was sufficient to authorize a sentence within the general 10–year sentence for Class B felonies, noting that under Washington law, the judge was *required* to find additional facts in order to impose the greater 90–month sentence. Our precedents, we explained, make clear "that the 'statutory maximum' for *Apprendi* purposes is the maximum sentence a judge may impose *solely on the basis of the facts reflected in the jury verdict or admitted by the defendant.*" (emphasis in original). The determination that the defendant acted with deliberate cruelty, like the determination in *Apprendi* that the defendant acted with racial malice, increased the sentence that the defendant could have otherwise received. Since this fact was found by a judge using a preponderance of the evidence standard, the sentence violated Blakely's Sixth Amendment rights.

[T]here is no distinction of constitutional significance between the Federal Sentencing Guidelines and the Washington procedures at issue in that case. This conclusion rests on the premise, common to both systems, that the relevant sentencing rules are mandatory and impose binding requirements on all sentencing judges.

If the Guidelines as currently written could be read as merely advisory provisions that recommended, rather than required, the selection of particular sentences in response to differing sets of facts, their use would not implicate the Sixth Amendment. We have never doubted the authority of a judge to exercise broad discretion in imposing a sentence within a statutory range. See *Apprendi*, 530 U.S., at 481, 120 S.Ct. 2348; *Williams v. New York,* 337 U.S. 241, 246, 69 S.Ct. 1079, 93 L.Ed. 1337 (1949). Indeed, everyone agrees that the constitutional issues presented by these cases would have been avoided entirely if Congress had omitted from the SRA the provisions that make the Guidelines binding on district judges; it is that circumstance that makes the Court's answer to the second question presented possible. For when a trial judge exercises his discretion to select a specific sentence within a defined range, the defendant has no right to a jury determination of the facts that the judge deems relevant.

The Guidelines as written, however, are not advisory; they are mandatory and binding on all judges. * * *

The availability of a departure in specified circumstances does not avoid the constitutional issue * * *. The Guidelines permit departures from the prescribed sentencing range in cases in which the judge "finds that there exists an aggravating or mitigating circumstance of a kind, or to a degree, not adequately taken into consideration by the Sentencing Commission in formulating the guidelines that should result in a sentence different from that described." 18 U.S.C.A. § 3553(b)(1) (Supp.2004). At first glance, one might believe that the ability of a district judge to depart from the Guidelines means that she is bound only by the statutory maximum. Were this the case, there would be no *Apprendi* problem. Importantly, however, departures are not available in every case, and in fact are unavailable in most. In most cases, as a matter of law, the Commission will have adequately taken all relevant factors into account, and no departure will be legally permissible. In those instances, the judge is bound to impose a sentence within the Guidelines range. * * *

Booker's case illustrates the mandatory nature of the Guidelines. The jury convicted him of possessing at least 50 grams of crack * * * based on evidence that he had 92.5 grams of crack in his duffel bag. Under these facts, the Guidelines specified an offense level of 32, which, given the defendant's criminal history category, authorized a sentence of 210-to-262 months. Booker's is a run-of-the-mill drug case, and does not present any factors that were inadequately considered by the Commission. The sentencing judge would therefore have been reversed had he not imposed a sentence within the level 32 Guidelines range.

Booker's actual sentence, however, was 360 months, almost 10 years longer than the Guidelines range supported by the jury verdict alone. To reach this sentence, the judge found facts beyond those found by the jury: namely, that Booker possessed 566 grams of crack in addition to the 92.5 grams in his duffel bag. The jury never heard any evidence of the additional drug quantity, and the judge found it true by a preponderance of the evidence. Thus, just as in *Blakely*, "the jury's verdict alone does not authorize the sentence. The judge acquires that authority only upon finding some additional fact." There is no relevant distinction between the sentence imposed pursuant to the Washington statutes in *Blakely* and the sentences imposed pursuant to the Federal Sentencing Guidelines in these cases.

In his dissent, Justice BREYER argues on historical grounds that the Guidelines scheme is constitutional across the board. He points to traditional judicial authority to increase sentences to take account of any unusual blameworthiness in the manner employed in committing a crime, an authority that the Guidelines require to be exercised consistently throughout the system. This tradition, however, does not provide a sound guide to enforcement of the Sixth Amendment's guarantee of a jury trial in today's world.

It is quite true that once determinate sentencing had fallen from favor, American judges commonly determined facts justifying a choice of a heavier sentence on account of the manner in which particular defendants acted. In 1986, however, our own cases first recognized a new trend in the legislative regulation of sentencing when we considered the significance of facts selected by legislatures that not only authorized, or even mandated, heavier sentences than would otherwise have been imposed, but increased the range of sentences possible for the underlying crime. See *McMillan v. Pennsylvania*, 477 U.S. 79, 8788, 106 S.Ct. 2411, 91 L.Ed.2d 67 (1986). Provisions for such enhancements of the permissible sentencing range reflected growing and wholly justified legislative concern about the proliferation and variety of drug crimes and their frequent identification with firearms offences.

The effect of the increasing emphasis on facts that enhanced sentencing ranges, however, was to increase the judge's power and diminish that of the jury. It became the judge, not the jury, that determined the upper limits of sentencing, and the facts determined were not required to be raised before trial or proved by more than a preponderance.

As the enhancements became greater, the jury's finding of the underlying crime became less significant. And the enhancements became very serious indeed. * * *

As it thus became clear that sentencing was no longer taking place in the tradition that Justice BREYER invokes, the Court was faced with the issue of preserving an ancient guarantee under a new set of circumstances. The new sentencing practice forced the Court to address the question how the right of jury trial could be preserved, in a meaningful way guaranteeing that the jury would still stand between the individual and the power of the government under the new sentencing regime. And it is the new circumstances, not a tradition or practice that the new circumstances have superseded, that have led us to the answer * * * developed in *Apprendi* and subsequent cases culminating with this one. It is an answer not motivated by Sixth Amendment formalism, but by the need to preserve Sixth Amendment substance.

III

* * *

[T]he principles we sought to vindicate [in *Apprendi*] * * * are unquestionably applicable to the Guidelines. They are not the product of recent innovations in our jurisprudence, but rather have their genesis in the ideals our constitutional tradition assimilated from the common law. The Framers of the Constitution understood the threat of "judicial despotism" that could arise from "arbitrary punishments upon arbitrary convictions" without the benefit of a jury in criminal cases. The Founders presumably carried this concern from England, in which the right to a jury trial had been enshrined since the Magna Carta. * * *

IV

* * * We recognize * * * that in some cases jury factfinding may impair the most expedient and efficient sentencing of defendants. But the interest in fairness and reliability protected by the right to a jury trial—a common-law right that defendants enjoyed for centuries and that is now enshrined in the Sixth Amendment—has always outweighed the interest in concluding trials swiftly. * * *

Accordingly, we reaffirm our holding in *Apprendi:* Any fact (other than a prior conviction) which is necessary to support a sentence exceeding the maximum authorized by the facts established by a plea of guilty or a jury verdict must be admitted by the defendant or proved to a jury beyond a reasonable doubt.

Justice BREYER delivered the opinion of the Court in part.[5]*

* * *

We * * * turn to the second question presented, a question that concerns the remedy. We must decide whether or to what extent, "as a matter of severability analysis," the Guidelines "as a whole" are "inapplicable ... such that the sentencing court must exercise its discretion to sentence the defendant within the maximum and minimum set by statute for the offense of conviction."

* * *

I

[W]e must determine which of the two following remedial approaches is the more compatible with the legislature's intent as embodied in the 1984 Sentencing Act.

One approach, that of Justice STEVENS' dissent, would retain the Sentencing Act (and the Guidelines) as written, but would engraft onto the existing system today's Sixth Amendment "jury trial" requirement. The addition would change the Guidelines by preventing the sentencing court from increasing a sentence on the basis of a fact that the jury did not find (or that the offender did not admit).

The other approach, which we now adopt, would (through severance and excision of two provisions) make the Guidelines system advisory while maintaining a strong connection between the sentence imposed and the

---

5. * THE CHIEF JUSTICE, Justice O'CONNOR, Justice KENNEDY, and Justice GINSBURG join this opinion.

offender's real conduct—a connection important to the increased uniformity of sentencing that Congress intended its Guidelines system to achieve.

Both approaches would significantly alter the system that Congress designed. But today's constitutional holding means that it is no longer possible to maintain the judicial factfinding that Congress thought would underpin the mandatory Guidelines system that it sought to create and that Congress wrote into the Act * * *.

II

Several considerations convince us that, were the Court's constitutional requirement added onto the Sentencing Act as currently written, the requirement would so transform the scheme that Congress created that Congress likely would not have intended the Act as so modified to stand. First, the statute's text states that "[t]he court" when sentencing will consider "the nature and circumstances of the offense and the history and characteristics of the defendant." 18 U.S.C.A. § 3553(a)(1) (main ed. and Supp.2004). In context, the words "the court" mean "the judge without the jury," not "the judge working together with the jury." * * *

Second, Congress' basic statutory goal—a system that diminishes sentencing disparity—depends for its success upon judicial efforts to determine, and to base punishment upon, the *real conduct* that underlies the crime of conviction. * * * Judges have long looked to real conduct when sentencing. Federal judges have long relied upon a presentence report, prepared by a probation officer, for information (often unavailable until *after* the trial) relevant to the manner in which the convicted offender committed the crime of conviction.

Congress expected this system to continue. * * *

To engraft the Court's constitutional requirement onto the sentencing statutes, however, would destroy the system. It would prevent a judge from relying upon a presentence report for factual information, relevant to sentencing, uncovered after the trial. In doing so, it would, even compared to pre-Guidelines sentencing, weaken the tie between a sentence and an offender's real conduct. It would thereby undermine the sentencing statute's basic aim of ensuring similar sentences for those who have committed similar crimes in similar ways.

* * *

* * * Congress' basic goal in passing the Sentencing Act was to move the sentencing system in the direction of increased uniformity. That uniformity does not consist simply of similar sentences for those convicted of violations of the same statute—a uniformity consistent with the dissenters' remedial approach. It consists, more importantly, of similar relationships between sentences and real conduct, relationships that Congress' sentencing statutes helped to advance and that Justice STEVENS' approach would undermine. * * *

Third, the sentencing statutes, read to include the Court's Sixth Amendment requirement, would create a system far more complex than Congress could have intended. How would courts and counsel work with an indictment and a jury trial that involved not just whether a defendant robbed a bank but also how? Would the indictment have to allege, in addition to the elements of robbery, whether the defendant possessed a firearm, whether he brandished or discharged it, whether he threatened death, whether he caused bodily injury, whether any such injury was ordinary, serious, permanent or life threatening, whether he abducted or physically restrained anyone, whether any victim was unusually vulnerable, how much money was taken, and whether he was an organizer, leader, manager, or supervisor in a robbery gang? * * *

Fourth, plea bargaining would not significantly diminish the consequences of the Court's constitutional holding for the operation of the Guidelines. Rather, plea bargaining would make matters worse. Congress enacted the sentencing statutes in major part to achieve greater uniformity in sentencing, *i.e.,* to increase the likelihood that offenders who engage in similar real conduct would receive similar sentences. The statutes reasonably assume that their efforts to move the trial-based sentencing process in the direction of greater sentencing uniformity would have a similar positive impact upon plea-bargained sentences, for plea bargaining takes place *in the shadow of* (*i.e.,* with an eye towards the hypothetical result of) a potential trial.

That, too, is why Congress, understanding the realities of plea bargaining, authorized the Commission to promulgate policy statements that would assist sentencing judges in determining whether to reject a plea agreement after reading about the defendant's real conduct in a presentence report (and giving the offender an opportunity to challenge the report). This system has not worked perfectly; judges have often simply accepted an agreed upon account of the conduct at issue. But compared to preexisting law, the statutes try to move the system in the right direction, *i.e.,* toward greater sentencing uniformity.

The Court's constitutional jury trial requirement, however, if patched onto the present Sentencing Act, would move the system backwards in respect both to tried and to plea-bargained cases. In respect to tried cases, it would effectively deprive the judge of the ability to use post-verdict-acquired real-conduct information; it would prohibit the judge from basing a sentence upon any conduct other than the conduct the prosecutor chose to charge; and it would put a defendant to a set of difficult strategic choices as to which prosecutorial claims he would contest. The sentence that would emerge in a case tried under such a system would likely reflect real conduct less completely, less accurately, and less often than did a pre-Guidelines, as well as a Guidelines, trial.

Because plea bargaining inevitably reflects estimates of what would happen at trial, plea bargaining too under such a system would move in the wrong direction. That is to say, in a sentencing system modified by the Court's constitutional requirement, plea bargaining would likely lead to sentences that gave greater weight, not to real conduct, but rather to the skill of counsel, the policies of the prosecutor, the caseload, and other factors that vary from place to place, defendant to defendant, and crime to crime. Compared to pre-Guidelines plea bargaining, plea bargaining of this kind would necessarily move federal sentencing in the direction of diminished, not increased, uniformity in sentencing. It would tend to defeat, not to further, Congress' basic statutory goal.

Such a system would have particularly troubling consequences with respect to prosecutorial power. Until now, sentencing factors have come before the judge in the presentence report. But in a sentencing system with the Court's constitutional requirement engrafted onto it, any factor that a prosecutor chose not to charge at the plea negotiation would be placed beyond the reach of the judge entirely. Prosecutors would thus exercise a power the Sentencing Act vested in judges: the power to decide, based on relevant information about the offense and the offender, which defendants merit heavier punishment.

* * *

For all these reasons, Congress, had it been faced with the constitutional jury trial requirement, likely would not have passed the same Sentencing Act. It likely would have found the requirement incompatible with the Act as written. Hence the Act cannot remain valid in its entirety. Severance and excision are necessary.

III

We now turn to the question of *which* portions of the sentencing statute we must sever and excise as inconsistent with the Court's constitutional requirement. * * * [W]e must retain those portions of the Act that are (1) constitutionally valid, (2) capable of "functioning independently," and (3) consistent with Congress' basic objectives in enacting the statute.

Application of these criteria indicates that we must sever and excise two specific statutory provisions: the provision that requires sentencing courts to impose a sentence within the applicable Guidelines range (in the absence of circumstances that justify a departure), see 18 U.S.C. § 3553(b)(1) (Supp.2004), and the provision that sets forth standards of review on appeal, including *de novo* review of departures from the applicable Guidelines range, see § 3742(e) (main ed. and Supp.2004). * * *

* * * Without the "mandatory" provision, the Act nonetheless requires judges to take account of the Guidelines together with other sentencing goals. The Act nonetheless requires judges to consider the Guidelines "sentencing range established for ... the applicable category of offense committed by the applicable category of defendant," the pertinent Sentencing Commission policy statements, the need to avoid unwarranted sentencing disparities, and the need to provide restitution to victims. And the Act nonetheless requires judges to impose sentences that reflect the seriousness of the offense, promote respect for the law, provide just punishment, afford adequate deterrence, protect the public, and effectively provide the defendant with needed educational or vocational training and medical care.

Moreover, * * * the Act continues to provide for appeals from sentencing decisions (irrespective of whether the trial judge sentences within or outside the Guidelines range in the exercise of his discretionary power * * *). We concede that the excision of § 3553(b)(1) requires the excision of a different, appeals-related section, namely § 3742(e) (main ed. and Supp. 2004), which sets forth standards of review on appeal. That section contains critical cross-references to the (now-excised) § 3553(b)(1) and consequently must be severed and excised for similar reasons.

Excision of § 3742(e), however, does not pose a critical problem for the handling of appeals. That is because * * * a statute that does not *explicitly* set forth a standard of review may nonetheless do so *implicitly*. We infer appropriate review standards from related statutory language, the structure of the statute, and the "sound administration of justice." And in this instance those factors, in addition to the past two decades of appellate practice in cases involving departures, imply a practical standard of review already familiar to appellate courts: review for "unreasonable[ness]."

[W]e read the statute as implying this appellate review standard—a standard consistent with appellate sentencing practice during the last two decades. * * *

Finally, the Act without its "mandatory" provision and related language remains consistent with Congress' initial and basic sentencing intent. Congress sought to "provide certainty and fairness in meeting the purposes of sentencing, [while] avoiding unwarranted sentencing disparities ... [and] maintaining sufficient flexibility to permit individualized sentences when warranted." The system remaining after excision, while lacking the mandatory features that Congress enacted, retains other features that help to further these objectives.

As we have said, the Sentencing Commission remains in place, writing Guidelines, collecting information about actual district court sentencing decisions, undertaking research, and revising the Guidelines accordingly. The district courts, while not bound to apply the Guidelines, must consult those Guidelines and take them into account when sentencing. The courts of appeals review sentencing decisions for unreasonableness. These features of the remaining system, while not the system Congress enacted, nonetheless continue to move sentencing in Congress' preferred direction, helping to avoid excessive sentencing disparities while maintaining flexibility sufficient to individualize sentences where necessary. We can find no feature of the remaining system that tends to hinder, rather than to further, these basic objectives. Under these circumstances, why would Congress not have preferred excision of the "mandatory" provision to a system that engrafts

today's constitutional requirement onto the unchanged pre-existing statute—a system that, in terms of Congress' basic objectives, is counterproductive?

* * *

Ours, of course, is not the last word: The ball now lies in Congress'
court. The National Legislature is equipped to devise and install, longterm,
the sentencing system, compatible with the Constitution, that Congress
judges best for the federal system of justice.

IV

* * *

In respondent Booker's case, the District Court applied the Guidelines
as written and imposed a sentence higher than the maximum authorized
solely by the jury's verdict. The Court of Appeals held *Blakely* applicable to
the Guidelines, concluded that Booker's sentence violated the Sixth Amendment, vacated the judgment of the District Court, and remanded for
resentencing. We affirm the judgment of the Court of Appeals and remand
the case. On remand, the District Court should impose a sentence in
accordance with today's opinions, and, if the sentence comes before the
Court of Appeals for review, the Court of Appeals should apply the review
standards set forth in this opinion.

* * *

[W]e must apply today's holdings—both the Sixth Amendment holding
and our remedial interpretation of the Sentencing Act—to all cases on
direct review. That fact does not mean that we believe that every sentence
gives rise to a Sixth Amendment violation. Nor do we believe that every
appeal will lead to a new sentencing hearing. That is because we expect
reviewing courts to apply ordinary prudential doctrines, determining, for
example, whether the issue was raised below and whether it fails the
"plain-error" test. It is also because, in cases not involving a Sixth
Amendment violation, whether resentencing is warranted or whether it will
instead be sufficient to review a sentence for reasonableness may depend
upon application of the harmless-error doctrine.

It is so ordered.

■ JUSTICE STEVENS, with whom JUSTICE SOUTER joins, and with whom JUSTICE
SCALIA joins except for [portions omitted here], dissenting in part.

* * *

The principal basis for the Court's chosen remedy is its assumption
that Congress did not contemplate that the Sixth Amendment would be
violated by depriving the defendant of the right to a jury trial on a factual
issue as important as whether Booker possessed the additional 566 grams
of crack that exponentially increased the maximum sentence that he could

receive. I am not at all sure that that assumption is correct, but even if it is, it does not provide an adequate basis for volunteering a systemwide remedy that Congress has already rejected and could enact on its own if it elected to.

[O]ver 95% of all federal criminal prosecutions are terminated by a plea bargain, and * * * in almost half of the cases that go to trial there are no sentencing enhancements * * *.

[T]he fact that a statute, or any provision of a statute, is unconstitutional in a portion of its applications does not render the statute or provision invalid, and no party suggests otherwise. The Government conceded at oral argument that 45% of federal sentences involve no enhancements. And, according to two U.S. Sentencing Commissioners who testified before Congress * * *, the number of enhancements that would actually implicate a defendant's Sixth Amendment rights is even smaller. Simply stated, the Government's submissions to this Court and to Congress demonstrate that the Guidelines could be constitutionally applied in their entirety, without any modifications, in the "majority of the cases sentenced under the federal guidelines." On the basis of these submissions alone, this Court should have declined to find the Guidelines, or any particular provisions of the Guidelines, facially invalid.

Accordingly, the majority's claim that a jury factfinding requirement would "destroy the system" would at most apply to a *minority* of sentences imposed under the Guidelines. In reality, given that the Government and judges have been apprised of the requirements of the Sixth Amendment, the number of unconstitutional applications would have been even smaller had we allowed them the opportunity to comply with our constitutional holding. This is so for several reasons.

First, it is axiomatic that a defendant may waive his Sixth Amendment right to trial by jury. * * * As the majority concedes, only a tiny fraction of federal prosecutions ever go to trial. If such procedures were followed in the future, our holding * * * would be consequential only in the tiny portion of prospective sentencing decisions that are made after a defendant has been found guilty by a jury.

Second, in the remaining fraction of cases that result in a jury trial, I am confident that those charged with complying with the Guidelines—judges, aided by prosecutors and defense attorneys—could adequately protect defendants' Sixth Amendment rights without this Court's extraordinary remedy. In many cases, prosecutors could avoid [a] problem simply by alleging in the indictment the facts necessary to reach the chosen Guidelines sentence. * * * Enhancing the specificity of indictments would be a simple matter, for example, in prosecutions under the federal drug statutes (such as Booker's prosecution).

Third, even in those trials in which the Guidelines require the finding of facts not alleged in the indictment, such factfinding by a judge is not unconstitutional *per se.* To be clear, our holding in Parts I–III (STEVENS, J. opinion of the Court) does not establish the "impermissibility of judicial factfinding." Instead, judicial factfinding to support an offense level determination or an enhancement is *only unconstitutional when that finding raises the sentence beyond the sentence that could have lawfully been imposed by reference to facts found by the jury or admitted by the defendant.* This distinction is crucial to a proper understanding of why the Guidelines could easily function as they are currently written.

* * *

Rather than engage in a wholesale rewriting of the SRA, I would simply allow the Government to * * * prove any fact that is *required* to increase a defendant's sentence under the Guidelines to a jury beyond a reasonable doubt. * * * [A] requirement of jury factfinding for certain issues can be implemented without difficulty in the vast majority of cases.

* * *

As a matter of policy, the differences between the regime enacted by Congress and the system the Court has chosen are stark. Were there any doubts about whether Congress would have preferred the majority's solution, these are sufficient to dispel them. First, Congress' stated goal of uniformity is eliminated by the majority's remedy. True, judges must still *consider* the sentencing range contained in the Guidelines, but that range is now nothing more than a suggestion that may or may not be persuasive to a judge when weighed against the numerous other considerations listed in 18 U.S.C.A. § 3553(a). The result is certain to be a return to the same type of sentencing disparities Congress sought to eliminate * * *. Those disparities will undoubtedly increase in a discretionary system in which the Guidelines are but one factor a judge must consider in sentencing a defendant within a broad statutory range.

Moreover, the Court has neglected to provide a critical procedural protection that existed prior to the enactment of a binding Guidelines system. Before the SRA, the sentencing judge had the discretion to impose a sentence that designated a minimum term "at the expiration of which the prisoner shall become eligible for parole." Sentencing judges had the discretion to reduce a minimum term of imprisonment upon the recommendation of the Bureau of Prisons. Through these provisions and others, all of which were effectively repealed in 1984, it was the Parole Commission—not the sentencing judge—that was ultimately responsible for determining the length of each defendant's real sentence. Prior to the Guidelines regime, the Parole Commission was designed to reduce sentencing disparities and to provide a check for defendants who had received excessive sentences. Today, the Court reenacts the discretionary Guidelines system that once existed without providing this crucial safety net.

* * *

I respectfully dissent.

■ JUSTICE SCALIA, dissenting in part.

I join the portions of the opinion of the Court that are delivered by Justice STEVENS. I also join Justice STEVENS's dissent * * *. I write separately mainly to add some comments regarding the change that the remedial majority's handiwork has wrought (or perhaps—who can tell?—has not wrought) upon appellate review of federal sentencing.

* * *

Until today, appellate review of sentencing discretion has been limited to instances prescribed by statute. Before the Guidelines, federal appellate courts had little experience reviewing sentences for anything but legal error. "[W]ell-established doctrine," this Court said, "bars [appellate] review of the exercise of sentencing discretion." *Dorszynski v. United States,* 418 U.S. 424, 443, 94 S.Ct. 3042, 41 L.Ed.2d 855 (1974). "[O]nce it is determined that a sentence is within the limitations set forth in the statute under which it is imposed, appellate review is at an end." *Id.,* at 431–432, 94 S.Ct. 3042 (citing cases). * * *

Today's remedial opinion does not even pretend to honor this principle that sentencing discretion is unreviewable except pursuant to specific statutory direction. * * *

The Court claims that "a statute that does not *explicitly* set forth a standard of review may nonetheless do so *implicitly.*" Perhaps so. But we have before us a statute that *does* explicitly set forth a standard of review. The question is, when the Court has *severed* that standard of review (contained in § 3742(e)), does it make any sense to look for some congressional "implication" of a *different* standard of review in the remnants of the statute that the Court has left standing? * * * The Court's need to create a new, "implied" standard of review however "linguistically" "fair"—amounts to a confession that it has exceeded its powers. * * *

Even assuming that the Court ought to be inferring standards of review to stanch the bleeding created by its aggressive severance of § 3742(e), its "unreasonableness" standard is not, as it claims, consistent with the "related statutory language" or with "appellate sentencing practice during the last two decades." * * *

There can be no doubt that the Court's severability analysis has produced a scheme dramatically different from anything Congress has enacted since 1984. Sentencing courts are told to "provide just punishment" (among other things), and appellate courts are told to ensure that district judges are not "unreasonable." The worst feature of the scheme is that no one knows and perhaps no one is meant to know how advisory Guidelines and "unreasonableness" review will function in practice. * * *

* * * Will appellate review for "unreasonableness" preserve *de facto* mandatory Guidelines by discouraging district courts from sentencing

outside Guidelines ranges? Will it simply add another layer of unfettered judicial discretion to the sentencing process? Or will it be a mere formality, used by busy appellate judges only to ensure that busy district judges say all the right things when they explain how they have exercised their newly restored discretion? Time may tell, but today's remedial majority will not.

I respectfully dissent.

■ JUSTICE THOMAS, dissenting in part.

I join Justice STEVENS' opinion for the Court, but I dissent from Justice BREYER's opinion for the Court. While I agree with Justice STEVENS' proposed remedy and much of his analysis, I disagree with [some of his discussion], and thus write separately.

* * *

[N]othing except the Guidelines as written will function in a manner perfectly consistent with the intent of Congress, and the Guidelines as written are unconstitutional in some applications. While all of the remedial possibilities are thus, in a sense, second-best, the solution Justice STEVENS and I would adopt does the least violence to the statutory and regulatory scheme.

* * *

I would hold that § 3553(b)(1) [and certain] provisions of the Guidelines * * *, are unconstitutional as applied to Booker, but that the Government has not overcome the presumption of severability. Accordingly, the unconstitutional application of the scheme in Booker's case is severable from the constitutional applications of the same scheme to other defendants. I respectfully dissent from the Court's contrary conclusion.

■ JUSTICE BREYER, with whom THE CHIEF JUSTICE, JUSTICE O'CONNOR, and JUSTICE KENNEDY join, dissenting in part.

The Court today applies its decisions in *Apprendi v. New Jersey,* 530 U.S. 466, 120 S.Ct. 2348, 147 L.Ed.2d 435 (2000), and *Blakely v. Washington,* 542 U.S. 296, 124 S.Ct. 2531, 159 L.Ed.2d 403 (2004), to the Federal Sentencing Guidelines. The Court holds that the Sixth Amendment requires a jury, not a judge, to find sentencing facts—facts about the *way* in which an offender committed the crime—where those facts would move an offender from lower to higher Guidelines ranges. I disagree with the Court's conclusion. I find nothing in the Sixth Amendment that forbids a sentencing judge to determine (as judges at sentencing have traditionally determined) the *manner* or *way* in which the offender carried out the crime of which he was convicted.

* * *

■ THE CHIEF JUSTICE, JUSTICE O'CONNOR, JUSTICE KENNEDY, and I have previously explained at length why we cannot accept the Court's constitutional analysis. * * *

Although [these] considerations * * * did not dissuade the Court from its holdings in *Apprendi* and *Blakely,* I should have hoped they would have dissuaded the Court from extending those holdings to the statute and Guidelines at issue here. Legal logic does not require that extension, for there are key differences.

First, the Federal Guidelines are not statutes. The rules they set forth are *administrative,* not statutory, in nature. Members, not of Congress, but of a Judicial Branch Commission, wrote those rules. The rules do not "establis[h] minimum and maximum penalties' for individual crimes, but guide sentencing judges to do what they have done for generations—impose sentences within the broad limits established by Congress." The rules do not create a new set of legislatively determined sentences so much as they reflect, organize, rationalize, and modify an old set of judicially determined pre-Guidelines sentences. Thus, the rules do not, in *Apprendi's* words, set forth a "prescribed *statutory* maximum," (emphasis added), as the law has traditionally understood that phrase.

* * *

More importantly, there is less justification for applying an *Apprendi*-type constitutional rule where administrative guidelines, not statutes, are at issue. The Court applies its constitutional rule to statutes in part to avoid what *Blakely* sees as a serious problem, namely, a legislature's ability to make of a particular fact an "element" of a crime or a sentencing factor, at will. That problem—that legislative temptation is severely diminished when Commission Guidelines are at issue, for the Commission cannot create "elements" of crimes. It cannot write rules that "bind or regulate the primary conduct of the public." Rather, it must write rules that reflect what the law has traditionally understood as sentencing factors. That is to say, the Commission cannot switch between "elements" and "sentencing factors" at will because it cannot write substantive criminal statutes at all.

At the same time, to extend *Blakely's* holding to administratively written sentencing rules risks added legal confusion and uncertainty. Read literally, *Blakely's* language would include within *Apprendi's* strictures a host of nonstatutory sentencing determinations, including appellate court decisions delineating the limits of the legally "reasonable." (Imagine an appellate opinion that says a sentence for ordinary robbery greater than five years is unreasonably long unless a special factor, such as possession of a gun, is present.) Indeed, read literally, *Blakely's* holding would apply to a single judge's determination of the factors that make a particular sentence disproportionate or proportionate. (Imagine a single judge setting forth, as a binding rule of law, the legal proposition about robbery sentences just mentioned.) Appellate courts' efforts to define the limits of the "reasonable" of course would fall outside *Blakely's* scope. But they would do so, *not because they escape Blakely's literal language,* but because they are not *legislative* efforts to create limits. Neither are the Guidelines *legislative* efforts.

Second, the sentencing statutes at issue in *Blakely* imposed absolute constraints on a judge's sentencing discretion, while the federal sentencing statutes here at issue do not. As the *Blakely* Court emphasized, the Washington statutes authorized a higher-than-standard sentence on the basis of a factual finding *only if* the fact in question was a new fact—*i.e.,* a fact that did not constitute an element of the crime of conviction or an element of any more serious or additional crime. A judge applying those statutes could not even consider, much less impose, an exceptional sentence, unless he found facts " 'other than those which are used in computing the standard range sentence for the offense.' "

The federal sentencing statutes, however, offer a defendant no such fact-related assurance. As long as "there exists an aggravating or mitigating circumstance of a kind, or to a degree, not adequately taken into consideration by the Sentencing Commission," they permit a judge to depart from a Guidelines sentence based on facts that constitute elements of the crime (say, a bank robbery involving a threat to use a weapon, where the weapon in question is nerve gas). Whether departure-triggering circumstances exist in a particular case is a matter for a court, not for Congress, to decide.

Thus, as far as the federal *statutes* are concerned, the federal system, unlike the state system at issue in *Blakely,* provides a defendant with no guarantee that the jury's finding of factual elements will result in a sentence lower than the statutory maximum. Rather, the statutes put a potential federal defendant on notice that a judge conceivably might sentence him anywhere within the range provided by *statute*—regardless of the applicable Guidelines range. Hence as a practical matter, they grant a potential federal defendant less assurance of a lower Guidelines sentence than did the state statutes at issue in *Blakely.*

* * *

For these reasons, I respectfully dissent.

Page 1189.   Insert the following new notes after *Booker*:

1. Is a sentencing guideline scheme advisory or mandatory? The California Determinate Sentencing Law (DSL) provides three terms of imprisonment for offenses—a lower, middle, and upper term sentence. A judge is to impose the middle term unless "there are circumstances in aggravation or mitigation of the crime." In *Cunningham v. California*, 549 U.S. 270, 127 S.Ct. 856, 166 L.Ed.2d 856 (2007), three members of the Supreme Court argued that the California scheme was no different than the post-*Booker* federal scheme and thus constitutionally acceptable. They reasoned in part that the California scheme does not require the finding of an aggravating *fact* as is required to trigger *Apprendi's* rule as applied in *Booker*. 549 U.S. at 307–08, 127 S.Ct. at 879 (Alito, J., dissenting). The *Cunningham* majority, however, concluded that as a practical matter the DSL requires factual findings for imposition of the upper term sentence. Further:

California's DSL does not resemble the advisory system the *Booker* Court had in view. Under California's system, judges are not free to exercise their "discretion to select a specific sentence within a defined range."

549 U.S. at 292, 127 S.Ct. at 870. Thus the California statutory scheme was unconstitutional.

2. Appellate review of federal sentences after *Booker*. Contrary to the material in Note 4 on page 1187 of the casebook, in a post-*Booker* world federal appellate courts no longer review for conformity with the guidelines, but rather appellate review is limited to determining whether sentences are "reasonable" under an abuse-of-discretion standard.

3. Appellate presumptions of reasonableness. In *Rita v. United States*, 551 U.S. 338, 127 S.Ct. 2456, 168 L.Ed.2d 203 (2007) , the majority concluded such a presumption was permissible although it may encourage district judges to impose Guidelines sentences. This does not *forbid* district judges from imposing—on the basis of jury-determined facts alone—a sentence higher than the Guidelines provide. Moreover, neither trial nor appellate courts may presume that outside Guideline range sentences are unreasonable, as this would transform the now-advisory Federal Sentencing Guidelines back into mandatory ones. 551 U.S. at 351–53, 127 S.Ct. at 2465–66.

In *Gall v. United States*, 552 U.S. 38, 128 S.Ct. 586, 169 L.Ed.2d 445 (2007) (slip op. at 8–11), the district court's below Guideline drug trafficking conspiracy sentence (probation rather than 37 months), based on defendant's youth, rehabilitation, and voluntary withdrawal from the conspiracy, was reversed by the Eighth Circuit on the ground that a sentence outside the Federal Sentencing Guideline range must be supported by "extraordinary circumstances." A seven-member majority of the Supreme Court reinstated the original sentence after concluding that "applying a heightened standard of review ... is inconsistent with the rule that the abuse-of-discretion standard of review applies to appellate review of all sentencing decisions—whether inside or outside the Guidelines range." 552 U.S. at 49, 128 S.Ct. at 596.

4. District court disagreement with policy positions reflected in Guidelines. The Supreme Court has emphasized that district courts are entitled to reject and vary categorically from at least some of the Guidelines based on policy disagreements with those guidelines. Spears v. United States, 555 U.S. 261, 129 S.Ct. 840, 172 L.Ed.2d 596 (2009) (per curiam); Kimbrough v. United States, 552 U.S. 85, 128 S.Ct. 558, 169 L.Ed.2d 481 (2007). Both *Spears* and *Kimbrough* involved district judges who declined to follow the Guideline provision subjecting a defendant dealing in crack cocaine to the same sentence as one dealing in 100 times more powder cocaine. *Booker*, the Court made clear, established that the district judges were entitled to do this. Further, the district judge in *Spears* did not err in explicitly adopting a 20:1 ratio to replace the Guidelines 100:1 ratio.

5. Facts necessary for multiple sentences to run consecutively rather than concurrently. Jurisdictions differ on the making of the decision as to whether sentences for multiple offenses imposed on a defendant run concurrently or consecutively. Some leave this completely within the discretion of the sentencing judge. Some provide that sentences are to run concurrently unless the sentencing judge finds good cause for, and orders, them to run consecutively. Others, including

Oregon, require that a sentencing judge find certain facts before making multiple sentences run consecutively.

In Oregon v. Ice, 555 U.S. 160, 129 S.Ct. 711, 172 L.Ed.2d 517 (2009), the Supreme Court considered whether in jurisdictions of the last sort *Apprendi* gives a defendant a right to have a jury find the facts essential to imposition of consecutive sentences. In applying *Apprendi*, the *Ice* majority stressed, the Court has "considered whether the finding of a particular fact was understood as within 'the domain of the jury . . . by those who framed the Bill of Rights.' In undertaking this inquiry, we remain cognizant that administration of a discrete criminal justice system is among the basic sovereign prerogatives States retain."

Historically, *Ice* noted, juries have had no role in deciding whether sentences run consecutively. The Court continued:

> In light of this history, legislative reforms regarding the imposition of multiple sentences do not implicate the core concerns that prompted our decision in *Apprendi*. There is no encroachment here by the judge upon facts historically found by the jury, nor any threat to the jury's domain as a bulwark at trial between the State and the accused. Instead, the defendant-who historically may have faced consecutive sentences by default-has been granted by some modern legislatures statutory protections meant to temper the harshness of the historical practice.

555 U.S., at ___, 129 S.Ct., at 718. States' prerogative to fashion criminal justice systems also argued against construing *Apprendi* to bar consecutive sentences on judge-made factual determinations:

> [S]tate legislative innovations like Oregon's seek to rein in the discretion judges possessed at common law to impose consecutive sentences at will. Limiting judicial discretion to impose consecutive sentences serves the "salutary objectives" of promoting sentences proportionate to "the gravity of the offense," and of reducing disparities in sentence length. All agree that a scheme making consecutive sentences the rule, and concurrent sentences the exception, encounters no Sixth Amendment shoal. To hem in States by holding that they may not equally choose to make concurrent sentences the rule, and consecutive sentences the exception, would make scant sense. Neither *Apprendi* nor our Sixth Amendment traditions compel straitjacketing the States in that manner.

555 U.S., at ___, 129 S.Ct., at 719. Consequently, a 5–to–4 majority held, *Apprendi* does not apply to the finding of facts necessary to imposing consecutive sentences.

C. PROCEDURAL ISSUES IN SENTENCING

1. DEVELOPMENT OF SENTENCING INFORMATION

Page 1193. Add the following after Rule 32:

NOTE

Federal Rules of Criminal Procedure Rule 32.1. On April 29, 2002, the Court transmitted to Congress a proposed Rule 32.1 to specify procedures for the revocation of probation or supervised release—conditional release from prison. Rule 32.1 became effective December 1, 2002:

Rule 32.1. Revoking or Modifying Probation or Supervised Release

(a) Initial Appearance

(1) *Person In Custody.* A person held in custody for violating probation or supervised release must be taken without unnecessary delay before a magistrate judge.

(A) If the person is held in custody in the district where an alleged violation occurred, the initial appearance must be in that district.

(B) If the person is held in custody in a district other than where an alleged violation occurred, the initial appearance must be in that district, or in an adjacent district if the appearance can occur more promptly there.

(2) *Upon a Summons.* When a person appears in response to a summons for violating probation or supervised release, a magistrate judge must proceed under this rule.

(3) *Advice.* The judge must inform the person of the following:

(A) the alleged violation of probation or supervised release;

(B) the person's right to retain counselor to request that counsel be appointed if the person cannot obtain counsel; and

(C) the person's right, if held in custody, to a preliminary hearing under Rule 32.1(b)(1).

(4) *Appearance in the District With Jurisdiction* [omitted]

(5) *Appearance in a District Lacking Jurisdiction* [omitted].

(6) *Release* or *Detention.* The magistrate judge may release or detain the person under 18 U.S.C. § 3143(a) pending further proceedings. The burden of establishing that the person will not flee or pose a danger to any other person or to the community rests with the person.

(b) Revocation.

(1) *Preliminary Hearing.*

(A) *In General.* If a person is in custody for violating a condition of probation or supervised release, a magistrate judge must promptly conduct a hearing to determine whether there is probable cause to believe that a violation occurred. The person may waive the hearing.

(B) *Requirements.* The hearing must be recorded by a court reporter or by a suitable recording device. The judge must give the person:

(i) notice of the hearing and its purpose, the alleged violation, and the person's right to retain counselor to request that counsel be appointed if the person cannot obtain counsel;

(ii) an opportunity to appear at the hearing and present evidence; and

(iii) upon request, an opportunity to question any adverse witness, unless the judge determines that the interest of justice does not require the witness to appear.

(C) *Referral.* If the judge finds probable cause, the judge must conduct a revocation hearing. If the judge does not find probable cause, the judge must dismiss the proceeding.

(2) *Revocation Hearing.* Unless waived by the person, the court must hold the revocation hearing within a reasonable time in the district having jurisdiction. The person is entitled to:

(A) written notice of the alleged violation;

(B) disclosure of the evidence against the person;

(C) an opportunity to appear, present evidence, and question any adverse witness unless the court determines that the interest of justice does not require the witness to appear; and

(D) notice of the person's right to retain counsel or to request that counsel be appointed if the person cannot obtain counsel.

(c) Modification.

(1) *In General.* Before modifying the conditions of probation or supervised release, the court must hold a hearing, at which the person has the right to counsel.

(2) *Exceptions.* A hearing is not required if:

(A) the person waives the hearing; or

(B) the relief sought is favorable to the person and does not extend the term of probation or of supervised release; and

(C) an attorney for the government has received notice of the relief sought, has had a reasonable opportunity to object, and has not done so.

(d) Disposition of the Case [omitted].

D. ALTERNATIVES OR SUPPLEMENTS TO INCARCERATION

1. PROBATION

Page 1213. Add the following to Note 3:

The respondent in United States v. Knights, 534 U.S. 112, 122 S.Ct. 587, 151 L.Ed.2d 497 (2001) was placed on probation by a California state court on conditions that included a search condition similar to that of People v. Mason. Subsequently, a law enforcement officer was investigating respondent for various acts of vandalism against the property of a public utility. With knowledge of that probation condition, and upon reasonable suspicion that incriminating evidence would be found in Knights' apartment, the officer conducted a warrantless search of the apartment that resulted in the seizure of incriminating evidence. The seizure lead to a federal criminal prosecution, but the United States District Court suppressed the evidence seized in the apartment search on the ground that the search was conducted for investigatory rather than probationary purposes and, therefore, was required to meet normal Fourth Amendment standards rather than the lesser standard of Griffin v. Wisconsin. The Ninth Circuit affirmed, but the Supreme Court in an opinion by The Chief Justice, reversed.

The Court avoided ruling on the constitutionality of the search condition as a waiver of Fourth Amendment rights. Instead, it confined its ruling to situations in which a probation or law enforcement officer has reasonable suspicion of criminal activity. In that circumstance, an officer may conduct a warrantless search of the probationer's residence:

> The State has a dual concern with a probationer. On the one hand is the hope that he will successfully complete probation and be integrated back into the community. On the other is the concern, quite justified, that he will be more likely to engage in criminal conduct than an ordinary member of the community. The view of the Court of Appeals in this case would require the State to shut its eyes to the latter concern and concentrate only on the former. But we hold that the Fourth Amendment does not put the State to such a choice. Its interest in apprehending violators of the criminal law, thereby protecting potential victims of criminal enterprise, may therefore justifiably focus on probationers in a way that it does not on the ordinary citizen.

> We hold that the balance of these considerations requires no more than reasonable suspicion to conduct a search of this probationer's house. The degree of individualized suspicion required of a search is a determination of when there is a sufficiently high probability that criminal conduct is occurring to make the intrusion on the individual's privacy interest reasonable. * * * Although the Fourth Amendment ordinarily requires the degree of probability embodied in the term "probable cause," a lesser degree satisfies the Constitution when the balance of governmental and private interests makes such a standard reasonable. See, e.g., Terry v. Ohio, 392 U.S. 1, 88 S.Ct. 1868, 20 L.Ed.2d 889 (1968); United States v. Brignoni-Ponce, 422 U.S. 873, 95 S.Ct. 2574, 45 L.Ed.2d 607 (1975). Those interests warrant a lesser than probable-cause standard here. When an officer has reasonable suspicion that a probationer subject to a search condition is engaged in criminal activity, there is enough likelihood that criminal conduct is occurring that an intrusion on the probationer's significantly diminished privacy interests is reasonable.

534 U.S. at 120–21, 122 S.Ct. at 592–93, 151 L.Ed.2d at 506–07. The Court held that the same circumstances justified dispensing with the requirement of a warrant for a residential search.

The officer in *Knights* was aware of the probationer's search condition. Under the rationale of the Court, should the result be different if he had not been aware of it? If he had been unaware even that the target of the search was on probation? If there had been no such search condition?

The Court upheld a completely suspicionless search of a parolee by a police officer where as required by statute the parolee had agreed to submit to such searches as a condition of parole. Samson v. California, 547 U.S. 843, 126 S.Ct. 2193, 165 L.Ed.2d 250 (2006), discussed in the material supplementing page 279 of the text. But this holding rested at least in part on the Court's conclusion that parole is more akin to imprisonment than is probation and therefore parolees "have fewer expectations of privacy than probationers." 547 U.S. at 848–50, 126 S.Ct. at 2197.

4. INVOLUNTARY COMMITMENT OF "SEXUAL PREDATORS"

Page 1247. Add the following before Section 5:

NOTES

1. **Determining that confinement is civil.** In Seling v. Young, 531 U.S. 250, 121 S.Ct. 727, 148 L.Ed.2d 734 (2001), the Washington Supreme Court had declared that its state's commitment of sexual predators statute, which is similar to the Kansas statute, is civil in nature. Nevertheless, the Ninth Circuit held that double jeopardy and *ex post facto* standards could be used to evaluate the constitutionality of the statute on an "as applied" basis. The United States Supreme Court, in an opinion by Justice O'Connor, reversed the Ninth Circuit. Once it has been determined under the analysis used in Kansas v. Hendricks that the statute is civil, that precludes using double jeopardy and *ex post facto* analyses of the scheme as applied. An as applied approach is unworkable:

> We hold that respondent cannot obtain release through an "as-applied" challenge to the Washington Act on double jeopardy and ex post facto grounds. We agree with petitioner that an "as-applied" analysis would prove unworkable. Such an analysis would never conclusively resolve whether a particular scheme is punitive and would thereby prevent a final determination of the scheme's validity under the Double Jeopardy and Ex Post Facto Clauses. * * * Unlike a fine, confinement is not a fixed event. As petitioner notes, it extends over time under conditions that are subject to change. The particular features of confinement may affect how a confinement scheme is evaluated to determine whether it is civil rather than punitive, but it remains no less true that the query must be answered definitively. The civil nature of a confinement scheme cannot be altered based merely on vagaries in the implementation of the authorizing statute.

531 U.S. at 263, 121 S.Ct. at 735, 148 L.Ed.2d at 746–47. Respondent was complaining primarily about the conditions of confinement. The Court noted that he has state remedies available to address those concerns:

> Our decision today does not mean that respondent and others committed as sexually violent predators have no remedy for the alleged conditions and treatment regime at the Center [where respondent is confined]. The text of the Washington Act states that those confined under its authority have the right to adequate care and individualized treatment. * * * As petitioner acknowledges, if the Center fails to fulfill its statutory duty, those confined may have a state law cause of action. * * * It is for the Washington courts to determine whether the Center is operating in accordance with state law and provide a remedy.

531 U.S. at 265, 121 S.Ct. at 736, 148 L.Ed.2d at 748.

2. **The requirement of difficulty in controlling behavior.** The respondent in Kansas v. Crane, 534 U.S. 407, 122 S.Ct. 867, 151 L.Ed.2d 856 (2002) was committed under the same statute that the Court in Kansas v. Hendricks upheld. In this litigation, the Kansas Supreme Court interpreted *Hendricks* to require a showing the person lacks any ability to control the prohibited behavior as a predicate to commitment. The Supreme Court, in an opinion by Justice Breyer, disagreed with that interpretation. Total inability to control is not required.

Instead, the State must show that the person has difficulty in controlling that behavior but need not show a total absence of volition. Total lack of control might be impossible to prove if it were required as a predicate to commitment: "Insistence upon absolute lack of control would risk barring the civil commitment of highly dangerous persons suffering severe mental abnormalities." 534 U.S. at 412, 122 S.Ct. at 870, 151 L.Ed.2d at 862.

The State argued that no requirement of lack of control is constitutionally required to be shown for civil commitment. However, the Court also rejected that position. Instead, it adopted a constitutional requirement of a showing of some (although not total) impairment:

> *Hendricks* underscored the constitutional importance of distinguishing a dangerous sexual offender subject to civil commitment "from other dangerous persons who are perhaps more properly dealt with exclusively through criminal proceedings." * * * That distinction is necessary lest "civil commitment" become a "mechanism for retribution or general deterrence"—functions properly those of criminal law, not civil commitment. * * * The presence of what the "psychiatric profession itself classifie[d] ... as a serious mental disorder" helped to make that distinction in *Hendricks*. And a critical distinguishing feature of that "serious ... disorder" there consisted of a special and serious lack of ability to control behavior.
>
> In recognizing that fact, we did not give to the phrase "lack of control" a particularly narrow or technical meaning. And we recognize that in cases where lack of control is at issue, "inability to control behavior" will not be demonstrable with mathematical precision. It is enough to say that there must be proof of serious difficulty in controlling behavior. And this, when viewed in light of such features of the case as the nature of the psychiatric diagnosis, and the severity of the mental abnormality itself, must be sufficient to distinguish the dangerous sexual offender whose serious mental illness, abnormality, or disorder subjects him to civil commitment from the dangerous but typical recidivist convicted in an ordinary criminal case. * * *

534 U.S. at 412–13, 122 S.Ct. at 870, 151 L.Ed.2d at 862–63.

3. **Sex offender treatment in prison.** The respondent in McKune v. Lile, 536 U.S. 24, 122 S.Ct. 2017, 153 L.Ed.2d 47 (2002) was incarcerated in a Kansas state prison. Officials offered him the opportunity to participate in an in-prison sex offender treatment program. As a prerequisite to participating, respondent was required to acknowledge all prior sex offenses. The state offered no immunity for doing so and made no promises not to prosecute, although it had never done so based on such disclosures. Lile refused to participate, claiming Fifth Amendment grounds. As a result, his privilege status was reduced, which adversely impacted his visitation rights, earnings, work opportunities, ability to send money to family, canteen expenditures, access to a personal television and other privileges. In addition, he was transferred from a medium security to a maximum security unit and from a two-person to a four-person cell. He refused to participate knowing of those consequences for failing to acknowledge prior sex offenses. A United States District Court and the Court of Appeals held that placing those burdens on waiver of the Fifth Amendment privilege against compelled self-incrimination was unconstitutional. However, the Supreme Court, in a plurality opinion by Justice Kennedy, reversed.

Justice Kennedy stated that there are valid penological reasons for the incentive system created by prison officials. Transfer was to make room for inmates who wished to participate in the program. The sex offender treatment program was a good faith rehabilitation program, not a sham to gather information for criminal prosecution. It does not create an unconstitutional burden on the exercise of the privilege against compelled self-incrimination. Justice Kennedy explained the logic of the Kansas incentive system:

> Acceptance of responsibility is the beginning of rehabilitation. And a recognition that there are rewards for those who attempt to reform is a vital and necessary step toward completion. The Court of Appeals' ruling would defeat these objectives. If the State sought to comply with the ruling by allowing respondent to enter the program while still insisting on his innocence, there would be little incentive for other SATP participants to confess and accept counseling; indeed, there is support for Kansas' view that the dynamics of the group therapy would be impaired. If the State had to offer immunity, the practical effect would be that serial offenders who are incarcerated for but one violation would be given a windfall for past bad conduct, a result potentially destructive of any public or state support for the program and quite at odds with the dominant goal of acceptance of responsibility. If the State found it was forced to graduate prisoners from its rehabilitation program without knowing what other offenses they may have committed, the integrity of its program would be very much in doubt. If the State found it had to comply by allowing respondent the same perquisites as those who accept counseling, the result would be a dramatic illustration that obduracy has the same rewards as acceptance, and so the program itself would become self-defeating, even hypo-critical, in the eyes of those whom it seeks to help. The Fifth Amendment does not require the State to suffer these programmatic disruptions when it seeks to rehabilitate those who are incarcerated for valid, final convictions.
>
> The Kansas SATP represents a sensible approach to reducing the serious danger that repeat sex offenders pose to many innocent persons, most often children. The State's interest in rehabilitation is undeniable. There is, further-more, no indication that the SATP is merely an elaborate ruse to skirt the protections of the privilege against compelled self-incrimination. Rather, the program allows prison administrators to provide to those who need treatment the incentive to seek it.

536 U.S. at 47–48, 122 S.Ct. at 2032. Justice O'Connor concurred in the judgment. Justice Stevens, joined by Justices Souter, Ginsburg and Breyer, dissented.

4. **Federal Sexual Predator Statute.** A federal statute, similar to the state sexual predator statutes, authorizes the United States Department of Justice to obtain civil commitment of a sexually dangerous person about to be released from federal confinement resulting from conviction for a federal crime. 42 U.S.C. § 4248. The authority of Congress to enact this provision was at issue in United States v. Comstock, ___ U.S. ___, 130 S.Ct. 1949, 176 L.Ed.2d 878 (2010). By a 7 to 2 vote, the Supreme Court held Congress has this power under Article I, section 8's authorization to make all law necessary and proper for carrying into execution the powers vested in the federal government. Essentially, the majority reasoned, the power to enact specific federal crimes also includes the power to provide for those who commit such offenses and remain dangerous at the expiration of their term of imprisonment. "We do not reach or decide," the Court noted, "any claim that the statute or its application denies equal protection of the laws, procedural or substan-tive due process, or any other rights guaranteed by the Constitution." ___ U.S. at ___, 130 S.Ct. at 1965.

5.   ENHANCED PUNISHMENT UNDER RECIDIVIST PROVISIONS

Page 1256.   Add the following Note at the end of the page:

NOTE

In Shepard v. United States, 544 U.S. 13, 125 S.Ct. 1254, 161 L.Ed.2d 205 (2005), the Supreme Court construed the Armed Career Criminal Act (the "ACCA"), 18 U.S.C. § 922. Under the ACCA, a mandatory minimum sentence must be imposed upon conviction of a defendant for possession of a firearm after three prior convictions for serious drug offenses or violent felonies. Burglary is defined as a violent felony only if it is committed in a building or enclosed space. At issue in *Shepard* was how a sentencing court must go about determining whether a prior conviction for burglary, resting on a plea of guilty, was for a burglary that constitutes a violent felony under the Act. A majority of the Court held that a sentencing court is generally limited to considering the statutory definition of the crime, the charging instrument, any written plea agreement, a transcript of the plea colloquy, any explicit factual findings by the trial to judge to which the defendant assented, or "some comparable judicial record." The sentencing court may not consider such sources as police reports or complaint applications. In a portion of Justice Souter's opinion joined by only three other Justices, he defended this position as based in part on the need to so construe the ACCA to avoid a serious risk of the Act being unconstitutional under *Apprendi v. New Jersey,* reprinted in Chapter 23 of this Supplement.

If the ACCA permitted consideration of sources such as police reports, Justice Souter reasoned, it would create a factual issue on which defendants might, under *Apprendi* and despite *Almendarez–Torres,* have a right to jury trial:

> While the disputed fact here can be described as a fact about a prior conviction, it is too far removed from the conclusive significance of a prior judicial record, and too much like the findings subject to *Jones* and *Apprendi,* to say that *Almendarez–Torres* clearly authorizes a judge to resolve the dispute.

544 U.S. at 25, 125 S.Ct. at 1262.

Three *Shepard* dissenters commented that this was a "hint at extending the *Apprendi* rule to the issue of ACCA prior crimes * * *." 544 U.S. at 38, 125 S.Ct. at 1270 (O'Connor, J., dissenting). Justice Thomas opined that *Amendarez–Torres* has been eroded by the Court's Sixth Amendment jurisprudence, a majority of the Court recognizes that it was wrongly decided, and "in an appropriate case, this Court should consider *Almendarez–Torres'* continued viability." 544 U.S. at 27, 125 S.Ct. at 1264 (Thomas, J., concurring in part and concurring in the judgment).

Page 1256.   Add the following two new sections at the bottom of the page:

6.   REMOVAL OF A RESIDENT ALIEN FROM THE UNITED STATES

Padilla v. Kentucky

Supreme Court of the United States, 2010.
___ U.S. ___, 130 S.Ct. 1473, 176 L.Ed.2d 284.

■ JUSTICE STEVENS delivered the opinion of the Court.

Petitioner Jose Padilla, a native of Honduras, has been a lawful permanent resident of the United States for more than 40 years. Padilla served this Nation with honor as a member of the U.S. Armed Forces during the Vietnam War. He now faces deportation after pleading guilty to the transportation of a large amount of marijuana in his tractor-trailer in the Commonwealth of Kentucky.

In this postconviction proceeding, Padilla claims that his counsel not only failed to advise him of this consequence prior to his entering the plea, but also told him that he " 'did not have to worry about immigration status since he had been in the country so long.' " Padilla relied on his counsel's erroneous advice when he pleaded guilty to the drug charges that made his deportation virtually mandatory. He alleges that he would have insisted on going to trial if he had not received incorrect advice from his attorney.

Assuming the truth of his allegations, the Supreme Court of Kentucky denied Padilla postconviction relief without the benefit of an evidentiary hearing. The court held that the Sixth Amendment's guarantee of effective assistance of counsel does not protect a criminal defendant from erroneous advice about deportation because it is merely a "collateral" consequence of his conviction. In its view, neither counsel's failure to advise petitioner about the possibility of removal, nor counsel's incorrect advice, could provide a basis for relief.

We granted certiorari to decide whether, as a matter of federal law, Padilla's counsel had an obligation to advise him that the offense to which he was pleading guilty would result in his removal from this country. * * *

I

The landscape of federal immigration law has changed dramatically over the last 90 years. While once there was only a narrow class of deportable offenses and judges wielded broad discretionary authority to prevent deportation, immigration reforms over time have expanded the class of deportable offenses and limited the authority of judges to alleviate the harsh consequences of deportation. The "drastic measure" of deportation or removal, is now virtually inevitable for a vast number of noncitizens convicted of crimes.

The Nation's first 100 years was "a period of unimpeded immigration." * * * It was not until 1875 that Congress first passed a statute barring convicts and prostitutes from entering the country. In 1891, Congress added to the list of excludable persons those "who have been convicted of a felony or other infamous crime or misdemeanor involving moral turpitude."

The Immigration and Nationality Act of 1917 (1917 Act) brought "radical changes" to our law * * * because it authorized deportation as a consequence of certain convictions, [but] the Act also included a critically important procedural protection to minimize the risk of unjust deportation:

At the time of sentencing or within 30 days thereafter, the sentencing judge in both state and federal prosecutions had the power to make a recommendation "that such alien shall not be deported." This procedure, known as a judicial recommendation against deportation, or JRAD, had the effect of binding the Executive to prevent deportation; the statute was "consistently . . . interpreted as giving the sentencing judge conclusive authority to decide whether a particular conviction should be disregarded as a basis for deportation." Thus, from 1917 forward, there was no such creature as an automatically deportable offense. Even as the class of deportable offenses expanded, judges retained discretion to ameliorate unjust results on a case-by-case basis.

Although narcotics offenses—such as the offense at issue in this case—provided a distinct basis for deportation as early as 1922, the JRAD procedure was generally available to avoid deportation in narcotics convictions. Except for "technical, inadvertent and insignificant violations of the laws relating to narcotics," it appears that courts treated narcotics offenses as crimes involving moral turpitude for purposes of the 1917 Act's broad JRAD provision.

[T]he JRAD procedure is no longer part of our law. Congress first circumscribed the JRAD provision in the 1952 Immigration and Nationality Act (INA), and in 1990 Congress entirely eliminated it. In 1996, Congress also eliminated the Attorney General's authority to grant discretionary relief from deportation, an authority that had been exercised to prevent the deportation of over 10,000 noncitizens during the 5-year period prior to 1996. Under contemporary law, if a noncitizen has committed a removable offense after the 1996 effective date of these amendments, his removal is practically inevitable but for the possible exercise of limited remnants of equitable discretion vested in the Attorney General to cancel removal for noncitizens convicted of particular classes of offenses.[6] Subject to limited exceptions, this discretionary relief is not available for an offense related to trafficking in a controlled substance.

These changes to our immigration law have dramatically raised the stakes of a noncitizen's criminal conviction. The importance of accurate legal advice for noncitizens accused of crimes has never been more important. These changes confirm our view that, as a matter of federal law, deportation is an integral part—indeed, sometimes the most important part—of the penalty that may be imposed on noncitizen defendants who plead guilty to specified crimes.

II

Before deciding whether to plead guilty, a defendant is entitled to "the effective assistance of competent counsel." [*Strickland v. Washington*, 466

---

6. The changes to our immigration law have also involved a change in nomenclature; the statutory text now uses the term "removal" rather than "deportation."

U.S. 668, 686, 104 S.Ct. 2052, 80 L.Ed.2d 674 (1984).] The Supreme Court of Kentucky rejected Padilla's ineffectiveness claim on the ground that the advice he sought about the risk of deportation concerned only "collateral matters, *i.e.,* those matters not within the sentencing authority of the state trial court. In its view, collateral consequences are outside the scope of representation required by the Sixth Amendment," and, therefore, the "failure of defense counsel to advise the defendant of possible deportation consequences is not cognizable as a claim for ineffective assistance of counsel." The Kentucky high court is far from alone in this view.

We, however, have never applied a distinction between direct and collateral consequences to define the scope of constitutionally "reasonable professional assistance" required under *Strickland.* Whether that distinction is appropriate is a question we need not consider in this case because of the unique nature of deportation.

We have long recognized that deportation is a particularly severe "penalty," but it is not, in a strict sense, a criminal sanction. Although removal proceedings are civil in nature, deportation is nevertheless intimately related to the criminal process. Our law has enmeshed criminal convictions and the penalty of deportation for nearly a century. And, importantly, recent changes in our immigration law have made removal nearly an automatic result for a broad class of noncitizen offenders. Thus, we find it "most difficult" to divorce the penalty from the conviction in the deportation context. Moreover, we are quite confident that noncitizen defendants facing a risk of deportation for a particular offense find it even more difficult.

Deportation as a consequence of a criminal conviction is, because of its close connection to the criminal process, uniquely difficult to classify as either a direct or a collateral consequence. The collateral versus direct distinction is thus ill-suited to evaluating a *Strickland* claim concerning the specific risk of deportation. We conclude that advice regarding deportation is not categorically removed from the ambit of the Sixth Amendment right to counsel. *Strickland* applies to Padilla's claim.

III

Under *Strickland,* we first determine whether counsel's representation "fell below an objective standard of reasonableness." Then we ask whether "there is a reasonable probability that, but for counsel's unprofessional errors, the result of the proceeding would have been different." The first prong—constitutional deficiency—is necessarily linked to the practice and expectations of the legal community * * *.

The weight of prevailing professional norms supports the view that counsel must advise her client regarding the risk of deportation. "[A]uthorities of every stripe-including the American Bar Association, criminal defense and public defender organizations, authoritative treatises, and state and city bar publications-universally require defense attorneys to advise as to the risk of deportation consequences for non-citizen clients. . . .'' Brief for Legal Ethics, Criminal Procedure, and Criminal Law Professors as *Amici Curiae* 12–14 (footnotes omitted).

We too have previously recognized that " '[p]reserving the client's right to remain in the United States may be more important to the client than any potential jail sentence.' " Likewise, we have recognized that "preserving the possibility of" discretionary relief from deportation under § 212(c) of the 1952 INA, 66 Stat. 187, repealed by Congress in 1996, "would have been one of the principal benefits sought by defendants deciding whether to accept a plea offer or instead to proceed to trial." [INS v. St. Cyr, 533 U.S. 289, 323, 121 S.Ct. 2271, 150 L.Ed.2d 347 (2001).] We expected that counsel who were unaware of the discretionary relief measures would "follo[w] the advice of numerous practice guides" to advise themselves of the importance of this particular form of discretionary relief.

In the instant case, the terms of the relevant immigration statute are succinct, clear, and explicit in defining the removal consequence for Padilla's conviction. See 8 U.S.C. § 1227(a)(2)(B)(i) ("Any alien who at any time after admission has been convicted of a violation of (or a conspiracy or attempt to violate) any law or regulation of a State, the United States or a foreign country relating to a controlled substance . . ., other than a single offense involving possession for one's own use of 30 grams or less of marijuana, is deportable"). Padilla's counsel could have easily determined that his plea would make him eligible for deportation simply from reading the text of the statute, which addresses not some broad classification of crimes but specifically commands removal for all controlled substances convictions except for the most trivial of marijuana possession offenses. Instead, Padilla's counsel provided him false assurance that his conviction would not result in his removal from this country. This is not a hard case in which to find deficiency: The consequences of Padilla's plea could easily be determined from reading the removal statute, his deportation was presumptively mandatory, and his counsel's advice was incorrect.

Immigration law can be complex, and it is a legal specialty of its own. Some members of the bar who represent clients facing criminal charges, in either state or federal court or both, may not be well versed in it. There will, therefore, undoubtedly be numerous situations in which the deportation consequences of a particular plea are unclear or uncertain. The duty of the private practitioner in such cases is more limited. When the law is not succinct and straightforward * * *, a criminal defense attorney need do no more than advise a noncitizen client that pending criminal charges may carry a risk of adverse immigration consequences. But when the deportation consequence is truly clear, as it was in this case, the duty to give correct advice is equally clear.

Accepting his allegations as true, Padilla has sufficiently alleged constitutional deficiency to satisfy the first prong of *Strickland*. Whether Padilla is entitled to relief on his claim will depend on whether he can satisfy

Strickland 's second prong, prejudice, a matter we leave to the Kentucky courts to consider in the first instance.

IV

The Solicitor General has urged us to conclude that *Strickland* applies to Padilla's claim only to the extent that he has alleged affirmative misadvice. In the United States' view, "counsel is not constitutionally required to provide advice on matters that will not be decided in the criminal case . . .," though counsel is required to provide accurate advice if she chooses to discusses these matters.

Respondent and Padilla both find the Solicitor General's proposed rule unpersuasive. * * * [W]e agree that there is no relevant difference "between an act of commission and an act of omission" in this context.

A holding limited to affirmative misadvice would invite two absurd results. First, it would give counsel an incentive to remain silent on matters of great importance, even when answers are readily available. Silence under these circumstances would be fundamentally at odds with the critical obligation of counsel to advise the client of "the advantages and disadvantages of a plea agreement." When attorneys know that their clients face possible exile from this country and separation from their families, they should not be encouraged to say nothing at all. Second, it would deny a class of clients least able to represent themselves the most rudimentary advice on deportation even when it is readily available. It is quintessentially the duty of counsel to provide her client with available advice about an issue like deportation and the failure to do so clearly satisfies the first prong of the *Strickland* analysis.

* * *

[I]nformed consideration of possible deportation can only benefit both the State and noncitizen defendants during the plea-bargaining process. By bringing deportation consequences into this process, the defense and prosecution may well be able to reach agreements that better satisfy the interests of both parties. As in this case, a criminal episode may provide the basis for multiple charges, of which only a subset mandate deportation following conviction. Counsel who possess the most rudimentary understanding of the deportation consequences of a particular criminal offense may be able to plea bargain creatively with the prosecutor in order to craft a conviction and sentence that reduce the likelihood of deportation, as by avoiding a conviction for an offense that automatically triggers the removal consequence. At the same time, the threat of deportation may provide the defendant with a powerful incentive to plead guilty to an offense that does not mandate that penalty in exchange for a dismissal of a charge that does.

* * *

V

[W]e now hold that counsel must inform her client whether his plea carries a risk of deportation. Our longstanding Sixth Amendment precedents, the seriousness of deportation as a consequence of a criminal plea, and the concomitant impact of deportation on families living lawfully in this country demand no less.

Taking as true the basis for his motion for postconviction relief, we have little difficulty concluding that Padilla has sufficiently alleged that his counsel was constitutionally deficient. Whether Padilla is entitled to relief will depend on whether he can demonstrate prejudice as a result thereof, a question we do not reach because it was not passed on below.

The judgment of the Supreme Court of Kentucky is reversed, and the case is remanded for further proceedings not inconsistent with this opinion.

It is so ordered.

■ JUSTICE ALITO, with whom THE CHIEF JUSTICE joins, concurring in the judgment.

I concur in the judgment because a criminal defense attorney fails to provide effective assistance * * * if the attorney misleads a noncitizen client regarding the removal consequences of a conviction. In my view, such an attorney must (1) refrain from unreasonably providing incorrect advice and (2) advise the defendant that a criminal conviction may have adverse immigration consequences and that, if the alien wants advice on this issue, the alien should consult an immigration attorney. I do not agree with the Court that the attorney must attempt to explain what those consequences may be. As the Court concedes, "[i]mmigration law can be complex;" "it is a legal specialty of its own;" and "[s]ome members of the bar who represent clients facing criminal charges, in either state or federal court or both, may not be well versed in it." The Court nevertheless holds that a criminal defense attorney must provide advice in this specialized area in those cases in which the law is "succinct and straightforward"—but not, perhaps, in other situations. This vague, halfway test will lead to much confusion and needless litigation.

* * *

■ JUSTICE SCALIA, with whom JUSTICE THOMAS joins, dissenting.

* * * I dissent from the Court's conclusion that the Sixth Amendment requires counsel to provide accurate advice concerning the potential removal consequences of a guilty plea. For the same reasons, but unlike the concurrence, I do not believe that affirmative misadvice about those consequences renders an attorney's assistance in defending against the prosecution constitutionally inadequate; or that the Sixth Amendment requires counsel to warn immigrant defendants that a conviction may render them removable. Statutory provisions can remedy these concerns in a more

targeted fashion, and without producing permanent, and legislatively irreparable, overkill.

* * *

There is no basis in text or in principle to extend the constitutionally required advice regarding guilty pleas beyond those matters germane to the criminal prosecution at hand—to wit, the sentence that the plea will produce, the higher sentence that conviction after trial might entail, and the chances of such a conviction. Such matters fall within "the range of competence demanded of attorneys in criminal cases." We have never held, as the logic of the Court's opinion assumes, that once counsel is appointed all professional responsibilities of counsel—even those extending beyond defense against the prosecution—become constitutional commands. Because the subject of the misadvice here was not the prosecution for which Jose Padilla was entitled to effective assistance of counsel, the Sixth Amendment has no application.

Adding to counsel's duties an obligation to advise about a conviction's collateral consequences has no logical stopping-point. * * *

The Court's holding prevents legislation that could solve the problems addressed by today's opinions in a more precise and targeted fashion. If the subject had not been constitutionalized, legislation could specify which categories of misadvice about matters ancillary to the prosecution invalidate plea agreements, what collateral consequences counsel must bring to a defendant's attention, and what warnings must be given. Moreover, legislation could provide consequences for the misadvice, nonadvice, or failure to warn, other than nullification of a criminal conviction after the witnesses and evidence needed for retrial have disappeared. Federal immigration law might provide, for example, that the near-automatic removal which follows from certain criminal convictions will not apply where the conviction rested upon a guilty plea induced by counsel's misadvice regarding removal consequences. Or legislation might put the government to a choice in such circumstances: Either retry the defendant or forgo the removal. But all that has been precluded in favor of today's sledge hammer.

In sum, the Sixth Amendment guarantees adequate assistance of counsel in defending against a pending criminal prosecution. We should limit both the constitutional obligation to provide advice and the consequences of bad advice to that well defined area.

NOTE

The Attorney General's discretionary authority to cancel removal is limited to situations in which the noncitizen has not been convicted of an aggravated felony. 8 U.S.C. § 1229b. Whether a state conviction is for an aggravated felony depends on whether it is punishable as a felony under federal law. Generally, a first-time possession of a controlled substance offense is a misdemeanor. Simple possession becomes a felony if a prior conviction is alleged and proved. The manner of determining whether a noncitizen convicted in state court is eligible for cancellation of removal under this scheme was at issue in Carachuri–Rosendo v. Holder, ___ U.S. ___, 130 S.Ct. 2577, 177 L.Ed.2d 68 (2010).

Carachuri–Rosendo was convicted in 2004 in a Texas court of misdemeanor possession of less than two ounces of marijuana and was sentenced to jail for 20 days. In 2005, he was charged with misdemeanor possession of less than 28 grams (one tablet) of alprazolam (Xanax). The local Texas prosecutor could have but did not invoke a Texas recidivist statute by alleging the prior conviction. Invoking this provision would have made the second offense a felony. Carachuri–Rosendo was convicted on the second misdemeanor charge and sentenced to 10 days in jail. Removal proceedings were begun and he sought discretionary cancellation of removal. The Court of Appeals held he was not eligible for cancellation of removal because the facts of his case would have permitted his conviction for a felony and thus his Texas conviction was for an aggravated felony under federal immigration law.

The Supreme Court held that whether the Texas conviction was for an aggravated felony did not turn on whether the facts could have permitted a felony conviction under federal law. Rather, he must have been actually convicted of a crime that is itself punishable as a felony under federal law. Since Carachuri–Rosendo had not been actually convicted of an offense punishable as a felony under federal law, he was eligible for cancellation of removal. This was in part because the structure and design of drug laws gives prosecutors discretion whether to seek recidivist enhancement of drug offenses. The position of the Court of Appeals, the *Carachuri–Rosendo* majority reasoned, would have permitted a federal immigration judge to apply his own recidivist enhancement after the fact where a state prosecutor had decided against such a course of action. This "would denigrate the independent judgment of state prosecutors to execute the laws of those sovereigns." ___ U.S. at ___, 130 S.Ct. at 2588.

7. SEX OFFENDER REGISTRATION

Connecticut Department of Public Safety v. Doe

Supreme Court of the United States, 2003.
538 U.S. 1, 123 S.Ct. 1160, 155 L.Ed.2d 98.

■ CHIEF JUSTICE REHNQUIST delivered the opinion of the Court.

We granted certiorari to determine whether the United States Court of Appeals for the Second Circuit properly enjoined the public disclosure of Connecticut's sex offender registry. The Court of Appeals concluded that such disclosure both deprived registered sex offenders of a "liberty interest," and violated the Due Process Clause because officials did not afford registrants a predeprivation hearing to determine whether they are likely to be "currently dangerous." *Doe v. Department of Public Safety ex rel. Lee,* 271 F.3d 38, 44, 46 (2001). Connecticut, however, has decided that the registry requirement shall be based on the fact of previous conviction, not the fact of current dangerousness. Indeed, the public registry explicitly states that officials have not determined that any registrant is currently dangerous. We therefore reverse the judgment of the Court of Appeals because due process does not require the opportunity to prove a fact that is not material to the State's statutory scheme.

"Sex offenders are a serious threat in this Nation." *McKune v. Lile,* 536 U.S. 24, 32, 122 S.Ct. 2017, 153 L.Ed.2d 47 (2002) (plurality opinion). "[T]he victims of sex assault are most often juveniles," and "[w]hen convicted sex offenders reenter society, they are much more likely than any other type of offender to be re-arrested for a new rape or sex assault." *Id.,* at 32–33, 122 S.Ct. 2017. Connecticut, like every other State, has responded to these facts by enacting a statute designed to protect its communities from sex offenders and to help apprehend repeat sex offenders. Connecticut's "Megan's Law" applies to all persons convicted of criminal offenses against a minor, violent and nonviolent sexual offenses, and felonies committed for a sexual purpose. Covered offenders must register with the Connecticut Department of Public Safety (DPS) upon their release into the community. Each must provide personal information (including his name, address, photograph, and DNA sample); notify DPS of any change in residence; and periodically submit an updated photograph. The registration requirement runs for 10 years in most cases; those convicted of sexually violent offenses must register for life. Conn. Gen.Stat. §§ 54–251, 54–252, 54–254 (2001).

The statute requires DPS to compile the information gathered from registrants and publicize it. In particular, the law requires DPS to post a sex offender registry on an Internet Website and to make the registry available to the public in certain state offices. §§ 54–257, 54–258. Whether made available in an office or via the Internet, the registry must be accompanied by the following warning: " 'Any person who uses information in this registry to injure, harass or commit a criminal act against any person included in the registry or any other person is subject to criminal prosecution.' " § 54–258a.

Before the District Court enjoined its operation, the State's Website enabled citizens to obtain the name, address, photograph, and description of any registered sex offender by entering a zip code or town name. The following disclaimer appeared on the first page of the Website:

> " 'The registry is based on the legislature's decision to facilitate access to publicly-available information about persons convicted of sexual offenses. [DPS] has not considered or assessed the specific risk of reoffense with regard to any individual prior to his or her inclusion within this registry, and has made no determination that any individual included in the registry is currently dangerous. Individuals included within the registry are included solely by virtue of their conviction record and state law. The main purpose of providing this data on the Internet is to make the information more easily available and accessible, not to warn about any specific individual.' " 271 F.3d, at 44.

Petitioners include the state agencies and officials charged with compiling the sex offender registry and posting it on the Internet. Respondent Doe is a convicted sex offender who is subject to Connecticut's Megan's Law. He filed this action pursuant to Rev. Stat. § 1979, 42 U.S.C. § 1983, on behalf of himself and similarly situated sex offenders, claiming that the law violates, *inter alia,* the Due Process Clause of the Fourteenth Amendment. Specifically, respondent alleged that he is not a " 'dangerous sexual offender,' " and that the Connecticut law "deprives him of a liberty interest—his reputation combined with the alteration of his status under state law—without notice or a meaningful opportunity to be heard." 271 F.3d, at 45–46. The District Court granted summary judgment for respondent on his due process claim. 132 F.Supp.2d 57 (D.Conn.2001). The court then certified a class of individuals subject to the Connecticut law, and permanently enjoined the law's public disclosure provisions.

The Court of Appeals affirmed, 271 F.3d 38 (C.A.2 2001), holding that the Due Process Clause entitles class members to a hearing "to determine whether or not they are particularly likely to be currently dangerous before being labeled as such by their inclusion in a publicly disseminated registry." *Id.,* at 62. Because Connecticut had not provided such a hearing, the Court of Appeals enjoined petitioners from " 'disclosing or disseminating to the public, either in printed or electronic form (a) the Registry or (b) Registry information concerning [class members]' " and from " 'identifying [them] as being included in the Registry.' " *Ibid.* The Court of Appeals reasoned that the Connecticut law implicated a "liberty interest" because of: (1) the law's stigmatization of respondent by "implying" that he is "currently dangerous," and (2) its imposition of "extensive and onerous" registration obligations on respondent. *Id.,* at 57. From this liberty interest arose an obligation, in the Court of Appeals' view, to give respondent an opportunity to demonstrate that he was not "likely to be currently dangerous." *Id.,* at 62. We granted certiorari, 535 U.S. 1077, 122 S.Ct. 1959, 152 L.Ed.2d 1020 (2002).

In *Paul v. Davis,* 424 U.S. 693, 96 S.Ct. 1155, 47 L.Ed.2d 405 (1976), we held that mere injury to reputation, even if defamatory, does not constitute the deprivation of a liberty interest. Petitioners urge us to reverse the Court of Appeals on the ground that, under *Paul v. Davis,* respondent has failed to establish that petitioners have deprived him of a liberty interest. We find it unnecessary to reach this question, however, because even assuming, *arguendo,* that respondent has been deprived of a liberty interest, due process does not entitle him to a hearing to establish a fact that is not material under the Connecticut statute.

In cases such as *Wisconsin v. Constantineau,* 400 U.S. 433, 91 S.Ct. 507, 27 L.Ed.2d 515 (1971), and *Goss v. Lopez,* 419 U.S. 565, 95 S.Ct. 729, 42 L.Ed.2d 725 (1975), we held that due process required the government to accord the plaintiff a hearing to prove or disprove a particular fact or set of facts. But in each of these cases, the fact in question was concededly relevant to the inquiry at hand. Here, however, the fact that respondent seeks to prove—that he is not currently dangerous—is of no consequence under Connecticut's Megan's Law. As the DPS Website explains, the law's requirements turn on an offender's conviction alone—a fact that a convicted offender has already had a procedurally safeguarded opportunity to contest. 271 F.3d, at 44 (" 'Individuals included within the registry are included *solely* by virtue of their conviction record and state law' " (emphasis added)). No other fact is relevant to the disclosure of registrants' information. Conn. Gen.Stat. §§ 54–257, 54–258 (2001). Indeed, the disclaimer on the Website explicitly states that respondent's alleged nondangerousness simply does not matter. 271 F.3d, at 44 (" '[DPS] has made no determination that any individual included in the registry is currently dangerous' ").

In short, even if respondent could prove that he is not likely to be currently dangerous, Connecticut has decided that the registry information of *all* sex offenders—currently dangerous or not—must be publicly disclosed. Unless respondent can show that that *substantive* rule of law is defective (by conflicting with a provision of the Constitution), any hearing on current dangerousness is a bootless exercise. It may be that respondent's claim is actually a substantive challenge to Connecticut's statute "recast in 'procedural due process' terms." *Reno v. Flores,* 507 U.S. 292, 308, 113 S.Ct. 1439, 123 L.Ed.2d 1 (1993). Nonetheless, respondent expressly disavows any reliance on the substantive component of the Fourteenth Amendment's protections, Brief for Respondent 44–45, and maintains, as he did below, that his challenge is strictly a procedural one. But States are not barred by principles of *"procedural* due process" from drawing such classifications. *Michael H. v. Gerald D.,* 491 U.S. 110, 120, 109 S.Ct. 2333, 105 L.Ed.2d 91 (1989) (plurality opinion) (emphasis in original). See also *id.,* at 132, 109 S.Ct. 2333 (STEVENS, J., concurring in judgment). Such claims "must ultimately be analyzed" in terms of substantive, not procedural, due process. *Id.,* at 121, 109 S.Ct. 2333. Because the question is not properly before us, we express no opinion as to whether Connecticut's Megan's Law violates principles of substantive due process.

Plaintiffs who assert a right to a hearing under the Due Process Clause must show that the facts they seek to establish in that hearing are relevant under the statutory scheme. Respondent cannot make that showing here. The judgment of the Court of Appeals is therefore

Reversed.

■ JUSTICE SCALIA, concurring.

I join the Court's opinion, and add that even if the requirements of Connecticut's sex offender registration law implicate a liberty interest of respondent, the categorical abrogation of that liberty interest by a validly enacted statute suffices to provide all the process that is "due"—just as a state law providing that no one under the age of 16 may operate a motor vehicle suffices to abrogate that liberty interest. Absent a claim (which respondent has not made here) that the liberty interest in question is so fundamental as to implicate so-called "substantive" due process, a properly enacted law can eliminate it. That is ultimately why, as the Court's opinion demonstrates, a convicted sex offender has no more right to additional "process" enabling him to establish that he is not dangerous than (in the analogous case just suggested) a 15-year-old has a right to "process" enabling him to establish that he is a safe driver.

■ Justice Souter, with whom Justice Ginsburg joins, concurring.

I join the Court's opinion and agree with the observation that today's holding does not foreclose a claim that Connecticut's dissemination of registry information is actionable on a substantive due process principle. To the extent that libel might be at least a component of such a claim, our reference to Connecticut's disclaimer, * * *, would not stand in the way of a substantive due process plaintiff. I write separately only to note that a substantive due process claim may not be the only one still open to a test by those in the respondents' situation.

Connecticut allows certain sex offenders the possibility of avoiding the registration and reporting obligations of the statute. A court may exempt a convict from registration altogether if his offense was unconsented sexual contact, Conn. Gen.Stat. § 54–251(c) (2001), or sexual intercourse with a minor aged between 13 and 16 while the offender was more than two years older than the minor, provided the offender was under age 19 at the time of the offense, § 54–251(b). A court also has discretion to limit dissemination of an offender's registration information to law enforcement purposes if necessary to protect the identity of a victim who is related to the offender or, in the case of a sexual assault, who is the offender's spouse or cohabitor. §§ 54–255(a), (b).* Whether the decision is to exempt an offender from registration or to restrict publication of registry information, it must rest on a finding that registration or public dissemination is not required for public safety. §§ 54–251(b), 54–255(a), (b). The State thus recognizes that some offenders within the sweep of the publication requirement are not dangerous to others in any way justifying special publicity on the Internet, and the legislative decision to make courts responsible for granting exemptions belies the State's argument that courts are unequipped to separate offenders who warrant special publication from those who do not.

The line drawn by the legislature between offenders who are sensibly considered eligible to seek discretionary relief from the courts and those who are not is, like all legislative choices affecting individual rights, open to

* To mitigate the retroactive effects of the statute, offenders in these categories who were convicted between October 1, 1988, and June 30, 1999, were allowed to petition a court for restricted dissemination of registry information. §§ 54–255(c)(1)–(4). A similar petition was also available to any offender who became subject to registration by virtue of a conviction prior to October 1, 1998, if he was not incarcerated for the offense, had not been subsequently convicted of a registrable offense, and had properly registered under the law. § 54–255(c)(5).

challenge under the Equal Protection Clause. See, *e. g.*, 3 R. Rotunda & J. Nowak, Treatise on Constitutional Law § 17.6 (3d ed.1999); L. Tribe, American Constitutional Law § 16–34 (2d ed.1988). The refusal to allow even the possibility of relief to, say, a 19–year-old who has consensual intercourse with a minor aged 16 is therefore a reviewable legislative determination. Today's case is no occasion to speak either to the possible merits of such a challenge or the standard of scrutiny that might be in order when considering it. I merely note that the Court's rejection of respondents' procedural due process claim does not immunize publication schemes like Connecticut's from an equal protection challenge.

NOTE

On the same day the Court decided the Connecticut case, it decided Smith v. Doe, 538 U.S. 84, 123 S.Ct. 1140, 155 L.Ed.2d 164 (2003), holding that retroactive application of Alaska's sex offender registration statute to persons who were convicted before enactment of the law does not violate the *ex post facto* clause of the United States Constitution. Writing for the Court, Justice Kennedy acknowledged a two-step process in analyzing an *ex post facto* claim:

> This is the first time we have considered a claim that a sex offender registration and notification law constitutes retroactive punishment forbidden by the *Ex Post Facto* Clause. The framework for our inquiry, however, is well established. We must "ascertain whether the legislature meant the statute to establish 'civil' proceedings." *Kansas v. Hendricks,* 521 U.S. 346, 361, 117 S.Ct. 2072, 138 L.Ed.2d 501 (1997) [Casebook p. 1233]. If the intention of the legislature was to impose punishment, that ends the inquiry. If, however, the intention was to enact a regulatory scheme that is civil and nonpunitive, we must further examine whether the statutory scheme is " 'so punitive either in purpose or effect as to negate [the State's] intention' to deem it 'civil.' " *Ibid.* * * * Because we "ordinarily defer to the legislature's stated intent," * * * " 'only the clearest proof' will suffice to override legislative intent and transform what has been denominated a civil remedy into a criminal penalty," *Hudson v. United States,* 522 U.S. 93, 100, 118 S.Ct. 488, 139 L.Ed.2d 450 (1997) * * *.

538 U.S. at 92, 123 S.Ct. at 1146–47. The Court accepted that the intent of the Alaska legislature was to establish a non-punitive regulatory scheme. The Court also concluded that the scheme in effect did not negate the legislature's non-punitive purpose. Justice Thomas, concurred, as did Justice Souter. Justice Stevens issued an opinion in which he dissented in Smith v. Doe, but concurred in Connecticut Department of Public Safety v. Doe.

CHAPTER 26

APPEAL AND COLLATERAL ATTACK

B.   APPEAL

Page 1264.   Add the following before Note 2:

1a.   **Right to representation where any appeal is discretionary.** Michigan's Constitution provides that where a criminal defendant pleads guilty or *nolo contendere*, the defendant has no appeal as a matter of right but appeal "shall be by leave of court." Mich. Const., Art. I, § 20. Implementing this, the state has denied a right to appointed appellate counsel to defendants who enter such pleas. In Halbert v. Michigan, 545 U.S. 605, 125 S.Ct. 2582, 162 L.Ed.2d 552 (2005), the Supreme Court held that this situation was governed by *Douglas* rather than *Ross* and thus violated Equal Protection. In *Ross* situations, the defendant will already have had the assistance of appellate counsel in reviewing the record, researching the issues, and formulating and presenting those issues. Further, the decision on whether to grant review will not focus on whether there was error in the particular case but on such considerations as whether the case presents an important issue of public import. In the Michigan situations, in contrast, the defendant will have had no prior assistance of appellate counsel. Moreover, and "of critical importance," the appellate court sits as an error-correction court and its decision will therefore be more influenced by whether the defendant's application demonstrates error in the case. The Court added that many persons who might wish to appeal after a plea of guilty or nolo contendere are poorly educated and possibly illiterate or impaired. They "are particularly handicapped as self-representatives." 545 U.S. at 607, 125 S.Ct. at 2585.

The *Halbert* majority also rejected Michigan's contention that the case involved waiver:

> Michigan contends that, even if Halbert had a constitutionally guaranteed right to appointed counsel for first-level appellate review, he waived that right by entering a plea of *nolo contendere*. We disagree. At the time he entered his plea, Halbert, in common with other defendants convicted on their pleas, had no recognized right to appointed appellate counsel he could elect to forgo. Moreover, * * * the trial court did not tell Halbert, simply and directly, that in his case, there would be no access to appointed counsel.

545 U.S. at 623–24, 125 S.Ct. at 2594. It added:

> We are unpersuaded by the suggestion that, because a defendant may be able to waive his right to appeal entirely, Michigan can consequently exact from him a waiver of the right to government-funded appellate counsel. Many legal rights are "presumptively waivable," and if Michigan were to require defendants to waive all forms of appeal as a condition of entering a plea, that condition would operate against moneyed and impoverished defendants alike. A

required waiver of the right to appointed counsel's assistance when applying for leave to appeal to the Michigan Court of Appeals, however, would accomplish the very result worked by [the present statute]: It would leave indigents without access to counsel in that narrow range of circumstances in which, our decisions hold, the State must affirmatively ensure that poor defendants receive the legal assistance necessary to provide meaningful access to the judicial system.

545 U.S. at 624 n. 8, 125 S.Ct. at 2594 n. 8.

1b. **Is there a right not to have a lawyer on appeal?** In Faretta v. California [Casebook p. 1132] the United States Supreme Court held that the Sixth Amendment creates a right for a person to represent himself in criminal trial proceedings—that the government cannot require representation by an attorney over the objection of a criminal defendant. Does the right to self-representation extend to the appellate process?

Appellant in Martinez v. Court of Appeal of California, 528 U.S. 152, 120 S.Ct. 684, 145 L.Ed.2d 597 (2000) was a paralegal charged with theft and embezzlement. He represented himself at trial, was convicted of embezzlement, and sought to represent himself of appeal. The California appellate courts refused his waiver of counsel and request to represent himself on appeal. The United States Supreme Court, in an opinion by Justice Stevens, held that a criminal appellant has no constitutional right to pro se representation in his first appeal. In an opinion that Justice Kennedy accused of attempting to cast doubt on the wisdom and continued validity of *Faretta*, Justice Stevens said that Fourteenth Amendment Due Process does not require a right of self-representation for the appellate process to be fair:

> Under the practices that prevail in the Nation today ... we are entirely unpersuaded that the risk of either disloyalty or suspicion of disloyalty [of appointed counsel to his or her client] is a sufficient concern to conclude that a constitutional right of self-representation is a necessary component of a fair appellate proceeding. We have not doubt that instances of disloyal representation are rare. In both trials and appeals there are, without question, cases in which counsel's performance is ineffective. Even in those cases, however, it is reasonable to assume that counsel's performance is more effective than what the unskilled appellant could have provided for himself.

528 U.S. at 160, 120 S.Ct. at 690–91, 145 L.Ed.2d at 606. He continued that the autonomy interests that are the underpinning of *Faretta* are less significant after the defendant is convicted of a criminal offense, yet the interest of the government in the efficient administration of justice is as great. Finally, States are free to recognize a right of pro se representation in appeals if they choose to do so.

Page 1266. Add the following after Note 3:

3a. **Frivolous appeal procedures.** In Smith v. Robbins, 528 U.S. 259, 120 S.Ct. 746, 145 L.Ed.2d 756 (2000), the question was raised whether the procedure specified in Anders v. California for relief from representation when appointed counsel concludes an appeal is frivolous is the sole constitutionally-acceptable procedure. That procedure requires counsel to brief any arguable grounds for reversal and serve a copy of that brief on the appellant, informing the client of his or her right to file a pro se brief. If the appellate court concludes the appeal lacks merit, it may permit counsel to withdraw from representation and dismiss the appeal or affirm the trial court's judgment. If it concludes that a ground of review has possible merit, it must take steps to assure that the indigent appellant has assistance of counsel in arguing that ground.

The California Supreme Court in People v. Wende, 25 Cal.3d 436, 158 Cal.Rptr. 839, 600 P.2d 1071 (1979) authorized a different procedure under which counsel is not required to brief arguable grounds for reversal but instead summarizes the case and submits a brief to the court without a claim the appeal is frivolous. The appellate court is obligated to examine the record to determine whether arguable grounds exist. If any are found, counsel is then required to brief them.

In this case, the Ninth Circuit held that those procedure violated requirements of the Fourteenth Amendment under *Anders*. The Supreme Court, in an opinion for a five-justice majority authored by Justice Thomas, reversed, holding that the California procedure is constitutional. The *Anders* procedure is not constitutionally mandated, but merely one way of achieving the constitutionally-mandated objective of assuring that an indigent's first appeal is adequate and effective. To hold that the *Anders* procedure is constitutionally required would be to contravene the Court's policy of "allowing the States wide discretion, subject to the minimum requirements of the Fourteenth Amendment, to experiment with solutions to difficult problems of policy." 528 U.S. at 272, 120 S.Ct. at 757, 145 L.Ed.2d at 772. The Court found that the procedures established by *Wende* provide protections at least a great as those established by the *Anders* opinion.

Justice Souter, joined by Justices Stevens, Ginsburg and Breyer, dissented on the ground, among others, that excusing the *Anders* step that counsel brief possible grounds of reversal was a substantial reduction in the protections provided to indigent appellants.

Page 1271.   Add the following new notes:

7a.   **The *Teaque* exceptions.** Since the Court's decision in *Teague v. Lane*, 489 U.S. 288, 109 S.Ct. 1060, 103 L.Ed.2d 334 (1989), the Court has regularly refused to apply a new constitutional rule of criminal retroactively to cases on federal habeas review on the ground that it falls within the second exception for "watershed rules of criminal procedure." *See, e.g., Whorton v. Bockting*, 549 U.S. 406, 127 S.Ct. 1173, 167 L.Ed.2d 1 (2007); *Schriro v. Summerlin*, 542 U.S. 348, 353–354, 124 S.Ct. 2519, 159 L.Ed.2d 442 (2004); *Sawyer v. Smith*, 497 U.S. 227, 243–245, 110 S.Ct. 2822, 111 L.Ed.2d 193 (1990); *Penry v. Lynaugh*, 492 U.S. 302, 318–319, 109 S.Ct. 2934, 106 L.Ed.2d 256 (1989).

7b.   ***Teague* constrains only federal habeas cases.** The Court in *Danforth v. Minnesota*, 552 U.S. 264, 128 S.Ct. 1029, 169 L.Ed.2d 859 (2008) explained that the *Teague* rules were tailored to the federal habeas context and thus had no bearing on whether States could provide broader relief in their own postconviction proceedings. Petitioner in *Danforth* sought state postconviction relief on the ground that he was entitled to a new trial because admitting the victim's taped interview at his trial violated *Crawford*. The State Supreme Court refused because *Crawford* does not apply retroactively under *Teague* and concluded that state courts are not free to give a decision of the Supreme Court announcing a new rule of criminal procedure broader retroactive application than given by the Court. The *Danforth* majority explained that *Teague* was based on statutory authority that extends only to federal courts applying a federal statute, and it cannot be read as imposing a binding obligation on state courts. The Court remanded for Minnesota to determine whether it wishes to provide broader remedies for federal constitutional violations than mandated by *Teague*.

8. **Application of "unexpected" appellate rulings to parties.** In Rogers v. Tennessee, 532 U.S. 451, 121 S.Ct. 1693, 149 L.Ed.2d 697 (2001) the petitioner was convicted of homicide in a case in which the death occurred more than a year and a day after the injuries were inflicted. The Tennessee Supreme Court in petitioner's case abolished the common law rule that death must occur within that time and affirmed petitioner's conviction. The United States Supreme Court, in an opinion authored by Justice O'Connor, affirmed. Bouie v. City of Columbia, 378 U.S. 347, 84 S.Ct. 1697, 12 L.Ed.2d 894 (1964) held that a totally unexpected interpretation of a state criminal statute cannot consistent with Due Process be applied to the parties. The ruling complained of here was not an interpretation of a statute but the abolition of a common law rule. That requires a different application of the *Bouie* principle:

> In the context of common law doctrines (such as the year and a day rule), there often arises a need to clarify or even to reevaluate prior opinions as new circumstances and fact patterns present themselves. Such judicial acts, whether they be characterized as "making" or "finding" the law, are a necessary part of the judicial business in States in which the criminal law retains some of its common law elements. Strict application of *ex post facto* principles in that context would unduly impair the incremental and reasoned development of precedent that is the foundation of the common law system. The common law, in short, presupposes a measure of evolution that is incompatible with stringent application of *ex post facto* principles. It was on account of concerns such as these that *Bouie* restricted due process limitations on the retroactive application of judicial interpretations of criminal statutes to those that are "unexpected and indefensible by reference to the law which had been expressed prior to the conduct in issue." Bouie v. City of Columbia, 378 U.S., at 354, 84 S.Ct. 1697 (internal quotation marks omitted).

> We believe this limitation adequately serves the common law context as well. It accords common law courts the substantial leeway they must enjoy as they engage in the daily task of formulating and passing upon criminal defenses and interpreting such doctrines as causation and intent, reevaluating and refining them as may be necessary to bring the common law into conformity with logic and common sense. It also adequately respects the due process concern with fundamental fairness and protects against vindictive or arbitrary judicial lawmaking by safeguarding defendants against unjustified and unpredictable breaks with prior law. Accordingly, we conclude that a judicial alteration of a common law doctrine of criminal law violates the principle of fair warning, and hence must not be given retroactive effect, only where it is "unexpected and indefensible by reference to the law which had been expressed prior to the conduct in issue." Ibid.

532 U.S. at 461–62, 121 S.Ct. at 1700, 49 L.Ed.2d at 107–08.

9. **Application of rule clarifications to previous prosecutions.** The petitioner in Bunkley v. Florida, 538 U.S. 835, 123 S.Ct. 2020, 155 L.Ed.2d 1046 (2003) was convicted of burglary in 1989 in a case in which he received a life sentence because he committed the offense with a dangerous weapon. The weapon in question was a pocketknife with a blade of two and one-half to three inches. The knife was not used in any manner in commission of the offense. If the pocketknife

was not a weapon, the maximum Bunkley could have received for the burglary would have been five years. In 1997, in a different case, the Florida Supreme Court decided that a pocketknife with blade of three and three-quarters inches was not a weapon. The Florida Supreme Court rejected Bunkley's claim that he should benefit from the 1997 ruling, characterizing the ruling as part of a century-long evolutionary process of interpreting these statutes, not a new rule.

The United States Supreme Court reversed in a *per curiam* opinion. The question is whether Bunkley's knife was a weapon under the law in 1989 when the burglary was committed. The Florida Supreme Court has never addressed that question. If the knife was not a weapon, then Bunkley's conviction violated due process of law. The Court remanded for the Florida Supreme Court to determine where in the evolutionary process the law was in 1989. The Chief Justice, joined by Justices Kennedy and Thomas, dissented on finality grounds in that petitioner had before 1997 without success presented this claim to Florida courts in direct appeal and collateral proceedings.

C.   COLLATERAL ATTACK

Page 1276.   Add the following to Note 1:

The Supreme Court in Woodford v. Garceau, 538 U.S. 202, 123 S.Ct. 1398, 155 L.Ed.2d 363 (2003), again reversing the Ninth Circuit and expanding on *Lindh*, held that the 1996 amendments apply to a federal habeas petition filed after their effective date even though a federal district court had earlier appointed counsel for the proceedings and issued a stay of execution.

Page 1278.   Add the following at the bottom of the page:

4a.   **Attacking prior convictions.** Under what circumstances may an inmate serving a sentence enhanced by a prior conviction use federal habeas to seek to invalidate the prior conviction? In a pair of cases decided on the same day, the Supreme Court in opinions authored by Justice O'Connor held that with very limited exceptions, federal habeas cannot be used for those purposes.

In Daniels v. United States, 532 U.S. 374, 121 S.Ct. 1578, 149 L.Ed.2d 590 (2001), petitioner was convicted in federal court and given a sentenced that was enhanced by prior state convictions. Building on Custis v. United States, 511 U.S. 485, 114 S.Ct. 1732, 128 L.Ed.2d 517 (1994), holding that a federal criminal defendant may not at sentencing challenge the constitutional validity of a state conviction the government proposes to use to enhance punishment, Justice O'Connor said the same interests in avoiding judicial burdens and in achieving conviction finality recognized in *Custis* apply when the attack is by federal habeas under 2255. The same rule applies:

> After an enhanced federal sentence has been imposed pursuant to the ACCA [Armed Career Criminal Act of 1984], the person sentenced may pursue any channels of direct or collateral review still available to challenge his prior conviction. In *Custis*, we noted the possibility that the petitioner there, who was still in custody on his prior convictions, could "attack his state sentences [in state court] or through federal habeas review." Ibid. If any such challenge to the underlying conviction is successful, the defendant may then apply for